ENCYCLOPEDIA OF THE UNITED STATES CONSTITUTION

ENCYCLOPEDIA OF THE UNITED STATES CONSTITUTION

VOLUME II
M–Z

David Schultz

Facts On File
An imprint of Infobase Publishing

For Helene

Encyclopedia of the United States Constitution

Copyright © 2009 David Schultz

Facts On File, Inc.
An imprint of Infobase Publishing
132 West 31st Street
New York NY 10001

Library of Congress Cataloging-in-Publication Data

Schultz, David A. (David Andrew), 1958–
Encyclopedia of the United States Constitution / David Schultz.—1st ed.
p. cm.
Includes bibliographical references and index.
ISBN 978-0-8160-6763-3 (hc : alk. paper) 1. Constitutional law—United States—Encyclopedias. I. Title.
KF4548.5.S38 2009
342.730203—dc22   2008023349

Facts On File books are available at special discounts when purchased in bulk quantities for businesses, associations, institutions, or sales promotions. Please call our Special Sales Department in New York at (212) 967-8800 or (800) 322-8755.

You can find Facts On File on the World Wide Web at http://www.factsonfile.com

Text design by Annie O'Donnell
Cover design by Alicia Post
Illustrations by Sholto Ainslie

Printed in the United States of America

VB Hermitage 10 9 8 7 6 5 4 3 2 1

This book is printed on acid-free paper and contains 30 percent postconsumer recycled content.

Contents

NOTE

When a case has been decided, but not yet published in the case reporter, the citation may note the volume but leave blank the page of the case reporter until it is determined. For example, *Meredith v. Jefferson*, 551 U.S. ___ (2007).

M

Madison, James (1751–1836) *fourth U.S. president*

James Madison, Jr., is often called the "father" of the U.S. Constitution. Few individuals have had more influence on the writing, recording, ratification, amendment, implementation, and interpretation of that document.

Born at his mother's homestead at Port Conway, Virginia, in March 1751, Madison was the son of a wealthy Virginia planter whose name he bore and who was a leading citizen of Orange County. Madison went to boarding school and studied under private tutors before entering the College of New Jersey (today's Princeton). Although Madison completed his undergraduate degree quickly, he spent additional time studying under President John Witherspoon before returning to Virginia.

After his return, Madison tutored his siblings and became involved with politics. He was perturbed by the actions of local officials who were imprisoning Baptist ministers for their views. Madison also joined his father in opposing what he believed to be British abuses of colonial liberties. As Virginia edged toward independence, Madison was appointed to the state Constitutional Convention, where he served on the committee that formulated the Virginia Bill of Rights. He helped revise language introduced by George Mason so that the Declaration recognized religious freedom not simply as a matter of "toleration" but as a natural right. Madison and THOMAS JEFFERSON later battled Patrick Henry for the complete disestablishment of church and state in Virginia.

Although subsequently losing an election to the Virginia legislature, Madison served as a member of the Governor's Council and went from there to the Continental Congress and then to the Virginia legislature. Madison was a leader in both bodies. He developed an unfavorable view of the weak government under the Articles of Confederation. He recognized that this government lacked adequate powers to promote domestic prosperity, to defend itself against foreign enemies, and to rectify abuses of individual liberties and other excesses that he saw at that level. He soon began advocating a stronger national government.

Madison had been selected to attend the Mount Vernon meeting to discuss common problems between Maryland and Virginia, but the governor did not inform him of his appointment in time for him to attend. By contrast, he appears to have been a leading figure at the Annapolis Convention in September 1786. With the help of ALEXANDER HAMILTON and other nationalists, Madison pushed for what was to become the CONSTITUTIONAL CONVENTION of 1787; he subsequently got the Virginia legislature to lend its support.

Madison was the first delegate from Virginia to arrive in Philadelphia. He masterminded the VIRGINIA PLAN, which got the 55 delegates who were attending to think about formulating a new plan of government rather than simply revising the existing government of the Articles of Confederation. The Virginia Plan proposed replacing a government centered on Congress with one based on separate legislative, executive, and judicial branches. He proposed a bicameral Congress in which states would be represented in both houses by population to replace the unicameral Congress, in which each state had a single vote; in addition to being more consistent with majority rule, this proposal favored states, like Virginia, with larger populations. Madison favored a unitary president and an independent judiciary. He had to compromise

James Madison *(Library of Congress)*

on most issues. Contrary to his hopes, the Convention eventually settled on a Congress where only one house was apportioned according to population. The convention also defeated other pet measures of Madison's, like a Council of Revision that would combine executive and judicial officers, and a congressional VETO of state legislation.

Although the Convention met in secret, Madison took comprehensive notes of the proceedings. These were not published until after his death. They remain the best record of Convention deliberations.

Even before the Convention adjourned, some distrusted its work. As it was sent to the states for ratification, Madison supported Federalist proponents of the document over anti-Federalist opponents. Madison joined Alexander Hamilton and JOHN JAY as one of three authors of *The FEDERALIST,* a series of newspaper articles, later collected in book form, explaining and defending the new document. Madison's more important contributions included: *Federalist* 10, where he advanced the idea that a republican, or representative, government spread over a large land area would embrace more factions, making it less likely that any one would destroy the liberties of the others; *Federalist* 39, where he defended the new government as being "partly national" and "partly federal"; and *Federalist* 51, where he argued for the advantages of a system of separated powers.

A key argument raised during the debates centered on whether a bill of rights was necessary. In time, Madison—who may have been influenced on the subject by correspondence from Thomas Jefferson, and who most certainly viewed the adoption of such a bill as a way of heading off a second convention that might undo the work of the first—agreed to work for a bill of rights once the new constitution was adopted. Blocked by Governor Patrick Henry from the U.S. SENATE, Madison defeated James Monroe to gain a seat in the HOUSE OF REPRESENTATIVES, where he introduced the BILL OF RIGHTS and was its strongest supporter. Madison did not succeed in getting an amendment that would protect the rights of conscience against state intervention, but the first 10 amendments did protect many fundamental liberties against federal abuse.

Although Madison had united with Hamilton in defense of the new Constitution, he quickly parted ways with the ambitious financial program that Hamilton introduced on behalf of increasing national powers. Madison unsuccessfully joined his friend Secretary of State Thomas Jefferson in opposing the establishment of a national bank. He also opposed the initiatives that the Washington administration was taking in foreign affairs, arguing that the House of Representatives should have more say in TREATY implementation. In time, Jefferson and Madison helped found the Democratic-Republican Party, which opposed Federalist expansion of the national government and increasingly stressed the importance of states' rights. In 1794, Madison married a widow, Dolley Todd Payne, who would later establish herself as one of the most influential first ladies. In the interim, Madison served again in the Virginia legislature.

When the Federalists adopted the Alien and Sedition Acts of 1798, the latter of which restricted freedom of speech, Madison and Jefferson responded by secretly authoring the Virginia and Kentucky Resolutions. Madison's words were more temperate than Jefferson's, but Madison's suggestion that states should be able to "interpose" themselves against unconstitutional legislation set the stage for more divisive theories of FEDERALISM that followed. In his famed Report of 1800, Madison later built on these resolutions by stressing the powers reserved to the states and by denying that the national government had any authority to restrict freedom of speech or press.

Madison served as Jefferson's secretary of state from 1801 through 1809, a time during which the United States purchased the Louisiana Territory, and in which Madison became the defendant in the case of *MARBURY V. MADISON*, 1 Cranch (5 U.S.) 137 (1803) that established the right of the judiciary to void unconstitutional federal legislation. Madison then served two terms as president. His presidency was marked by the War of 1812. Despite extreme peril, including the sacking of the White House, Madison did not request legislation, like the Alien and Sedition Acts, to restrict individual liberties. Over time, Madison accepted the constitutionality of the national bank, but he vetoed other measures that he did not think the Constitution had granted to the national government.

In retirement at his plantation at Montpelier, Madison entertained numerous guests. He served on the board of trustees for the University of Virginia, which Thomas Jefferson had established; was a delegate to the Virginia Constitutional Convention of 1829–30; and grew particularly concerned about the growing movement for nullification of state laws. He died on June 28, 1836, the last delegate to the Constitutional Convention to do so. In words published after his death, he urged his fellow countrymen to cherish national unity.

For more information: Meyers, Marvin, ed. *The Mind of the Founder: Sources of the Politi-*

cal Thought of James Madison. Indianapolis, Ind.: Bobbs-Merrill, 1973; Miller, William L. *The Business of May Next: James Madison and the Founding*. Charlottesville: University Press of Virginia, 1992; Rakove, Jack N. *James Madison and the Creation of the American Republic*. Glenview, Ill.: Scott, Foresman, 1990; Rutland, Robert Allen. *James Madison: The Founding Father*. New York: Macmillan Publishing Company, 1987; Sheldon, Garrett Ward. *The Political Philosophy of James Madison*. Baltimore, Md.: Johns Hopkins University Press, 2001.

—John Vile

Madsen v. Women's Health Center, Inc.
512 U.S. 753 (1994)

In *Madsen v. Women's Health Center*, the Supreme Court decided whether anti-abortion protestors had the right to conduct protests at women's health centers that performed abortions by blocking access to the building and preventing women from pursuing their constitutional right to obtain abortions.

The protest activity took place at the Aware Woman Center for Choice in Melbourne, Florida, with protestors blocking doors and marching in front of the building, using bullhorns to spread their message. They approached patients to attempt to dissuade them from getting ABORTIONS and demonstrated at the homes of clinic staff. When the Center filed suit in September 1992, a state court judge ordered the protestors not to trespass on Center property, block its entrances, or physically abuse anyone entering or leaving the clinic; the judge specifically noted that the order was not intended to limit protestors from exercising their FIRST AMENDMENT rights.

About six months later, as the protestors violated the court order, the court created a 36-foot buffer zone around the clinic entrances and driveways (including the public sidewalk) within which all anti-abortion speech was banned. It also prohibited protestors from making excessive noise and showing images that could be heard or seen by patients during surgery and recovery. Additionally, the court established a 300-foot zone to maintain a distance between protestors and clinic patients and a 300-foot barrier around the homes of clinic staff.

The Florida Supreme Court unanimously upheld the order, declaring that the state's concern for public safety as well as women's right to abortion outweighed the demonstrators' right to protest against the performance of abortions.

On appeal to the U.S. Supreme Court, although the anti-abortion protestors did not challenge the 300-foot zone in which only invited speech was allowed, they claimed that the rest of the state court order violated their First Amendment rights. They also argued that the court order targeted anti-abortion expression because pro-choice demonstrators were allowed within the buffer zone. The Center contended that the court order promoted a number of interests, including public safety of clinic staff and patients. They further maintained that the regulation was a proper crowd control measure that was unrelated to opinions on abortion.

When the case reached the Court, it directed most of its attention to the constitutionality of the 36-foot buffer zone. The 6-3 ruling, announced by Chief Justice WILLIAM HUBBS REHNQUIST, found that the court order was content-neutral and applied to all persons engaged in clinic protests, regardless of their message. The Court determined that the burden imposed by the order was no greater than necessary to further the government's interest in preserving order and upheld the 36-foot buffer zone around the clinic entrances and driveway to allow access to the clinic and allow street traffic. It found, however, that the restrictions forbidding protestors from showing images were unjustified because they were an unnecessary burden on the protestors' constitutional rights. Similarly, it found the 300-foot zone around the clinic and at staff residences too broad, because it prevented protestors from expressing their views peacefully and exceeded the government's interest in ensuring access to the clinic and preventing intimidation of patients and staff.

For more information: Hagan, Melanie C. "The Freedom of Access to Clinic Entrances Act and the Nuremberg Files Web Site: Is the Site Properly Prohibited or Protected Speech?" *Hastings Law Journal* 51 (2000): 411–444; Hare, Ivan. "Method and Objectivity in Free Speech Adjudication: Lessons from America." *International & Comparative Law Quarterly* 54 (2005): 49–87; Keast, Tiffany. "Injunction Junction: Enjoining Free Speech after *Madsen, Schenck,* and *Hill.*" *American University Journal of Gender, Social Policy & the Law* 12 (2004): 273–307; Zick, Timothy. "Speech and Spatial Tactics." *Texas Law Review* 84 (2006): 581–651.

—Susan Gluck Mezey

Magna Carta

The Magna Carta is an important English legal document that also had a big impact upon the American Constitution.

Magna Carta means "Great Charter" in Latin (the language in which it was originally written) and was granted by King John in 1215 under the duress of a potential civil war. Magna Carta limited certain key powers of the king and was revised several times over the following years. The 1225 version remains today as what many refer to as Magna Carta, because King Edward I of England included it in his 1297 statute rolls, thus concluding the evolution of Magna Carta itself.

King John, a Plantagenet, had come to the throne upon a legitimate but disputed claim. The expensive campaign that he waged to regain his lost interests in Normandy required heavy taxation upon the aristocracy during a time of vexing inflation. King John's decisive defeat at the Battle of Bouvines in 1214 inflamed the already discontented aristocracy. A powerful group of barons directed by Stephen Langdon, archbishop of Canterbury, forced the issue of liberties to be granted by the king. The Articles of the Barons, as it was known, was sealed by King John in a field at Runnymede, England, on June 12, 1215. The formal version of Magna Carta was agreed upon by the barons and the king on June 19, 1215.

Clearly, the significance of Magna Carta far exceeds most of its actual wording. The majority of the document had to do with largely feudal issues benefiting the aristocracy from which little modern constitutional law could be gleaned. After this has been removed, however, what remains in its provisions is nothing short of monumental, ensuring that the king would not be above legal retribution. He would also be required to consult with the barons in important state matters, including taxation. This would ultimately lead to the rise of the British Parliament. For the United States, the beginnings of representation by the people can be traced through our English legal heritage directly to Magna Carta.

Also important to Anglo-American legal history, Magna Carta established several specific requirements upon the courts of the day. These are enumerated in Clauses 17–22. Among them, courts would have to be held in a fixed location, instead of traveling from place to place. Further pertinent jurisdictional issues of the time were addressed. Clause 40 seems somewhat modern and fundamental, though it of course must be taken in historical context. It stated, "To no one will we sell, to no one will we refuse or delay right or justice."

Looking specifically to the United States Constitution (and subsequently to state constitutions), the legacy of Magna Carta is readily apparent. It can be argued that the entire U.S. Constitution belies a philosophy deeply steeped in limiting the powers of government when basic individual liberties are at issue, as seen in Magna Carta. Clearly, these rights are particularly visible in the BILL OF RIGHTS.

Clause 39 of Magna Carta is of great significance to the U.S. Constitution. It actually contained what modern Americans might call a DUE PROCESS clause. It stated that "No free man shall be arrested or imprisoned or disseised or outlawed or exiled or in any way victimized, neither will we attack him or send anyone to attack him, except by the lawful judgment of his peers or by the law of the land." The Fifth Amendment of the U.S. Constitution clearly harkens to this concept with the language "No person shall . . . be deprived of life, liberty, or property, without due process of law."

Further, the FOURTEENTH AMENDMENT applies due process rights to the states and says "No State shall make or enforce any law which shall abridge the privileges or immunities of citizens of the United States; nor shall any State deprive any person of life, liberty, or property, without due process of law."

Also pertaining to the Bill of Rights, though clearly the 13th century had different standards and mores than today's constitutional climate, one can see the beginnings in Clause 20 of Magna Carta the prohibition against CRUEL AND UNUSUAL PUNISHMENT. The U.S. Constitution has such a clause in the Eighth Amendment. Moreover, Clause 21 of Magna Carta shows the beginnings of the right to a jury of our peers, which is presented in the SIXTH AMENDMENT of the U.S. Constitution.

Of further interest, a few clauses remain directly in force today as British law.

Please note: Magna Carta is historically more often and correctly referred to without the article "The" in its name. In other words, "Magna Carta" and not "The Magna Carta" is preferable.

For more information: Blake, Robert, ed. *The English World: History, Character, and People.* New York: Harry N. Abrams, Inc., Publishers, 1982; Lyon, Ann. *Constitutional History of the United Kingdom.* Portland, Oreg.: Cavendish Publishing Limited, 2003.

—Maria Collins Warren

Mann Act

The Mann Act, or White Slave Traffic Act, was a federal statute enacted in 1910 to address the fear of "white slavers" coercing young women living in cities into prostitution. The statute made it a felony to knowingly transport in INTERSTATE COMMERCE or persuade or coerce the interstate travel of "any woman or girl for the purpose of prostitution, debauchery, or for any other immoral purpose" with or without her consent. Conviction could bring a fine up to $5,000 and imprisonment up to five years.

The U.S. Supreme Court upheld the statute's constitutionality in *Hoke v. United States*, 227 U.S. 308 (1913). The next year, in *Wilson v. United States*, 232 U.S. 563 (1914), a commercial prostitution case, the Court held that a person violated the statute when the woman was transported in interstate commerce with an immoral purpose or intent, even though no sexual activity subsequently occurred. Then, in *Caminetti v. United States,* 242 U.S. 470 (1917), the Court extended the statute's reach to non-commercial, consensual activity, because the conduct fell within the meaning of "any other immoral purpose."

The Mann Act was used by U.S. attorneys to prosecute pimps and madams who transported prostitutes across state lines to engage in their profession, and for two other purposes. Blackmailers used the statute to extort money from men for a weekend dalliance, and wives, such as Frank Lloyd Wright's, to extort a favorable divorce settlement. Federal prosecutors also used the statute to selectively prosecute non-commercial sexual activity. *Caminetti* permitted them to obtain convictions by proving that a state line had been crossed, a man had enticed and transported a woman, and he had an immoral purpose at the time of the transportation. The Supreme Court's *United States v. Holte* (1915) decision even allowed them to prosecute the woman for conspiring to arrange her own transportation by agreeing to make the interstate trip.

Men were convicted for crossing state lines with their girl friends and mistresses, as were high-profile defendants: gangsters, political dissidents, or black men consorting with white women. Jack Gebardi, an Al Capone gangster, was prosecuted in 1932, because the government lacked the evidence to charge him with a gang-related crime, but his conviction was reversed on appeal. Charlie Chaplin, the well-known actor and communist sympathizer, was prosecuted in 1944, but the jury acquitted him. In 1960, however, Chuck Berry, a black rock and roll star, was convicted for crossing the state line with a white woman and served a 20-month sentence.

Congress amended the Mann Act in 1986 by replacing "debauchery and any other immoral purpose" with "any sexual activity for which any person can be charged with a crime." The new language severely limited the statute's use to prosecute consensual, non-commercial sexual activity. No generally applicable federal criminal laws pun- ish illegal sexual activity. State prosecutions for illegal sexual activity are unlikely, because most states have repealed their fornication statutes and decriminalized adultery. Still, the Mann Act is applicable to interstate transportation for rape and prostitution.

For more information: Grittner, Frederick K. *White Slavery: Myth, Ideology, and American Law.* New York: Garland Publishing, 1990; Langum, David J. *Crossing Over the Line: Legislating Morality and the Mann Act.* Chicago: University of Chicago Press, 1994.

—William Crawford Green and Martin Gruberg

Marbury v. Madison 5 U.S. 137 (1803)
One of the pinnacle decisions under the tenure of Chief Justice JOHN MARSHALL, *Marbury v. Madison* greatly enhanced the stature of the judiciary by firmly establishing JUDICIAL REVIEW, giving the courts the power to determine whether acts of Congress were constitutional. *Marbury* is perhaps the most important decision ever issued by the Supreme Court, and its impact has been significant in term of augmenting judicial power and establishing the concepts of separation of powers and checks and balances within the American constitutional system.

The case arose amid much political controversy. In the last day President JOHN ADAMS served in office, William Marbury was appointed a justice of the peace in the DISTRICT OF COLUMBIA. However, with such a late term appointment, Adams's Secretary of State John Marshall (who was also Supreme Court chief justice) failed to deliver the commission. William Marbury asked President THOMAS JEFFERSON's Secretary of State JAMES MADISON to deliver the commission. President Jefferson, who was not pleased with the last minute federal judicial appointments, ordered Madison not to deliver the commission, and 23 of the 45 commissions issued on inauguration day were voided. After this decision, Marbury and three other Adams appointees in the same situation filed a writ of mandamus with the Supreme Court requesting that Madison be forced to deliver their commissions.

Chief Justice Marshall and President Jefferson were political opponents, and before the Supreme Court heard the case, President Jefferson threatened to ignore the order of the Court. At this point, the Supreme Court had not been very extensive in exercising its powers. Marshall did not want to endanger the power of the Court by issuing a ruling that the executive branch would not acknowledge.

The Supreme Court issued a unanimous 4-0 decision on February 24, 1803. Focusing on the tensions with Jefferson, Marshall determined that although Marbury and others were entitled to their commissions, the Supreme Court lacked the power to force the commissions to be delivered. William Marbury did not receive his commission, and the Supreme Court limited its power by declaring it did not have the power to force the executive to issue the commission.

However, this portion of the decision did not have the long-term effects of the rest of the opinion. Marshall invalidated the JUDICIARY ACT OF 1789 enacted by Congress because it was found to violate the Constitution. The Judiciary Act of 1789 established the operation and structure of the federal court system. In addition, the Supreme Court was granted ORIGINAL JURISDICTION for writs. Marshall determined this act was a violation of Article III, Section 2 of the Constitution.

In the opinion, Marshall declared, "It is emphatically the province and duty of the judicial department to say what the law is." With this statement, the basis of the exercise of judicial review was established in precedent, and in the future the Supreme Court frequently exercised its power to determine the constitutionality of acts of Congress, the executive branch, and the states.

The lasting legacy of *Marbury v. Madison* extends beyond the facts in the case to establishing the power of judicial review for the courts. After *Marbury*, in COHENS V. VIRGINIA, 19 U.S. 264 (1821), the Court would also assert its judicial review power to examine the constitutionality of state laws. However, the Court would not overturn another congressional statute until DRED SCOTT V. SANDFORD, 60 U.S. 393 (1857). This case invalidated the MISSOURI COMPROMISE and was a major precipitant in launching the United States into the Civil War. After the Civil War, the Supreme and lower federal courts used the power of judicial review in cases such as LOCHNER V. NEW YORK, 198 U.S. 45 (1905), to invalidate many state and federal laws that enacted economic regulation. Since the New Deal of the 1930s, the federal courts have used judicial review to protect individual rights, such as free speech, or strike down discriminatory laws, such as in BROWN V. BOARD OF EDUCATION, 347 U.S. 483 (1954).

Overall, the Supreme Court's assertion of judicial review in *Marbury v. Madison* helped make it a coequal player in the national government. Through the power of judicial review, the federal courts have been able to place checks on the powers of the presidency and Congress, and the judiciary has also developed its own unique constitutional powers distinct from those held by these other two branches.

For more information: Clinton, Robert. *Marbury v. Madison and Judicial Review.* Lawrence: University Press of Kansas, 1989; Graber, Mark, and Michael Perhac, eds. *Marbury versus Madison.* Washington, D.C.: CQ Press, 2002; Kahn, Paul. *The Reign of Law:* Marbury v. Madison *and the Construction of America.* New Haven, Conn.: Yale University Press, 1997; Nelson, William. Marbury v. Madison: *The Origins and Legacy of Judicial Review.* Lawrence: University Press of Kansas, 2000.

—Carol Walker

Marshall, John (1755–1835) *chief justice of the Supreme Court*

John Marshall was chief justice of the U.S. Supreme Court from 1801–35, appointed by President JOHN ADAMS, and is considered the strongest proponent of constitutionally derived rights and the constructor behind methodology used to address American constitutional law. John Marshall is also considered by many the greatest and most important chief justice to ever sit on the

Supreme Court. Marshall read WILLIAM BLACK-STONE's early legal works and the philosophy of JOHN LOCKE, but was taught mostly by his father, who also led him into the Revolutionary War, where he became an officer in some of the most notable battles in the war. Marshall was known to have greatly admired General George Washington, and he penned a book while serving as the deputy judge advocate of the Revolutionary Army. Marshall received only two years of formal education and developed a disdain for political hubris, state isolationism, and ineffective government. Further education for Marshall came in the form of lectures at William and Mary College. Financial pressures limited his tenured political impact in localized politics, but his knowledge of the law and his sharp intellect allowed him to rise in the eyes of several nationalists. He sold real estate and entered other business ventures to afford his public service and, in order to provide for his family, often turned political office down. His service to the country included the posts of secretary of state, U.S. attorney general, minister to France, congressman, member of the Council for the State of Virginia, member of the Virginia House of Delegates, and associate justice on the Supreme Court before taking his place as chief justice. His allies were ALEXANDER HAMILTON, Washington, and Adams, and his championing of the Federalist causes and national unity proved prophetic in his later writings as he battled THOMAS JEFFERSON's allies in the courts.

Interestingly, Marshall brought one case, WARE V. HYLTON (1796), to the Supreme Court and lost after arguing for states' rights. As the chief justice, Marshall pushed for the move by the Court away from individual opinions and toward a consolidated voice for the Court. Two years after taking the helm as chief justice, Marshall led the court in the MARBURY V. MADISON (1803) decision, which fundamentally altered the manner in which Congress could create acts. The JUDICIAL REVIEW of where authority would derive from was a contentious battlefield, as there were voices wishing it to be mostly from the people on an ad hoc basis versus based upon interpretation of a constitutional document.

The *Marbury* decision, amazingly unanimous, set that the Constitution, particularly ARTICLE III, held authority over the JUDICIAL ACT OF 1789. The voiding of the congressional act resulted in a maelstrom of criticism, and the decision was suggested to have created an atmosphere of absolute authority by the Court over constitutional matters and interpretations. Judicial review authority was cited as stemming from this decision in later years.

In *McCulloch v. Maryland* (1819) and *Cohens v. Virginia* (1821), the Court reaffirmed its right to expand the understanding of what the Constitution was meant to be and the limitations of the state courts versus the power of the Supreme Court derived from the Constitution. The NECESSARY AND PROPER CLAUSE (ARTICLE I, Section 8 of the Constitution) established the implied powers concept of CONSTITUTIONAL INTERPRETATION. Individual rights and a faith in the agrarian system of democracy, whereby the people's rights are guaranteed as inherent in the right to own property, a Jeffersonian ideal, followed with the *Fletcher v. Peck* (1810) decision. Drawing from his real estate experiences, Marshall believed it was his duty to stabilize the contractual issues related to land speculation and potential abuse by the devaluing of a state's contractual duties. Despite the fact that the underlying issue would allow for an illegal contract based upon bribery to stand, the MARSHALL COURT went against the state of Georgia to bring a sense of stability to the real estate market and thus protect citizens' rights related to current ownership practices. Thus the branching out of contracts as they related to both public and private understandings was rooted in Article I, Section 10 of the Constitution, but judicial review now was able to protect the greater good of society, deriving support for such through interpretations related to the spirit of the Constitution. Marshall also read and referenced quietly the *FEDERALIST PAPERS*, and often the treatises set out within them for the young nation were the basis of some of his constitutional arguments and within the spirit of his writings.

Thus contract law was born to protect the underlying stability of the system of capitalism, and the protections attributed to the contract clause would stave off state government creep as it related to individual rights. Marshall championed that the people's rights would trump the states' rights and that the protection of those rights was mandated through the Supreme Court. In the ABRAHAM LINCOLN presidency this concept would again be challenged, both directly and indirectly, with the advent of the CIVIL WAR.

In the Court's decision in DARTMOUTH COLLEGE V. WOODWARD (1819), the Court recognized that there would need to be inherent language captured in a contract, implied or directly stated within, that allowed for a significant private dissolution of the charter of that entity. In not allowing the state of New Hampshire to dissolve the private status of Dartmouth College, private education was allowed and businesses were now placed in a stronger position to thwart EMINENT DOMAIN challenges by the state. Marshall furthered the diminishment of the state sovereignty arguments present at the time with the Jeffersonian political approach through the compelling of a separation of states from the affairs of INTERSTATE COMMERCE, as in the GIBBONS V. OGDEN (1824) case, and thus upheld the understood power of the Congress to regulate the states.

In Marshall's later term years, he and the other justices struggled with the question of whether the Court should set the course directly through decision-making or if the de facto attention paid by the Court was enough to keep the Constitution alive. The internal pressure to keep the Court unified weakened some decisions and created some of the furor surrounding the BILL OF RIGHTS in later years with the BARRON V. MAYOR AND CITY COUNCIL OF BALTIMORE (1833) case, which allowed states' rights to trump the federal government.

For more information: Beveridge, Albert J. *The Life of John Marshall.* Atlanta, Ga.: Cherokee Publishing Company, 1998; Hobson, Charles F. *The Great Chief Justice: John Marshall and the Rule of Law.* Lawrence: University Press of Kansas, 1996; Robarge, David Scott. *A Chief Justice's Progress: John Marshall.* Westport, Conn.: Greenwood, 2000; Smith, Jean Edward. *John Marshall: Definer of a Nation.* New York: Holt, 1996.

—Ernest Alexander Gómez

Marshall Court (1801–1835)

JOHN MARSHALL, a leader of the Federalist Party, was a jurist who is considered by many to have shaped American constitutional law and the Supreme Court's power more than any other individual in U.S. history. Under Marshall, the Supreme Court issued many opinions that gave broad power to the national government, as well as giving the Court itself important legal and political powers.

Marshall was the fourth chief justice of the Supreme Court, having previously served in the HOUSE OF REPRESENTATIVES (1799–1800) and as Adams's Secretary of State (June 1800–March 1801). As the longest serving chief justice in the history of the Supreme Court, Marshall served for over three decades, from 1801 until his death in 1835. The Supreme Court under Marshall played a significant role in the development of the American legal system and the role the Supreme Court would play from that period onward in the governing of the country. The Marshall Court was best known for making significant changes to the structure and decision-making processes of the Court, as well as for its support of values such as national supremacy (increasing the powers of the national government in respect to states' powers and legislation, thereby perpetuating a Federalist ideal of centralization of government), economic competition, and judicial power. Throughout his term as chief justice, Marshall was in the minority of the Court's decisions on only seven occasions, although he sat on the court for 1,127 decisions during this period.

Upon taking up his post as chief justice, Marshall made revolutionary changes to the manner in which the Court presented its decisions, sweeping aside the authoring of separate opinions by each justice and adopting the practice of handing down a single decision from the Court (in addition to any dissenting opinions).

Some of the most important cases decided by the Supreme Court during Marshall's term as chief justice were significant in shaping the legal system—shaping the relationship between federal and state levels of government (strengthening the national government and weakening the states)—confirming the supremacy of federal law over state law; taking a more expansive view of the enumerated powers within the Constitution (expanding the powers of Congress); and establishing the authority of the Supreme Court, thereby cementing the independence and influence of the judicial branch in relation to the other branches of government (establishing the doctrine of JUDICIAL REVIEW).

The first important case handled by the Marshall Court was MARBURY V. MADISON, 5 U.S. 137 (1803), which saw the Court invalidating a provision of the JUDICIARY ACT OF 1789 on grounds that it violated the Constitution. *Marbury v. Madison* was significant, as it was the first case where the Court ruled a congressional act as unconstitutional, creating the doctrine of judicial review and expansion of the authority of the Supreme Court. This case revolved around undelivered justice of the peace commissions that were approved by Congress and signed by President JOHN ADAMS during his last hours in office. One of the intended commissions that went undelivered was meant for William Marbury, who applied to the Court for a writ of mandamus to obtain his commission from the new secretary of state (JAMES MADISON). Marshall found he had difficulties with the new government under JEFFERSON—because the Court's prestige was at stake, Marshall found his decision could have a lasting impact on the Supreme Court and his own position as chief justice. The result of the case was that the Constitution defined the Court's ORIGINAL JURISDICTION and that Congress could not change this through legislation. Therefore, the particular provision of the Judiciary Act was invalid, thereby setting precedent for the supremacy of the Constitution over any conflicting law.

Other cases that followed would further solidify the Court's expanding authority, such as *United States v. Peters*, 9 U.S. 115 (1809), MARTIN V. HUNTER'S LESSEE, 14 U.S. 304 (1816), and COHENS V. VIRGINIA, 19 U.S. 264 (1821). In *Martin v. Hunter's Lessee*, the Supreme Court confirmed its position and its right to override a state court's decision. Similarly, the case of *Cohens v. Virginia* confirmed federal jurisdiction over state courts, thereby extending the Supreme Court's authority and jurisdiction in various ways.

Other cases of significance handled by the Supreme Court during Marshall's tenure as chief justice included MCCULLOCH V. MARYLAND, 17 U.S. 316 (1819), and GIBBONS V. OGDEN, 22 U.S. 1 (1824). Both of these cases involved the strengthening of the federal government—more specifically, they dealt with the expansion of congressional powers. For example, in *McCulloch v. Maryland,* the Court found in favor of McCulloch and the federal government, finding the federal government's powers to be supreme over state powers (although the government was limited in its sphere of power). This particular case involved a dispute between the state of Maryland and McCulloch, who, as a cashier of the Baltimore branch of the established Bank of the United States, issued notes in noncompliance with state law. The state of Maryland sued for the taxes it was due, claiming that a sovereign state had concurrent power to tax and that the creation of the Bank of the United States in the first instance was unconstitutional, as it misused the NECESSARY AND PROPER CLAUSE of the Constitution. Another case that expanded governmental sovereignty over state legislation was demonstrated in *Gibbons v. Ogden.* This case provided the federal government with undisputed control over INTERSTATE COMMERCE when the Supreme Court ruled that a charter the state of New York provided to a specific company allowed for the development of a monopoly in the steamboat industry, which the Court ruled as invalid.

Other important cases that undermined and weakened state powers occurred with the Court rulings made in FLETCHER V. PECK, 10 U.S. 87 (1810), DARTMOUTH COLLEGE V. WOODWARD, 17 U.S. 518 (1819), and *Martin v. Mott*, 25 U.S. 19 (1827). *Fletcher v. Peck* is viewed as a significant case as it established the principle and practice of invalidating state laws that conflicted with the Constitution. This allowed for CONSTITUTIONAL INTERPRETATION by the Court and judgment as to whether the state law in question actually conflicted with the text and intentions of the Constitution.

While *Fletcher v. Peck* established the supremacy of the Constitution over state laws, *Dartmouth College v. Woodward* focused on the perceived and actual powers of the state via legislation it has passed and its relationship to the upholding of prior contracts. In this particular case in 1819, the Supreme Court held and established that a college's charter could be construed as a contract, and therefore, state legislation could not impair or alter a college charter (in this case Dartmouth College's charter), as it would then be altering a contract's created obligations as previously entered into by the college. The case was brought to the courts by the trustees of Dartmouth College after the state of New Hampshire passed a law in 1816 making the private college into a public state university and changing its name to Dartmouth University from its given name of Dartmouth College as chartered in 1769 by the English monarch prior to the Revolution.

The last case mentioned as having weakened state powers was *Martin v. Mott*. The Court in this particular case denied a state's right to withhold its militia from service, thus further cementing the weakening of state powers in comparison to government and the Court itself (the judicial branch of government).

The significance of the cases heard by the Court during Marshall's tenure was that they illustrated Marshall's own values and his goals for the Supreme Court while chief justice. As a Federalist supporter and chief justice of the U.S. Supreme Court, Marshall perpetuated the Federalist principle of centralization through development of doctrines supporting the supremacy of government, the Supreme Court as interpreter and arbitrator of arising conflicts with the Constitution, and the weakening of states' powers in decisions that overturned and abolished legislation passed by the states.

For more information: Johnson, Herbert Alan. *The Chief Justiceship of John Marshall, 1801–1835.* Columbia, S.C.: University of South Carolina Press, 1998; Lipkin, Robert Justin. *Constitutional Revolutions: Pragmatism and the Role of Judicial Review in American Constitutionalism.* Durham, N.C.: Duke University Press, 2000; Newmyer, R. Kent. *The Supreme Court under Marshall and Taney.* Arlington Heights, Ill.: Harlan Davidson, 1986; O'Brien, David M. *Storm Center: The Supreme Court in American Politics.* New York: W. W. Norton, 2000.

—Jack Waskey

Marsh v. Alabama 326 U.S. 501 (1946)

In *Marsh v. Alabama*, the Supreme Court ruled that the state of Alabama could not prohibit a citizen from distributing religious literature in a company-owned town. The Court held that the FIRST AMENDMENT rights of the town's citizens outweighed any ownership interests of the corporation.

When this case was brought before the Supreme Court, the town of Chickasaw, Alabama, was owned and operated by Gulf Shipbuilding Corporation. Chickasaw had all the characteristics of a typical American town, except that its governmental functions were managed and performed by employees of Gulf. Marsh, a Jehovah's Witness, was convicted under the state's criminal trespass law for distributing religious literature to residents of the town.

Justice HUGO BLACK wrote on behalf of the majority, which refused to correlate the company's ownership of the town to that of a homeowner and his house. He stated that the town's center shopping district is essentially a PUBLIC FORUM and that "[t]he more an owner, for his advantage, opens up his property for use by the public in general, the more his rights become circumscribed by the statutory and constitutional rights of those who use it." He also noted that people must be well-informed to be good citizens, and distribution of literature is a primary means of keeping people informed.

This case represents one branch of the Supreme Court's "state action" doctrine. Usually, the Court finds otherwise legal private conduct to be unconstitutional because the state is sufficiently implicated with the private party (see *Shelly v. Kraemer*, 334 U.S. 1 [1948]). Here, however, the Court found a violation because the private party was acting as a substitute for the state. In essence, the private party was performing a "public function."

Marsh has been reviewed multiple times since it was decided. The Court originally expanded its ruling to cover distribution of literature in modern shopping malls in *Amalgamated Food Employees Union v. Logan Valley Plaza,* 391 U.S. 308 (1968), but it has since overruled itself (see *Hudgens v. NLRB,* 424 U.S. 507 [1976]). Today, *Marsh* only applies to company-owned town scenarios.

For more information: Askin, Frank. "Free Speech, Private Space, and the Constitution." *Camden Rutgers Law Journal* 29 (Summer 1998): 947–961.

—Dylan R. Kytola

Martin v. Hunter's Lessee 14 U.S. 304 (1816)
In *Martin v. Hunter's Lessee,* the U.S. Supreme Court ruled that it had jurisdiction over the decisions of state appellate courts in cases involving federal law or the Constitution. The case was a result of a tug-of-war between the U.S. Supreme Court (with Justice JOSEPH STORY at the helm) and the Virginia Court of Appeals (led by Virginia jurist Spencer Roane). At issue in *Martin* was Section 25 of the Judiciary Act that granted the Supreme Court jurisdiction to hear appeals from state courts in cases where a federal law or the Constitution was involved.

The complex history of *Martin* began in the early 1780s as a dispute over a title to land in Virginia and turned into a dispute over state sovereignty and nationalism. Specifically, the Virginia Supreme Court (also known as the Virginia Court of Appeals) had approved the seizing of land that was covered under a federal TREATY. In *Fairfax's Devisee v. Hunter's Lessee,* 7 Cranch (U.S.) 602 (1813), the U.S. Supreme Court disagreed and ordered the Virginia court to reverse its decision. In *Hunter v. Martin, Devisee of Fairfax,* 4 Munford 1 (1814), the Virginia court strongly objected on the grounds that the states were sovereign and, therefore, not subject to federal judicial control.

The Virginia court's refusal to obey the Court's mandate resulted in a writ of error to the Supreme Court (the *Martin* case). Virginia argued that the appellate power of the U.S. Supreme Court did not extend to its court and that Section 25 of the Judiciary Act violated the Constitution. Virginia argued that it was sovereign and, therefore, had every right to interpret the Constitution and not have its judgments reviewed and overturned by the U.S. Supreme Court.

Justice Joseph Story rejected Virginia's contention that the U.S. Supreme Court had no appellate power over state court decisions. The Constitution was ordained and established not by the states, but by "the people of the United States." As such, the people were free to invest in the national government all the powers deemed necessary and proper to limit the exercise of federal power and to prohibit the exercise of state powers that were incompatible with the Union. The states were subordinate to the nation and the people. Therefore, the people had the right to prohibit the states from exercising powers that violated the Constitution. As for judicial power, Story called it "the voice of the whole American people, solemnly declared in establishing one great department which was, in many respects, national, and in all, supreme" (328). Hence, if "it is the duty of Congress to vest the judicial power of the United States, it is a duty to vest the *whole judicial power*" (330). Congress's decision to vest the Supreme Court with the power to hear appeals from state courts was consistent with the national demand for uniformity and necessary to maintaining the supremacy of the Constitution.

The decision in *Martin* set off a political firestorm in the nation and provided the impetus for states to begin a full-fledged attack on the constitutionality of Section 25.

For more information: Hobson, Charles F. "John Marshall and the Fairfax Litigation: The Background of *Martin v. Hunter's Lessee.*" *Journal of Supreme Court History* 2 (1996): 36–50; Miller, F. Thorton. "John Marshall Versus Spencer Roane: A Reevaluation of *Martin v. Hunter's Lessee.*" *The Virginia Magazine of History and Biography* 96

(1988): 297–314; Warren, Charles. "Legislative and Judicial Attacks on the Supreme Court of the United States: A History of the Twenty-Fifth Section of the Judiciary Act." *American Law Review* 47 (1913): 1–47 and 161–189.

—Randa Issa

Masson v. New Yorker Magazine 501 U.S. 496 (1991)

In this decision, the Supreme Court made important clarifications to the scope of FIRST AMENDMENT protection for allegedly defamatory publications about public figures.

In the seminal case of *New York Times Co. v. Sullivan*, 376 U.S. 254 (1964), the Supreme Court established that "actual malice" was necessary to constitutionally hold a speaker liable for DEFAMATION of a public official (a doctrine later extended to cover public figures in general). "Actual malice" is a legal term of art: It refers not to the speaker's wicked state of mind or vicious motivations, but to the speaker's knowledge. Ordinarily, a plaintiff in a defamation case need only prove that false, damaging statements were made: The fact that the speaker did not know the statements were false is irrelevant. If the plaintiff is a public figure, however, he or she must also show that the defendant knew his or her statements were false or acted with reckless disregard of their truth or falsity. That knowledge or recklessness comprises the actual malice doctrine.

Over time, the lower courts developed a variety of extensions to the *New York Times* actual malice doctrine. One of the more prominent extensions was the "incremental harm" doctrine. In many cases, a publisher would create a publication with a substantial amount of nonactionable content that was detrimental to the plaintiff's reputation on its own, but with several actionable statements in addition. The incremental harm doctrine was developed to establish that a defendant would not be held liable if the additional actionable statements did very little harm to the plaintiff's reputation beyond the harm already inflicted by the nonactionable portions of the publication. For example, if a published

article truthfully reported that the plaintiff was a convicted bank robber, tax cheat, and mugger, an additional false accusation of shoplifting, even though made with actual malice, would not be sufficient to give rise to liability. The defendant's reputation would already be ruined by the true accounts of his criminality.

Masson ringingly rejected the incremental harm doctrine. In the words of the Court, "Here, we reject any suggestion that the incremental harm doctrine is compelled as a matter of First Amendment protection for speech."

The incremental harm doctrine had, like many extensions to the Supreme Court's First Amendment jurisprudence on defamation law, been initially developed by the Second Circuit. The doctrine had its most well-known exposition in *Herbert v. Lando*, 781 F.2d 298 (2nd Cir. 1996). (Because of its jurisdiction over New York, the hub of the U.S. publishing industry, many seminal defamation cases can be found in the Second Circuit.) Later, in *Church of Scientology Intnl. v. Behar*, 238 F.3d 168 (2nd Cir. 2001), the Second Circuit appears to have reestablished a similar doctrine, under the name of the "subsidiary meaning doctrine," notwithstanding the Supreme Court's explicit repudiation in *Masson* of incremental harm.

According to the Second Circuit, the subsidiary meaning doctrine establishes that when the defendant's "overall view" of the plaintiff rests on a series of nonactionable statements, additional otherwise actionable statements that bolster that overall view are not made with actual malice. The Second Circuit thus distinguished the subsidiary meaning doctrine from the incremental harm doctrine by asserting that subsidiary meaning is merely a test for the presence of actual malice, rather than a separate First Amendment doctrine on its own behalf like incremental harm. However, the Second Circuit's defense is somewhat implausible, since the substantive import of the subsidiary meaning appears to be identical to that of incremental harm. Moreover, it is difficult to see what the subsidiary meaning doctrine has to do with a finding of actual malice. It is unclear whether the new doctrine will survive Supreme Court scrutiny.

Masson also importantly clarified the scope of defamation law as it applies to quotations: Words in a publication, attributed to the plaintiff, outside of quotation marks are protected from defamation liability if they represent a "rational interpretation" of the plaintiff's actual words. However, words in quotation marks are protected only if they are substantially true.

For more information: Forde, Kathy Roberts. "How *Masson v. New Yorker* Has Shaped the Legal Landscape of Narrative Journalism." *Common Law & Policy* 10 (2005): 101–133.

—Paul Gowder

McCleskey v. Kemp 481 U.S. 279 (1987)

In *McCleskey v. Kemp,* a sharply divided Supreme Court held, in a 5–4 decision, that statistical evidence of race-based disparities in Georgia's system of CAPITAL PUNISHMENT did not violate either the CRUEL AND UNUSUAL PUNISHMENT clause of the Eighth Amendment or the EQUAL PROTECTION clause of the FOURTEENTH AMENDMENT. Instead, the *McCleskey* majority required particularized evidence of intentional racial discrimination, in the individual case, to satisfy constitutional claims under either the Eighth or Fourteenth Amendments. The significance of this decision was to insulate states from race-based challenges to their capital punishment policies and practices where those challenges were based upon the statistical analyses of aggregate data. *McCleskey* would demand instead that criminal defendants provide evidence that *their* arrest, conviction, or sentencing was racially discriminatory.

In 1978, Warren McCleskey, an African-American man, was convicted in a Fulton County, Georgia, trial court on charges that he participated in the robbery of a local furniture store and in the murder of a white police officer during the course of that robbery. McCleskey was sentenced to life imprisonment for the armed robbery by a jury comprised of 11 white jurors and one black juror; he received the death penalty for his involvement in the murder of the police officer.

Subsequent to the Georgia Supreme Court's affirmation of his conviction and sentence, McCleskey's lawyers filed a petition for HABEAS CORPUS review in the United States District Court. Arguing that the Georgia system of capital punishment was unconstitutionally tainted by racial discrimination, McCleskey's lawyers contended that racially disparate capital sentencing outcomes were causally, and unconstitutionally, related to both the race of the victim and the race of the defendant. Both the United States District Court and the Circuit Court of Appeals rejected McCleskey's arguments.

In 1986, the United States Supreme Court granted McCleskey's request for review. In support of his claim of systemic racial discrimination in Georgia's criminal justice system, McCleskey's attorneys relied heavily upon the Baldus Study—what was then considered to be a landmark social scientific study of the impact of race in the Georgia criminal justice system. Relying upon the findings of Professor Baldus and his colleagues, McCleskey's attorneys argued that, in capital cases, a criminal defendant was statistically more likely to be convicted, to receive the death penalty, and to be executed if the defendant was black and the victim was white. Although the district court questioned the validity and relevance of the Baldus Study, the Court of Appeals for the Eleventh Circuit assumed the validity of the study itself but found the statistics insufficient to support either Fourteenth or Eighth Amendment claims.

Although his biographer would observe that Justice LEWIS POWELL later came to regret the decision in this case, in his opinion for the Court, Powell rejected McCleskey's arguments and affirmed the lower court's decision. Instead, Justice Powell followed the Eleventh Circuit's lead and began his analysis by first accepting the validity and basic conclusions of the Baldus Study. Nonetheless, Powell concluded that statistical evidence of racially disparate treatment of whites and blacks in Georgia's criminal justice system was not sufficient to prove that McCleskey's conviction and sentencing were themselves tainted by racial discrimination. Justices WILLIAM J.

BRENNAN, JR., Blackmun and JOHN PAUL STEVENS wrote sharply worded dissents, contending that the Court had elided the reality of racial discrimination in the Georgia criminal justice system, compelling evidence of which having been provided in the Baldus Study.

Warren McCleskey was executed on September 25, 1991, in the Georgia electric chair—a method of execution the Georgia Supreme Court would, 10 years later, hold to be unconstitutional.

For more information: Baldus, David. "Comparative Review of Death Sentences: An Empirical Study of the Georgia Experience." *Journal of Criminal Law & Criminology* 74 (1983): 661–753; Baldus, David. "Monitoring and Evaluating Contemporary Death Sentencing Systems: Lessons from Georgia." *University of California Davis Law Review* 18 (1985): 1,375–1,407; Banner, Stuart. *The Death Penalty: An American History.* Cambridge, Mass.: Harvard University Press, 2003; Jeffries, John C. Jr. *Justice Lewis F. Powell: A Biography.* New York: Fordham University Press, 2001.

—William Rose

McConnell v. FEC 540 U.S. 93 (2003)

In *McConnell v. FEC*, the Supreme Court reviewed the constitutionality of the Bipartisan Campaign Finance Reform Act of 2002 (BCRA). In a strongly divided opinion, the Supreme Court upheld key provisions of BCRA and ruled that several other provisions were unconstitutional, holding that they violated the FIRST AMENDMENT's freedom of speech protections.

Congress passed BCRA (also known as McCain-Feingold) in 2002 in response to concerns that campaign contributions were being made in exchange for political favors. Further, supporters of BCRA believed that BCRA was necessary to prevent donors from using contributions to political parties and other groups to get around already existing CAMPAIGN FINANCE restrictions on candidates.

Opponents of campaign finance reform believed that restrictions on campaign contributions interfered with citizens' constitutional right to participate in the electoral process and violated their First Amendment free speech rights. Opponents argued that by limiting campaign contributions, BCRA limited the citizens' ability to fund and participate in political communication, thereby impinging those citizens' ability to speak on such matters.

The stated purpose of BCRA was to eliminate the potential for corruption, or the appearance of corruption, that comes with large unregulated political contributions. To this end, BCRA attempted to limit the influence of money that was not subject to the limits and reporting requirements of the Federal Election Campaign Act (FECA) and to ensure that all communications designed to influence elections are financed through money subject to FECA's limitations and disclosure requirements.

In a lengthy opinion, the Supreme Court ruled that many of the provisions of BCRA were constitutional. The Court also concluded, however, that some provisions were not constitutional.

The Supreme Court ruled that many of the provisions of BCRA were constitutional because the government's interest in "preventing the actual or apparent corruption of federal candidates and officeholders" was sufficiently important to justify the restrictions. Further, these provisions were also necessary to prevent circumvention of the rules. These provisions include banning national party committees, federal candidates and officeholders, and state and local party committees from soliciting, receiving, directing, or spending any funds that were not subject to FECA's limits and reporting requirements to finance "federal election activity."

Other provisions of BCRA that the Court upheld based on this reasoning include prohibitions on national, state, and local committees' solicitation of contributions for or making donations to certain tax-exempt organizations that engaged in election activity. (The Court did clarify, however, that party committees could make donations to these tax-exempt organizations if the funds donated were subject to FECA's limits and reporting requirements.) A more narrow restriction prevents state and local candidates and officeholders from raising or spending funds unregulated by FECA to pay for public communications that promote or attack federal candidates.

BCRA placed disclosure requirements on "electioneering communications" and prohibited unions or corporations from financing electioneering communications. Before BCRA, only communications that contained words of "express advocacy," i.e., "vote for," "vote against," "elect," "defeat," were subject to any limits. BCRA barred corporations or unions from funding any broadcast, cable, or satellite communication mentioning a clearly identifiable federal candidate within 30 days of a primary or 60 days of a general election that is directed at that candidate's electorate. This definition attempted to capture the spirit of the express advocacy restrictions, though opponents argued that it covered a far more broad category of communications and would unreasonably restrict the right of citizens to engage in lobbying. The Supreme Court upheld the electioneering communications provisions, reasoning that the definition of "electioneering communication" would better capture those ads that really were aimed at influencing an election, although active litigation continues over this provision.

The Supreme Court ruled that two key provisions of BCRA were unconstitutional. First, the Court found that a provision of BCRA requiring parties to choose between making coordinated expenditures with a candidate in a general election and making "independent expenditures" in support of candidates was unconstitutional. The Supreme Court has repeatedly invalidated restrictions on parties' expenditures and again held that independent expenditures by parties were entitled to First Amendment protection.

Second, the Supreme Court ruled that a minor's First Amendment rights extend to campaign contributions, and therefore, BCRA's prohibition on political contributions from minors was unconstitutional. Proponents of this provision argued that contributions from minors were a mere cover for larger contributions from their parents. The Supreme Court ruled that so long as a contribution really was from a minor, it was constitutionally protected.

Subsequently in *FEDERAL ELECTION COMMISSION v. WISCONSIN RIGHT TO LIFE, INC.,* U.S. ___ (2007), the United States Supreme Court ruled that Section 203 of the Bipartisan Campaign Reform Act of 2002 was an unconstitutional violation of the First Amendment as applied to certain forms of political speech.

For more information: Malbin, Michael, ed. *Life after Reform: When the Bipartisan Campaign Reform Act Meets Politics.* Lanham, Md.: Rowman and Littlefield, 2003; Urofsky, Melvin I. *Money and Free Speech: Campaign Finance Reform and the Courts,* Lawrence: University of Kansas Press, 2005.

—Karen Blackistone

McCreary County, Kentucky v. American Civil Liberties Union 545 U.S. 844 (2005)

In a 5-4 decision, the Supreme Court in *McCreary County v. ACLU* declared TEN COMMANDMENTS displays on the walls of two Kentucky county courthouses to be unconstitutional. This occurred on the same day that the Court, also in a 5-4 decision, upheld a Ten Commandments monument in Texas (*VAN ORDEN V. PERRY*).

The Kentucky counties had originally posted framed copies of an abbreviated King James version of the Commandments. Following a complaint by the ACLU, they added eight other documents, all with religious references, such as the national motto, "In God we trust," and the "endowed by their creator" reference in the DECLARATION OF INDEPENDENCE. Following a court INJUNCTION, they replaced that display with a new set of nine documents, including a more complete version of the Ten Commandments. Other items ranged from the MAGNA CARTA to a picture of "Lady Justice." Collectively titled "The Foundations of American Law and Government Display," the documents all had statements about their legal and historical significance. The Ten Commandments were credited with providing the "moral background for the

Declaration of Independence and the foundation of our legal tradition."

Using the standard that government actions must have a secular purpose, Justice DAVID H. SOUTER, writing for the majority, chided the counties that "the secular purpose required has to be genuine, not a sham, and not merely secondary to a religious objective." He also rejected the proposal to ignore the previous displays: "The Counties' position just bucks common sense: reasonable observers have reasonable memories." Souter then provided a detailed textual and contextual analysis of the three displays as well as the Ten Commandments display contested two decades earlier in *Stone v. Graham*, 449 U.S. 39 (1980), also from Kentucky. Particularly since more explicitly religious language in the Commandments was included in the third display, Souter concluded, incredulously, "No reasonable observer could swallow the claim that the Counties had cast off the objectives so impermissible in the earlier displays." He was also baffled by the third display's mix of documents purporting to educate about American government. For example, the Magna Carta was included, but not the Constitution.

Souter then turned his attention to the dissenting opinion in which Justice ANTONIN GREGORY SCALIA called for a return to the original intent of the ESTABLISHMENT CLAUSE. He reminded Scalia that it had meant different things to different Founders but clearly had the still relevant goal of keeping government free from religious divisiveness. Scalia, in equally pointed tones, rebuked Souter for reaching a new level of "false assumptions" by insisting on a neutrality that did not fit with American history. He reminded the majority that even the Court had deviated occasionally for what he labeled "self preservation." Scalia also used his space to attack Justice JOHN PAUL STEVENS's dissent in *Van Orden* for Stevens's expansive and flexible interpretation of the establishment clause.

In light of the extremely polarized tone of both sides in this case, it is noteworthy that Justice STEPHEN G. BREYER, part of the *McCreary* majority, joined the *McCreary* dissenters to form the *Van Orden* voting majority.

For more information: Boston, Rob. "Decalogue Divide." *Church and State* July/August 2005, 7–9; Hester, Joseph P. *The Ten Commandments: A Handbook of Religious, Legal, and Social Issues.* Jefferson, N.C.: McFarland and Co., 2003; Irons, Peter. *God on Trial: Dispatches from America's Religious Battlefields.* New York: Viking, 2007.

—Jane G. Rainey

McCulloch v. Maryland 17 U.S. 316 (1819)

In *McCULLOCH V. MARYLAND*, the Supreme Court upheld the power of Congress to create a national bank under the NECESSARY AND PROPER CLAUSE of the Constitution, and it also ruled that the state of Maryland had no authority to tax the bank. This opinion by JOHN MARSHALL ranks as one of the most important cases in American constitutional history.

The underlying facts of the case began to develop from what were believed to be unfair competitive advantages enjoyed by the Bank of the United States, which had been chartered by Congress in 1816. The financial practices of the Bank of the United States often disallowed market and pricing opportunities. Maryland believed this to be an egregious abuse of national power by the Bank of the United States, and in an approach to restrict banking operations within the state and specifically the Bank of the United States, the state of Maryland imposed a tax on the bank. The Bank of the United States refused to accept that this tariff was valid and refused to pay. In doing so, their sovereign rights were called into question, and the rights of the states and their abilities to impact the federal government would be challenged for years to come. The case then moved to court. Maryland argued that the federal government and especially the Congress did not have the authority to establish a bank, because that power was not delegated to either of them in the Constitution.

The Supreme Court's unanimous decision upheld the authority of Congress to establish a national bank, and thus Maryland lost its challenge. Chief Justice John Marshall's opinion does in some manner concede that the Constitution does not explicitly grant Congress the right to establish a national bank, but noted that the action by Congress does in spirit fall within the necessary and proper clause (ARTICLE I, Section 8, Clause 18) of the Constitution. This necessary and proper clause gives Congress the authority to do whatever is required so as to exercise its enumerated powers, and so the Court recognized the existence of implied powers within the Constitution. According to Marshall:

> This clause is nothing more than a declaration of the authority of congress to make laws, to execute the powers expressly granted to it, and the other departments of the government. But the laws which they are authorized to make, are to be such as are necessary and proper for this purpose. No terms could be found in the language, more absolutely excluding a general and unlimited discretion than these. It is not "necessary or proper," but "necessary and proper." The means used must have both these qualities. It must be, not merely convenient—fit—adapted—proper, to the accomplishment of the end in view; it must likewise be necessary for the accomplishment of that end. Many means may be proper, which are not necessary; because the end may be attained without them.

Marshall also crushed Maryland's attempt at taxation of the U.S. government bank. Marshall offered that, within the issue as it relates to the authority of Maryland to tax the national bank, the Court understood that "the power to tax involves the power to destroy. . . . If the states may tax one instrument [of the federal government] they may tax any and every other instrument . . . the mail . . . the mint . . . patent rights . . . judicial process." The Court stated also that this was not believed to be the intention of the American people. Also, the Court believed that the intention of the people and framers of the Constitution did not design the government to be dependent upon the respective states. With this statement, Chief Justice Marshall again defined himself to be a staunch supporter of the Constitution, further establishing within the law the rights of Congress and thereby limiting the rights of the states in action against the federal government.

Overall, *McCulloch v. Maryland* offered an important statement about the power of the national and state governments, and it defined how the Constitution would be interpreted in this regard.

For more information: Killenbeck, Mark Robert. McCulloch v. Maryland: *Securing a Nation.* Lawrence: University Press of Kansas, 2006; White, G. Edward. *The Marshall Court and Cultural Change, 1815–1835.* New York: Oxford University Press, 1991.

—Ernest Gomez

Megan's Law

Megan's Law is a term used to denote a number of state laws in the United States that require law enforcement authorities to identify sex offenders to the public. States must implement some form of sex- and child-offender registration and community-notification legislation in order to receive 10 percent of anticrime funds as well as to protect children from sex offenders.

Since 1996, every state has enacted legislation requiring sex offenders to register with law enforcement and have their personal information available to the community, often for life. Registration must take place upon release from custody. Slightly over half of all states require registration and community notification for juveniles adjudicated delinquent for sex offenses. The first Megan's Law was passed in New Jersey in 1994 after the rape and murder of Megan Kanka by Jesse Timmendequas. Timmendequas was a convicted sex offender who had lived across the street from Megan. Timmendequas had twice been convicted of sexual offenses against children and raped and murdered his neighbor, seven-year-old Megan Kanka. Megan's mother claimed that her daughter would still be alive if she had known about her neighbor's history of sexual offenses. Megan's mother and thousands of supporters implored the New Jersey legislature to help citizens identify sexual offenders in their neighborhoods.

The basic intention of Megan's Law is to give parents and guardians the ability to protect their children by making them aware of the presence of convicted sex offenders in their neighborhood. The individual who murdered Megan Kanka was a convicted sex offender whose background the Kanka family claims not to have been aware of. Supporters of Megan's Law maintain that the law is imperative because of the inability of sex offenders to be "cured." Additionally, supporters contend that sex offenders have extremely high recidivism rates, so passing the legislation might combat sexual abuse recidivism. Supporters oppose using the law for the purpose of harassing or violating the rights of sex offenders, even if only to prevent the law from being repealed on the grounds that it may facilitate such illegal behavior.

Megan's Law is not such an unusual law, since information about convicted criminals has always been public information. In fact, sex offender registration laws had existed in five states since 1986 and in almost half of the states by 1993. Most of these laws limited the release of registration information to law enforcement agencies to facilitate the location of subjects when new crimes occurred. One prominent federal law stood out as a means to combat sexual abuse recidivism. In 1994, Congress passed the Jacob Wetterling Act, which required states to create registries of sexually violent offenders, including offenders who targeted children. These registries were required to annually track offenders' residences for a minimum of 10 years after their release from custody. Recidivistic offenders were lifetime registers. Due to several high-profile rape and murder cases involving children in the 1990s, sex registration laws were again reviewed. The state of Washington lobbied the legislature for community notification as a citizen's tool for protecting children and was successful by 1990. Many states followed suit, with Megan's Law becoming the formal policy. Megan's Law basically enhanced the Wetterling Act by requiring community notification of sex offenders.

Megan's Law simply makes it easier for parents and guardians to access information about sex offenders in lieu of tiresome research. The intent of Megan's Law is not to punish sex offenders but to facilitate in the quest for public safety, particularly where children are concerned. Megan's Law provides an easy way for schools, churches, day-care centers, and volunteer youth organizations to screen applicants for positions. Parents and guardians can also check babysitters or live-in domestics against a registry database. On May 17, 1996, President Bill Clinton signed into law the first federal version of Megan's Law. According to this version, every state in the country is required by law to tell a community when a dangerous sexual predator is a resident. The law was written by Congressman Dick Zimmer and has been amended several times since the original bill was passed. Different states have different procedures for making the required disclosures.

Despite the successful passage of Megan's Law, it is not without criticism. For example, not all state agencies agree that juveniles should be treated as adults under Megan's Law. The argument is that states have failed to consider the distinct characteristics of juvenile sex offending, such as exceptionally low recidivism rates and culpability complications arising from age-of-consent laws. Additionally, while most felony convictions infringe, in part, a released individual's rights and opportunities, no other type of offense results in such pervasive post-release requirements as do sexual offenses, particularly those perpetrated against minors. As a result, there have been at least two important constitutional challenges to sex offender registry laws.

In the first case, SMITH V. DOE, 538 U.S. 84 (2002), the Court heard arguments as to whether Alaska's sex offender registration and notification law and the implementation of community notification through the Internet imposes punishment in violation of the EX POST FACTO CLAUSE of the U.S. Constitution. The argument on behalf of the United States was that Megan's law was a remedial measure designed to protect the public, not to punish offenders. The argument against registering on the Internet was that the posting of sex offenders' criminal history and personal information on the Internet available to the general public constitutes a form of punishment that violates the constitutional rights of those offenders who committed their crimes prior to the enactment of the law.

The second notable challenge in 2002, *Connecticut Department of Public Safety v. Doe*, 538 U.S. 1 (2002), involved the DUE PROCESS clause. Connecticut's "Megan's Law" requires persons convicted of sexual offenses to register with the Department of Public Safety (DPS) upon their release into the community and requires DPS to post a sex offender registry containing registrants' names, addresses, photographs, and descriptions on an Internet Web site and to make the registry available to the public in certain state offices. One convicted sex offender claimed that the law violates the FOURTEENTH AMENDMENT's due process clause. The district court and Second Circuit Court concluded that such disclosure both deprived registered sex offenders of a "liberty interest" and violated the due process clause because officials did not afford registrants a predeprivation hearing to determine their level of dangerousness. This ruling was reversed on the grounds that mere injury to reputation does not constitute the deprivation of liberty interest. Additionally, even if that offender has been deprived of a liberty interest, due process does not entitle him to a hearing to establish a fact—that he is not currently dangerous—that is not material under the statute.

For more information: Garfinkle, Elizabeth. "Coming of Age in America: The Misapplication of Sex-Offender Registration and Community-Notification Laws to Juveniles." *California Law Review* 91 (2003): 163–206.

—Kim MacInnes

Metro Broadcasting, Inc. v. FCC 497 U.S. 547 (1990)

In *Metro Broadcasting, Inc. v. FCC*, the U.S. Supreme Court upheld the Federal Communications Commission's use of race as a factor in awarding certain types of broadcast licenses to minority-owned companies in order to increase diversity in on-air programming.

The 5-4 decision, written by Justice WILLIAM J. BRENNAN, JR., reflected the deep divisions in the Court over the issue of AFFIRMATIVE ACTION, a rift that spanned 25 years.

One aspect of the rift was reflected in a short-lived portion of the *Metro Broadcasting* decision, that affirmative action programs implemented by the federal government should be afforded more deference under the Constitution than similar programs of state and local governments. This portion of the ruling held that federal affirmative action should be measured under an intermediate constitutional standard—whether there was an important governmental objective and whether the means of achieving it was substantially related to the goal—instead of the stricter standard applied to state and local affirmative action programs. But five years later, in *ADARAND CONSTRUCTORS, INC. v. PENA*, 515 U.S. 200 (1995), the Supreme Court overruled this portion of *Metro Broadcasting* and said that any use of race by a government at any level is inherently suspect and must be subjected to the strictest standard of review in court.

The case had its origins in 1978, when the FCC announced that it would consider minority ownership as one of many factors when comparing competing applicants for radio or television broadcast licenses. The FCC also said that licensees facing loss of their broadcast outlet in what is known as a "distress sale" may assign their licenses to minority-owned broadcast companies. Both of these new policies were designed to increase minority participation in broadcasting.

Metro Broadcasting challenged the FCC's award of a license to a minority-owned company, Rainbow Broadcasting, for a new UHF television station in Orlando, Florida. The Rainbow license was upheld by the U.S. Court of Appeals for the DISTRICT OF COLUMBIA Circuit, and Metro appealed to the Supreme Court. In a related case, Shurberg Broadcasting objected to a distress sale of a Hartford, Connecticut, license to a minority-owned company, Astroline Communications Co. The D.C. Circuit struck down the FCC distress sale policy, and Astroline appealed to the Supreme Court, where the two appeals were combined.

Justice Brennan concluded that "the diversity of views and information on the airwaves serves important FIRST AMENDMENT values" and said the Court should defer to the FCC's view that "there is an empirical nexus between minority ownership and broadcasting diversity." He also concluded that Congress had endorsed FCC efforts to promote minority ownership.

Justice SANDRA DAY O'CONNOR wrote the main dissent, joined by Chief Justice WILLIAM HUBBS REHNQUIST and Justices ANTONIN GREGORY SCALIA and ANTHONY M. KENNEDY. Accusing the majority of departing from established principles, O'Connor said, "This departure marks a renewed toleration of racial classifications and a repudiation of our recent affirmation that the Constitution's EQUAL PROTECTION guarantees extend equally to all citizens."

It was O'Connor who wrote the subsequent *Adarand* decision. That ruling, focused on federal highway contracts, overruled *Metro's* use of a lower standard to judge federal affirmative action programs. But the *Adarand* decision had no occasion to reconsider the goal of broadcast diversity as a rationale to justify the use of racial classifications.

For more information: Baynes, Leonard M. "Life after Adarand: What Happened to the Metro Broadcasting Diversity Rationale for Affirmative Action in Telecommunications Ownership?" *University of Michigan Journal of Law Reform* 33 (2000): 87–132.

—Stephen Wermiel

Miami Herald v. Tornillo 418 U.S. 241 (1974)

In *Miami Herald Publ'g. Co. v. Tornillo,* the Supreme Court ruled that newspapers cannot be required to publish materials by political candidates responding to published criticisms. The decision enhanced the doctrine under the freedom of expression provisions of the FIRST AMENDMENT that government generally may not require individuals or entities to say or print particular matters.

The case arose out of a state statute in Florida that granted political candidates a right to equal space in newspapers to reply to criticisms and attacks on their records. A candidate for local office in Florida sought to activate the "right reply" law after he was criticized by a newspaper editorial.

The Florida measure was intended to allow political candidates who are harmed or defamed by published matter to respond or reply to the publication. It paralleled a doctrine that had been established by the Federal Communications Commission (FCC), which regulates the broadcast industry. Under FCC's "FAIRNESS DOCTRINE," broadcast media, which are subject to government licensure, were required for many years to provide an opportunity for those who were attacked in the media to respond. The Equal Time Law, a federal law, also requires broadcasters to give parity to candidates for political offices during election campaigns.

The candidate's claim was upheld by the state court, but the ruling was reversed by the U.S. Supreme Court, which held that the law violated the freedom of press and speech provision of the First Amendment by forcing publication of undesired speech. The Court struck down the statute on several grounds: (1) because it "exacts a penalty on the basis of the content of a newspaper"; (2) it encourages newspapers to "avoid controversy"; and (3) it results in compelled "intrusion into the function of editors."

While the case involved only the "right of reply" for newspapers, its impact is much broader. The effect of the ruling prohibits government from requiring anyone—traditional media, electronic communications like bloggers, or others—to publish material that responds to criticisms. The *Tornillo* doctrine does not proscribe DEFAMATION claims, but limits remedies for claims to damages, rather than requiring the publishers of defamatory materials to furnish the subject of the defamation the opportunity to reply.

For more information: Bezanson, Randall P. *How Free Can the Press Be?* Champaign: University of Illinois Press, 2003; Schwartz, Bernard. *A History of the Supreme Court.* New York: Oxford University Press, 1993.

—Marshall Tanick

military and the Constitution

The military or armed forces are subject to numerous constitutional limitations, raising issues regarding which branches of the national government have control over them.

Having just been through a major war, the framers of the Constitution were skeptical of standing armies. Thus, the SECOND AMENDMENT discusses the importance of a "well regulated Militia," while the THIRD AMENDMENT makes it illegal to quarter soldiers in civilian homes during peacetime. Despite this, the Framers vested considerable war-making powers in the hands of the Congress (including the power to declare war, raise and support armies, and maintain a navy) and the president (who is the COMMANDER IN CHIEF of the army and navy).

At the same time, the framers were unclear about the Supreme Court's power to review military acts. ALEXANDER HAMILTON, in *Federalist* 78, spoke of a natural presumption favoring JUDICIAL REVIEW but in other places suggested that issues of war and peace were beyond the judiciary's scope. The Supreme Court appeared to adopt this view in *MARBURY v. MADISON,* 5 U.S. (1 Cranch) 137 (1803), when it refused to rule on "political questions"—a category that specifically included military matters. Chief Justice JOHN MARSHALL reasoned that such questions were best discussed by the political branches (Congress and the president).

Although the antebellum period saw some constitutional debate surrounding the War of 1812 and the Mexican-American War, it was the Civil War that put the constitutional arrangements governing military power to the test. President ABRAHAM LINCOLN suspended HABEAS CORPUS, blockaded Southern ports, silenced dissenting voices, and established military tribunals. During this time, the Court deferred to Lincoln—usually over the dissent of Chief Justice ROGER TANEY. When Taney argued that only Congress could suspend the writ of habeas corpus, Lincoln responded that it was meaningless to enforce all the laws if the government fell to pieces.

Reconstruction saw a more assertive Court. Facing an unpopular president (Andrew Johnson), the Supreme Court, in *EX PARTE MILLIGAN,* 71 U.S. (4 Wall.) 2 (1866), granted habeas corpus to an Indiana citizen sentenced to death by a military commission for conspiracy. In reaching this decision, the Court explained that unlike during the Civil War, "public safety is assured." However, this newfound assertiveness had limits. The Supreme Court did not challenge the basis of military governments in Southern states and, in *EX PARTE McCARDLE,* 74 (7 Wall.) 505 (1868), agreed that Congress could strip the Court's jurisdiction to hear a case involving criticism of Mississippi's military government.

Although the First World War saw a number of prosecutions brought against critics of conscription, it did not generate a constitutional crisis. World War II, however, was another matter. In *Ex parte Quirin,* 317 U.S. 1 (1942), the Supreme Court upheld the power of the president to establish military commissions to try "enemy combatants"—in this case Nazi saboteurs. The main conflict, however, centered on President Franklin Roosevelt's order deporting Japanese Americans

This 1941 photograph shows President Franklin D. Roosevelt asking Congress to declare war on Japan the day after the Japanese attack on Pearl Harbor. *(Library of Congress)*

living on the West Coast of the United States to internment camps. Although the deportation order was issued in early 1942—shortly after the attack on Pearl Harbor—the Supreme Court did not rule on its constitutionality until 1944. In KOREMATSU V. UNITED STATES, 325 U.S. 219 (1944), the Supreme Court upheld the order, noting that "the properly constituted military authorities" feared an invasion. Later, however, in *Ex parte Endo,* 323 U.S. 283 (1944), issued the day after Roosevelt announced the closing of the camps, the Court held that an individual could challenge her deportation to a camp. Significantly, by this time, the administration of the internment camps had been turned over to a civilian organization—a factor that may have made the Court more willing to rule against the military.

More recently, the Supreme Court has, in a series of cases related to the war on terror, limited the state's power to detain enemy combatants. In *HAMDI V. RUMSFELD,* 542 U.S. 507 (2004), the Court held that the government cannot indefinitely detain an enemy combatant. In *Rasul v. Rumsfeld,* 542 U.S. 466 (2004), the Court held that civilian courts can hear habeas challenges from Guantánamo Bay prisoners. Finally, *Hamdan v. Rumsfeld,* 126 S.Ct. 2749 (2006)—a highly technical ruling—saw the Court invalidate President George W. Bush's plan to use military commissions to try enemy combatants as going beyond the power he had been given by Congress.

While these cases appear to break from the pattern of judicial deference on military matters, they can also be understood as responses to a weak president at a time (2004–06) when the fear of terrorism had begun to dissipate. Furthermore, none of the decisions have (so far) struck a mortal blow against the Bush administration's detention of enemy combatants. (For example, after *Hamdan,* President Bush was able to go back and gain congressional authorization for military commissions.)

Questions of the constitutional position of the military also arise in the wide variety of cases that force the Court to review some aspect of military life. Here, as well, courts treat the military with great deference. In part, this is because the military, like other professional groups, possesses specialized knowledge. But while courts are occasionally willing to challenge the norms of doctors, lawyers, and accountants, they tend to treat the military as a separate society with its own rules.

Deference to the military often trumps other constitutional rights. For example, in *Goldman v. Weinberger,* 475 U.S. 503 (1986), the Court held that the FIRST AMENDMENT right to free expression did not cover an air force doctor who sought to wear a yarmulke while on active duty. The similar argument was used in *ROSTKER V. GOLDBERG,* 453 U.S. 57 (1981), which held that male-only draft registration did not violate the constitution.

At the same time, deference to the military does not always lead to a rollback of CIVIL RIGHTS. In *GRUTTER V. BOLLINGER,* 539 U.S. 306 (2005), the armed forces submitted an amicus brief which stated that the ROTC and service academies would be unable, without race-conscious admissions standards, to field a military that was highly qualified and racially diverse. Justice SANDRA DAY O'CONNOR quoted from this brief repeatedly in her plurality opinion upholding AFFIRMATIVE ACTION in higher education.

For more information: Lichtman, Steven B. "The Justices and the Generals: A Critical Examination of the U.S. Supreme Court's Tradition of Deference to the Military, 1918–2004." *Maryland Law Review* 65 (2006): 907–949; Neely, Mark E., Jr. *The Fate of Liberty: Abraham Lincoln and Civil Liberties.* Oxford: Oxford University Press, 1992; O'Connor, John F. "Statistics and the Military Deference Doctrine: A Response to Professor Lichtman." *Maryland Law Review* 66 (2007): 668–706; Pilon, Roger. "The War Powers in Brief: On the Irreducible Politics of the Matter." *Cardozo Public Law, Policy and Ethics Journal* 2 (2003) 49–58; Pushaw, Robert J. "The 'Enemy Combatant' Cases in Historical Context: The Inevitability of Pragmatic Judicial Review." *Notre Dame Law Review* 82 (2007): 1,005–1,083; Vagts, Detlev F. "Military Commissions: A Concise History." *American Journal of International Law* 101 (2007): 35–48.

—Robert A. Kahn

Miller-El v. Cockrell 537 U.S. 322 (2003)

In *Miller-El v. Cockrell,* the Supreme Court held that the Fifth Circuit Court of Appeals improperly denied petitioner Thomas Joe Miller-El's Certificate of Appealability by failing to properly review the district court's decision to deny petitioner's HABEAS CORPUS petition for relief based on the Dallas county prosecutor's discriminatory use of peremptory strikes to remove African Americans from Miller-El's state capital murder trial.

In this case, the petitioner, Miller-El, sought relief from a 1986 Texas state court capital murder conviction through a habeas corpus petition based on a violation of his EQUAL PROTECTION rights. Miller-El's petition was based on his claim that prosecutors had used 10 of 11 peremptory strikes to eliminate African Americans from the jury hearing Miller-El's case in a purposeful and discriminatory manner.

At the state trial court level, Miller-El had asked the judge to strike the jury due to the prosecutor's improper and discriminatory use of peremptory strikes. The trial court denied Miller-El's request, and subsequently, he was convicted by the jury of capital murder. Miller-El filed both direct appeals and habeas relief before the Texas state courts. During the time period when Miller-El filed his state court appeals, the U.S. Supreme Court, in BATSON V. KENTUCKY, 476 U.S. 79, 106 S.Ct. 1712, 90 L.Ed.2d 69, created a new standard for analyzing equal protection claims. Under *Batson,* the Supreme Court established a three-step process for evaluating claims that prosecutors had exercised PEREMPTORY CHALLENGES in violation of a defendant's equal protection. Under the new three-step process: (1) the defendant must show with prima facie evidence that the peremptory challenges had been exercised on the basis of race; (2) if the defendant succeeds with step one, then the prosecution must offer a "race-neutral basis" for striking jurors; and (3) the trial court must determine if the defendant has shown purposeful discrimination.

After failing at the state court level, Miller-El filed a habeas petition with the federal district court raising a *Batson* claim. The federal court denied his petition in deference to the state court decision. The Fifth Circuit Court of Appeals subsequently denied a Certificate of Appealability to Miller-El, required before that court can take control of the case.

In its decision, the Supreme Court found that Miller-El's case was entitled to review by the Fifth Circuit Court of Appeal, because he had presented overwhelming evidence that the prosecution had improperly exercised peremptory strikes against potential African-American jurors. Under the *Batson* standard, the Supreme Court found that Miller-El had convincingly established that peremptory strikes used by the prosecution in his state trial were exercised in a discriminatory manner. Specifically, Miller-El showed that prosecutors had exercised peremptory strikes and removed 91 percent of the eligible African-American jurors and only removed 13 percent of other, non-black jurors. Also, under *Batson,* the Court found that the prosecution did not provide a credible race-neutral basis for striking African-American jurors. Miller-El also presented evidence showing that the prosecutor asked jurors different questions regarding CAPITAL PUNISHMENT and minimum sentences during voir dire, depending on their race. Miller-El also showed that one of the prosecutors in his case had access to a Dallas County policy to strike minorities from juries.

Justice CLARENCE THOMAS was the lone dissent in this case. In his separate opinion, Thomas claimed that petitioner had not shown by clear and convincing evidence that the prosecution's striking African Americans from the jury was done due to race.

On remand to the Fifth Circuit Court of Appeals, this court again ruled against Miller-El on the merits of his *Batson* claim that prosecutors had exercised peremptory strikes in a discriminatory manner. The Supreme Court heard on certiorari Miller-El's subsequent appeal of his case in *Miller-El v. Dretke,* 545 U.S. 231 (2005), not on the question on whether the court of appeals had improperly failed to issue a Certificate of Appealability, but this time on the direct issue of discrimination. In this case, the Supreme Court reversed the Fifth Circuit's decision.

The two Miller-El decisions were part of a group of cases in which the Supreme Court expressed dissatisfaction with the decisions of the Fifth Circuit Court of Appeals and Texas district courts that approved of death penalty convictions in light of prosecutorial misconduct.

For more information: Johnstone, Mattie, and Joshua M. Zachariah. "Peremptory Challenges and Racial Discrimination: The Effects of *Miller-El v. Cockrell.*" *Georgetown Journal of Legal Ethics* 17 (Summer 2004): 863–886.

—Lydia Brashear Tiede

Miller v. California 413 U.S. 15 (1973)

In *Miller v. California*, the Supreme Court, in a 5-4 decision, stipulated three legal tests for determining if material was considered obscene. First, material is obscene, according to the Court, if the work, taken in its entirety, appeals to the prurient interest in sex. In other words, if the material is intended for the sole purpose of arousing a distasteful interest in sexual activity, then the material is considered obscene. Second, if the work depicts in a "patently offensive way, sexual conduct specifically defined by the applicable state law," then it is obscene. Third, the work is obscene if, taken in its entirety, it lacks any "serious literary, artistic, political, or scientific value." The significance of this case was that it was seen as an answer to a previous case, *ROTH V. UNITED STATES*, 354 U.S. 476 (1957), a case that set the "average person" OBSCENITY standard. In the Roth case, Justice WILLIAM J. BRENNAN, JR., noted the standard for obscenity as "whether to the average person, applying contemporary community standards, the dominant theme of the material taken as a whole appeals to prurient interests."

Marvin Miller, the appellant in this case, had been arrested, tried, and convicted pursuant to California Penal Code Section 311.2(a) for distributing obscene material. Miller sent through the mail an advertisement for the sale of adult books that depicted men and women engaging in sexual activity. Five of these brochures ended up at a restaurant located in Newport Beach, California, where the manager and his mother opened the material and subsequently made a complaint to local law enforcement.

Chief Justice WARREN BURGER delivered the opinion of the Court. He was joined by Justices White, Blackmun, LEWIS POWELL, and WILLIAM HUBBS REHNQUIST (Justices WILLIAM O. DOUGLAS, Brennan, Stewart, and Marshall dissented). In addition to setting the three tests discussed above, the Court noted that it was "not our function to propose regulatory schemes for the sates. That must await their concrete legislative efforts. It is possible, however, to give a few plain examples of what a state statute could define for regulation." They then proceed to provide examples of lewd sexual conduct that the Court considered to be obscene. In addition, the Court noted that the "FIRST AMENDMENT protects works which, taken as a whole, have serious literary, artistic, political, or scientific value, regardless of whether the government or a majority of the people approve of these ideas the works represent." Basically, the protection of speech and press is done in order to bring about free and open discourse in the marketplace of ideas. The publication of hard-core sexual activity for nothing more than commercial gain for the vendor or just for the sake of depicting hard-core sexual activity is a different matter and may not be protected by the First Amendment to the Constitution of the United States of America.

After the decision was rendered by the Court, law enforcement agencies saw this as an opportunity to close various pornographic establishments. However, they soon learned that the *Miller* decision did not provide them with carte blanche to pursue even those people who displayed "four-letter" words. The Court, as previously stipulated, held that only hard-core pornography lay outside the purview of the First Amendment.

For more information: Farber, Daniel A., William N. Eskridge, Jr., and Philip P. Frickey. *Cases and Materials on Constitutional Law: Themes for the Constitution's Third Century.* St. Paul, Minn.: Thompson/West, 1993; Wayne, Stephen J., G. Calvin Mackenzie, and Richard L. Cole. *Conflict and*

Consensus in American Politics. Belmont, Calif.: Thomson Wadsworth, 2007.

—Dan Krejci

Miller v. Johnson 515 U.S. 900 (1995)

In *Miller v. Johnson*, the Supreme Court ruled that the use of race in the apportionment of congressional districts violated the FOURTEENTH AMENDMENT, even when done to comply with the 1965 Voting Rights Act.

Between 1980 and 1990, only one of Georgia's 10 congressional districts was majority black. However, according to the 1990 decennial census, Georgia's black population of 27 percent clearly would have entitled the state to an additional congressional seat. This observation prompted Georgia's legislature to create a majority-black district through the formation of an 11th congressional district. The new district, which extended from Atlanta to the Atlantic Ocean, was in Georgia's most recent congressional districting plan that included three majority-black districts redrawn after the Department of Justice refused to "preclear" two earlier plans. Voters in the new 6,784.2 square mile Eleventh District—which included metropolitan black neighborhoods and the poor black population of coastal areas 260 miles away—challenged the new district on the grounds that it was a "racial gerrymander," which violates the EQUAL PROTECTION CLAUSE as interpreted in *Reno v. Shaw* (1993). The district court agreed, holding that evidence of the state legislature's purpose, as well as the new district's irregular borders, show that race was the overriding and predominant factor in the redistricting plan. The district court reasoned that, while compliance with the Voting Rights Act of 1965 is a compelling state interest, Georgia's redistricting plan was not narrowly tailored to meet that interest.

On certiorari to the Supreme Court, the Court was confronted with the question of whether a racially gerrymandered congressional redistricting order made pursuant to Department of Justice's preclearance scheme required by the VOTING RIGHTS ACT was a violation of the equal protection clause. In a 5-4 decision, the Supreme Court held that a bizarre shape is not a requirement for a "racial gerrymander" claim, and that all plaintiffs must prove is that race was a "predominant factor" in the drawing of the district lines. Once this is shown, STRICT SCRUTINY is triggered to determine whether the redistricting plan is narrowly tailored to achieve the state's interest. In *Shaw*, decided two years before, the Supreme Court articulated the principles that govern the drawing of congressional districts. Specifically, the Court held (a) that laws that explicitly distinguish between individuals on racial grounds fall within the equal protection clause's prohibition against race-based decision-making; (b) that this prohibition extends to laws "neutral on their face" but unexplainable on grounds other than race; and (c) that redistricting legislation that is so bizarre on its face that it is unexplainable on grounds other than race demands the same strict scrutiny given to other state laws that classify citizens by race.

Writing for a split Court in affirming and remanding the district court's decision, Justice ANTHONY M. KENNEDY maintained that, while in some instances a reapportionment plan may be so highly irregular and bizarre in shape that it rationally cannot be understood as anything other than an effort to segregate voters based on race, applying *Shaw* requires strict scrutiny whenever race is the "overriding, predominant force" in redistricting. Kennedy reasoned that "just as the state may not, absent extraordinary justification, segregate citizens on the basis of race in its public parks, buses, golf courses, beaches, and schools," it may not "separate its citizens into different voting districts on the basis of race" alone. As the Court saw it, because Georgia's 11th congressional district had been drawn primarily for racial reasons, the conclusion that the redistricting decision was not motivated solely by race can be overcome only if the state legislature had a compelling interest. For example, if the drawing of three majority-black districts had really been necessary to redress past discrimination, the requisite compelling interest to do so would have been found. But the only interest found, the Court continued, was Georgia's interest to satisfy the Department of Justice's rules, one of which implicitly required the state to engage in presumptively unconstitutional race-based districting to bring the Voting Rights Act (once upheld as a proper exercise of Congress's FIFTEENTH AMENDMENT authority) into tension with the Fourteenth Amendment equal protection.

In a concurring opinion, which supplied the vital fifth vote for the 5-4 majority to strike down Georgia's districting plan, Justice SANDRA DAY O'CONNOR suggested that she would have made it harder for plaintiffs to win challenges predicated on strict scrutiny. With the burden shifted to the plaintiffs challenging a districting plan to show that race was a "predominant factor" in the drawing of the district lines, she observed that the standard for those challenging race-conscious districts was a "demanding one," since plaintiffs must show that the state "relied on race in substantial disregard of customary and traditional districting practices." Thus, under Justice O'Connor's scheme, only "extreme instances of gerrymandering" would be subjected to strict scrutiny. In a cogent dissent, Justice Ginsburg argued, however, that the majority was unduly expanding *Shaw*. She objected to the use of strict scrutiny as a linchpin whenever race was a "predominant factor." She argued that such a use would open the door to federal litigation over the legitimacy of any districting plans that even slightly took account of race as in AFFIRMATIVE ACTION cases. She sees legislation enacted for the purpose of protecting minorities as fundamentally different from and less needful of strict scrutiny than actions taken to advance the interests of the white majority. White voters in Georgia, she argued, do not lack the means to exert strong pressure on their state legislators. In the minority view, O'Connor's majority decision raised more issues than they resolved in *Shaw*, which continues in the instant case. The perceived danger of *Shaw* and *Miller* is their potential to open new cause to reverse what for many so far are considered as the "great gains" for blacks and Hispanics resulting from the Voting Rights Act of 1965.

In summary, the Court held in *Miller v. Johnson* that Georgia's congressional redistricting plan violates the equal protection clause and that, while it is not expected that state legislators should ignore race in their decision to redraw congressional district lines, they may not, absent a compelling interest, be motivated solely by race in their decision. Justice Kennedy delivered the opinion of the Court, in which Chief Justice WILLIAM HUBBS REHNQUIST, Associate Justices O'Connor, ANTONIN GREGORY SCALIA, and CLARENCE THOMAS joined, with O'Connor filing a separate concurring opinion. Justice JOHN PAUL STEVENS filed a dissenting opinion separately. Justice Ginsburg also filed a dissenting opinion, in which Justice STEPHEN G. BREYER joined and in which Justice DAVID H. SOUTER joined with an excerpt in part III-B.

For more information: Kousser, J. Morgan. *Colorblind Injustice: Minority Voting Rights and the Undoing of the Second Reconstruction*. Chapel Hill: University of North Carolina Press, 1999; Ryden, David K., *The U.S. Supreme Court and the Electoral Process*. Washington, D.C.: Georgetown University Press, 2002.

—Marc G. Pufong

Millikin v. Bradley 418 U.S. 717 (1974)

In *Millikin v. Bradley,* 418 U.S. 717 (1974), the Supreme Court ruled that court-ordered busing programs aimed at DESEGREGATION could not include adjacent school districts that had no history of racial discrimination. Interdistrict remedies to eliminate segregated schools are acceptable only if the districts involved have committed constitutional violations by taking actions intended to perpetuate segregation. A district must be shown to be the perpetrator of a constitutional violation in order to be included in a court-ordered remedy.

Three years earlier, the Supreme Court approved the practice of court-ordered busing in order to achieve racial balance in public schools (SWANN V. CHARLOTTE-MECKLENBURG BOARD OF EDUCATION, 402 U.S. 1 [1971]). The Court said that race-conscious remedies were appropriate when governmental entities had previously taken actions to promote racial segregation. This intent to segregate, labeled de jure segregation, violated the Constitution, and the students involved were entitled to equitable relief. Thus, in order to rectify this violation, lower federal courts enjoyed equitable powers that included the use of race-conscious techniques such as busing.

A suit was brought in Michigan against Governor William G. Millikin, charging that official actions by state and local officials had perpetuated racial segregation in the public schools of Detroit. For example, busing had been used to take African-American children to predominately black schools, even when white schools were closer. The federal court overseeing the desegregation effort concluded that any efforts to desegregate the schools within Detroit itself would make "the Detroit system more identifiably Black . . . thereby increasing the flights of whites from the city and the system." The result would be a predominately black school district surrounded by overwhelmingly white suburban districts. Therefore, the district court concluded, the remedy for desegregation must include 53 of the surrounding suburban school districts. Both white and black students would be bused across various district lines in order to achieve racially balanced schools.

By a 5-4 vote, the Supreme Court rejected this interdistrict remedy, arguing that the constitutional violation had occurred only within the Detroit school system. Chief Justice WARREN BURGER, writing for the majority, maintained "that the scope of the remedy is determined by the nature and extent of the constitutional violation." An interdistrict remedy would be appropriate, he wrote, if it were shown that officials in several districts engaged in racially discriminatory acts that resulted in interdistrict segregation. However, "without an interdistrict violation and interdistrict effect, there is no constitutional wrong calling for an interdistrict remedy." In this case, there was neither evidence of constitutional violations by the 53 districts surrounding Detroit nor evidence of an interdistrict violation, so an interdistrict remedy was unsupportable. Furthermore, the majority insisted that "the constitutional right of the Negro respondents residing in Detroit is to attend a unitary school system in that district." There is not a constitutional right to attend a school district with any specific racial balance, said Chief

Justice Burger. Finally, the majority saw the interdistrict remedy as impracticable, causing massive logistical problems and forcing the district court to become a de facto school superintendent.

The four justices in dissent protested that there was nothing sacred in the boundaries of school districts. "Under Michigan law 'a school district is an agency of the State government.'" School district lines were malleable boundaries under control of the state. The relevant actor here, wrote Justice Thurgood Marshall, was the state of Michigan. There was abundant evidence that the state legislature had encouraged and perpetuated the segregation of Detroit schools through the selection of school sites, restrictions on busing, and prohibiting the implementation of the desegregation plan designed by the Detroit School Board. Justice Marshall argued, "Racial discrimination by the school district, an agency of the State, is therefore racial discrimination by the State itself, forbidden by the FOURTEENTH AMENDMENT." The state of Michigan could create new districts or consolidate old ones as it chose; therefore there was no reason to limit remedies along district boundaries.

As a result of the *Millikin* decision, interdistrict desegregation remedies were limited to areas in which past de jure segregation could be demonstrated in all of the school districts involved.

For more information: Clotfelter, Charles. *After Brown: The Rise and Retreat of School Desegregation.* Princeton, N.J.: Princeton University Press, 2004; Orfield, Gary, Susan E. Eaton, and the Harvard Project on Desegregation. *Dismantling Segregation: The Quiet Reversal of* Brown v. Board of Education. New York: New Press, 1996; Stave, Sondra Astor. *Achieving Racial Balance: Case Studies of Contemporary School Desegregation.* Westport, Conn.: Greenwood Press, 1995.

—Gwyneth I. Williams

Minnesota v. Dickerson 508 U.S. 366 (1993)

In *Minnesota v. Dickerson,* the U.S. Supreme Court held that, although police may seize contraband they detect through the sense of touch during a protective patdown of a suspect for weapons, in this case the seizure was unconstitutional because the police ascertained the incriminating nature of the object only by going beyond the permissible scope of the patdown.

After leaving a known "crack house," Dickerson was stopped by two officers who conducted a protective patdown search of his outer clothing. The officer found no weapons, but during the course of this search an officer felt a small lump through the outer material of Dickerson's jacket pocket. Although he knew the object was not a weapon, he was not able to ascertain the nature of the object until he further manipulated it through the material. Suspecting then that the object was crack cocaine, the officer reached into the pocket and retrieved a small amount of the drug. After Dickerson attempted unsuccessfully to have the evidence excluded from the case, he was tried and convicted of possession of a controlled substance.

On appeal, the U.S. Supreme Court observed that a warrantless search, such as the one in this case, is presumptively invalid unless it fits into a recognized exception. One such exception is established in TERRY V. OHIO, 392 U.S. 1 (1968), where the Court held that a police officer may (1) stop and briefly detain a person if the officer has reasonable suspicion that he was engaging or about to engage in criminal activity and (2) conduct a protective patdown search of the suspect for weapons if the officer has reasonable suspicion that he is armed and dangerous. The Court made it clear that this patdown is for weapons, not for evidence.

Another exception is the PLAIN VIEW rule, which permits police to seize any contraband they observe during the course of a lawful search so long as it can be identified as contraband from the permissible scope of the search. Using this rule as an analogy, the Court held that contraband detected through the sense of touch in the course of a patdown can likewise be seized without a warrant. The Court reasoned that, as with the plain view rule, the seizure of contraband detected through plain touch or feel constitutes no intrusion into the suspect's PRIVACY beyond the intrusion already permitted by *Terry* in the patdown, and requiring the officer in this situation to obtain a search warrant from a judicial official would not be practical. The Court made it clear, however, that the sensory information that forms the basis of probable cause—the belief necessary to justify searching for and seizing the contraband—must be obtained within the permissible scope of the patdown.

Having concluded that a warrantless seizure of contraband was permissible based on probable cause acquired through touch or feel during the course of a patdown, the Court proceeded to apply the doctrine to the facts of Dickerson's case. The officer was within the scope of the patdown for weapons when he felt the lump through the outer material of Dickerson's jacket, but at that point the nature of the object was not readily apparent. The incriminating nature of the object became apparent only after the officer manipulated it through the material, but that manipulation in a pocket that the officer knew contained no weapon was beyond the scope of the patdown permitted under *Terry*. Inasmuch as this further search was invalid, the seizure was unconstitutional and the evidence found was, therefore, inadmissible under the EXCLUSIONARY RULE.

For more information: LaFave, Wayne R., Jerold H. Israel, and Nancy J. King. *Criminal Procedure.* 4th ed. St. Paul, Minn.: Thomson/West, 2004; MacIntosh, Susanne M. "Fourth Amendment: The Plain Touch Exception to the Warrant Requirement." *Northwestern School of Law Journal of Criminal Law & Criminology* 84 (1994): 743–768.

—Steven B. Dow

Minor v. Happersett 88 U.S. 162 (1874)

In *Minor v. Happersett,* the Supreme Court determined that women were citizens under the Constitution of the United States, but that even as citizens, the PRIVILEGES AND IMMUNITIES clause of the FOURTEENTH AMENDMENT did not grant them the RIGHT TO VOTE. The decision in *Minor* repudiated the attempt of the women's suffrage movement to secure women's right to vote through judicial interpretation of Section 1 of the

Fourteenth Amendment, and it reaffirmed the Court's narrow construction of the privileges and immunities clause in the *Slaughter-House Cases,* 83 U.S. 36 (1873).

Congress passed and the states ratified the Fourteenth Amendment in 1868. Section 1 of the Fourteenth Amendment stated in relevant part: "No State shall make or enforce any law which shall abridge the privileges or immunities of citizens of the United States." On the basis of this broad language, women, led by Francis and Virginia Minor, claimed a constitutional right to vote. Minor contended that the clause did not limit the privileges or immunities to men, and since the Fourteenth Amendment made African Americans citizens of the United States, it surely made women citizens as well.

Chief Justice Waite, writing for a unanimous Supreme Court, rejected both arguments. Addressing the citizenship claim, the Court held that women did not need the Fourteenth Amendment to give them the status of citizens. Instead, women, as part of the membership body that associated to form the new nation, were citizens of the United States at the adoption of the Constitution. The Court cited, as additional support for its view that women were always citizens, the fact that federal statutes allowed alien women to naturalize as citizens, that women were able to sue or be sued in courts under the diversity-of-citizenship clause of ARTICLE THREE OF THE U.S. CONSTITUTION, and that women were allowed to settle public land.

Addressing the voting claim, the Court held that the Fourteenth Amendment's privileges and immunities clause did not expand the privileges and immunities of citizens beyond those contained in the original Constitution. Looking to the history of the thirteen original colonies, the Court determined that the right to vote was not one of the privileges or immunities that citizens were entitled to in the original Constitution. None of the original colonies granted all citizens the vote, and only the state of New Jersey granted women the vote at the time of the adoption of the Constitution. The Court also supported its holding that the privileges-and-immunities clause

did not create a broader right to vote for citizens, and particularly women, by looking to the penalty provision of Section 2 of the Fourteenth Amendment, which reduced representation by the number of "male" voters denied the vote, and the FIFTEENTH AMENDMENT, passed one year after the Fourteenth Amendment, which prohibited the denial of the vote on account of race, color, or condition of servitude. If the privileges-and-immunities clause was intended to extend the vote to all citizens, then, the Court reasoned, the Fifteenth Amendment would have been unnecessary.

It would be another 44 years after the Court's holding in *Minor* before women secured the right to vote with the passage and ratification of the NINETEENTH AMENDMENT. The narrow construction of the privileges-and-immunities clause first elaborated by the Court in cases such as *Minor* has continued to the present.

For more information: Siegel, Reva B. "She the People: The Nineteenth Amendment, Sex Equality, Federalism, and the Family," *Harvard Law Review* 115 (2002): 947–1,046; Winkler, Adam. "A Revolution Too Soon: Woman Suffragists and the 'Living Constitution,'" *New York University Law Review* 76 (2001): 1,456–1,526.

—Bertrall Ross

Miranda v. Arizona 384 U.S. 436 (1966)

In *Miranda v. Arizona,* 384 U.S. 436 (1966), the Supreme Court ruled 5 to 4 that, when an individual is subjected to custodial interrogation, the statements he or she makes cannot be used against him or her unless the prosecution demonstrates the defendant was aware of the RIGHT AGAINST SELF-INCRIMINATION. These rights have become known as "Miranda rights," of which there are four: (1) the defendant has the RIGHT TO REMAIN SILENT; (2) anything the defendant says can be used against him or her; (3) the defendant has the right to an attorney; and (4) if the defendant cannot afford an attorney, one will be provided. In the Court's analysis, these rights are derived from the Fifth Amendment, which states, in part, that no person "shall be compelled in any criminal case to be a witness against himself."

Miranda is a compilation of four cases. Each involved a defendant who, during custodial interrogation, i.e., questioning by law enforcement after one's liberty is circumscribed in some way, was questioned and admitted the crime without access to counsel. At the trial court level, each defendant was convicted. These appeals followed, with the Supreme Court hearing them together.

The foundation of the majority opinion's analysis, written by Chief Justice Warren, is an assessment of the nature of police interrogations. Studies, cases, and manuals on interrogation are cited to describe an environment of psychological isolation and manipulation and occasional physical abuse to facilitate a confession; however, while psychological manipulation is criticized by the opinion, nothing in the opinion proscribes its use. This finding has been called "noteworthy."

The environment created by these coercive techniques is then compared to the custodial environment of the cases before the Court. The Court stated that while the confessions of the four defendants may have been admissible under previous Fifth Amendment jurisprudence, the Court now interprets the Fifth Amendment differently, and confessions such as these no longer pass constitutional muster.

For a confession to be admissible, the Court outlines what must occur prior to a custodial interrogation. First, the individual must be informed of his right to remain silent. The Court mandates that this must be an express warning, calling this an "absolute prerequisite" and saying it "will not pause to inquire in individual cases whether the defendant was aware of his rights without a warning being given."

Second, the individual must be told that "anything said can and will be used against" him or her. This is necessary to make the defendant aware of the privilege and to show the defendant the consequences of disregarding the warning in the adversarial system.

Third, the individual must be told that he or she has the right to consult with an attorney. This is "to assure that the individual's right to choose

between silence and speech remains unfettered throughout the interrogation process." This right also militates against police coercion and ensures the accuracy of the defendant's statement. The defendant may waive this right, but it is difficult. For instance, silence is not considered waiver. If the state argues waiver in its prosecution, the state has burden of proof.

Fourth, the RIGHT TO COUNSEL exists, notwithstanding the defendant's financial ability to pay. The defendant must be told that if he or she cannot afford a lawyer, one will be appointed. The Court states that it is the poor who may be in most need of counsel.

After the warnings have been given, the Court says the procedure is clear. If the defendant wants to remain silent, the questioning must stop. If the defendant desires an attorney, the questioning must stop until one is present. The burden is placed on the government to show that any statement obtained without an attorney was obtained voluntarily, though it goes on to say that nothing in the opinion should be construed to state that all confessions are inadmissible. The Court wants any admissions to be made voluntarily, and they define voluntary as being free from the coercive effects of custodial interrogation.

Though the procedure may have been clear to Chief Justice Warren, what constituted the procedure was less so to those ruling on future cases. Questions arose over the terms "custodial interrogation" and "knowing and intelligent waiver." For example, one may be in "custodial interrogation" outside the confines of a police station, as in *Mathias v. United States*. In this case, the defendant was questioned in the state prison, where he was an inmate, regarding a crime unrelated to the crime for which he was then serving a sentence; however, in *Oregon v. Mathiason*, the Court held that one may not be in "custodial interrogation" where the accused is questioned in a police station, whether or not he or she was "invited," presented himself of his own volition, or was able to leave after questioning. Regarding "knowing and intelligent waiver," while the language of the opinion seemed to demand an express waiver of rights before a statement could be obtained from the defendant, the Court later held in *North Carolina v. Butler:* "An express written or oral statement of waiver of the right to remain silent or of the right to counsel . . . is not inevitably either necessary or sufficient to establish waiver."

The opinion devotes space to addressing whether the Court has achieved the proper balance between the rights of the accused and the rights of the victim and society to have the assailant brought to justice. The Court asserted it had achieved the proper balance because government cannot demand respect for the law if it is a law breaker; the FBI had already generally adhered to the rules set forth in *Miranda* in its dealing with suspects, so other law enforcement agencies should be able to do so as well; and in other common law countries, such as Scotland and India, the accused are afforded similar rights.

The dissents take issue with these reasons. Justice Clark's dissent argues that the law enforcement duties the FBI performs are substantially different from what the state authorities perform, and the laws affording rights to the accused in Scotland and India are counterbalanced by prosecutorial advantages not present in the United States. The dissents also argue that the cases should have been decided on different constitutional grounds. Justice Clark argues that the DUE PROCESS clauses of the Fifth and FOURTEENTH AMENDMENTs are better suited to determine whether a confession was voluntary. This was the test used to determine the admissibility of statements made by the accused prior to *Miranda.* It was called the "totality of the circumstances" test, where the trier of fact, often the jury, would assess the voluntariness of the statements made by the accused.

Justice JOHN MARSHALL HARLAN II argues in dissent that the previous precedents do not support the rights enumerated in *Miranda.* He argues that the majority opinion is not balanced, but tips too far toward the accused. In doing this, it does not defend against the police brutality criticized by the majority, but instead "negate[s] all pressures, to reinforce the nervous or ignorant suspect, and ultimately to discourage any confession at all." More important, Justice Harlan criticizes the majority's Fifth Amendment rea-

soning, calling it a "trompe l'oeil," or something that deceives the eye. Finally, he reasons that the Court's rationale is drawn from SIXTH AMENDMENT precedents dealing with the right to counsel, which should not weigh on Fifth Amendment cases such as *Miranda.*

Justice White's dissent adds that, prior to this ruling, there was nothing "inherently wrong" with the police's getting information on the crime from the accused himself, while the "not so subtle overtone of the opinion" is that, now, it is. Additionally, he posits, "In some unknown number of cases the Court's rule will return a killer, a rapist or other criminal to the streets . . . to repeat his crime whenever it pleases him." This results in a net societal loss.

The impact of *Miranda* is debatable. Some authors posit that the worst fears of the dissenters were unfounded. Others state that the effect is mitigated by the use of certain police tactics, such as having officers reading the Miranda rights off cards in ways that minimize its impact. Ultimately, it is difficult to get an accurate assessment of the impact due to the lack of reliable empirical data and the differing interpretations one can make based on the data. What is known is that *Miranda* has been and continues to be the subject of litigation.

For more information: LaFave, Wayne R., Jerold H. Israel, and Nancy J. King. *Criminal Procedure.* 4th ed. St. Paul, Minn.: Thomson/West, 2004; Stuart, Gary L. *Miranda: The Story of America's Right to Remain Silent.* Tucson: University of Arizona Press, 2004; Weaver, Russell L., Leslie W. Abramson, John M. Burkoff, and Catherine Hancock. *Principles of Criminal Procedure.* St. Paul, Minn.: Thomson/West, 2004.

—Rob DeWees

Mississippi University for Women v. Hogan
458 U.S. 718 (1982)

In *Mississippi University for Women v. Hogan,* the U.S. Supreme Court revisited the subject of sex discrimination, specifically focusing on publicly funded higher education and sex-based admission practices. The Court invalidated a public university's single-sex admission policy to one of its undergraduate programs.

A state-supported university relied upon applicants' sex in rendering admission decisions to its undergraduate nursing program, routinely rejecting otherwise qualified applicants because they were men. Joe Hogan was a resident of the city in which Mississippi University for Women (MUW) was located and wanted to further his nursing education at the school. MUW was the nearest institution offering this training; he applied and was denied admission. Hogan filed suit, challenging the constitutionality of MUW's single-sex admission policy, arguing that it constituted sex discrimination prohibited by the EQUAL PROTECTION clause of the FOURTEENTH AMENDMENT.

The Supreme Court agreed with Hogan, throwing out the school's policy. Speaking through Justice SANDRA DAY O'CONNOR, the Court concluded that the State of Mississippi failed to demonstrate an "exceedingly persuasive justification" for the single-sex admission policy; that is, the policy did not serve an important governmental objective, nor was the means employed by the state substantially related to achieving that objective. These criteria comprise the intermediate scrutiny standard, which the Court has applied in sex discrimination cases since the 1970s.

In defense of MUW's admission policy, the state specifically argued that it constituted "educational AFFIRMATIVE ACTION" for women—a historically disadvantaged group subjected to stereotypes and discrimination. The Court rejected this contention, concluding that such a program actually perpetuated harmful stereotypical generalizations, namely that nursing was a "woman's job." The state's position was further compromised by the fact that MUW permitted male students to attend nursing classes under an audit provision even though they could not take them for credit. Therefore, it could not be argued persuasively that women would be adversely affected by male attendance in their classes; men were present, but could not receive credit for their work.

Since the state's policy failed to survive constitutional scrutiny, the Court struck it down as offensive to the equal protection requirement of the Fourteenth Amendment. This case is one in a series of decisions issued by the Supreme Court over the past 30 years involving gender discrimination. The level of scrutiny articulated in O'Connor's opinion echoes many sex discrimination decisions handed down by the Court since the 1970s. Although this demonstrates consistency—the justices again applied the intermediate scrutiny test in a sex discrimination case—the majority opinion was also somewhat controversial because the case involved discrimination against men rather than women. Many critics argued that intermediate scrutiny should be applied in instances where women allege discrimination, not men; where men allege discrimination, they contend, a lower burden should be applied in determining the constitutionality of the practice at issue. According to a majority of the Supreme Court, however, sex discrimination—regardless of who is advantaged or disadvantaged by the policy—must be evaluated according to the same level of constitutional rigor.

For more information: Kirp, Donald L., et al. *Gender Justice*. Chicago: University of Chicago Press, 1986.

—Melanie K. Morris

Mississippi v. Johnson 71 U.S. 475 (1867)

Mississippi v. Johnson concerns the issue of presidential immunity and whether the president can be sued to enjoin (prevent) the enforcement of congressional enactments believed to be unconstitutional. The Supreme Court ruled unanimously that it is the president's executive responsibility to execute the law and not his duty to question the constitutionality of laws enacted by Congress. The president is therefore immune from such litigation.

At the close of the Civil War, Congress passed a series of laws known collectively as the Reconstruction Acts of 1867. Among their many provisions, the acts divided the states of the former Confederacy into military districts, authorized military personnel to appoint and remove state officials, promoted voter registration of black males, and required the rebel states to ratify the FOURTEENTH AMENDMENT as a condition for readmission to the Union. President Andrew Johnson, a Southerner from Tennessee, vetoed the acts, but Congress overrode his VETO. Although President Johnson felt that the measures were too harsh, he nevertheless maintained that it was his constitutional duty to enforce the new laws.

The State of Mississippi immediately sought an INJUNCTION to prevent President Johnson from enforcing the Reconstruction Acts. Mississippi averred that Congress had no constitutional underpinning to interfere with state governance and that the president possessed no authority to enforce an unconstitutional law. The argument, however, fell on deaf ears, as the Supreme Court unanimously dismissed the suit on grounds of separation of powers. Justice Salmon P. Chase, delivering the majority opinion, ruled that "the President of the United States cannot be restrained by injunction from carrying into effect an act alleged to be unconstitutional, nor will a bill having such a purpose be allowed to be filed." Joining the opinion were Justices David Davis, Nathan Clifford, Stephen Field, Robert Grier, Samuel Miller, Noah Swayne, and James Wayne.

This case must also be viewed from a political perspective. Before the case was filed, there was widespread rumor that at least five Supreme Court justices considered the Reconstruction Acts unconstitutional. Thus, Mississippi officials had reason to hope that a majority of the Supreme Court might enjoin President Johnson from enforcing the acts. But members of the Supreme Court were also under severe political pressure. Indeed, Justice Chase recognized that any attempt to thwart the president or Congress would prove futile, because the Supreme Court would be without power to enforce its own process.

For more information: Donald, David Herbert, Jean Harvey Baker, and Michael F. Holt. *The Civil War and Reconstruction.* New York: Norton, 2001; Kutler, Stanley I. *Judicial Power and Reconstruction Politics.* Chicago: University of Chicago Press, 1968; McKitrick, Eric L. *Andrew Johnson and Reconstruction.* Chicago: University of Chicago Press, 1970; Simpson, Brooks D. *The Reconstruction Presidents.* Lawrence: University Press of Kansas, 1998.

—Richard J. Hardy

Missouri Compromise

The Missouri Compromise (1820) ended the first national crisis over the expansion of slavery into the territories of the Louisiana Purchase. By admitting Missouri as a slave state and prohibiting slavery above 36°30′ N, it averted a sectional division that could have ended the Union. The passage, and more importantly, the Supreme Court's declaring it unconstitutional, triggered a major constitutional crisis for the country that led to the Civil War. The Supreme Court decision is also considered to be one of the worst in history.

In 1819, Missouri, which already had a large slave population, petitioned Congress for statehood as a slave state. It appeared that admission would be routine and Missouri, carved out of the vast territory of the Louisiana Purchase, would become the first state west of the Mississippi. That expectation changed, however, when Representative James Tallmadge of New York proposed an amendment that would make Missouri a free state by gradually ending slavery. The amendment required that, after statehood, all slaves born in Missouri would be emancipated at the age of 25, and it banned the importation of new slaves.

The amendment, adopted by the HOUSE OF REPRESENTATIVES and rejected by the SENATE, sparked a contentious debate that brought sectional divisions to the fore. At the heart of the debate was disagreement over several fundamental issues that were essential to the stability of the Union. First was the constitutional question of whether Congress had the power to place antislavery restrictions on a new state at the time of its entry into the Union. Although it was generally agreed that Congress had no power to interfere with slavery in the original states, the antislavery forces argued that the Founding Fathers had provided the constitutional means for Congress to regulate the expansion of slavery. Among the proofs of the Founders' intentions they cited the

Northwest Ordinance of 1787 (renewed by the first Congress in 1791), which prohibited the importation of slaves into the Northwest Territories; the 1808 date set in ARTICLE I, Section 9 of the Constitution for ending the Atlantic slave trade; and Article IV, Sections 3 and 4 of the Constitution. Section 3 gave Congress the power "to make all needful Rules and Regulations respecting the Territory and property of the United States," and Section 4 guaranteed a "republican form of government" to every state.

The South, which viewed any attempt to restrict slavery as a conspiracy to destroy the Union, responded with a straightforward states' rights position, arguing that if Congress had no right to interfere with slavery where it originally existed, it had no right to impose its will on new states seeking admission to the Union. They also pointed out that statehood had been granted to other new slave states.

Related to the role of Congress was the issue of western expansion. This raised two issues. The first was moral. Could a free nation continue to support the expansion of slavery? The second was economic, pitting the use of slave labor against the value of free labor essential to the industrial development in the North.

The final issue concerned the balance of power in the Senate between North and South. When Missouri applied for statehood in 1819, there were 11 free and 11 slave states. If Missouri entered as a slave state it would upset that sectional balance. This was unacceptable to the North, which already felt that the three-fifths compromise (Article I, Section 2) in the Constitution worked to the South's advantage in the House of Representatives and in the ELECTORAL COLLEGE.

The deadlock in Congress was broken in 1820, when moderate Northerners and Southerners agreed to a compromise that allowed Missouri to enter as a slave state, Maine to enter as a free state, and barred slavery above 36°30′ N (the southern border of Missouri). Almost immediately there was a second crisis to threaten disunion. Missouri submitted a state constitution that barred free blacks from immigrating to the state. The Senate approved statehood, but added the stipula-tion that Congress had not approved anything in the charter that would violate Article IV, Section 2, the PRIVILEGES AND IMMUNITIES clause of the Constitution. Southerners argued that, since Missouri was already a state, there could be no conditions. That crisis was resolved with a second compromise that called for admission if the Missouri legislature promised never to pass a law that would bar a U.S. citizen from settling in the state.

The Missouri Compromise lasted until 1854, when it was nullified by the KANSAS-NEBRASKA ACT. In 1857, Chief Justice ROGER TANEY, in the *DRED SCOTT* decision, 60 U.S. (19 Howard) 393, 15 L.Ed. 691 (1857), declared the Missouri Compromise unconstitutional.

For more information: Kohn, Alfred H., Herman Bolz, and Winifred A. Hanbinson. *The American Constitution: Its Origin and Development.* Vol. 2. New York: W.W. Norton, 1991.

—Nedda C. Allbray

Missouri v. Holland 252 U.S. 416 (1920)

In *Missouri v. Holland*, the Supreme Court upheld a federal law passed pursuant to a TREATY between Great Britain and the United States against Missouri's claim that the Tenth Amendment reserved to it the power to regulate wildlife within the state. *Missouri v. Holland* affected the distribution of powers between the federal and state governments and expanded the scope for federal legislation made pursuant to a treaty by relying on the SUPREMACY CLAUSE (Article VI, Section 2): Congress might, in order to implement a treaty, pass legislation that otherwise lay beyond its constitutional powers.

On December 8, 1916, the United States entered into a treaty with Great Britain to protect migratory birds in Canada and the United States. To give effect to that treaty, Congress subsequently passed the Migratory Bird Treaty Act on July 3, 1918, which prohibited the "killing, capturing or selling" of any of the birds mentioned in the treaty except according to regulations made by the Secretary of Agriculture (252 U.S. 416, 431 [1920]). The state of Missouri sought to prevent enforcement of the act within Missouri, claiming that it infringed on the sovereign powers reserved to the states through the Tenth Amendment and that, as owner of the wildlife, Missouri had a financial interest in the wild birds. Noting that an earlier act of Congress that attempted to regulate bird populations within the states had failed in the district court, Missouri argued that Congress could not claim powers pursuant to the implementation of a treaty that it otherwise would not have—specifically, powers reserved to the states.

The opinion of the Court, delivered by Justice OLIVER WENDELL HOLMES, rebuffed the state's claims and held that the act was constitutional. ARTICLE II, Section 2 expressly gives to the president the power to make treaties (with the advice and consent of the SENATE), while Article VI, Section 2 proclaims that treaties made "under the Authority of the United States, shall be the supreme Law of the Land," state laws or constitutions to the contrary notwithstanding. Further, legislation passed pursuant to a valid treaty is itself a valid exercise of Congress's powers under the NECESSARY AND PROPER CLAUSE (ARTICLE I, Section 8).

In considering the state's interest in regulating wild birds and its claims of an exclusive title to do so, the Court had recourse to the severity of the problem with which the treaty dealt. Because the birds are migratory, Missouri could not claim exclusive title to regulate them. And because the problem of dwindling bird populations was "a national interest of very nearly the first magnitude," the federal government properly may address the issue: "We see nothing in the Constitution that compels the Government to sit by while a food supply is cut off and the protectors of our forests and our crops are destroyed" (252 U.S. 416, 435 [1920]).

Justices Van Devanter and Pitney dissented without an opinion.

For more information: Healy, Thomas. "Is *Missouri v. Holland* Still Good Law?: Federalism and the Treaty Power." *Columbia Law Review* 98, no. 7 (1998): 1,726–1,756; Henkin, Louis. *Foreign Affairs and the U.S. Constitution.* 2d ed. Oxford:

Oxford University Press, 1996; Lofgren, Charles A. "*Missouri v. Holland* in Historical Perspective." *The Supreme Court Review* (1975): 71–122; Richberg, Donald R. "The Bricker Amendment and the Treaty Power." *Virginia Law Review* 39, no. 6 (1953): 753–764.

—Lorna M. Dawson

Missouri v. Jenkins 495 U.S. 33 (1990)

In *Missouri v. Jenkins,* the Supreme Court ruled that federal courts may order local governments to levy a tax increase of their own property taxes to remedy segregation in public schools. The significance of *Missouri v. Jenkins* is that federal judges have the "power of the purse" to enter into tax finance and budgeting processes of local governments and order that they levy specific tax increases in order to effect compliance with the Constitution, such as DESEGREGATION of public schools. The decision expands the remedial powers of federal judges under equity law.

In 1984, the district court ruled that the Kansas City, Missouri, School District (KCMSD) was segregated by race/ethnicity. In 1986, the court of appeals upheld the findings and ordered that the costs be divided between the state of Missouri and KCMSD. The district court ordered a detailed desegregation plan with "magnet schools" that would attract more white students from the suburbs. However, state law limited the tax increase that was necessary to fund the remedies. The district court ordered property taxes in the school district doubled, as well as a capital bond for new school buildings. In 1988, the court of appeals affirmed the district court, but limited future tax-increase orders from directly setting the tax rate itself. Instead, courts should direct the school district to do so. The opinion of the Court affirmed the court of appeals limit on future tax-increase orders, but reversed the court of appeals by upholding the tax increase actually ordered by the district court.

Justice White, joined by Justices WILLIAM J. BRENNAN, JR., Marshall, Blackmun, and JOHN PAUL STEVENS, signed the opinion of the Court. First, the Supreme Court granted a limited writ of certiorari to review only the property tax increase, but not the appropriateness of the desegregation plan. Second, White reasoned that "the District Court abused its discretion in imposing the tax increase," because the order violated principles of comity—the manner by which the tax increase was ordered. Comity requires that local governments should not be dictated to by courts, but should have the opportunity to devise their own solutions. Third, in the future, the district court should order the school district to levy the property tax increase itself. The remedial order itself was not excessive, and the state and school district should each be responsible for funding their share of the remedies. Court orders were not invalid under the Tenth Amendment, reserving nondelegated powers to the states, because the case involved express prohibitions of unlawful state conduct under the FOURTEENTH AMENDMENT. The SUPREMACY CLAUSE can require local governments to fulfill the requirements of the Constitution, including the remedial power of a federal court to direct a local government to levy its own taxes.

Justice ANTHONY M. KENNEDY, joined by Chief Justice WILLIAM HUBBS REHNQUIST and Justices SANDRA DAY O'CONNOR and ANTONIN GREGORY SCALIA, signed an opinion that concurs in part and dissents in part. Although it seems a unanimous decision, these four agreed only that the district court should not have directly ordered specific tax increases. But they go on to specify that the "power of taxation is one that the federal judiciary does not possess," even by the indirect route authorized by the majority.

For more information: Schultz, David. *Leveraging the Law: Using the Courts to Achieve Social Change.* New York: Peter Lang Publishing, 1998.
—Bradley Chilton and Mary Welek Atwell

Mistretta v. United States 488 U.S. 361, 102 L.Ed 2d 714, 109 S.Ct. 647 (1989)

In *Mistretta v. United States*, the Supreme Court held that the power of the United States Sentencing Commission (USSC) to set SENTENCING GUIDELINES for federal courts was neither an unconstitutional delegation of legislative authority nor a violation of the SEPARATION OF POWERS doctrine.

Congress, after over a decade of debate and research, created the United States Sentencing Commission (USSC) as an independent agency of the judicial branch in the Sentencing Reform Act (SRA), Title II of the Comprehensive Crime Control Act of 1984. The primary purposes of the USSC are to establish sentencing policies and procedures for ARTICLE III district courts through the enactment of sentencing guidelines and policy statements; to advise Congress and the executive branch on the establishment of crime prevention policy; and to collect and analyze data on federal crimes and sentencing as a resource for the three branches of government and the public.

Prior to the enactment of the sentencing guidelines by the USSC, there was growing concern among legislators, criminal law practitioners, and the public about the disparity in judges' decisions in similar criminal cases (USSC Guideline Manual §1A1.1 2005). As noted by the USSC, prior to the guidelines, district court judges could issue sentences ranging from probation to the maximum penalty for a particular offense. In establishing the USSC and the sentencing guidelines, Congress sought honesty, uniformity, and proportionality in sentencing (USSC Guideline Manual §1A1.1 2005). By establishing guidelines, the USSC specifically chose to limit federal judges' discretion by requiring judges to sentence defendants to prison time that fell within a certain sentence range for the vast number of crimes, taking into account various differences in crimes and defendants' criminal history background.

The original case was brought by a defendant indicted in the United States District Court for the Western District of Missouri. This defendant argued that the guidelines established by the USSC were invalid, because the manner in which the USSC had been created violated the doctrine of separation of powers, and that Congress had delegated excessive legislative authority to the USSC in relation to its powers to set guidelines. The district court upheld the constitutionality of the guidelines. Although the defendant originally filed a notice of appeal to the U.S. Court of

Appeals for the Eighth Circuit, both the defendant and the prosecution subsequently petitioned the United States Supreme Court for certiorari.

In an opinion by Blackmun, joined by WILLIAM HUBBS REHNQUIST, White, Marshall, JOHN PAUL STEVENS, SANDRA DAY O'CONNOR, ANTHONY M. KENNEDY, and in pertinent part WILLIAM J. BRENNAN, JR., the Supreme Court held that in establishing the USSC and allowing it to create sentencing guidelines, Congress had not violated the nondelegation doctrine, because Congress itself had previously defined important criminal offenses and established gradations of punishment. As to the nondelegation doctrine, the Supreme Court indicated the following:

> [The guidelines] do not bind or regulate the primary conduct of the public or vest in the Judicial Branch the legislative responsibility for establishing minimum or maximum penalties for every crime. They do no more than fetter the discretion of sentencing judges to do what they have done for generations—impose sentences within the broad limits set by Congress [*Mistretta* at 396].
>
> . . . [The] judicial contribution to the enterprise of creating rules to limit the discretion of sentencing judges does not enlist the resources or reputations of the Judicial Branch in either the legislative business of determining what conduct should be criminalized or the executive business of enforcing the law [*Mistretta* at 407].

According to the Supreme Court, the USSC's guidelines were similar to internal regulations enacted by courts (*Mistretta* at 391).

ANTONIN GREGORY SCALIA was the lone justice to dissent to the substance of the majority opinion. His dissent was based only on the nondelegation doctrine. In his dissent to the majority opinion, Scalia wrote that the Sentencing Reform Act that established the USSC was an invalid delegation of legislative power and authority because the USSC's rule-making power in establishing guidelines was a legislative power and not a part of a valid exercise of judicial or executive power. Scalia opined that Congress established the com-

mission only to exercise law-making powers that are exclusively reserved for the legislature.

The majority also ruled that the establishment of the USSC in the judicial branch did not violate the separation-of-powers doctrine for several reasons, but most importantly because the functions of the USSC to establish rules and make judgments about sentencing were deemed appropriate for the judicial branch. Furthermore, the creation of the USSC did not violate the separation-of-powers doctrine because the USSC was not a court and did not hear individual cases and thus did not improperly unite judicial and political power.

The effect of the *Mistretta* decision has been far-reaching. Sentencing guidelines established by the USSC and upheld by *Mistretta* and their amendments were applied to approximately 700,000 federal criminal cases between 1989 and 2005, when the Supreme Court, in UNITED STATES V. BOOKER, 125 S.Ct. 738 (2005), found that the guidelines were unconstitutional and rendered their further use as advisory, rather than mandatory, constraints on district court judges.

For more information: Cohen, Mark. "Explaining Judicial Behavior, or What's Unconstitutional about the Sentencing Commission?" *Journal of Law, Economics and Organization* 71 (1991): 183–199; Epstein, Lee, and Thomas G. Walker. *Constitutional Law for a Changing America: Institutional Powers and Constraints.* 5th ed. Washington, D.C.: CQ Press, 2004.

—Lydia Brashear Tiede

Monell v. Department of Social Services
436 U.S. 658 (1978)

In *Monell v. Dept. of Social Services,* the United States Supreme Court held that municipalities, such as cities and counties, could be sued under 42 U.S.C. §1983 for violations of citizens' CIVIL RIGHTS.

Prior to *Monell,* the Court had established in *Monroe v. Pape,* 365 U.S. 167 (1961), that municipalities were not "persons" for purposes of SECTION 1983, and could not be sued under this statute. Thus, although individual employees of municipalities, such as police officers, could be sued for violations of citizens' civil rights, the municipalities themselves could not. The Supreme Court overturned this decision in *Monell*, making possible a much wider range of litigation under Section 1983 against municipalities and municipal agencies.

The petitioners in *Monell* were a group of women employed by the Department of Social Services and the Board of Education of the city of New York. The department and the board had a policy requiring any pregnant employee to take an unpaid leave of absence after the fifth month of pregnancy, regardless of whether such leave was medically necessary. The female employees sued the Department of Social Services and its commissioner, the Board of Education and its chancellor, and the city of New York and its mayor, alleging claims under 42 U.S.C. §1983. This statutory provision provides a civil cause of action to individuals whose civil rights have been violated under color of state law. The petitioners sought both monetary damages and an INJUNCTION to ensure that the policy would not continue to be applied. The United States District Court for the Southern District of New York found that the damages were not available, because any monetary damages awarded would have to be paid by the city of New York, which would not honor the rule of municipality immunity established in *Monroe*. On appeal, the United States Court of Appeals for the Second Circuit affirmed the district court's finding, ruling against the petitioners. The petitioners then appealed on a writ of certiorari to the United States Supreme Court.

In an opinion written by Justice WILLIAM J. BRENNAN, JR., for a majority of the Court, the justices considered the prior rule set out in *Monroe* establishing absolute immunity for municipalities under Section 1983 and rejected it. The Court analyzed the legislative history of Section 1983 and concluded that Congress had intended to allow for municipalities to be sued under the statute. Although it overruled the holding that municipalities were entirely immune from suit under Section 1983, *Monell* did not disturb the rule that municipalities could not be held respon-

sible for the torts of their employees under a theory of respondeat superior—a theory that holds the municipality liable simply because it employs a person who has caused some injury.

Under the rule set out in *Monell*, municipalities do not have absolute immunity and may be sued under Section 1983 for violations of civil rights that they have caused. Although stressing that municipalities may be sued only for violations for which they are actually responsible, the Court declined to express any view as to the potential scope of municipal liability under Section 1983. Subsequent decisions, such as *City of Canton v. Harris,* 489 U.S. 378 (1989), have refined this holding, establishing the types of actions that may give rise to liability under Section 1983 for municipalities.

For more information: Gerhardt, Michael. "The *Monell* Legacy: Balancing Federalism Concerns and Municipal Accountability under Section 1983." *Southern California Law Review* 62 (1989): 539, 542–543; Nahmod, Sheldon. *Civil Rights and Civil Liberties Litigation: The Law of Section 1983.* 3d ed. New York: McGraw-Hill, 1991.

—Johanna Hickman

Montesquieu and the Constitution

The baron de Montesquieu's ideas on the separation of powers as a constitutional device for achieving liberty influenced the authors of the Constitution of the United States. Their version of his ideas is embodied in the Constitution in the Legislative Article (ARTICLE I), the Executive Article (ARTICLE II), and the Judicial Article (ARTICLE III) and institutionally in the Congress, president, and the judiciary.

Charles-Louis de Secondat, baron de le Brède et de Montesquieu, was born on January 18, 1689, at the castle of La Brède near Bordeau. In 1716, he inherited the barony of Montesquieu and the presidency of the Bordeaux Parlement, which was basically the post of chief justice of a local court, from his uncle. In this role, he championed provincial rights against the centralized power of the king.

In 1721, Montesquieu published anonymously *The Persian Letters (Les lettres persanes)*, which was an immediate and sensational success. When his authorship was discovered, it won him literary acclaim. The book pretended to be letters written by two Persian travelers. Using the sensuality of their imagined harems as a backdrop, he engaged in severe social criticism of Europe and France.

In 1729, Montesquieu began traveling in search of political liberty. When he journeyed to England, he discovered the liberty he was seeking. Because he was a nobleman and a famous man of letters, he was royally received, elected to the Royal Society, and for two years given thorough explanations of England's system of government. He eventually concluded that separation of powers was the cause of English liberties. In 1731, Montesquieu returned to Bordeaux, where he began a series of studies that culminated in 1748 with the publication of *The Spirit of Laws (De l'esprit des lois)*. *The Spirit of Laws* is divided into 33 books (*livres*) of chapter length. For Montesquieu, the "spirit" of the law lay in the origin and development of the law through custom. This included the development of the meaning of legal terms, rules, and adoption of laws.

For Montesquieu, the key to liberty lay in moderate governments. He expounded on this in Book XI, Section 4, of *The Spirit of Laws*. In Section 6 of Book XI, Montesquieu discusses separation of powers, that is, the division of government into three branches with each having only legislative, only executive, or only judicial powers. For Montesquieu, every government chooses a goal such as dominion, war, religion, or commerce as the guide to its actions. The delegates at the CONSTITUTIONAL CONVENTION chose political liberty as the American goal due to his influence.

Montesquieu's ideas are discussed in three articles in the *FEDERALIST PAPERS*. In *Federalist 9* and 43, his ideas are used to expound the idea of a federal union. His views on separation of powers are discussed at length in *Federalist 47*.

For more information: Courtney, Cecil Patrick. *Montesquieu and Burke*. Oxford: Blackwell & Mott, 1963; Pangle, T. L. *Montesquieu's Philoso-*phy of Liberalism: A Commentary on "The Spirit of the Laws." Chicago: University of Chicago Press, 1973; Shackleton, Robert. *Montesquieu: A Critical Biography*. London: Oxford University Press, 1961.

—Andrew J. Waskey

Morse v. Frederick 551 U.S. ___ (2007)

In *Morse v. Frederick*, the Supreme Court, by a 5-4 vote, held that public school officials were not barred by the FIRST AMENDMENT from restricting students' drug-related speech.

The case arose from an incident in which high school senior Joseph Frederick refused to remove his 14-foot banner reading "BONG HiTS 4 JESUS" during a school-sponsored outing to watch the Olympic torch parade. The principal, Deborah Morse, thinking this an endorsement of drug use, confiscated the banner and suspended him. Frederick said the words were nonsensical and meant to get him on television. He thought the actions taken against him violated his First Amendment free speech rights, and the principal should be held liable for damages. The district court supported Morse. The Ninth Circuit Court of Appeals supported Frederick.

The Supreme Court was divided in its reasons as well as its votes. Chief Justice JOHN G. ROBERTS, JR., writing for the majority, dismissed Frederick's argument that the circumstances did not make this a "school speech" case and agreed with Morse that the message might be interpreted as pro-drug. While not repudiating the landmark case, *TINKER V. DES MOINES*, 393 U.S. 503 (1969), he employed two principles from a later school speech case, *Bethel School District v. Fraser*, 478 U.S. 675 (1986): (1) Students do not automatically have the same rights as adults or as they themselves might have outside of school; and (2) the *Tinker* standard—protecting student speech except when clearly disruptive of the school's educational mission—was not the only criterion for deciding school speech cases. Roberts drew on FOURTH AMENDMENT cases, congressional spending, and school board policies to demonstrate that combating student drug use was a government priority. Finally he clarified that this ruling supported school officials' power to discipline specifically pro-drug speech and did not address more generally "offensive" speech.

This provided the point of departure for Justice SAMUEL ALITO's concurring opinion. Alito expressed continued support for the *Tinker* standard and a reluctance to deviate from it. His vote was based on the specific circumstances of this case and was not intended to empower schools to censor any student speech inconsistent with their educational mission.

In sharp contrast, Justice CLARENCE THOMAS, also concurring, wholeheartedly endorsed the Court's opinion, while arguing that the *Tinker* standard "is without basis in the Constitution" and student speech has no constitutional protection. He described disciplinary powers of early American private schools, arguing that when public schools appeared, they inherited these powers. "In the earliest public schools, teachers taught and students listened." Thomas believed the Court rejected this tradition in *Tinker* but was restoring it piecemeal. He joined the Court to help "erode" *Tinker,* preferring, however, to abandon the *Tinker* principle entirely.

Justice JOHN PAUL STEVENS, dissenting, took Frederick at his word as to his motivation and argued that by bowing to Morse's interpretation, the Court trivialized *Tinker* and endorsed viewpoint discrimination. To Stevens, it was "implausible" that Frederick's banner would lead to increased student drug use. He feared that there would be "no stopping point" after this ruling, with schools silencing perfectly legal mention of drugs as in classroom debates about legalizing marijuana for medical uses.

Justice STEPHEN G. BREYER agreed with the Court's position that Morse's "qualified immunity" protected her from liability for monetary damages. However, reminding the Court in his concurring/dissenting opinion of the tradition of avoiding constitutional questions if a narrower ruling was possible, he would have decided for Morse on that basis alone.

The conservative American Committee for Law and Justice (ACLJ) and other religious right organizations filed amicus curiae briefs on behalf of Frederick, putting them uncharacteristically on the same side as the AMERICAN CIVIL LIBERTIES UNION (ACLU) and in opposition to the Bush administration. Their concern was that a ruling giving broad power to school officials could endanger student religious speech.

The case also attracted attention because of the presence of former independent prosecutor Kenneth Starr, who volunteered his time to represent Morse.

For more information: Johnson, John W. *The Struggle for Student Rights.* Lawrence: University of Kansas Press, 1997; Raskin, Jamin B. *We the Students: Supreme Court Cases for and about Students.* 2d ed. Washington, D.C.: CQ Press, 2003.

—Jane G. Rainey

Mueller v. Allen 463 U.S. 388 (1983)

In *Mueller v. Allen,* the Supreme Court ruled that a Minnesota statute (290.09, subd. 22) did not violate the ESTABLISHMENT CLAUSE of the U.S. Constitution's FIRST AMENDMENT. The statute allowed Minnesota taxpayers to deduct expenses for tuition, textbooks, and transportation for their children attending public or private elementary and secondary schools. The 5-4 decision set the standard for determining the constitutionality of state aid for parents who send their children to parochial schools.

Justice WILLIAM HUBBS REHNQUIST, joined by Justices WARREN BURGER, White, LEWIS POWELL, and SANDRA DAY O'CONNOR, delivered the opinion of the court. In this opinion, Rehnquist applied the three-part *Lemon* test, set forth in *LEMON V. KURTZMAN,* 403 U.S. 602 (1971), to determine whether the statute violates the establishment clause. The *Lemon* test requires that a statute (a) must have a legitimate secular purpose, (b) must not have the primary effect of either advancing or inhibiting religion, and (c) must not result in an "excessive entanglement" with religion. Rehnquist explained that the Minnesota legislation had the secular purpose of educating the populace, and it did so by defraying the cost of educational expenses. The statement also stressed the important role that private schools play in relation to public schools by providing educational alternatives and competition and offsetting operating costs.

In applying the second part of the *Lemon* test, advancing or inhibiting religion, the court ruled that, since the deductions were available to all parents, including those whose children go to public school, the statute was not subject to challenge under the establishment clause. They also found that this case was different from earlier cases, because the aid was provided to the parents rather than directly to the schools. Lastly, Rehnquist explained that the statute did not result in excessive entanglement with religion just because state officials determine the eligibility of textbooks that qualify as legitimate deductions. Making decisions to disallow deductions for books and materials used in teaching religious tenets, doctrines, or worship is insufficient evidence of entanglement.

Dissenting justices Marshall, WILLIAM J. BRENNAN, JR., Blackmun, and JOHN PAUL STEVENS asserted that the establishment clause prohibits states from subsidizing religious education, whether directly or indirectly, and that the Minnesota statute tax deductions were a form of subsidy for sectarian schools. They countered the majority's opinion of the secular purpose of the law by explaining that, although the deductions are available to all parents, in practice the bulk of the benefit goes to parents who send their children to religious schools, because those are the schools that charge tuition. Furthermore, they did not agree with the majority's view that there was significant difference between this case and precedent set forth in earlier cases, particularly *Committee for Public Education v. Nyquist*, 413 U.S. 756 (1973). The dissenting opinion also held that allowing tax deductions for any textbooks used exclusively in religious schools violates the establishment clause.

The significance of the *Mueller v. Allen* decision was the potential impact on future legislation concerning tax credits for religious schooling. Rehnquist's application of the *Lemon* test and the clarification that tax deductions for education

benefit all parents establish criteria for new laws to follow.

For more information: Connolly, John W. "*Mueller v. Allen*: A New Standard of Scrutiny Applied to Tax Deductions for Educational Expenses." *Duke Law Journal* (1984): 983–1,001; Renstrom, Peter G. *Constitutional Rights Sourcebook.* Santa Barbara, Calif.: ABC-CLIO, 1999.

—Jocelyn Tipton

Muller v. Oregon 208 U.S. 412, 28 S.CT. 324 (1908)

In *Muller v. Oregon,* the United States Supreme Court upheld an Oregon statute limiting the number of hours per day women could work and setting the minimum wage they must be paid. Curt Muller challenged his conviction under the statute as a deprivation of his DUE PROCESS rights under the FOURTEENTH AMENDMENT, inviting the court to apply its SUBSTANTIVE DUE PROCESS analysis to find the Oregon statute unconstitutional, as it had done three years previously in *LOCHNER V. NEW YORK*, 198 U.S. 45, 25 S.Ct. 539 (1905).

In *Lochner,* the Court had held that a maximum hour law for bakers in New York unconstitutionally infringed the DUE PROCESS rights of owners of bakeries and their employees. Although the Supreme Court did apply the same substantive due process analysis to the Oregon statute as it had with that of New York, unlike with the New York statute, the Court found the Oregon statute to have passed its test of constitutionality, i.e., that the statute served a public interest that outweighed the individual right.

As the 19th century came to an end and the 20th began, the Progressive Era of American politics dawned as well, bringing with it numerous state and federal statutes seeking protection for the American worker. In light of the Supreme Court's substantive due process doctrine requiring all statutes that posed regulations on business to pass the Court's test of constitutionality, to wit, that they were serving a public interest that outweighed the private property right, the defense of such statutes necessarily required evidence that the challenged statutes were, in fact, within the authority of the government to enact as a health, safety, or morals code.

In *Muller,* the Progressive Movement sought to defend the Oregon maximum hour/minimum wage law for women by proving that it was a true public health law for women. To this end, the National Consumers' League hired future Supreme Court Justice Louis D. Brandeis to make its case. Filing what later came to be known as a BRANDEIS BRIEF, Brandeis wrote a 113-page argument that consisted of two pages of legal citation and 111 pages of social science research on the impact of long working hours and low pay on the health and well-being of women and, by extension, the family.

Although the state of New York had asserted that it, too, was seeking to protect the health and well-being of its bakers in *Lochner,* the assertion that the New York law was a health code had fallen on deaf ears only three years previously. Brandeis's strategy of focusing on proving that the law was, in fact, a health code and not simply the "protectionist" legislation struck down in *Lochner* proved compelling to the Court. Although this case stands as a victory for progressive forces and the use of the Brandeis brief in court, it must also be understood in the context of the political culture of the times with its structure of sexism that pervaded both Brandeis's argument and the resulting Court opinion. The only significant difference between the statutes challenged in *Lochner* and *Muller* is that, in the former case, men were to be protected from sweatshop conditions, and in the latter case, women were the subject of the law. The structure of gender discrimination that these two cases, taken together, highlight would continue to permeate both legislation and court doctrine until the last quarter of the 20th century, ultimately disadvantaging both men and women.

In the end, *Muller* was only a quite small ray of hope for those concerned with conditions faced by the American worker in the early years of the 20th century. Within 15 years of the *Muller* decision, the Court returned to its *Lochner* view of worker protective legislation, overturning a congressional statute governing Washington, D.C., that set a minimum wage for women in the district (*ADKINS v. CHILDREN'S HOSPITAL,* 261 U.S. 525 [1923]). It would take almost 15 more years before the Court would accept the judgment of the nation that had elected and reelected Franklin D. Roosevelt and his "New Deal" of progressive legislation and cease using its substantive due process analysis to second-guess elected legislative action in the economic realm.

For more information: Bickel, Alexander M. *The Least Dangerous Branch: The Supreme Court at the Bar of Politics.* New Haven, Conn.: Yale University Press, 1986; Cardozo, Benjamin N. *The Nature of the Judicial Process* (The Storrs Lecture Series). New Haven, Conn.: Yale University Press, 1960; Ely, John Hart. *Democracy and Distrust: A Theory of Judicial Review.* Cambridge, Mass.: Harvard University Press, 2004.

—Phyllis Farley Rippey

Munn v. Illinois 94 U.S. 113 (1876)

In *Munn v. Illinois,* the United States Supreme Court upheld an Illinois statute requiring grain elevators to have operating licenses and setting maximum rates chargeable for storage of grain. After being found in violation of the statute, Ira Munn challenged the law as an infringement of his DUE PROCESS rights. Although the Supreme Court rejected Munn's argument in this case, at the same time, it opened the door to the possibility that there were cases where Munn's FOURTEENTH AMENDMENT analysis would prevail with the Court. In so doing, the Court established and legitimated in all but explicit language the doctrine of SUBSTANTIVE DUE PROCESS.

Munn's argument reasserted the framework of analysis of the Fourteenth Amendment first urged on the Supreme Court in *The Slaughterhouse Cases* in 1867, 10 years previously. That argument was based on a reading of the Fourteenth Amendment as having two significant features: (1) that the amendment offered constitutional protection to all Americans, not just to newly freed slaves and black Americans and (2) that the due process clause was intended as a check on overreaching protectionism by state governments.

The due process clause forbids the states from writing laws that deprive individuals of life, liberty, or property without due process. Beginning with *The Slaughterhouse Cases* (see BUTCHERS' BENEVOLENT ASSOCIATION OF NEW ORLEANS . . .), two years after ratification of the Fourteenth Amendment, lawyers for business corporations introduced a CONSTITUTIONAL INTERPRETATION of the Fourteenth Amendment that, in time, came to be endorsed by the Supreme Court as the doctrine of substantive due process. The structure of the argument is as follows: (a) Due process protections include more than ensuring that laws are properly enacted and enforced; (b) even if legislative rules are properly followed, the resulting law may, itself, be a deprivation of liberty or property without due process; (c) consequently, the appropriate constitutional role for the Court is to look beyond the process of legislation to the substance of the law to determine its constitutionality; and (d) should the substance of the law violate due process, the Court must strike it down as unconstitutional. This reading of the Fourteenth Amendment's due process clause greatly enhances the power of the Supreme Court and expands its role in American politics and, consequently, significantly undermines the authority of government to enact economic (private property–related) legislation.

In *The Slaughterhouse Cases,* the Supreme Court majority rejected this argument, but the four-justice minority opinion embraced it, giving it significant credibility and encouraging lawyers for business clients to continue to urge the argument on the Court in succeeding cases, which Ira Munn's attorneys did in *Munn v. Illinois* in 1876. In the intervening 10 years between these two cases, the Supreme Court majority came to join the view of the dissenting minority of *The Slaughterhouse Cases.* In *Munn,* the Supreme Court made two statements of enormous significance to governments seeking to regulate business in some measure as well as to the businesses subject to the regulations.

First, the Court reaffirmed the traditional view that it is legitimate for government to regulate private property "clothed in a public interest," and thus, under the Fourteenth Amendment, it cannot be assumed that, in all cases of government regulation of private property, there has necessarily been a deprivation of property without due process. Had the Supreme Court ended its opinion here, both Ira Munn and business interests generally would have lost the war against the regulation of business, perhaps for all time. But to the delight of business, the Court continued its opinion with the statement that "[u]nder some circumstances they [government regulations on business] may [amount to a deprivation], but not under all."

With these words in *Munn,* substantive due process was full born as a constitutional doctrine. Because the Court acknowledged that there were some cases where government regulation of private property may constitute a deprivation of property or liberty without due process, the holding necessarily begged the question: Under what circumstances was this the case? To answer this question, the Supreme Court necessarily had to assume the task of looking at the substance of legislation to determine whether the government had overstepped its authority under the Fourteenth Amendment's due process clause.

Beginning with *Munn* and continuing for the next 60 years, the Supreme Court imposed its substantive due process analysis on economic legislation, finding more times than not that the government had exceeded its powers. As part of its substantive due process doctrine, the Court constructed a "test of constitutionality" that required all legislation challenged as infringing due process protections to make the case that the enactment served a public interest that outweighed the individual right. Failing this test, state and federal laws were struck down by the Court. It was entirely within the power of the Court to determine both what the purpose of the challenged law was and whether that purpose outweighed the individual right. In the vast majority of cases over the 60 years after *Munn,* the Supreme Court routinely found public policy regulating business to be constitutionally invalid. Consequently, the lawyers for Ira Munn lost his battle but won business's war against government regulation.

Although the Supreme Court ultimately backed away from imposing its substantive due process analysis on economic legislation by the late 1930s, its authority to review the substance of legislative enactment continues apace today.

For more information: Currie, David P. *The Constitution in the Supreme Court: The First Hundred Years, 1789–1888.* Chicago: University of Chicago Press, 1986; Kelly, Alfred H., Winfred A. Harbison, and Herman Belz. *The American Constitution: Its Origins and Development.* New York: W.W. Norton & Company, 1991.

—Phyllis Farley Rippey

music censorship

Music censorship refers to changing, eliminating, or otherwise suppressing individual songs or musical genres based on the content of the lyrics. Music censorship, if undertaken by the government, is generally a violation of the FIRST AMENDMENT free speech clause. However, there are some circumstances when the government may regulate musical lyrics on television and radio.

The First Amendment to the U.S. Constitution says that "Congress shall make no law . . . abridging the freedom of speech." This explicit restriction on Congress's power has thus far prevented legislation that would permit or require music censorship, and no Supreme Court decisions expressly deal with efforts to censor music. The Court has, however, explicitly stated that obscene speech is not protected under the First Amendment, and this would be the standard applied to music.

Under MILLER V. CALIFORNIA, 413 U.S. 15 (1973), speech is obscene (1) if the average person, applying contemporary community standards, would find that the material appeals to prurient interests; (2) if the material depicts or describes sexual conduct in a patently offensive way; and (3) if it lacks literary, artistic, political, or scientific value. As discussed briefly below, most music censorship has been the result of either intense public pressure, or indirect governmental pressure, to restrict certain music in order to protect young people from offensive lyrics.

Popular music has long been the bane of the older generation. In the early 20th century, ragtime, jazz, and blues were viewed with alarm because they expressed, among other things, the sexual side of human nature. By the 1950s, the influence of radio and the emergence of rock and roll combined to raise adult fears that sexually suggestive lyrics were fostering perversion and delinquency in young people. Radio disc jockeys increasingly banned certain songs, often at the suggestion of, or with the support of, local authorities and religious groups. As television became more prevalent in American society, efforts to censor certain types of music spread to TV. For example, when the Rolling Stones appeared on the Ed Sullivan Show in 1967, they changed the words of "Let's Spend the Night Together" to "Let's Spend Some Time Together" in response to Sullivan's belief that the original phrase was objectionable.

The 1960s and 1970s ushered in parental fears of illicit drug use, as well as public outcries against song lyrics that alluded to drugs. Among the more controversial actions of the 1970s was a widespread ban on John Denver's "Rocky Mountain High" because radio stations thought "high" would be perceived as a reference to drug use. Otherwise, lyrics deemed objectionable were often bleeped or otherwise obscured by radio stations, sometimes without the consent of the artists. In general, music censorship was a local affair, with scant attention paid by national public figures.

While, in general, the government cannot censor music sold in CDs or in other formats, it may restrict what is broadcast on public airwaves. In FEDERAL COMMUNICATIONS COMMISSION V. PACIFICA FOUNDATION, 438 U.S. 726 (1978), the Supreme Court upheld a decision by the Federal Communications Commission to fine a radio station for the broadcast of George Carlin's "Seven Dirty Words" comedy routine because it contained several four-letter words. Even though these words were speech under the First Amendment, the Court ruled that the FCC could prohibit the use of these words on broadcast television and radio in order to protect captured audiences and children from hearing them. In general, as a result of this decision, the FCC can censor broadcasts of some objectionable materials, and it has fined individuals, such as Howard Stern, for using certain words or because of their content. However, the FCC has also permitted more adult language to be used on cable and in nonfamily hours.

The music censorship landscape changed dramatically in 1985 with the formation of the Parents' Music Resource Center (PMRC), a group composed mainly of the wives of some of the most influential public figures in Washington, D.C., including Tipper Gore, wife of former Vice President Al Gore. The group aimed to inform parents that much of the popular music enjoyed by their children explicitly glorified drugs, alcohol, violence, and sex. They wanted the music industry to voluntarily label recordings containing explicit lyrics to help parents determine whether certain music was suitable for their children. A key part of their strategy was convincing the SENATE to hold a hearing in 1985 on the content of rock music. Much of the testimony was combative, with statements from members of the PMRC that linked various social ills to music lyrics, and testimony by musicians that called the hearing a censorship charade. Ultimately, the music industry agreed to place "Parental Advisory: Explicit Content" stickers on CDs according to their own internal standards.

Since 1990, some major retail chains, including Wal-Mart, have refused to sell CDs containing warning labels, and some stores restrict sales of labeled music to people over 18 years old. Some recording companies have marketed "clean" versions of songs in order to get the music on the shelves. A number of states have debated legislation that would prevent the sale of labeled music, and some have considered taxing recordings that contain warning labels. Over the years, Music Television (MTV) has chosen to ban certain music videos based on both lyrical and visual content. Although no music censorship cases have been heard by the U.S. Supreme Court, one came close. In 1990, a Florida judge declared 2 Live Crew's album *As Nasty as They Want to Be* obscene, and the Broward County sheriff ordered it removed from stores. Although three retailers were arrested, charges were eventually dropped, and on appeal, a federal court found that the recording was not obscene; the Supreme Court did not grant certiorari. As the Internet becomes more integral to the music industry in the 21st century, actions against the content of music are likely to move in new directions.

For more information: Chastagner, Claude. "The Parents' Music Resource Center: From Information to Censorship." *Popular Music* 18 (May 1999): 179–192; Cohen, Ronald D. "The Delinquents: Censorship and Youth Culture in Recent U.S. History." *History of Education Quarterly* 37 (Autumn 1997): 251–270; Paulson, Kenneth A. "Regulation through Intimidation: Congressional Hearings and Political Pressure on America's Entertainment Media." *Vanderbilt Journal of Entertainment Law and Practice* 7 (Winter 2004): 61–89.

—Margaret Tullai

Muskrat v. United States 219 U.S. 346 (1911) In *Muskrat v. United States,* the Court reversed and dismissed the claims of David Muskrat that challenged the constitutionality of a series of congressional restrictions imposed on land owned by Cherokees. More broadly, however, this decision acknowledged that ARTICLE III OF THE U.S. CONSTITUTION limits the exercise of federal judicial power to actual cases and controversies that are brought to the courts for resolution.

In this opinion, the Court put words to a tradition that had guided its decision making for more than a century, but one that had never before been clearly stated: namely, that it would not hear friendly suits, nor issue hypothetical opinions, nor address any questions beyond those contained in real cases or controversies.

The *Muskrat* case has its origin in a long list of disputes that grew out of the complexities of Indian treaties and the congressional struggle at the turn of the 19th to the 20th century to address them. The General Allotment Act of 1887 pronounced a new federal Indian policy: Former tribal lands were to be subdivided, then individually bought and sold. This initiated a complex process wherein Indian claims to land titles became a critical element in determining federal allotments, tribal boundaries, TREATY provisions, and corporate and personal ownership.

Subsequent congressional legislation, in order to clarify the factual questions that arose as well as to remedy the bureaucratic inadequacies that a multitude of these disputes revealed, often would invite suits against the government. The legislation specified that these cases were to be tried in federal courts of claims to determine the details and resolve the differences in these matters, and that such decisions could be reviewed by the Supreme Court.

Muskrat v. United States bears all of these characteristics. It was born of a 1907 statute, wherein Muskrat and others were individually named and authorized to bring suit in the court of claims "to determine the validity of any acts of Congress" (Opinion of the Court, p. 360) that since 1902 had regulated Cherokee lands. The legislation instructed the attorney general to represent the federal government in the case, and the U.S. Treasury to pay the lawyers' fees for the attorneys who represented Muskrat and Cherokee citizens. Muskrat's suit was, in short, orchestrated, planned, and paid for by Congress.

In delivering the opinion for a unanimous (7-0) court, Justice Day highlighted the lack of genuine adversarial interests that existed between the Cherokees and the United States, the transparent objective to garner Supreme Court approval for the "doubtful character" of congressional legislation in these matters, and the unofficial practice of the Court only to hear actual cases and controversies. Faced with an unabashed congressional invitation to render an advisory opinion here, Day declared, "Is such a determination within the judicial power conferred by the Constitution . . . ? We think it is not" (361).

Day's opinion traced the development of this tradition to Washington's presidency, when the administration and Congress asked for the justices' advice and counsel on a wide range of issues from treaty matters with France and Britain to settling Revolutionary War pensions for widows and orphans. In correspondence, Chief Justice JOHN JAY and his associates declined to assist on the grounds that such action would violate the unique power that was vested only in the judiciary by Article III of the U.S. Constitution (see appendix).

Declaring that this was neither a case nor a controversy and, as such, fell outside its constitutional jurisdiction, Justice Day laid the foundation for the gradual development of the modern court's limitation of congressional attempts to place issues before the court. The holdings of *Muskrat* were reaffirmed in *Aetna Life Insurance Co. v. Haworth,* 300 U.S. 227 (1937), and further sharpened in *LUJAN V. DEFENDERS OF WILDLIFE,* 504 U.S. 555 (1997), which said it is the Court, not the Congress, that ultimately determines what is a true case or controversy.

For more information: Casto, William R. "The Early Supreme Court Justices' Most Significant Opinion." *Ohio Northern University Law Review* 29 (2002): 173–207; Kannan, Phillip M. "Advisory Opinions by Federal Courts." *University of Richmond Law Review* 32 (1998): 769–798.

—George Peery

Myers v. United States 272 U.S. 52, 47 S. Ct. 21, 71 L. Ed. 160 (1926)

Myers v. U.S. established the president's authority unilaterally to remove inferior executive officers appointed "by and with the Advice and Consent of the SENATE" (ARTICLE II, Section 2). The Court thereby resolved a question long debated: When the Constitution is explicit about the mode of appointing officials, but silent about the mode of their removal, who may remove officials jointly appointed? The Court's answer established a sweeping executive authority and derived a substantial power from his obligation to "take Care that the Laws be faithfully executed" (Article II, Section 3).

Although the TENURE OF OFFICE ACT (1867), which sought to restrict the executive's removal power, had been repealed in 1887, an 1876 statute that required Senate consent to the removal of all first-, second-, and third-class postmasters remained on the books. In January 1920, President Wilson removed Postmaster First-Class

Frank S. Myers before his term expired and without Senate consent, in violation of that law. After Myers sought unsuccessfully to recover his lost salary in the U.S. Court of Claims, he appealed to the Supreme Court.

In a 6-3 decision, authored by Chief Justice William Howard Taft, the Court entered the fray and held the 1876 statute unconstitutional. A lengthy review of history led the Court to conclude that "the executive Power" (Article II, Section 1) was a broad grant of substantive power, and that the appointing provisions of Article II, Section 2 were to be understood as limitations to this power which were to be construed strictly. Congress's power to determine the mode of appointment of "inferior officers" (Article II, Section 2) thus does not extend to it the power to limit their removal once appointed. The power to remove is inherently executive: The president must be able to remove officials in whom he has lost confidence in order to fulfill his own obligation to "take Care that the Laws be faithfully executed" (Article II, Section 3).

In dissent, Justice McReynolds followed Taft's foray into history to conclude that the president had no such "illimitable" power (272 U.S 52, 192 [1926]), one inconsistent with a Constitution of limited and enumerated powers. The obligation to ensure faithful execution of the laws cannot justify infraction of some of those laws. Further, the Court's holding had been "expressly repudiated" (272 U.S. 52, 202 [1926]) in *Marbury v. Madison,* 5 U.S. (I CR.) 137 (1803), and consistently denied in subsequent cases.

Agreeing with McReynolds's conclusions, Brandeis added pointedly that there is "no express grant to the President of incidental powers resembling those conferred upon Congress by clause 18 of *Article I, 8*" (272 U.S. 52, 246 [1926]).

Finally, Justice Oliver Wendell Holmes, Jr. argued that because Congress had created the office and had conferred upon the president the power to appoint its officers, its assent was required for their removal. The president's obligation to ensure the faithful execution of the laws "does not go beyond the laws or require him to achieve more than Congress sees fit to leave within his power" (292 U.S. 52, 295 [1926]).

For more information: Corwin, Edward S. *The President's Removal Power under the Constitution.* New York: National Municipal League, 1927; Entin, Jonathan L. "The Pompous Postmaster and Presidential Power: The Story of *Myers v. United States.*" Case Legal Studies Research Paper No. 05-39 (November 2005); Fisher, Louis. *Constitutional Conflicts between Congress and the President.* 4th ed. Lawrence: University Press of Kansas, 1997.

—Lorna M. Dawson

National Endowment for the Arts v. Finley
524 U.S. 569 (1998)

In *National Endowment for the Arts v. Finley*, the Supreme Court rejected the notion that Congress was barred by the FIRST AMENDMENT from conditioning federal arts funding on adherence to a vague standard of decency.

After taxpayer-subsidized grants from the National Endowment for the Arts were awarded to controversial artists Robert Mapplethorpe and Andres Serrano in 1989, angry congressional conservatives inserted an amendment in the NEA's 1990 reauthorization, directing the NEA to "take into consideration general standards of decency." Subsequently, the NEA denied the grant application of performance artist Karen Finley, who was renowned for reenacting rape by stripping to the waist and smearing her body with chocolate. Finley and three other rejected applicants then challenged the new directive as violating the First Amendment's bar against viewpoint discrimination.

By an 8-1 vote, the Supreme Court disagreed, with SANDRA DAY O'CONNOR characterizing the decency amendment as in fact viewpoint neutral. However, Justice O'Connor arrived at this conclusion in tortuous fashion, by declaring that the amendment was "merely hortatory." While the NEA was entitled to use decency as a factor in evaluating grant proposals, O'Connor argued, it was not compelled to do so.

This interpretation of the new directive stunned observers. The amendment's congressional sponsors had fully intended to make the new rule mandatory, and to reinforce that desire, Congress had slashed the NEA's budget by $45,000—the precise total of the grants provided for the Mapplethorpe and Serrano exhibits. Legal scholars were likewise unsatisfied. Prominent First Amendment commentator Frederick Schauer described O'Connor's handiwork as "an implausible doctrinal structure."

But perhaps O'Connor's most trenchant critic was a colleague. In his concurring opinion, ANTONIN GREGORY SCALIA excoriated O'Connor's disingenuousness about the amendment, as well as what he saw as fealty to a flawed vision of freedom of speech. Headlining his argument with an all-capital-letters scold, "THE STATUTE MEANS WHAT IT SAYS," Scalia argued that the government is free to require that the money it hands out be used the way it wants it used. Whereas O'Connor had ducked the question of whether whoever pays the piper gets to call the tune by essentially declaring that no tune was actually being "called," Scalia embraced government's ability to discriminate against disfavored viewpoints whenever it was subsidizing speech.

Scalia's doctrinaire argument may have been more consistent with the intentions of Congress, but it has never found favor with a majority of the justices. Indeed, the Court once again declined to embrace it in UNITED STATES V. AMERICAN LIBRARY ASSOCIATION, 539 U.S. 194 (2003), in which it upheld the federal government's power to forbid federal finding for libraries that refused to install anti-pornography filtering software on public computers. Yet two of the four justices who signed on to the plurality opinion (ANTHONY M. KENNEDY and STEPHEN G. BREYER) specifically noted that their approval was based on the fact the libraries were free to turn the filters off at patrons' request, thus indicating the continuing unacceptability of the kind of unabashedly mandatory scheme that Scalia would countenance.

For more information: Finley, Karen. *A Different Kind of Intimacy: The Collected Writings of Karen Finley.* New York: Thunder's Mouth Press, 2000; Grazia, Edward de. *Girls Lean Back Everywhere: The Law of Obscenity and the Assault on Genius.* New York: Random House, 1992.

—Steven B. Lichtman

National Labor Relations Board v. Jones and Laughlin Steel Corp. 301 U.S. 1

(1937)

In *NLRB v. Jones and Laughlin Steel Corp.*, the U.S. Supreme Court ruled 5 to 4 that the National Labor Relations Act (NLRA) was constitutional under Congress's power to regulate commerce among the states. The ruling by the Court was significant in that it signified an important shift in the Court's approach to the commerce power of Congress.

In previous cases, such as UNITED STATES V. E.C. KNIGHT CO., 156 U.S. 1 (1895), and CARTER V. CARTER COAL CO., 298 U.S. 238 (1936), the Court had reasoned that labor practices, as elements of production rather than distribution, were activities outside of congressional authority because they had only an indirect effect on INTERSTATE COMMERCE. Distributive activities, so long as they did not infringe upon states' reserved powers, were under the regulatory authority of Congress, as those activities would have a direct effect on commerce among the states. The Court's decision in *NLRB v. Jones and Laughlin Steel Corp.* did away with both the production/distribution distinction as well as the direct/indirect effects test established by the Court in the earlier cases.

In 1935, Congress passed the NLRA in response to the Court's striking down a collective bargaining protection provision of the National Industrial Relations Act (NIRA) in SCHECHTER POULTRY CORP. V. UNITED STATES, 295 U.S. 495 (1935). The NLRA, known as the WAGNER ACT, provided for the establishment of the National Labor Relations Board (NLRB) to guarantee collective bargaining rights for workers and granted the NLRB authority to compel action by employers who ran afoul of fair labor practices that would affect interstate commerce. A claim was brought to the NLRB by workers at Jones and Laughlin Steel Corporation, charging that the company had discouraged workers from unionizing and had fired 10 workers who had engaged in union activities. The board upheld the charges against the company and ordered the company to reinstate the employees. Jones and Laughlin refused to abide by the board's order and challenged the constitutionality of the Wagner Act, which granted authority to the NLRB. The company argued that, consistent with U.S. Supreme Court precedent, labor practices were primarily elements of production, had only an indirect effect on interstate commerce, and were therefore beyond the scope of congressional authority to regulate. The NLRB responded by seeking enforcement of its order in a U.S. district court, but that petition was rejected. The NLRB appealed to the U.S. Supreme Court, which granted certiorari.

Justice Hughes wrote the opinion for the Court. Hughes reasoned that the National Labor Relations Act's grant of authority to the NLRB was constitutional, because labor disputes and labor unrest may give rise to strikes and other acts "which directly burden or obstruct interstate or foreign commerce, or its free flow." Consequently, such acts are "within the reach of the congressional power" to regulate. "Acts having that effect are not rendered immune because they grow out of labor disputes." According to the Court, the Jones and Laughlin Steel Corporation had substantial commercial dealings on a national scale, "making their relation to interstate commerce the dominant factor in their activities," which led the Court to the conclusion that the labor disputes that would arise without NLRB protections would lead to substantial barriers to the free flow of interstate commerce.

The dissent in the case argued that the majority had simply rejected, without due consideration, the line of precedent established in production-related cases. They noted that the indirect effect on interstate commerce of labor practices in manufacturing steel was so remote as not to fall under congressional authority to regulate. Discontent among a few workers might lead to a strike, which may lead to a reduction in goods traveling interstate. But, Justice McReynolds wrote, "By this chain of indirect and progressively remote events we finally reach the evil" with which the legislation purports to deal. "A more remote and indirect interference with interstate commerce or a more definite invasion of the powers reserved to the states is difficult, if not impossible, to imagine."

NLRB v. Jones and Laughlin Steel Corp. is an important case to consider in light of its contribution to the development of the Court's approach to the COMMERCE CLAUSE. This case signaled a new direction for the Court in commerce clause cases, away from the tests established earlier to limit congressional authority in manufacturing and toward a much more broad understanding of the scope of congressional power to regulate interstate commerce.

Moreover, the case is viewed as a turning point in constitutional development. From 1933 to 1937, the Court had repeatedly turned back major New Deal legislation aimed at regulating the national economy. In this case, the Court rejected those limits it had embraced prior to President Roosevelt's court-packing proposal (in which Roosevelt proposed to increase the number of Supreme Court judges from nine to 15). Though the proposal was rejected by Congress, the "switch in time that saved nine" is remembered for its profound contribution to constitutional development and a greater role for Congress in the nation's economy. As the Court became dominated by appointees of President Franklin Roosevelt, subsequent cases, like UNITED STATES V. DARBY LUMBER Co., 312 U.S. 100 (1941), and WICKARD V. FILBURN, 317 U.S. 111 (1942), consolidated that constitutional revolution.

For more information: Cortner, Richard C. *The Jones and Laughlin Case.* New York: Knopf, 1970; Hardin, Patrick, et al. *The Developing Labor Law: The Board, the Courts, and the National Labor Relations Act.* 4th ed. Washington, D.C.: Bureau of National Affairs, 2001.

—Brian M. Harward

National League of Cities v. Usery 426 U.S. 833 (1976)

In *National League of Cities v. Usery,* the Supreme Court, in a closely divided decision, held that a federal law that required states to pay a minimum wage to state and local employees violated the Tenth Amendment because it "operate[s] to directly displace the States' freedom to structure integral operations in areas of traditional governmental functions." *Usery* is the only decision of the Supreme Court between 1937 and 1990 to strike down a federal law as unconstitutional under the Tenth Amendment. The Court subsequently overruled *Usery* in GARCIA V. SAN ANTONIO METROPOLITAN TRANSIT AUTHORITY, 469 U.S. 528 (1985).

At issue in *Usery* was whether Congress had the power, pursuant to the COMMERCE CLAUSE of ARTICLE I OF THE U.S. CONSTITUTION, to enact the Fair Labor Standards Act, which required that states pay their state and local employees a minimum wage. The issue arose when a consortium of cities and states brought suit against the secretary of labor, Mr. Usery, contending that Congress could not exercise its commerce power "so as to force directly upon the States its choices as to how essential decision[s] regarding the conduct of integral governmental functions are to be made." In the view of appellant National League of Cities, the Tenth Amendment reserved to the states decisions regarding traditional state and local functions, such as the setting of minimum wages for state employees.

In an opinion written by then-Justice WILLIAM HUBBS REHNQUIST for four other justices, the Court agreed that the states retained the power to set minimum wages for state employees. Justice Rehnquist reasoned that, although it is "beyond peradventure that the commerce clause . . . is a grant of plenary authority to Congress," the power is not without limits. "Congressional enactments which may be fully within the grant of legislative authority contained in the commerce clause may nonetheless be invalid if they offend" particular constitutional provisions, such as the SIXTH AMENDMENT'S RIGHT TO TRIAL BY JURY or the Fifth Amendment's guarantee of DUE PROCESS. The *Usery* Court held that the Tenth Amendment reflects one such limitation: it limits the federal government from interfering with traditional state or local functions. Forcing states to pay their employees a federal minimum wage would require the states to raise taxes or cut services to pay increased wages and, in turn, may force states to "substantially restructure traditional ways in which the local governments have arranged their affairs."

Justice Blackmun penned a short concurrence downplaying the possible implications of the majority's opinion. In his view, the majority opinion adopted a balancing approach that would "not outlaw federal power in areas such as environmental protection, where the federal interest is demonstrably greater and where state facility compliance with imposed federal standards would be essential."

In dissent, Justice WILLIAM J. BRENNAN, JR., joined by Justices White and Marshall, contended that the Tenth Amendment did not affirmatively limit Congress's power under the commerce clause and assailed the majority for setting forth an unworkable standard for ascertaining the limits of congressional power. In a separate dissent, Justice JOHN PAUL STEVENS argued that the Court had failed to articulate a principled basis to determine whether a particular federal law violates the Tenth Amendment.

Following *Usery,* the Court struggled to define what powers were reserved to the states under the Tenth Amendment. A decade later, the Court, in an opinion by Justice Blackmun, expressly overruled *Usery* in *Garcia v. San Antonio Metropolitan Transit Authority,* rejecting as "unsound in principle and unworkable in practice, a rule of state immunity from federal regulation that turns on a judicial appraisal of whether a particular government function is 'traditional' or 'integral.'"

For more information: McAffee, Thomas B., Jay S. Bybee, and A. Christopher Bryant. *Powers Reserved for the People and the States: A History of the Ninth and Tenth Amendments.* Westport, Conn.: Praeger Publishers, 2006.

—Andre Mura

national security and the Constitution

The making of national security under the Constitution is assigned primarily to the president in ARTICLE II as COMMANDER IN CHIEF of the armed forces and to Congress under its various powers outlined in ARTICLE I. While both of these branches of government have historically shared responsibility in the creation of national security policy, at different times Congress and the president have sought to assume more responsibility, thereby setting up conflict and competition between the two. Moreover, the making of national security policy also raises issues regarding the scope of protection for individual rights when the United States faces a security threat. The competition between Congress and the president and the balance of freedom versus security can especially be seen since the events of 9/11, as the president has sought to assume more authority in the making of national security and foreign policy, and as critics contend that many of his actions violated the Constitution and the BILL OF RIGHTS.

The authors of the Constitution of the United States created a system of ordered liberty, in which the Constitution distributes powers for securing national security among the three branches of government. To the president and the Congress were given the major portions of power and responsibility, including law enforcement and war powers as outlined in Articles I and II. Article I, Section 8 of the Constitution describes several exclusive powers of Congress in the area of war making and foreign policy, including the authority to declare war, to raise and support an army and navy, and to make regulations for the military. Article II, Section 2 makes the president exclusively the commander in chief of the armed forces. Finally, Article II, Section 2 gives Congress and the president joint authority to nominate and confirm ambassadors and to negotiate and ratify treaties. In general, the courts have had the responsibility to settle disputes between them and to protect the liberties of the people, deciding cases between order and liberty.

Throughout American history there has been a continuing debate regarding where the lines are drawn to divide the constitutional authority of the president from that of the Congress. While during the Civil War, President ABRAHAM LINCOLN and Congress often clashed, the Supreme Court generally endorsed Lincoln's authority to act. For example, in the *Prize Cases,* 67 U.S. 635 (1863), the Court upheld Lincoln's order to blockade the South's ports, ruling that the president's power as commander in chief was broad enough to permit this action. However, in *EX PARTE MILLIGAN,* 71 U.S. 4 Wall. 2 (1866), the Supreme Court ruled that an American citizen could not be tried by military commission when the civil federal courts were open and operational. The significance of the *Milligan* decision was that it limited the ability of the president to try American citizens without all the constitutionally protected guarantees when accused of a crime. Finally, in *EX PARTE MCCARDLE,* 74 U.S. 506 (1869), the Supreme Court ruled that it lacked the jurisdiction to hear a HABEAS COR-PUS petition by an individual even though it had already heard oral arguments in his case. These three Civil War–era cases seem to suggest that the courts will defend or ignore individual rights, presidential power, and congressional authority at different times when the United States is facing security threats.

Congress and the president competed for rival influence in foreign and national security policy after the Civil War and through World Wars I and II, but individual rights were challenged in a series of cases, such as *SCHENCK V. UNITED STATES,* 249 U.S. 47 (1919), and *WHITNEY V. CALIFORNIA,* 274 U.S. 357 (1927). The Supreme Court upheld laws criminalizing individuals who criticized World War I or who otherwise were deemed to have engaged in subversive activity. Similarly, during the cold war after World War II, in cases such as *Dennis v. United States,* 341 U.S. 494 (1951), the Court upheld the conviction of a member of the Communist Party for a violation of the Smith Act, which had made it illegal to "knowingly or willfully advocate, abet, advise or teach the duty, necessity, desirability or propriety of overthrowing the Government of the United States or of any State by force or violence, or for anyone to organize any association which teaches, advises or encourages such an overthrow, or for anyone

to become a member of or to affiliate with any such association." The Smith Act and other policies such as LOYALTY OATHS, during the Cold War and McCarthy eras, effectively make it illegal simply to be a communist. All these actions were taken as necessary to protect national security, and the Supreme Court displayed a mixed record in upholding or voiding them on constitutional (generally FIRST AMENDMENT) grounds.

One of the most important Court cases examining the relationship between the powers of these two branches is found in *YOUNGSTOWN SHEET & TUBE V. SAWYER,* 343 U.S. 579 (1952). Here President Truman stepped in via executive order and had the steel mills of the nation seized in order to avert a strike during the Korean War. The Supreme Court overturned the seizure. Justice Robert Jackson's concurrence in the case suggested that the president's or commander in chief's authority is limited in scope, and he cannot act on his own without the consent of Congress on most matters that offer other methods for recourse.

Jackson described three categories of presidential power: (1) "When the President acts pursuant to an express or implied authorization of Congress, his authority is at its maximum"; (2) "When the President acts in absence of either a congressional grant or denial of authority, he can only rely upon his own independent powers, but there is a zone of twilight in which he and Congress may have concurrent authority, or in which its distribution is uncertain"; and (3) "When the President takes measures incompatible with the expressed or implied will of Congress, his power is at its lowest ebb, for then he can rely only upon his own constitutional powers minus any constitutional powers of Congress over the matter." Jackson's concurrence sets up a trifold analysis of presidential and congressional power in national security based on whether the two branches are cooperating or in conflict.

The lines between congressional and presidential power were again tested in the Vietnam War. Here, Presidents Lyndon Johnson and RICHARD NIXON deployed hundreds of thousands of troops without a formal declaration of war by Congress. They instead relied upon the Gulf of Tonkin Resolution, which was adopted by Congress on August 7, 1964, in response to an alleged attack on the United States by North Vietnam. The resolution seemed to empower the president to take any steps necessary to protect the United States. Many contended that the Vietnam War and the deployment of troops was unconstitutional, but in cases such as *Mora v. McNamara,* 389 U.S. 934 (1967), the Supreme Court refused to address this question.

In 1973, Congress sought to close the gap between the lines of authority of Congress to make war versus the president's power as commander in chief by adopting the WAR POWERS ACT. This act provides for limited presidential engagement of troops for up to 60 days, and it also mandates that the president must consult with Congress when possible before deploying troops. Congress, by joint resolution, could also require the president to bring the troops home sooner. However, the act has thus far been invoked by the president only once—in 1975, when Gerald Ford sent troops in to rescue members of the *Mayaguez* who had been captured by Cambodia—and the constitutionality of it is in question, since it relies upon a LEGISLATIVE VETO. In *INS v. Chada,* 462 U.S. 919 (1983), the Supreme Court declared unconstitutional a one-house legislative veto, leaving open whether even a two-house VETO would be upheld.

The terrorist attacks of September 11, 2001, on the United States have yet again raised questions about what powers the president as commander in chief has. Similarly to what happened in Vietnam, Congress authorized the president to respond to the attacks with the authorization to use military force (AUMF) of September 14, 2001, "to use all necessary and appropriate force against those nations, organizations, or persons he determines planned, authorized, committed or aided the terrorist attacks that occurred on September 11, 2001, . . . in order to prevent any future acts of international terrorism against the United States by such nations, organizations, or persons." The authorization appeared, or has been invoked, to give him extensive power to respond to terrorist attacks. President Bush has invoked AUMF, as well as claims of inherent executive authority as commander in chief, to undertake a variety of actions,

including electronic surveillance of overseas communications without warrants issued by the courts and the detaining of suspected terrorists without arraignments. These claims of presidential authority, along with AUMF and the adoption of the PATRIOT ACT, have raised concerns that the war on terrorism is both threatening individual liberties and producing a usurping of congressional power by the president.

The Supreme Court has addressed some of the constitutional issues arising out of the actions taken by the president and Congress since 9/11. In *HAMDI V. RUMSFELD,* 542 U.S. 507 (2004), *RASUL V. BUSH,* 545 U.S. 466 (2004), *RUMSFELD V. PADILLA,* 542 U.S. 426 (2004), and *Hamdan v. Rumsfeld,* 126 S.Ct. 2749 (2006), the Supreme Court has generally ruled that the president lacks the authority to detain indefinitely both American citizens and aliens without hearings, and the Court has also ruled that the tribunals and procedures set up so far have not complied with the Constitution. In addition, in *American Civil Liberties Union v. National Security Agency,* 438 F. Supp. 2d 754 (D. Mich. 2006), a Michigan district court struck down as unconstitutional the president's warrantless electronic surveillance program, finding that it violated both the First and FOURTH AMENDMENTS. More important, this case rejected the

President George W. Bush speaks to members of the armed forces, Department of Defense, and Department of State in the Pentagon auditorium on March 19, 2008.

government's claims that the president has inherent authority for this type of surveillance. However, a Sixth Circuit decision overturned the Michigan court, ruling that the plaintiffs lacked STANDING because they had failed to demonstrate an injury.

Overall, recent post-9/11 debates and litigation continue to highlight the tension between the powers of the president and Congress and the status of individual rights that are constitutionally raised when national security issues are implicated.

For more information: Ball, Howard. *The USA Patriot Act of 2001: Balancing Civil Liberties and National Security: A Reference Handbook.* Santa Barbara, Calif.: ABC-CLIO, 2004; Dycus, Stephen, et al. *National Security Law.* New York: Aspen Law and Business, 2006; Graham, Edward M., and David M. Marchick. *U.S. National Security and Foreign Direct Investment.* Washington, D.C.: Institute for International Economics, 2006; Moore, John Norton, and Robert F. Turner, eds. *National Security Law.* Durham, N.C.: Carolina Academic Press, 2005; Posner, Richard A. *Not a Suicide Pact: The Constitution in a Time of National Emergency.* New York: Oxford University Press, 2006; Shanor, Charles A., and L. Lynn Hogue. *National Security and Military Law in a Nutshell.* St. Paul, Minn.: Thomson/West, 2003.

—David Schultz and Andrew J. Waskey

natural law

Natural laws (also known as the laws of nature) are principles, conditions, or patterns that are not of human making or human design; rather, natural laws are those laws that exist independently of human will and that have as their origin nature itself or a divine entity. For some, such as Justice CLARENCE THOMAS, natural laws are the basic rules or principles that should guide the constitution and interpretation of human laws, including the Constitution.

Theories of natural law generally claim that natural law is morally superior to positive law (law made by governments) and that positive laws should be evaluated in relation to the standards set by the laws of nature. Theories of natural law also tend to argue that natural laws have a universal claim to our obedience. That is, natural law theory tends to conceptualize natural law as a law that imposes obligations that form the boundaries of acceptable human choices and actions. Furthermore, natural law theorists have generally taught that humans know natural law by virtue of a special human attribute, usually reason (or, for theologically minded natural law theorists, reason assisted by revelation). A belief in natural law is a prevalent theme in ancient, medieval, and early modern political and moral philosophy. Theories of natural law have also influenced American political thought and jurisprudence since the colonial period, including the writing of the DECLARATION OF INDEPENDENCE and the Constitution. In fact, many of the rights found in the BILL OF RIGHTS were thought of as natural rights, and the limitations on the powers of the government found in the Constitution may have had natural law origins.

The roots of natural law theory can be traced to antiquity. Arguments grounded in assumptions about the existence of natural law can be found in the classical Greek political theories of Plato (427?–347 B.C.) and Aristotle (384–322 B.C.) and in the teachings of Greek and Roman Stoics (Zeno, Cicero, Seneca, Marcus Aurelius). While disagreeing about the specific content of the best political life or the best political system, for example, both Plato and Aristotle taught that there are certain standards (of justice, virtue, goodness, etc.) that are transcendent and objective, in that the substance of such standards are not reducible to the mere opinions of humans, but, rather, exist in a realm of truth more enduring and reliable than the fads or whims of the moment.

Indeed, Aristotle wrote that humanness itself was identifiable by means of its natural (objectively true) and lawlike qualities. Aristotle taught, for example, that man was, by nature, a creature who, according to his very essence as a man, could live fully only as a member of a polis (political community). Someone who might appear to be a man but who lived outside the polis would be essentially (i.e., naturally) of a different character—such a creature might superficially look like a man, but he would have to be either a beast or a god. It is important to see in this example from Aristotle a crucial element associated with natural law theory: An observed or hypothetical difference that departs from what is regarded as the "natural" order/law/pattern is not interpreted as an alternative choice made by a being with a shared nature (i.e., two men making different choices, but neither choice makes the chooser any less a man), but is, instead, interpreted as indicative of a different nature (i.e., man in contrast to beast or god). In the medieval period, Thomas Aquinas (1224–74) continued the natural law tradition in a manner that synthesized classical teachings and Christian doctrine. Aquinas taught that God's reason was manifest in what humans could understand as laws of nature.

Modern writers, like English philosophers John Locke (1632–1704) and William Blackstone (1723–80), offered elaborate theories based on natural law, and both Locke and Blackstone influenced many American thinkers on matters relating to natural law, natural rights, individualism, the right of revolution, and the need for limited government. Locke argued that laws of nature were simply "rules of reason" (i.e., principles that could be deduced by rational human beings); specifically, Locke asserted that rational people could figure out for themselves three common-sense rules to live by: Take care of yourself; do not harm others; and assist others in taking care of themselves when doing so does not impose self-harm. Governments did not need to indoctrinate such rules, Locke concluded. Blackstone concurred, noting that the laws of nature "are performed in a wondrous involuntary manner" insofar as they truly do come naturally to rational people. Locke explicitly linked the concept of natural law with advocacy of limited government and the right of revolution.

According to Locke, people had the capacity for knowing natural law (by virtue of their capacity to reason) on their own, and, therefore, in most instances, governments should be limited to the role of "umpirage," that is, stepping in to resolve disputes when conflict arose but then immediately stepping back and leaving rational people alone to live as they choose within the rules of reason/natural law. What if government exceeds its bounds as umpire and violates the laws of nature? Locke's answer was both philosophically logical and politically radical: If the government rebels against nature/the laws of nature, it is the people's right to resist/revolt against the government.

The writings of John Locke and William Blackstone, as well as their theories of natural law, were of tremendous influence on the constitutional framers. Thomas Jefferson, for example, invoked Locke and natural law in the writing of the Declaration of Independence. Similarly, the idea of natural law was behind the idea of a bill of rights, with many of the first 10 amendments representing basic rights many thought were natural or God-given. In particular, the Ninth Amendment, which states that the "enumeration in the Constitution, of certain rights, shall not be construed to deny or disparage others retained by the people," clearly recognized that individuals had a list of natural rights that the government could not restrict.

Throughout American history, the concept of natural law was important in constitutional interpretation. The idea of natural rights supported the concepts of economic or substantive due process in the late 19th and early 20th centuries, as the Supreme Court invoked these doctrines to limit the ability of state and federal governments to interfere with the economic rights of individuals and corporations. Since the New Deal, natural law, while not explicitly invoked, is behind many of the claims to protect individual rights, such as those guaranteeing privacy. Most recently, Justice Clarence Thomas has invoked natural law in his constitutional interpretation.

For more information: Blackstone, William. *Commentaries on the Laws of England.* Chicago: The University of Chicago Press, 1979; Locke, John. "Second Treatise of Government." In *Classics of Moral and Political Theory.* 4th ed. Cambridge, Mass.: Hackett Publishing Company, 2005; Wright, B. F., Jr. "American Interpretations of Natural Law." *The American Political Science Review* 20 (1926): 524–547.

—Ellen Grigsby

Near v. Minnesota 283 U.S. 697 (1931)

In *Near v. Minnesota,* the Supreme Court struck down as a violation of the FIRST AMENDMENT a Minnesota statute known as a "public nuisance" law that allowed authorities to close down any "malicious, scandalous and defamatory newspaper, magazine, or other periodical." A local prosecutor sought to halt publication of a newspaper that published virulent anti-Semitic charges and that also accused the police chief of improprieties. The state courts upheld the measure and it closed down the newspaper.

But the U.S. Supreme Court, in a narrow 5-4 ruling, held that the statute was unconstitutional. It violated the protection of freedom of speech and the press in the First Amendment. The Court drew upon age-old English law proscribing "censorship of the press," which was then enshrined in the Constitution and was a predicate of the freedom of expression provisions in the Constitution. The Minnesota statute was constitutionally infirm, because it required newspapers charged with statutory offenses to prove that their publications were true and published for good motives and justifiable ends, which the court characterized as "the essence of censorship." The decision, in addition to creating a barrier to prior suppression of freedom of expression, was significant because it was the first time that the Supreme Court had ever applied any of the provisions of the BILL OF RIGHTS, the first ten amendments of the U.S. Constitution, to the states. In previous cases, the Supreme Court and other tribunals had held that the protections under the Bill of Rights, including the First Amendment, applied only to the federal government and not to state and local units of government. But the *Near* case parted from that restriction and began a process by which most of the provisions of the Bill of Rights were applied to state and local governments through a process known as "selective INCORPORATION."

The prohibition against prior restriction in the *Near* case was not absolute. The Court suggested that government could obtain "previous restraint . . . in exceptional cases." It offered examples such as national security, actual obstruction to "recruiting" of the military, or publications giving details of military actions. It also mentioned "obscene publications" as subject to prior restraint.

Although the decision was a fragile one, decided by a single vote, the prohibition against prior restraint has become a bedrock principle of First Amendment law. As a result of *Near,* courts are almost always disinclined to prohibit publication of offensive or objectionable material. The prohibition, however, does not extend to post-punishment sanctions that may be imposed for violation of laws.

An application of the doctrine was tested. The protection of national security, as alluded to in the *Near* decision, was at the forefront in another Supreme Court ruling in *The Pentagon Papers* case 40 years later. In *New York Times v. United States,* 403 U.S. 713 (1971), the Supreme Court rejected an effort by the government to prohibit publication of an internal classified report of government decisions regarding the Vietnam War, which was reflective of various flaws and defects in the way the war had been conducted. Relying upon the proscription in *Near,* the majority of the Court, by a 6-3 vote, held unconstitutional the effort of the government to stop two newspapers, the *New York Times* and the *Washington Post.* The decision fortified the barrier against prior restraint erected in the *Near* case.

For more information: Friendly, Fred W. *Minnesota Rag: The Dramatic Story of the Landmark Court Case That Gave New Meaning to Freedom of the Press.* New York: Random House, 1981.

—Marshall Tanick

Nebbia v. New York 291 U.S. 502 (1934)

In *Nebbia v. New York,* the Supreme Court upheld a New York law that fixed prices for the retail sale of milk. The Court ruled that it was not a violation of the DUE PROCESS clause of the FOURTEENTH AMENDMENT for the state legislature to regulate the price of a necessary good such as milk, as long as the regulation was not arbitrary or unreasonable.

In the early 1930s, due to a variety of economic conditions, dairy farmers in New York struggled to sell their milk for a price greater than their cost of production. Milk retailers began buying directly from farmers, rather than from large milk distributors, allowing them to bypass the high storage and delivery costs associated with moving a perishable item such as milk through the distribution chain, and thus increasing their own profits. As a result, farmers were forced to sell milk to both retailers and distributors at a lower price. The state feared that the drop in price would cause farmers to loosen up on their health inspections, so the legislature passed a bill that fixed the minimum price at which a quart of milk could be sold at 10 cents for distributors and nine cents for retailers. Nebbia, a grocery store owner, was convicted for selling two quarts of milk and a five-cent loaf of bread for 18 cents.

Nebbia argued that the government was violating the Fourteenth Amendment by interfering with his right to contract with another private party. Justice JOHN G. ROBERTS, JR., writing on behalf of the majority, responded by stating that such rights, even if protected, can be infringed upon if proper regard to due process is given. He found the state health concerns to be legitimate and ruled that there is no freedom of contract in the Fourteenth Amendment sufficient to supersede the right of the state to promote public welfare. He noted that any industry affecting the public interest is subject to control for the public good.

Justice McReynolds dissented, arguing that there was no evidence that this law would help achieve the ends sought. He noted that consumers were also struggling and doubted that putting the price of milk out of reach for a great number of consumers would help increase returns for dairy farmers.

Nebbia v. New York stands as a departure from precedent set by the Supreme Court in *LOCHNER V. NEW YORK*, 198 U.S. 45 (1905), which invalidated a state law restricting work hours for bakers. Many other economic regulations were challenged and upheld in the face of *Lochner* before *Nebbia* was decided, but most, if not all, of those decisions lacked the breadth and clout of the decision in *Nebbia*. Today, *Nebbia* remains influential, while *Lochner* defines a bygone era of Supreme Court doctrine.

For more information: Cushman, Barry. "Lost Fidelities," *William and Mary Law Review* 41 (December 1999): 95–145; Gillman, Howard. *The Constitution Besieged: The Rise and Demise of* Lochner *Era Police Powers Jurisprudence.* Durham, N.C.: Duke University Press, 1993.

—Dylan R. Kytola

Nebraska Press Association v. Stuart 427 U.S. 539 (1976)

In *Nebraska Press Association v. Stuart,* a court order restricting media coverage of a murder suspect's trial was held to be an unconstitutional infringement on FREEDOM OF THE PRESS. The decision recognized the potential for conflict between the accused's SIXTH AMENDMENT right to a fair trial and the FIRST AMENDMENT rights of the news media. Nevertheless, the Court held that a restraining order against media coverage was an unwarranted response to this conflict, reaffirming that prior restraints are not constitutional except in the most extraordinary of circumstances.

In October 1975, Erwin Charles Simants was arrested and charged with the murder of six members of a family in Sutherland, Nebraska, a town of about 850 people. The prosecutor and defense jointly requested a restraining order limiting news coverage in order to ensure that the county court would be able to find an impartial jury and provide a fair trial. The county court issued an order prohibiting the publication or broadcast of accounts suggesting that Simants was guilty in the killings. The order was to remain in effect until a jury was impanelled.

Attorneys for the media petitioned the state district court to lift the order, while simultaneously requesting that the Nebraska Supreme Court hear their petition on an expedited basis. The district court issued its own order prohibiting reporting on evidence of Simants's guilt, as well as details about the order itself, and the Nebraska Supreme Court upheld the restraining order.

The U.S. Supreme Court agreed to hear the case. Oral arguments were held on April 19, 1976, and the court's decision was announced on June 30. The restraining order expired before oral arguments were heard, and Simants was convicted and sentenced to death. (Simants was granted a new trial in 1979 and found not guilty by reason of insanity.)

Attorneys for the media argued that the restraining order was an unconstitutional restriction on freedom of the press. Attorneys for Hugh Stuart, the Nebraska district judge, argued that extensive pretrial publicity would have made it impossible for Simants to receive a fair trial and that therefore Stuart had acted properly in issuing the order to protect Simants's rights under the Sixth and FOURTEENTH AMENDMENTS. They also argued that the case was moot because the restraining order was no longer in effect.

The Court ruled that the restraining order was an unconstitutional restriction on the press. Chief Justice WARREN BURGER wrote for the majority and was joined by Justices White, Blackmun, LEWIS POWELL, and WILLIAM HUBBS REHNQUIST. Justices White, Powell, and JOHN PAUL STEVENS filed separate concurrences, and Justice WILLIAM J. BRENNAN, JR., filed a concurring opinion that was joined by Justices Stewart and Marshall.

In the majority opinion, Burger rejected the argument that the case was moot because, while the controversy was no longer active, it was "capable of repetition, yet evading review" (546). The Court agreed that the case was certain to be the subject of a great deal of pretrial publicity. Nevertheless, it ruled that a prior restraint on the press was an inappropriate remedy that was unlikely to be more effective than less-objectionable alternatives. "If it can be said that a threat of criminal or civil sanctions after publication 'chills' speech, prior restraint 'freezes' it at least for the time," Burger wrote, explaining why there must be a heavy presumption against prior restraint.

For more information: Russomanno, Joseph. *Speaking Our Minds: Conversations with the People behind Landmark First Amendment Cases.* Mahwah, N.J.: Lawrence Erlbaum Associates, 2002; Stack, Richard A. *Courts, Counselors and Correspondents: A Media Relations Analysis of the Legal System.* Littleton, Colo.: Fred B. Rothman and Co., 1998.

—Thomas C. Ellington

necessary and proper clause

The necessary and proper clause is found in ARTICLE I, Section 8 of the United States Constitution, which reads, "The Congress shall have power . . . to make all laws which shall be necessary and proper for carrying into execution the foregoing powers, and all other powers vested by this Constitution in the government of the United States, or in any department or officer thereof."

The necessary and proper clause is subject to interpretation. Those who take a strict constructionist view of the Constitution argue that Congress's power is limited to laws directly related to their specific powers listed in Article I, Section 8. If a power is not listed, Congress does not have it. Those who take a broad view of the clause suggest that it is practically impossible to list every single congressional power in the Constitution. Nor is it feasible to continually amend the Constitution each time Congress wants to exercise its power. Furthermore, the clause is found in the same section of the Constitution granting (not limiting) Congress's powers. Article I, Section 8 lists all of Congress's explicit powers and ends with the necessary and proper clause, which can be read as yet another one of Congress's enumerated powers. Therefore, the necessary and proper clause serves an elasticity function in that it allows Congress to pass laws not expressly enumerated in Article I, but are nevertheless pursuant to one of their expressly enumerated powers.

The necessary and proper clause was at the heart of a number of debates during the early American Republic over the scope of federal power with respect to the states. One of the most famous cases was *MCCULLOCH V. MARYLAND*, 4 Wheaton 316 (1819), which involved the right of the federal government to create a national bank. In 1791, Secretary of the Treasury ALEXANDER

HAMILTON, a Federalist, invoked the necessary and proper clause to establish the bank on the grounds that the Constitution did not expressly give Congress the power to establish it. Hamilton argued that Congress not only had those powers that were expressly enumerated in the Constitution, but under a broad reading of the clause, Congress also had those powers that were not expressly denied to it. The bank charter expired after 20 years, but in 1816, Congress chartered the Second Bank of the United States, mainly to help finance in part the War of 1812. The clause was also paired with Congress's explicit constitutional power to regulate commerce—the bank was necessary to facilitate the flow of INTERSTATE COMMERCE. Opponents of the bank argued that the Constitution did not expressly give Congress the authority to establish a national bank. The state of Maryland imposed a tax on any bank not chartered by the state, which included the Bank of the United States. Maryland argued that the bank was unconstitutional because the Constitution did not specifically authorize the federal government to charter a bank.

In *McCulloch,* Chief Justice JOHN MARSHALL argued that Congress had the authority to incorporate a national bank. Even though such power was not expressly enumerated in the Constitution, it was an implied power that stemmed from Congress's other enumerated financial powers, such as the power to collect taxes, to borrow money, to regulate commerce, and to declare and conduct a war. In this case, the bank was necessary in order to implement Congress's enumerated powers.

Marshall wrote, "Let the end be legitimate, let it be within the scope of the Constitution, and all means which are appropriate, which are plainly adapted to that end, which are not prohibited, but consistent with the letter and spirit of the Constitution, are constitutional" (420). In this case, the end was the establishment of a strong national economy under the auspices of the taxing and spending power, which was within the purview of Congress's delegated powers. By virtue of the necessary and proper clause, Congress was authorized to use its best judgment to carry into execution its constitutional powers. And as long as that judgment (i.e., the means) did not violate the Constitution, Congress was acting within the scope of its authority. The bank, therefore, was made in pursuance of the Constitution and could not be subject to a tax by the state of Maryland, which in and of itself violated the supremacy of the Constitution. With this decision, the necessary and proper clause became the basis for the expansion of federal authority.

For more information: Gunther, Gerald. *John Marshall's Defense of* McCulloch v. Maryland. Stanford, Calif.: Stanford University Press, 1969; McCloskey, Robert G. *The American Supreme Court.* 3d ed. Chicago: University of Chicago Press, 2000.

—Randa Issa

neutral principles

Professor Herbert Wechsler coined the term "neutral principles" in his 1959 Holmes Lecture at Harvard Law School. This lecture became one of the most cited and controversial pieces of legal scholarship.

Wechsler began the lecture by arguing, contra Judge LEARNED HAND, that because the Constitution grants the Supreme Court the power of JUDICIAL REVIEW, the Court may, and indeed must, exercise this power whenever a matter is properly within its jurisdiction. According to Wechsler, a corollary to the duty to review the constitutionality of legislation is the duty to act differently from "a naked power organ." Therefore, to distinguish constitutional adjudication from "the *ad hoc* in politics," the Court must apply neutral principles to cases. For Wechsler, a neutral principle consists of two elements: content generality and equal applicability. Wechsler thus defined a principled decision as one resting on "reasons quite transcending the immediate result that is achieved" and applying to all parties equally, "whether a labor union or a taxpayer, a Negro or a segregationist, a corporation or a Communist." At the end of his lecture, Wechsler shocked many by using this neutrality framework to criticize some of the Supreme Court's most progressive decisions, particularly those of the WARREN COURT. Most famously, Wechsler argued that BROWN V. BOARD OF EDUCATION, 347 U.S. 483 (1954), was not a principled decision because the Court's use of education-specific social science to invalidate the "separate but equal" doctrine was motivated, not by a general principle of race equality, but by a bare desire to integrate public education.

Wechsler's attack on the Warren Court elicited harsh responses. Shortly after Wechsler's lecture, the then professor and later judge Louis Pollack drafted an opinion explaining how the *Brown* opinion did rest on a neutral principle—the "anti-subordination" principle that the government may not discriminate against any racial minority (Louis H. Pollack, *Racial Discrimination and Judicial Integrity: A Reply to Professor Wechsler,* 108 U. Pa. L. Rev. 1 [1959]). Political scientist Martin Shapiro modified Wechsler's thesis by arguing that, because the Court is just another political actor whose function is to achieve results that the people accept, the Court must *appear* neutral, but need not *be* neutral (Martin Shapiro, *The Supreme Court and Constitutional Adjudication: Of Politics and Neutral Principles,* 31 Geo. Wash. L. Rev. 587 [1963]). Some conservative scholars, seeking to add an originalist element to Wechsler's thesis, argued that neutrality must guide the Court, not only in the application of principles, but also in their derivation (ROBERT H. BORK, *Neutral Principles and Some First Amendment Problems,* 47 Ind. L.J. 1 [1971]). Many liberals sought to abandon Wechsler's project altogether, some characterizing it as naive because judges could not and would not transcend their political preferences (Addison Mueller & Murray L. Schwartz, *The Principle of Neutral Principles,* 7 UCLA L. Rev. 571, 577 [1960]), and others making the sweeping claim that there is no such thing as a constitutionally neutral principle (Mark V. Tushnet, *Following the Rules Laid Down: A Critique of Interpretivism and Neutral Principles,* 96 Harv. L. Rev. 781 [1983]).

Despite these criticisms, Wechsler's neutralism remains extremely important to constitutional theory and practice. Neutralism provides a powerful rebuttal to the legal realist claim that law is just another name for politics; antirealists see neutralism as a way to restore the objectivity and reason that had once distinguished law as a discipline. Moreover, the ideal of neutrality still animates constitutional doctrine: Procedural DUE PROCESS guarantees a hearing before a neutral arbiter; religious disestablishment and liberty compel religion-neutrality; EQUAL PROTECTION commands race-neutrality; and free speech analysis turns on whether a speech restriction is content- or viewpoint-neutral. Undeniably, no matter what one thinks of Wechsler's neutralist framework and application, his lecture on neutral principles has profoundly influenced the insoluble debate over the essence of law, and will continue to play a role in efforts to depoliticize constitutional law.

For more information: Friedman, Barry. "Neutral Principles: A Retrospective," *Vanderbilt Law Review* 50 (1997): 503–535.

—Jesse R. Merriam

New Jersey Plan (1787)

The New Jersey Plan, a governmental outline proposed by William Patterson at the CONSTITUTIONAL CONVENTION, was created primarily not only to replace the defunct Articles of Confederation, but also to allay smaller states' fears about being dominated in the new government. Ultimately, it was not officially adopted entirely but formed an integral part of the government structure decided upon as a result of the CONNECTICUT COMPROMISE engineered by Roger Williams.

William Patterson was born in Ireland but immigrated to New Jersey as a young man and graduated from the College of New Jersey, which was to later become Princeton University. He studied law and became a citizens' rights activist, greatly influenced by Enlightenment philosophers. His background; his active participation before, during, and after the Revolution; and his resulting renown and influence allowed him to make significant contributions to the Constitutional Convention.

His most important contribution, the New Jersey Plan, was structured in response to the VIRGINIA PLAN proposed by JAMES MADISON. The New Jersey Plan, which he proposed on June 15, 1787, called for the creation of a three-branch government composed of legislative, executive, and judicial branches. The legislative branch contained only a single house in which states would have equal voting power, regardless of size or population. The unicameral legislation was empowered to elect those who were to serve in the multi-executive branch. In turn, the executive selected the justices for the Supreme Court, which made up the judicial branch. Interestingly, the executives could have been recalled not only by the legislature, but also by state governors. The New Jersey Plan also called for the supremacy of the national government, making all state laws subordinate to the laws and directions imposed by the central government.

Most importantly, the New Jersey Plan offered smaller states a hope of not being dominated by more populous states like Virginia and Pennsylvania. Some smaller northern states even feared an expected rise in southern populations due to a temporary economic boom at the time. The equal representation scheme in the unicameral legislation was seen as a protection for smaller states and contrasted directly with the Virginia Plan, which proposed a bicameral legislation based entirely upon population-based representation. In this way, Patterson's proposal was a direct rebuttal of the Virginia Plan, somewhat throwing the Constitutional Convention into turmoil, as delegates and states were split between the plans.

From a legal standpoint, the New Jersey Plan was more similar to the Articles of Confederation, since it guarded certain powers for states and protected smaller ones. As a result, the proposal reheated arguments over whether or not to rework or scrap the former confederation system. Impasse reigned over the Convention until the Connecticut Compromise was decided upon, leading to a mixing of the Virginia and New Jersey plans.

For more information: Berkin, Carol. *A Brilliant Solution: Inventing the American Constitution.* New York: Harcourt, 2002; Collier, Christopher. *All Politics Is Local: Family, Friends, and Provincial Interests in the Creation of the Constitution.* Hanover, N.H.: University Press of New England, 2003; Collier, Christopher. *Decision in Philadelphia: The Constitutional Convention of 1787.* New York: Ballantine Books, 1987; Solberg, Winton U., ed. *The Constitutional Convention and the Formation of the Union.* 2d ed. Urbana: University of Illinois Press, 1990.

—Arthur Holst

New Jersey v. T.L.O. 469 U.S. 325 (1985)

In *New Jersey v. T.L.O.* the Supreme Court ruled that public school officials do not need a warrant or probable cause before conducting a search. For a search to be valid, all they need is reasonable grounds to suspect that the search will produce evidence that a student has violated either the law or a school rule.

A teacher at a New Jersey high school discovered T.L.O., a 14-year-old freshman, and her friend smoking in the school restroom in violation of a school rule. The two girls were brought to the vice-principal's office and questioned about the incident. T.L.O. denied she had been smoking and claimed that she never smoked. The vice-principal then opened T.L.O.'s purse and saw a pack of cigarettes and a package of cigarette rolling papers commonly associated with marijuana use. A further search of the purse produced a small quantity of marijuana, a pipe, plastic bags, a substantial amount of money, an index card with the names of students who owed T.L.O. money, and two letters implicating her in the sale of marijuana. This evidence was turned over to police, and T.L.O. was charged with delinquent conduct. The juvenile court denied T.L.O.'s motion to suppress the evidence found in her purse, holding that the search by the vice-principal was reasonable. T.L.O. was subsequently adjudicated delinquent. The state appellate court affirmed the juvenile court's ruling, but the New Jersey Supreme Court reversed, holding that the search was unreasonable and that the evidence should be suppressed.

The United States Supreme Court held that, although students are constitutionally protected from illegal searches and seizures while at school, school officials are not bound by the same restrictions as law enforcement officers. Police need "probable cause" before they can conduct a search, but teachers and other school officials are permitted to search a student when they have "reasonable suspicion" to believe that the student has violated the law or broken a school rule. The Court noted that school officials have an important interest in maintaining a safe and orderly learning environment; thus school officials need not obtain a warrant before searching a student. However, the Court warned that such searches, when conducted by school officials, must be reasonable and not excessively intrusive in light of the student's age and sex and the nature of the violation.

The Court cited two considerations in determining whether a warrantless search of a student by a school official is "reasonable" or not. First, "one must consider whether . . . the action was justified at its inception." Second, "one must determine whether the search . . . was reasonably related in scope to the circumstances which justified the interference in the first place." In short, the first criterion involves the justification, or grounds, for initiating the search, while the second relates to the intrusiveness of the search.

For more information: Beger, Randall. "The Worst of Both Worlds: School Security and the Disappearing Fourth Amendment Rights of Students." *Criminal Justice Review* 28, no. 3 (2003): 336–354; Hemmens, Craig, Benjamin Steiner, and David Mueller. *Criminal Justice Case Briefs: Significant Cases in Juvenile Justice.* Los Angeles: Roxbury Publishing Company, 2004; Lawrence, Richard. *School Crime and Juvenile Justice.* New York: Oxford University Press, 1998.

—David Mueller

New State Ice Co. v. Liebmann 285 U.S. 262 (1932)

New State Ice Co. v. Liebmann, a Depression-era Supreme Court decision, is both a historical curiosity and a significant precursor. The majority opinion is an artifact of pre–New Deal DUE PROCESS jurisprudence. The dissent foreshadows the eclipse of that jurisprudence after 1937. *Liebmann* thus provides an instructive window into ongoing debates over the constitutional relationship between government POLICE POWER and the rights of property.

This case arose from a dispute between two competing Oklahoma City ice companies. The New State Ice Company sued one Liebmann, another ice purveyor, seeking an INJUNCTION prohibiting Liebmann from selling ice without the license required by state law. At trial, the federal district court dismissed New State's bill of complaint. That court's reasoning is grounded in a reading of the FOURTEENTH AMENDMENT due process clause then prevailing—a reading derived from an 1877 U.S. Supreme Court decision, MUNN V. ILLINOIS, 94 U.S. 113. *Munn* ties the constitutionality of government economic regulations to the character of the business being regulated. As Justice George Sutherland, author of the *New State* opinion, put it: "The question here is whether the business is so charged with a public use as to justify the particular restriction."

By a 6-2 vote (recently appointed Justice Cardozo did not participate), the Supreme Court held that the Oklahoma statute failed the *Munn* test. It was clear to the majority that the ice business is an "ordinary business . . . essentially private in its nature." Consequently, following *Munn* and citing a long list of subsequent progeny, Sutherland concluded: "A regulation which has the effect of denying or unreasonably curtailing the common right to engage in a lawful private business, such as that under review, cannot be upheld consistent with the Fourteenth Amendment."

Famously, Justice Brandeis disagreed. He supported the legitimacy of legislative discretion, and urged judicial restraint in second-guessing such judgments. Brandeis also rejected the *Munn* doctrine: "[T]he true principle is that the state's power extends to every regulation of any business reasonably required and appropriate for the public protection." He then placed the Oklahoma statute squarely within the context of the Great

Depression. "The people of the United States are now confronted with an emergency more serious than war." Social misery is rife, Brandeis wrote, and proposed governmental responses are problematical. Nevertheless: "There must be power in the states and the nation to remould, through experimentation, our economic practices and institutions to meet changing social and economic needs." To this Sutherland had replied: "It is plain that unreasonable or arbitrary interference or restrictions cannot be saved from . . . condemnation . . . merely by calling them experimental."

Accordingly, *New State Ice Co. v. Liebmann* illustrates the clash between "garden-variety" *Munn*-era economic due process (1877–1937), on the one hand, and the competing view—portraying each state "as a laboratory . . . try[ing] novel social and economic experiments"—that displaced (without destroying) the previous vision.

For more information: Krishnakumar, Anita A. "On the Evolution of the Canonical Dissent." *Rutgers Law Review* 52 (Spring 2000): 781–825; Sanders, Anthony B. "The 'New Judicial Federalism' before Its Time: A Comprehensive Review of Economic Substantive Due Process under State Constitutional Law since 1940 and the Reasons for Its Recent Decline." *American University Law Review* 55 (December 2005): 457–540.

—James C. Foster

New York Times v. Sullivan 376 U.S. 254 (1964)

In *New York Times v. Sullivan,* the Supreme Court struck down the application of a state DEFAMATION law to a newspaper and in the process issued a constitutional rule for the protection of FREEDOM OF THE PRESS.

Defamation was not subject to any protection under the freedom of press and speech provision of the FIRST AMENDMENT of the U.S. Constitution until 1964, when the Supreme Court decided the landmark case of *New York Times Co. v. Sullivan.* In that case, a full-page fund-raising advertisement was published in the *New York Times* magazine by a CIVIL RIGHTS organization, asserting abuse

and inappropriate behavior by law enforcement authorities in Montgomery, Alabama, during the height of the Civil Rights movement. The police commissioner of the city sued the newspaper for defamation for libel based on some minor inaccuracies in the advertisement, such as the statement that Dr. Martin Luther King Jr. had been arrested seven times, when, in fact, he had been arrested on only four occasions.

A state court jury in Alabama awarded $500,000, which the state supreme court upheld. The U.S. Supreme Court reversed the ruling, holding that because the commissioner was a "public official," he could not prevail unless he could prove that the newspaper published the inaccuracies with "knowing falsity or reckless disregard for the truth," which the Court referred to as "actual malice." The Court reasoned that the right of freedom of press and speech under the First Amendment of the U.S. Constitution requires some "breathing space" for errors, and that allowing defamation actions for inaccurate statements about public officials would deter the media and others from speaking out on important matters of public concern.

The "actual malice" referred to by the Supreme Court differs from the traditional notion of "malice," which consists of ill will or spite. Under the "actual malice" standard of *New York Times*, a claimant must prove that the person making the defamatory statements knew of their falsity with reckless disregard for the truth.

In subsequent decisions, the Supreme Court extended the *New York Times* rule to "public figures," persons who are in the limelight or voluntarily inject themselves into controversial matters (*Curtis Publishing Co. v. Butts* and *Associated Press v. Walker*, 388 U.S. 130 [1967]). It also ruled that "actual malice," knowing falsity and reckless disregard of the truth, must be established by clear and convincing evidence and cannot be based on shoddy or careless investigation or reporting, but generally must consist of a "purposeful avoidance of the truth" (*Harde-Hanks Communications, Inc., v. Connaughton*, 491 U.S. 657 [1989]). Punitive damages against the media also were restricted to instances where there is "knowing falsity or reckless disregard of the truth" (*Gertz v. Robert Welch, Inc.,* 418 U.S. 323 [1974]).

The standards established in *New York Times* do not apply in all instances. Those rules are limited to claims involving "public officials," elected or appointed government personnel, "public figures," and in some instances, matters of high-level public concern. These high standards make it very difficult for government personnel, well-known people, or those involved in high-profile controversies to prevail in defamation cases.

But private figures, individuals who do not fall within these categories, can pursue defamation claims without complying with the high standards of the *New York Times* doctrine. They can prevail if they prove that the defamatory statement was made carelessly or negligently. In these situations, a claimant need not prove that the falsity was intentional or done with recklessness.

For more information: Kalven, Harvey. *A Worthy Tradition: Freedom of Speech in America.* New York: Harper & Row, 1988; Lewis, Anthony, ed. *Make No Law: The Sullivan Case and the First Amendment.* New York: Random House, 1991.

—Marshall Tanick

Nineteenth Amendment

The Nineteenth Amendment to the Constitution states, "The rights of citizens of the United States to vote shall not be denied or abridged by the United States or by any state on account of sex. Congress shall have power to enforce this article by appropriate legislation." The amendment was ratified on August 18, 1920, giving American women the RIGHT TO VOTE in both state and federal elections.

The campaign to win women's suffrage dates from the 1848 SENECA FALLS Convention, where the delegates approved a resolution stating "that it is the duty of the women of this country to secure to themselves their sacred right to the elective franchise." The 19th-century movement, under the leadership of Elizabeth Cady Stanton and Susan B. Anthony, developed two major arguments to support voting rights for women. They made the case that full citizenship included the suffrage and that to be true to its egalitarian principles the United States must include women in the electorate. They and their followers also argued that women would use the franchise to improve society—to abolish slavery, to reform working conditions, to protect children, to enact prohibition—and that women would bring their unique perspective to address existing social problems.

Until the Civil War, women's rights organizations were mostly indistinguishable from antislavery groups. Many suffragists hoped that their interests would be considered as part of the constitutional changes that followed the war. Specifically, advocates of votes for women believed that the FIFTEENTH AMENDMENT, prohibiting denial of voting rights on the basis of "race, color, or previous condition of servitude," might be improved by adding the word "sex" to the list of forbidden discriminators. However, they were disappointed when their former allies in the abolitionist cause asked them to wait their turn for the vote. According to the Republicans who controlled Congress and supported the amendment, it was "the Negro's hour." Women's suffrage would be delayed another 50 years.

Supporters of votes for women, if united in their goal, were divided in their strategy. The National Women's Suffrage Association advocated an amendment to the U.S. Constitution, while the American Women's Suffrage Association worked more at the state level. The two groups united in the late 1890s to form the National American Women's Suffrage Association (NAWSA). In 1916, their leader, Carrie Chapman Catt, developed her "Winning Plan," which involved a tight hierarchical organization; extensive fund-raising, education and lobbying of politicians; and eventually winning the support of President Woodrow Wilson for a constitutional amendment.

NAWSA's efforts were undoubtedly aided by a rival organization, the more militant Women's Party. Members of the latter group picketed outside the White House, holding banners that offered mild criticisms of Wilson for his tepid interest in women's suffrage. During a crackdown on dissidents during World War I, scores of those women pickets were arrested and held in unspeakable conditions. To draw attention to their cause, a number of the suffrage women went on hunger strikes. When jailers brutally force-fed these middle-class political protesters, much public interest and sympathy turned in their direction. The Women's Party gained publicity for the suffrage; NAWSA organized the political process.

The HOUSE OF REPRESENTATIVES passed the suffrage amendment by exactly the required two-thirds majority on January 10, 1918. Four members of Congress left their sick beds to cast crucial votes in support. It passed the SENATE with 66 votes in May 1919. Much of the opposition to women's suffrage came from southern states, where politicians were reluctant to allow the federal government to get involved in deciding who should and should not vote for fear it would reopen the "Negro question." In addition, powerful lobbies such as the liquor industry (fearing women would support prohibition), business interests (fearing women would try to reform working conditions), and conservative religious groups, such as the Catholic hierarchy, also fought passage of the amendment.

After Congress assented to the suffrage amendment, ratification by three-fourths of the states took another year. Supporters assumed most southern states would refuse to ratify, but Tennessee ultimately provided the final approval. The deciding vote was cast by a young legislator whose mother had told him to "be a good boy" and vote for the suffrage. On August 26, 1920, 26 million women became enfranchised. Ten states—Delaware and nine in the South—refused to ratify the amendment.

The results of the Nineteenth Amendment delighted and disappointed both supporters and opponents. Women were not able to transform politics, as their advocates had hoped. On the other hand, their participation did not destroy the home, as some anti-suffragists had predicted. Ultimately, women's suffrage should be viewed as a vital step in the evolution of the relationship of American women with the state, a stage on the road to full citizenship.

For more information: Flexner, Eleanor. *Century of Struggle: The Woman's Rights Movement in the United States.* Cambridge, Mass.: Belknap Press of Harvard University, 1975; Kerber, Linda K. *No Constitutional Right to Be Ladies: Women and the Obligations of Citizenship.* New York: Hill and Wang, 2000.

—Mary Welek Atwell

Ninth Amendment

The Ninth Amendment guarantees rights to the people of the United States otherwise not stated or enumerated in the Constitution. This amendment is one of the original ten, the BILL OF RIGHTS that amended the Constitution in 1791, proposed by JAMES MADISON in the HOUSE OF REPRESENTATIVES. The Ninth Amendment is the result of intense debates that took place both between the Federalists and anti-Federalists during the debates over the RATIFICATION OF THE CONSTITUTION in 1787 and later, between James Madison and ALEXANDER HAMILTON.

In criticizing the proposed Constitution, the anti-Federalists argued that it was flawed because it lacked a Bill of Rights and therefore threatened the rights and liberties of individuals. In response, Federalist defenders of the document, such as Alexander Hamilton in *Federalist* 84, argued against a bill of rights. Hamilton offered two reasons. First, he noted that the proposed constitution did in fact contain many provisions that limited the power of the national government, such as bans on ex post facto laws and bills of attainder. Second, and more importantly, Hamilton argued that a bill of rights was not necessary because the Constitution did not grant any powers to limit rights and therefore no bill of rights, was necessary to limit the power of the federal government to do that. For Hamilton:

> Bills of rights, in the sense and to the extent in which they are contended for, are not only unnecessary in the proposed Constitution, but would even be dangerous. They would contain various exceptions to powers not granted; and, on this very account, would afford a colorable pre-

text to claim more than were granted. For why declare that things shall not be done which there is no power to do? Why, for instance, should it be said that the liberty of the press shall not be restrained, when no power is given by which restrictions may be imposed?

Hamilton saw the Constitution as a document containing only expressed powers. By that, unless the Constitution actually stated that the federal government had a specific power, it lacked it. Thus, why have a bill of rights that stated that Congress cannot limit freedom of speech if it lacked the authority to restrict expression?

Despite Hamilton's arguments in *Federalist 84*, many state legislatures during the ratification process demanded that a bill of rights be added to the Constitution. Eventually, in part, ratification of the Constitution was secured when some Federalists, such as James Madison, agreed to propose a bill of rights in Congress. In proposing the Bill of Rights in 1789, the Ninth Amendment was meant to protect any other rights not already enumerated either in the original text of the Constitution or in the rest of the Bill of Rights. Inspired perhaps by the natural rights theory of JOHN LOCKE and other political theorists, the Ninth Amendment seems to protect any inherent rights of the people. Alternatively, perhaps it was meant to defend rights found in the common law. In either case, the amendment was meant to protect unenumerated rights. The question, however, is what these unenumerated rights are.

From 1791, when the Ninth Amendment was ratified, until 1965, the Ninth Amendment was not cited as the basis of any Supreme Court decisions. Thus, for over 170 years, there was no clear indication regarding what the Ninth Amendment protected. However, in GRISWOLD V. CONNECTICUT, 381 U.S. 479 (1965), the Supreme Court cited the Ninth along with several other amendments as protecting a right to PRIVACY. In *Griswold*, it protected a right of married couples to secure and use birth control. Similarly, in ROE V. WADE, 410 U.S. 113 (1973), the Ninth Amendment was also cited to support a woman's right to secure an ABORTION, and in a footnote in *Richmond Newspa-*

pers, Inc. v. Virginia, 448 U.S. 555 (1980), Justice WARREN BURGER cites the amendment in ruling that the media has a right to attend criminal trials. Justice WILLIAM O. DOUGLAS also cited this amendment in a separate concurrence in *Lubin v. Panish*, 415 U.S. 709 (1974), contending that the right of the people to vote in state elections is one of the unenumerated rights protected by the Ninth. Beyond these references, this amendment has not been employed as a constitutional clause to find and protect rights.

The use of the Ninth Amendment to find a right to privacy has been controversial. Its use to support abortion rights and at one time to support GAY AND LESBIAN RIGHTS has pitted social conservatives against liberals, as well as those who believe in using the INTENT OF THE FRAMERS in the interpretation of the Constitution against those who use other techniques. Thus, the use of the Ninth Amendment has become netted in political disputes that question the scope of the authority of the judiciary to protect individual rights.

For more information: Barnett, Randy, ed. *The Rights Retained by the People.* Fairfax, Va.: George Mason University Press, 1989; Shaw, Stephen K. *The Ninth Amendment: Preservation of the Constitutional Mind.* New York: Garland, 1990.

—David Schultz

Nixon, Richard (1913–1999) *U.S. vice president, 37th U.S. president*

Richard Milhous Nixon was the 37th president of the United States. His keen political skill allowed him to resurrect a political career thought by many to be long defunct. He holds the dubious distinction of being the only president in U.S. history to resign from office. During the course of his career, and especially during his presidency, he left both a direct and an indirect impact upon the Constitution.

Richard Nixon was born in Yorba Linda, California, on January 13, 1913. He was the son of Francis "Frank" Nixon and Hannah Milhous. His father held a variety of jobs, including working as an orange farmer, an occupation Nixon often referred to years later to demonstrate his hard-scrabble roots. During his formative years, Nixon suffered the loss of two brothers.

Nixon attended college at nearby Whittier College from 1930 to 1934 and went on to, and graduated from, Duke University Law School in 1937. In an odd historical footnote, upon graduating from law school, Nixon applied for a job with the Federal Bureau of Investigation and was turned down. Like many of his generation, Nixon served in the armed forces during the Second World War. Lieutenant Commander Nixon served in the Pacific Fleet from 1942 to 1945.

Following the war, Nixon returned to Whittier, California, and ran for Congress. In his first campaign for office, Nixon sought to unseat Democratic incumbent Jerry Voorhis. The election of 1946 was a strong year for Republican candidates, although not a presidential election year. One of the main issues in the election of 1946 was the effectiveness and propriety of many of the New Deal programs implemented under Franklin Roosevelt and Harry Truman. Many were concerned that these programs bordered on, if not actually being, socialist. In retrospect, it seems appropriate that in Nixon's first election, socialism and communism would be the most prominent issues of the campaign.

Nixon served in the HOUSE OF REPRESENTATIVES from 1946 to 1950. While in the House, Nixon served on the House Un-American Activities Committee (HUAC). This committee was notable for its active investigation into alleged communist spying and infiltration in American government and the entertainment industry. As a result of some of the more zealous activities of this and other congressional committees, the Supreme Court, in cases such as *Watkins v. United States*, 354 U.S. 178 (1957), and *Barrenblatt v. United States*, 360 U.S. 109 (1959), was required to define the limits on these investigations.

Additionally, during his tenure on this committee, Nixon began his first foray onto a national stage with the investigation of Whittaker Chambers and Alger Hiss. Hiss was charged with being a communist spy infiltrating the federal bureau-

cracy. Under the Truman administration, Alger Hiss served as the secretary-general of the United Nations Charter Conference. Nixon's committee investigations led to Hiss's indictment and subsequent conviction. Following these events, Nixon was forever maligned as a "red baiter" and often likened to Senator Joe McCarthy. Not until the mid-1990s and the fall of the Soviet Union was Nixon somewhat exonerated, when it was discovered that Alger Hiss had, in fact, been an agent of the Soviet Union.

Nixon was elected to the United States SENATE in 1950, again defeating a Democratic incumbent, Helen Gahagan Douglas. Nixon's career in the Senate was cut short, however, due to his selection as General Dwight D. Eisenhower's vice presidential running mate in 1952. Nixon's selection was the result of an agreement between Eisenhower and the other front runner to be his running mate, California Governor Earl Warren. To preserve party unity and placate Warren, Eisenhower promised Warren the first appointment to the Supreme Court if he was elected.

For eight years, Nixon served as Eisenhower's VICE PRESIDENT. Nixon's most recognizable contribution as vice president was his participation in what was known as the "kitchen debate" with Soviet premier Nikita Khrushchev. In 1956, Eisenhower contemplated dropping Nixon from the reelection ticket due to a CAMPAIGN FINANCE scandal involving Nixon. Nixon avoided removal by appearing with his wife Pat on national television and disclosing his family's personal finances in the famous "Checkers speech."

Nixon ran for office in 1960 and lost to John F. Kennedy in one of the closest elections in the nation's history. Following the assassination of Kennedy and the decision of Lyndon Johnson not to run for reelection in 1968, Nixon once again ran for president. Nixon defeated Vice President (and former Minnesota senator) Hubert H. Humphrey in a close election.

Nixon's presidency, like Johnson's, was mired in Vietnam. Nixon had promised to bring "peace with honor" to the United States, but the war continued for the next five years. Nixon's policies showed a great amount of social conscience; he signed into law clear-air legislation and founded the Environmental Protection Agency (EPA). President Nixon also approved dramatic changes to American Indian policy, which recognized the sovereign status of Indian tribes for the first time in 175 years. Perhaps Nixon's greatest achievement as president was his decision to travel to China and formalize relations with the communist country. This policy was responsible for bringing about peace negotiations in Vietnam and cooling cold war tensions between the United States and the Soviet Union.

Perhaps Nixon's most significant constitutional legacies were twofold. First, he had a major impact on the Supreme Court by appointing WARREN EARL BURGER to replace Earl Warren as chief justice, and Nixon also appointed WILLIAM HUBBS REHNQUIST, a future chief justice, and Harry Blackmun and LEWIS POWELL JR. Through his four appointments he created a more conservative Supreme Court, especially in regard to criminal DUE PROCESS issues.

The second major impact was through the case UNITED STATES V. NIXON, 418 U.S. 683 (1974), which grew out of Watergate. Nixon's presidency began to unravel in August of 1973, when burglars broke into the Democratic National Committee headquarters in the Watergate Hotel in Washington, D.C. This activity was linked back to the White House and ultimately led to the House of Representatives' voting to draft articles of IMPEACHMENT against the president, resulting in his resignation from office. The Watergate investigations produced two important constitutional moments. First, Archibald Cox had been appointed to be a special prosecutor to investigate the break-in, and during the course of both his and congressional investigations, it was revealed that Nixon had secretly taped many of his Oval Office conversations. Cox sought to obtain these tapes in his investigation. On October 20, 1973, in what has come to be known as the "Saturday Night Massacre," Nixon ordered Cox fired. Both Attorney General Elliot Richardson and Deputy Attorney General William Ruckelshaus refused to fire Cox and instead resigned. The solicitor general, ROBERT BORK, ultimately fired Cox.

The dispute over the tapes came to a head in *United States v. Nixon,* where the Supreme Court in an 8-0 decision ruled that, while the concept of separation of powers recognized executive privilege, it had to give way to the demands and needs of a criminal investigation. What this meant was that Nixon had to turn the tapes over to the special prosecutor. Shortly after turning over the tapes, on August 9, 1974, Richard Nixon became the first president in U.S. history to resign from office. This led to Gerald Ford's assuming the presidency. Ford subsequently pardoned Nixon for any crimes arising out of Watergate.

Nixon died in 1999 in Yorba Linda, California. He was preceded in death by his wife Patricia.

For more information: Kurland, Phillip. *Watergate and the Constitution.* Chicago: University of Chicago Press, 1978; Small, Melvin. *The Presidency of Richard Nixon.* Lawrence: University Press of Kansas, 2003.

—R. Reid LeBeau

Nixon v. Shrink Missouri Government PAC
528 U.S. 377 (2000)

In *Nixon v. Shrink Missouri Government PAC,* the Supreme Court upheld a state law limiting the size of contributions that could be made to candidates for state office.

Missouri's CAMPAIGN FINANCE system had a series of ceilings on contributions to candidates for state offices, with the highest ceiling being $1,075. In 1997, Shrink Missouri Government PAC gave $1,025 to Zev David Fredman, a Republican candidate for state auditor; they added another $50 gift in 1998. Shrink Missouri argued that they would have given more to Fredman had they been so allowed, and Fredman himself contended that the gift ceiling was so low that it made effective campaigning impossible. Consequently, they argued, the statute unduly limited political expression.

By a vote of 6 to 3, the Court upheld the Missouri law—the first time in 18 years that the Court had completely upheld a campaign finance law. DAVID H. SOUTER's majority opinion turned aside the argument that the Missouri ceiling was too low. Even though the seminal campaign finance opinion, BUCKLEY V. VALEO, 424 U.S. 1 (1976), made it more difficult for restrictions on political money to survive constitutional scrutiny, it did not necessarily follow that a low contribution limit ran afoul of the FIRST AMENDMENT. What Souter argued was that, so long as there was sufficient evidence of corruption as a result of the money in politics, the courts should defer to the legislative branches in the setting of contribution limits, so long as they were not so low that they made it difficult for a candidate to run an effective campaign.

The nature of Souter's opinion stood in stark contrast to the angry words in both the dissents and the concurrences. *Shrink* revealed conclusively that the Court was bitterly divided on some of the most basic assumptions undergirding its campaign finance jurisprudence. In separate dissents, both ANTHONY M. KENNEDY and CLARENCE THOMAS stridently called for *Buckley* to be overruled. Calling the earlier case a "half-way house," Justice Kennedy flatly stated that "*Buckley* has not worked." Justice Thomas bemoaned "the analytic fallacies of our flawed decision in *Buckley v. Valeo*" and specifically urged that it be struck from the books as a means of precluding any future attempts at campaign finance reform.

However, it was not only skeptics about the campaign finance project who pronounced themselves unhappy with the existing structure. Concurring in the result, STEPHEN G. BREYER gently argued that *Buckley* should be replaced with an opinion that would allow for more regulations on political money. Yet it was JOHN PAUL STEVENS who put the sword to *Buckley* most dramatically. In his own concurrence, Stevens countered that opinion's core holding with his own declaration that "money is property; it is not speech," and he decried how *Buckley* had created a system of non-transparent political "mercenaries" whose cash paid for misleading "speech by proxy."

Ultimately, Stevens came much closer to winning the argument than Kennedy and Thomas. In late 2003, in *McCONNELL V. FEDERAL ELECTION COMMISSION*, 540 U.S. 93 (2003), Stevens cowrote (with SANDRA DAY O'CONNOR) an opinion

preserving the more comprehensive campaign finance restrictions embodied by the Bipartisan Campaign Reform Act of 2002.

For more information: Redish, Martin H. *Money Talks: Speech, Economic Power, and the Values of Democracy.* New York: New York University Press, 2001; Urofsky, Melvin I. *Money and Free Speech: Campaign Finance Reform and the Courts.* Lawrence: University of Kansas Press, 2005.

—Steven B. Lichtman

Northwest Ordinance

The adoption of the Northwest Ordinance, also called the Ordinance of 1787, was one of the most significant achievements of the Continental Congress under the Articles of Confederation. The Ordinance, officially titled "An Ordinance for the Government of the Territory of the United States, Northwest of the River Ohio," was adopted on July 13, 1787. Following the adoption of the Constitution, the Ordinance was affirmed by the U.S. Congress with minor changes.

Following the 1783 Treaty of Paris, which ended the Revolutionary War, the United States was left in possession of the Ohio Country, an area west of Pennsylvania, bounded by the Great Lakes on the north, the Ohio River on the south, and the Mississippi River on the west. The region, which had previously been closed to colonial settlement, was subject to both continuing British interference and conflicting claims by Connecticut, Massachusetts, New York, and Virginia.

The Ordinance established a civil government in the territory, with a territorial governor, secretary, and three judges appointed by Congress. When the population of the territory reached 5,000 free adult male inhabitants, the people would elect a general assembly, which would send a non-voting delegate to Congress. When the population increased to 60,000, the territorial legislature would draft a constitution and petition Congress for admission as a state.

Although the Articles of Confederation did not include a bill of rights, the Northwest Ordinance guaranteed that "[n]o person . . . shall ever be molested on account of his mode of worship or religious sentiments." It provided for "the benefits of the writ of HABEAS CORPUS, and of trial by jury." The Ordinance barred cruel or unusual punishments and forbade laws that would "interfere with or affect private contracts." It recognized that "the means of education shall forever be encouraged." Many of the protections contained in the Northwest Ordinance were later carried over to the BILL OF RIGHTS.

The Ordinance prohibited slavery and involuntary servitude in the territory at a time when slavery was still permitted in several northern states. Later legislative acts continued to recognize the Ohio River as the boundary between free and slave states. The Ordinance also noted that "[t]he utmost good faith shall always be observed towards the Indians; their lands and property shall never be taken from them without their consent."

The Ordinance provided for the formation of "not less than three nor more than five states" out of the Northwest Territory. Ultimately, the territory was organized into the present-day states of Ohio, Indiana, Illinois, Michigan, and Wisconsin.

A part of the organic laws of the United States, the Northwest Ordinance served as the model for the admission of all future states to the Union.

For more information: Onuf, Peter S. *Statehood and Union: A History of the Northwest Ordinance.* Bloomington: Indiana University Press, 1987.
—Mark W. Podvia

nude dancing

Nude dancing is a form of expression that the Supreme Court has given communities wide latitude to restrict. This is true even though the Court has stated that nude dancing implicates some FIRST AMENDMENT concerns.

From the burlesque shows of the 1920s and 1930s to the current "gentlemen's clubs," establishments that offer women dancing in stages of undress have been popular with customers and unpopular with government officials. Since the 1970s, communities have tried various means of shutting down or covering up such establishments. The Supreme Court has been reluctant to give any protection to the practice of nude dancing and has given communities a great deal of latitude in prohibiting such activities.

The central constitutional question is whether nude dancing is expressive activity that communicates a message and thus is entitled to First Amendment protection, or whether it is conduct that can be prohibited by local governments. In a series of cases, the Supreme Court has addressed the protection that nude dancing enjoys and does not enjoy.

California v. LaRue, 409 U.S. 109 (1972), allowed the state of California to deny a liquor license to any club that allowed nude dancing. The Court's decision upheld the law on the basis of the TWENTY-FIRST AMENDMENT and did not directly answer the question of First Amendment rights. Many states across the nation adopted this tactic along with zoning regulations in attempts to discourage nude dancing establishments.

In the case of *Barnes v. Glen Theatre Inc.,* 501 U.S. 560 (1991), the Court ruled that nude dancing was "within the outer perimeters of the First Amendment, although only marginally so." However, the five-person majority upheld the Indiana law on the basis that the intent was not to suppress an erotic message but was a general prohibition against public indecency. Justice DAVID H. SOUTER, in a concurring opinion, argued that harmful secondary effects of nude dancing (e.g. crime, sexual assaults) could be used as a basis for the prohibition of such conduct. The four-person dissent argued that the regulation was aimed at expressive conduct and that nudity was an essential part of the message.

The issue of harmful secondary effects was expanded on in the case of *City of Erie v. PAP's A.M.,* 529 U.S. 227 (2000). In this decision, the Court reaffirmed that nude dancing had symbolic meaning but upheld a law banning all nude dancing because of harmful secondary effects that accrue to areas with adult entertainment. Among the effects cited were crime, prostitution, and drug use. The Court did not require government officials to prove that such harmful effects were in fact taking place or that regulating nude dancing would ameliorate them. The Court said the government could assume such premises. Justice ANTONIN GREGORY SCALIA concurred in the majority's decision, attacking the *Barnes* majority's reasoning and arguing that cities had the right to protect morals through such regulations. Justice JOHN PAUL STEVENS dissented, arguing that a total ban on nude dancing was unnecessary and that zoning laws could achieve the same results.

While nude dancing has not fared well with the Supreme Court, less explicit forms of adult entertainment (i.e., topless dancing) have been left relatively unregulated. Despite efforts at regulation, "gentlemen's clubs" proliferated during the 1980s and 1990s.

For more information: Manuto, Ron, and Sean Patrick O'Rourke. "Dances with Wolves: Nudity, Morality and the Speech Conduct Doctrine." *Free Speech Yearbook* 43 (1994): 86–109.

—Charles Howard

Nullification Controversy

The Nullification Controversy stemmed from a debate during the early American republic over whether states had the right to nullify federal laws. Nullification had its roots in the Tariff of 1828 (also known as the Tariff of Abominations), passed by Congress to protect industries in the North against European competition. The tariff and its economic repercussions worried the South and provided the impetus for a sectional conflict.

The Nullification movement was led by VICE PRESIDENT JOHN C. CALHOUN of South Carolina, who authored the *South Carolina Exposition and Protest*. At its core was the belief that the Union was a compact of the sovereign states that came together to form the Constitution. Since the federal government was a result of a compact among the several states, the states had the final say over the scope of their own authority, as well as that of the federal government. The nullifiers believed that, since the Constitution did not provide for an independent arbiter to settle disputes

between the states and the federal government, only the parties to the constitutional compact (the states) could judge constitutional infractions.

The *Exposition* proclaimed that the tariff was unconstitutional and identified a remedy for such a breach of federal power. The remedy did not lie in the federal judiciary, since that would raise the judiciary above the states who created the Constitution. Rather it lay in the states themselves, as sovereign parties to the constitutional compact.

Calhoun's *Exposition* shifted its focus from the role of the states in the creation of the constitutional compact and in checking federal authority to the right of a single state to nullify a federal law. Accordingly, South Carolina was a sovereign party to the constitutional compact, and it alone (through its state legislature) had the right to preserve its sovereignty and impose a VETO on any laws that threatened its sovereignty.

The prospect of nullification loomed large as a SENATE debate over the fate of public lands (the Foote Resolution) turned into one of the most famous debates over nullification and who had the right to interpret the Constitution and veto unconstitutional laws. On January 21, 1830, Senator Robert Hayne (South Carolina) changed the focus from the resolution to an attack on the tariffs and the evils of national consolidation, in particular the federal government (and the judiciary) being the sole judge of its own powers.

Senator Daniel Webster's (Massachusetts) response was geared toward defending the Supreme Court as vital to the Union. According to Webster, the Constitution did not authorize a single state, in particular, a state legislature, to nullify a federal law. He argued that the government was created by the people, not by the state legislatures. The people declared that the Constitution was the supreme law of the land, and if each state legislature was permitted to nullify federal laws, then the Union would no longer exist. Webster felt that it was impossible to live under a government of uniform laws if each state had the right to judge for itself constitutional infractions. As for the resolution of constitutional disputes, Webster noted that the people had already vested in the Constitution such a tribunal—the federal judiciary.

On November 24, 1832, the "people of the State of South Carolina" issued an Ordinance of Nullification and declared the Tariff Act "null, void, and no law, nor binding on this State, its officers or citizens." The Ordinance also declared that any promises, contracts, obligations, and judicial proceedings made in pursuance of the act to be "utterly null and void." In addition, it stipulated, "no case decided by the courts of the State regarding the Ordinance or acts of the legislature made in pursuance of it, could be appealed to the U.S. Supreme Court." Finally, the Ordinance provided that, with the exception of members of the legislature, all civil and military officers were required to take an oath to obey, enforce, and execute the Ordinance. "No allegiance is due to any power or authority but this State" (South Carolina Ordinance of Nullification, 28–31).

The final aspect of this interpretive struggle involved the rejection of nullification throughout the country. President Andrew Jackson, one of the strongest advocates of states' rights, was also one of the most ardent critics of nullification. Northern and southern states issued resolves condemning the ordinance and pronouncing it as destructive to the Union. Many states' rights advocates believed in the compact theory, but they did not subscribe to nullification. Even Georgia, Virginia, and Ohio, which were continually involved with their own struggles against the national government, and in particular the federal judiciary, condemned the ordinance.

For more information: Bancroft, Frederic. *Calhoun and the South Carolina Nullification Movement.* Baltimore, Md.: The Johns Hopkins Press, 1928; Freehling, William W. *Prelude to Civil War: The Nullification Controversy in South Carolina 1816–1836.* New York and London: Harper and Row, 1966; Houston, David Franklin. *A Critical Study of Nullification in South Carolina.* Gloucester, U.K.: Peter Smith, 1968; *State Papers on Nullification.* New York: Da Capo Press, 1970.

—Randa Issa

obscenity

Obscenity is a category of speech or expression that is not protected by the FIRST AMENDMENT. This stands in contrast to material that is pornographic and does receive constitutional protection. However, defining exactly what is considered obscene has been a problem for the courts.

The Supreme Court has been grappling with a workable definition of obscenity for over half a century. By the late 1960s, the Supreme Court had already heard dozens of obscenity-pornography cases. Justice JOHN HARLAN II called this deluge of litigation "the intractable obscenity problem" in *Interstate Circuit, Inc. v. Dallas*, 390 U.S. 676, 704 (1968). Justice WILLIAM J. BRENNAN, JR., referred to the issue of obscenity as "the vexing problem," and in his dissent in *Paris Adult Theatre I v. Slaton*, 413 U.S. 49 (1973), wrote that "no other aspect of the First Amendment has, in recent years, demanded so substantial a commitment of our time, generated such disharmony of views, and remained so resistant to the formulation of stable and manageable standards."

Obscenity cases are difficult because they involve First Amendment rights. Freedom of speech is a fundamental right, one that this country greatly cherishes and that shall not be permitted to slowly erode. Balancing the First Amendment rights of the people against the government's power to restrict certain types of speech in order to protect particular segments of the population and maintain order and decency will always be a formidable task.

These cases can also be complex. Although the primary constitutional question revolves around the First Amendment, obscenity cases may involve several constitutional issues. Alleging that a statute is too vague to give notice of the proscribed action may bring the DUE PROCESS clause of the FOURTEENTH and Fifth AMENDMENTs into focus. Federal obscenity laws may be challenged on the basis that they invade the sovereignty of a state, requiring NINTH and Tenth AMENDMENT inquiries.

Criminal obscenity laws were recorded as early as 1726. The Acts and Laws of Massachusetts Bay Colony expressly prohibited "composing, writing, printing or publishing, of any filthy obscene or profane song, pamphlet, libel or mock-sermon, in imitation or in mimicking of preaching, or any other part of Divine Worship." A majority of states made blasphemy or profanity punishable offenses, despite having ratified the Constitution and the First Amendment guarantee that "Congress shall make no law . . . abridging the freedom of speech, or of the press." An in-depth historical analysis of the various forms of unprotected speech, including obscenity, was undertaken by the Supreme Court and became the foundational premise for every obscenity case. The Court found in *BEAUHARNAIS V. ILLINOIS*, 343 U.S. 250 (1952), that the unconditional phrasing of the First Amendment was not intended to protect every utterance.

Beginning with *ROTH V. UNITED STATES*, 354 U.S. 476 at 484–485 (1957), the Court undertook the task of defining what constituted constitutionally protected speech and what did not. Five justices joined in the opinion. The majority concluded that the test for obscenity was whether, to the average person, applying contemporary community standards, the dominant theme of the material, taken as a whole, appeals to the prurient interest.

This test was an improvement over the existing English common law rule developed in *Regina v. Hicklin,* L.R. 3 Q.B. 360 (1868), which defined obscenity as material intended to "deprive and corrupt those whose minds are open to such immoral influences."

However, in subsequent analyses, *Roth* would become unworkable due to the difficulty in determining "community standards." The Court clearly exhibited its disparate views and the insufficiency of the *Roth* test in JACOBELLIS V. OHIO, 378 U.S. 184 (1964), finding that the motion picture in question was not obscene but not being completely able to agree on the reasoning. Justice Stewart penned his famous words, "I shall not today attempt further to define the kinds of materials I understand to be embraced within that shorthand description; and perhaps I could never succeed in intelligibly doing so. But I know it when I see it, and the motion picture involved in this case is not that."

Two years later, the Court edited the *Roth* test in *Memoirs v. Massachusetts,* 383 U.S. 413 (1966). This time, only three justices joined in the plurality opinion. Elaborating on the *Roth* definition, the Court held that before speech could be considered obscene, "it must be established that (a) the dominant theme of the material taken as a whole appeals to a prurient interest in sex; (b) the material is patently offensive because it affronts contemporary community standards relating to the description or representation of sexual matters; and (c) the material is utterly without redeeming social value." The Court would eventually disparage the plurality opinion in *Memoirs* in later years, and eventually none of the members of the Court would support the *Memoirs* formulation of obscenity.

An opportunity to reformulate and agree on the definition of obscenity presented itself in *MILLER v. CALIFORNIA,* 413 U.S. 15 (1973). At last, the Court would establish a standard for identifying obscene material that would remain viable even today. Miller was a commercial purveyor of adult material. As part of an advertising campaign, he conducted a mass mailing intended to publicize the availability and sale of four books entitled "Intercourse," "Man-Woman," "Sex Orgies Illustrated," and "An Illustrated History of Pornography." The Court described the books as containing some descriptive printed material, but consisting primarily of pictures and drawings very explicitly depicting men and women in groups of two or more engaging in a variety of sexual activities, with genitals often prominently displayed.

One of the brochures was sent to a restaurant. The manager of the restaurant and his mother opened the envelope and were apparently upset by the contents. They lodged a formal complaint with the local police department. Miller was arrested pursuant to a violation of the California Penal Code and later convicted by a jury for knowingly distributing obscene material. On appeal, the Appellate Division of the Superior Court of Orange County, California, summarily dismissed his action, and Miller appealed to the United States Supreme Court.

Justice WARREN BURGER delivered the opinion of the Court, which held that (1) obscene material is not protected by the First Amendment, citing *Roth v. United States;* (2) the basic guidelines for the trier of fact in deciding whether a work is obscene must be: (a) whether "the average person, applying contemporary community standards would find that the work, taken as a whole, appeals to the prurient interest," (b) whether the work depicts or describes, in a patently offensive way, sexual conduct specifically prohibited by the applicable state law, and (c) whether the work, taken as a whole, lacks any serious literary, artistic, political, or scientific value; (3) the jury may measure the factual issue of "prurient appeal and patent offensiveness" by the prevailing standard in the forum community, and need not employ a national standard. In footnote two, the Court noted that pornography is a subgroup of obscene expression.

This was the first time since *Roth* that the majority could agree on a standard. Various members of the Court voiced their dissatisfaction with previous standards. Justice White wrote, "While *Roth* presumed obscenity to be 'utterly without redeeming social importance,' *Memoirs* required that it be affirmatively established by the prosecution, a burden that is virtually impossible to discharge under our criminal statutes." Justice Brennan criticized the prior national "community standard" element as an exercise in futility. The Court also reaffirmed some basic underlying ideas espoused in their earlier cases, emphasizing the importance of a free and robust exchange of ideas. Citing *Roth,* they reiterated that the First Amendment was to protect the exchange of ideas for the purpose of bringing political and social changes desired by the people, and that public portrayal of hard-core sexual conduct for commercial gain falls outside the protection of the Constitution.

The dissenters in *Miller,* Justices WILLIAM O. DOUGLAS, Brennan, Stewart, and Marshall, felt that the law was still too vague and overbroad. Justice Douglas wrote that "what shocks me may be sustenance for my neighbor" and that "obscenity—which even we cannot define with precision—is a hodge-podge. To send men to jail for violating standards they cannot understand, construe, and apply is a monstrous thing to do in a Nation dedicated to fair trials and due process."

Despite the concerns of the dissenting justices, the *Miller* test remains alive and well. It was last utilized by the Court in deciding *ASHCROFT V. ACLU,* 535 U.S. 564 (2002). Some legal scholars see the application of *Miller* as an affirmation of its continued viability and an indication that the Court has no intention of reformulating an obscenity test any time soon.

Obscenity laws apply to all forms of publications, printed or recorded, on paper, tape, or in cyberspace. The widespread availability and use of the Internet in the late '90s prompted Congress to pass several forms of legislation intended to keep obscene materials from being easily viewed by children. All of the laws enacted were challenged and have been struck down in whole or in part. The Court found that the 1996 COMMUNICATIONS DECENCY ACT and portions of the 1998 Child Online Protection Act and the Child Pornography Prevention Act were unconstitutionally overbroad in several cases, including *Ashcroft v. ACLU.*

The Court acknowledged the government's compelling interest in protecting minors from commercial pornographers, but found that all three laws were overbroad and that there were less restrictive alternatives available that would not unduly interfere with an adult's constitutional right to view this type of materials.

The Supreme Court has been diligent and steadfast in upholding the First Amendment. It should also be noted that state law, federal law, and the Supreme Court have never set their sights on punishing or limiting private, individual, in-home possession of obscene materials. In all the cases, the focus of attention was on the distribution and sale of materials by dealers for commercial gain. However, the mere possession of child pornography is in violation of the law. The Court has noted that CHILD PORNOGRAPHY can constitutionally be totally proscribed because of the state's interest in protecting the children exploited in the production process.

For more information: Kalven, Harvey. *A Worthy Tradition: Freedom of Speech in America.* New York: Harper & Row, 1988.

—Loretta M. Young

O'Connor, Sandra Day (1930–) *Supreme Court justice*

Sandra Day O'Connor was sworn in as the first female Supreme Court justice on September 25, 1981, after being nominated by President Ronald Reagan and confirmed 99–0 by the SENATE. On July 1st, 2005, O'Connor announced that her retirement from the Supreme Court would occur upon the confirmation of her successor. However, with the death of Chief Justice WILLIAM HUBBS REHNQUIST, JOHN G. ROBERTS, JR., who was nominated to assume O'Connor's position, instead took the place of Rehnquist. The retirement of Sandra Day O'Connor from the Supreme Court became official on January 31, 2006, when SAMUEL ALITO was sworn in as associate justice.

On March 26, 1930, Sandra was born to Henry and Ada Day in El Paso, Texas. She spent most of her childhood on a cattle ranch in southeastern Arizona, where she worked on the ranch and read in her spare time.

The intelligent Sandra Day headed to Stanford University in California for college. In 1950, she graduated with a bachelor's degree in economics and headed off to Stanford Law School. Her performance in law school was stellar. She completed the course work in two years instead of three, served on the *Stanford Law Review,* was inducted into the legal honor society Order of the Coif, and graduated third in a class of 102. The person who graduated first in that class was future Chief Justice William Hubbs Rehnquist. Rehnquist and Sandra Day formed a close friendship during law school that including a brief period of dating. They would become lifelong friends. While in law school, Sandra did meet the man that she would eventually marry, John Jay O'Connor III. The couple married on December 20, 1952, about six months after Sandra graduated law school.

Since the beginning of her legal career, being female played a major role. Despite stellar performance in law school, the only job Sandra Day O'Connor was offered was a secretarial position in Los Angeles. At that time, there were very few women in the legal industry, and law firms were not willing to hire a woman to be an attorney. Women in law firms generally worked only in secretarial and administrative positions. Given her training and intellectual capabilities, O'Connor continued searching for a position as an attorney. She turned to a district attorney in San Mateo County, California, who had previously hired a female attorney, and she sought any position as an attorney. The district attorney gave her an attorney position, even though it was unpaid initially. In this position, O'Connor found that she loved being a lawyer and the fulfillment of a career in public service.

The following year, in 1953, O'Connor's husband John graduated from law school and took a position with the army's Judge Advocate General Corps stationed in Frankfurt, Germany. Sandra Day O'Connor went with her husband, but once again found difficulties gaining employment. In Germany, she worked as a civilian lawyer with the Quartermaster Corps. After a few years in Germany, John O'Connor found a good job with a large law firm in Phoenix, Arizona, in 1957. Despite having higher grades and class ranking than her husband, Sandra once again had difficulties finding a position and eventually ended

Associate Justice Sandra Day O'Connor *(United States Supreme Court)*

up forming her own law firm with another person. Within the first six years of living in Phoenix, the O'Connors had three sons, and Sandra decided to become a full-time mother and part-time volunteer in 1962, when her second son was born. In 1965, she decided to return to full-time legal work and found a position in the Arizona attorney general's office. After excelling in the attorney general's office, she was appointed to the Arizona state senate in 1969. Starting in 1974, she served as a judge on the Maricopa County Superior Court. Five years later, Governor Bruce Babbitt appointed her to the Arizona Court of Appeals.

At a time when women faced many barriers in the legal industry, she excelled and eventually earned an appointment to the United States Supreme Court.

When O'Connor became the first female justice, the Court adopted the term "Justice" instead of addressing each other as "Mr. Justice." Observers assumed that she would become one of the most conservative members of the Court. As a justice on the Supreme Court, she often voted with other conservatives such as Chief Justice Rehnquist. Generally, she opposed extending new rights to those accused of committing crimes, and she was also a reliable vote in supporting states rights and FEDERALISM, such as in UNITED STATES V. LOPEZ, 514 U.S. 549 (1995), seeking to place some limits upon the ability of the federal government to regulate states or tell them what to do. Over time, O'Connor seemed to change or moderate her conservative views. For example, while in WEBSTER V. REPRODUCTIVE HEALTH SERVICES, 492 U.S. 490 (1990), she voted to uphold some restrictions on the use of state funds to provide for ABORTION services, in PLANNED PARENTHOOD OF SOUTHEASTERN PENNSYLVANIA V. CASEY, 505 U.S. 833 (1992), she wrote the majority opinion reaffirming ROE V. WADE, 410 U.S. 113 (1973), affirming the right of women to terminate pregnancies. Additionally, in cases such as SHAW V. RENO, 509 U.S. 690 (1993), she was very critical of the use of race in the drawing of district lines, but in GRUTTER V. BOLLINGER, 539 U.S. 306 (2003), she wrote the majority opinion affirming the use of race in a law school admissions process in order to promote diversity. Finally, while in BOY SCOUTS OF AMERICA V. DALE, 530 U.S. 640 (2000), she upheld the right of the Boy Scouts to exclude a gay leader from their organization, in LAWRENCE V. TEXAS, 539 U.S. 558 (2003), she wrote a separate concurrence striking down, on EQUAL PROTECTION grounds, a state law that criminalized consensual homosexual sodomy.

In her last couple of years on the Supreme Court, Justice O'Connor became a critical swing vote. With the Court often deadlocked 4-4 between liberals and conservatives, her fifth vote was highly sought and generally decided the outcome in the case.

After leaving the Court in 2006, she toured the country speaking, and also served as a senior judge in some lower federal court cases.

For more information: Maveety, Nancy. *Justice Sandra Day O'Connor.* New York: Rowman & Littlefield Publishers, 1996; McFeatters, Ann Carey. *Sandra Day O'Connor: Justice in the Balance.* Albuquerque: University of New Mexico, 2005.

—Carol Walker

Ogden v. Saunders 25 U.S. 213 (1827)

In *Ogden v. Saunders,* the Supreme Court upheld a state bankruptcy law against claims that it violated the CONTRACT CLAUSE of the Constitution.

Article I, Section 10, Clause 1 of the Constitution states, "No State shall enter into any TREATY, Alliance, or Confederation; grant LETTERS OF MARQUE AND REPRISAL; coin Money; emit Bills of Credit; make any Thing but gold and silver Coin a Tender in Payment of Debts; pass any BILL OF ATTAINDER, ex post facto Law, or Law impairing the Obligation of Contract, or grant any Title of Nobility." Article I, Section 8, Clause 4 notes that Congress has the power "to establish an uniform Rule of Naturalization, and uniform laws on the subject of Bankruptcies throughout the United States." *Ogden v. Saunders* focuses on portions of these two sections—the issue of making laws "impairing the Obligation of Contracts" and laws on the subject of bankruptcies. This case involved a citizen of Kentucky named Saunders who was suing a Louisiana citizen named Ogden over a contract dispute. Ogden had been a resident of Louisiana when the two agreed to the contract. Ogden subsequently moved to New York. Saunders claimed in the suit that Ogden had not made payment on the obligation. Ogden, as a resident of New York, claimed bankruptcy as his defense on an 1801 New York bankruptcy law.

In a 4-3 decision, Justice Washington, in his discussion of the case, posed an intriguing question. The first and most important point to be decided in this cause turns essentially upon the question whether the obligation of a contract is impaired by a state bankruptcy law or insolvent law, which discharges the person from his liability under a contract entered into in that state after the passage of the act.

The key question here was whether Congress had the sole power to pass bankruptcy laws, which hinged on what was meant by the phrase regarding the enactment of laws "impairing the Obligation of Contracts." The Court found that the New York law was not in violation of the contract clause contained in the U.S. Constitution. In other words, for any contract that is made after the enactment of a bankruptcy law, any obligations set forth in the contract are subject to the provisions of that law. In other words, once a bankruptcy law is enacted, that law becomes part of any contract that is entered into after the date of enactment. However, even though the Court upheld the legality of the 1801 New York law, it restricted its applicability to the state in which the law was enacted.

For more information: Hall, Kermit L., and Kevin T. McGuire, eds. *The Judicial Branch.* New York: Oxford University Press, 2005.

—Dan Krejci

Olmstead v. United States 277 U.S. 438 (1928)

In *Olmstead v. United States,* the Court ruled that using evidence from wiretaps without a warrant is not an illegal search and seizure violating the FOURTH AMENDMENT. This decision promotes the physical trespass theory, which says that the Fourth Amendment prevents the government only from physically seizing tangible items, not intangible items like conversations. Forty years later, the Court overruled *Olmstead* in *Katz v. United States,* 389 U.S. 347 (1967).

Roy Olmstead was a successful bootlegger who was indicted and convicted for importing and selling liquor during Prohibition. At his trial, prosecutors introduced incriminating evidence from wiretaps placed on Olmstead's and his partner's telephone lines without a warrant. Olmstead unsuccessfully sought to exclude this evidence on the grounds that it was an illegal search and seizure under the Fourth Amendment and that it violated his Fifth Amendment RIGHT AGAINST SELF-INCRIMINATION. The appellate court affirmed the conviction, and the Supreme Court upheld WIRETAPPING in a 5-4 decision.

Writing for the majority, Chief Justice Taft promoted the physical trespass theory, which says that the Fourth Amendment protects only tangible things such as houses, persons, papers, etc., from physical intrusion and literal seizure. Since the police did not enter the house or office of the accused and they cannot seize the spoken word, there was no search and no seizure. The police simply tapped lines outside the house and wrote down the conversations they heard, making the wiretap the equivalent of overhearing a conversation in public. Moreover, since there was no illegal search, there was no Fifth Amendment violation against self-incrimination.

In dissent, Justice Brandeis objected to the literal interpretation of the Constitution, claiming that constitutional doctrine must change as technology changes. He believed that physical intrusion and seizure is immaterial, because the Fourth Amendment protects against "every unjustifiable intrusion by the government upon the PRIVACY of the individual." Wiretapping violated Olmstead's privacy, and the evidence should be thrown out.

In a separate dissent, Justice Butler used a literal approach infused with property rights principles to protect the conversations. He claimed that the parties on the phone own their conversation, because the wires belong solely to the parties communicating at that time. Thus, any seizure violates the Fourth Amendment.

In response to this decision, Congress prohibited the warrantless wiretapping of telephones and telegraphs by passing the Federal Communications Act in 1934. However, the physical trespass theory still allowed the police to intercept conversations by listening through walls as long as they did not physically invade the individual's home or office. Eventually, the Supreme Court replaced the physical intrusion standard with the "reasonable expectation of privacy" standard in *Katz,* providing greater protection to persons, conversations, homes, businesses, papers, etc.

For more information: Diffie, Whitfield, and Susan Landau. *Privacy on the Line: The Politics of Wiretapping and Encryption.* Cambridge, Mass.: MIT Press, 1998; Kerr, Orin S. "The Fourth Amendment and New Technologies: Constitutional Myths and the Case for Caution." *Michigan Law Review* 102 (March 2004): 801–888.

—Sean Evans

one person, one vote

"One person, one vote" is a voting principle that emphasizes political equality which was first pronounced as a constitutional rule by the Supreme Court in REYNOLDS V. SIMS, 377 U.S. 533 (1964). It gives assurance to citizens that their political preference is equal in weight to those of all others. Such equality is politically fair, because it preserves the core ideal of universal suffrage by incorporating the respect due, and the responsibilities owed, to each citizen in a democracy.

In the United States, the concept of one person, one vote originates from two sources: the Constitution and the Supreme Court's articulation of relevant constitutional provisions. First, from the Constitution, the concept of one person, one vote is drawn from ARTICLE I, Section 2 and the FOURTEENTH AMENDMENT EQUAL PROTECTION clause. While the Constitution states that congressional apportionment of "representatives and direct taxes shall be apportioned among the several states . . . according to their respective numbers," the equal protection clause has been the source of making the one person, one vote principle applicable to states, since the Constitution vests primary responsibility to allocate legislative districts to states. Second, in American constitutional law and the politics of representation, the Supreme Court has been instrumental in making the one person, one vote principle a currency in political conversations. It has done so in a series of landmark decisions rendered between 1960 and 1969 that challenged serious population inequities on how congressional and state districting were drawn.

Prior to 1960, the Supreme Court did not show much interest in reviewing state districting and apportionment practices despite serious complaints of population inequality in congressional and state legislative districts. Before then, the Supreme Court had ruled only in one case that issues of state legislative apportionments were political questions not appropriate for judicial resolution. Its position on this matter is reflected in the plurality opinion in COLEGROVE V. GREEN (1946), a case in which members of the Illinois electorate challenged provisions of Illinois law governing the apportionment of congressional districts. Illinois voters claimed that, due to subsequent changes in population, the congressional districts for the election of representatives lacked approximate equality of population. Three members of that Court agreed that equal protection required the election of congressmen from districts that were generally equal in population. Justice Frankfurter wrote for the 4-3 undermanned Court majority decision, where he warned against the judiciary entering a "political thicket" of congressional districting. He viewed the case as one that did not present justiciable questions. Accordingly, "the basis for the suit is not a private wrong, but a wrong suffered by Illinois as a polity," Frankfurter wrote, and "the remedy for unfairness in districting is to secure State legislatures that will apportion properly, or invoke the ample powers of Congress."

Sixteen years later, the Supreme Court surprisingly entered the very political thicket it previously deemed not to present justiciable questions in 1946. Reversing *Colegrove* in a 6-2 decision in BAKER V. CARR, 369 U.S. 186 (1962), the Court held that apportionment issues were indeed reviewable under the Fourteenth Amendment. More specifically, that "the mere fact the suit seeks protection of political right does not mean that it presents a political question." This decision reflected a significant change in the Court's jurisprudence and a new development that facilitated the application of the equality principle of one person, one vote in subsequent cases. As exemplified in *Gray v. Sanders* (1963), *Wesberry v. Sanders* (1964), *Reynolds v. Sims* (1964), and *Kirkpatrick v. Preisler* (1969) discussed below, the principle of one person, one vote would emerge as a fundamental political right, empowering citizens to partake in the process of self-government.

Pioneering this principle in an 8-1 decision in *Gray v. Sanders,* 372 U.S. 368 (1963), the Supreme Court assuredly equated the concept of political equality to one person, one vote. The case involved Georgia's notorious county unit system of nominating candidates to statewide offices in which each county was assigned a unit vote that had little relation to its population. Invalidating Georgia's congressional districts on the grounds of population inequality, the Court declared that "[t]he conception of political equality from the DECLARATION OF INDEPENDENCE, to LINCOLN's Gettysburg Address, to the FIFTEENTH, Seventeenth, and NINETEENTH AMENDMENTs can mean only one thing—one person, one vote." Said the Court, "Once the geographical unit for which a representative is to be chosen is designated, all who participate in the election are to have an equal vote—whatever their race, whatever their sex, whatever their occupation, whatever their income, and wherever their home may be in the geographical unit. This is required by the Equal Protection Clause of the Fourteenth Amendment." While the case dealt with the weight of a person's vote within a previously designated geographical unit, the principle of "one person, one vote" announced would later be extended to subsequent cases examining constitutional challenges of congressional redistricting (*Wesberry,* 1964) and congressional and state legislative redistricting (*Reynolds,* 1964). In these two cases, the Court established definitively that the United States Constitution imposed a fundamental requirement on those charged with congressional and state legislative redistricting to approximate their population as "practicable" or make them as "substantially" equal relative to the population as possible.

Wesberry v. Sanders, 376 U.S. 1 (1964), was the next case in the Court's development of the one person, one vote criterion. It involved a congressional redistricting in the state of Georgia. Citing the principle articulated a year before in *Gray* as authority in a 6-3 decision, the Court ordered that districts in Georgia be redrawn more evenly. Holding that gross disparities in Georgia's congressional districts were a violation of the U.S. Constitution, the Court concluded that "Article I, Section 2 of the Constitution requires that representatives shall be chosen by the people of the several states" and be "apportioned among the several States . . . according to their respective Numbers." Although in this case the Court recognized the impossibility of drawing congressional districts with mathematical precision, its dictum revealed the expectation that "as nearly as is practicable one man's vote in a congressional election is to be worth as much as another's." Emphasizing the importance for a universally fair system of election that incorporates the respect due and the responsibilities owed to each citizen, the Court observed further that "no right is more precious in a free country than that of having a voice in the election of those who make the laws under which, as good citizens, we must live." Other rights, even the most basic, the Court added, "are illusory if the RIGHT TO VOTE is undermined."

In *Reynolds v. Sims* (1964), a related case decided four months after *Wesberry* but this time focusing on state legislative districts alone, the Supreme Court held that both houses of a state legislature must be apportioned on the basis of population equality and that "population" will hence be the controlling factor in the construction of legislative districts. Upholding a lower court decision invalidating Alabama's legislative apportionment, the Court observed that the equal protection clause of the Fourteenth Amendment requires that a state make an honest and good-faith effort to construct districts, in both houses of its legislature, as nearly equal in population as is practicable. Put differently, the apportionment of seats and boundary for legislative districts for both houses of state legislatures had to be arranged so that the number of inhabitants per legislator in any one district is substantially equal or roughly equal to the number of inhabitants per legislator in any other district in the same state. Indeed, in *Baker v. Carr* (1960), a case that in hindsight set the stage for the development of the concept of one person, one vote, the Supreme Court also held that issues relative to state legislative apportionment were appropriate for JUDICIAL REVIEW.

Until *Kirkpatrick v. Preisler*, 394 U.S. 526 (1969), a case that challenged a Missouri congressional redistricting plan, there were no clear standards to achieve the one person, one vote objectives clearly stated in previous cases. Surely, *Gray, Wesberry,* and *Reynolds* strove to end the pattern of gross rural overrepresentation and urban underrepresentation. However, the conclusion that emerged from these cases was that the principle of proportionality should be practiced in the strictest way possible to achieve political equality. But how? The answer was at best unclear, and perhaps was made deliberately so.

In announcing the one person, one vote rule in June 1964, the Court left a considerable amount of flexibility to the lower courts in working out standards so long as population equality was the general pattern. Refining that rule for Missouri's congressional redistricting plan in *Kirkpatrick*, the Supreme Court held that states are required to "come as nearly as practicable to population equality," provided that doing so (a) does not offend the principle of one person, one vote; and (b) so long as the ratio of representatives to voters remain equal. Article I, Section 2, the Court reasoned, requires states to create congressional districts that provide equal representation for equal numbers of people with possible minimum population variances that are unavoidable, despite good-faith effort and for which a compelling justification can be presented.

In the Court's view, setting an acceptable minimum range is arbitrary and inconsistent with the "as nearly as practicable" standard—a rule more likely to encourage legislators to strive for the minimum rather than promote equality. The Court concluded that even where population variances among the districts were shown to be unavoidable despite a state's good-faith effort to achieve population equality, the state must justify each variation, no matter its size. Lastly, for each contested redistricting plan to prevail, states must prove that the population deviation at issue is necessary to achieve a legitimate state objective.

In *Karcher v. Daggett*, 462 U.S. 725 (1983), the Supreme Court went further than before to provide needed clarity. It placed the burden on states

relative to any contested redistricting scheme that undermines the one person, one vote principle or political equality. Specifically, the Court concluded that:

> States must show with some specificity that a particular objective requires the specific deviations in its plan, rather than simply relying on general assertions. The showing required to justify population deviation is flexible, depending on the size of the deviations, the importance of the State's interests, the consistency with which the plan as a whole reflects those interests, and the availability of alternatives that might substantively vindicate those interests yet approximate population equality more closely.

States must show with clear specificity, rather than make generalized assertions, the objective they intend to accomplish for each deviation in their apportionment and redistricting plans.

The overall effect of the Supreme Court's reapportionment decisions from the 1960s is that they altered forever the substantive nature of political representation in the United States. They created more equity in congressional and state legislative districting and apportionments by requiring that states alter their priorities to make the political process fair and more inclusive. To be sure, the principle of one person, one vote as developed so far remains fundamentally one that assures all voters the right to cast a theoretically equal ballot. However, to the extent that it matters, it allows the vote of each citizen to exert an equal influence on the forming of representation regardless of the constituency in which the citizen votes.

Thus, where the right to vote has been restricted, the principle is used to advocate universal suffrage, thereby broadening the electoral base to include everyone, particularly minorities and all others who are disenfranchised. Support for a wide and more equal participation in the political systems also meant steadfast opposition to voting schemes that undermined the integrity of electoral systems. For example, the theoretical right to vote cannot be realized under electoral schemes that allow "winner-take-all districts," since widespread use of such districts undermines the validity of votes cast by citizens.

Lastly, within representative political systems such as the United States, the concept of one person, one vote is often linked to calls for more direct democracy, where representatives are selected through electoral schemes hinged on making equal representation for equal numbers of people. Although historically contested, this view is now settled in American constitutional law and the Supreme Court's interpretation of relevant constitutional provisions. Today, any understanding at odds with ARTICLE I, Section 2 and the equal protection clause that connotes anything other than one person, one vote is unconvincing. The Court has said this much, clearly, in its decisions from the early 1960s.

For more information: Bybee, Keith J. *Mistaken Identity: The Supreme Court and the Politics of Minority Representation.* Princeton, N.J.: Princeton University Press, 1998; Dixon, Robert. "The Court, the People Voting and One Man One Vote." In *Reapportionment in the 1970s Rights.* Berkeley and Los Angeles, Calif.: University of California Press, 1971; Grofman, Bernard, and Chandler Davidson, eds. *Controversy in Minority Voting: The Voting Rights Act in Perspective.* Washington, D.C.: Brookings Institute, 1992; Guinier, C. Lani. "[E]racing Democracy: The Voting Rights Cases." *Harvard Law Review* 108 (1994): 109–137; Levinson, Sanford. "Gerrymandering and the Brooding Omnipresence of Proportional Representation: Why Won't It Go Away?" *UCLA Law Review* 33 (1985): 257–281.

—Marc G. Pufong

original jurisdiction

Original jurisdiction refers to cases that ARTICLE III OF THE U.S. CONSTITUTION gives to the Supreme Court to hear directly and not on appeal. These cases include disputes involving ambassadors and where states are parties, among other types of cases. Cases on original jurisdiction are far less than 1 percent of all the cases the Court hears.

The United States Constitution provides original and appellate jurisdictional rules under Article III, and Congress has several important jurisdictional powers. The Constitution provides the federal courts with original jurisdiction in Article III. Section 2 provides that the Supreme Court has original jurisdiction "in cases affecting ambassadors, other public ministers and consuls, and those in which a state shall be a party." The Supreme Court usually hears cases upon appellate review from a lower federal court or a state supreme court. The cases or controversies listed in Article III, Section 2 allow for petitioners to bypass lower courts and have the Supreme Court hear the dispute from the first instance. The JUDICIARY ACT OF 1789 outlined original jurisdiction and allowed the Court to have original and exclusive jurisdiction in disputes between states. For all other Section 2 disputes, the Court has original but concurrent jurisdiction.

When the Supreme Court hears an original jurisdiction case, it acts similarly to a trial court. The chief justice appoints a special master to hear evidence and compose factual findings. The Court will issue an opinion after reviewing the report of the special master and hearing oral arguments. The Court treats the report of the special master in a similar fashion as it does an appealed lower court ruling, and procedurally issues a final opinion in the case as accepting, modifying, or rejecting the recommendations of the special master as reported. Unlike other disputes, original jurisdiction cases offer no opportunity for appeal, because the United States Supreme Court is the highest judicial authority.

Chief Justice JOHN MARSHALL gave the first interpretation of original jurisdiction for the Court in *MARBURY V. MADISON*, 5 U.S. 137 (1803), and in the majority opinion he outlined that original jurisdiction could not be enlarged or restricted by Congress. Original jurisdiction has limited fungibility with regard to jurisdictional questions. As legal scholar Herbert Johnson has noted, "Unfortunately for Marbury, the Constitution does not give this original jurisdiction to the Supreme Court, and the question then becomes whether Congress can do so in the absence of a constitutional grant."

In the case of *Utah v. United States*, 394 U.S. 89 (1969), the Court restricted its own original jurisdiction powers in a per curiam opinion by stating, "Our original jurisdiction should be invoked sparingly." The Court has also explained that original jurisdiction is not a mandate on the Supreme Court to hear every case involving a dispute between two states. In *Texas v. New Mexico*, 462 U.S. 554 (1983), Justice WILLIAM J. BRENNAN, JR. explained the unanimous opinion of the Court and offered this statement: "We have consistently interpreted 28 U.S.C. 1251(a) as providing us with substantial discretion to make case-by-case judgments as to the practical necessity of an original forum in this Court for particular disputes within our constitutional original jurisdiction." The standard for accepting original jurisdiction cases was determined in *Illinois v. City of Milwaukee*, 406 U.S. 91, 93 (1972), where the Court decided the appropriateness of the claim by examining (1) the "seriousness and dignity of the claim" and (2) the "availability of another forum where there is jurisdiction over the named parties, where the issues tendered may be litigated, and where appropriate relief may be had." If relief can be provided in another forum, then the Court has routinely refused to hear original jurisdiction cases to "avoid impairing its ability to administer its appellate docket."

For more information: Johnson, Herbert. *American Legal and Constitutional History.* London: Austin & Winfield, 1994; Marbach, Joseph R., Ellis Katz, and Troy E. Smith, eds. *Federalism in America.* Westport, Conn.: Greenwood Publishing, 2005; Wood, Gordon. *The Creation of the American Republic 1776–1787.* New York: W.W. Norton & Co., 1969.

—Michael W. Hail and Brian Weber

original package doctrine

The original package doctrine was one rule fashioned by the Supreme Court to determine if states could regulate the shipment of goods without violating the COMMERCE CLAUSE. The doctrine, although it is no longer used, was first pronounced in *Brown v. Maryland*, 12 Wheat 419 (1827).

The Constitution of the United States granted Congress the power to regulate commerce with foreign nations, the Indian tribes, and between the states (Article I, Section 8, Paragraph 3). It also gave to Congress the power to supervise the importing and exporting of goods (Article I, Section 10) and forbade states from taxing imported goods without congressional approval.

In *Brown v. Maryland,* the Maryland state legislature had enacted a law that required all importers to spend $50 for a license before they could handle or sell foreign articles or commodities. In contrast, no such license fee was required of merchants handling only domestic goods. Alexander Brown and other importers refused to pay the license fee. He and the other importers took the $100 fine to the Court of Appeals of Maryland and then to the United States Supreme Court.

Chief Justice JOHN MARSHALL delivered the Court's opinion. He reasoned that Maryland had every right to tax goods that had become commingled with domestic goods. However, as long as the goods were in their original package in the warehouse of the importer and still the property of the importer, they could not be taxed, because the tax would be a duty on imports, specifically forbidden by the Constitution.

In *Leisy v. Hardin*, 135 U.S. 100 (1890), the Court ruled that goods in interstate shipments could not be regulated by a state until the original package had been delivered to the consignee and the original package had been broken open.

The Court used the original package doctrine to prevent the states from imposing an ad valorem tax on imported goods and on goods imported from one state into another in domestic INTERSTATE COMMERCE. When "dry" states tried to prevent the importation of alcohol into their borders, they were blocked by the original package doctrine, which viewed liquor as still in interstate commerce even though being consumed locally out of its original container.

Beginning in the 1940s, the Supreme Court began to limit the scope of the doctrine. By the 1950s, it allowed states to tax raw materials imported for manufacturing, arguing that they immediately became an essential part of the manufacturing process. In *Michelin Tire Corp. v. Wages,* 423 U.S. 276 (1976), the Court allowed Gwinnett County, Georgia, to tax goods imported from France and Nova Scotia, even though still in their original packages. In *Limbach v. Hooven & Allison Co.,* 466 U.S. 352 (1984), the Court expressly announced the death of the original package doctrine. It allowed Ohio to impose a tax on imported fibers used for tire cordage even when stored in their original package, before the package was opened for spinning into tire cordage.

For more information: Corwin, Edward S. *The Commerce Power Versus States' Rights.* Princeton, N.J.: Princeton University Press and London: H. Milford, Oxford University Press, 1936; Ribble, F. D. G. *State and National Power over Commerce.* New York: Columbia University Press, 1937.

—Andrew J. Waskey

overbreadth doctrine

The overbreadth doctrine is a legal concept used to evaluate laws that may restrict FIRST AMENDMENT free speech rights.

The Supreme Court has used the overbreadth doctrine in cases to overturn laws that hinder free expression of ideas. The overbreadth doctrine, on the surface, appears simplistic in nature, yet is rather ingenious in its application. This doctrine stipulates that if a law is written in an overbroad fashion, then the law faces the possibility of being overturned, even if the law, according to *Black's Law Dictionary,* "prohibits acts that may legitimately be forbidden." Two cases provide examples of how the Court applies the overbreadth doctrine.

The first case is *BROADRICK V. OKLAHOMA,* 413 U.S. 601 (1973). This case involved three appellants who were employees of the state of Oklahoma. The state of Oklahoma filed charges against these state employees for violating Section 818 of the Oklahoma Merit System of Personnel Administration Act. According to Paragraph 6 of this act, no classified state employee "shall directly or indi-

rectly, solicit, receive, or in any manner be concerned in soliciting or receiving any assessment . . . or contribution for any political organization, candidacy or other political purpose." Paragraph 7 of this act states that no employee shall be a member of "any national, state or local committee of a political party." In other words, an Oklahoma state employee may not be involved in politics "except to exercise his right as a citizen privately to express his opinion and . . . vote."

In a 5-4 decision, written by Justice White, the Court upheld the law under the First Amendment of the Constitution. The Court noted:

> Although such laws, if too broadly worded, may deter protected speech to some unknown extent, there comes a point where that effect—at best a prediction—cannot, with confidence, justify invalidating a statute on its face and so prohibiting a State from enforcing the statute against conduct that is admittedly within its power to proscribe. To put the matter another way, particularly where conduct and not merely speech is involved, we believe that the *overbreadth* [emphasis added] of a statute must not only be real, but substantial as well, judged in relation to the statute's plainly legitimate sweep. It is our view that 818 is not substantially overboard and that whatever overbreadth may exist should be cured through case-by-case analysis of the fact situations to which its sanctions, assertedly, may not be applied.

The Court stressed two key points to this doctrine of overbreadth. A law that focuses on conduct and not mere speech must (1) be real and (2) be substantial. In this case, the Court determined that the law focused on conduct and not merely speech and that the law was not substantial enough to be overbroad. However, the Court appears to have left the issue open with the comment "that whatever overbreadth may exist should be cured through case-by-case analysis."

The second case, *Board of Airport Commissioners v. Jews for Jesus, Inc.,* 482 U.S. 569 (1987), revolved around a resolution that had been adopted by the Board of Airport Commissioners

(Resolution No. 13787) that stipulated, in part, "NOW, THEREFORE, BE IT RESOLVED by the Board of Airport Commissioners that the Central Terminal Area at Los Angeles International Airport is not open for First Amendment activities by any individual and/or entity." Alan Snyder, a minister of the Gospel for Jews for Jesus (a nonprofit organization), was caught distributing free pamphlets at the Los Angeles International Airport. An airport police officer approached Snyder and informed Snyder of Resolution No. 13787, and then the police officer warned Snyder to leave the airport or face legal action by the City of Los Angeles. Snyder complied with the order and left.

Jews for Jesus and Snyder filed an action challenging the constitutional nature of Resolution No. 13787. In a 9-0 decision, Justice SANDRA DAY O'CONNOR ruled that the resolution was overbroad—it went too far. The Court recognized that the law addressed some legitimate concerns the Board of Airport Commissioners may have had for the safety of people using the airport—congestion, disruption of services, and so forth. However, this does not mitigate the importance of and the right to free expression. In other words, the law was so broad it prohibited constitutionally protected activities.

For more information: Garner, Bryan A., ed. *Black's Law Dictionary.* 8th ed. St. Paul, Minn.: Thomson/West, 2004.

—Dan Krejci

P

Pacific Gas & Electric Company v. State Energy Resources Conservation and Development Commission 461 U.S. 190 (1983)

In *Pacific Gas & Electric Company v. State Energy Resources Conservation and Development Commission,* the Supreme Court ruled that a state law regulating the placement of nuclear power plants did not conflict with the 1954 Atomic Energy Act that had been passed by Congress. The importance of this case is that it dealt with the issue of PREEMPTION.

Preemption is a legal concept that addresses the issue of the scope of authority to legislate. Under the United States Constitution's SUPREMACY CLAUSE (Article VI), it, along with federal laws, is the supreme law of the land, and any state or local law in direct conflict with it is preempted, so long as the issue is one that the federal government has authority over. If federal legislation, especially when it comes to the regulation of commerce, is so pervasive as to leave states no room to act on their own, then the issue is deemed preempted by federal action.

In this case, the California Public Resources Code Section 25524.1(b) and Section 25524.2 stipulated that the State Energy Resources Conservation and Development Commission must determine whether a proposed nuclear power plant will have "adequate capacity" for "interim storage of the plant's spent fuel at the time the plant requires such storage." According to Section 25524.1(b), this decision must be made prior to the building of the plant. Section 25524.2 imposed a moratorium on any certification of new nuclear plants "until the State Commission finds that there has been developed, and that the

United States through its authorized agency has approved, a demonstrated technology or means for the permanent and terminal disposal of high-level nuclear wastes." Pacific Gas & Electric filed an action in the federal district court, claiming that these sections of the Public Resources Code were invalid because the Atomic Energy Act preempted these sections of the Public Resources Code. The federal district court found that the two sections were ripe for adjudication and found both sections to be preempted by the Atomic Energy Act.

The case made its way to the United States Court of Appeals for the Ninth Circuit. The court of appeals agreed with the notion that Section 25524.2 was ripe for adjudication but not Section 25524.1(b) "because it could not be known whether the State Commission will ever find a nuclear plant's storage capacity to be inadequate." In addition, the court of appeals noted that Section 25524.2

[W]as not designed to provide protection against radiation hazards but was adopted because uncertainties in the nuclear fuel cycle make nuclear power an uneconomical and uncertain source of energy, and therefore that the section was not pre-empted because 271 and 274(k) of the Atomic Energy Act constituted authorization for States to regulate nuclear powerplants for purposes other than protection against radiation hazards.

Furthermore, the court stated that Section 25524.2 was not unconstitutional because it was not an impediment to the "fulfillment of the federal goal of encouraging the development of atomic energy."

The Supreme Court, in a 9-0 decision, affirmed the court of appeals decision. It ruled that the Atomic Energy Act, which dealt with the safety of nuclear power plants, left room to states to regulate the issue of the disposal of spent nuclear waste. Therefore, the California law was not preempted by the act.

For more information: Farber, Daniel A., William N. Eskridge Jr., and Philip P. Frickey. *Cases and Materials on Constitutional Law: Themes for the Constitution's Third Century.* St. Paul, Minn.: West Publishing Company, 1993.

—Dan Krejci

Palko v. State of Connecticut 302 U.S. 319 (1937)

In *Palko v. State of Connecticut*, the Supreme Court case defined what protections in the BILL OF RIGHTS should be applied to limit the actions of individual states.

Frank Palko was a poor Connecticut factory worker who burglarized a store one night. Fleeing on foot with a stolen radio, Palko was interrupted by two police officers who tried to stop him, but he shot one of them to death. He was captured a little over a month later.

Palko was indicted in Fairfield County by the State of Connecticut for murder in the first degree. He was tried before a jury that had only two legal options. Either it could have acquitted Palko, or it had to sentence him to death. However, the jury found Palko guilty of murder not in the first degree but guilty of murder in the second degree. The sentence for second degree murder was life in prison.

With the permission of the trial judge, which was required by Connecticut law, the state prosecutor appealed the conviction on the grounds that the jury had erred by returning a verdict of murder in the second degree rather than acquittal or murder in the first degree. The Supreme Court of Errors for Connecticut ordered a new trial (*State v. Palko,* 121 Conn. 669, 186 Atl. 657) on grounds there had been errors of law to the prejudice of the state in the lower court, including the exclu-

sion of Palko's confession and flawed instructions to the jury, as well as the improper conviction.

At Palko's second trial, the jury returned a verdict of first degree murder. Palko was then sentenced to death. Palko appealed the legality of his second trial to the Connecticut Court of Errors (122 Conn. 529, 191 Atl. 320), which ruled against him. He then appealed to the United States Supreme Court under the DUE PROCESS clause of the FOURTEENTH AMENDMENT, claiming that the Fifth Amendment prohibition against DOUBLE JEOPARDY had been violated.

The case was argued on November 12, 1937, and decided December 6, 1937. The 8-1 majority opinion, written by Justice Benjamin N. Cardozo, was probably his most famous decision. He concluded that the question of double jeopardy was not the controlling issue. The state of Connecticut, in seeking a trial without prejudicial errors, was not engaged in double jeopardy.

While the Court was unwilling to apply the Fifth Amendment prohibition of double jeopardy to Palko's case, Cardozo announced a test for determining which rights were to be applied to the states or incorporated. It was to be those "so rooted in the traditions and conscience of our people as to be ranked as fundamental."

Justice Pierce Butler dissented. Palko was executed in the electric chair at the Connecticut State Prison at Wethersfield on April 12, 1938.

For more information: Cortner, Richard C. *The Supreme Court and the Second Bill of Rights: The Fourteenth Amendment and the Nationalization of Civil Liberties.* Madison: University of Wisconsin Press, 1981; Harrison, Maureen, and Steve Gilbert. *Criminal Justice Decisions of the United States Supreme Court.* Carlsbad, Calif.: Excellent Books, 2003.

—Andrew J. Waskey

Panama Refining Co. v. Ryan 293 U.S. 388 (1935)

In *Panama Refining Co. v. Ryan,* the Supreme Court held that Section 9(c) of the National Industrial Recovery Act of 1933 was an unconstitutional delegation of authority from Congress to the president. The importance of the *Panama Refining* ruling, coupled with the Court's decision in SCHECHTER POULTRY V. UNITED STATES, 295 U.S. 495 (1935), handed down the same year, was that the Court emphasized Congress could not delegate authority to the executive branch unless the legislative branch issued standards to guide the exercise of this authority.

The National Industrial Recovery Act was one of the first pieces of New Deal legislation, proposed by the Roosevelt administration and approved by Congress, to deal with the depression affecting the United States in the early 1930s. At issue in this case was Section 9(c), which gave the president the authority to prohibit the transportation of petroleum in excess of the amount permitted by various state laws. In short, this section of the act would help control the supply of petroleum, in hope that by doing so prices would stabilize. Panama Refining Company, the owner of an oil refining plant in Texas, challenged the law on the grounds that it was an unconstitutional delegation of legislative authority to the president and that it exceeded Congress's COMMERCE CLAUSE authority.

The Court, in an 8-1 vote, held that Section 9(c) was an unconstitutional delegation of legislative authority. Presuming for the purposes of this case that Congress had the authority under the commerce clause to pass such a law, the Court looked to the law to determine if Congress had declared a policy, and if so, whether Congress had set up a standard to guide executive branch action or required any finding by the president before exercising the authority found in the law. In the end, the Court concluded that Congress had left to the president's discretion as to when the industry violated state regulations, imposing upon the executive no standard to guide his actions in enforcing the law nor requiring the president to find certain facts in evidence before acting.

The larger issue in this case was what the Constitution required of the political branches as the administrative state grew dramatically in the 1930s and 1940s. While the Court acknowledged that the Constitution afforded Congress the ability to pass legislation that adapted to complex situations that the legislative branch could not foresee, the Court also stressed that the Constitution firmly rests legislative authority in Congress. For Congress to delegate authority to the executive branch without standards and guidance would violate the separation of powers written into the Constitution.

In a lone dissenting opinion, Justice Cardozo claimed that the Court misread the law. In particular, Cardozo stated that Congress made clear the intent of the policy, and it did not give the president limitless discretion, as he could not act unless the industry violated established state regulations. For Cardozo, the Court should have looked at the law in its entirety, not just Section 9(c), to determine whether Congress clearly pronounced a policy to guide the president.

As a number of scholars have pointed out, the Court's rulings in *Panama Refining* and *Schechter Poultry* were the last two times that the Court limited the delegation of authority from Congress to the executive branch. The nondelegation doctrine, as these rulings came to be known, gave way to the Court's typically ratifying broad congressional delegations of authority to the executive branch throughout the 20th century. In a number of contexts, whether foreign affairs (see *United States v. Curtiss-Wright*, 299 U.S. 304 [1936]) or the U.S. Sentencing Commission (see MISTRETTA V. UNITED STATES, 109 S.Ct. 647 [1989]), the Court has held the non-delegation doctrine to be dead.

For more information: Warren, Kenneth F. *Administrative Law in the Political System.* 3d ed. Upper Saddle River, N.J.: Prentice Hall, 1997.
—John M. Aughenbaugh

parades

Parades raise several constitutional concerns under the FIRST AMENDMENT right to freedom of association.

First, there is the place the parade takes place. HAGUE V. COMMITTEE FOR INDUSTRIAL ORGANIZATIONS, 307 U.S. 496 (1939), established that streets are PUBLIC FORUMS, which have traditionally allowed a broad range of debate—including parades. In a public forum, the state cannot discriminate against speech without a compelling interest. For most of the 20th century, this interest was hard to find. For example, in *Collin v. Smith,* 578 F.2d 1197 (7th Cir. 1978), the case that spawned the Skokie affair, the Seventh Circuit held that concerns about HATE SPEECH were not sufficient to uphold a ban against a proposed Nazi march through a neighborhood of Holocaust survivors.

However, courts tend to be more lenient toward the state when the state's regulations do not appear on their face to discriminate against a particular type of speech. In resolving these cases, courts apply the "time, place, and manner" test, which asks (1) whether the restrictions are content neutral, (2) whether they are narrowly tailored to meet the state's concerns, and (3) whether there are alternative means of communication.

Applying these tests, courts have held that the state can require the group to seek a permit, provided that the process is timely, does not vest too much authority in the hands of state officials, and allows for JUDICIAL REVIEW. Likewise, the state can limit the number of people who can attend the parade, change the parade route, or restrict the activities that parade goers can undertake. Finally, most courts that have considered the issue have also upheld laws banning masked demonstrations.

Disputes sometimes arise over whether state regulations are in fact neutral. In *Clark v. Community for Creative Non Violence,* 468 U.S. 288 (1984), the Court upheld a ban on sleeping during an overnight demonstration as a valid, content-neutral restriction on speech. In a sharp dissent, however, Justice Thurgood Marshall argued that given the context—the demonstration was an encampment on the Capitol Mall intended to call attention to the plight of the homeless—the ban on sleeping discriminated against the protesters.

In the post 9/11 era, courts have tended to defer to state restrictions on parades—especially when national security can be invoked. For example, in *United for Peace & Justice v. City of New York,* 243 F. Supp. 2d 19 (S.D.N.Y. 2003), a lower court, citing fears of terrorism, upheld New York City's refusal to allow an antiwar group to stage a parade in front of the United Nations to protest the impending invasion of Iraq. Courts also approved the use of "protest pens" and "free speech" zones at the 2004 Democratic and Republican national conventions.

A separate issue involves whether parade organizers can, consistent with the antidiscrimination laws, exclude parade goers. This issue has arisen repeatedly where gay and lesbian groups have sought to march openly in St. Patrick's Day parades. In *HURLEY V. IRISH-AMERICAN GAY, LESBIAN AND BISEXUAL GROUP OF BOSTON, INC.,* 515 U.S. 557 (1995), the Supreme Court held that parades were per se an expressive activity, and, therefore, parade organizers were free to exclude messages they opposed.

For more information: Duncan, Dwight G. "Parading the First Amendment through the Streets of Boston." *New England Law Review* 30 (1996): 664–694; Nanes, Susan Rachel. "Comment: 'The Constitutional Infringement Zone': Protest Pens and Demonstration Zones at the 2004 National Conventions." *Louisiana Law Review* 66 (2005): 189–232; Suplina, Nick. "Note: Crowd Control: The Troubling Mix of First Amendment Law, Political Demonstrations, and Terrorism." *George Washington Law Review* 73 (2005): 395–428.

—Robert A. Kahn

parental notification and abortion

Parental notification and ABORTION refer to laws passed by states requiring women under the age of 18 to obtain parental consent before terminating a pregnancy. These laws raise important questions about the right to PRIVACY of minors as well as the rights of parents.

Shortly after 1973, when the Supreme Court declared that the right to privacy included the right to abortion, states began to impose restrictions on a minor's access to abortion, either by requiring her to notify her parents or by requiring their consent. Advocates of such laws say that parents have a right to be involved in her decision, and that their involvement would reduce teenage pregnancies. Opponents say that pregnant teenagers usually inform their parents anyway, and parents do not provide support and comfort in every case. Beginning in 1976, the Court decided the parameters of the minor's right to privacy, weighing it against the parents' interest in their child's welfare and the state's interest in the child's health and in the integrity of the family.

In *H.L. v. Matheson*, 450 U.S. 398 (1981), the first case on the constitutionality of a notice law, the Court upheld a Utah statute requiring a physician to notify the parents of a minor before performing an abortion. The law was challenged by a 15-year-old pregnant and unmarried teenager living at home who wanted to obtain an abortion without notifying her parents. The Court held that a state may require a physician to notify the parents of an immature and dependent minor such as this. In a 6-3 opinion, it found that the law fostered the state's interest in promoting the family and protected the teenager by allowing her parents to apprise her physician about her medical and psychological history.

In June 1990, the Court addressed the issue of parental notice in two cases arising out of Minnesota and Ohio. Subdivision Two of the Minnesota law, with few exceptions, required a doctor to notify both parents. Another section, Subdivision Six, specified that a judicial bypass procedure would take effect if Subdivision Two were declared unconstitutional by a court. The bypass would allow the minor to try to convince a judge that she was mature enough to decide for herself about having an abortion or that it was not in her best interests to notify her parents. In *Hodgson v. Minnesota*, 497 U.S. 417 (1990), a majority of the Court found Subdivision Two unconstitutional because it had no reasonable relationship to a legitimate state interest. A different five-justice majority sustained Subdivision Six, thereby upholding the entire law.

Speaking for the Court on Subdivision Two, Justice JOHN PAUL STEVENS stressed that none of the Court's earlier rulings addressed the constitutionality of a notice or consent requirement that applied to both parents. He denied that the two-parent notice furthered the state's interests in

the teenager or the family. The state could protect the minor by requiring one parent to be notified and allowing that parent to decide whether to notify the other. He rejected the state's argument that it was best for the family if both parents were involved in a teenager's abortion decision, saying that the state cannot try to mold a family into its idealized image.

With respect to Subdivision Six, Stevens explained how the Minnesota judicial bypass procedure differed from those upheld in previous cases. A bypass is intended to allow exceptions from a reasonable general rule and thereby preserve its constitutionality. This bypass requires the minor to ask the court to excuse her from complying with a rule that does not further the state interest. In her concurring opinion, Justice SANDRA DAY O'CONNOR agreed that Subdivision Two was unconstitutional. But she believed that Subdivision Six was constitutional, because the bypass procedure allowed the minor to avoid notifying both her parents.

Similarly, in *Ohio v. Akron Center for Reproductive Health*, 497 U.S. 502 (1990), the Court upheld an Ohio law with a one-parent notice requirement and a bypass procedure. The law specified that, in most cases, before performing an abortion, the physician was required to give 24 hours notice to a parent; the law also allowed the teenager to show that she was sufficiently mature and could make the decision without notifying her parent or simply that notification was not in her best interests. The lower courts declared the law unconstitutional, but the majority declared the Ohio law constitutional because it did not place an undue burden on the young woman seeking an abortion.

Since *Hodgson*, the Court has ruled on challenges to parental notification laws in Montana, Virginia, and Arizona, among others and, in most cases, has upheld them. In 2006, the SENATE and HOUSE OF REPRESENTATIVES each approved legislation that would make it illegal to transport a minor child across a state line to obtain an abortion that would avoid complying with parental involvement laws in the minor's home state. No final vote was taken after the bill came out of the conference committee before the 109th Congress adjourned.

For more information: Friedman, Jennifer C. "Parental Notice in State Abortion Statutes: Filling the Gap in Constitutional Jurisprudence." *Columbia Human Rights Law Review* 29 (1998): 437–464; Liebman, Joanna S. "The Underage, the 'Unborn,' and the Unconstitutional: An Analysis of the Child Custody Protection Act." *Columbia Journal of Gender & Law* 11 (2002): 407–425; Mezey, Susan Gluck. *Elusive Equality: Women's Rights, Public Policy, and the Law.* Boulder, Colo.: Lynne Rienner Publishers, 2003.

—Susan Gluck Mezey

Parker v. Brown 317 U.S. 341 (1943)

In *Parker v. Brown,* the Supreme Court recognized an important exception to federal antitrust law. The Court unanimously upheld a state program intended to restrict competition among California raisin producers in an opinion by Chief Justice Harlan Stone. Although the state policy was attacked on three separate grounds, the primary impact of the case has been within antitrust law, through the development of "state action" or "*Parker* immunity."

Brown, a producer and packer of raisins, was subject to state sanctions for failing to participate in a price maintenance program that, he claimed, would prevent him from marketing existing crops and fulfilling previously entered sales contracts. He challenged the enforcement of the State Agricultural Prorate Advisory Commission's program as a violation of the Sherman Act, as preempted by a federal statute regulating agricultural marketing, and as inconsistent with the DORMANT COMMERCE CLAUSE, which prohibits the states from imposing unreasonable restraints on INTERSTATE COMMERCE. A three-judge district court ruled for Brown on the dormant commerce clause, and the case was accepted by the Court on that basis, but after other issues arose during oral argument, the case was scheduled for additional briefs and reargument. The justices rejected all proposed challenges, however, concluding that California's

prorate program was not subject to the Sherman Act because its operation is directed by the state, acting as a sovereign government, and the Sherman Act does not indicate that Congress intended to restrain such activities.

The Sherman Act prohibits the restraint of trade by contract, conspiracy, or the act of monopolization, and Chief Justice Stone's opinion grants that the prorate program, which combines raisin production in California for the purposes of controlling output and price, would be illegal if it were performed by private actors. The majority opinion also granted that Congress could forbid such a program by legislation if it chose. However, the Court's interpretation of the Sherman Act concluded that Congress did not intend to displace the states' power to enact programs like the one at issue in the case. The chief justice also made reference to the substantial issues of FEDERALISM raised by any subtraction of state authority by congressional action, and this line of support has contributed more to the subsequent development of *Parker* doctrine.

The California proration program also survived the other two challenges to its legal enforcement. The Court concluded that the state program did not conflict with the federal Agricultural Marketing Agreement Act of 1937 (7 U.S.C. 601–674), nor was it preempted by the dormant commerce clause, as the district court had declared.

Although *Parker v. Brown* was litigated primarily as a PREEMPTION case and initially accepted by the Court for review on that question, its primary impact has been as the foundation for "state action immunity" from antitrust enforcement, which took its modern form in *California Retail Liquor Dealers Association v. Midcal Aluminum, Inc.,* 445 U.S. 97 (1980). This doctrine has been subject to considerable criticism, within and outside the judiciary, and the justices have struggled for some time to articulate the distinction between regulatory or regulated activity conducted by or under color of state authority immune from antitrust law and illegal market behavior that states cannot immunize.

For more information: Patrizia, Charles A. "*Parker v. Brown*: A Preemption Analysis." *Yale*

Law Journal 84 (1975): 1,164–1,177; Philips, Dirk C. "Putting *Parker v. Brown* and its Progeny in Perspective: An Assessment of the Supreme Court's Role in the Development of Antitrust Federalism." *Journal of Law and Politics* 16 (2000): 193–229; Squire, Richard. "Antitrust and the Supremacy Clause." *Stanford Law Review* 59 (2006): 77–130.

—Scott E. Graves

partisan gerrymandering

Partisan gerrymandering refers to the drawing of political representation district lines for partisan purposes or advantage. While the Supreme Court has stated that partisan gerrymandering is a potential violation of the FOURTEENTH AMENDMENT's EQUAL PROTECTION clause, there is significant dispute and disagreement over whether this is the type of issue the judiciary should hear.

The role of the Supreme Court and lower federal courts in resolving redistricting issues is a continuing source of controversy. In *Colgrove v. Green,* 328 U.S. 549 (1946), the Supreme Court was asked to hear a case alleging the malapportionment or drawing of district lines to benefit one party of a community at the expense of another. Justice Felix Frankfurter, writing for the Court, ruled that questions about reapportionment were political questions that the judiciary should not hear. Instead, they should be resolved by the political branches, such as by Congress. However, in *BAKER V. CARR,* 369 U.S. 186 (1962), the Court reversed itself and ruled that reapportionment questions were justiciable. By justiciable, the Court meant that the federal judiciary would no longer consider them to be political questions, but, instead, would be willing to hear them.

As a result of *Baker,* in cases such as *REYNOLDS V. SIMS,* 377 U.S. 533 (1963), the Supreme Court was increasingly drawn into redistricting issues, ruling that the apportioning of district lines could violate the ONE PERSON, ONE VOTE standard. This would occur if some districts contained more individuals than another, such that the votes of some would have more weight than others. If this dilution of voting strength occurred, then it would constitute a violation of the equal protection clause of the Fourteenth Amendment.

While the Supreme Court had ruled, in cases such as *Reynolds* and in *GOMILLION V. LIGHTFOOT,* 364 U.S. 339 (1960), that the drawing of district lines contrary to the one person, one vote standard, or for racial purposes, was unconstitutional, these cases did not address whether it was permissible to consider partisan motives when undertaking apportionment. Some allege that it is a common practice for political parties in control to attempt to draw district lines to their advantage, so that it will be easier for them to get reelected and stay in office. Beginning in *Davis v. Bandamer,* 478 U.S. 109 (1986), the Supreme Court attempted to address this issue to decide if partisan gerrymandering or redistricting was also a constitutional violation.

In *Davis v. Bandamer,* at issue was a suit brought by Indiana Democrats, contesting the constitutionality of a 1981 state redistricting plan. The specific allegation was that the plan drew legislative lines and seats in such a way as to disadvantage Democrats. It did so by dividing up cities such as South Bend in arguably unusual ways. The Democrats filed suit, contending that these districts violated their rights as Democrats under the Fourteenth Amendment equal protection clause. The district court had ruled in favor of the Democrats, in part because of evidence and testimony suggesting that the Republican Party had in fact drawn the lines in its favor. When the case reached the Supreme Court, a central issue was whether this was a justiciable controversy under the equal protection clause. The Court held that it was.

The Court articulated several stipulations that had to be met to sustain a political gerrymandering claim. First, there had to be proof of INTENTIONAL DISCRIMINATION against the one party, here, the Democrats. Second, "a group's electoral power is not unconstitutionally diminished by the simple fact of an apportionment scheme that makes winning elections more difficult. A failure of proportional representation alone does not constitute impermissible discrimination under the equal protection clause." Instead, the Court stated that the political process must frustrate political activity in a systematic fashion that frustrates the will of the voters. Finally, the Court contended that showing frustration or dilution of political influence in one election was also insufficient. Instead, it would need to be shown that it took place over several elections.

While the *Bandamer* decision ruled that partisan gerrymandering was justiciable and laid out a test to determine if an apportionment was a constitutional violation, no court had held in favor of such claims. Instead, some contended that *Bandamer* was wrongly decided and that partisan gerrymanders should not be heard by the courts. There were calls to revisit the decision in *Bandamer.* The Supreme Court did that, first in *Vieth v. Jubelirer,* 541 U.S. 267 (2004), and again in League of United Latin American Citizens v. Perry, 126 S.Ct. 2594 (2006).

In *Vieth,* at issue was the constitutionality of a Pennsylvania districting plan that drew the seats for its congressional delegation after the 2000 census. Prior to the census, the state had 21 representatives, but after 2000 it was entitled to only 19 seats. Republicans controlled both houses of the Pennsylvania legislature as well as the governor's office. State Democrats contended that the district lines drawn violated Article I, Sections 2 and 4, and the equal protection clause, thereby constituting both a violation of the one person, one vote standard and, more importantly here, a partisan gerrymander. The district court dismissed the partisan or political gerrymandering claim (with some of the other issues addressed or resolved in other litigation in the case), and it was appealed to the Supreme Court.

In a split decision, the Supreme Court ruled several things. First, a four-person plurality opinion written by Justice ANTONIN GREGORY SCALIA reviewed the history of partisan gerrymandering in the United States, concluding that such a practice went back to the early days of the republic. Given this history, there had also been numerous efforts to address it, and they all had failed. Scalia next argued that the standards for addressing partisan gerrymandering in *Bandamer* had proved unworkable. He criticized the three-prong test

enunciated there, contending that it was unmanageable and arbitrary and that it would fall into a simple proportionality test between voting percentages and seats won by a particular party. But more importantly, based on the employment of the test in the lower courts, the *Bandamer* opinion provided no guidance to the Court.

Overall, a four-justice plurality ruled that partisan gerrymanders were not justiciable, and therefore, in the case before them, the claims of the Democrats should be rejected. However, five justices agreed that the Democrats had not proved that a partisan gerrymander existed in the case before them, and that this type of issue was not justiciable. Justice ANTHONY M. KENNEDY concurred that there was no partisan gerrymander here, but he refused to go along with overruling *Bandamer.* He agreed that neutral rules for resolving and adjudicating partisan gerrymanders were needed, but he did not agree with the majority that it would never be possible to find them. This thus created a five-justice majority to reject the plaintiffs' claims. However, five justices in several dissents, including Kennedy, refused to overrule *Bandamer,* continuing to make partisan gerrymanders justiciable issues. What the dissenters could not agree on were what constituted acceptable or manageable standards for adjudicating a partisan gerrymander dispute. The hope was that *League of United Latin American Citizens v. Perry (LULAC)* would do that, but it did not.

LULAC arose from a high-profile partisan battle in the Texas legislature that involved U.S. Representative Tom DeLay and a battle for the state legislature and its congressional delegation. The 2000 census indicated that the state of Texas should receive two additional seats in the HOUSE OF REPRESENTATIVES beyond the current 30 that it had. At the time of redistricting the Texas Republican Party controlled the state senate and governor's office, but the Democrats controlled the state house of representatives. With the legislature unable to agree to adopt a redistricting scheme, litigation eventually led to the creation of a court-ordered one. This plan produced a 17 to 15 Democratic majority in the Texas congressional delegation. But in 2003, state elections gave

Republicans control of both houses of the state legislature as well as control of the governor's office. With the encouragement of Tom DeLay, and after a long struggle, including Democrats in the legislature hiding out in Oklahoma to avoid a special session, the state passed a new redistricting plan in 2003.

In 2004, elections using this new plan gave Republicans 58 percent of the statewide vote, compared to 41 percent for Democrats. Republicans also captured 21 of the congressional seats to the 11 won by the Democrats. The 2003 plan was challenged in court, claiming, inter alia, that it was a partisan gerrymander and that the state and federal constitutions barred a second redistricting scheme following a decennial census. Judgment was for the appellees, but in light of the *Vieth v. Jubelirer* decision, the Supreme Court vacated and remanded it to reconsider. The district court then solely considered the political gerrymandering claim and again ruled in favor of the appellees. Before the Supreme Court were arguments that the 2003 redistricting schema was a partisan or political gerrymander, that it violated the VOT-ING RIGHTS ACT (VRA), and that the mid-decade redistricting violated the one person, one vote requirement under the Fourteenth Amendment. While the Court did find that one of the districts did violate the VRA, it rejected claims that the mid-decade redistricting violated the Constitution, and it also ruled that the appellants had failed to state a claim upon which relief could be granted for the political gerrymander.

Justice Kennedy, writing for yet another divided Court when it came to the partisan gerrymander claim, specifically noted that the theory of the plaintiffs was that mid-decade redistricting, when solely motivated by partisan objectives, violated the Fourteenth Amendment. A majority of the Court rejected this claim, stating that not every line drawn was done based on partisan objectives. Yet, even if mixed motives were not present in this case, Kennedy asserted that one challenging a gerrymander as partisan would have to show how it burdened, according to a reliable standard, their representational rights. The simple fact that a mid-decade redistricting schema took place is rejected

as a per se standard to show burden. Similarly, the claim that a mid-decade redistricting violates the one person, one vote requirement if done for partisan purposes is also rejected. While Kennedy clearly stated that this decision did not revisit the JUSTICIABILITY of partisan gerrymandering, it rejected the tests offered in this case to define a standard for resolving disputes averring this as a claim.

As with *Vieth*, *LULAC* produced a divided Court that failed to mend the split over partisan gerrymandering. Kennedy wrote the opinion for the Court, with various justices concurring with parts of the decision. The splits occurred over whether partisan gerrymanders are justiciable (five justices agreed that they were), whether there was a VRA violation in the drawing of district 23 (five agreed there was), and over what constituted manageable standards for resolving a political gerrymander. Kennedy rejected the plaintiff's proposed standard, four justices rejected all standards, and four other justices splintered over various possible standards.

LULAC left the Court no better off than before, despite a change in two justices since the *Vieth* decision and with four justices saying political gerrymanders are nonjusticiable, four saying they are and proposing different standards, and Kennedy in the middle saying the issue is justiciable but still in search of a standard.

Overall, in theory, partisan gerrymanders are justiciable issues that can be heard by the courts. However, lacking a clear set of standards to determine what constitutes a partisan gerrymander, it is unclear how these issues will be resolved in the near future.

For more information: Schultz, David. "The Party's Over: Partisan Gerrymandering and the First Amendment." *Capital University Law Review* 36 (2007): 1–52.

—David Schultz

patents

A patent is the grant by a federal government to an inventor of the exclusive property right to make, use, or sell an invention for a specific period of time, generally 20 years—essentially a monopoly over the invention for a limited time.

In the United States, Congress is given the power by the United States Constitution, Article I, Section 8, Clause 8, to grant rights to inventors to "promote the progress of science and useful arts, by securing for limited times to authors and inventors the exclusive right to their respective writings and discoveries." The United States Patent and Trademark Office is the agency of the United States Department of Commerce charged with the duty of examining patent applications. There, patent examiners ensure that each patent application meets with all of the requirements of the United States Patent Act.

There are three types of patents available in the United States: utility, design, and plant patents. The Patent Act, codified in 35 United States Code §101 et al., defines patentable subject matter for a utility patent and requires that the invention be useful, novel, and nonobvious.

In order for a patent application to progress to a patent, the invention must be useful or have utility. Such utility needs only to be sufficient to convince one skilled in the art or technology that the invention has the inventor's asserted utility (*In re Brana*, 51 F.3d 1560 [Fed. Cir. 1995]). An invention claimed in a patent must be new or novel at the time of invention, meaning, among other requirements, that the invention was not known or used by others in the United States or described in a printed publication anywhere in the world (35 U.S.C §102). An invention that is not novel is described as anticipated by the art. Even if the invention is not anticipated at the time of invention, the subject matter of the application as a whole must not be such that it would have been obvious to a person having ordinary skill in the art or technology (35 U.S.C §103).

The United States patent system defines rights on a first-to-invent basis, as opposed to almost entirely the rest of the world, which uses a first-to-file basis. Courts have interpreted the concept of invention to include conception, diligence, and reduction to practice (*Marhurkar v. C.R. Bard, Inc.*, 79 F.3d 1572, 1577 [Fed. Cir. 1996]). If an inventor works with reasonable diligence to actually demonstrate that the invention is suitable for its intended purpose (reduction to practice), then the inventor may establish rights back to the date that he or she had such a fully formed thought (conception) that such thought only need be constructed (*Brown et al. v. Barbacid et al.*, 436 F.3d 1376 [Fed. Cir. 2006]).

The Patent Act allows inventors to seek protection for "any new, original, and ornamental design for an article of manufacture" (35 U.S.C. §171). Also, one who "invents or discovers and asexually reproduces any distinct and new variety of plant" may be entitled to protection of such as a plant patent (35 U.S.C. 161).

Philosophical bases for the grant of a patent include that an inventor is entitled to the fruits of his or her intellectual labor and that the grant of such a monopoly fosters technological innovation.

For more information: Durham, Alan L. *Patent Law Essentials: A Concise Guide*. Westport, Conn.: Praeger Press, 2005.

—Nathan H. Cristler

PATRIOT Act (USA PATRIOT Act)

The PATRIOT Act refers to a law and its subsequent reauthorization in 2006 that was enacted to detect terrorist activity after the events of 9/11. While many believe the act is an important tool to enhance American security, others argue that portions of it violate the Constitution.

On September 11, 2001, al-Qaeda terrorists hijacked four commercial airplanes, using them to attack the United States, ending in a huge loss of life and numerous injuries. In the weeks following the terrorist attacks, the U.S. government took several steps—proactive and preventive measures—to avoid a repeat of the terrible events that occurred on September 11.

In addition to providing the president with unprecedented authorization in the fight against terrorism, Congress took steps to provide law enforcement and intelligence agencies with expanded powers for countering terrorist activities against the United States, both within the country and abroad. One of the most visible and perhaps controversial steps taken by Congress was the passage of the PATRIOT Act, signed into law by the president on October 26, 2001, only 45 days after the terrorist attacks in New York and Washington, D.C.

The Uniting Strengthening America by Providing Appropriate Tools Required to Intercept and Obstruct Terrorism Act of 2001 (Public Law 107-56), more commonly known as the PATRIOT Act, originated in the HOUSE OF REPRESENTATIVES as Bill H.R. 2975 (the PATRIOT Act) and in the SENATE as S. 1510 (the USA Act). These bills passed through both houses in the early half of October 2001. Due to some unresolved discrepancies between the original text and previous legislation on money laundering and intelligence gathering, the House subsequently passed a clean bill H.R. 3162 on October 24, 2001, incorporating changes that expanded and amended the previously passed FOREIGN INTELLIGENCE SURVEILLANCE ACT (FISA) OF 1978, and also passed on October 26, 2001, the Financial Anti-Terrorism Act. The Senate agreed to the changes with only one dissenting voice (Senator Russ Feingold, D-Wisconsin) and one nonvoting member (Senator Mary Landrieu, D-Louisiana). The bill was then sent to the president and signed into law on October 26, 2001.

In particular, the PATRIOT Act provided federal officials with sweeping powers for tracking and intercepting communications for law enforcement and intelligence-gathering purposes. It seeks to close off American borders to foreign terrorists, to detain and remove those terrorists already within our borders, and to shut down their financial resources with expanded money laundering powers. The PATRIOT Act has created new procedures, penalties, and definitions of crimes to combat domestic and international terrorism. Despite garnering majority support and quick passage through Congress, the act was surrounded by controversy, with those supporting it claiming that the provisions have not gone far enough to ensure the United States is protected from future terrorist acts. Opponents have argued against the act on the grounds that it treads heavily on citizens' CIVIL LIBERTIES in the fight against terrorism.

For example, the PATRIOT Act has eased government access to confidential information and authorizes so-called sneak-and-peak search warrants to be issued for "reasonable cause" rather than "probable cause." However, there were also a number of safeguards included within the text of the act, specifying notification periods and requirement of authorization for particular provisions on surveillance, wiretaps, and the issuance of warrants. These safeguards also included providing additional review, clarification, and public reporting, as checks built into the reforms to avoid actual or perceived abuse of power.

Due to the impact the act would have on individual liberties and the sweeping reforms it implements, a sunset clause was added, requiring that Congress take active steps to reassess the act after its implementation and testing over time. Several of the surveillance sections of the original act would have expired on December 31, 2005, but these were extended until March 10, 2006. Congress reauthorized the PATRIOT Act without much reform, with President Bush signing it into law on March 9, 2006, a day before the extension was due to expire. The reauthorized act has included a four-year sunset clause on three specific provisions covering attainment of records (such as library records), use of wiretaps to monitor communications, and secret surveillance of non-U.S. citizens within the country—all without probable cause or suspicion—an important reform with regard to protection of civil liberties and FIRST AMENDMENT rights.

Although the PATRIOT Act has had a large impact on First Amendment rights and civil liberties since its passage in 2001, the debate surrounding it has also expanded over the past four years about the balance between security and preemptive measures for combating terrorism versus protection of individual rights. This is perhaps most evident in the fact that while only one senator voted against the original PATRIOT Act in 2001, during Senate debate in mid-December 2005, a bipartisan group of 52 senators filibustered the reauthorization. In the end, 10 senators opposed the reauthorization of the PATRIOT Act without substantial reform in early 2006. Moreover, the

AMERICAN CIVIL LIBERTIES UNION has tried to challenge the act in court, claiming it violates either the First Amendment freedom of speech clause or the FOURTH AMENDMENT's protection against unreasonable searches and seizures. While some district courts have ruled in favor of the ACLU, appellate courts have either thrown the suits out or refused to rule on the issues. For the most part, core challenges to the PATRIOT Act have faced mixed success.

For more information: Abdolian, Lisa Finnegan, and Harold Takooshian. "The USA PATRIOT Act: Civil Liberties, the Media, and Public Opinion." *Fordham Urban Law Journal* 30 (May 2003): 1,429–1,453; Cole, David. "The Priority of Morality: The Emergency Constitution's Blind Spot." *Yale Law Journal* 113 (June 2004): 1,753–1,800; Etzioni, Amitai. *How Patriotic Is the Patriot Act?: Freedom versus Security in the Age of Terrorism.* New York: Routledge, 2004; Gudridge, Patrick O., and Laurence H. Tribe. "The Anti-Emergency Constitution." *Yale Law Journal* 113 (June 2004): 1,801–1,870; Heymann, Philip B. "Civil Liberties and Human Rights in the Aftermath of September 11." *Harvard Journal of Law & Public Policy* 25 (Spring 2002): 441–456.

—Dale Mineshima-Lowe

Payne v. Tennessee 501 U.S. 111 (1991)

In *Payne v. Tennessee*, the United States Supreme Court was asked to decide whether the CRUEL AND UNUSUAL PUNISHMENT clause of the Eighth Amendment to the United States Constitution barred the introduction of victim impact testimony during the sentencing phase of a death penalty trial.

The Eighth Amendment states: "Excessive bail shall not be required, nor excessive fines imposed, nor cruel and unusual punishments inflicted." Prior to the decision in *Payne*, in *Booth v. Maryland*, 482 U.S. 496 (1987), and *Carolina v. Gathers*, 490 U.S. 805 (1989), the Supreme Court had ruled that victim impact evidence—evidence concerning a victim's personal characteristics and the emotional impact of the crime on the victim's

family—could not be relied upon by the prosecution when seeking the death penalty, because it would create an unacceptable risk that the jury would impose an arbitrary and capricious death sentence. In *Payne,* the Court revisited the issue, overruled *Booth* and *Gathers,* and held that the Eighth Amendment does not bar the introduction of victim impact testimony.

The issue arose during the death penalty murder trial of Purvis Payne. Payne brutally killed a mother and her two-year-old daughter and attempted to kill her three-year-old son, but the son survived his wounds. After being found guilty, Payne sought to mitigate his sentence with evidence of his good personal characteristics. He called his parents, his girlfriend, and a clinical psychologist to testify that he was a docile, law-abiding man of limited mental abilities who attended church, did not use drugs and alcohol, and was good with children. In rebuttal, the prosecution called the surviving son's grandmother to testify about the emotional impact that the murders had on the victim and his family. Then, during closing arguments, the prosecutor relied upon that testimony in asking the jury to impose a sentence of death.

Payne challenged the admission of the victim impact testimony as a violation of the Eighth Amendment's prohibition against cruel and unusual punishments, relying upon the Supreme Court's decisions in *Booth* and *Gathers.* However, the Tennessee Supreme Court rejected Payne's claim, concluding that the impact of the crimes on the surviving victim was relevant to determining Payne's blameworthiness and that any violation of Payne's constitutional rights was harmless beyond a reasonable doubt. Thereafter, Payne sought review in the United States Supreme Court.

The Supreme Court accepted the case in order to reevaluate its prior decisions. Ultimately, the court rejected the rule that had prohibited the introduction of victim impact evidence. The Court concluded that consideration of the nature and extent of the harm caused by a particular crime had always been included in the determination of the appropriate punishment for a particular crime. Moreover, the court rejected the premise of *Booth* and *Gathers* and concluded that "a State may properly conclude that for the jury to assess meaningfully the defendant's moral culpability and blameworthiness, it should have before it at the sentencing phase evidence of the specific harm caused by the defendant." In reaching this decision, the Court recognized that the prosecution has a legitimate interest in counteracting the defendant's mitigating evidence with evidence about the individual character of the victim and the impact of the crime on the victim's family. Accordingly, victim impact evidence is an integral part of the jury's sentencing decision, and its admission does not violate the Eighth Amendment's cruel and unusual punishment clause.

For more information: Coyne, Randall, and Lyn Entzeroth. *Capital Punishment and the Judicial Process.* Durham, N.C.: Carolina Academic Press, 2006.

—Mark A. Fulks

Penn, William (1644–1718) *Quaker leader, founder of Pennsylvania*

William Penn, founder of the colony of Pennsylvania, symbol of religious tolerance, and an inspirational figure in the formation of the U.S. Constitution, was born on October 14, 1644, to a wealthy Anglican family living in London. Although raised as an Anglican, Penn became a Quaker when he was 22 years old, joining the Religious Society of Friends. Penn's conversion alarmed his father, Admiral Sir William Penn, whose military prowess had earned his family fame and extensive property in Ireland, not least because his son's new religious affiliation did not allow him to go to war.

Although Penn never went to war, he did get into trouble with the law rather frequently as a result of his religious convictions, nor was he able to pursue his studies at Oxford. In London, the Quakers drew the ire of the Lord Mayor for leading Quaker meetings, resulting in numerous arrests, but Penn was never convicted. During one of his self-defended trials, Penn won a landmark case, which established the precedent of jury nullification, freeing juries from the views of the judge.

Penn's continued troubles and the persecution of Quakers made him look across the Atlantic. Some Quakers had already established themselves in America but also faced hard treatment from Puritans in the Massachusetts colony and in the Caribbean. Penn, however, was able to negotiate a land deal with King Charles II, because the king needed to repay a loan made by Penn's father. On March 4, 1681, the king officially granted Penn land west and south of New Jersey, along the Delaware River.

Quickly, Penn worked to assure that his colony became a successful venture. He composed the colony's "Frame of Government" which established a democratic governmental structure based on representation, religious tolerance, and a fair legal system. He publicized his colony throughout Europe, attracting numbers of Dutch Quakers, French Huguenots, and German Lutherans to his promise of religious freedom.

This painting shows William Penn negotiating a treaty with Native Americans. *(Library of Congress)*

Beginning in 1682, Penn came to America and established the plans for his capital city of Philadelphia. Soon after, he traveled inland, making treaties with local Native American tribes and even learning native languages. Penn's treatment of the Natives was unlike that of any other English colony, leading to fair payment for the land, fair trials in disputes between Natives and colonists, and a lengthy period of peace. Additionally, Penn received praise from European intellectuals like Voltaire for his fair treatment of the Natives and his religious-tolerance principle.

The colony developed rapidly, but Penn did not earn enough money from his colony to pay his debts in England (caused by mismanagement by a financial adviser), forcing him to return to England in 1684. He returned to America briefly in 1699, but passed most of the remainder of his life facing his economic difficulties in England. After suffering a stroke in 1712, Penn passed away six years later in Ruscombe, England, as a poor man. His accomplishments however, inspired the Founding Fathers to build upon his principles of religious tolerance and separation of powers, ultimately espousing them in the U.S. Constitution.

For more information: Kroll, Steven, and Ronald Himler. *William Penn: Founder of Pennsylvania.* New York: Holiday House, 2000; Soderlund, Jean R. *William Penn and the Founding of Pennsylvania: 1680–1684.* Philadelphia: University of Pennsylvania Press, 1983.

—Arthur Holst

Pennsylvania v. Nelson 350 U.S. 497 (1956)

In *Pennsylvania v. Nelson,* the Supreme Court held by a 6-3 vote that federal antisedition legislation preempted the prosecution of a communist under a state sedition law. The case aroused great interest because, when *Nelson* was decided, 42 states had such laws. In addition, critics of the Court's school DESEGREGATION case, BROWN V. BOARD OF EDUCATION, 347 U.S. 483 (1954), saw *Nelson* as another instance of the Court's intruding on states' rights.

Steve Nelson, a Communist Party organizer, was convicted of violating the Pennsylvania Sedition Act, which made it illegal to threaten the overthrow of the federal government or of Pennsylvania's government. The Pennsylvania Supreme Court reversed on PREEMPTION grounds, pointing out that Nelson had not uttered a "single word . . . against the Government of Pennsylvania."

The United States Supreme Court affirmed. Writing for the majority, Chief Justice Earl Warren noted the many federal laws targeting sedition, including the Smith Act (1940), the Internal Security Act of 1950, and the Communist Control Act (1954). Although none of these acts directly excluded state prosecutions, taken together, they demonstrated a congressional intent to "occupy the field" of sedition law. Chief Justice Warren added that state sedition laws posed "a serious danger of conflict" with federal antisedition laws. Here he drew on testimony from FBI director J. Edgar Hoover, who—writing in 1940—stressed the importance of "meeting the spy or saboteur" with the "experienced men" of the FBI.

Chief Justice Warren pointed to another danger. Unlike the Smith Act, which left the power to prosecute in the hands of government officials, the Pennsylvania law let private individuals file charges. Other laws criminalized mere membership in subversive organizations—unlike the Smith Act, which explicitly rejected this basis of liability. The concern with the scope of sedition laws foreshadowed *Yates v. United States,* 354 U.S. 298 (1957), which interpreted the Smith Act narrowly to exclude statements that abstractly advocated the overthrow of the government.

Justice Reed, joined by Justices Burton and Minton, dissented. Justice Reed argued that none of the laws passed by Congress explicitly rejected state regulation of sedition. Nor should the court preempt based on "[m]ere fear . . . of possible difficulties." Finally, Justice Reed rejected the notion that state officials were "less alert to ferret out . . . subversion."

The reaction to *Nelson* was quite negative. States felt a threat both to their ability to fight subversion and to their dignity. There was widespread agreement among scholars, the media, and federal legislators themselves that Congress had never intended to overrule state sedition laws. Representative Howard Smith, author of the Smith Act, proposed legislation limiting preemption of state legislation to those situations where Congress explicitly stated its intent to occupy the field. The legislation was reported out of the HOUSE and SENATE but never brought to a vote.

The occupation of the field test survived to remain a pillar of federal preemption doctrine. Meanwhile, *Nelson* remains noteworthy as the moment during the Cold War when the Court began to return to the libertarian approach that dominated the 1930s and 1940s.

For more information: Belknap, Michael R. *Cold War Political Justice: The Smith Act, the Communist Party, and American Civil Liberties.* Westport, Conn.: Greenwood Press, 1977; Caute, David. *The Great Fear: The Anti-Communist Purge under Truman and Eisenhower.* New York: Simon & Schuster, 1978; Hunt, Alan Reeve. "State Control of Sedition: The Smith Act as the Supreme Law of the Land." *Minnesota Law Review* 41 (1958): 287–332.

—Robert A. Kahn

Penry v. Lynaugh 492 U.S. 302 (1989)

In *Penry v. Lynaugh,* the Supreme Court ruled that a jury should be instructed to consider mental retardation as a mitigating circumstance during the sentencing phase of a trial. The Court also held that the execution of the mentally retarded did not violate the Eighth Amendment's prohibition against CRUEL AND UNUSUAL PUNISHMENT.

On October 22, 1979, Pamela Carpenter was raped, beaten, and stabbed with a pair of scissors in her home in Livingston, Texas. Although she later passed while receiving medical treatment at the hospital, Pamela was able to describe her assailant to the local sheriff. Penry, who had just been released on parole after being convicted on another rape charge, matched the description. Two local sheriffs apprehended the suspect and, while in custody, Penry confessed to the crime and was charged with capital murder.

At trial, Penry was found competent to stand trial, even though a psychologist had testified that Penry was mentally retarded and had the mental age of a 6½-year-old. Penry raised an insanity defense, arguing that he suffered from brain damage and moderate retardation, but the jury rejected his claim and found him guilty of capital murder. During the penalty phase, the jury was not instructed that it could consider the mitigating circumstances of Penry's mental retardation, and he was sentenced to death. Penry appealed to the Texas Court of Criminal Appeals, which rejected his claim and affirmed his conviction. The federal district court then denied his HABEAS CORPUS petition, and the court of appeals affirmed. The Supreme Court partially affirmed and partially reversed the lower court's decision, holding that, although the jury should have been instructed to consider Penry's mental deficiencies during the sentencing phase, the Eighth Amendment did not categorically prohibit the execution of the mentally ill.

Justice SANDRA DAY O'CONNOR wrote the opinion of the Court, in which Justices WILLIAM J. BRENNAN, JR., Marshall, Blackman and JOHN PAUL STEVENS joined, with respect to the first issue raised by Penry. In her opinion, she argued that the Texas death penalty statute was applied unconstitutionally, because the jury was not allowed to consider Penry's mitigating circumstances during the sentencing phase of his trial. O'Connor went on to argue that, although the jury should have considered his mental retardation and history of abuse, this decision would not create a new rule requiring juries to always consider mental retardation and child abuse before imposing the death penalty.

Justice O'Connor also wrote the opinion of the Court with respect to Penry's second claim, in which Chief Justice WILLIAM HUBBS REHNQUIST and Justices White, ANTONIN GREGORY SCALIA, and ANTHONY M. KENNEDY joined. O'Connor argued that the execution of the mentally retarded does not violate the Eighth Amendment, because opinion surveys and state statutes did not establish the required societal consensus banning such practice. Although a "national consensus against execution of the mentally ill may someday emerge reflecting the 'evolving standards of decency that mark a maturing society,'" at the time Perry was brought before the Court, Justice O'Connor could not find sufficient consensus to rule such practice unconstitutional.

In two separate concurring opinions, Justice Brennan (joined by Marshall) and Justice Stevens (joined by Blackmun) agreed with O'Connor that the jury should have been instructed to consider those mitigating circumstances but argued that the Eighth Amendment did prohibit the execution of the mentally retarded.

Justice Scalia authored the last concurring opinion, which Chief Justice Rehnquist and Justices White and Kennedy joined. Although Scalia agreed with O'Connor concerning the constitutionality of the death penalty, he argued that the jury should not be required to consider these mitigating factors when considering whether to impose the death penalty.

Overall, *Penry* made it clear that the Court was not willing to create a new rule prohibiting the execution of the mentally retarded until a larger national consensus against such practice could be shown. It would take another 13 years for the Court to rule that the "evolving standards of decency" were sufficient, and in 2002 the Court ruled in *ATKINS V. VIRGINIA* that the Eighth Amendment to the Constitution prohibited the execution of the mentally retarded.

For more information: Latzer, Barry. *Death Penalty Cases: Leading U.S. Supreme Court Cases on Capital Punishment.* Woburn, Mass.: Butterworth-Heinemann, 1998.

—Katherine M. Miller

people with disabilities

The Americans with Disabilities Act (ADA), enacted on July 26, 1990, is the nation's most far-reaching attempt to combat discrimination on the basis of disabilities. The law emerged out of the disability rights movement of the 1970s and 1980s and was intended to establish a "national mandate" to end discrimination against people with disabili-

ties and to guarantee that the federal government would play a major role in enforcing the law.

In enacting the ADA, Congress guaranteed CIVIL RIGHTS protection to persons with disabilities in employment, in the delivery of state and local government services, including public transportation, in public accommodations, and in telecommunications. At the time of its passage, Congress estimated that there were at least 43 million people with disabilities in the United States and that this number would increase as the population aged. The law allowed individuals complaining of discrimination to sue private businesses as well as state and local governments. Although Congress had enacted laws to protect the rights of disabled persons in the past—the Architectural Barriers Act of 1968; the Urban Mass Transportation Act of 1970; the Rehabilitation Act of 1973; the Education of All Handicapped Children Act of 1975, later amended and renamed the Individuals with Disabilities Education Act; the Air Carrier Access Act of 1986; and the Fair Housing Act Amendments of 1988—it was not until the ADA was passed that the nation adopted a comprehensive approach to combating discrimination on the basis of disabilities, producing a law that drew on well-established principles of civil rights guarantees.

In the late 1960s, people with disabilities began to be recognized as a civil rights group, following in the path of women and racial minorities. For the most part, however, their claims were not based on constitutional rights, but on federal laws enacted by Congress.

The first major piece of disability rights legislation was the 1973 Rehabilitation Act. Its most important provision was Section 504, which prohibits discrimination in federally assisted programs on the basis of disability. Shortly after the passage of the Rehabilitation Act, Congress enacted the Education of All Handicapped Children Act (EAHCA) in 1975; in 1990, it was renamed the Individuals with Disabilities Education Act (IDEA). The heart of the bill was a grants-in-aid program that required states to allocate significant resources for the education of children with disabilities if they wished to receive federal funding; they could avoid the requirements of the act by refusing the federal funds. Subsequent amendments to the EAHCA expanded the state's responsibility to children from birth to 21, guaranteed a wide range of educational and support services, and specified that all children were covered, whether they lived at home or in a foster care or institutional setting.

During the 1980s and 1990s, Congress continued to enact laws affecting the rights of people with disabilities. Perhaps the most comprehensive legislation predating the ADA was the Fair Housing Act Amendments (FHAA) of 1988, amending the 1968 Fair Housing Act (FHA). The 1968 FHA prohibited discrimination in the sale and rental of public and private housing on the basis of race, religion, and national origin. The 1988 FHAA extended the law to include discrimination based on disability in selling, renting, financing, zoning, new construction design, and advertising.

During the 1970s, there had been a good deal of support for ending discrimination against people with disabilities, in part fueled by the disability community's association with the ideology and rhetoric of the Civil Rights movement. Throughout the 1980s, disability rights groups became adept at political mobilization, demanding equality for people with disabilities, reminiscent of the earlier struggles for civil rights. By the end of the decade, as disability advocates became convinced that Section 504 was inadequate to achieve their goal of removing barriers to their full participation in society, they began to press members of Congress to enact a successor to Section 504.

It became increasingly clear that more comprehensive legislation was needed when, in 1985, the United States Supreme Court decided *City of Cleburne v. Cleburne Living Center,* 473 U.S. 432 (1985), a case establishing the boundaries of the EQUAL PROTECTION guarantee of the FOURTEENTH AMENDMENT for people with disabilities. In this case, the Court held that the Constitution permitted states latitude in enacting laws based on disability, merely requiring them to act rationally. Although the plaintiffs succeeded in challenging the zoning regulation, the Court ruled that laws based on disability were consistent with

the Fourteenth Amendment as long as they were reasonable.

As a result of wide-ranging lobbying efforts by disability rights advocates, Congress enacted the ADA, a wide-ranging law, banning discrimination on the basis of disabilities in employment (Title I), in the delivery of state and local government services, including public transportation (Title II), in public accommodations (Title III), and in telecommunications (Title IV). Title V consists of miscellaneous provisions, including attorneys' fees, alternative dispute resolution, retaliation, consistency with state laws, and insurance underwriting. The law defines a disability with a broad stroke, classifying "an individual with a disability" as a person with "a physical or mental impairment that substantially limits one or more of the major life activities" of an individual. The second part of the definition, "has a record of such an impairment," refers to an individual "who has a history of, or has been misclassified as having, a mental or physical impairment that substantially limits one or more major life activities." The third, "regarded as," prong applies to individuals who have no substantially limiting impairments but are treated as if they do, or their substantially limiting impairments result from the attitudes of others.

For more information: Fleischer, Doris Zames, and Frieda Zames. *The Disability Rights Movement: From Charity to Confrontation.* Philadelphia: Temple University Press, 2001; Mezey, Susan Gluck. *Disabling Interpretations: Judicial Implementation of the Americans with Disabilities Act.* Pittsburgh: University of Pittsburgh Press, 2005; O'Brien, Ruth. *Crippled Justice: The History of Modern Disability Policy in the Workplace.* Chicago: University of Chicago Press, 2001; Percy, Stephen L. *Disability, Civil Rights, and Public Policy.* Tuscaloosa: University of Alabama, 1989.

—Susan Gluck Mezey

peremptory challenges
Peremptory challenges refer to the right that parties are given during jury selection to remove potential jurors without being required to offer a

reason. These challenges have come under constitutional scrutiny in the last few years because of allegations they are used in a racially biased fashion or on account of gender.

The process of jury selection is known as voir dire, which means "to speak the truth" in French. In the process of selecting a jury, each side in a trial wishes to remove jurors who are biased against their client, and they also seek to find jurors who will be sympathetic towards their client. Potential jurors, also known as veniremen, who are removed based on the sole discretion of the attorney (usually with the consent of his or her client) are excused through a process called peremptory challenges or peremptory strikes during jury selection. Other jurors who are removed for a particular reason by the judge are excused based on a cause challenge. Usually, this is because of an obvious reason, such as that the potential juror is related to a party or the potential juror states that he or she cannot be fair and impartial in this case. There is no maximum number of cause challenges.

One concern with the use of peremptory challenges is using them due to bias. In the South, prior to the CIVIL RIGHTS era of the 1950s and 1960s, it was not uncommon for all-white juries to convict African Americans of crimes. This was the case in the famous SCOTTSBORO CASE of the 1930s. In BATSON V. KENTUCKY, 476 U.S. 79 (1986), the Supreme Court ruled that race was an impermissible basis for using a peremptory challenge by the state against an African-American juror. Other United States Supreme Court cases have further solidified this decision. Among others, *Edmonson v. Leesville Concrete Co.,* 500 U.S. 614 (1991), applied *Batson* to juries in civil trial, and *Georgia v. McCollum,* 505 U.S. 42 (1992), extended *Batson* to disallow the discriminatory use of a criminal defendant's own peremptory strikes based on race. Later, in *J.E.B. V. ALABAMA,* 511 U.S. 127 (1994), the high court applied *Batson* to gender.

Many critics of peremptory challenges see their potential abuse as so great that they advocate eliminating them or turning the process of jury selection over to the presiding judge. Former Associate Justice of the United States Supreme Court Thurgood Marshall made this argument in his concurring opinion in the *Batson* case, in fact. Many attorneys feel, however, that peremptory strikes are absolutely necessary to ensure a fair trial.

For more information: Klarman, Michael J. *From Jim Crow to Civil Rights: The Supreme Court and the Struggle for Racial Equality.* New York: Oxford University Press, 2004; Mauet, Thomas A. *Trial Techniques.* 4th ed. Frederick, Md.: Aspen Publishing, Inc., 1996.

—Maria Collins Warren

Philadelphia v. New Jersey 437 U.S. 617 (1978)

The Supreme Court ruled on the case of the *City of Philadelphia v. New Jersey* that New Jersey's waste importation restriction laws were unconstitutional, because they violated the Constitution's COMMERCE CLAUSE by discriminating against another state's goods.

In 1973, the government of the state of New Jersey passed a law forbidding the importation of waste "solid or liquid which was originated or was collected outside of the territorial limits of the State." For New Jersey, this law carried great importance, as the state was seen regionally and nationally as a receiving center for garbage and waste originating from nearby states, especially New York and Pennsylvania. The law was passed in order to counteract what was seen as an unacceptable amount of waste being disposed of within the state boundaries of New Jersey.

Almost immediately, this new law caused serious logistical waste disposal issues for cities near New Jersey, such as New York and Philadelphia, that had traditionally shipped their waste to landfill operators located there. As a result, cities and landfill operators began to sue the state of New Jersey in order to challenge the constitutionality of the law. The major case was spearheaded by the city of Philadelphia.

A positive verdict for the city was received from the original trial, because the judge was convinced that the law violated the commerce clause of the

Constitution by restricting interstate trade. The ruling was soon challenged by the state of New Jersey, leading to a case in the Supreme Court of New Jersey. The state supreme court reversed the original verdict, claiming that the law had other benefits, which outweighed the minor interstate commercial issues related to the law. In their decision, the court stated that the public health of the citizens of New Jersey and the protection of the state's environment was more important than absolute protection of the commerce clause. In response, the city of Philadelphia's legal team decided to appeal the decision of the state supreme court to the U.S. Supreme Court.

The U.S. Supreme Court accepted the appeal, and arguments began on March 27, 1978. The Court delivered its decision roughly three months later on June 23, 1978, overturning the Supreme Court of New Jersey's reversal of the original decision. Justice Potter Stewart wrote the 7 to 2 majority opinion, rejecting New Jersey's claims that waste was not a matter of INTERSTATE COMMERCE, since it believed it to be "worthless." Stewart stated that this argument was false and was not an exception to the commerce clause, since waste has an economic value, whether it is positive or negative. Ultimately, New Jersey's 1973 waste restriction law was overturned as unconstitutional for discriminating against products from another state and violating interstate commerce clauses and precedents.

Justice WILLIAM HUBBS REHNQUIST wrote the dissenting opinion, arguing that products that may cause public health issues should fall subject to quarantine laws, which prohibit exportation and importation of harmful products. Nevertheless, New Jersey has since tried to find other ways to cope with its waste importation issues and high population density, promoting waste reduction efforts in Philadelphia and creating waste incinerators in numerous counties throughout the state.

For more information: Corwin, Edward S. *The Commerce Power Versus States' Rights*. Princeton, N.J.: Princeton University Press, 1936; Schwartz, Bernard. *A History of the Supreme Court*. New York: Oxford University Press, 1993.

—Arthur Holst

Pierce v. Society of the Sisters of the Holy Names of Jesus and Mary 268 U.S. 519 (1925)

Pierce v. Society of the Sisters of the Holy Names of Jesus and Mary is a U.S. Supreme Court decision upholding economic and personal liberty against government regulation. As such, two major strands of the constitutional doctrine known as SUBSTANTIVE DUE PROCESS intersect in the judgment. *Pierce* also is doubly ironic, first, because of its origins and, second, because of its author.

Pierce originated in a challenge to a 1922 initiative measure adopted by Oregon voters. The Oregon compulsory public school law required all children under 16 to be educated in public schools. What spawned this mandate was an incongruous—not untypical American—mix of aspirations and anxieties: populist support for universal education, civic literacy, and curricular reform commingled with bias, bigotry, and fear of the Red Menace. Groups supporting the initiative included Scottish Rite Masons, the American Legion, the Federation of Patriotic Societies, and the Ku Klux Klan, which had close to 15,000 Oregon members in the 1920s and controlled the state legislature during that decade.

A primary target of the compulsory public school movement was Catholic parochial education. Appellant Walter M. Pierce, 16th governor of Oregon, personified the blend of intolerance and ideals underlying the Oregon law. The Roman Catholic Church, Pierce believed, was "an authoritarian institution bent upon subverting democratic thought and human progress." He also believed that public school education could teach even Catholic children to be good Americans. From these thorny circumstances came a decision affirming FUNDAMENTAL RIGHTS.

Justice James C. McReynolds wrote the unanimous opinion. More bigoted than Governor Pierce, McReynolds was an unlikely champion of liberty. Nevertheless, in his *Pierce*, opinion, McReynolds defined "liberty" expansively. In *Pierce,* McReynolds relied on a decision he had authored two years previously, *Meyer v. Nebraska*, 262 U.S. 390, where he had written that liberty was not merely freedom from bodily restraint but also the right of the individual to contract, to engage in any of the common occupations of life, to acquire useful knowledge, to marry, establish a home and bring up children, to worship God according to the dictates of his own conscience, and generally to enjoy those privileges long recognized at common law as essential to the orderly pursuit of happiness by free men.

McReynolds drew upon this blend of economic and personal liberty to nullify the Oregon initiative. He held that the law "unreasonably interferes with the liberty of parents and guardians to direct the upbringing and education of children under their control," as well as being an "arbitrary, unreasonable, and unlawful interference with [the Society of Sisters'] patrons and the consequent destruction of their business and property."

With its reliance on economic and personal liberty, *Pierce* exemplifies substantive due process. This doctrine holds that certain fundamental rights constrain government—regardless of what regulatory procedures government employs. Although the economic strand of substantive due process went into judicial eclipse in the late 1930s, the personal liberty strand remains influential, albeit controversial, in areas such as child welfare, contraception, ABORTION, and sexual preference.

For more information: Ross, William G. *Forging New Freedoms: Nativism, Education, and the Constitution, 1917–1927*. Lincoln: University of Nebraska Press, 1994; Woodhouse, Barbara Bennett. "Child Abuse, the Constitution, and the Legacy of *Pierce v. Society of Sisters*," *Mercy Law Review* 78 (Spring 2001): 479; ———. "'Who Owns the Child?': *Meyer* and *Pierce* and the Child as Property," *William and Mary Law Review* 33 (Summer 1992): 995–1,122.

—James C. Foster

plain view doctrine

The plain view doctrine states that an item: (1) within the sight of a police officer (2) who is legally in a position to see the item may be seized without a search warrant, (3) so long as the item is immediately recognizable evidence subject to seizure. Plain view is a recognized exception to the search warrant requirement of the FOURTH AMENDMENT.

For the plain view doctrine to apply, the police must be "lawfully present." This means the police must have a legal right to be where they are when they observe an item in plain view. This is sometimes referred to as a "valid prior intrusion" (Carmen, 2006). Some examples of situations in which a law enforcement officer is lawfully present include a traffic stop or the pursuit of a fleeing suspect.

Under the plain view doctrine, police may seize an item only if it is "immediately apparent" that the item is subject to seizure (Hemmens et al., 2004). This means that the police must have probable cause that an item is subject to seizure without conducting any further examination of the object. While the plain view doctrine does not allow a police officer to conduct a further search of an object to determine its incriminating nature, an officer may use mechanical aids (such as flashlights) to assist in observing items of evidence, and alter his or her position to gain a better view.

It was once thought that the discovery of evidence in plain view must be "inadvertent" to satisfy the "immediately apparent" requirement. In *Horton v. California*, 496 U.S. 128 (1990), the Supreme Court held that an item seen in plain view need not have been discovered inadvertently or by accident.

Some courts have expanded the plain view doctrine to the senses of smell and touch. These courts frequently cite *United States v. Johns*, 469 U.S. 478 (1985), in which the Supreme Court said in dicta that it was "debatable" whether there is a PRIVACY interest in a package "reeking of marijuana." It is unclear whether the Supreme Court currently endorses this expansion of the plain view doctrine. In *MINNESOTA v. DICKERSON*, 508 U.S. 366 (1993), the Supreme Court stated that the plain view doctrine "has an obvious application by analogy" to instances involving the discovery of contraband through the sense of touch, but disallowed a seizure of crack cocaine found during a frisk because the officer manipulated the jacket containing crack cocaine before determining it was seizable. It is unclear whether it could ever be "immediately apparent" that an unseen item is seizable without some manipulation.

The plain view doctrine is an important, and logical, exception to the search warrant requirement. It allows police officers to seize evidence without a warrant so long as they are lawfully present and the item seized is clearly subject to seizure. Since the police are lawfully present, requiring them to obtain a warrant before seizing an item that they have seen and know is subject to seizure would unnecessarily complicate the search process without protecting any reasonable expectation of privacy.

For more information: Carmen, Rolando del. *Criminal Procedure: Law and Practice.* 7th ed. Belmont, Calif.: Wadsworth/Thomson, 2006; Hemmens, Craig, John Worrall, and Alan Thompson. *Criminal Justice Case Briefs: Significant Cases in Criminal Procedure.* Los Angeles: Roxbury, 2004; *Horton v. California,* 496 U.S. 128 (1990); *Minnesota v. Dickerson,* 508 U.S. 366 (1993); *United States v. Johns,* 469 U.S. 478 (1985).

—Craig Hemmens

Planned Parenthood v. Casey 505 U.S. 833 (1992)

In *Planned Parenthood v. Casey*, the Supreme Court rebuffed efforts to overturn Roe v. Wade, 410 U.S. 113 (1973) by upholding restrictions on ABORTION as long as they did not unduly burden women seeking abortions. The significance of this case is that it upheld the basic finding of *Roe* that women have a constitutional right to have an abortion while jettisoning the trimester framework for the UNDUE BURDEN STANDARD.

After the Supreme Court upheld several restrictions on abortion in WEBSTER V. REPRODUCTIVE HEALTH SERVICES, 492 U.S. 490 (1989), Pennsylvania passed even a more restrictive abortion law that required doctors to discuss the risks and alternatives to abortion, provided for informed consent, required minors to receive parental or judicial consent before receiving an abortion, imposed reporting and public disclosure requirements on doctors, and required spousal consent for abortions. Planned Parenthood immediately challenged the law, and the Third Circuit upheld all provisions of the law except for spousal consent. The Supreme Court affirmed in a 5-4 decision, even though the justices split into three camps.

Writing for the plurality, Justices SANDRA DAY O'CONNOR, ANTHONY M. KENNEDY, and DAVID H. SOUTER claimed that stare decisis and public opinion demand that they uphold the essence of *Roe,* which is that women have a constitutional right to an abortion. They claimed that to do otherwise would negatively impact the Court's legitimacy and the nation's commitment to the rule of law. However, the Court replaced the trimester approach with the undue burden test, because medical technology has changed the point of viability and rendered the trimester approach ineffectual. The Court said that an undue burden exists when a law's purpose or effect "is to place a substantial obstacle in the path of a woman seeking an abortion before the fetus attains viability." Laws that do not do this must have a rational basis. The Court concluded by saying that the informed consent, 24-hour waiting period, and parental notification have a rational basis but that spousal notification places an undue burden on women and is unconstitutional.

Concurring with the result, Justice Blackmun would maintain the original ruling of *Roe* and use STRICT SCRUTINY to strike down all provisions. Surprisingly, he ended his concurrence by noting his mortality and calling on political forces to fight in the coming elections to ensure that his successor would be a supporter of abortion rights.

Dissenting, Chief Justice WILLIAM HUBBS REHNQUIST claimed that stare decisis should not be controlling, because the plurality rejected *Roe*'s holdings that abortion is a fundamental right, strict scrutiny should apply, and states must follow the trimester approach. This meant there was nothing to uphold. Moreover, public opinion should not be used to justify upholding bad law, because it would require the Court to uphold discredited principles, such as separate but equal. In a separate dissent, Justice ANTONIN GREGORY SCALIA rejected the right to an abortion because the Constitution does not mention the right, and history shows that states have proscribed it in the past.

Contrary to many people's expectations, the Court refused to overturn *Roe* and upheld the right to an abortion while allowing restrictions. This decision seems to be a good example of the Court's "following the election returns." Polls consistently show that the public supports the general right to an abortion, but their discomfort with it leads to support for commonsense restrictions.

For more information: Baer, Judith. *A Historical and Multicultural Encyclopedia of Women's Reproductive Rights in the United States.* Westport, Conn.: Greenwood Publishing, 2001; Hull, N. E. H., and Charles Hoffer. *Roe v. Wade: The Abortion Rights Controversy in American History.* Lawrence: University of Kansas Press, 2001.
—Sean Evans

Plessy v. Ferguson 163 U.S. 537 (1896)

Plessy v. Ferguson was one of the most landmark CIVIL RIGHTS cases in American history. In this case, the Supreme Court upheld a state law segregating blacks from whites on railroad cars. As a result of the U.S. Supreme Court's decision, segregation became the federal government's de facto policy toward civil rights and race relations in the United States for many difficult decades.

In 1865, the United States found itself wounded by years of war, destruction, and harsh and inhumane treatment of a significant portion of its population who had formerly lived under slavery. In order to address these problems, the federal government began a string of programs known today as Reconstruction, which involved sending the U.S. military into defeated Southern states to rebuild farms and infrastructure, to guarantee that peace was respected, and to ensure a very basic protection of freed slaves' civil rights.

Reconstruction ended in 1877, and the military was withdrawn as a result, leaving some Southern states with the ability to pass more repressive legislation than was possible before. The laws that came about became known as Jim Crow laws, which prohibited African Americans from using the same facilities as whites, among other discriminatory practices. As the civil rights struggle continued, in 1883 the Supreme Court overruled most of the Civil Rights Act of 1875 by stating that the FOURTEENTH AMENDMENT applied only to the actions of state governments, not to individual citizens or their businesses.

In Louisiana, a state law was passed that required separate passenger cars for blacks and whites on all state railways. In response, a multiracial group of concerned citizens organized a small movement to fight the law in New Orleans, a focal point of the civil rights struggle at the time. The group persuaded a local, Homer Plessy, who was only one-eighth black, to purchase a ticket and place himself in a car reserved for whites. Once he boarded the train and took his seat, he informed the conductor of his racial background and was soon after asked to move to a car reserved for blacks. Plessy denied this request and the police were called to place him under arrest.

Plessy and the group of concerned citizens argued their case all the way to the U.S. Supreme Court. Plessy and his lawyer, Albion W. Tourgee, based their case on the argument that Louisiana's law denied U.S. citizens all of their privileges and rights guaranteed by the Constitution, as well as denying DUE PROCESS and EQUAL PROTECTION of law for all citizens regardless of race. Additionally, they argued that the law implied that blacks were racially inferior.

The U.S. Supreme Court ruled 7-1, voting to uphold Louisiana's segregation law. The overwhelming majority of the justices rejected Plessy and Tourgee's arguments; they claimed that the law did not violate the Constitution, nor imply the inferiority of blacks. Interestingly, the only dissenting justice, JOHN HARLAN, himself a former slave-owner, wrote that the law violated the Constitution since it was not color-blind and equal, like the Constitution itself.

In the aftermath of the ruling, segregation was legitimized and became more widespread. Finally,

A drinking fountain on the county courthouse lawn, Halifax, North Carolina, 1938 *(Library of Congress)*

in January 1897, Plessy paid the $25 fine assessed to him by the police for refusing to leave his seat many years earlier.

In 1954, *Plessy* was overturned by Brown v. Board of Education.

For more information: Fireside, Harvey. Plessy v. Ferguson: *Separate but Equal.* Berkeley Heights, N.J.: Enslow Publishers, 1997; Thomas, Brook. Plessy v. Ferguson: *A Short History with Documents.* New York: Bedford, St. Martins, 1996.
—Arthur Holst

Plyler v. Doe 457 U.S. 202 (1982)

In *Plyler v. Doe,* the Supreme Court held that state and local policies that denied children without legal immigration status (undocumented children) free public education violated the EQUAL PROTECTION clause of the FOURTEENTH AMENDMENT.

In 1975, Texas amended its Education Code so that local school districts were allowed to deny enrollment of undocumented children or to condition enrollment upon the payment of full tuition. Constitutional challenges against the Texas code as well as local school district policies implementing the code were brought across the state by parents and guardians of children who were thus denied public education. These challenges were eventually consolidated into this case. The Court had ample precedents, dating back to 19th-century cases regarding discrimination against Chinese immigrants, to hold that the Fourteenth Amendment extended its protection to all persons who were within the territory of the United States, regardless of citizenship.

But extensive discussion ensued over the application of the equal protection clause to the Texas statute in question. Under the equal protection clause analysis, the government is given wide latitude in making distinctions and classifications in the course of conducting policy, unless it involves a suspect classification (such as race) or it touches upon a fundamental right of a person. In *Plyler*, the Court had trouble deciding what level of scrutiny should apply. While the Court rejected the claim that illegal aliens were a suspect class, it nonetheless held that the children in this case were special members of this underclass. They were brought to the United States as young members of their family, and they had no control over their parents' decisions to do so. It was unfair to punish these children for their parents' acts, just like it was unfair to discriminate against children born out of wedlock. And while the Court did not find that education was a fundamental right, it distinguished education from other forms of social welfare legislation where the government had wide discretion. Citing BROWN V. BOARD OF EDUCATION, 347 U.S. 483 (1954), the Court emphasized that the inestimable toll on the social, economic, intellectual, and psychological well-being of the individual in being deprived of education was difficult to reconcile with the framework of equality embodied in the equal protection clause.

For these reasons—special consideration for children, and special consideration for deprivation of education—the Court adopted a quasi-suspect class and quasi-fundamental rights analysis (in the words of the dissenting opinion), and held that the denial must be justified by showing that it furthers some substantial state interest. The Court found that none of the justifications offered by Texas withstood this scrutiny. Accordingly, the law was in violation of the equal protection clause.

The dissenting opinion argued that undocumented status itself was sufficient justification for denial of public benefits. However, the majority held that states could act with respect to illegal aliens when it mirrored federal objectives, and that in this case it perceived no national policy that supported depriving undocumented children of elementary education.

There are important contextual factors behind the case. The trial courts had found as a matter of fact that most undocumented children were likely to stay in the United States permanently through various forms of legalization. Given this context, the Court found that deprivation of education for these children would create a permanent underclass within the United States and that the Fourteenth Amendment was meant to prevent such second-class citizens from emerging. On the other hand, the Court had been struggling with school finance litigations across the nation, and had held in *San Antonio School District v. Rodriguez*, 411 U.S. 1 (1973), that education was not a fundamental right. This is why the Court had to emphasize that *Plyler* involved a deprivation of education, not the relative quality of education, as in school finance cases, in invoking a heightened scrutiny.

Although *Plyler* could be narrowly construed to apply only to the special circumstances of the case, it has resonated throughout debates over the rights of immigrants, the role of federal and state governments, and the manner of judicial intervention. State initiatives (such as Proposition 187, which sought to deny government services to illegal aliens in California) containing provisions contradicting *Plyler* have been repeatedly proposed. *Plyler* continues to be a guiding case for judicial scrutiny of such actions.

For more information: Hutchinson, Dennis J. "More Substantive Equal Protection?: A Note on *Plyler v. Doe*." *The Supreme Court Review* 1982 (1982): 167–194; Petronicolos, Loucas, and William S. New. "Anti-Immigrant Legislation, Social Justice, and the Right to Equal Educational Opportunity." *American Educational Research Journal* 36, no. 3 (Autumn 1999): 373–408.

—Takeshi Akiba

Poe v. Ullman 367 U.S. 497 (1961)

In *Poe v. Ullman*, the Supreme Court again dismissed a constitutional challenge to Connecticut's long-standing yet unenforced 1879 law criminalizing the use and distribution of CONTRACEPTIVES as well as medical advice about their use. The Court had earlier denied STANDING to a doctor's challenge to the law in *Tileston v. Ullman*, 318 U.S. 44 (1943). In *Poe*, two anonymous married couples who faced possible health complications from future pregnancies and their physician challenged the law. None had been arrested or prosecuted, but all argued the law's existence denied them liberty without DUE PROCESS of law in violation of the FOURTEENTH AMENDMENT.

The Supreme Court again considered the case nonjusticiable. Justice Felix Frankfurter, writing for a plurality, called the parties' fears of criminal liability "chimerical." No one had ever been prosecuted under this law; thus there is a "tacit agreement" not to enforce it, and "this Court cannot be umpire to debates concerning harmless, empty shadows" (508). WILLIAM J. BRENNAN, JR., concurred in the judgment, noting that the "true controversy" would concern the opening of birth control clinics in the state (509).

This case is significant for the dissenting opinions by Justices WILLIAM O. DOUGLAS and JOHN MARSHALL HARLAN. Douglas found standing, asking "What are these people—doctor and patients—to do? Flout the law and go to prison? Violate the law surreptitiously and hope they will not get caught?" (513). He found that the law violated the free speech rights of the doctor and a right to PRIVACY of the married couple that "emanates from the totality of the constitutional scheme under which we live," including the THIRD AMENDMENT (521).

Harlan also found standing, claiming the married couples are saved only by "the whim of the prosecutor" (536). On the merits, Harlan argued that constitutional liberty protected by the Fourteenth Amendment is not reducible to the specific protections stated in the BILL OF RIGHTS; rather, it is "a rational continuum which, broadly speaking, includes a freedom from all substantial arbitrary impositions and purposeless restraints" (543). He admits that the right of marital privacy "most manifestly is not an absolute." Nevertheless, the novel nature of Connecticut's broad law constitutes an "imminent threat to the privacy of the households of the State" (552, 553).

Justice HUGO BLACK dissented without opinion. Justice Potter Stewart also briefly dissented from the dismissal, stating "I in no way imply that the ultimate result I would reach on the merits of these controversies would differ from the conclusions of my dissenting Brothers" (555).

Four years later, in GRISWOLD V. CONNECTICUT, 381 U.S. 479 (1965), the Court would hear a challenge from a physician who was convicted for distributing contraceptives. By a 7-2 vote, the Court struck the law. Douglas wrote the majority opinion, articulating a constitutional right to marital privacy based on penumbra formed by emanations from the several of the first 10 amendments. Harlan wrote a concurring opinion that reiterated his argument in *Poe*. Black—joined, surprisingly, by Stewart—dissented.

For more information: Garrow, David J. *Liberty & Sexuality: The Right to Privacy and the Making of* Roe v. Wade. New York: Macmillan, 1994; Johnson, John W. Griswold v. Connecticut: *Birth Control and the Constitutional Right of Privacy*. Lawrence: University of Kansas Press, 2005.

—Frank J. Colucci

police civil liability

Police civil liability is granted to citizens under the Constitution both directly and indirectly from actions by the government that are determined to be illegal or wrongful in nature. Generally, the more common claims for relief come from the protections derived under the FIRST, FOURTH, SIXTH, and FOURTEENTH AMENDMENTs, individually or in sum. Intrusion by the government or its agents can be challenged by both criminal and civil action, if it is deemed that the conduct of the officer was committed "under color of law." In more common terms, the officer must have been acting in an official government capacity and retained the authority of the state in his/her actions.

Unreasonable intrusions into the PRIVACY of persons, even with a compelling government reason, is generally deemed an unacceptable practice. In *Katz v. United States*, one of the most notable Fourth Amendment cases in criminal law, the Court questioned whether there were protections included against unreasonable searches and seizures that required the police or agents of the government to obtain a search warrant in order to wiretap a public pay phone and record the personal and private conversations of the accused. The decision offered that Katz was entitled to Fourth Amendment protection for his conversations. This concept of accepted protections and police liability grew further, as the courts reviewed aspects of the amendments that included violations of 42 U.S.C. 1983 (Section 42 of the United States Code, a law banning the violation of the constitutional rights of individuals) and other rights of the accused.

In *Paul v. Davis,* 424 U.S. 693 (1976), Davis sought civil restitution under the Fourteenth Amendment's protections for the actions of Paul, the Louisville police chief, for the distribution of a flyer identifying Davis as a "shoplifter." The court ruled against relief and stated privacy and liberty under the DUE PROCESS clause was not violated, which further narrowed the interpretation of when relief could be instituted.

In *Barnes v. Gorman,* 536 U.S. 181 (2002), Gorman sued police officials in Kansas for punitive damages due to alleged discrimination against him on the basis of his disability, which was prohibited within the Americans with Disabilities Act of 1990 (ADA) and the Rehabilitation Act of 1973 (RA). In a conservative opinion and to further the stare decisis, Justice ANTONIN GREGORY SCALIA wrote that, because punitive damages could not be awarded in private suits brought under Title VI of the CIVIL RIGHTS ACT OF 1964, it is within precedent that similar restrictions be followed for suits brought under the ADA and the RA. Therefore, through the above examples, it should be understood that there are specificities of the cases that must be considered in totality of the circumstances, and that relief is not deemed an automatic response to a suit.

Additional police liability falls under violations of 42 U.S. §1983, further making available other CIVIL RIGHTS remedies, if clearly there is a violation of a statute that has conferred substantive rights to the citizen and is not just a congressional declaration of policy. In addition, the statute must not expressly foreclose the use of a civil rights remedy. In order to recover, the officer must have been acting under the color of law, and it must be proven that the officer's conduct was not only the cause in fact of injuries or damages and the proximate cause (it was reasonable and foreseeable that the officer's actions could have caused the damage) of constitutional or statutory loss. The final aspect of considering whether or not the police acted in proper manner, and thus are eligible for a defense, lies in the understanding related to a police officer's reasonable belief as measured objectively that his actions were allowable under the law and that he had utilized all available information.

Relief is granted for violations of the statutes for recovery of out-of-pocket expenses sustained as a result of the defendant's conduct, such as in the case of medical expenses, lost wages or lost earnings, losses of potential or future income, and for damages suffered from pain and suffering, emotional distress, humiliation, and injury to reputation. If the conduct by the officer was reckless or egregious, then punitive damages may be awarded as well as attorney's fees.

For more information: Kappeler, Victor. *Critical Issues in Police Civil Liability.* Long Grove, Ill.: Waveland Press, 2006.

—Ernest Gomez

police interrogations
See *MIRANDA V. ARIZONA.*

police power
Police power is the power of states to make laws to protect the health, safety, welfare, and morals of their inhabitants. While the 50 different states have inherent police power, neither the federal nor local governments have this authority. The federal government must rely upon its COMMERCE CLAUSE power to perform police power–type functions, while local governments

may receive this authority from their respective states.

Police power is the general power of state governments to act on behalf of their citizens. Police power, EMINENT DOMAIN, and taxation are the basic three powers of state governments. In the case of police power, it is the authority used by states to build schools; to enact health codes, construction codes, and criminal laws; and to regulate a host of other activities. As stated by Chief Justice JOHN MARSHALL in *GIBBONS V. OGDEN*, 22 U.S. 1 (1824), of police powers:

> They form a portion of that immense mass of legislation which embraces everything within the territory of a State not surrendered to the General Government; all which can be most advantageously exercised by the States themselves. Inspection laws, quarantine laws, health laws of every description, as well as laws for regulating the internal commerce of a State, and those which respect turnpike roads, ferries, &c., are component parts of this mass.

States do not need to have police power granted to them in their own constitutions. Instead, it is assumed that every state has inherent policing authority.

However, the federal government does not have inherent police power authority. Instead, its power to act in this area is located in the commerce clause, according to the Court in *New York v. Miln*, 36 U.S. 102 (1837). There is a tension between the authority of Congress to regulate commerce and the police power authority of states. While Congress has the general authority to regulate commerce, necessitating that states refrain from discriminating against it, there are some situations where state police power functions may permit the state to interfere with it. For example, while states cannot enact taxes or other laws to discriminate against goods imported from other states in order to protect their own products, they may enact laws out of health or safety concerns, even if those laws in effect make it more difficult to import out-of-state goods. This is the justification that Michigan and New York gave in

GRANHOLM V. HEALD, 544 U.S. 460 (2005), in their effort to prevent the shipment of out-of-state wine into their state. The Supreme Court ruled that this type of legislation exceeded the police power authority of the states and instead discriminated against INTERSTATE COMMERCE.

Conversely, in cases such as *PRINTZ V. UNITED STATES*, 521 U.S. 898 (1997), and *Lopez v. United States,* 514 U.S. 549 (1995), the Supreme Court invalidated laws regulating handgun possession, ruling that Congress had exceeded its commerce clause authority to act in areas traditionally relegated to states under their police power.

Finally, while states' police power has traditionally extended to protect the health, safety, welfare, and morals of their people, some have argued that this authority to regulate morality is archaic, or that the rights of personal PRIVACY limit states' ability to regulate, in the areas of sexual behavior, for example.

For more information: Barros, D. Benjamin. "The Police Power and the Takings Clause." *University of Miami Law Review* 58, no. 2 (2004): 471–524; Novak, William J. *The People's Welfare: Law and Regulation in Nineteenth-Century America.* Chapel Hill: University of North Carolina Press, 1996; Reynolds, Glenn H., and David B. Kopel. "The Evolving Police Power: Some Observations for a New Century." *Hastings Constitutional Law Quarterly* 27 (2000): 511–536.

—Kim Mac Innis and David Schultz

Pollock v. Farmers' Loan and Trust Company 157 U.S. 429, 158 U.S. 601 (1895)

In *Pollock v. Farmers' Loan and Trust Company,* the Supreme Court invalidated the 1894 income tax as an unconstitutional direct tax. Two provisions of the Constitution require that direct taxes must be apportioned among the states according to population. The framers anticipated that most federal revenue would be raised by indirect levies, such as tariff duties and excise taxes. The apportionment rule limited the power of Congress to impose direct taxes. Designed to prevent abuses of taxing authority and to make direct taxes geographically fair, the impact of the apportionment rule turned upon the definition of "direct tax."

Congress enacted the first income tax in 1862 to help pay for the Civil War. The levy became increasingly unpopular after the war, and Congress allowed it to expire in 1872. Thereafter, the Supreme Court in *Springer v. United States*, 102 U.S. 586 (1881), upheld the levy as applied to professional earnings against the contention that it was a direct tax that had to be apportioned among the states.

In the 1890s, the Populists spearheaded a drive to revive the income tax. They argued that an alternative source of revenue would bring about tariff reductions and shift more of the national tax burden to the wealthy. Congress enacted the first peacetime income tax as part of the Wilson-Gorman Tariff Act. The measure imposed a flat tax rate on individual incomes above $4,000 a year as well as a levy on corporate profits. It was estimated that the tax would fall upon less than 1 percent of the nation's population, with most taxpayers living in the Northeast. The 1894 income tax triggered a bitter public debate. Critics charged that the levy amounted to class legislation, because it burdened only one segment of society and constituted a direct tax that had to be apportioned among the states according to population.

Charles Pollock, a stockholder of Farmers' Loan and Trust Company, sued to prevent the company from paying the income tax on grounds that the levy was unconstitutional. This complex case was argued twice before the Supreme Court, and leading attorneys appeared for both sides. In April of 1895, Chief Justice Melville W. Fuller, speaking for the majority, ruled that a tax on income from land was a direct tax requiring apportionment. He insisted that the apportionment requirement was intended to confine the use of direct taxation to extraordinary emergencies. Fuller explained that this "rule of protection" was "one of the great landmarks" defining the boundary between the national government and the states, and a safeguard of private property (*Pollock* I, 583). He also held that the federal income tax on state and municipal bonds was unconstitutional as a viola-

tion of the doctrine of INTERGOVERNMENTAL TAX IMMUNITY. In a forceful concurring opinion, Justice Stephen J. Field pictured the income tax as a step toward class warfare.

The Court was unable to resolve the validity of other aspects of the income tax. The case was reargued in May, when a previously absent justice was present. Two weeks later, Fuller delivered the second *Pollock* opinion, striking down the entire income tax. He determined that a tax on income from personal property, such as stocks and bonds, was also a direct tax that must be apportioned according to population. This left only an income tax on earnings. Fuller maintained that the scheme must be considered as a whole, and that Congress did not intend a tax on just occupational earnings. He noted that the Constitution could be amended to authorize a federal income tax and that states could tax incomes. Four justices vigorously dissented, arguing that the majority ignored precedent and inappropriately protected invested wealth from taxation.

The underlying issue in *Pollock* was the legitimacy of using federal tax power to redistribute wealth. The SIXTEENTH AMENDMENT, adopted in 1913, empowered Congress to levy a federal income tax, and in effect overturned the *Pollock* decisions.

For more information: Ely, James W., Jr. *The Chief Justiceship of Melville W. Fuller, 1888–1910.* Columbia: University of South Carolina Press, 1995; Fiss, Owen M. *Troubled Beginnings of the Modern State, 1888–1910.* New York: Macmillan Publishing, 1993; Jensen, Erik M. "Interpreting the Sixteenth Amendment (By Way of the Direct-Tax Clauses)," *Constitutional Commentary* 21 (2004): 355–404.

—James Ely, Jr.

Posadas de Puerto Rico v. Tourism Company of Puerto Rico 478 U.S. 328 (1986)

In *Posadas de Puerto Rico v. Tourism Company of Puerto Rico,* the Supreme Court upheld a ban on the advertising of gambling to residents of Puerto

Rico. This decision was important regarding what it had to say about COMMERCIAL SPEECH.

Posadas de Puerto Rico Associates, consisting of Condado Holiday Inn Hotel and Sands Casino, filed a suit against the Tourism Company of Puerto Rico, a state regulatory agency. The Posadas, an American company, obtained a gambling license to operate in the Condado Holiday Inn Hotel and Sands Casino. Since 1978, the Posadas de Puerto Rico had been fined $1500 and again $500 on two separate occasions by the Tourism Company of Puerto Rico for transgressing advertisement restrictions as enshrined in the Gambling Act of 1948, as interpreted by the Tourism Company of Puerto Rico.

An amendment of the Gambling Act of 1948 (15 R. & R. P. R. § 76a-1[7] [1972]) restricts advertisements by gambling parlors to the public. Any advertisement promoting a Puerto Rico game of chance has to be first approved by the Tourism Development Company. As a result of a one-page advertisement in the *New York Times Magazine* that highlighted the casino as one of its features, Posadas was found guilty by the state agency. In another case, workers at the casinos went on strike and carried pickets suggesting the casino was closed. The Posadas management then placed a sign outside the establishment that read: "Casino is opened." Additionally, in a correspondence to the Tourism Company of Puerto Rico, the letterhead contained the word "casino." For all of these deeds, the Posadas de Puerto Rico was issued a series of fines by the Tourism Company of Puerto Rico.

Having paid the fines, albeit reluctantly, the Posadas started a court proceeding at the superior court to challenge the interpretation of the Gambling Act of 1948 by the Tourism Company of Puerto Rico. The Posadas argued that these advertisement restrictions violated its commercial speech as protected by the U.S. FIRST AMENDMENT. The superior court ruled that the act was constitutional. However, the court judged that the interpretation of the regulations was excessively strict and passed that advertisements are permissible as long as they are aimed at tourists and that they could appear even in the mass market of Puerto Rico, so long as words like "casino"

were not emphasized. Failing to get a favorable ruling from the Supreme Court of Puerto Rico, the Posadas filed for a review with the Supreme Court of the United States. The arguments were heard in April 1986, and the judgment, in July 1986 in favor of the Tourism Company of Puerto Rico, upheld the decision of the Puerto Rico Supreme Court.

Justice WILLIAM J. BRENNAN, JR., and Justice JOHN PAUL STEVENS, representing two other judges, dissented on the basis that commercial speech should be accorded protection by the First Amendment, as it serves societal interest to have access to full information on a transaction that is not illegal. One of the key arguments of the dissenting bench was based on the fact that commercial interests are allowed to advertise horse racing, cockfighting, and the Puerto Rico lottery, with the exception of casino gambling. Therefore, the dissenting voices of the Court suggested that, since other forms of gambling advertisements, particularly the Puerto Rico lottery, are allowed, the state cannot claim to have a substantial interest and override the casino's right to advertise in the public domain, unless it could be proven that such advertisements would result in harmful effects on the society. Justice Stevens in particular opposed discrimination on the basis that tourists and commuters may be entitled to the advertisements but not the residents themselves.

WILLIAM HUBBS REHNQUIST of the Supreme Court, presenting the Court's verdict, opined that the Puerto Rican government's interest was substantial in protecting its residents and that the freedom of commercial speech was limited from misleading or fraudulent acts. Advertisements in any form or manner that are visible or have a reach to the Puerto Rico populace were deemed as violating the Gambling Act.

For more information: Biskupic, Joan, and Elder Witt, eds. *Guide to the Supreme Court of the United States.* Washington, D.C.: Congressional Quarterly Inc., 1997; Kurland, Philip B. "*Posadas de Puerto Rico v. Tourism Company*: 'Twas Strange, 'Twas Passing Strange, 'Twas Pitiful, 'Twas Wondrous Pitiful," *Supreme Court Review*

(1986): 1–17; Langvardt, Arlen W., and Eric L. Richards. "The Death of Posadas and the Birth of Change in Commercial Speech Doctrine: Implications of 44 Liquormart." *American Business Law Journal* (Summer 1997) 483–559; Richards, Jeff I. "Is 44 Liquormart a Turning Point?" *Journal of Public Policy & Marketing* (Spring 1997): 156.

—K. Thirumaran

postal power

ARTICLE I, Section 8 of the Constitution gives Congress the power to establish post offices. For much of U.S. history, the federal government chiefly restricted itself to providing for a military, conducting foreign policy, and delivering the mail. While the military and foreign policy have attracted considerable scholarly attention, postal power is largely ignored.

The maintenance of postal facilities has been a recognized function of the state since the days of ancient Rome. In the American colonies, the General Court of Massachusetts established the first mail service in 1639, but only for the transmission and delivery of foreign mail. A domestic post did not begin until 1673, when Massachusetts established one. In 1692, the Lords of Trades and Plantation created the first postmaster general for America. Postal facilities expanded over the next decades, but not by much. However, the mails were seen as essential to communication. The Continental Congress considered the establishment of postal facilities to be critical to the transmission of intelligence from one end of the nation to the other. On July 26, 1775, Congress appointed BENJAMIN FRANKLIN as postmaster general for the United Colonies. Franking privileges, or free postage, were almost immediately established for members of Congress and for the army commanders. Yet Congress viewed the post as a matter of war policy more than the exercise of a government function.

The Articles of Confederation limited the extent of postal power. Congress had the sole right and power to establish post offices and set postal rates from one state to another. Rates were only to cover the expenses of the system. Intrastate postal facilities were beyond the purview of Congress. At the creation of the Constitution, the framers were more concerned with the survival of the nation than with postal power. With travel extremely difficult and likely to remain so, it did not appear that the mails would ever attract much attention. THE FEDERALIST PAPERS contain only a single reference to the power lodged in Congress to establish post offices and post roads, in No. 42. JAMES MADISON, its author, declared the postal power to be a harmless power that with good management could produce great public convenience. He noted that nothing which aids communication between the states can be deemed unworthy of the public care. Giving postal power to the federal government would contribute to prosperity. The anti-Federalists, while concerned about the dangers of power, did not bother to address postal power.

In succeeding decades, as transportation improved, the post office became a critical part of the U.S. government. The U.S. Supreme Court, *IN RE DEBS*, 158 U.S. 564 (1895), upheld broad congressional power to prevent and punish interference with the mails. By this point, the postal power had become generally accepted as critical to the nation's ability to conduct commerce and gather information.

For more information: Rogers, Lindsay. *The Postal Power of Congress: A Study in Constitutional Expansion.* Baltimore, Md.: Johns Hopkins University, 1916.

—Caryn E. Neumann

Powell, Lewis Franklin, Jr. (1907–1998)
Supreme Court justice

Lewis Franklin Powell Jr. was an associate justice on the United States Supreme Court for the 16-year period between 1971 and 1987. He was the 103rd justice to serve on the Court. During his time on the Court, he was known for his moderate beliefs and ability to create consensus among his fellow justices.

Powell was born in Suffolk, Virginia, and did both his undergraduate and law education at Washington and Lee University, receiving degrees in 1929 and 1931. During World War II, Powell served as a colonel in the Army Air Force. His service took him around the world, and he spent time in England, North Africa, and Sicily. Toward the end of his service, he was also part of a secret team that worked to decipher encrypted German radio messages.

After the war, Powell returned to private legal practice and served as the chairman of the Richmond School Board from 1952 to 1961. This position was controversial for Powell, as he was embroiled in the bitter conflict over segregation in public schools, which the Supreme Court had ruled unconstitutional in its 1954 landmark decision of BROWN V. BOARD OF EDUCATION, 347 U.S. 483. Powell later went on to serve as president of the American Bar Association, a national professional organization for lawyers.

In 1971, President RICHARD NIXON nominated Powell to fill the vacancy created by the retirement of Justice HUGO L. BLACK. Nixon had sought to nominate Powell earlier, in 1969, but Powell had turned him down. The SENATE confirmed Powell by a vote of 89 to 1 (WILLIAM HUBBS REHNQUIST was confirmed as an associate justice on the same day by a slightly closer vote of 68 to 26.) Confirmed at the age of 64, Powell was the oldest person to be confirmed in over 40 years (in 1930, Charles E. Hughes was confirmed at age 67).

While on the Court, Powell was known not for his major contributions to the development of the law, but rather for his pragmatism and collegiality. A former clerk called him the intellectual balance wheel of the Court, mediating the philosophical extremes and brokering consensus. Data concerning Powell's service on the Court seem to support this claim. Powell voted with the majority nearly 90 percent of the time. Ideologically, he tended to be more conservative than he was liberal, but not by a tremendous amount (he voted conservatively approximately 60 percent of the time). By contrast, Justice Rehnquist, who was confirmed the same day as Powell, tended to be both more divisive and more ideological.

Among his major decisions, his concurrence in REGENTS OF THE UNIVERSITY OF CALIFORNIA V. BAKKE, 438 U.S. 265 (1978), is perhaps the most significant. In that case, the Court was divided 4-4 over the constitutionality of a separate admissions policy for people of color for the medical school at the University of California at Davis than for white applicants. While Powell ruled that this policy did violate the FOURTEENTH AMENDMENT's EQUAL PROTECTION clause, he also argued that race may be one of several factors to consider in an admissions policy in order to help schools promote diversity. Powell's opinion thus was an important vote upholding the use of race in some AFFIRMATIVE ACTION programs.

A second major opinion was Powell's providing the fifth vote in the 5-4 BOWERS V. HARDWICK, 478 U.S. 186 (1986), decision that upheld a Georgia law that criminalized same-sex sodomy among consenting adults. Later, after he left the Court, Powell told biographers that this vote was the one he most regretted. Finally, in *McCleskey v. Kemp*, 481 U.S. 279 (1987), Powell wrote the majority opinion in a death penalty case upholding a CAPITAL PUNISHMENT penalty, even though statistical evidence suggested a racial disparity in how this sentence was awarded.

Due to increasing health concerns, Powell retired from the Court in 1987. Justice ANTHONY M. KENNEDY was confirmed as his successor. After retiring, Powell remained active in public life and the legal field, which included occasional service as a judge on the courts of appeal. Powell created a significant controversy when, after retiring from the Court, he renounced his votes in two crucial cases. Powell stated that he should have opposed a death penalty decision and should have also opposed a state law that banned homosexual sodomy. He died at the age of 91 in 1998.

For more information: Jeffries, John, Jr. *Justice Lewis F. Powell, Jr.* New York: Fordham University Press, 2001.

—Ryan Black

Powell v. McCormack 395 U.S. 486 (1969)

In *Powell v. McCormack,* the Supreme Court set limits on Congress's ability to judge fitness to serve of elected members.

Adam Clayton Powell, Jr., was elected to the New York City Council in 1941 by an American

Labor Party-City Fusion ticket. (Having the same name as his minister-father did not hurt.) In 1944, he received the endorsement of the Democratic, Republican, and American Labor parties when he ran for Congress. Powell took his seat as a Democrat.

In 1956, Powell supported Eisenhower, claiming that the latter had staged a "quiet revolution" for CIVIL RIGHTS, whereas the Democrats had rejected Powell's requests for a strong civil rights plan. Opponents held that he had made a deal with the Republicans to avoid prosecution on his income tax. The flamboyant Powell could not stay out of trouble, ranging from marital (divorcing Hazel Scott to marry a young member of his congressional staff, whose salary then escalated) to official (taking a junket with Labor Committee staffers to Paris, calling a Harlem critic a "bag lady," and then seeking to evade the DEFAMATION judgment she won against him).

In 1966, Powell won reelection with more than 70 percent of the votes. He had been in the House 22 years. He became chair of the Education and Labor Committee in 1961. The previous chair, a South Carolina segregationist, never gave Powell a chance to chair a subcommittee.

In 1961 and 1962, Powell took some female staffers with him to study equal job opportunities for women in Common Market nations. They used counterpart funds. (In filing reports, Powell listed substantially lower sums than the amounts he had spent.) He was not the only one going on taxpayer-funded junkets. Powell was also accused of misusing funds appropriated for his Education and Labor Committee (e.g., airline tickets for private vacations, payroll padding). (A member of his staff, a Miss Universe contestant, was his sometime traveling companion.)

A House subcommittee, chaired by Wayne L. Hays, had had a cursory investigation of the travel and payroll charges right after the 1966 election. (Ironically, a few years later, Hays was accused of having his mistress on his congressional payroll. As Powell said in his defense, "He who is without sin should cast the first stone.") Powell was then investigated by a Select Committee, chaired by Emanuel Celler. (Later it was learned that Celler

had written clients of his law firm on his Judiciary Committee stationery. Subliminal message: Pay my firm; I can do a lot for you.)

The Select Committee heard from Powell's by-then estranged wife, who acknowledged that she had not done much staff work and that Powell, not herself, took the money. The Select Committee recommended that Powell be seated but censured and fined $40,000. Others said he should be seated but expelled on a two-thirds vote. It was easier to exclude him by majority vote. In fact, more than two-thirds voted to exclude Powell (307 to 116).

The House was nominally Democratic. In fact, a coalition of conservative Republicans and Democrats was in control. The Select Committee's recommendation was rejected (222 to 202), and the House voted Powell's exclusion. In April 1967, Powell won a special election to fill his seat but waited till the outcome of the Supreme Court appeal. He won the regular election in 1968. In 1969 the Supreme Court (in Chief Justice Earl Warren's last decision) ruled (7-1) that Powell had been removed from Congress illegally. He returned to the House but without his seniority or his committee chairmanship. Since a fixed amount was withheld from his paycheck each month to pay the fine, Powell announced he was a part-time congressman. He spent most of his time away from Washington.

In 1970, the Supreme Court refused to hear a second Powell case in which he requested $55,000 in back salary for the two years that he had been excluded, recovery of a $25,000 fine imposed on him when he was seated in 1969, and reestablishment of his House seniority.

For more information: Dionisopoulos, P. Allen. *Rebellion, Racism & Representation: The Adam Clayton Powell Case and Its Antecedents.* Dekalb: Northern Illinois University Press, 1970; Hamilton, Charles V. *Adam Clayton Powell, Jr.: The Political Biography of an American Dilemma.* New York: Atheneum, 1991; Haygood, Wil. *King of the Cats: The Life and Times of Adam Clayton Powell, Jr.* New York: Houghton Mifflin, 1993; Jacobs, Andy. *The Powell Affair: Freedom Minus One.* Indianapolis, Ind.: Bobbs-Merrill, 1973;

Weeks, Ken M. *Adam Clayton Powell and the Supreme Court.* New York: Dunellen, 1971.
—Martin Gruberg

Preamble to the Constitution

The Preamble to the United States Constitution, while notable for its prose, has no legally binding effect. The Preamble reads, "We the People of the United States, in Order to form a more perfect Union, establish Justice, insure domestic Tranquility, provide for the common defense, promote the general Welfare, and secure the Blessings of Liberty to ourselves and our Posterity, do ordain and establish this Constitution for the United States of America."

The purpose of the Preamble is to introduce the Constitution and the rationale behind it. Although the Preamble does not grant or inhibit power, the phrase "We the People" represents one of the Constitution's core values—the idea that power emanates from the people. One of the most profound changes in the history of the constitutional order involved the transfer of sovereign authority from a single monarch to the people as a whole. During their struggle for independence from England, the colonists contended with an overzealous king and Parliament, and the framers of the Constitution were determined not to repeat history. Through the Preamble, the Constitution and all laws stemming from it embodied the fundamental will of the people.

The phrase "We the People" was a point of contention throughout early American history between the states and the federal government, in particular, the scope of federal judicial power over the states. Did the phrase mean "We the People" of the Union or "We the People" of the states? During the early years of the Republic, the United States Supreme Court invoked "We the People" as a Union as a means of consolidating federal power. In McCULLOCH V. MARYLAND, 4 Wheaton 316 (1819), the Court upheld the power of the Congress to incorporate a national bank on the grounds that the Union was formed by the people as a whole and, as such, the people of one state (Maryland) had no right to impose their will

(by taxing a national institution) on the whole. In MARTIN V. HUNTER'S LESSEE, 14 U.S. 304 (1816), and COHENS V. VIRGINIA, 19 U.S. 264 (1821), the MARSHALL COURT argued that state courts do not have final interpretive authority over the Constitution, which was a product of one people. Therefore, any state laws repugnant to the Constitution were void.

States' rights advocates invoked the Preamble to support their contention that the Constitution was "ordained and established" by "We the People" of the states, and if the federal government exceeded its constitutional authority, the states as representatives of the people, not the federal courts, had the right to police the boundaries of federal power. The idea of "We the People" of the states was invoked by South Carolina during the NULLIFICATION CONTROVERSY in the 1830s to justify the right of one state to nullify a federal law it felt was in contradiction to the Constitution. Similar logic was used by the South to justify secession from the Union. The Constitution was a compact among the people of the several states, and as sovereign and independent entities, the states had the right to leave the Union if the federal government (created by the states) exceeded its authority.

The issue of secession and the sanctity of the Union was finally put to rest by the Supreme Court in *Texas v. White,* 74 U.S. 700 (1868), a case involving the federal government's pre-War sale of bonds to Texas. The Court affirmed that the Constitution created "an indestructible Union, composed of indestructible States" (725). "We the People" as a Union was indissoluble.

For more information: Bailyn, Bernard, ed. *The Debate on the Constitution: Federalist and Antifederalist Speeches, Articles, and Letters during the Struggle over Ratification.* New York: Literary Classics of the United States, 1993.

—Randa Issa

preemption

The doctrine of preemption is used by courts to decide whether a federal statute, based on a valid exercise of the constitutional powers of Congress and the SUPREMACY CLAUSE, supersedes a valid state law addressing the same subject. In making a decision, courts will articulate the meaning of FEDERALISM by defining the limits on federal and state power.

Whether a federal law will invalidate a state law addressing the same subject is guided by two principles created by the Supreme Court. First, a court will try to avoid finding that a federal law preempts state law, because it will presume that state and federal law can coexist, and that Congress will tolerate any tension created by its statutes and state law. In *Silkwood v. Kerr-McGee* (1984), the Court decided that Congress was willing to allow any conflicts created by the Atomic Energy Act that regulated nuclear safety and a state law that permitted the punitive damage award for radiation injuries.

Second, a court will consider the subject of the state and federal laws. If the case involves a subject traditionally reserved to the states, such as health and safety regulation, preemption is less likely. In *Silkwood*, a state award of punitive damages against a manufacturer of atomic fuel rods for its failure to protect its employees from radiation hazards was not preempted by the Atomic Energy Act. If, however, the case involves a subject delegated to the national government, such as foreign relations, bankruptcy, PATENTS, trademarks, and immigration, preemption is more likely. In *Crosby v. National Foreign Trade Council* (2000), a federal statute imposing sanctions on Myanmar for its human rights abuses preempted a Massachusetts statute barring state agencies from purchasing goods from any company that did business with Myanmar, because it intruded upon the ability of the president to speak with one voice in foreign affairs.

The Supreme Court has created two tests to decide preemption cases: congressional intent and actual conflict. When Congress expressly declares its intention to displace state law, a court will find that federal law has preempted state law. Since this rarely happens, courts have had to determine whether congressional action has by implication superseded state law. When a con-gressional statute creates a pervasive and detailed regulatory scheme, addresses a field in which the federal interest is dominant, or creates an agency and grants it regulatory powers, a court is inclined to find that these actions indicate a congressional intent to preempt the field. *San Diego Buildings and Trades Council v. Garmon* (1959) held that the National Labor Relations Act preempted a state tort law action for damages based on a union's organizing activity, because Congress had bestowed labor policymaking on the National Labor Relations Board.

Where Congress has not expressly or impliedly intended to preempt state law, a court will find preemption if there is an actual conflict between the federal and state laws that makes compliance with both laws physically impossible or frustrates the achievement of the purpose of the federal law. *McDermott v. Wisconsin* (1913) held that the federal Food and Drug Act preempted the Wisconsin syrup labeling rules, because out-of-state syrup producers could not physically comply with the federal law without violating the state law.

In *Silkwood*, the Supreme Court relied on both intent and conflict theories to find that the Atomic Energy Act did not preempt state tort law recovery for nuclear radiation injuries. First, the Court held that Congress, in creating the Atomic Energy Commission, did not intend to so completely occupy the field of nuclear safety that it foreclosed state negligence and strict liability remedies for persons injured by nuclear incidents. Second, the Court held there was no actual conflict between federal and state civil remedies. It was not physically impossible for Kerr-McGee to pay both federal fines and state punitive damage awards, nor did the state punitive damage remedy frustrate the desire of Congress to encourage nuclear power development.

Overall, preemption decisions are a matter of statutory interpretation. A court will ask whether the federal law addresses a subject matter traditionally delegated to Congress, whether Congress intended to permit state regulation of the subject, and if it did not, whether the federal and state laws conflict. In answering these questions, a court will scrutinize the text of the federal statute, examine its legislative history, and then determine the practical effect of its implementation on the state law.

For more information: Sullivan, Kathleen, and Gerald Gunther. *Constitutional Law.* 15th ed. New York: Foundation Press, 2004; Tribe, Laurence. *American Constitutional Law.* 3d ed. New York: Foundation Press, 2000.

—William Crawford Green

presentment clause

The presentment clause of the United States Constitution is located in Article I, Section 7. It provides the fundamental guidelines for passing federal legislation, which involve both chambers of Congress as well as the president. Specifically, this clause requires every bill or resolution passed by a majority vote by the HOUSE OF REPRESENTATIVES and the SENATE to be presented to the president for his signature or VETO. In instances where the president approves of the legislation, the bill or resolution is enacted into law. Bills or resolutions vetoed by the president are required to be returned to their chamber of origin, where the veto may be overruled by a two-thirds vote in each chamber. In short, this clause requires legislation passed in both chambers of Congress to be presented to the president for his approval or veto.

The primary consequence of the presentment clause concerns the significant involvement of the president in the legislative process. While the Constitution generally constructs a federal system based on separated powers among the three branches of government, this clause provides that the legislative process is one that involves both the legislative and executive branches.

Contrary to other constitutional provisions that have provided the basis for controversy, debate, and adjudication, the presentment clause has been mostly noncontroversial throughout American history. As this clause clearly specifies what types of legislation require presentation to the president, the president's limited options to approve or veto legislation, and the legislative process necessary to override instances of presidential vetoes, a noticeable lack of ambiguity often leads to different conceptualizations regarding the original INTENT OF THE FRAMERS. However, in recent decades the presentment clause has been the basis of the controversy over the increased use of the LEGISLATIVE VETO, the line-item veto, and PRESIDENTIAL SIGNING STATEMENTS.

Legislative vetoes are statutory provisions that authorize either or both houses of Congress, or specific committees or subcommittees from either or both houses, to approve or disapprove of certain bureaucratic decisions, actions, or policies. By coupling the delegation of authority to bureaucratic agencies with veto provisions, Congress can utilize bureaucratic expertise and provide latitude in administrative decision making while reserving veto powers over certain administrative actions. This particular oversight device allows Congress to take actions that are legislative in function without presidential approval, as required by the presentment clause. First adopted in 1932, congressional use of the legislative veto substantially increased in the 1970s and 1980s in association with the growth of the federal bureaucracy. In 1983, however, the Supreme Court declared the legislative veto unconstitutional in *INS v. Chadha,* 462 U.S. 919 (1983), by declaring that legislative veto provisions violated prescribed policy-making procedures that the Constitution stipulated as necessary in the legislative process—namely, the presentment clause. Despite this ruling, Congress has continued the practice of including various types of legislative veto provisions in legislation.

The presentment clause has also been part of the debate over the presidential use of the line-item veto. As part of the Republican "Contract with America" following the 1994 elections in which the Republicans assumed congressional majorities in both chambers, Congress passed the Line-Item Veto Act of 1996 (2 U.S.C. § 683). This legislation empowered the president to strike out certain provisions of appropriations bills as a means toward fiscal responsibility. The constitutional permissibility of this act was challenged in *CLINTON V. CITY OF NEW YORK,* 524 U.S. 417 (1998), wherein the Supreme Court ruled that the line-item veto violated the legislative process stipulated by the Constitution, which necessitated bicameral passage and presentment to the president.

Yet another issue concerns the applicability of presidential signing statements to the presentment clause. Modern presidents have increased the frequency of attaching statements when signing approved legislation into law. Signing statements are generally used to provide instructions to executive branch officials regarding the president's preferred means of policy implementation, to identify provisions that possibly violate the Constitution, or simply as rhetorical devices. As the affixation of presidential statements to approved legislation is not mentioned in ARTICLE I OF THE U.S. CONSTITUTION, some argue that this practice violates the presentment clause.

At its core, the presentment clause provides for a considerable role for the president in the legislative process. Although it has not been the subject of serious controversy for much of American history, modern political phenomena such as legislative vetoes, the line-item veto, and presidential signing statements have all raised interesting questions regarding what policy-making actions and procedures require presentment to the president as stipulated by the Constitution.

For more information: Eskridge, William N., and John Ferejohn. "The Article I, Section 7 Game." *Georgetown Law Journal* 80 (1992): 523–564; Korn, Jessica. "The Legislative Veto and the Limits of Public Choice Analysis." *Political Science Quarterly* 109, no. 5 (1994): 873–894; Spitzer, Robert J. "The Constitutionality of the Presidential Line-Item Veto." *Political Science Quarterly* 112, no. 2 (1997): 261–283.

—Michael John Berry

presidential pardoning power

ARTICLE II, Section 2 of the United States Constitution states that the president "shall have power to grant Reprieves and Pardons for Offenses against the United States, except in Cases of IMPEACHMENT." The pardon is a power that can be traced to the monarchy in England. This power, which has been made available to the U.S. president, is probably the most imperial of his powers. The president is able to grant a pardon to people who have committed crimes or offenses against the United States, except in cases of impeachment. Impeachment is virtually the only limitation that has been placed on the president by the Constitution. Other than impeachment, the president essentially has unlimited power when it comes to granting pardons, and this power has the potential for abuse. The Supreme Court has mentioned that abuse of this power could make the president susceptible to JUDICIAL REVIEW and even impeachment.

When the president grants someone a reprieve, the sentence is simply reduced and does not take away guilt. For instance, a death sentence may be reduced to a term of life imprisonment rather than execution. A presidential pardon relieves the accused of guilt in addition to the punishment. When a person is granted a presidential pardon, all of their rights are immediately restored, and it is as if nothing had ever occurred.

In *Federalist* 74, ALEXANDER HAMILTON made the argument that there are certain occasions where it is important for the president to have pardoning power. Hamilton stated that "in seasons of insurrection or rebellion, there are often critical moments when a well-timed offer of pardon to the insurgents or rebels may restore the tranquility of the commonwealth." While the power of pardon in England was granted to the monarch and offenses were deemed to be made against the monarch, in the U.S. crimes were made against the government and its laws and not simply the president. However, Alexander Hamilton argued that the legislative branch was not fit for this power, because the president would be better suited to act more quickly and with national and other interests in mind.

An example of the value of granting pardoning power to the president was during Reconstruction after the Civil War. The United States did not immediately calm down, and it took a long time for the two sides to get along. The people of the South eventually became a part of the political process again; they were given back their voting rights; and many even went on to hold federal political offices.

The first presidential pardon was granted by George Washington in 1792. President Washington attempted violence and demands in order to end the Whiskey Rebellion, but nothing worked until he handed out presidential pardons. The number of pardons granted has fluctuated over time. After the Civil War, Presidents ABRAHAM LINCOLN and Andrew Jackson granted amnesty to about 200,000 people. In *Ex parte Garland*, 71 U.S. 333 (1866), the Supreme Court upheld the broad scope of these pardons. President Harry Truman granted pardons to about 1,500 people, and in 1952, he restored CIVIL RIGHTS to about 9,000 peacetime deserters.

Presidential pardons have also created a great deal of controversy over time. One of the more famous presidential pardons was the one granted to RICHARD NIXON by President Gerald Ford. Shortly after taking over the presidency from Nixon, President Ford granted Richard Nixon a full pardon. The controversy did not surround the fact that President Ford granted Nixon a pardon, but rather the timing of the pardon: Nixon's pardon was granted before charges were even filed. It was suspected that Ford's pardoning of Nixon was a major factor in his loss to Jimmy Carter in 1976. Moreover, while some questioned the constitutionality of this pardon, in *Murphy v. Ford*, 390 F. Supp. 1372 (D. Mich. 1975), a federal district court judge upheld it, noting that the power is "unlimited" except for impeachment.

Presidents have continued issuing pardons. President Carter issued a pardon to all the individuals who evaded the draft during the Vietnam War. During his last hours in office, President George H. W. Bush granted pardons to six people from President Reagan's administration who had been implicated in the Iran-Contra scandal. President Bill Clinton issued many controversial pardons during his tenure in the White House; some have even referred to this as "pardon-gate." Some of Clinton's pardons had family and campaign ties to both the president and the First Lady. On his last day in office, President Clinton granted 140 pardons. Many presidents have chosen to grant a few pardons on their last day in office, but Clinton's far exceeded previous numbers. One of

President Clinton's last-minute pardons was for his half-brother, Roger Clinton, who was serving a sentence on drug-related charges. In 2007, President George Bush pardoned Lewis Libby, the chief of staff for the vice president, after he had been convicted for perjury. In this case, the pardon extended only to the prison sentence, but not to the fines.

Today, there is an office that is in charge of handling pardons. The Office of the Pardon Attorney was created by Congress in 1891. It is this office that reviews petitions that have been made for pardons and clemency. The pardon attorney then makes recommendations to the attorney general, who then advises the president.

For more information: Dorris, Jonathan T. *Pardon and Amnesty under Lincoln.* Westport, Conn.: Greenwood Press, 1977; Milkis, Sidney M., and Michael Nelson. *The American Presidency: Origins and Development 1776–2002.* 4th ed. Washington, D.C.: CQ Press, 2003; More, Kathleen D. *Pardons: Justice, Mercy and the Public Interest.* New York: Oxford University Press, 1989; Nelson, Michael, ed. *Guide to the Presidency.* 2d ed. Washington, D.C.: Congressional Quarterly, 1996; Pederson, William D., and Frank J. Williams. "America's Presidential Triumvirate: Qualitative Measures." In *George Washington. Foundation of Presidential Leadership and Character.* Westport, Conn.: Greenwood Press, 2001.

—William D. Pederson and
Jacqueline M. Loubet

presidential signing statements

A presidential signing statement is a written statement made by the president when he signs a piece of legislation. Presidents James Monroe and Andrew Jackson each used signing statements to challenge what they viewed as congressional encroachment on their executive powers. An 1899 Supreme Court decision recognized that "it has properly been the practice of the President to inform Congress by message of his approval of bills" (*La Abra Silver Mining Co. v. United States*, 175 U.S. 423). Even so, presidents in the late 19th and early 20th centuries rarely used signing statements, preferring to express their disagreements with Congress in other ways.

Professor Christopher Kelly grouped presidential signing statements into three categories: rhetorical signing statements, used to mobilize political support; political signing statements, used to interpret legislation and structure its implementation; and constitutional signing statements, used to point out perceived constitutional defects in legislation. Walter Dellinger, an assistant attorney general in the Clinton administration, identified three similar functions in 1993 and noted that a fourth had recently emerged: the use of signing statements to create an alternative "legislative history."

A memo prepared in 1986 by then-Deputy Assistant Attorney General SAMUEL ALITO, appointed to the Supreme Court in 2006, suggested that presidents could effectively use signing statements to address questions of interpretation and to express what he called "presidential intent." The contemporary use of signing statements first appeared during the Reagan presidency. Presidential signing statements, routinely published in the *Weekly Compilation of Presidential Documents,* began to be included in the legislative histories compiled by West Publishing Company for its *U.S. Code Congressional and Administrative News* in 1986.

According to the Congressional Research Service, President Ronald Reagan issued 276 signing statements during his eight years in office (1981–88). Most of them involved statutory interpretation, but 71 of them (26 percent) questioned the constitutionality of at least one provision of the bill being signed into law. President George H. W. Bush continued this trend, issuing 214 signing statements in his single term (1989–92); 146 of them (68 percent) raised constitutional objections. President Bill Clinton issued 391 signing statements during his two terms (1993–2000), but only 105 of them (27 percent) raised constitutional concerns.

President George W. Bush has used signing statements more than any previous president. The Congressional Research Service noted that "the nature and sheer number of provisions challenged or objected to indicates that there is . . . a qualitative difference" between the actions of previous administrations and those of President Bush. During his first term (2001–04), he issued 108 signing statements. After six years the number had risen to 149; 127 of them (85 percent) contained at least one constitutional challenge. By June 2007, the president had challenged over 1,100 separate legislative provisions, the majority of them on constitutional grounds.

Professor Phillip J. Cooper noted that the administration consistently gave its own executive powers "the widest possible scope" while giving legislative powers "the narrowest possible reading." President Bush's signing statements were characterized by "boilerplate" language that was not specific to the bill. As the Congressional Research Service report pointed out, presidential objections were "largely unsubstantive" or "so general as to appear to be hortatory assertions of executive authority." The most common claims of unconstitutional encroachment involved the president's power to supervise the unitary executive, his exclusive authority over foreign affairs, his right to control the information provided by the executive branch to Congress, his inherent authority to protect national security, and his powers as commander in chief. The concept of the "unitary executive" is particularly important. Under this theory, as developed by the Bush administration, the president has exclusive authority over all elements of the executive branch, including the independent regulatory agencies initially created by Congress. Relying on ARTICLE II, Section 3 of the Constitution, which states that the president "shall take care that the laws be faithfully executed," the unitary executive theory also asserts that the president has independent authority to interpret the law and to implement his views.

President Bush's use of signing statements drew little attention until Congress approved the McCain Anti-Torture Amendment to the Detainee Treatment Act in 2005, explicitly prohibiting the use of "cruel, inhuman or degrading treatment or punishment." President Bush first adamantly opposed this provision, then agreed to accept it. But after publicly signing the bill, he issued a written signing statement on December 30, 2005, that asserted his right to ignore provisions of the bill he had just signed:

> The executive branch shall construe Title X in Division A of the Act, relating to detainees, in a manner consistent with the constitutional authority of the President to supervise the unitary executive branch and as commander in chief and consistent with the constitutional limitations on the judicial power, which will assist in achieving the shared objective of the Congress and the President, evidenced in Title X, of protecting the American people from further terrorist attacks.

In spring 2006, Boston *Globe* reporter Charlie Savage reported on the president's frequent use of signing statements to challenge legislative provisions and transform the meaning of statutory language. The Congressional Research Service was asked to prepare a report on the constitutional implications of presidential signing statements. The American Bar Association created a Task Force on Presidential Signing Statements and the Separation of Powers Doctrine, which criticized President Bush's use of presidential signing statements as "tantamount to exercising the line-item veto power held unconstitutional by the Supreme Court." The General Accountability Office examined the impact of Bush's signing statements on the implementation of some of the specified provisions and found that several of them had not been implemented as the law directed.

All of the reports agreed that the issue was not the use of presidential signing statements per se, but the frequency with which they were now being issued and the broad scope of the claims being made. The Congressional Research Service report noted that "the broad and persistent nature of the claims of executive authority forwarded by President Bush appear designed to inure Congress, as well as others, to the belief that the President in fact possesses expansive and exclusive powers upon which the other branches may not intrude." Administrative spokesmen, in contrast, asserted that President Bush was simply making his interpretation of legislation clear, as previous presidents have done, and asserting his right—indeed, his obligation—to refuse to implement unconstitutional provisions. Both sides agree that the issues raised by these uses of presidential signing statements have the potential to reshape core constitutional principles relating to CHECKS AND BALANCES and the separation of powers.

For more information: Cooper, Phillip J. "George W. Bush, Edgar Allan Poe, and the Use and Abuse of Presidential Signing Statements." *Presidential Studies Quarterly* 35 (2005): 515–532; General Accountability Office [GAO]. Letter Opinion on Presidential Signing Statements Accompanying the Fiscal Year 2006 Appropriations Acts. Washington, D.C.: GAO, released June 18, 2007. Available online. URL: http://www.gao.gov/decisions/appro/308603.htm. Accessed May 14, 2008; Halstead, T. J. Presidential Signing Statements: Constitutional and Institutional Implications (updated version, document RL33667). Washington, D.C.: Congressional Research Service, released April 13, 2007. Available online. URL: http://www.fas.org/sgp/crs/natsec/RL33667.pdf. Accessed May 14, 2008.

—Barbara J. Hayler

presumption of innocence

The presumption of innocence is a bedrock principle of criminal law that describes the protection afforded a criminal defendant during the course of a prosecution. In essence, it stands for the proposition that all criminal defendants have the benefit of being viewed as innocent until such time as the prosecution can supply evidence of an appropriate weight such as to overcome that supposition.

The origins of the presumption of innocence are not to be found in the Constitution itself, but rather from time-honored tradition and the common law. In 1866, the United States Supreme Court recognized that the presumption of innocence was a recognized principle of common law, which was "supposed to be fundamental and unchangeable" (*Cumings v. Missouri*, 71 U.S. 277

[1866]). Ultimately, in 1895, the Supreme Court went even further in *Coffin v. United States,* 156 U.S. 432, and traced the origins of the presumption of innocence to Roman law, canon law, and the English common law. The English common law articulation of the presumption was, as asserted by WILLIAM BLACKSTONE, the belief that it is better that 10 guilty persons be acquitted than that one innocent person be convicted of a crime. As the Court in *Coffin* stated, "The principal that there is a presumption of innocence in favor of the accused is the undoubted law, axiomatic and elementary, and its enforcement lies at the foundation of the administration of our criminal law."

The Supreme Court concluded in *Taylor v. Kentucky,* 436 U.S. 478 (1978), that the very phrase "presumption of innocence" is a misnomer, and that the proper manner of articulating the principal should be as an "assumption of innocence." This distinction was made because a presumption is an evidentiary concept that carries with it implications beyond that of a simple "assumption of innocence." An evidentiary presumption, established either by statute or in common law, allows for inferences to be made from facts that are in evidence. This permits legal conclusions to be drawn even when direct evidence on the issue is not available. In the case of the presumption of innocence, however, there are no facts in evidence from which the inference can be made. Rather, the Supreme Court in *Taylor* concluded that the presumption of innocence is a shorthand description of the ability of a criminal defendant to compel the prosecution to put on evidence of guilt, with the defendant assumed to be innocent until such time as that evidence is presented and meets the burden of proof required.

While it may be axiomatic that a criminal defendant possesses a presumption of innocence, it is less clear how this protection is procedurally effected. The court in *Taylor* was forced to decide what purpose, if any, this assumption served in the modern criminal trial. Many had argued that the presumption of innocence was logically indistinguishable from the protections afforded criminal defendants by the requirement that the prosecution prove its case beyond a reasonable doubt. In fact, in *Taylor,* the Kentucky state court had refused to provide a special jury instruction on the presumption of innocence based on its belief that the instructions pertaining to the burden of proof adequately protected the defendant from the prejudices of lay jurors. The court concluded that, despite the fact that the presumption of innocence and the burden of proof are not logically separate and distinct, it may be necessary to provide a separate jury instruction on the presumption of innocence, in addition to the instructions dealing with the burden of proof, as a means of impressing upon the lay jury the importance of having findings of guilt or innocence based only upon evidence rather than suspicion. The *Taylor* court went so far as to conclude that the DUE PROCESS clause of the FOURTEENTH AMENDMENT required jury instructions on the presumption of innocence in the case in question.

Later, in *Kentucky v. Whorton,* 441 U.S. 786 (1979), the Court modified its due process finding to require courts to evaluate the necessity for such instructions on a case-by-case basis. A finding of a due process violation was not automatic, and, depending upon the content of the instructions provided as to the burden of proof, the arguments of counsel and the weight of the evidence may not always be necessary to ensure a fair trial. It is this notion of a fair trial, the *Whorton* Court noted, not a jury instruction on the presumption of innocence, that is constitutionally mandated. Thus, the presumption of innocence is a phrase that accurately characterizes more specific protections afforded criminal defendants and is also a concept that, in some circumstances, juries must be advised of as a means of ensuring a fair trial for the accused.

For more information: Fox, William F., Jr. "The 'Presumption of Innocence' as Constitutional Doctrine." *Catholic University Law Review* 28 (1979): 253–269; Thayer, James Bradley. "The Presumption of Innocence in Criminal Cases." *Yale Law Journal* 6, no. 4 (1897): 185–212.

—Bryan H. Ward

Price v. Vincent 538 U.S. 634 (2003)

In *Price v. Vincent,* the Supreme Court ruled that an individual convicted of first-degree murder after a judge had issued an order indicating that second-degree murder was an appropriate charge did not violate the DOUBLE JEOPARDY provision of the Fifth Amendment. *Black's Law Dictionary* defines double jeopardy as "the fact of being prosecuted or sentenced twice for substantially the same offense."

Markeis Jones was killed during an altercation between two groups of youths in Flint, Michigan. In a Michigan state court, Duyonn Andre Vincent was charged and convicted of first-degree murder for killing Jones. Eventually, the case made its way to the Federal District Court and to the U.S. Court of Appeals for the Sixth Circuit. Each federal court granted Vincent's habeas petition, noting that the continuation of prosecution for the first-degree murder charge was a violation of the constitutional right against double jeopardy. The question before the Supreme Court in this case was: Did the trial court violate the double jeopardy clause when the trial judge granted a motion for a directed verdict of acquittal, but failed to direct the verdict to the jury that eventually found the defendant guilty of the charge?

In a unanimous decision delivered by Chief Justice WILLIAM HUBBS REHNQUIST, the Court concluded that Vincent did not meet the basis for habeas relief. In the opinion, it is noted, "Double Jeopardy Clause is prohibition against multiple trials and corresponding prevention of oppression by the Government." The trial judge only granted the motion for a directed verdict of acquittal, yet never made a decision as to the motion. In other words, granting a motion is quite different from deciding the motion. Oyez, a noted site for Supreme Court opinion summations, notes,

> The Court stated that Vincent was entitled to relief only if he can demonstrate that the state court's adjudication of his claim was "contrary to" or an "unreasonable application of" the Court's clearly established precedents. Finding that the state court's adjudication of his claim was not, the Court reversed the Court of Appeals because

> "Even if we agreed with the Court of Appeals that the Double Jeopardy Clause should be read to prevent continued prosecution of a defendant under these circumstances, it was at least reasonable for the state court to conclude otherwise."

Price v. Vincent is an important case clarifying the double jeopardy clause. It stands for the proposition that a judge's comments on a motion, short of a directed verdict, do not constitute an acquittal that would implicate double jeopardy if one were retried.

For more information: Garner, Bryan A., ed. *Black's Law Dictionary.* 8th ed. St. Paul, Minn.: Thomson/West, 2004; Thomas, George C., III. *Double Jeopardy: The History, the Law.* New York: New York University Press, 1998.

—Dan Krejci

Printz v. United States 521 U.S. 898 (1997)

In *Printz v. United States,* the U.S. Supreme Court invalidated a federal law that required local officials to perform mandatory background checks on individuals wishing to purchase firearms. In reaching this conclusion, the Court ruled that Congress had exceeded its authority under the COMMERCE CLAUSE when it enacted this law. In addition, the Court stated that the law violated the Tenth Amendment.

In 1993, Congress passed the Brady Handgun Violence Prevention Act, which, among other things, required a five-day waiting period before purchasing guns. It also mandated local officials to perform background checks on potential buyers. Two separate county sheriffs sought enjoinment of the law that compelled their assistance during an interim period until a national instant background-check system was established.

Two United States district courts that heard the unconsolidated question held the statute unconstitutional. On appeal to the Ninth Circuit Court of Appeals, the cases were consolidated and reversed. The Supreme Court, per Justice ANTONIN GREGORY SCALIA, reversed the appellate court and reinstated much of the district court's decision that held that state executive officers were not obligated to execute federal laws.

To begin, Justice Scalia reviewed the question from a historical perspective. Early Congresses sometimes conferred upon state courts certain obligations to enforce federal laws, but there only were limited efforts dealing with state executive officials. Justice Scalia drafted this distinction. Courts differed from the roles of the state executives, as the "Constitution was originally understood to permit imposition on state *judges* to enforce federal prescriptions" (id. at 907). The lack of attempts by early Congresses to impress state executives into federal service "suggests an assumed *absence* of such power" (id. at 908). Those federal laws that did exist were primarily congressional recommendations to the states or authorizations for federal authorities to solicit state consent. This statute, by contrast, involved compelled assistance rather than consensual.

The Court continued by noting the Constitution envisioned dual sovereignties, wherein both federal and state governments have common power to regulate their citizens. However, the states have obligations only toward their own citizens, which potentially requires states to assert independence from the federal legislative schemes. While Congress does have authority under the NECESSARY AND PROPER CLAUSE, as well as the SUPREMACY CLAUSE, to enact broad-based federal legislation that may directly impact upon states, even under these provisions, there is no power to regulate the states, only power for the federal authority to enforce its own federal legislation. By contrast, this firearm law "effectively transfers this responsibility to thousands" of state officials. The federal government suggested that the state role in the firearm case only involved discrete, administerial tasks and had little to do with policy making. This argument assumes the Congress can shift nondiscretionary burdens upon the states. However, Justice Scalia disagreed, arguing that the burden and expense of enforcement is placed upon the states for a federal decision. If the law is unpopular, the states will suffer the blame during the enforcement phase for a legislative decision that the states did not enact. Whether this federal law merely is interim or permanent, and regardless if expensive or not, the principle is state sovereignty.

Printz is an important case in that it placed federal limits on the use of the commerce clause to legislate, but it also used the concept of FEDERALISM and states' rights to limit federal power.

For more information: Langran, Robert W. *The Supreme Court: A Concise History.* New York: Peter Lang, 2004; Vizzard, William J. *Shots in the Dark: The Policy, Politics, and Symbolism of Gun Control.* Lanham, Md.: Rowman & Littlefield, Inc., 2000.

—Daniel M. Katz

prisoners' rights

According to the Supreme Court's interpretations of the U.S. Constitution, people held in jails and prisons possess limited rights, including protections for FREEDOM OF RELIGION, access to lawyers and courts, and humane living conditions, as long as the exercise of those rights does not threaten safety and security at the jail or prison. If wardens or corrections officers violate these limited rights, prisoners may file lawsuits against them to seek financial compensation and enforcement of recognized rights.

For most of American history, judges followed a "hands-off" policy that permitted corrections officials to manage jails and prisons without supervision from courts. Prior to the 1960s, the U.S. Supreme Court rarely interpreted the Constitution as providing legal protections for prisoners. Thus, prisoners were usually powerless to challenge the policies and practices in jails and prisons. Two notable exceptions during this period were Supreme Court decisions condemning the use of torture in local jails as a means to extract confessions from criminal suspects (*Brown v. Mississippi,* 297 U.S. 278 [1936]) and prohibiting prison officials from intercepting legal documents that prisoners sought to mail to a court (*Ex parte Hull,* 312 U.S. 546 [1941]).

The Supreme Court's 1941 decision in *Ex parte Hull* provided the basis for cases in the 1960s and 1970s that clarified the existence of prisoners' right of access to the courts. In 1969, the Supreme Court ruled that prisoners must be permitted to help each other prepare legal cases unless prison officials provide other means of legal assistance (*Johnson v. Avery*, 393 U.S. 483). The right of access was later expanded when the Supreme Court declared that prisons must provide prisoners with either access to a law library or to assistance from someone trained in law (*Bounds v. Smith*, 430 U.S. 817 [1977]). Most corrections institutions chose to provide prisoners with law libraries as the means to fulfill the right of access to the courts. Critics note that very few prisoners have training in law, and thus access to a law library does not ensure that they have a realistic opportunity to prepare effective legal actions for filing in court.

For reasons of safety and security, prisoners and their cells must be searched on a regular basis. Thus the FOURTH AMENDMENT protection against unreasonable searches and seizures protects prisoners against only one kind of search: intrusive searches of their body cavities that are done without justification or for purposes of harassment.

An important Supreme Court decision in 1987 mandated that, when prisoners claim that particular prison rules or policies violate their constitutional rights, those rights must be weighed against the safety and security interests of the institution (*Turner v. Safley*, 482 U.S. 78). The Court's decision effectively narrowed the extent of prisoners' rights, as prison officials used security justifications in specific situations to block prisoners' access to books and magazines, visitors, and religious services. Congress enacted the Religious Land Use and Institutionalized Persons Act of 2000 in an effort to ensure that prisoners enjoy freedom of religion unless prison officials can provide a compelling reason to prohibit a specific religious practice.

The most significant controversies about prisoners' rights arose as the Supreme Court and lower federal courts interpreted the Eighth Amendment's prohibition on CRUEL AND UNUSUAL PUNISHMENT to guarantee certain standards for conditions of confinement. In the 1960s, lower federal courts interpreted the Eighth Amendment as protecting prisoners against whipping as a form of punishment (*Jackson v. Bishop*, 404 F.2d 371 [8th Cir. 1968]). Judges later expanded their use of the Eighth Amendment to establish minimum standards for humane living conditions, including nutrition, medical care, and personal safety for prisoners.

The U.S. Supreme Court's first significant interpretation of the Eighth Amendment as a source of prisoners' rights came in *Estelle v. Gamble*, 429 U.S. 97 (1976). In *Estelle*, the Court declared that a violation of the prohibition on cruel and unusual punishment occurs when prison officials show deliberate indifference to prisoners' serious medical needs. This is not a right to high-quality medical care, but merely a protection against enduring deliberate indifference to serious problems.

In 1978, the Supreme Court endorsed the power of lower court judges to use the Eighth Amendment to order changes in the conditions of confinement in prisons and jails (*Hutto v. Finney*, 437 U.S. 678). In many corrections institutions, overcrowding, violence, lack of sanitation facilities, and inadequate food created living conditions that fell below government standards for public health and human survival. Lawyers who advocated on behalf of prisoners filed successful lawsuits in many states to challenge such substandard conditions. As a result, federal judges throughout the United States ordered individual prisons and jails to improve living conditions in order to meet constitutional standards. Many states were forced to spend millions of dollars on jails and prisons in order to meet these standards. Governors and legislators complained that judges were interfering in the operation of prisons. Although judges continued to issue orders throughout the 1980s and 1990s, the U.S. Supreme Court slowed the process of recognizing additional rights for prisoners. In fact, the Court overruled several lower court decisions that sought to recognize new rights for prisoners, including a claimed right to assistance from a trained legal professional (*Lewis v. Casey*, 516 U.S. 804 [1996]) and a claimed right to receive visitors (*Overton v. Bazzetta*, 539 U.S. 126 [2003]). Congress also enacted a law called the Prison Litigation Reform Act of 1996 to make it more difficult for prisoners to file lawsuits seeking the recognition and protection of constitutional rights. Thus, most observers believe that the Supreme Court will continue to protect established rights for prisoners but will not expand those rights or interpret the Constitution to recognize additional rights.

For more information: Cripe, Clair, and Michael G. Pearlman. *Legal Aspects of Corrections Management.* 2d ed. Sudbury, Mass.: Jones and Bartlett Publishers, 2005; Smith, Christopher E. *Law and Contemporary Corrections.* Belmont, Calif.: Wadsworth Publishing, 2000.

—Christopher E. Smith

privacy

The right to privacy is a concept that developed gradually in the United States through the 19th century. While privacy is not mentioned explicitly in the Constitution, it has been deemed to be among the unenumerated rights guaranteed by the NINTH AMENDMENT.

There is no broadly accepted definition of privacy. Depending on the legal context, privacy refers to physical seclusion, informational secrecy, or a principle that protects one's ability to make decisions about certain fundamental matters. Privacy can pertain to individuals, families, groups, and businesses. The constitutional right to privacy currently protects the freedom of individuals from unwanted and unwarranted intrusion by government in such domains as human reproduction, familial relationships, sexuality, decisions about dying, personal autonomy, and personal information. The Supreme Court has made clear that the right to privacy is not absolute, since government has a degree of legitimate interest in each of these domains. The extent of one's privacy under the Constitution remains controversial and continues to be defined and modified by statute and by judicial interpretation.

Through the 19th century, privacy interests began to be recognized in the common law and protected by the courts. Protected privacy inter-

ests included the home, the person, confidential communications, and personal information.

In 1890, in one of the most influential law review articles in American history, Samuel D. Warren and Louis D. Brandeis (later a Supreme Court justice) suggested that the advance of civilization and the development of the law had led to the recognition of a right to privacy of the individual, understood as the "right to be let alone." They argued that common-law protections already afforded to individuals are in fact rooted in an underlying right to privacy, which is in turn "part of the more general right to the immunity of the person—the right to one's personality." As privacy scholar Richard Glenn observes, they called for common-law recognition of "a specific legal right to privacy, a right independent of property and liberty, a right unrelated to tort law." Such a right to privacy entered state constitutional law in *Pavesich v. New England Life Insurance Company*, 50 S.E. 68 (Ga. 1905), which was the first case in which privacy was "deemed by a state court to be an independent right under a state constitution" (Glenn).

Being let alone, however, is broader than privacy; it is the contemporary understanding of liberty, articulated most influentially by John Stuart Mill (*On Liberty* [1869]). Liberty or personal freedom may be enjoyed publicly or privately. If society is sufficiently tolerant, individuals may be able to engage in a large range of activities in the public sphere (e.g., COHEN V. CALIFORNIA, 403 U.S. 15 [1971]). Privacy creates a nonpublic sphere in which individuals are free to engage in activities that are concealed from others and hence are removed from public scrutiny. Hence, privacy is a narrower concept than liberty. For example, *Pavesich* recognized a "right of personal liberty" that encompasses "the right to withdraw from the public gaze at such times as a person may see fit, when his presence in public is not demanded by any rule of law." The difference between privacy and liberty is also recognized in WILLIAM HUBBS REHNQUIST's dissent in *ROE V. WADE*, 410 U.S. 113 (1973). Safeguarding privacy, then, is one way of protecting personal freedom, and hence privacy is instrumental to liberty.

A constitutional right to privacy was decisively established in *GRISWOLD V. CONNECTICUT*, 381 U.S.

479 (1965). Justice WILLIAM O. DOUGLAS argued that

> specific guarantees in the Bill of Rights have penumbras, formed by emanations from those guarantees that help give them life and substance. . . . Various guarantees create zones of privacy. The right of association contained in the penumbra of the FIRST AMENDMENT is one. . . . The THIRD AMENDMENT in its prohibition against the quartering of soldiers "in any house" in time of peace without the consent of the owner is another facet of that privacy.
>
> The FOURTH AMENDMENT explicitly affirms the "right of the people to be secure in their persons, houses, papers, and effects, against unreasonable searches and seizures." The Fifth Amendment in its Self-Incrimination Clause enables the citizen to create a zone of privacy which government may not force him to surrender to his detriment. The Ninth Amendment provides: "The enumeration in the Constitution, of certain rights, shall not be construed to deny or disparage others retained by the people." . . . We have had many controversies over these penumbral rights of "privacy and repose." . . . These cases bear witness that the right of privacy which presses for recognition here is a legitimate one.

This line of argument was used to strike down a Connecticut state law (that criminalized the use of drugs or articles to prevent conception) through INCORPORATION, wherein the BILL OF RIGHTS becomes binding upon the states through the FOURTEENTH AMENDMENT.

This right to privacy in *Griswold* was extended in *EISENSTADT V. BAIRD*, 405 U.S. 438 (1972). There the Court contended that if "the right to privacy means anything it is the right of the individual, married or single, to be free from unwarranted government intrusion into matters so fundamentally affecting a person as the decision whether to bear or beget a child." This broadening of privacy to protect intimate personal decisions, especially those pertaining to procreation, became one of the precedents upon which the landmark ABORTION case, *Roe v. Wade,* was decided.

The defendant in *Roe v. Wade* claimed that a Texas statute (which prohibited all abortions except in cases in which the health of the mother was at stake) "abridged her right of personal privacy, protected by the First, Fourth, Fifth, Ninth, and Fourteenth Amendments" as defined and protected in *Griswold* and *Eisenstadt*. More specifically, it was argued that this right to privacy created a right "possessed by the pregnant woman, to choose to terminate her pregnancy." Writing the majority opinion, Justice Blackmun found that "the Court has recognized that a right of personal privacy, or a guarantee of certain areas or zones of privacy, does exist under the Constitution." Based on previous cases, this right extends to marriage, procreation, contraception, family relationships, child rearing, and education. In reviewing these cases, the Court upheld the right to personal privacy as "founded in the Fourteenth Amendment's concept of personal liberty" and decided that it "is broad enough to encompass a woman's decision whether or not to terminate her pregnancy."

The Court made clear that this right is not absolute, since the state has legitimate interests in "safeguarding health, in maintaining medical standards, and in protecting potential life." Thus the right to personal privacy was reaffirmed and found to include the right to an abortion under certain circumstances. A limit on the right to privacy was set in *BOWERS V. HARDWICK*, 478 U.S. 186 (1986). In that case, the Court rejected the claim that the Constitution conferred a fundamental right to engage in homosexual sodomy in the privacy of one's home. "[T]he privacy right, which the Griswold line of cases found to be one of the protections provided by the DUE PROCESS Clause, did not reach so far." However, *Bowers* was repudiated and overruled by the Court in *LAWRENCE V. TEXAS*, 539 U.S. 558 (2003). There, the Court found that the laws in question and their penalties touch "upon the most private human conduct, sexual behavior, and in the most private of places, the home. They seek to control a personal relationship that, whether or not entitled to formal recognition in the law, is within the liberty of persons to choose without being punished as criminals. The liberty protected by the Constitution allows homosexual persons the right to choose to enter upon relationships in the confines of their homes and their own private lives and still retain their dignity as free persons." This further extended constitutional protection of privacy of intimate personal decisions. The Supreme Court further enlarged the right to privacy to include the right of competent patients to refuse life-sustaining medical treatment (CRUZAN V. DIRECTOR, MISSOURI DEPARTMENT OF HEALTH, 497 U.S. 261 [1990]).

In reviewing its decisions regarding privacy in Whalen v. Roe, 429 U.S. 589 (1977), the Supreme Court demarcated "at least two" categories of privacy interests. "One is the individual interest in avoiding disclosure of personal matters, and another is the interest in independence in making certain kinds of important decisions." The latter includes those matters discussed above. The former includes information privacy or data protection, including personal information such as one's name, the intimate details of one's life, one's likeness, finances, medical records, and educational records. Constitutional protections of this kind of privacy interest include the inviolability of the home (Third and Fourth Amendments), the confidentiality of communications such as the mail (Fourth Amendment), and the secrecy of self-incriminating evidence (Fifth Amendment).

A security camera in place across the street from the World Trade Center site on July 9, 2007, in New York City (Mario Tama/Getty)

In Katz v. United States, 389 U.S. 347 (1967), private communications during criminal investigations were afforded protection under the constitutional guarantee against unreasonable searches and seizures. Since "the Fourth Amendment protects people, not places," it "governs not only the seizure of tangible items, but extends as well to the recording of oral statements, over-heard without any 'technical trespass under . . . local property law.'" As a result, the Court deemed WIRETAPPING in public places without a warrant to be a violation of privacy, which has led subsequently to further state and federal protections that limit the use of electronic surveillance in both public and private areas.

Since the terrorist attacks of September 11, 2001, and the subsequent enactment of the USA PATRIOT ACT (Uniting and Strengthening America by Providing Appropriate Tools Required to Intercept and Obstruct Terrorism Act of 2001), concerns have been raised about potential governmental intrusions upon the privacy of citizens. Most provisions of the act extend existing governmental powers rather than establishing entirely new means of surveillance of suspects who are foreign nationals. However, some of these extensions are substantial, as is the case with the revisions of FISA (FOREIGN INTELLIGENCE SURVEILLANCE ACT OF 1978). For example, former narrow limits on the purpose of surveillance, its location, and what things can be observed, searched, and collected have been significantly broadened. As a result, there is a growing concern that the barrier between foreign intelligence gathering and domestic law enforcement, which FISA was meant to protect, has been breached, which may lead to direct incursions on the informational privacy of citizens in novel ways. Public deliberation, legislation, and jurisprudence surrounding these concerns and those of other kinds of privacy interests will continue to shape the definition of privacy as it evolves.

For more information: Glenn, Richard A. *The Right to Privacy: Rights and Liberties under the Law.* Santa Barbara, Calif.: ABC-CLIO, 2003; Jaeger, Paul T., John Carlo Bertot, and Charles R.

McClure. "The Impact of the USA Patriot Act on Collection and Analysis of Personal Information under the Foreign Intelligence Surveillance Act." *Government Information Quarterly* 20 (2003): 295–314; Warren, Samuel D., and Louis D. Brandeis. "The Right to Privacy." *Harvard Law Review* 4, no. 5 (December 15, 1890): 193–220.

—Stephen J. Lange

privileges and immunities

The Constitution refers to "privileges" and "immunities" in Article IV, Section 2 and in the FOURTEENTH AMENDMENT, Section 1. The meaning of the phrases has been hotly contested, and the Court has never exhaustively ruled on what those privileges and immunities actually are.

Justice Washington first interpreted the phrase in *CORFIELD V. CORYELL,* 4 Wash. (C.C. 3d) 6 Fed. Cas. 546, No. 3,230 C.C.E.D.Pa. (1823). In upholding a New Jersey law that prohibited nonresidents from harvesting oysters against the challenge that it violated Article IV, Section 2, Justice Washington gave an expansive reading of that clause. Protected were those privileges and immunities "which are, in their nature, fundamental; which belong, of right, to the citizens of all free governments . . ." (4 Wash. [C.C. 3d], 503 [1823]). Because the right to harvest oysters was not fundamental, New Jersey could discriminate against nonresidents.

However, in *Dred Scott v. Sandford,* 60 U.S. (19 How.) 393 (1857), Chief Justice ROGER TANEY distinguished between state citizenship and United States citizenship. Ruling that Scott, a slave who had temporarily resided in free territory, was not thereby made a free citizen, Taney held that state citizenship did not confer all the rights of national citizenship. States could abridge the privileges and immunities of their resident noncitizens, and since Scott was not an American citizen, Article IV, Section 2 offered him no protection.

The Fourteenth Amendment (1868) countered *Dred Scott,* establishing that citizens of the United States are also citizens of the states in which they reside and requiring that "No State shall make or enforce any law which shall abridge the privileges

or immunities of citizens of the United States . . ." (Amendment XIV, Section 1). The amendment's backers drew upon *Corfield* in their efforts to prevent state infringement of those privileges or immunities held by virtue of national citizenship (see *Adamson v. California,* 332 U.S. 46 [1947], Black, J., dissenting).

Five years later the Court offered its 5-4 decision in *BUTCHERS' BENEVOLENT ASSOCIATION OF NEW ORLEANS V. CRESCENT CITY LIVE-STOCK LANDING AND SLAUGHTER-HOUSE COMPANY* (*the Slaughterhouse Cases*), 83 U.S. 36 (1873). In ruling that Louisiana could create a "monopoly" on slaughterhouses, the Court interpreted extremely narrowly the privileges or immunities of United States citizenship. Article IV, Section 2's "sole purpose," declared Justice Miller, was to require states to extend to citizens of other states whatever rights they granted to their own citizens (83 U.S. 36, 77 [1873]). Aside from a few very limited exceptions, prior to the adoption of the Fourteenth Amendment the states determined the privileges and immunities of their citizens, and it was decidedly not the purpose of that amendment to transfer to the federal government the protection of the privileges and immunities of American citizens.

Although the Court declined to offer an exhaustive list of what those were, it identified some, including the right to petition government, free access to seaports and courts, protection abroad, HABEAS CORPUS, rights secured by the THIRTEENTH and FIFTEENTH AMENDMENTs, and the procedural guarantees of the Fourteenth. Other privileges or immunities, however, including the right to run a slaughterhouse, lay within the state's power to regulate or abridge.

In dissent, Justice Field observed that, if the Fourteenth Amendment was not intended to secure the privileges and immunities of American citizens against the states, "it was a vain and idle enactment, which accomplished nothing, and most unnecessarily excited Congress and the people on its passage" (83 U.S. 36, 96 [1873]). On the contrary, the phrase was properly elaborated in *Corfield,* and designated those "natural and inalienable rights" (83 U.S. 36, 96 [1873]) *"which of right belong to the citizens of all free governments"* (83

U.S. 36, 98 [1873], emphasis in original). As Article IV, Section 2 secures equality of privileges and immunities "between citizens of different States," the Fourteenth Amendment does so "between citizens of the United States" (83 U.S. 36, 101 [1873]). Also in dissent, Justice Bradley construed it as safeguarding "FUNDAMENTAL RIGHTS" (83 U.S. 36, 114 [1873]), those articulated in *Corfield,* those implied by other constitutional provisions, those in the BILL OF RIGHTS, and still others. Indeed, "even if the Constitution were silent, the fundamental privileges and immunities of citizens, as such, would be no less real and no less inviolable than they now are" (83 U.S. 36, 119 [1873]).

But the *Slaughterhouse Cases* "gutted" the privileges and immunities clause. A short-lived attempt to revivify it appeared in *Colgate v. Harvey,* 296 U.S. 404 (1935), when Justice Sutherland held that the right to do business in another state was a privilege of United States citizenship. Justice Stone dissented at the novelty—and "feeble[ness]"—of relying upon the clause, asserting that the narrow *Slaughterhouse* interpretation had been affirmed subsequently in "at least 44 cases" (296 U.S. 404, 445 and n. 2 [1935]). And in *Madden v. Kentucky,* 309 U.S 83 (1940), the Court expressly overturned *Colgate* and held that "the right to carry out an incident to a trade . . . is not a privilege of national citizenship" (309 U.S. 83, 92–93 [1940]). This retrenchment was reaffirmed in *Snowden v. Hughes,* 321 U.S. 1 (1944), where the Court held that the right to run for state office was not an aspect of national citizenship, and in many subsequent cases.

Thus, with the exception of *Colgate,* the *Slaughterhouse* interpretation was "good law" until SAENZ V. ROE, 526 U.S. 489 (1999). Striking down a California law establishing differential welfare payments to new residents, Justice JOHN PAUL STEVENS identified their right to the same privileges and immunities enjoyed by other citizens to be an aspect of the right to travel protected by both the Fourteenth Amendment and Article IV, Section 2. Dissenting, Chief Justice WILLIAM HUBBS REHNQUIST denied this connection and insisted that California could limit full benefits to those who were or intended to become Califor-

nia citizens. Also dissenting, Justice CLARENCE THOMAS argued that the history of the clause argued against both the *Slaughterhouse* interpretation and the majority's holding: "At the time the Fourteenth Amendment was adopted, people understood that 'privileges or immunities of citizens' were fundamental rights, rather than every public benefit established by positive law" (526 U.S. 489, 527 [1999]).

Both the narrow and broad constructions of these Delphic clauses are problematic. After the *Slaughterhouse Cases,* the Court employed SUBSTANTIVE DUE PROCESS and substantive EQUAL PROTECTION to secure citizens' (unwritten) rights. Equally problematic, however, is the attempt to secure (unwritten) "fundamental" rights—which may be simply what five members of the Court deem to be so at any particular time.

For more information: *Baldwin v. Fish and Game Commission of Montana,* 436 U.S. 371 (1978); Bogen, David S. *Privileges and Immunities: A Reference Guide to the United States Constitution.* Westport, Conn.: Praeger/Greenwood, 2003; Bork, Robert H. *The Tempting of America: The Political Seduction of the Law.* New York: The Free Press, 1990; Harrison, John. "Reconstructing the Privileges or Immunities Clause." *Yale Law Journal* 101, no. 7 (May 1992): 1,193, 1,224–1,225; Sunstein, Cass R. "Naked Preferences and the Constitution." *Columbia Law Review* 84, no. 7 (1984): 1,689–1,732; Tribe, Laurence H. "*Saenz* sans Prophecy: Does the Privileges or Immunities Revival Portend the Future or Reveal the Structure of the Present?" *Harvard Law Review* 113, no. 1 (1999): 110–198.

—Lorna M. Dawson

professional sports and the Constitution

Professional sports' collisions with the Constitution have mostly centered on antitrust questions, and by extension on the nature of INTERSTATE COMMERCE and the COMMERCE CLAUSE.

The first such collision arose out of the most serious challenge to the hegemony of the American and National Leagues in professional baseball:

the Federal League. After the FL's initial season in 1914, its owners launched an antitrust lawsuit against the AL and NL. That lawsuit was assigned to federal judge Kenesaw Mountain Landis, who adopted a gradualist strategy of inducing the parties to settle, rather than expediting the case. The delay proved fatal to the FL, whose overextended owners were forced to settle with the established leagues after the 1915 season (the delay also proved professionally advantageous for Landis, who would later be named baseball's commissioner). Of the eight FL ownership groups, four were bought out, two were allowed to buy clubs in the established leagues, and one had already declared bankruptcy. That left the owners of the Baltimore franchise, who rejected the buyout and pursued their own antitrust suit.

The Supreme Court disposed of the Baltimore club's claim in FEDERAL BASEBALL CLUB OF BALTIMORE V. NATIONAL LEAGUE OF PROFESSIONAL BASEBALL CLUBS, 259 U.S. 200 (1922). In a brief opinion for a unanimous Court, Justice OLIVER WENDELL HOLMES announced that, while professional baseball was certainly an interstate operation, "the exhibition, although made for money, would not be called trade or commerce in the commonly accepted use of those words." Although modern observers might deem it ridiculous that professional baseball does not count as commerce, Holmes's outlook was in line with the constricted view of interstate commerce that the Supreme Court held prior to 1937.

For decades, *Federal Baseball*'s holding was a major weapon for baseball's ownership in restricting players' ability to change teams of their own accord. It was reaffirmed in *Toolson v. New York Yankees,* 346 U.S. 356 (1953), with the Court leaving it to Congress to decide whether to define baseball as interstate commerce. Congressional inactivity enabled professional baseball to further enjoy—and exploit—its judicially granted exemption.

By the time the Supreme Court heard the complaint of St. Louis Cardinals center fielder Curt Flood, who was protesting the Cardinals' ability to unilaterally trade him to the Philadelphia Phillies, it had affirmatively subjected other professional

sports to antitrust law: *United States v. International Boxing Club of New York,* 348 U.S. 236 (1955); *Radovich v. National Football League,* 352 U.S. 445 (1957); and *Haywood v. National Basketball Association,* 401 U.S. 1204 (1971). Yet, in *Flood v. Kuhn,* 407 U.S. 258 (1972), the Court continued to insist that only Congress could bring baseball into the antitrust fold, and once again reaffirmed baseball's exemption. *Flood* stands as one of the Court's most embarrassing efforts, both for its stubborn adherence to a principle it had already undercut vis-à-vis other sports, and for the overall loopiness of the opinion, which reproduced F. P. Adams's verse "Tinker to Evers to Chance" and also featured an entire paragraph devoted only to listing several dozen great players.

Over the last quarter-century, the Court's pronouncements on professional sports and antitrust law have been more about substance than applicability. In *National Football League v. North American Soccer League,* 459 U.S. 1074 (1982), the Court let stand a lower court ruling invoking antitrust law to bar the NFL from enforcing its rule against owners having controlling interests in teams in other pro sports leagues, a decision that prompted a dissent from WILLIAM HUBBS REHNQUIST, who did not see antitrust problems in the "cross-ownership" rule. On the other hand, in *Brown v. Pro Football,* 518 U.S. 231 (1996), the Court declared that a "nonstatutory" antitrust exemption would apply when necessary to let the collective bargaining process function, thus shielding the NFL's wage scale for its "developmental squad," which was imposed after a labor impasse, from antitrust attack.

Professional sports have also found their way onto the Supreme Court's docket as vehicles for clarification of the Federal Rules of Civil Procedure (*National Hockey League v. Metropolitan Hockey Club,* 427 U.S. 639 [1976]), tax law (*United States v. Cleveland Indians Baseball Company,* 532 U.S. 200 [2001]), and the Americans with Disabilities Act (*PGA Tour v. Martin,* 532 U.S. 661 [2001]). In the latter case, the Court ordered the PGA Tour to allow Casey Martin, who suffered from a vascular disorder in his legs, to use a golf cart during tournaments, disregarding the

Tour's insistence that it could deem walking the course to be an integral part of the competition.

For more information: Snyder, Brad. *A Well-Paid Slave: Curt Flood's Fight for Free Agency in Professional Sports.* New York: Viking Adult Press, 2006; White, G. Edward. *Creating the National Pastime: Baseball Transforms Itself.* Princeton, N.J.: Princeton University Press, 1996.

—Steven B. Lichtman

prosecutorial discretion

Prosecutors possess great amounts of discretional authority—arguably more discretional authority than any other courtroom actor. The use of this discretion often raises constitutional issues, especially in terms of how it affects those accused of a crime.

Prosecutors possess discretion in many different ways. First, they possess discretion at the charging stage. They determine when to file a criminal charge, the degree of seriousness of those charges, and when to dismiss charges. Second, they have the discretional authority to enter into plea agreements—also known as "plea bargaining"—and to decide what consideration to give during these agreements. Third, prosecutors have the power to request capital sentencing within statutory considerations. Prosecutors have virtually unfettered discretion and ultimate power regarding the type(s) and frequency of charges and plea bargaining.

Throughout the last 30 years, the Supreme Court has slowly removed discretional authority from judges—the most recent instances being Supreme Court decisions in *Apprendi v. New Jersey,* 530 U.S. 466 (2000), *Blakely v. Washington,* 542 U.S. 296 (2004), and *UNITED STATES v. BOOKER,* 543 U.S. 220 (2005). Legislatures have had an interest in restricting judicial discretion in implementing SENTENCING GUIDELINES and statutory ranges to equalize sentences. However, as judges have experienced a restriction on their discretional authority, prosecutors have gained discretional authority. Since prosecutors possess the power to determine the type of charges to give to particular defendants, they can undercharge likable

defendants and overcharge unlikable defendants, ensuring that the unlikable defendants receive a harsher punishment. The real question, then, is: "Who is likable and who is unlikable in the eyes of the prosecutor?"

A major component of the prosecutorial discretionary power is placed in prosecutors' power to negotiate guilty pleas from defendants. When decision making is restricted, one's discretionary power is often displaced to someone else. In this situation, discretional authority of the judge is displaced to the prosecutor. Studies have indicated that, due to the restrictions created in sentencing guidelines, prosecutors have enforced their discretional authority by engaging in "hidden plea bargaining" to undermine the rigidity—and, ultimately, the uniformity—of the sentencing guidelines by enticing the defendant to engage in a plea agreement. Ninety-one percent of defendants plead guilty and, arguably, a majority of these pleas are a result of some type of plea negotiation. Researchers have determined that the implementation of sentencing guidelines has limited judicial discretion, and some would argue that the same could be concluded about prosecutorial discretion.

The restrictive nature of sentencing guidelines has actually increased prosecutorial discretion at the time of initial charging practices and charge bargaining. Because of the discretional authority of the prosecutor over the decision to decide the frequency and severity of charges—major determinants of sentencing—the key to sentencing may very well lie with the prosecutor, not the judge. Research indicates that there is less structure associated with prosecutorial discretion than with judicial discretion. Miehte and Moore (1988) also indicated that prosecutors possess the ability to manipulate not only the type of sentence but also the length of sentence through their discretionary charging and/or charge-bargaining decisions in sentencing-guideline states. Many scholars agree that the goal of obtaining equal justice is currently threatened by prosecutors, not judges, and the threat has increased as prosecutorial discretion has increased. Legal scholars such as Stuntz have indicated that, under a sentencing-guideline system, the prosecutor "is no longer the price taker but the price setter." Although sentencing guidelines were developed to limit discretion and unwarranted disparity, it seems that they actually empower prosecutorial discretion that can still lead to unwarranted disparity—a phenomenon that ought to be avoided with sentencing guidelines.

Under the new Supreme Court decisions (i.e., *Apprendi, Blakely,* and *Booker*), this power is increased to an even greater extent by limiting judicial discretion even further, requiring a jury to find facts beyond a reasonable doubt that might raise the sentence above the sentencing guideline range maximum. This discretion, therefore, is arguably displaced to the prosecutor, an agent with virtually unfettered discretionary power prior to the ruling in *Blakely.* Although discretion can be a very useful tool, discretion in the hands of agents who have free reign on their decision-making process can institute dangerous roadblocks to carrying out justice. Namely, unwarranted disparity—through individual discrimination or contextual discrimination—is a great possibility.

For more information: Albonetti, C. A. "Prosecutorial Discretion: The Effects of Uncertainty." *Law & Society Review* 21 (1987): 291–313; Albonetti, C. A., and J. R. Hepburn. "Prosecutorial Discretion to Defer Criminalization: The Effects of Defendant's Ascribed and Achieved Status Characteristics." *Journal of Quantitative Criminology* 12 (1996): 63–81; Spohn, C. *Thirty Years of Sentencing Reform: The Quest for a Racially Neutral Sentencing Process.* Washington, D.C.: National Institute of Justice, 2000; Tonry, M. *Sentencing Matters.* New York: Oxford University Press, 1996.

—Amanda Freeman and Jeremy D. Ball

Pruneyard Shopping Center v. Robins 447 U.S. 74 (1980)

In this decision, the United States Supreme Court ruled that the state of California could interpret its constitution to protect political protesters from being evicted from a shopping mall without running afoul of the property rights of the mall owner, including those rights protected under the TAKINGS CLAUSE of the Fifth Amendment to the United States Constitution.

Pruneyard permitted the states to carry forward a body of law that had been taken up, then abandoned, by the U.S. Supreme Court. In *Amalgamated Food Employees Union Local 590 v. Logan Valley Plaza, Inc.,* 391 U.S. 308 (1968), the U.S. Supreme Court ruled that shopping malls were the "functional equivalent" of a historical town square. Accordingly, vital FIRST AMENDMENT interests in preserving a vibrant political and public sphere, in the face of increasing replacement of public gathering spaces with private spaces, required that speakers be permitted to protest in those contexts. However, in *Lloyd Corp. v. Tanner,* 407 U.S. 551 (1972), the court de facto overruled *Logan,* leaving protesters in shopping malls and similar places with no guarantee of federal constitutional protection for their political speech.

In *Pruneyard,* the California court went beyond the federal rule and held that, under the California constitution, a shopping mall owner could not exclude citizens who engaged in political activity. Thereafter, several states, including Colorado (*Bock v. Westminster Mall Co.,* 819 P.2d 55 [1991]) and New Jersey (*New Jersey Coalition v. J.M.B.,* 138 N.J. 326, 650 A.2d 757 [1994]), adopted the California rule.

Other states, such as Massachusetts (*Batchelder v. Allied Stores Intl.,* 388 Mass. 83, 445 N.E.2d 590 [1983]), Oregon (*Lloyd Corporation v. Whiffen,* 315 Or. 500, 849 P.2d 446 [1993]), and Washington (*Southcenter Joint Venture v. Natnl. Dem. Policy Committee,* 113 Wash.2d 413, 780 P.2d 1282 [1989]), protect citizens gathering signatures for petitions (e.g., for referendum or recall campaigns) in shopping malls, but not speakers engaging in ordinary political speech. Massachusetts's reasoning is typical: The Massachusetts Supreme Judicial Court held that the free speech protection of the Massachusetts constitution is coextensive with that of the federal constitution. However, Massachusetts contains a separate provision guaranteeing the right to participate in direct democracy such as referenda, and that provision is broad enough to guarantee a right to solicit signatures in shopping malls. At least one state (*Western Penn. Socialist Workers 1982 Campaign v. Connecticut General Life Ins. Co.*, 515 A.2d 1331, 512 P.A. 23 [1984]) applies something like a "FAIRNESS DOCTRINE" to private landowners: If the landowner invites people to speak on one side of a political issue, opposing speakers are protected.

The *Pruneyard* doctrine is one of a handful of legal protections for speech interests against private economic interests. Other such protections include the Noerr-Pennington doctrine, which insulates political activists from certain business torts; the fair use doctrine, which privileges certain communicative uses of copyrighted and trademarked material; and the actual malice rule, which privileges speech about public figures from most DEFAMATION claims. *Pruneyard,* however, is particularly distinctive as a constitutional doctrine that requires private parties to surrender a portion of their traditionally sacrosanct private property rights.

Pruneyard represents a distinct analytic perspective on the relationship of political constitutional rights to private property rights. Its closest relative along that dimension is *SHELLEY V. KRAEMER*, 334 U.S. 1 (1948), which forbade the states from enforcing racially restrictive covenants in land, notwithstanding the private property rights of the landowners, because the state could not be a participant in racial discrimination. *Pruneyard* similarly subjects private property rights to constitutional checks, this time in the interest of preserving a vibrant political public sphere. Thus, it is likely to become increasingly important as more and more public sphere communication is carried out in spaces controlled by private economic interests, whether physically (as in shopping malls) or virtually (as on privately owned Internet servers, or using privately owned cultural artifacts such as trademarks).

Pruneyard's relatives are also becoming more important. For example, the Noerr-Pennington doctrine was originally developed in the context of antitrust law to protect businesses lobbying for advantageous government action. Now, solitary citizens and grassroots groups frequently use it to defend "SLAPP Suits" ("Strategic Lawsuits Against Public Participation"), which are brought by land developers and others in order to deter grassroots political opposition to their commercial projects.

For more information: Berger, Curtis. "Pruneyard Revisited: Political Activity on Private Lands." *New York University Law Review* 66, no. 633 (1991).

—Paul Gowder

public forum

The U.S. Supreme Court has declared that the free speech clause of the FIRST AMENDMENT to the U.S. Constitution includes a "public forum doctrine" that allows people to use public property for free speech activities.

The public forum doctrine has its origin in the historical fact that, before the existence of modern mass media, citizens would meet and engage in public discussion on the streets, sidewalks, and parklike areas of town squares. People would read the latest news posted on a wall or in a newspaper, share other news by word of mouth, and debate the issues involved in the news. According to the public forum doctrine, all government-owned (public owned) property can be divided into three types. First, a "traditional public forum" is government property that has historically been used for public gatherings and discussions. The Supreme Court regularly lists parks, streets, and sidewalks as public forums. Although the Court has never declared that those are the only types of government property that are traditional public forums, the Court has never declared that any other government property meets the definition of a traditional public forum. In other words, whether other types of property can be considered a traditional public forum is an open question.

The second type of government property is a "designated public forum." This occurs when government intentionally sets aside some type of government property for use as a public forum. For example, a bulletin board, a room, or an atrium might be designated for use by the public as a forum.

The third and final type of government property is all other government property; that is, property that is neither a traditional public forum nor a designated public forum is simply not a public forum. For example, office space in government buildings is not a public forum while in use by government workers; neither are courtrooms or legislative assemblies while in session, as well as public school classrooms during classtime. As another example, in the Court's most recent public forum case titled INTERNATIONAL SOCIETY FOR KRISHNA CONSCIOUSNESS (ISKCON) V. LEE, 505 U.S. 672 (1992), the Court declared that publicly owned airport terminals are not public forums.

Under the public forum doctrine, the type of speech regulations the First Amendment allows to regulate government property depend on whether the property is a traditional or designated public forum, or is not a public forum. If a speech regulation involves a traditional public forum, the government must show a "compelling" justification for any limits placed on free speech activities within that forum. Also, the government may not discriminate on the basis of the subject matter of the speech or the viewpoint of the speaker. As a practical matter, this means that few restrictions may be placed on speech in a traditional public forum, other than regulations to maintain public safety and order, known as "time, place, and manner" restrictions. For example, a person driving a car at 3:00 A.M. in a residential neighborhood using an electronic megaphone to ask people to support a particular presidential candidate is using a public street, but the government may nevertheless prohibit even political speech done in this manner and at this time and place.

If the government designates property to be used as a public forum, the government again must show a "compelling" reason for limiting free speech, and may enact time, place, and manner restrictions. In addition, the government may enact regulations to preserve the nature of the forum, even including limiting the subject matter of the speech if necessary, but government still may not discriminate against any single viewpoint among the topics it allows for discussion. For example, if government creates a bulletin board for use as a public forum, a regulation can restrict the size and number of flyers any one person or group may post, but may not prohibit only Democrats or only pro-environment groups from posting flyers. Or, if a public school district generally opens a classroom for meetings by after-school student groups, the school district may restrict the number of people that may be in the room according to the fire code, but the government may not prohibit only a religious group or only a GAY AND LESBIAN RIGHTS group from using the room.

However, if government sponsors a public debate on the death penalty, the government may prohibit a person from speaking who wants to discuss ABORTION and taxes, because that is not the designated purpose of the forum.

Finally, in government property that is not a public forum, the government can enact any restrictions on speech as long as those restrictions are "reasonable." Generally, this means that government acting as a property manager may restrict any speech activities that are incompatible with the government property functioning as its primary use. In other words, government has broad leeway to regulate property that is not a public forum for its intended use as something *other than* a forum for public discussion.

The Court's most recent description of the public forum doctrine in *ISKCON* has led many commentators as well as the dissenting justices in the *ISKCON* case to criticize the Court's narrowing of the definition of traditional public forums to seemingly include nothing other than parks, streets, and sidewalks. Critics argue that in a modern era where town squares are disappearing or do not serve as a primary meeting place for public discussion, other types of government property (such as airport terminals or government-leased shopping malls) must be recognized as "traditional" public forums to be used by people to directly confront a mass audience in person.

Otherwise, only those individuals or groups who can afford the use of the mass media will be able to communicate their ideas directly to a large audience, a concept that runs contrary to the basic purpose of the free speech clause: promoting robust public discourse. For this reason, several state supreme courts have interpreted the free speech provisions of their respective state constitutions as creating state public forum doctrines more protective of free speech than the federal public forum doctrine. For example, a few state supreme courts have decided that even some *privately owned* property within their states, such as large indoor shopping malls, are public forums to a limited degree.

For more information: Volokh, Eugene. *The First Amendment: Problems, Cases and Policy Arguments.* New York: Foundation Press, 2001.

—Rick A. Swanson

R

racial profiling

Racial profiling refers to the practice of stopping individuals or suspected criminals based upon their race or skin color.

Racial profiling involves the claim that police are detaining individuals in traffic enforcement simply because of their race or skin color. Oftentimes, the pretext for the stopping is the claim that the individual fits some profile of a person wanted for a crime, or individuals are stopped in their car on the basis that they have committed a minor traffic infraction.

The origins of profiling are rooted in four events. First, the practice of profiling goes back to the middle of the 20th century, when it was used to create sketches or psychological descriptions of individuals in a crime that had already been committed. In these cases, specialists did the profiling. Second, in the 1960s and 1970s, profiles were created to detect potential airplane hijackers (skyjackers) and then drug couriers. Third, the landmark case, *Terry v. Ohio,* 392 U.S. 1 (1968), which gave police the authority to STOP AND FRISK individuals, expanded the discretionary authority of law enforcement officials to approach individuals suspected of engaging in illegal activity. Finally, in cases such as *Whren v. United States,* 517 U.S. 806 (1996), the Supreme Court has given the police broad powers to stop, detain, and search individuals during routine traffic stops if they are suspected of engaging in illegal activity. According to the Court, so long as the police observe some illegal activity, such as speeding or a failure to signal a turn, they are permitted to stop and perhaps search individuals and their vehicles.

Evidence that racial profiling exists began to appear in the media in the middle to late 1990s when newspapers revealed that the New Jersey State Police were using racial profiles to stop and detain motorists. Since then, statistics gathered in other areas, such as New York City, Denver, Minneapolis and St. Paul, Minnesota, south Florida, and Maryland, as well as in other cities and states, demonstrate that people of color are disproportionately more likely to be stopped than are whites.

Those who point to profiling say that the issue raises important legal questions regarding racial discrimination. These issues may arise out of either the EQUAL PROTECTION or DUE PROCESS clauses of the FOURTEENTH AMENDMENT. In fact, racial profiling is sometimes referred to as "driving while black." The singling out of individuals based solely upon their race or skin color is unconstitutional. The statistics on who is stopped by the police are pointed to as evidence of either de jure or de facto discrimination or racial profiling.

Others deny that the statistics reveal discrimination, that these stops are not motivated by race but are simply a sign of aggressive policing and efforts to apprehend criminals. Police are thus stopping individuals on the basis of reasonable suspicion that a crime has been committed, or that the person stopped is a criminal. In fact, in *Brown v. City of Oneonta,* 195 F.3d 111 (2d Cir. 1999), a federal court ruled that in some cases race could be used as a reason to justify an investigatory stop.

While racial profiling has focused mostly on police stops, other statistics reveal that whites and people of color are treated very differently in the entire criminal justice system. For example, not only are people of color more likely to be stopped, they are also more likely to be detained longer, and searched. Statistics indicate that

Linda Sarsour, a social activist for the Arab American Association of New York, speaks to representatives from the FBI's Counter Terrorism Division's Joint Task Force and Immigration and Customs Enforcement in a discussion about post-9/11 relations on June 2, 2005, in New York City. *(Robert Nickelsberg/Getty)*

more than 70 percent of the searches produce no illegal substances. Overall, this means that the initial stopping of people of color makes it more likely that they will face additional interaction with the criminal justice process. All of these instances could be considered examples of racial profiling.

For example, whites are more likely to be offered BAIL than people of color. Whites are much less likely to receive prison than people of color, and whites are much less likely to be prosecuted—and more aggressively—for drug offenses than are people of color.

Prior to the terrorist attacks of 2001, racial profiling appeared to be under attack in the United States. However, since the events of 9/11, public opinion is mixed. There are indications that individuals who are Muslim or who look like they are from Arab countries are detained or discrimi-

nated against, especially when it comes to flying on airplanes.

Overall, racial profiling or racial disparities exist on several levels in the criminal justice system, raising questions regarding explanations and possible remedies for this different treatment.

For more information: Derbyshire, John. "In Defense of Racial Profiling: Where Is Our Common Sense?" *National Review* 53 (February 19, 2001); Heumann, Milton, and Lance Cassak. *Good Cop, Bad Cop: Racial Profiling and Competing Views of Justice.* New York: Peter Lang Publishing, 2003; N.A. "Civil Rights Commission Cites Improper Use of Racial Profiling by New York City Police." *Jet* 98, no. 4 (July 3, 2000): 4–5; Walker, Samuel, et al. *The Color of Justice: Race, Ethnicity, and Crime in America.* Belmont, Calif.: Wadsworth, 2000.

—David Schultz

racial quotas

Racial quotas are fixed numbers or percentages of a particular race or a select grouping of races that need to be present within either a student body or place of employment. In REGENTS OF THE UNIVERSITY OF CALIFORNIA V. BAKKE, 438 U.S. 265 (1978), the Supreme Court ruled that racial quotas used for the purposes of hiring or admissions decisions to schools violated the FOURTEENTH AMENDMENT.

Racial quotas were fashioned in an effort to implement AFFIRMATIVE ACTION programs in the 1960s and 1970s. The first mention of affirmative action was in Executive Order 10925 signed by President John F. Kennedy in 1961. At this time, it was not a program, but only a description of the type of outreach or recruiting action that needed to be taken to prevent EMPLOYMENT DISCRIMINATION based on race. What was created at that time was the Committee on Equal Employment Opportunity. This committee, which was created for the purpose of eliminating discrimination in hiring practices, was only the start of legislation supporting affirmative action. From 1961 to 2003, there have been a total of 19 acts, orders, or laws created supporting affirmative action.

The Office of Federal Contract Compliance began to gather data on the racial makeup of vendors in 1972 in order to ensure that federal contractors were complying with antidiscrimination laws. Out of these efforts to police compliance emerged quotas. One way to show nondiscrimination was to have hiring policies that recruited solely on the basis of race. Thus, hiring quotas were initiated. Eventually, schools began to consider race in admissions, with some setting up special admissions policies for people of color.

The case that has been a benchmark in how racial quotas should be addressed is the Bakke case. This case is Regents of the University of California v. Bakke, 438 U.S. 265 (1978). Allan Bakke had been rejected twice because he failed to meet the requirements set by the University of California medical school at the Davis campus. The admissions program used by the University of California was found to be operating as a racial quota. This program was considered to be in violation of the law, in that it took race into account in making admissions decisions. While this would seem to settle the issue of the use of racial quotas, it did not. For while the racial quotas that this university was using were considered in violation of the law, it did not consider all racial quotas to be illegal; the judgment of the Supreme Court stated that only "those racial classifications that would violate the EQUAL PROTECTION Clause if employed by a State or its agencies" are prohibited. Those uses, according to Justice LEWIS POWELL, would be when race alone is used as an admissions criterion. Race could be used as one of several criteria if the goal were to promote educational diversity. This decision was upheld further by the University of Michigan cases in 2003. There were two cases: GRATZ V. BOLLINGER, 539 U.S. 244 (2003), and GRUTTER V. BOLLINGER, 539 U.S. 306 (2003). The Gratz case dealt with the undergraduate program, the Grutter case with the graduate program. The law school (graduate) program was constitutional because it was a highly individualized, holistic review of each applicant's file, rather than a rigid formula. The undergraduate points scheme, by contrast, was a non-individualized, mechanical system and therefore not constitutionally acceptable because it looked more like a fixed racial quota system.

Finally, in Parents Involved in Community Schools v. Seattle Sch. Dist. No. 1, ___U.S.___ (2007), the use of race in school assignment and attendance plans was struck down as unconstitutional, in part because of the quota-like aspect to race when determining school compositions and attendance.

Overall, the Supreme Court has made it clear that the use of hard or fixed racial quotas is a violation of the equal protection clause, and it appears to be moving toward arguing that the Constitution does not permit any use of race, even for remedial purposes.

For more information: Schwartz, Bernard. *A History of the Supreme Court.* New York: Oxford University Press, 1993; Skrentny, John David. *The Ironies of Affirmative Action: Politics, Culture, and Justice in America.* Chicago: University of Chicago Press, 1996; Weiss, Robert J. *"We Want*

Jobs": A History of Affirmative Action. New York: Garland Publishing, 1997.

—Anne D. Reynolds

Rasul v. Bush 542 U.S. 466 (2004)

In *Rasul v. Bush,* the United States Supreme Court ruled that aliens being held in confinement at the American military base at Guantánamo Bay, Cuba, were entitled to have a federal court hear challenges to their detention under the federal HABEAS CORPUS statute. This decision represented an important limit upon the authority of the United States government to detain individuals captured as a result of the "war on terrorism" initiated by the president of the United States after the attacks on the United States on September 11, 2001.

On September 11, 2001, al-Qaeda terrorists hijacked four commercial airplanes and used them in several attacks against the United States. Subsequently, Congress authorized the president to use all "necessary and appropriate force" against any persons, organizations, and nations that aided or supported these acts of terrorism. The president then used this authorization to send troops to Afghanistan against al-Qaeda and the ruling Taliban regime that had supported them.

This military action led to the capture of approximately 640 non-Americans who were then relocated to the United States military base at Guantánamo Bay, Cuba, where they were being held indefinitely and without access to legal counsel or access to the federal courts. Among those detained, claiming innocence and wishing to be freed, were Shafiq Rasul and Fawzi Khalid Abdullah Fahad Al Odah, neither of whom were U.S. citizens.

Relatives of these two individuals filed actions in U.S. District Court for the DISTRICT OF COLUMBIA, challenging the detentions. First the federal district court and then the court of appeals for the District of Columbia dismissed the cases, claiming that the courts lacked jurisdiction to hear the challenges. In both of these cases, relatives of the detainees sought habeas corpus review. Habeas corpus is the constitutional right of individuals to

have a judge review the reasons why a person has been detained.

Habeas corpus is the legal means that individuals may use to challenge what they believe to be an illegal imprisonment by requesting that the person holding them explain to a judge the reasons for their confinement. Both ARTICLE I, Section 9, Clause 2 of the Constitution, as well as 28 United States Code section 2241, provide for habeas review. While the law is well established that American citizens being held in the United States are entitled to habeas corpus review, there seemed to be some uncertainty regarding whether noncitizens held at Guantánamo Bay enjoyed habeas review.

One issue is the status of Guantánamo Bay itself and whether it is sovereign territory of the United States. In 1934 Cuba granted the United States a lease to Guantánamo Bay so long as the base was being used. In turn, the United States recognized Cuba's sovereignty over Guantánamo Bay. Second, in *Johnson v. Eisentrager,* 339 U.S. 763 (1950), the Supreme Court had ruled that aliens detained outside the United States are not entitled to habeas review. Thus, President George W. Bush and his administration argued that they had legal authority to detain aliens at Guantánamo Bay, Cuba, indefinitely without granting them access to the courts to contest their confinement.

The United States Supreme Court granted certiorari to the relatives after they lost in the court of appeals. The Court, with Justice PAUL STEVENS writing the majority opinion, ruled 6-3 that the courts did have jurisdiction to hear the case and that the detainees did have a right to federal habeas review.

The Court first reviewed the history of federal habeas corpus law, noting how this right had significantly expanded since its original enactment in 1789. Justice Stevens noted that the Court had permitted habeas review in a wide variety of situations involving presidential detention of individuals, including those who were deemed enemy combatants. Second, Stevens examined the status and extent of the control the United States had over Guantánamo Bay. The Court found the control to be so pervasive that, while Guantánamo Bay was not sovereign territory of the United States, it was under its jurisdiction, and therefore the ruling in *Eisentrager* did not apply. This meant that habeas review was available to those at Guantánamo Bay, and all those detained there were entitled to challenge their detention.

Rasul v. Bush was an important decision. It was issued the same day as *HAMDI V. RUMSFELD*, 542 U.S. 507 (2004), which ruled that an American citizen could not be held indefinitely on American soil without a right to habeas review. Together, these cases placed significant limits upon the ability of the president and the government to detain individuals suspected of being terrorists. The cases represent a major affirmation of the right of citizens and noncitizens to challenge their confinement, even if they are suspected of being terrorists. Almost immediately after *Rasul* was decided, the United States government was forced to undertake procedures to permit the Guantánamo Bay detainees to bring habeas challenges to their confinement.

For more information: Adler, David Gray, and Robert George, eds. *The Constitution and the Conduct of American Foreign Policy.* Lawrence: University Press of Kansas, 1996; Henkin, Louis. *Foreign Affairs and the United States Constitution.* Oxford: Clarendon Press, 1996; Henkin, Louis. *Constitutionalism, Democracy, and Foreign Affairs.* New York: Columbia University Press, 1990.

—David Schultz

ratification of the Constitution

Ratification of the Constitution refers to the process whereby the original thirteen states approved the document written in 1787 in Philadelphia.

The CONSTITUTIONAL CONVENTION that met in Philadelphia in 1787 was called by the U.S. Congress to propose amendments to the Articles of Confederation. The convention reviewed proposals such as the NEW JERSEY PLAN, which would have essentially followed that congressional mandate. However, after long and considered deliberation, the delegates completed their work with a strong consensus for a new constitution that would serve as a new compact between the states and replace the Articles of Confederation. The Philadelphia Constitutional Convention submitted the new constitution to Congress in 1787, and Congress voted to forward it to the states for their consideration and ratification. The ratification debates that followed in each of the states were between the Federalists and the Anti-Federalists.

The Federalists supported the new constitution and wrote the *Federalist Papers,* under pseudonyms such as Publius, to articulate the need for and meaning of the new constitution. The newspapers in each of the states featured writers who debated the strengths and weaknesses of the Articles of Confederation and the 1787 constitution.

Among the controversies that were addressed in the ratification debates was the fact that the Articles of Confederation required unanimity to amend, whereas the Philadelphia Convention required only nine states to ratify. The Anti-Federalists vigorously objected in state after state as ratification was debated and voted upon. Though victorious in achieving a rejection vote in Rhode Island on more than one occasion, the Anti-Federalists witnessed ratification even in such hard-fought states as Virginia and New York. The Anti-Federalists provided crucial interpretive points throughout the debate, but the Federalists would ultimately prevail, and the present Constitution serves as an enduring legacy to their statesmanship.

The ratifications in several states were achieved with "conditions." For example, "conditional" approvals were included in Virginia (20) and in New York (31), and these conditions represented significant contributions of the Anti-Federalists to the ultimate design and interpretation of the Constitution. The deliberations and political compromises in the state ratification processes were significant as contributions that were part of the immediate amendments, proposed and passed by the first Congress under the new Constitution, that became known as the BILL OF RIGHTS.

On December 7, 1787, Delaware became the first state to ratify the new Constitution, with a unanimous vote in favor. Pennsylvania was second

RATIFICATION OF THE CONSTITUTION			
State	Date	Votes for	Votes against
Delaware	December 7, 1787	30	0
Pennsylvania	December 12, 1787	46	23
New Jersey	December 18, 1787	38	0
Connecticut	January 9, 1788	128	40
Georgia	February 2, 1788	26	0
Massachusetts	February 6, 1788	187	168
Maryland	April 28, 1788	63	11
South Carolina	May 23, 1788	149	73
New Hampshire	June 21, 1788	57	47
Virginia	June 25, 1788	89	79
New York	July 26, 1788	30	27
North Carolina	November 21, 1789	194	77
Rhode Island	May 29, 1790	34	32

to ratify on December 12, 1787, by a vote of 46 to 23, a vote scarcely indicative of the struggle that had taken place there. Two more states followed with unanimous votes: New Jersey ratified on December 19, 1787, and Georgia on February 2, 1788, and in between Connecticut ratified on January 9, 1788 (128 to 40). A fierce debate followed in Massachusetts, but on February 6, 1788, Massachusetts approved by a narrow margin of 187 to 168, but recommended that a bill of rights be added to protect the states from federal encroachment on individual liberties. Maryland ratified on April 28, 1788 (63 to 11) and South Carolina ratified on May 23, 1788 (149 to 73).

On June 21, 1788, New Hampshire became the ninth state to ratify, but, just as other states had done, New Hampshire suggested a bill of rights be added. By the terms outlined in the Constitution, nine states were sufficient for its establishment among the states so ratifying, but the Federalists realized the great importance of New York and Virginia, neither of which had ratified. The U.S. Congress passed a resolution on September 13, 1788, to put the new Constitution into operation. At that point, 11 states had ratified the Constitution, with North Carolina and Rhode Island remaining. North Carolina added its ratification on November 21, 1789 (194 to 77). Rhode Island ultimately ratified on May 29, 1790, with 34 (51.5 percent) in favor and 32 against.

The ratification process resulted in a broad national conversation about the nature of the Union, about the roles of national and state governments in our system of FEDERALISM, about what CIVIL LIBERTIES were most essential to protect, and about what restrictions should be placed upon government. The Federalist and Anti-Federalist papers that resulted from these debates over ratification have become classic expositions of American political theory and have significantly informed Supreme Court jurisprudence throughout the history of the Court.

For more information: Gillespie, Michael Allen, and Michael Lienesch, eds. *Ratifying the Constitution.* Lawrence: University of Kansas Press, 1989; Marbach, Joseph R., Ellis Katz, and Troy E. Smith, eds. *Federalism in America.* Westport, Conn.: Greenwood Publishing, 2005.

—Michael W. Hail

rational basis test

The rational basis test is one of the standards applied by the Supreme Court in determining the constitutionality of laws created by the elected branches of government. The rational basis test developed alongside the much higher standard of STRICT SCRUTINY and is applied to rights deemed to be less than fundamental. This differentiation between fundamental and non-FUNDAMENTAL RIGHTS has allowed the Supreme Court to pursue a two-tiered standard for the protection of rights.

In FOOTNOTE FOUR of the famous opinion in *United States v. Carolene Products* (304 U.S. 144 [1938]), Justice HARLAN FISKE STONE began the division of rights into those that are most protected and those to which a lower standard of scrutiny may be applied. In the second paragraph of that footnote, Justice Stone suggests that there is a difference between laws that restrict the most important freedoms and those that restrict less important, nonfundamental freedoms. While democracy could continue without the most vigorous protection of property rights, for instance, it could not long exist without freedom of speech or of the press because those rights are fundamental to the democratic enterprise.

Governmental action that impinges on these "fundamental" rights deserves far less judicial deference than legislation limiting the exercise of other, less important rights; such actions by the elected branches can more easily be struck down by the Supreme Court. This led, during the period of the WARREN COURT, to a two-tiered system for testing the constitutionality of laws passed by Congress or actions taken by the executive. Laws that limit the exercise of fundamental or "preferred" freedoms are subject to the highest standard and to strict scrutiny. Under strict scrutiny, the government must show that the law in question is tailored as narrowly and specifically as possible to accomplish its ends, that it is the least restrictive alternative capable of achieving those ends, and that the legal limitation of the right constitutes a "compelling state interest."

Laws that limit the exercise of nonpreferred or nonfundamental rights are judged on the basis of their reasonableness or rationality, subjected to only minimal scrutiny. If the law or regulation is reasonably related to a legitimate government purpose, then the law or regulation is normally presumed by the Supreme Court to be constitutional. Reasonableness represents a low standard for the government to meet and makes regulation of nonfundamental rights relatively easy.

Under the rational basis test, the Supreme Court is highly deferential to the elected branches of government, and legislation to which the rational basis test is applied is almost universally upheld. In only two instances since 1938 has the Supreme Court found irrational and ultimately struck down laws that sought to regulate economic activity. The first was in *Morey v. Dowd* (354 U.S. 459 [1957]) and the second was in *Allegheny Pittsburgh Coal Company v. County Commission* (488 U.S. 366 [1989]). These two cases represent the exceptions that effectively prove the rule that, when the rational basis test is applied, the Court will uphold the exercise of governmental power.

The rational basis test is most often applied in cases of economic regulation but it can also be used in some types of discrimination claims, including age discrimination, and some types of sex discrimination. It may also be applied in some cases that deal with laws regulating ABORTION.

For more information: O'Brien, David M. *Constitutional Law and Politics: Struggles for Power and Governmental Responsibility.* New York: W.W. Norton, 2005; Stephens, Otis H., and John M. Scheb II. *American Civil Liberties.* New York: West Publishing, 1999.

—David A. May

R.A.V. v. St. Paul 505 U.S. 377 (1992)

In *R.A.V v. St. Paul,* the Supreme Court struck down a city ordinance making it illegal to place an object "including . . . a burning cross or Nazi swastika" on public or private property that one reasonably knows will arouse "anger, alarm or resentment in others on the basis of race, color, creed, religion or gender."

Several teenagers were charged with burning a cross on the yard of an African-American family.

The trial judge invalidated the ordinance as overbroad and content-based, but the Minnesota Supreme Court reversed, arguing that the phrase "arouses anger, alarm, or resentment in others" could be limited to apply to "fighting words"—a category of speech that the Court held in CHAPLINSKY V. NEW HAMPSHIRE, 315 U.S. 568 (1942), was outside FIRST AMENDMENT protection. The Minnesota Supreme Court also recognized the city's compelling interest in "protecting the community against bias-motivated threats to public safety and order."

Writing for five justices, Justice ANTONIN GREGORY SCALIA held that the ordinance violated the First Amendment because it banned only that speech that offended "on the basis of race, color, creed, religion or gender." While the government can ban some types of speech—such as fighting words—no category of speech is "entirely invisible to the Constitution." Therefore, the government cannot single out speech for content-based reasons unrelated to the reason the speech was proscribable in the first place. For example, "the government may proscribe libel, but . . . not . . . only those libels critical of the government." However, the government may target the most severe forms of a given category of proscribable speech, or certain forms of speech—such as CHILD PORNOGRAPHY—that have secondary effects unrelated to the speech's content. In these circumstances "there is no realistic possibility that official suppression of ideas is afoot."

The ordinance did not fall into either of these exceptions. Instead, by targeting speech opposed to racial and religious tolerance, it allowed "one side of a debate to fight freestyle, while requiring the other to follow Marquis of Queensbury rules." Justice Scalia called CROSS BURNING "reprehensible" and agreed with the Minnesota Supreme Court about the importance of fighting bias crimes, but argued that an ordinance banning all fighting words would achieve the same goals.

There were three concurring opinions. Justice Byron White faulted the Court for applying content neutrality to speech outside the First Amendment and for creating a new category of "underinclusive" speech. However, he would have found the ordinance unconstitutional because "anger, alarm and resentment" amounted to hurt feelings, not fighting words. Justice Harry Blackmun echoed these concerns and accused the Court of yielding to the "temptation" of dabbling in the culture wars. Justice JOHN PAUL STEVENS, critical of both Justice Scalia and Justice White's adherence to "absolute principles," argued for a balancing approach, under which he would have found the ordinance constitutional (assuming it was not overbroad).

At the time, some commentators read *R.A.V.* as proof of the Court's absolutist rejection of HATE SPEECH laws. But *Virginia v. Black,* 538 U.S. 343 (2003), which upheld a law banning cross burning when done with an intent to intimidate, shows that the Court will sustain hate speech laws, provided they are content neutral.

For more information: Cleary, Edward J. *Beyond the Burning Cross: A Landmark Case of Race, Censorship and the First Amendment.* New York: Vintage, 1994.

—Robert A. Kahn

redistricting and reapportionment

The term "redistricting" denotes the process of changing political boundaries. Most commonly it is used to denote the drawing of new congressional or legislative election district boundaries within each U.S. state. "Reapportionment," on the other hand, denotes the process of allocating the 435 congressional seats among the 50 states. Though there is a difference in the meanings of the two terms, they are often used interchangeably.

Apportionment and congressional districting are closely related processes. Reapportionment occurs in every year ending in "1," the year after the decennial census. After seats have been reapportioned, each state determines the boundaries of congressional districts within the state—a process called redistricting. Both apportionment and districting serve the same purpose: adjusting the districts in response to the migrations and unequal growth of populations in various areas of the country, since the Constitution requires that each representative should represent approximately an equal number of people.

The Constitution directs that the representatives shall be apportioned among the several states "according to their respective Numbers," that is, proportionally. It does not state, however, how this proportionality is to be achieved. Over the past two centuries, Congress has used at least four different methods to apportion the seats among the states, and several others have been proposed. Each of the apportionment formulas has produced quite different results. Currently the Hill method, also known as the Hill-Huntington method, is used. It was proposed by University of Harvard mathematics professor Edward V. Huntington and statistician Joseph A. Hill.

During the first decades of the 20th century, migrations brought about huge inequalities in districts' populations. Congress, however—and many states—refused to redraw district boundaries. Voters in underrepresented districts often sought relief in courts as their voting strength was weaker than that of the voters in other districts. In COLE-GROVE V. GREEN, 328 U.S. 549 (1946), the Supreme Court held that redistricting cases were not within the Court's jurisdiction.

By the 1960s, differences among districts' populations swelled to larger than 1:100, but the courts followed *Colegrove* in holding that redistricting matters are nonjusticiable, meaning that the courts could not hear them. But in *Gomilion v. Lightfood,* 364 U.S. 339 (1960), the Supreme Court admitted for the first time that the redistricting plan could be a tool for discrimination on the basis of race. BAKER V. CARR, 369 U.S. 186 (1962), and *Gray v. Sanders,* 372 U.S. 368 (1963), finally overruled *Colegrove* and developed the "ONE PERSON, ONE VOTE" rule.

The principle of "one person, one vote" was followed in a series of Supreme Court cases. In these cases the principle was extended to all levels of government and was further defined. In *Wesberry v. Sanders,* 376 U.S. 1 (1964), the Court struck down the election of members of Congress from unequally populated districts. In REYNOLDS V. SIMS, 377 U.S. 533 (1964), the Court applied the EQUAL PROTECTION clause to invalidate

unequally weighted voting in state legislative elections; and in AVERY V. MIDLAND COUNTY, 390 U.S. 474 (1968), the principle of "one person, one vote" was extended to local elections.

Following these decisions, the Court defined different standards for congressional districts on the one hand and state and local election districts on the other. In state and local districting plans, population disparities under 10 percent generally require no justification from the state, and even an 89 percent deviation has been upheld for preserving county borders (see *Gaffney v. Cummings,* 412 U.S. 772 [1973], and *Brown v. Thompson,* 462 U.S. 835 [1983]). On the other hand, among congressional districts within a particular state, exact mathematical equality is required. This was confirmed in *Karcher v. Daggett,* 462 U.S. 725 (1983), when a deviation of less than 1 percent from population equality was not sustained due to the lack of a proof of a good-faith effort to achieve mathematically exact apportionment. In 2002, even a population discrepancy of as little as 19 people has been struck down following Supreme Court precedent (*Vieth v. Pennsylvania,* 195 F. Supp. 2d 672 [M.D. Pa. Apr 08, 2002], appeal dismissed by *Jubelirer v. Vieth,* 537 U.S. 801 [2002], and appeal dismissed by *Schweiker v. Vieth,* 537 U.S. 801 [2002]).

Some authors see this insistence on precise equality of district population as curious in light of the fact that distribution of 435 seats among the 50 states inevitably entails more than 70 percent deviations among districts of different states (see, for example, Baker, Gordon E., "Whatever Happened to the Reapportionment Revolution in the U.S.," in Grofman, Bernard, and Arend Lijphart, *Electoral Laws and Their Political Consequences* [New York: Agathon Press, 1986], 275–276).

The districts can be drawn in such a way that boundaries are manipulated for an unfair electoral advantage by a certain party, candidate, or racial, ethnic, or other group. Such manipulation is termed *gerrymandering.* Based on the type of group that is being advantaged or disadvantaged by the manipulation, one distinguishes between partisan, racial, or ethnic gerrymandering. In order to prevent gerrymandering, a number of rules and standards were developed on how districts should be drawn. Besides the equal population requirement, the standards include compactness, contiguity, respect to political subdivisions, racial fairness, partisan fairness, respect to ethnic, religious, and social interest groups, and more.

In 1965, Congress enacted the VOTING RIGHTS ACT (VRA), which prohibited election procedures that deny or dilute the RIGHT TO VOTE on account of race. The VRA inspired a flood of lawsuits challenging racially discriminatory election laws, including redistricting laws. The remedy most often sought was the creation of majority-minority districts (i.e., districts containing a voting majority of the racial minority group that brought the lawsuit). *Thornburg v. Gingles,* 478 U.S. 163 (1986), authorized the creation of such districts, but in the mid-1990s, decisions such as *SHAW V. RENO,* 509 U.S. 630 (1993), and *Bush v. Vera,* 517 U.S. 952 (1996), held that race may not be a "predominant" factor in the redistricting process.

In *Davis v. Bandemer* (478 U.S. 109 [1986]), the Supreme Court for the first time declared PARTISAN GERRYMANDERING justiciable. *Bandemer* created a standard for finding an unacceptable partisan gerrymander that was so difficult of application that no court in the United States had ever found a partisan gerrymander that violated the standard. Consequently, in *Vieth v. Jubelirer,* 541 U.S. 267 (2004), Justice ANTONIN GREGORY SCALIA, for a four-member plurality, wrote that the Court should declare all claims related to political (but not racial) gerrymandering nonjusticiable. Because no court had been able to find an appropriate remedy to political gerrymandering claims in the 18 years since the Court decided *Bandemer,* Scalia wrote that it was time to recognize that the solution simply did not exist.

Since the 1960s, researchers have been attracted by the idea of a so-called automated districting process. Such a process, composed of strict in-advance and legally prescribed rules, would be followed by either a computer system or by persons. There is no room for discretion in the drawing of districts. The idea is said to have been first introduced by Nobel Prize winner William

Vickrey (William Vickrey, "On the Prevention of Gerrymandering," *Political Science Quarterly* 76 [1961]: 105–110). Automated districting has often been proposed by academia but never yet used for real elections in the United States or elsewhere.

For more information: Balinski, Michael L., and H. Peyton Young. *Fair Representation: Meeting the Ideal of One Man, One Vote.* 2d ed. New Haven: Yale University Press, 2001; Hasen, Richard L. *The Supreme Court and Election Law: Judging Equality from* Baker v. Carr *to* Bush v. Gore. New York: New York University Press, 2003; Lowenstein, Daniel Hays, and Richard L. Hasen. *Election Law: Cases and Materials.* 3d ed. Durham, N.C.: Carolina Academic Press, 2004; Scher, Richard K., et al. *Voting Rights and Democracy: The Law and Politics of Districting.* Chicago: Nelson-Hall, 1997; Toplak, Jurij. *In Defense of Automated Districting: A Comparative Study of Redistricting Procedures and Gerrymandering Prevention Measures.* Boca Raton, Fla.: Dissertation.com, 2001.

—Jurij Toplak

Regents of the University of California v. Bakke 438 U.S. 265 (1978)

In *Regents of the University of California v. Bakke,* the U.S. Supreme Court confronted for the first time the issue of what constitutional standard should apply to so-called "affirmative action" racial classifications where the purpose is to remedy the effects of past racial discrimination, including substantial, chronic minority underrepresentation. In this case, while the Court ruled against the specific AFFIRMATIVE ACTION plan at issue, it upheld its use in education in order to promote diversity.

Allan Bakke was an applicant for admission to the medical school at the University of California at Davis. He was rejected in both 1973 and 1974 under the school's general admissions program when his "benchmark score" (consisting of interview ratings, overall grade point average, science courses grade point average, Medical College Admission Test [MCAT] scores, letters of recommendation, extracurricular activities, and other biographical data) was not sufficiently high compared to the scores of other applicants. However, under the school's special admissions program, an applicant that was considered "economically and/or educationally disadvantaged" and was a member of a minority group (defined as blacks, Chicanos, Asians, and American Indians) did not have to meet the grade-point cutoff imposed on applicants evaluated under the general admissions program and was not ranked against those applicants. Although many whites claimed disadvantaged status and applied under the special admissions program, none were admitted.

In both 1973 and 1974, Bakke was rejected while special applicants with scores significantly lower than his were admitted. He filed suit in state court, claiming, inter alia, that the special admissions program violated the EQUAL PROTECTION clause of the FOURTEENTH AMENDMENT. After the trial court found that the special admissions program operated as an unconstitutional RACIAL QUOTA, the California Supreme Court, applying a STRICT SCRUTINY standard, concluded that, while integrating the medical profession and increasing the number of doctors willing to serve minority communities was a compelling state interest, the special admissions program was not the least intrusive means of achieving these goals. The California Supreme Court found the program unconstitutional and ordered Bakke admitted.

In reviewing the California decision, the U.S. Supreme Court was unable to reach a consensus, or even a coherent majority opinion, on what constitutional standard should be applied in evaluating remedial, race-conscious state action. Justice LEWIS POWELL, announcing a plurality decision in which four of his fellow justices (WARREN BURGER, JOHN PAUL STEVENS, Stewart, and WILLIAM HUBBS REHNQUIST) agreed, upheld the California Supreme Court's judgment that the program was illegal and that Bakke had to be admitted. However, while the other four justices relied on statutory grounds for invalidating the program, Justice Powell found the program unconstitutional. Nevertheless, he envisioned that consideration of race in admissions decisions could be constitutionally permissible in some circumstances, and in this holding he was joined by Justices WILLIAM J. BRENNAN, JR., White, Marshall, and Blackmun. However, Justice Powell and his four brethren parted company on what the standard for determining this constitutionality would be.

Justice Powell adhered to the traditional strict scrutiny standard and held that racial and ethnic classifications are inherently suspect and must be justified by a compelling government interest, and there must be no less restrictive alternative available.

Justices Brennan, White, Marshall, and Blackmun, on the other hand, while confirming that strict scrutiny was the appropriate standard, concluded that in the case of remedial racial classifications, those classifications must "serve [only] important government objectives and . . . be substantially related to achievement of those objectives." Thus, while claiming to "define with precision the meaning of that inexact term, 'strict scrutiny,'" the justices actually championed use of the "intermediate scrutiny" standard used previously with gender-based classifications. Furthermore, they found that under this standard the Davis program, which responded to the historical underrepresentation of minorities in the medical profession (mostly attributable to past and present discrimination), was constitutional.

Ultimately, while a majority of justices could not agree on the proper standard for remedial race-conscious state action, they did agree that "a properly devised admissions program involving the competitive consideration of race and ethnic origin" could meet constitutional muster. In so holding, Justice Powell gave a nod to Harvard's admissions program, which had no quotas or two-track processes, but rather considered race or ethnic background as just one of many factors. As a consequence, universities around the country adopted similar programs, and it would be some 25 years until the next major Supreme Court pronouncement on the constitutionality of educational affirmative action, when the Court confronted the University of Michigan program in the *GRUTTER v. BOLLINGER*, 539 U.S. 306 (2003), case.

For more information: Anderson, Terry H. *The Pursuit of Fairness: A History of Affirmative Action.* New York: Oxford University Press, 2005.
—Virginia Mellema

regulatory taking

The concept of regulatory taking developed as an attempt to protect property rights under the Constitution more robustly by expanding interpretation of the Fifth Amendment TAKINGS CLAUSE. The central insight of the approach is that whenever the government regulates, the regulation affects the free use of property in some manner. Whenever a regulation negatively affects the value or use of private property, the government must provide compensation, just as it would to private property owners for the building of a road, under traditional EMINENT DOMAIN principles.

Generally the Supreme Court has required compensation for physical, or complete, takings, not for regulations that less substantially impinge upon private property rights. The doctrine thus potentially transforms takings jurisprudence from a mostly government, action-preferred approach, to one that protects private property rights absolutely at the expense of public goods. Indeed, many of the proponents of the idea see it as a way to substantially diminish the modern regulatory state through the takings clause. The leading legal scholar of this approach is Richard Epstein. Epstein argues that a law that interferes with property in any way invokes the takings clause, a concept known as "partial takings." This was viewed by many conservative and libertarian legal actors as a way to reenergize property rights jurisprudence in light of the Supreme Court's abandonment of property rights protection during the New Deal.

Advocates of regulatory taking point to Justice OLIVER WENDELL HOLMES's opinion in *Pennsylvania Coal Co. v. Mahon*, 260 U.S. 393 (1922), where Holmes declared that "if a regulation goes too far it will be recognized as a taking." But Holmes also recognized that some interference with private property was a necessary and inevitable consequence of legitimate regulation. Thus, Holmes was not calling for a radically new takings jurisprudence. The Supreme Court generally reflected the Holmes approach in *Penn Central Transportation Company v. City of New York*, 438 U.S. 104 (1978), where it favored a local historic preservation law over the right of the owners of Penn Station to develop the property, including the construction of a modern office tower over the station.

However, some justices on the Supreme Court were receptive to the new arguments, especially in the 1980s and 1990s. This approach reached its high point in the case of *Lucas v. South Carolina Coastal Council*, 505 U.S. 1003 (1992). A state regulation protecting coastlines from development prevented Lucas from building houses on his property. Writing for the majority, Justice ANTONIN GREGORY SCALIA, an advocate of using the takings clause to more robustly protect property rights, held the regulation to be a "total taking" that required compensation. In dissent, Justice JOHN PAUL STEVENS noted the departure from the Court's traditional deferential stance toward regulations that interfered with private property, noting the "elastic nature of property rights." Even Scalia, however, favored compensation only if the regulation resulted in the deprivation of "all economically beneficial use." More aggressive advocates of regulatory takings doctrine, like Epstein, would require compensation for less than full takings, and it was hoped that this decision would lead the Court in that direction. Indeed, conservative and libertarian public interest groups aggressively pursued a litigation strategy to strengthen the takings clause protection of property rights, a movement that has been referred to as the "Takings Project."

The Court ultimately backed away from this more aggressive approach, likely because of the potential implications for undermining the modern regulatory state. However, cases such as *Lucas* have given greater leverage to property owners in conflicts with government regulatory efforts, particularly in the area of ENVIRONMENTAL REGULATION.

For more information: Epstein, Richard. *Takings: Private Property and the Power of Eminent*

Domain. Cambridge, Mass.: Harvard University Press, 1985; Tushnet, Mark. *A Court Divided: The Rehnquist Court and the Future of Constitutional Law.* New York: W.W. Norton, 2005.

—Jason Pierceson

Rehnquist, Hubbs William (1924–2005)
Supreme Court justice

William Donald Rehnquist was born on October 1, 1924, in Milwaukee, Wisconsin. While a teenager, he changed his name to Hubbs, his grandmother's maiden name. In 1942 he attended Kenyon College and then joined the Army Air Force. His military service was at a number of stateside bases. In the summer of 1945 he was sent to North Africa as a meteorologist.

After the war, Rehnquist moved to California where he attended Stanford University on the G.I. Bill. He received a bachelor's degree from Stanford (1948) and a master's degree in political science (1950). He then attended Harvard University where he earned a master's degree in government. Returning to California to enter Stanford Law School, he graduated in the same class with future associate justice Sandra Day O'Connor. After graduating in 1952 he served as law clerk (1952–53) for Justice Robert H. Jackson. During this time he wrote a memorandum arguing against school DESEGREGATION, which was then being considered by the Court in BROWN V. BOARD OF EDUCATION (1954). His memorandum was entitled "A Random Thought on the Segregation Cases."

From 1953 until 1969 Rehnquist practiced law in Phoenix, Arizona, and was active in Republican Party politics. In 1964 he served as legal adviser to Barry Goldwater's presidential campaign. President RICHARD NIXON appointed Rehnquist an assistant attorney general in the Justice Department in 1969. He was nominated to the Supreme Court as an associate justice by Nixon on December 10, 1971, to fill one of two vacancies. He was quickly confirmed and took his seat on January 7, 1972, replacing JOHN MARSHALL HARLAN II.

Rehnquist was the most conservative of the Nixon appointees serving on the Burger Court.

He gave strict interpretations to the FOURTEENTH AMENDMENT and wide latitude to state power. He voted against the expansion of the school desegregation plans of the Justice Department. He was also opposed to legalizing ABORTION in *ROE V. WADE* (1973). Rehnquist's conservatism was expressed in many cases, such as *Trimble v. Gordon* (1977), where he commented on the EQUAL PROTECTION clause. He considered it a mere device in the hands of the Court for endless tinkering with the legislative judgments of the states. His dissents were to influence the conservative majorities that eventually gathered around him.

President Ronald Reagan nominated Rehnquist to succeed Chief Justice WARREN E. BURGER when the latter retired in 1986. Despite liberal opposition, Rehnquist was confirmed and became the 16th chief justice of the Supreme Court on September 26, 1986.

Chief Justice Rehnquist wrote many notable majority decisions, including *Hustler Magazine v. Falwell* (1988) and *BOY SCOUTS OF AMERICA V. DALE* (2000). In the former case the conservative justice upheld freedom of a press that was libelous against the leader of the very conservative religious body, the Moral Majority. In the latter case he sided with the right of an organization to set moral standards. In *DICKERSON V. UNITED STATES* (2000) he refused to overrule the *Miranda* decision because it was not statutory law for Congress to resolve. In *PLANNED PARENTHOOD V. CASEY* (1992) Rehnquist was able to reverse some of *Roe v. Wade* (1973). He also concurred in *BUSH V. GORE* (2000), setting the stage for George W. Bush to become president of the United States.

Rehnquist was an author of several important books on legal matters. These include *The Centennial Crisis: The Disputed Election of 1876* (2004); *All the Laws but One: Civil Liberties in Wartime* (1998); *Grand Inquests: The Historic Impeachments of Justice Samuel Chase and President Andrew Johnson* (1992); and *The Supreme Court: How It Was, How It Is* (1987). His writings were almost prophetic because he was to preside at the IMPEACHMENT trial of President William Jefferson Clinton. Since the beginning of the War on Terror following the terrorist attacks of September

11, 2001, his thoughts on censorship have been stimulating to many chafing under expanded powers to engage in intercepting communications.

In October of 2004 Rehnquist was diagnosed with anaplastic thyroid cancer, the rarest and most fatal of thyroid cancers. On Saturday, September 3, 2005, Chief Justice Rehnquist died in his home at the age of 80.

For more information: Cameron, Scott. *William H. Rehnquist: Chief Justice of the U.S. Supreme Court.* New York: Ferguson Publishing, 2005; Schwartz, Herman. *The Rehnquist Court: Judicial Activism on the Right.* New York: Hill and Wang, 2002; Yarborough, Tinsley E. *The Rehnquist Court and the Constitution.* New York: Oxford University Press, 2000.

—Andrew J. Waskey

Rehnquist Court (1986–2005)

The Rehnquist Court began on September 26, 1986, when WILLIAM HUBBS REHNQUIST was sworn in as the 16th chief justice of the U.S. Supreme Court. It ended with his death of thyroid cancer on September 3, 2005, in Washington, D.C.

Rehnquist was appointed chief justice by President Ronald Reagan to succeed Chief Justice WARREN E. BURGER when the latter retired in 1986. He had already served for 15 years (sworn in on January 7, 1972) as an associate justice appointed by President RICHARD M. NIXON to replace JOHN MARSHALL HARLAN II.

Serving at the beginning of the Rehnquist Court were justices appointed by President Dwight D. Eisenhower (WILLIAM J. BRENNAN, JR., 1956), President John F. Kennedy (Byron R. White, 1962), President Lyndon B. Johnson (Thurgood Marshall, 1967), President Richard Nixon (1972), President Ford (JOHN PAUL STEVENS, 1975), and President Ronald Reagan (SANDRA DAY O'CONNOR, 1981). Added to the Rehnquist Court almost immediately was ANTONIN GREGORY SCALIA (1986) to fill the vacancy left by Rehnquist as an associate justice.

LEWIS POWELL retired in 1987 and was replaced by ANTHONY M. KENNEDY in 1988 as a Reagan appointee. William J. Brennan, Jr., retired

in 1990 and was replaced by DAVID H. SOUTER, a George W. Bush appointee. Thurgood Marshall retired in 1991 and was replaced by CLARENCE THOMAS, also a Bush appointee. Byron R. White retired in 1993 and was replaced by Ruth Bader Ginsburg, while Harry A. Blackmun retired in 1994 and was replaced by STEPHEN G. BREYER. Both were appointed by President William Jefferson Clinton.

The Rehnquist Court, in the view of many observers, became more conservative as the more liberal justices were replaced with more conservative appointees. Two exceptions were Ginsburg and Breyer, both Clinton appointees. The degree of shift from liberal to conservative depends upon the view of each observer of the Court. In general, the more conservative members did seek, under the leadership of the chief justice, to undo many of the liberal interpretations of the Court since the New Deal.

Important to the conservative members of the Rehnquist Court was the idea of "strict" interpretation of the Constitution. He was opposed to the idea of the Constitution as a "living document," which he viewed as a license for judicial activism. He was eventually joined by Scalia and Thomas in developing the doctrine that the Court should follow the "original intent" of the framers of the Constitution.

Outstanding in the many cases decided by the court was its interpretation of the sovereign immunity of the states (ELEVENTH AMENDMENT) against suits by citizens from other states. In several cases the conservatives, led by Rehnquist, restricted federal agencies from compelling state governments to follow federal guidelines in a variety of areas such as the Americans with Disabilities Act. In 2002 a 5-4 decision recognized the right of South Carolina to refuse berthing spaces in its ports to gambling ships that would sail out to sea to permit the gambling that was forbidden on shore by the state. The liberal minority harshly dissented, saying the conservatives were destroying "progressive" decisions made since the 1930s.

The conservative majority was composed of Rehnquist, Scalia, Thomas, and the swing votes of O'Connor and Kennedy. However, the first three were joined on some issues by other justices. While the Rehnquist Court claimed to be adhering to the text of the Constitution, it also cited at times its "spirit."

On other issues the majority moved toward positions that favored using the death penalty, preventing reverse discrimination, restricting the CIVIL RIGHTS claims of homosexuals, and religious rights. It also used FEDERALISM to restrict the actions of Congress in efforts to restrain the states. It restricted the use of the FOURTEENTH AMENDMENT in a way not done by the Court since the Great Depression.

A major decision was the flag desecration case (TEXAS V. JOHNSON, 491 U.S. 397 [1989]). The decision was 5-4 but joining the liberals on the Court were Scalia and Kennedy. The decision pointed to the independence of the members of the Court on some issues such as freedom of speech.

Perhaps its most controversial decision was BUSH V. GORE (2000), settling the 2000 presidential election in favor of George W. Bush.

For more information: Bradley, Craig M., ed. *Rehnquist Legacy.* Cambridge: Cambridge University Press, 2006; Hensley, Thomas R., Kathleen Hale, and Carl Snook. *The Rehnquist Court: Justices, Rulings, and Legacy.* Santa Barbara, Calif.: ABC-CLIO, 2006; Hudson, David L. *Rehnquist Court: Understanding Its Impact and Legacy.* Westport, Conn.: Greenwood Publishing, 2006.

—Andrew J. Waskey

religious displays on public property

Religious expression is protected speech. Under the free speech clause of the FIRST AMENDMENT, religious expression, like other forms of free expression, may not be excluded from public fora if the reason for the exclusion is the content of the expression. This means that in some cases religious displays on public property may place the establishment and free speech clauses of the First Amendment in conflict, forcing the courts to reconcile conflicting constitutional demands.

If religious expression is protected speech, then efforts to ban religious displays on public property are content-based discrimination, subject to STRICT SCRUTINY. For example, in *Widmar v. Vincent,* 454 U.S. 263 (1981), the Supreme Court held that a university, having generally opened its facilities to expressive activity by students, could not exclude expressive religious activities based on the religious content of the expression. Religious or other expression may be excluded from nonpublic fora for reasons related to the content of the expression. However, the state may not exclude expression even from a nonpublic forum if the reason for the exclusion is the viewpoint of the expression.

In *LAMB'S CHAPEL V. CENTER MORICHES UNION FREE SCHOOL DIST.,* 508 U.S. 384 (1993), the Court struck down a policy permitting the use of school facilities after hours for social, civic, and recreational purposes, but barring the use of the facilities for religious purposes. The Court assumed without deciding that the policy did not create a PUBLIC FORUM, but held that the ban on religious use was impermissible viewpoint discrimination. For the same reason, in *GOOD NEWS CLUB V. MILFORD CENTRAL SCHOOL,* 533 U.S. 98 (2001), the Court struck down a policy that permitted religious use of school facilities but prohibited the use of the facilities for religious instruction.

Although religious expression in public is protected under the First Amendment's free speech clause, the First Amendment's ESTABLISHMENT CLAUSE arguably requires the exclusion of expressive religious displays from some public places. The establishment clause prohibits government endorsement of religion, or government acts that create the appearance of endorsement of religion. Justice SANDRA DAY O'CONNOR expounded upon that principle in a concurring opinion in *LYNCH V. DONNELLY,* 465 U.S. 668 (1984), in which the Court held that a city's annual Christmas display, which included a combination of secular figures and a crèche, did not violate the establishment clause. According to Justice O'Connor, the display was not unconstitutional because the display of the crèche did not have the purpose or effect of conveying a message of state endorsement of religion. In subsequent cases involving religious displays on public property, the Court has followed Justice

O'Connor's approach and focused on the purpose and effect of the challenged display. Where the Court has found that a reasonable, objective observer would view the display as communicating a message of state endorsement of religion, the Court has held the display unconstitutional; where the Court has found that the hypothetical observer would not view the display as an endorsement of religion, the Court has not held the display unconstitutional. For example, in *Allegheny County v. American Civil Liberties Union,* 492 U.S. 573 (1989), the Court upheld the display of a menorah next to a Christmas tree underneath a sign reading "Salute to Liberty." The Court emphasized that, in combination, the menorah, tree, and sign did not have the effect of endorsing religion. In the same case, however, the Court held unconstitutional another crèche display—this one unaccompanied by secular seasonal figures—because "nothing in the context of the display detract[ed] from the crèche's religious message."

An expressive religious display on public property potentially brings the free speech clause and the establishment clause into conflict. Arguably, the mere presence of a religious symbol on public property conveys a message of state endorsement of religion. If the display violates the establishment clause, and if the relevant public property is a public forum, excluding the display from the public forum because of the religious content of its message would be content-based discrimination against religious expression, impermissible under the free speech clause. And even if the property is not a public forum, excluding the display for reasons related to its content would be viewpoint discrimination—equally impermissible under the free speech clause.

However, the Court has held that the free speech clause forbids content-based discrimination against religious expression, and that the establishment clause does not necessarily require the exclusion of religious expression from public fora. In *Capitol Square Review Board v. Pinette,* 515 U.S. 753 (1995), the Court held that a city could not deny the Ku Klux Klan permission to erect a cross in a public square, and that the cross did not convey a message of state endorsement of religion.

For more information: Hitchcock, James. *The Odyssey of the Religion Clauses.* Vol. 1 of *The Supreme Court and Religion in American Life.* Princeton, N.J.: Princeton University Press, 2004; Witte, John. *Religion and the American Constitutional Experiment: Essential Rights and Liberties.* Boulder, Colo.: Westview Press, 2000.

—Nathan M. Ingebretson

Religious Freedom Restoration Act (1993)

The Religious Freedom Restoration Act was Congress's attempt to restore religious freedom to the way it was before the Supreme Court's narrow interpretation of the free exercise clause in *Employment Division, Department of Human Resources of Oregon v. Smith,* 494 U.S. 892 (1990).

The Constitution provides for freedom of religious expression in the FIRST AMENDMENT, where it says: "Congress shall make no law respecting an establishment of religion, or prohibiting the free exercise thereof." Since these and other words in the Constitution are vague, the Supreme Court has been given primary responsibility as the interpreter of the Constitution. But the Supreme Court did not get a chance to interpret the free exercise clause until 1878, when it decided in *Reynolds v. United States* (98 U.S. 145) that religious freedom extends only to religious conscience. Religious conduct, if in violation of a law, cannot be exempted by the free exercise clause. Since that time, the Court has had many opportunities to interpret the free exercise clause, and has extended exemptions on religious conduct to laws that are blatantly discriminatory to religion.

In 1963 the Court extended freedom of religious conduct further in *Sherbert v. Verner* (374 U.S. 398), in which the Court ruled that the government cannot infringe upon religious freedoms unless it has a "compelling interest" that infringes upon those freedoms in the "least restrictive means" possible. This means that many laws that are generally applicable to the public at large could unintentionally place a burden on the free exercise of religion.

In 1990, the Supreme Court ruled in *EMPLOYMENT DIVISION V. SMITH,* 494 U.S. 872, that laws of "general applicability" still apply to people whose religious conduct comes into conflict with such laws, a much narrower interpretation of the free exercise clause than before. The Court reasoned that, if they did not rule in this way, people could exempt themselves from all kinds of general laws for religious reasons and could become a law unto themselves, something that was intolerable in the Court's view. This ruling overturned almost 30 years of the compelling interest test.

A coalition of religious groups, other concerned citizens groups, and academics petitioned Congress to enact a law that would overturn *Smith.* The result was the Religious Freedom Restoration Act (RFRA), which was passed by both houses of Congress with little opposition. President Clinton signed the bill into law on November 16, 1993.

RFRA creates a right granted by the legislature to exemptions from government laws and regulations for conduct generated by religion. It states that "Government shall not substantially burden a person's exercise of religion." This right is invalidated only if government has a COMPELLING GOVERNMENTAL INTEREST and the government is using the "least restrictive means of furthering that compelling governmental interest."

RFRA generated concern among legal circles, some arguing that the law was an unconstitutional legislative incursion into the judicial system's domain as interpreter of the Constitution. They also reasoned that Congress had unconstitutionally applied RFRA to the states through Section 5 of the FOURTEENTH AMENDMENT. Some concerns have also been raised about the effect that RFRA has on the ESTABLISHMENT CLAUSE. The establishment clause prohibits government from favoring religion, and this law appears to favor religion because it protects only religiously motivated conduct and not other kinds of conduct.

In 1997, the Supreme Court in CITY OF BOERNE V. FLORES, 521 U.S. 507, ruled RFRA unconstitutional as it applies to the states because it goes beyond Congress's Section 5 powers. The act is still in force as it applies to federal law.

After the Court's unconstitutional declaration, Congress again attempted to pass religious freedom legislation with the Religious Liberty Protection Act, but this legislation failed to pass in the SENATE. In 2000, Congress passed the Religious Land Use and Institutional Persons Act, a law narrower in scope than RFRA, but an indication that Congress and the Supreme Court are still trying to battle over what the free exercise clause means and who has the authority under the Constitution to decide what it means.

For more information: Adamczyk, Amy, John Wybraniec, and Roger Finke. "Religious Regulation and the Courts: Documenting the Effects of Smith and RFRA." *Journal of the Church and State* 46, no. 2 (Spring 2004): 237–262; Gressman, Eugene, and Angela C. Carmella. "The RFRA Revision of the Free Exercise Clause." *Ohio State Law Journal* 57 (1996): 66–143; Idleman, Scott C. "Religious Freedom Restoration Act." *Encyclopedia of the American Constitution.* 2d ed. New York: Macmillan Reference, 2000; Laycock, Douglas, and Oliver S. Thomas. "Interpreting the Religious Freedom Restoration Act." *Texas Law Review* 73, no. 2 (December 1994): 209–245; Magarian, Gregory P. "How to Apply the Religious Freedom Restoration Act to Federal Law without Violating the Constitution." *Michigan Law Review* 99 (August 2001): 1,903–1,998.

—Dennis B. Miles

Republican Party of Minnesota v. White
536 U.S. 765 (2002)

The Supreme Court in *Republican Party of Minnesota v. White* held that a Minnesota prohibition on judicial candidates announcing their views on disputed legal and political issues during a campaign violated their FIRST AMENDMENT rights to freedom of speech. The holding invalidated similar provisions in eight other states and has left unclear the extent to which states can limit the speech of judicial candidates.

The Minnesota Code of Judicial Conduct included an "announce clause," which stated that a "candidate for judicial office, including an incumbent judge," shall not "announce his or her views on disputed legal or political issues." Gregory Wersal, a candidate in the 1998 election for associate justice of the Minnesota Supreme Court, challenged the restriction, claiming that it forced him to refrain from announcing his views on issues in violation of his First Amendment rights. The Republican Party of Minnesota joined the suit, asserting that the law prevented voters from learning the views of candidates to enable them to make decisions on whether to support candidates for judicial office. In a 5-4 opinion, the Court struck down the "announce clause" under the First Amendment.

Justice ANTONIN GREGORY SCALIA, writing for the majority, determined that the "announce clause" prohibited speech on the basis of the content of the message and burdened political speech, a category of speech "at the core of our First Amendment freedoms." The Court applied STRICT SCRUTINY, examining whether the clause was narrowly tailored to serve a COMPELLING GOVERNMENTAL INTEREST. The state respondents had argued that the clause furthered the state's compelling interest in judicial impartiality. The Court, however, held that, depending on how impartiality was interpreted, the clause was either not narrowly tailored to serve the objective or impartiality was not a compelling state interest.

First, the "announce clause" was not narrowly tailored to serve the interest of impartiality, understood as ensuring the lack of bias by judges for or against a party to the proceeding, because "it does not restrict speech for or against parties, instead it restricts speech for or against particular issues." Second, an understanding of impartiality as a "lack of preconception in favor of or against a particular legal view" was not a compelling state interest. Justice Scalia explained that it is impossible to find a judicial candidate that does not have any preconceptions about the law, and even if it were possible, it would be undesirable for such a judge to be selected because this likely evidenced a lack of qualifications for the job. Third, Justice Scalia determined that the Minnesota Supreme Court did not intend for the "announce" clause to achieve impartiality understood as open-mindedness, the willingness of a judge "to consider views that oppose his preconceptions, and remain open to persuasion, when the issues arise in a pending case." Justice Scalia explained that the objective of impartiality as open-mindedness is implausible because judges often have committed themselves on legal issues that they must later rule upon.

The dissents of Justice JOHN PAUL STEVENS and Justice Ginsburg identified two flaws in the majority opinion. First, the majority failed to recognize the importance of judicial independence and impartiality. Second, the majority failed to distinguish the election of judges from other policy-making officials. The dissenters explained that in the American democratic system, the objective of legislative and executive officials is to be popular, while the function of judges is "to be indifferent to unpopularity." The dissenters contended "[j]udges are not politicians and the First Amendment does not require that they be treated as politicians simply because they are chosen by popular vote." Instead, to the extent that judicial candidates seek to enhance their popularity by campaigning for particular popular issues, it "evidence[s] a lack of fitness for the office."

The decision in *White* has required all 39 states with judicial elections to reexamine their judicial code to ensure that there are sufficient safeguards for the First Amendment rights of judicial candidates while maintaining protections for the states' interests in judicial impartiality.

For more information: Caulfield, Rachel P. "In the Wake of *White*: How States Are Responding to *Republican Party of Minnesota v. White* and How Judicial Elections Are Changing." *Akron Law Review* 38 (2005): 625–647; Ifill, Sherrilyn A. "Through the Lens of Diversity: The Fight for Judicial Elections after *Republican Party of Minnesota v. White*." *Michigan Journal of Race and Law* 10, no. 55 (2004): 84–85; Morrison, Alan B. "The Judge Has No Robes, Keeping the Electorate in the Dark about What Judges Think about the Issues." *Indiana Law Review* 36, (2003): 719, 739.
—Bertrall Ross

Republicanism

The concept of a republican form of government is guaranteed to all the states in Article IV, Section 4 of the Constitution. However, what this type of government requires is unclear because the federal courts have refused to hear suits on this matter.

In the United States, republicanism denotes limited government in the form of representative democracy. Citizens elect representatives who govern on their behalf, but within the constraints of the rule of law. Republican governments have nonhereditary leadership for fixed terms, are dependent upon the will of the people, and aim at promoting the collective public interest.

American (modern) republicanism is a modification of classical republicanism. Originally, republicanism was simply opposed to hereditary monarchies and tyrannies. Increasingly it came to mean a commitment to popular self-government. Popular self-government, if it is to be just, requires devotion by the citizens to the common good of the whole polity. Therefore, classical republicanism was demanding of the citizenry, requiring individual self-interest to be subordinated to the public interest. This entailed a state that was small (to eliminate anonymity and to make feasible collective decision making), homogenous (to produce a genuine common good), and committed to the cultivation of civic excellence in its citizens. As a result, classical republicanism required a strict rearing and education in virtue, in the form of prudence in deliberation, martial courage for the defense of the state, moderation, and justice. The early Roman Republic is a good example of classical republicanism.

The chief aim of American republicanism is to secure the fundamental natural rights of citizens. Human beings are deemed to be fundamentally free, equal, and independent (JOHN LOCKE, *Second Treatise*, section 95). As a result, governments are formed by consent, for the sole purpose of protecting people's inalienable rights, including the rights to life, liberty, and the pursuit of happiness (DECLARATION OF INDEPENDENCE). Consequently, the rights of citizens come before their duties. Rather than aiming at cultivating virtue in the citizenry, modern republicanism aims at achieving security and liberty, in which citizens pursue their individual conceptions of their private

good. In modern republicanism, then, civic virtue is instrumental to this aim, helping to secure the conditions that make the individual pursuit of happiness possible.

Avoiding exclusive reliance upon the virtue of the citizenry, the American framers of the Constitution devised a republic in which formal constitutional provisions and institutional arrangements would be the primary means of achieving security, liberty, and the public interest. These include a written constitution, the election of representatives, an extended republic, the separation of powers, a system of CHECKS AND BALANCES among institutions and offices, together with explicit protections of the rights of the people and a guarantee of republican government in all the states.

In *The Federalist*, Publius distinguishes a republic from a pure democracy. A pure democracy is "a society consisting of a small number of citizens, who assemble and administer the government in person," whereas a republic is "a government in which the scheme of representation takes place" (No. 10). Pure democracy is, in principle, an unlimited form of government. The will of the majority is supreme and thus can violate the interest and the good of any of its citizens in the minority. American republicanism is distinctive in its concern about such majority faction or tyranny of the majority. The Constitution's framers used primarily two mechanisms to limit injustice toward minorities in democratic decision making. First, they constructed a system of representation in which the people elect representatives who will "refine and enlarge the public views, by passing them through the medium of a chosen body of citizens, whose wisdom may best discern the true interest of their country, and whose patriotism and love of justice will be least likely to sacrifice it to temporary or partial considerations" (No. 10). Second, they enlarged the size of the republic, thereby increasing the number of factions and making it unlikely that any one faction or temporary alliance of factions would dominate contrary to the public interest.

Additionally, the separation of all political power into legislative, executive, and judicial branches of government ensures that power will not be concentrated in any one institution or office that could become tyrannical. Similarly, each branch of government is granted some overlapping powers. This creates a system of checks and balances that enables each branch both to protect itself from the encroachments of other branches and to protect the public interest from bad laws and poor administration. Other explicit constitutional protections uphold the equal rights of all citizens, such as the absolute prohibition on TITLES OF NOBILITY and the guarantees to writs of HABEAS CORPUS, to no ex post facto laws, to trial by a jury of one's peers, as well as the provisions in the BILL OF RIGHTS.

Finally, Article 4, Section 4 of the Constitution, which is known as the GUARANTEE CLAUSE, provides that "[t]he United States shall guarantee to every State in this Union a Republican form of Government." This provision has been invoked primarily in the admission of new states into the Union and during Reconstruction after the Civil War. It has not been the subject of extensive judicial scrutiny, as the Supreme Court has consistently ruled that the guarantee is a political rather than a judicial responsibility (*LUTHER V. BORDEN*, 48 U.S. 1 [1849]). The Court therefore has refused jurisdiction and assigned responsibility to Congress to determine if a state government is republican in character.

For more information: Kurland, Philip B., and Ralph Lerner, eds. *The Founders' Constitution.* Chicago: University of Chicago Press, 1987; Mansfield, Harvey C., Jr. *America's Constitutional Soul.* Baltimore, Md.: Johns Hopkins University Press, 1987.

—Stephen J. Lange

revenue bill

A revenue bill is an essential part of legislating, as it ostensibly funds most congressional activities. In order for the military to defend this country; bureaucrats to run necessary programs such as Social Security, Medicare, or Medicaid; and law enforcement officials to maintain peace within this country, money is required. Without these bills that determine revenue levels, congressional actions would be quite limited, since government programs could not function. Given their importance, these bills must originate in the HOUSE OF REPRESENTATIVES.

The origin of the revenue bill can be found in Article I, Section 7 of the U.S. Constitution. Here, the House of Representatives alone is given the explicit jurisdiction over revenue bills. However, revenue bills in this sense refer only to increases in existing forms of revenue, not the creation of new sources of revenue. The House was given responsibility over revenue bills for multiple reasons. In their continuous attempts to enshrine CHECKS AND BALANCES, the Founding Fathers saw this arrangement as a way to prevent an excessive concentration of power. Specifically, the control of revenue bills sought to limit the power held by the other branches, since they were unable to generate their own revenue independent of the House of Representatives. Also, because they were held accountable to the electorate, House members were given control over revenue bills. Because the Founding Fathers thought revenue bills were vitally important, they also felt that those responsible for these bills should be directly accountable to voters. While the SENATE cannot initiate a revenue bill, it does retain the power to either concur with or propose amendments to revenue bills. In the event that the Senate's amendments conflict with those of the House, a conference committee can be formed to resolve these differences.

Within the House of Representatives, the Ways and Means Committee (a standing committee in the House) is in charge of revenue bills. When discussing revenue bills, the House of Representatives is considering whether or not to increase existing levels of revenue. In other words, they consider increases in: individual or corporate, excise, estate, or other types of taxes. The Ways and Means Committee also has jurisdiction over payroll taxes, which are an especially important form of income for the House. Without these funds, essential government programs would be unable to function. Historically, these taxes have not always been the primary source of revenue;

years ago, tariffs comprised a much larger proportion of Congress's annual revenue than they do today. Although the House is solely responsible for revenue bills, the Senate can amend these bills. And, though the Senate cannot create revenue bills, senators are not powerless when it comes to the "powers of the purse." The committee primarily responsible for amending revenue considerations in the Senate is the Finance Committee. Each chamber's appropriations committee is also involved in this process. Senators can generate new sources of revenue—but they cannot increase extant revenue sources. Like numerous other issues, this discussion of the Senate's authority in revenue matters has been controversial, as evidenced by the number of court cases addressing this division of labor.

Revenue bills are possibly the most important form of legislation the House can produce. Without these bills, and the funds they provide, countless essential government programs could not perform the everyday functions that deliver services to millions of Americans.

For more information: Schick, Allen, and Felix LoStracco. *The Federal Budget: Politics, Process, Policy.* Washington, D.C.: Brookings Institution Press, 2000; Wildavsky, Aaron B., and Naomi Caiden. *The New Politics of the Budgetary Process.* New York: Longman, 2001.

—Joseph W. Robbins

Reynolds v. Sims 377 U.S. 533 (1964)

In *Reynolds v. Sims* the Supreme Court declared that an apportionment scheme that failed to allocate seats on the basis of the ONE PERSON, ONE VOTE standard violated the EQUAL PROTECTION clause of the FOURTEENTH AMENDMENT. This decision was an important precedent and the impetus for states redrawing political subdivisions to give equal representation.

The 1901 Alabama state constitution apportioned representation in the state legislature on the basis of equal numbers of representatives and senators per county. In the early 1960s, the Alabama legislature proposed to remedy the malapportionment that had occurred as a result of the unequal population growth of the state's counties. The U.S. Supreme Court reviewed this case on the grounds that such malapportionment violated the equal protection clause of the Fourteenth Amendment. The Court followed the decision set in *BAKER V. CARR*, 369 U.S. 186 (1962), that such a review of state legislative institutions does not present a political question. By stating that apportionment in the Alabama case should be based on population, the Court did not rule out the ability of the states to develop their own apportionment plans. Chief Justice Warren's opinion implies that when malapportionment results in "invidious discrimination," apportionment based on population is most equitable. The Court also noted that the federal legislature is unique in light of the historical background of the United States and is not a model for the states.

Representation in the Alabama legislature, pursuant to the 1901 constitution, was to consist of 106 representatives and 35 senators for the state's counties and senatorial districts. Counties were to have at least one representative and each county was to have one senator. The 1901 constitution also provided that the state reapportion the legislature decennially. However, this legislative apportionment plan was problematic due to the uneven growth of counties and the failure to reapportion decennially. The population of urban counties grew while the population of rural counties did not, leading to a situation where political representation was concentrated in rural counties. For example, "Bullock County, with a population of only 13,462, and Henry County, with a population of 15,286 each were allocated two seats in the Alabama House, whereas, Mobile County, with a population of 314,301, was given only three seats, and Jefferson County, with 634,864 people, had only seven representatives. Jefferson County with over 600,000 people, was given only one senator, as was Lowndes County, with a 1960 population of only 15,417, and Wilcox County, with only 18,739 people (208 F. Supp., at 450)."

Reapportionment plans to remedy the unequal representation between rural and urban counties were presented in the early 1960s. The Alabama legislature proposed a constitutional amendment called the 67-Senator Amendment, which did not differ much from the existing apportionment plan. The other reapportionment plan, called the Crawford Webb Act, was adopted by the legislature and signed by the governor. The Crawford Webb Act was designed as a backup to the 67-Senator Amendment, should voters not approve the constitutional amendment. The Crawford Webb Act apportioned the state House by giving each county one seat and apportioning the remaining seats on a population basis. Senate apportionment would remain one seat per county. The district court held that the Alabama legislature violated the equal protection clause of the Fourteenth Amendment by finding that the 67-Senator Amendment and the Crawford Webb Act did not provide an effective remedy to the existing malapportionment. The district court stated, "We find each of the legislative acts, when considered as a whole, is so obviously discriminatory, arbitrary and irrational that it becomes unnecessary to pursue a detailed development of the relevant factors of the [federal constitutional] test (208 F. Supp., at 437)." However, the district court allowed the apportionment plan of the 67-Senator Amendment and Crawford Webb Act to be used in the 1962 general elections as a temporary measure.

The U.S. Supreme Court ruled that representation of House and Senate in the states' BICAMERAL LEGISLATUREs must be apportioned by population as a requirement of the equal protection clause of the Fourteenth Amendment. The Court stated, "An individual's RIGHT TO VOTE for state legislators is unconstitutionally impaired when its weight is in a substantial fashion diluted when compared with votes of citizens living in other parts of the State" (*Reynolds* 377 U.S., at 568). As a result of the Court's decision in this case, most of the states developed reapportionment plans based on population. However, the Court did not determine a specific method of reapportionment, resulting in many states arbitrarily redrawing their legislative districts.

For more information: Hasen, Richard. *The Supreme Court and Election Law: Judging Equal-*

ity from Baker v. Carr *to* Bush v. Gore. New York: New York University, 2003.

—J. David Granger

Rice v. Cayetano 528 U.S. 495 (2000)

In *Rice v. Cayetano,* the Supreme Court ruled that limiting the RIGHT TO VOTE in elections for trustees of the Office of Hawaiian Affairs (OHA) violates the FIFTEENTH AMENDMENT. The significance of the *Rice* decision is that it threatens all programs and institutions that afford preferential treatment for Hawaiians and Native Hawaiians.

In 1996, Harold "Freddy" Rice, a rancher residing on the big island of Hawaii, applied for an OHA election ballot. Because he was unable to prove his legal status as a Hawaiian or Native Hawaiian, his application was denied. Subsequently, Rice filed suit in the U.S. District Court in Hawaii, asserting that the denial of his right to vote in the OHA election violated the Fourteenth and Fifteenth Amendments, which guarantee EQUAL PROTECTION under the law and voting rights irrespective of race. The state responded with three defenses to the voting restriction. First, the state argued that OHA is analogous to an American Indian tribe. As such, it is a quasi-sovereign entity and therefore entitled to limit participation in its governance to those of Hawaiian ancestry. Second, the state contended that the FOURTEENTH AMENDMENT does not apply in the case of special-purpose districts. OHA serves as a special-purpose district in its capacity as manager of a ceded land trust that benefits Hawaiians and Native Hawaiians, so it is not a violation of the Fourteenth Amendment to limit who is able to vote in its elections. Finally, the inclusion of Hawaiian and Native Hawaiian voters only is based on their beneficiary status and not on race, as only those defined by law as Hawaiian or Native Hawaiian may benefit from the trust.

Both the U.S. District Court and the Ninth Circuit ruled against Rice. In the district court opinion, Judge David Ezra upheld the voting restriction, asserting its validity on the basis of the unique status of Hawaiians and Native Hawaiians as OHA's only direct beneficiaries. The Ninth Circuit upheld Ezra's ruling, finding that the OHA voting restriction was legal and political rather than racial, arising from the unique history of the Hawaiian people.

Rice appealed the decision to the U.S. Supreme Court, which decided that the OHA voting restriction was indeed unconstitutional and reversed the decision of the lower courts. In his opinion, Justice ANTHONY M. KENNEDY, writing for Chief Justice WILLIAM HUBBS REHNQUIST and Justices SANDRA DAY O'CONNOR, ANTONIN GREGORY SCALIA, and CLARENCE THOMAS, stated that the OHA election is a state election; therefore, the state does not have the right to create a voting scheme that limits voting rights to one group of people. Furthermore, the argument—that limiting voting to Hawaiians and Native Hawaiians affiliates the interests of the trustees with those of the beneficiaries—was refuted on the grounds that no one group of people is more qualified than another to vote on specific matters. Justice STEPHEN G. BREYER filed a concurring opinion; Justices JOHN PAUL STEVENS and Ginsburg filed separate dissenting opinions.

For more information: Klarman, Michael. *From Jim Crow to Civil Rights.* Oxford: Oxford University Press, 2004.

—Cheryl Crozier Garcia

right against self-incrimination

The right against self-incrimination is found in the Fifth Amendment of the Constitution, which states that a person cannot be ". . . compelled in any criminal case to be a witness against himself." "Its roots go back to ancient times," the Supreme Court stated in *MIRANDA V. ARIZONA* (1996), finding historical antecedents in the Bible and in the aftermath of Great Britain's Star Chamber proceedings in the mid-1600s.

While the language of the Fifth Amendment has not changed, its scope has. The Supreme Court began outlining the parameters of the right in the 1807 case, *United States v. Burr, In re Willie.* Aaron Burr was charged with TREASON. The government sought to put Burr's clerk on the stand before the grand jury to verify Burr's handwriting on a document. The witness refused, invoking his Fifth Amendment right against self-incrimination. Chief Justice JOHN MARSHALL, sitting in the District of Virginia Circuit Court, wrote that compelling the clerk's testimony would violate his Fifth Amendment right against self-incrimination. "[T]he court ought never to compel a witness to give an answer which discloses a fact that would form a necessary and essential part of a crime which is punishable by the laws."

The right is not, however, all encompassing. In the late 1800s, the Court decided the right did not protect one called to testify under a statute where the statute provided immunity for such testimony. "In view of the constitutional provision, a statutory enactment, to be valid, must afford absolute immunity against future prosecutions for the offence to which the question relates." If there is no danger of self-incrimination, there is no need for the protection. But it did extend beyond criminal trials to grand jury proceedings. The Court stated, "The privilege is limited to criminal matters, but it is as broad as the mischief against which it seeks to guard."

As the 1900s progressed, the Court continued to expound on the jurisprudence of the right. It decided self-incrimination issues regarding corporations (a corporate agent could not claim the privilege so as to not incriminate his corporation, since the privilege is personal), the language required (a defendant before the House Un-American Activities Committee did not need to use specific language to invoke the privilege), and admission of evidence (a defendant who was required to testify in state court under a grant of immunity on a check-kiting charge could not invoke the privilege to prevent the evidence from being used against him on a federal mail fraud charge).

The 1960s brought about even more changes regarding this right. The Court expanded the right, and the language in the opinions reflected this view. In different opinions, the Court wrote, "[The right against self-incrimination] reflects many of our fundamental values and most noble aspirations," and the protections guaranteed by the Fifth Amendment right reflect "the concern of our society for the right of each individual to be let alone."

As this decade progressed, the Court tried to articulate exactly what the right should provide. The Court enunciated the "totality of the circumstances" test at one point. It was used when there was no warning given against self-incrimination and placed the burden on the state to prove the defendant voluntarily and intelligently waived his right. In 1964, the Court, in *Malloy v. Hogan*, held the constitutional right against self-incrimination was applicable to the states via the FOURTEENTH AMENDMENT's DUE PROCESS clause. The quintessential self-incrimination decision followed soon thereafter.

Miranda v. Arizona radically expanded the scope of the privilege. From the Fifth Amendment language of no person "shall be compelled in any criminal case to be a witness against himself, a 5-4 majority held that the right against self-incrimination included the following rights: (1) the defendant has the RIGHT TO REMAIN SILENT, (2) anything the defendant says can be used against him or her, (3) the defendant has the right to an attorney, and (4) if the defendant cannot afford an attorney, one will be provided.

In reaction to the decision in *Miranda*, Congress enacted legislation making statements admissible if they were voluntarily given. This law was tantamount to reinstating the "totality of the circumstances test" used prior to *Miranda*. But was this law valid? If *Miranda* announced a constitutional decision, changing the law would require a constitutional amendment. If *Miranda* was simply the Supreme Court exercising its right to supervise the procedures of the lower courts, the law would be valid.

The language in *Miranda* seemed to announce a constitutional decision. The Court stated it wanted to "give concrete constitutional guidelines for law enforcement agencies and courts to follow," and the confessions obtained in *Miranda* "did not meet constitutional standards for protection of the privilege." Subsequent decisions obscured the answer. For instance, the Court at times called the *Miranda* rights "prophylactic," "not themselves rights protected by the Constitution," and "safeguards [that] are not constitutional in character."

This question was finally answered in 2000. In *DICKERSON V. UNITED STATES* the Court held *Miranda* was a constitutional decision, largely because the Court reversed a state court decision. "Federal courts hold no supervisory authority over state judicial proceedings and may intervene only to correct wrongs of constitutional dimension," stated the opinion. Therefore, it had to be constitutional in nature. The concept of stare decisis, a doctrine where courts defer to previous decisions, also played a role. "Whether or not we would agree with Miranda's reasoning and its resulting rule, were we addressing the issue in the first instance, the principles of *stare decisis* weigh heavily against overruling it now," the Court wrote.

The limits of the right may be clearer now, but there are still conflicts. For instance, there are splits amongst the circuit courts over such issues as whether the government can use as evidence a defendant's silence post-arrest but pre-*Miranda* warnings and whether a defendant must be told during interrogation he has a RIGHT TO COUNSEL. The right continues to develop. As Chief Justice Warren stated in *Miranda*, "Thus we may view the historical development of the privilege as one which groped for the proper scope of governmental power over the citizen."

For more information: LaFave, Wayne R., Jerold H. Israel, and Nancy J. King. *Criminal Procedure*. 4th ed. New York: West Publishing, 2004; Weaver, Russell L., Leslie W. Abramson, John M. Burkoff, and Catherine Hancock. *Principles of Criminal Procedure*. New York: West Publishing, 2004.

—Rob DeWees

right to a speedy and public trial

The right to a speedy trial is a provision within the SIXTH AMENDMENT pertaining to all criminal prosecutions, whereby the defendant has the right to demand a trial within a short time. This right is protected, as to be held in jail without trial is a violation of the DUE PROCESS provision of the Fifth Amendment, and protected also by the due process clause of the FOURTEENTH AMEND-

MENT. Each state has a statute or constitutional provision limiting the time an accused person may be held before trial (e.g., usually 45 days). If the period expires without a trial, charges against the defendant must be dismissed and the defendant released. However, defendants often waive the right to a speedy trial in order to have time for their lawyers to prepare a stronger defense, and if the accused is free on BAIL he or she will not be hurt by the waiver of this right.

Originally, the right to a speedy trial can be seen to be derived from a provision of the MAGNA CARTA that was later incorporated into the VIRGINIA DECLARATION OF RIGHTS of 1776 and then into the Sixth Amendment of the U.S. Constitution. The right to a speedy trial is only one of the provisions of the Sixth Amendment (the other provisions being: the right to a public trial; the right to a trial by jury; the right to be informed about the nature and cause of the accusation; the CONFRONTATION CLAUSE, whereby the defense in the case must have the opportunity to "confront" and cross-examine witnesses; and the right of defendants to procure the assistance of counsel or to represent themselves).

The Supreme Court of the United States further ensured the protection of this particular provision of the Sixth Amendment when it laid down a four-point test for determining whether or not a defendant's right to a speedy trial had been violated or not, with its (the Court's) ruling in the case of *Barker v. Wingo* [407 U.S. 514 (1972)]. In this particular case, the Supreme Court determined not only a four-point test, but also that future decisions of whether a defendant's right to a speedy trial had been violated were to be on a case-by-case basis.

Unlike the other provisions of the Sixth Amendment, the right to a speedy trial is related to the rights of and infliction of harms to both defendants and society. The provision is meant to serve as a safeguard on three different points: firstly, against undue and/or oppressive incarceration prior to trial; secondly, against lengthy delays in a trial that would impair the ability of the accused to defend himself; and thirdly, to ensure that the concern and anxiety associated with public accusations are

minimized (in case proven false). Point two (limiting delay of a trial) is especially important, as lengthy delays could mean the loss of witnesses through death or other reasons, as well as the loss of reliable witness memories—thereby hindering both prosecution and defense in the case.

A speedy trial, aside from providing protection of the rights of the accused, also ensures that justice and societal interest are maintained. This is because of the public expense of lengthy trials, as well as the fact that, in many cases, long delays and backlogs within the criminal justice system mean that persons let free can jump bail and are then lost to the system. What also sometimes occurs is plea bargaining for a reduction in charges and sentences in order to move the case along through the system; this does not guarantee or provide society with justice, nor does this plea bargaining serve as a future deterrent for further criminal activities by the accused.

The use of this provision by a defendant does not need to wait for indictment or any formal charge, but can begin from the time of arrest if this precedes formal charges. In order to prevent any possible prejudice that can result from delays between evidence gathering and the institution of proceedings, there is usually in place a statute of limitations to outline and monitor what are permissible periods of delay, thus protecting the rights of the accused under the speedy-trial provision.

It was in *Barker v. Wingo* (1972) that the Court decided that decisions of this nature were to be strictly on a case-by-case basis and also devised the four-point test for determining whether a violation had occurred.

One of the main factors identified by the Court in its decision, setting the way for its four-point test, was the length of any delay. The Court, in its judgment, felt that a delay of a year or more from the date on which a right to a speedy trial "begins" (this being the date of arrest or indictment, whichever occurs first) could prejudice a case against a defendant. Despite this observation by the Court, it has never explicitly outlined any absolute time limit to be applied, but has left this to a case-by-case basis. The other three factors identified by the Court are also related to any delay, as with looking at the reason for the delay (so as not to disadvantage the defense when the prosecution asks for a delay of the trial for its own advantage; however, a delay can be made to secure absent witnesses or for other practical considerations). The final factors the Court considered important in deciding whether a defendant's right to a speedy trial had been violated were: the time and manner in which a defendant has asserted his/her right and the degree of prejudice any delay has caused to the defendant.

In cases where the reviewing court finds that a defendant's right to a speedy trial was violated (under any part of the four-point test), the Supreme Court has adopted an ad hoc approach to balance the rights of the accused with justice for the public. In its outline of the four-point test, the Court recognizes that these four points are merely some of the factors that courts should take into account in their determination as to whether a defendant has been deprived of his right to a speedy trial under the Sixth Amendment. The Court has also pointed out that a failure of the defendant to demand the right to a speedy trial cannot be construed as a waiver of this right, but any acquiescence to a delay on the defendant's part, when it works to his/her advantage, should and can be used against any later assertion that she has been denied this right. Overall, in determining whether a violation has occurred, the Court recommends that courts should also look to the possible prejudices and disadvantages suffered by a defendant during any delay.

In such cases where a violation has been deemed to have occurred, the Supreme Court has held that in these instances the only appropriate remedy would be for the indictment to be dismissed and/or the conviction to be overturned. After the reversal or dismissal of a criminal case on the grounds that there has been a violation of a defendant's right to a speedy trial, no further prosecution for the alleged offense can take place again.

For more information: Ellard, Patrick. "Learning from Katrina: Emphasizing the Right to a Speedy Trial to Protect Constitutional Guarantees in Disasters." *American Criminal Law Review* 44, no. 3 (2004): 1,207–1,238; Freedman, Warren. *The Constitutional Right to a Speedy and Fair Criminal Trial*. Westport, Conn.: Quorum Books/ Greenwood Publishing Group, 1989; Herman, Susan N. *The Right to a Speedy and Public Trial: A Reference Guide to the United States Constitution*. 3d ed. Westport, Conn.: Praeger, 2006; Misner, Robert L. *Speedy Trial: Federal and State Practice*. Contemporary litigation series. Charlottesville, Va.: Michie, 1983.

—Dale Mineshima-Lowe

right to bear arms (Second Amendment) (1791)

The Second Amendment of the Constitution, part of the BILL OF RIGHTS, establishes the right to keep and bear arms. Scholars disagree over whom the right applies to and exactly what it means.

The amendment reads: "A well regulated militia, being necessary to the security of a free state, the right of the people to keep and bear arms, shall not be infringed." Because its meaning is strongly contested, the Second Amendment continues to be one of the most controversial parts of the Constitution. Controversy stems from attempts to interpret the meaning of each of the clauses, to understand the original INTENT OF THE FRAMERS, and to interpret the contemporary relevance of the amendment in the context of changes in the nature of the militia, the increasing deadliness of firearms, and fierce debates over firearms in U.S. society. While two broad approaches—the collective rights perspective and the individual rights perspective—have dominated interpretations of the Second Amendment, newer approaches have recently emerged.

According to the collective rights interpretation, the Second Amendment confers a collective right to bear arms in a governmentally organized, "well regulated militia," not an individual right to personal ownership. Emphasizing the first two clauses of the amendment, advocates of this position argue that the founders were not arguing over the individual right to own and carry arms but were concerned with giving states the right

Columbine High School teacher Patty Nielson speaks at a Senate policy committee hearing on gun safety legislation, as Senator Tom Daschle looks on, May 15, 2000, in Washington, D.C. *(Smith/Newsmakers)*

to have organized militias as a counterbalance to federal power. Supporters of the collective rights interpretation stress that the Second Amendment, however interpreted, does not preclude gun regulation. Up until the 1970s, the majority of law review articles tended to support this approach, as have the courts.

The individual rights interpretation, emphasizing the last clause of the amendment, argues that the Second Amendment establishes a constitutionally protected right for individuals to own and bear arms. Advocates of this approach sometimes refer to it as the "standard model," emulating the standard model in physics and apparently trying to put their interpretation beyond disputation. This is now the dominant interpretation of the Second Amendment in terms of the number of law review articles. Many supporters of this perspective acknowledge that reasonable restrictions may be imposed on gun ownership. This approach received powerful support in 2001 when then Attorney General John Ashcroft endorsed it in a letter to the National Rifle Association. The Justice Department subsequently reversed its longstanding collective rights interpretation of the meaning of the Second Amendment in two briefs to the U.S. Supreme Court.

Four Supreme Court decisions, as well as numerous lower court decisions, touching most directly on the Second Amendment have all supported the collective rights interpretation. Three of the Supreme Court cases dealing with Second Amendment issues date to the 19th century: *United States v. Cruikshank,* 92 U.S. 542 (1876); *Presser v. Illinois,* 16 U.S. 252 (1886); and *Miller v. Texas,* 153 U.S. 535 (1894). Advocates of collective and individual rights interpretations have both claimed support for their position in the only 20th-century decision, *United States v. Miller* (1939). In that case, the Court ruled that a sawed-off shotgun has no utility as a firearm in a militia, thus supporting the view that the amendment referred to militias rather than individuals. Some legal scholars expect the Court to take up a Second Amendment case in the near future.

More recent interpretations have attempted to reconcile differences between collective and individual interpretations. Constitutional scholar Akhil Reed Amar has offered a "republican" reading of the Second Amendment. He argues that collective, or states rights, interpreters fail to give enough weight to the Founders' equation of the militia with much of the adult, white male citizenry, while he faults individual rights advocates for ignoring that this was a right of all the "people," rather than persons, and of failing to note that the phrase *bear Arms* has a military meaning and does not refer to individual gun ownership for activities such as hunting or protection. Amar suggests that the FOURTEENTH AMENDMENT (1868) freed the Second Amendment from its connection to the militia and established it as an individual right. Disagreeing with Amar, Uviller and Merkel argue that while the Second Amendment originally referred to an individual right to bear arms in an organized, governmentally sponsored militia, they suggest that the amendment "fell silent" with the decay of the old militia and its eventual displacement by the National Guard. Thus, they argue that the conditions under which the Second Amendment made sense no longer exist and that the amendment is now irrelevant, although they acknowledge that it could become relevant again under changing circumstances.

The Supreme Court finally resolved this debate between individualist or a collective reading of the Second Amendment in *District of Columbia v. Heller,* ___ U.S. ___ (2008). In that case, Justice ANTONIN GREGORY SCALIA wrote for a 5-4 majority holding that the right to bear arms conferred an individual right. How that decision will affect gun laws is critical.

Moreover, the Second Amendment has never been incorporated through the Fourteenth Amendment to be binding on individual states. This means that states are free to regulate, if not ban, guns if they so wish.

For more information: Amar, Akhil Reed. *For the People: What the Constitution Really Says about Your Rights.* New York: Free Press, 1998; Malcolm, Joyce Lee. *To Keep and Bear Arms: The Origins of an Anglo-American Right.* Cambridge, Mass.: Harvard University Press, 1994; Uviller, H. Richard, and William G. Merkel. *The Militia and the Right to Arms, or, How the Second Amendment Fell Silent.* Durham, N.C.: Duke University Press, 2002.

—Walter F. Carroll

right to counsel

The SIXTH AMENDMENT to the U.S. Constitution guarantees anyone accused of a crime the right to "the Assistance of Counsel for his defense." The JUDICIARY ACT OF 1789 confirmed this guarantee in statute law, giving all parties in federal court the right to "manage and plead" their cases with the assistance of counsel. Another federal statute, enacted in 1790, authorized federal judges to appoint counsel for indigent defendants in capital cases, and there is evidence that federal judges also did so in some noncapital cases. Not until *Johnson v. Zerbst,* 304 U.S. 458 (1938), did the Supreme Court require counsel to be provided to all indigent federal defendants, stating: "The Sixth Amendment withholds from federal courts, in all criminal proceedings, the power and authority to deprive an accused of his life or liberty unless he has or waives the assistance of counsel."

While many state constitutions contained language similar to the Sixth Amendment, state interpretations varied. Some states adopted statutes requiring courts to provide counsel in at least some criminal cases, while others did not. The FOURTEENTH AMENDMENT, ratified in 1868, required states to provide DUE PROCESS of law in criminal prosecutions but did not specify what that meant. The Supreme Court did not consider the right to counsel in state courts until *Powell v. Alabama,* 287 U.S. 45 (1932), a capital case also known as the "Scottsboro Boys" case. Justice Sutherland, writing for the majority, concluded that "the right to the aid of counsel" was a fundamental aspect of due process: "The right to be heard would be, in many cases, of little avail if it did not comprehend the right to be heard by counsel." In *BETTS v. BRADY,* 316 U.S. 455 (1942), a closely divided Supreme Court declined to extend this principle to all state criminal cases, ruling that the state was required to provide counsel in noncapital cases only when "special circumstances" made the appointment of counsel necessary for a fair trial.

The landmark decision of *GIDEON V. WAINWRIGHT,* 372 U.S. 335 (1963), rejected this approach. The Supreme Court unanimously held that states must provide counsel to all indigents facing serious charges: "The right of one charged with crime to counsel may not be deemed fundamental and essential to fair trials in some countries, but it is in ours." Later cases applied this principle to misdemeanor cases (*Argersinger v. Hamlin,* 407 U.S. 25 [1972]), but only where the actual punishment included incarceration, either directly (*Scott v. Illinois,* 440 U.S. 367 [1979]) or as part of a suspended sentence (*ALABAMA V. SHELTON,* 535 U.S. 654 [2002]). In 1967 the right to counsel was also extended to most juvenile court proceedings (*IN RE GAULT,* 387 U.S. 1). On the same day that *Gideon* was decided, the Supreme Court extended the right to counsel to the initial appeal, basing its decision on the Fourteenth Amendment's EQUAL PROTECTION clause as well as the due process clause. The Supreme Court has declined to extend this right to other appeals, although some states provide additional legal assistance to indigent appellants.

In 1970 the Supreme Court began to address the issue of effective counsel, noting in *McMann v. Richardson,* 397 U.S. 759, that "it has long been recognized that the right to counsel is the right to effective assistance of counsel." But the standard announced in *Strickland v. Washington,* 466 U.S. 668 (1984), changed little. To be considered ineffective, a lawyer's performance must be so unreasonably deficient that it "undermines the proper functioning of the adversarial process." As late as 2000, a federal appellate court found that even though a defendant's lawyer slept through "substantial portions" of his capital murder trial, proof that this prejudiced the trial's outcome was also required for an ineffective assistance of counsel claim (*Burdine v. Johnson,* 231 F.3d 950 [5th Cir. 2000]). In recent years the Supreme Court has looked more closely at ineffective counsel claims, particularly in capital cases. In *Wiggins v. Smith,* 539 U.S. 510 (2003), counsel's failure to investigate and present mitigating evidence in the sentencing phase was held to be ineffective assistance of counsel. In *Rompilla v. Beard,* 545 U.S. 374 (2005), a divided Supreme Court ruled that counsel's failure to obtain and review prosecutorial materials also constituted ineffective assistance of counsel.

Justice Sutherland noted in *Powell v. Alabama* (1932) that the pretrial period includes the most critical stages of the prosecution, and that defendants are "as much entitled to such aid [of counsel] during that period as at the trial itself." As early as 1959 (in *Spano v. New York,* 360 U.S. 315), four of the nine Supreme Court justices agreed that interrogating a defendant in the absence of his lawyer was a denial of his right to counsel. The Supreme Court adopted this view in *Miranda v. Arizona,* 384 U.S. 436 (1966), but based its decision primarily on the Fifth Amendment RIGHT AGAINST SELF-INCRIMINATION rather than the Sixth Amendment right to counsel.

The Supreme Court soon expanded the right to counsel to other nontrial settings, including the preliminary hearing, the arraignment, lineups occurring after charges had been brought, plea bargaining, and sentencing. During such "critical stages," where "substantial rights" of an accused might be affected, due process required that the "guiding hand of counsel" be available. In *United States v. Wade,* 388 U.S. 218 (1967), a case dealing with the right to counsel during lineups, Justice WILLIAM J. BRENNAN, JR., wrote: "It is central to that principle [right to counsel] that in addition to counsel's presence at trial, the accused is guaranteed that he need not stand alone against the State at any stage of the prosecution, formal or informal, in court or out, where counsel's absence might derogate from the accused's right to a fair trial."

Even so, the right to have counsel provided by the state does not extend to all stages where a person with resources may choose to have counsel present. In cases decided primarily in the 1970s, the Supreme Court has ruled that noncustodial investigative questioning, lineups that precede a formal charge, initial BAIL hearings, and most parole hearings are not "critical stages."

For more information: Baker, Liva. *Miranda: Crime, Law and Politics.* New York: Antheneum, 1983; Bright, Stephen W. "Turning Celebrated Principles into Reality." *The Champion* (January/February 2003): 6–18. Available online. URL: http://www.schr.org/indigentdefense/champion02.htm. Accessed May 14, 2008; Carter, Dan T. *Scottsboro: A Tragedy of the American South.* Rev. ed. Baton Rouge: Louisiana State University Press, 1979; Lewis, Anthony. *Gideon's Trumpet.* New York: Random House/Vintage, 1966.

—Barbara J. Hayler

right to die

The debate over the right to die is part of the Supreme Court's struggle to define liberty and the right to PRIVACY. While the Court has not held that a right to die exists, it recognizes a liberty interest in control over our bodily integrity and the administration of medicine. The problem is complicated by those who are incapable of acting on their own behalf and those who wish to accelerate death.

The contemporary debate over a constitutional right to die is part of a long-standing discussion over euthanasia. Euthanasia is the purposeful and often dignified act of ending a human life. It is differentiated from suicide by the role of a medical practitioner in relieving a person from suffering brought on by debilitating disease or late-stage terminal illness. In modern times euthanasia is accomplished through minimally disruptive means such as the ingestion of powerful barbiturates. Although the Supreme Court has ruled that the Constitution includes a right to refuse or withhold medical treatment, it does not extend to euthanasia.

Euthanasia is morally and politically controversial. The policy debate involves many nuances as revealed in emerging terminology. Active euthanasia is where the physician administers the lethal drug. Passive euthanasia typically involves medical cooperation with a hospitalized patient's wish to have life-sustaining treatment withdrawn at some point—a matter increasingly addressed by living wills. Physician-assisted suicide is where a patient self-administers a lethal potion while being medically attended. The term *mercy killing* increasingly connotes incomplete consent, possibly because of mental disability, to allow for assisted suicide. Euthanasia can take two forms. Passive euthanasia involves the withholding of medicine, including nutrition. Active euthanasia involves administering drugs to hasten death. The situations arise when life is unbearable or unrecognizable to the patient. This may be due to complete incompetence—including loss of brain function—or a terminal illness.

In many of these instances, advocates have worked to change state laws to allow for doctors' assistance in ending life. Dr. Jack Kevorkian challenged the legal prohibitions to assisted suicide and helped people end their lives. Opponents of euthanasia raise several concerns. Some are religious—only God can take a life. Others make a similar argument but focus on the biology; if the heart beats and the patient can breathe—even though through a machine—the patient lives. These groups debate life defined by its quality versus life defined by its existence or defined by forces transcending the individual. In political terms, the pro-euthanasia followers favor the autonomy of the individual to control her bodily integrity,

while the latter group looks to society (and the government) to create conditions that favor and foster continuing life, sometimes referred to as a "culture of life."

Constitutional controversies follow from two aspects of this debate. The first involves the removal of various life support systems. This issue is settled if the person is able to state a preference or has stated one in an ironclad way. The Supreme Court recognizes, as an aspect of liberty found in the DUE PROCESS clause, a long-standing common law right to refuse medical treatment. Forced feeding and ventilation are considered medical treatment. If the person cannot exercise that choice, how then should that decision be made? An incompetent patient is assigned a guardian—usually a close family member such as a spouse or parent—who acts on his behalf. He may also have left instructions while competent. Other acquaintances may be able to speak to those wishes. States have required that evidence of these previous beliefs be clear and compelling. That is a demanding legal standard. Those states choose to make biological life the default position even if it means opposing the apparent wishes of the patient.

The Court first confronted these issues in CRUZAN V. DIRECTOR, MISSOURI DEPARTMENT OF HEALTH, 497 U.S. 261 (1990). Nancy Cruzan, a healthy 25-year-old woman, suffered severe brain damage as a result of a car accident. She slipped into a persistent vegetative state; after it was clear that she would not regain her mental faculties, her parents, acting as her guardian, asked the hospital to withdraw her feeding tube. The hospital staff refused. The state of Missouri allowed for the removal of medical support only under conditions where there was clear and convincing evidence that the patient had expressed a desire for this. The state courts ruled that Nancy had not made such a declaration clearly and convincingly.

In this case, the U.S. Supreme Court reiterated the due process liberty right to refuse medical treatment but refused to bring it under the umbrella of privacy rights. This leaves the right to die as implied (but not stated) and strongest in the case of a competent person who chooses to refuse medication. But this case involved a mentally incompetent person, and the Court ruled that the state law requiring clear and convincing evidence of her previous views was reasonable. Consequently, the Court left it to the states to determine the mechanism of how the liberty interest is exercised in the case of an incapacitated/incompetent patient. This set the stage for Terri Schiavo. In this gruesome case, Ms. Schiavo collapsed in 1990 and fell into a persistent vegetative state. Her parents challenged her husband's right to be her legal guardian. Several times a court ordered Ms. Schiavo's feeding tube to be removed, and the order was either stayed or reversed at the behest of her parents. The case revolved around a fight over who best represented her interests—who should be her guardian—and also a profound disagreement over the meaning of being alive. The questions became reduced to "whose life is it?" Who can make a claim on it? Eventually, in 2005, the husband prevailed.

The second aspect of the right to die controversy involves the request by a patient to accelerate death or to escape a debilitating condition, such as profound dementia. This is the Dr. Kevorkian story. Most states view the ingestion or injection of drugs intended to bring about death as different from the withdrawal of nutrition that may also lead to death. Consequently, most states outlaw this use of drugs. These laws are based on a long tradition of opposition to suicide.

In 1997, the Supreme Court ruled on suits against laws prohibiting assisted suicide in New York (*Vacco v. Quill,* 521 U.S. 793 [1997]) and Washington (*Washington v. Glucksberg,* 521 U.S. 702 [1997]). In both cases, the Supreme Court upheld the laws. The Court reasoned that a longstanding tradition rejecting suicide and assisted suicide supported these laws. Many critics of the right to die look to laws rejecting assisted suicide as examples of how the state should exert an interest in life and try to persuade the patient of the possibility for a meaningful life. So far, only one state has challenged this trend.

In 1994, Oregon passed the Death with Dignity Act, which allows for doctors to assist their patients to end their lives when death is imminent. When the Oregon law reached the Supreme

Court, the Court did not address the constitutional issues. Instead the Court focused on the national Controlled Substances Act, which dealt with trafficking illegal drugs. Oregon's law did not fall under this, and thus the Court upheld the law. The right to die remained neither constitutionally rejected nor accepted, but and a state matter.

A liberty right in refusing medicine allows for control over one's body. Claiming a right to die suggests a more active and interventionist right. Critics fear that this right may turn into a duty: Do not burden the system with those hopelessly ill. Supporters of the right to die see it as ensuring control over our lives and selves. Religious concerns, individual autonomy, control over one's life, and a commitment to a "culture of life" are among the large, competing themes that ensure that this will remain a contentious issue. The Court has implied a right to die through ratifying a right to refuse medication, but it refuses to extend constitutional protection to a robust right to die. The Supreme Court has left the right to die debate to the states.

For more information: Caplan, Arthur L., James J. McCartney, and Dominic Sisti, eds. *The Case of Terri Schiavo: Ethics at the End of Life.* Amherst, N.Y.: Prometheus Books, 2006; Cohen-Almagor, Raphael. *The Right to Die with Dignity: An Argument in Ethics, Medicine, and Law.* Piscataway, N.J.: Rutgers University Press, 2001; Colby, William. *Unplugged: Reclaiming Our Right to Die in America.* Chicago: American Management Association, 2006; Dowbiggin, Ian. *A Merciful End: The Euthanasia Movement in Modern America.* New York: Oxford University Press, 2003; Eisenberg, Jon B. *Using Terri: The Religious Right's Conspiracy to Take Away Our Rights.* New York: Harper, 2005; Lavi, Shai. *The Modern Art of Dying: A History of Euthanasia in the United States.* Princeton, N.J.: Princeton University Press, 2005; Rosenfeld, Barry. *Assisted Suicide and the Right to Die.* Chicago: American Psychological Association, 2004.

—Timothy J. Barnett and Martin Gruberg and Douglas C. Telling

right to petition the government

The "right of the people . . . to petition the Government for a redress of grievances" concludes the First Amendment and overlaps with rights to speech and assembly. While petitioning originally involved direct appeals to and responses from the legislature, it now generally includes any legal method of communicating political opinions regarding government actions, whether legislative, executive, or judicial: writing letters to, e-mailing, or lobbying officials; organizing or supporting popular referenda or ballot initiatives; engaging in peaceful marches or protests; as well as testifying before tribunals, filing lawsuits, and suing government.

The Supreme Court repeatedly describes petitioning as "among the most precious liberties safeguarded by the Bill of Rights," implicit in "the very idea of a government, republican in form" (*United States v. Cruikshank*, 92 U.S. 542, 552 [1876], *United Mine Workers of America v. Illinois State Bar Association*, 389 U.S. 217 [1967], *BE&K Construction Co. v. National Labor Relations Board*, 536 U.S. 516 [2002]). In constitutional theory, petitioning constitutes a nexus between expressive and political rights. Petitioning is sometimes described as a source of rights to speech, press, and assembly. Likewise, petitioning is linked to the development of popular sovereignty and rights to democratic participation and control of government, with roots in English common law, Magna Carta, and the English Bill of Rights of 1689.

The right to petition creates incentives and protections for individuals and groups to communicate, act politically, and seek political change—by conveying citizens' opinions directly to governing officials, placing issues on the political agenda, and pressuring government to respond to political problems. The petition clause helps channel political information, goals, and grievances into the political process and promotes government accountability and responsiveness.

Drawing on their English heritage, some American colonial charters included rights to petition that were usually enjoyed more broadly than voting rights. Colonial assemblies heard and responded to petitions from women, Native Americans, felons, the indigent, and slaves, as well as white male property owners. Much colonial legislation consisted of responses to petitions on issues as varied as religious establishment; debt; property, and tax disputes; criminal appeals; emancipation; and public corruption. The Declaration of Independence illustrates the revolutionaries' attachment to petitioning, asserting that the patriots' "repeated Petitions have been answered only by repeated injury." During the founding, petitioning remained a prevalent concern, earning inclusion in the First Amendment.

Following the practice of many colonial legislatures, Congress initially attempted to respond to all petitions, but this was not sustainable. The right to petition and other expressive rights were curtailed by the Sedition Acts of 1798 and 1918, which prohibited writing, printing, uttering, or publishing criticisms of the U.S. government. Petitioning rights rose most prominently when abolitionists flooded Congress with antislavery petitions in the 1830s, leading to congressional "gag rules" that shelved these petitions. The Supreme Court never heard any cases involving congressional restrictions on petitioning.

The right to petition nearly always entails other expressive rights, and the Court has not developed a specific approach to petition, but instead treats petitioning in conjunction with speech and assembly. In *Cruikshank* (1876), for example, the Court conflated petition and assembly, holding that citizens may "assemble for the purpose of petitioning Congress for a redress of grievances." Even in cases that directly implicate the right to petition, including lobbying, suing, libel actions involving government officials, and lawsuits against citizens who speak critically on political issues before governing bodies (Strategic Lawsuits Against Public Participation or "SLAPP" suits), the Court discusses petitioning only tangentially or in connection with other expressive rights.

Although the Court repeatedly asserts the centrality of the right to petition, it also permits considerable limitations on petitioning. In *NAACP v. Button*, 371 U.S. 415 (1963), the Court affirmed that the right to petition supports litigating, noting that lawsuits can be a form of political expression and may provide minority groups with the ability to "petition for a redress of grievances." In the area of antitrust, the Court's "Noerr-Pennington doctrine" protects those who lobby or litigate from prosecution under antitrust law (*Eastern Railroad Presidents Conference v. Noerr Motor Freight Inc.,* 365 U.S. 127 [1961], *United Mine Workers v. Pennington,* 381 U.S. 657 [1965], *California Motor Transport v. Trucking Unlimited,* 404 U.S. 508 [1972]). In other cases, however, the Court has limited the right to petition. It rejects arguments that petitions require any form of government response: the right to petition does not require "government policymakers to listen or respond to individuals' communications on public issues" (*Minnesota Board for Community Colleges v. Knight,* 465 U.S. 271 [1984]). And, in *McDonald v. Smith,* 472 U.S. 479 (1985), the Court held that the right to petition is subject to limits, arguing that defamatory statements in a petition to government are not immune from libel.

For more information: Higginson, Stephen A. "A Short History of the Right to Petition Government for the Redress of Grievances." *Yale Law Journal* 96, no. 1 (November 1986): 142–166; Lawson, Gary, and Guy Seidman. "Downsizing the Right to Petition." *Northwestern University Law Review* 93 (Spring 1999): 739–766; Mark, Gregory A. "The Vestigial Constitution: The History and Significance of the Right to Petition." *Fordham Law Review* 66 (May 1988): 2,153–2,231.

—Elizabeth Beaumont

right to remain silent

The right to remain silent when being questioned by the police is now a constitutional protection, and this right and others are recognized as a set of CIVIL LIBERTIES for those that are accused of a crime, are being considered as a potential suspect by the police, or are being detained as a possible suspect in a crime.

The rights contained within the warning, which is mandatory for all police agencies to be read to persons under criminal arrest, are derived from several cases that were decided by the Supreme Court. *MIRANDA V. ARIZONA,* 384 U.S. 436 (1966), and *ESCOBEDO V. ILLINOIS,* 378 U.S. 478 (1964), are two of the more famous cases that allowed these protections to be drawn from.

The Fourth, Fifth, and FOURTEENTH AMENDMENTS to the Constitution support these rights both implicitly and through judicial interpretations. The rights as defined in *Miranda* are "You have the right to remain silent. Anything you say can and will be used against you in a court of law. You have the right to speak to an attorney, and to have an attorney present during any questioning. If you cannot afford a lawyer, one will be provided for you at government expense." That warning is now known among the law enforcement community and populace as the "Miranda warning," and once the person has been "read their rights," they have been "Mirandized." The restrictions of when a law enforcement officer must give the warning and in what circumstances are now well defined as when a person is placed in custodial interrogation.

There are some situations where the reading of the warning is not necessary unless the scenario calls for it and the officer intends for the answers to his questioning to be utilized within a criminal prosecution. These rights are compiled to avoid the situation where a person may unintentionally incriminate himself, by allowing them some aspect of personal freedom in that they may refuse to answer questions, thus the right to remain silent. The right to remain silent begins at the very moment of the suspension of freedom of movement, or at the time of arrest, through to the end of any criminal proceedings against the accused. In 1963, Ernesto Miranda, a grade-school drop out, was arrested by the police in Arizona for allegedly kidnapping and raping an 18-year-old woman of special needs who reportedly had challenged intelligence levels. Miranda was not informed that he had any rights to counsel, to remain silent, or to refuse questioning; thus Miranda signed a written confession, thereby incriminating himself. Miranda was convicted and his appeals went to the Supreme Court. At that stage the case was enjoined by three others, one being the Danny *ESCOBEDO V. ILLINOIS* case. The

Escobedo case involved a murder suspect who was denied his RIGHT TO COUNSEL and not advised that he could remain silent during the interrogations. Escobedo did not remain silent and he confessed to his complicity in the crime and was convicted. The decisions by the Supreme Court in both cases threw out the confessions for basically denying the defendant the rights aforementioned and established that the police could not use statements made by defendants while in police custody unless the police had advised these defendants of their rights.

In *UNITED STATES V. DICKERSON*, 530 U.S. 428 (2000), the Supreme Court recognized that the *Miranda* rules were constitutional and not advisory in nature. Moreover, they worked for both those under police scrutiny and those arrested. In addition, the decision further cemented the practice within the eyes of the Court by defining that the Congress cannot alter or rule over the applications made by the Court, and thus the likelihood that the *Miranda* rule will ever be overturned is even smaller. Yet the trade-off is that a guilty person can go free if there is a procedural error within the arrest process. If seen through the eyes of the *Miranda* case, if the prosecution can corroborate information outside of the excluded confession or other evidence about the crime in question, then the person will more than likely be convicted. Miranda never quite got his freedom, in that a girlfriend of his testified that he had admitted to her that he had committed the rape and kidnapping. Miranda went to jail and never quite got his life on track, as he was arrested several times. Upon his release from jail, Miranda was killed in a bar fight by a man who was out of jail allegedly because he was not read his rights and suffered some self-incrimination. The man that killed Miranda never self-incriminated himself in the Miranda murder and remained silent on the issue, and thus was never convicted for the crime of murder.

For more information: LaFave, Wayne R., Jerold H. Israel, and Nancy J. King. *Criminal Procedure*. St. Paul, Minn.: Thomson/West, 2004.

—Ernest Gomez

right to trial by jury

In the United States every person accused of a crime has a constitutional right to a trial by jury under the SIXTH AMENDMENT. The right to a trial by jury was later extended to defendants in state courts under the DUE PROCESS clause of the FOURTEENTH AMENDMENT.

A trial by jury in the United States is applicable in both criminal and civil cases, where the use of a jury in a trial has often been viewed as an important check against state power and is believed to provide a fairer hearing for parties. The right to a jury trial has always been dependent on the nature of the offense with which the defendant is charged; for example, petty offenses are not covered by the jury requirement under the Sixth Amendment. An exception to the petty offenses and jury requirement was passed by the Supreme Court with *Blanton v. North Las Vegas*, 489 U.S. 538 (1989), in which it ruled that "offenses for which the maximum period of incarceration is six months, or less, are presumptively petty . . . a defendant can overcome this, and become entitled to a jury trial, . . by showing that additional penalties [such as monetary fines] . . . are . . . so severe [as to indicate] that the legislature clearly determined that the offense is a serious one." The lack of jury requirement also pertains to multiple petty offenses that exceed six month imprisonment, as well as proceedings in state juvenile courts.

Jurors are normally selected through the use of voter registration and drivers' licenses, and then prescreened as prospective jurors for specific cases, through answering questions regarding citizenship, disabilities, understanding of the English language, and whether there are any considerations that would excuse them from serving on a jury. These jurists are generally not legal professionals but are ordinary citizens who collectively form a panel that then forms a verdict regarding the case from the evidence presented by both the prosecution and defense. Normally, a jury has comprised 12 individuals, and verdicts had to be unanimous, according to traditions adopted by the Constitution from England. However, with the establishment of the Fourteenth Amendment, extending the right to trial by jury to defendants in state courts under the due process clause, the Supreme Court reevaluated these requirements for unanimity and number of jurors. The Supreme Court ruled that despite historical basis and precedent mandating unanimity in federal jury trials under the Sixth Amendment, the due process clause of the Fourteenth Amendment did not incorporate this and therefore did not require unanimity of decisions in state jury trials, and there juries could comprise six rather than 12 jurors.

Originally, the Constitution required that defendants be tried by juries from the state in which the crime was allegedly committed. The Supreme Court upheld this requirement in *Beavers v. Henkel,* 194 U.S. 73 (1904). Decisions regarding the location of a trial were based upon where the alleged offense occurred; if the offense occurred across multiple districts, the trial may then be held in any of those locations. Also in cases where offenses were alleged to be committed outside of any state (for example, at sea), Congress would determine the place of trial and jury.

Another important aspect of the right to jury trial is the impartiality of the jury. To establish impartiality, both the prosecution and defense are allowed to question potential jurors to determine any biases, challenging the inclusion of a particular juror, with the court having final determination on the validity of these challenges. An additional factor considered is the composition of a jury panel to ensure that it represents a fair cross-section of the community. In this regard, a defendant may establish that the requirement of impartiality has been violated, if it can be shown that the jury panel excludes a "distinctive" group from within the community, which exclusion then has an impact on the outcome of the case. The Supreme Court established impartiality as a deciding factor in *Taylor v. Louisiana,* 419 U.S. 522 (1975), where it invalidated a state law that exempted women from jury service, while it had not done the same for men. A further example regarding impartiality of juries arose in the Rodney King case (California, 1992). The infamous case raised questions about prejudice and the racial biases of jurors, when the jury (consisting mostly of whites without any black jurors) acquitted the white police officers of violently beating a black man (Rodney King), despite an incriminating videotape of the action. The decision in this case, while leading to further questioning about the nature of juries in trial cases, also led to violent riots and racial clashes.

Lastly, in a vast number of criminal cases, defendants choose to resolve the case by negotiation resulting in a plea bargain. Alternatively, defendants may choose to waive their right to a jury trial, in which case a bench trial (with the judge deciding) is held. However, in U.S. federal courts, there is no absolute right to waive a jury trial, although in most states, the defendant does have an absolute right to waive a jury trial without the need for the prosecution or court's consent.

For more information: Banaszak, Ronald, Sr., ed. *Fair Trial Rights of the Accused: A Documentary History.* Westport, Conn.: Greenwood Press, 2002; Butler, Jeff E. "Petty Offenses, Serious Consequences: Multiple Petty Offenses and the Sixth Amendment Right to Jury Trial." *Michigan Law Review* 94 (1995): 872–897; Cortner, Richard C. *The Supreme Court and Civil Liberties Policy.* Palo Alto, Calif.: Mayfield Publishing, 1975; Hoffman, Morris B. "The Case for Jury Sentencing." *Duke Law Journal* 52 (2003): 951–1,010; Dripps, Donald A. *About Guilt and Innocence: The Origins, Development, and Future of Constitutional Criminal Procedure.* Westport, Conn.: Praeger, 2003.

—Dale Mineshima-Lowe

right to vote

The right to vote refers to the constitutional right to choose elected officials among a range of candidates with competing views. While the Constitution does not explicitly grant individuals the right to vote, the United States Supreme Court has ruled that it is a fundamental right protected by this document.

Nowhere in the United States Constitution is there an explicit declaration of the right to vote. More specifically, ARTICLE II, Section 1 grants to the states the authority to determine how they will allow for the selection of electors to choose the

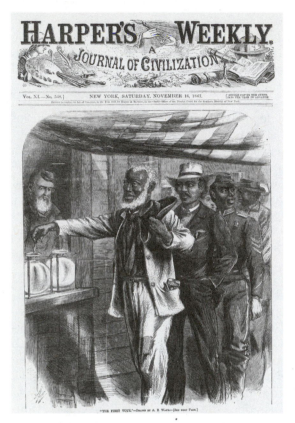

A cover of *Harper's Weekly* depicting blacks voting for the first time, 1867 *(Library of Congress)*

president. Originally, the Constitution permitted state legislatures to select U.S. senators, and members of the Supreme Court were to be appointed by the president, subject to confirmation by the SENATE. The only public officials whom the people could select were the members of the HOUSE OF REPRESENTATIVES, rendering rather thin any notion that the citizens had broad franchise rights in the selection of the national government.

Initially the Constitution appears to have left that right up to the states, which generally limited the franchise to white male property owners, who were citizens of a certain age and occasionally of a specific religious faith. For example, in *MINOR v. HAPPERSETT*, 88 U.S. 162 (1875), the United States Supreme Court rejected a claim by a Missouri woman that, as a citizen, the Constitution gave her a right to vote. The Court dismissed her claim, indicating that citizenship did not necessarily include the right to vote; states could decide who had that right.

Commencing after the Civil War, a series of constitutional amendments were adopted that addressed the right to vote. The FIFTEENTH AMENDMENT prohibited states from denying the right to vote on account of "race, color, or previous condition of servitude." The SEVENTEENTH AMENDMENT permitted the direct election of United States senators. The NINETEENTH AMENDMENT enfranchised women. The TWENTY-FOURTH banned poll taxes. The TWENTY-SIXTH directed states to allow qualified citizens who were age 18 or older to vote. Yet none of these amendments affirmatively granted the right to vote.

It was not until the 1940s that the Supreme Court affirmatively addressed the constitutional right to vote. In *UNITED STATES V. CLASSIC*, 313 U.S. 299 (1941), in a case arising out of vote fraud in a Louisiana federal election primary, the Court was faced with the issue of whether one has a right to vote as a primary question, and then whether depriving a person of that right came within the meaning of a federal criminal law that made it illegal to "injure a citizen in the exercise 'of any right or privilege secured to him by the Constitution or laws of the United States.'" The Court stated:

We come then to the question whether that right is one secured by the Constitution. Section 2 of Article I commands that Congressmen shall be chosen by the people of the several states by electors, the qualifications of which it prescribes. The right of the people to choose, whatever its appropriate constitutional limitations, where in other respects it is defined, and the mode of its exercise is prescribed by state action in conformity to the Constitution, is a right established and guaranteed by the Constitution and hence is one secured by it to those citizens and inhabitants of the state entitled to exercise the right.

In addition, in *REYNOLDS V. SIMS*, 377 U.S. 533 (1964), the Court embraced the principle of equal representation for equal numbers of people—ONE PERSON, ONE VOTE for the purposes of reapportionment. More importantly, in *Reynolds* the Supreme Court again reaffirmed that the Constitution protects the right to vote in federal elections. Furthermore, in *Reynolds* the Court drew a parallel between the right to vote and right to procreate in SKINNER V. OKLAHOMA, 316 U.S. 535 (1942), declaring the right to vote as fundamental.

Locating a constitutional text to support the right to vote in state elections is more problematic. In *Harper v. Virginia State Board of Elections*, 383 U.S. 663 (1966), in striking down the imposition of a poll tax in state elections, the Supreme Court ruled that the right to vote in state elections was located in the FIRST AMENDMENT by way of the FOURTEENTH AMENDMENT's DUE PROCESS and EQUAL PROTECTION clauses. Although the tax met traditional constitutional standards, it was neither racially discriminatory nor indefensible as rational policy, but the Court found that it unconstitutionally singled out the poor. More importantly, the Court yet again affirmed the importance of voting, stating that voting is a "fundamental political right, because preservative of all rights." The legacy of *Classic, Reynolds,* and *Harper* is that these three cases stand for the proposition that voting is a fundamental right that must be subject to STRICT SCRUTINY. Collectively, these cases would seem to suggest that interference with, or regulation of, the fundamental right to vote must be subject to strict scrutiny, and that only if COMPELLING GOVERNMENTAL INTERESTS are asserted, may it be limited.

Enfranchisement of African Americans

The battle by African Americans to obtain the right to vote was long and arduous. Originally, the Constitution was silent on the right of African Americans to vote; instead, ARTICLE I, section 2 referred to them only as "other persons" and counted them as only three-fifths of a free person. After the Civil War and during Reconstruction, African Americans were permitted to vote, and they elected several members of Congress in the South. In 1870 the Fifteenth Amendment made it unconstitutional to deny the right to vote on account of race.

When Reconstruction ended, so did effective franchise rights for African Americans. Many Southern states enacted a variety of restrictions on African-American voting rights. Some states instituted poll taxes that required African Americans to pay a fee to vote. Others imposed literacy tests upon African Americans that asked them to answer often arcane and trivial questions in order to vote. Still other states enacted laws that declared that individuals could vote only if their grandfather had that right, or used white primaries as a means to exclude African Americans from participating in elections. Through these laws, as well as by outright intimidation by the Ku Klux Klan and other groups, African Americans effectively were without franchise rights until the 1960s.

The Supreme Court initially upheld literacy tests and poll taxes as constitutionally permissible means by which to maintain a responsible and informed electorate, but in the 1920s Democratic Party primaries in which participation was restricted to whites began to crumble under judicial attack in cases such as *Smith v. Allwright*, 321 U.S. 649 (1944).

It was not until the 1960s that the Supreme Court and the federal government began to take serious steps to protect the right to vote for African Americans. The TWENTY-FOURTH AMENDMENT in 1964 made the poll tax illegal; reapportionment cases declared malapportionment on account of race to be unconstitutional, and these cases also established a constitutional right to vote at the state and federal levels.

However, it was the 1965 VOTING RIGHTS ACT that had the biggest impact on African-American franchise rights. The Voting Rights Act was enacted in 1965 and amended or reauthorized in 1970, 1975, 1982, and 2006. Section four of the act outlawed some practices such as literacy tests, section two precluded states from diluting voting on account of race, and other parts of the act provided for new legal remedies and powers of the federal government to intervene to protect the African-American franchise in the states.

In addition to African Americans, other groups have had their voting rights addressed by the courts, Congress, or the Constitution. In 1924,

Congress gave Indians the right to vote. In 1920 the Nineteenth Amendment enfranchised women, and in 1971 the Twenty-sixth Amendment directed states to allow qualified citizens who were age 18 or older to vote.

However, two groups still do not have constitutionally secure voting rights. Aliens may be denied the right to vote, and in *Richardson v. Ramirez,* 418 U.S. 24 (1974), the Supreme Court upheld a state law denying ex-felons franchise. As the Richardson case pointed out, many states deny ex-felons the right to vote, often for life, thereby affecting their rights to participate in elections and the political process. Estimates are that up to six million ex-felons, many of them people of color, are denied their right to vote.

Finally, while franchise is nearly universal in the United States, many individuals choose not to vote, often with a turnout of less than half the eligible voters for an election.

For more information: Grofman, Bernard, Lisa Handley, and Richard Niemi. *Minority Representation and the Quest for Voting Equality.* New York: Cambridge University Press, 1992; Keyssar, Alexander. *The Right to Vote: The Contested History of Democracy in the United States.* New York: Basic Books, 2001.

—David Schultz

Ring v. Arizona 536 U.S. 584 (2002)

In *Ring v. Arizona,* the U.S. Supreme Court ruled that the imposition of CAPITAL PUNISHMENT by a judge, rather than a jury, violates the SIXTH and FOURTEENTH AMENDMENTS of the Constitution. This case immediately impacted the sentences of at least 168 death row inmates in five states—Arizona, Colorado, Idaho, Montana, and Nebraska.

Timothy Stuart Ring and two other former law enforcement officers planned and executed the robbery of a Wells Fargo armored truck at a shopping mall in Glendale, Arizona, on November 28, 1994. During the robbery, Ring killed the security guard, John Magoch, with a single shot to the head at close range using a silencer.

The three accomplices stole an estimated $833,798. Approximately one month later, police received a tip from one of the accomplice's ex-girlfriends, suggesting that Ring and the others were involved in the heist. The FBI and Glendale police secured a warrant to tap the men's phones, which in turn yielded incriminating evidence. Police also observed that the three men went on wild spending sprees following the robbery, purchasing high-ticket items with cash. With a warrant, police searched Ring's home and found the murder weapon, a silencer, stolen cash, and incriminating notes. Ring was subsequently charged with first-degree murder, conspiracy to commit murder, armed criminal action, and burglary. The jury found Ring guilty on all counts, but under Arizona law the judge—not the jury—imposed the sentence. The judge ordered Ring to be executed by lethal injection.

In a 7-2 decision, the U.S. Supreme Court reversed and declared the Arizona law unconstitutional. Writing for the majority, Ruth Bader Ginsburg drew upon the Court's decision in *Apprendi v. New Jersey* (2000). In *Apprendi,* the Supreme Court struck down a state sentencing law that allowed trial judges to lengthen a penalty by two years if it was determined the crime was motivated by hate. According to Ginsburg, "The RIGHT TO TRIAL BY JURY guaranteed by the Sixth Amendment would be senselessly diminished if it encompassed the factfinding necessary to increase a defendant's sentences by two years, but not the factfinding necessary to put him to death." Joining Ginsburg were DAVID H. SOUTER, JOHN PAUL STEVENS, ANTHONY M. KENNEDY, ANTONIN GREGORY SCALIA, and CLARENCE THOMAS. Justice STEPHEN G. BREYER delivered a concurring opinion. The two dissenters were Arizonans SANDRA DAY O'CONNOR and Chief Justice WILLIAM HUBBS REHNQUIST. Justice O'Connor believed that the decision would have a destabilizing effect on the criminal justice system by opening the doors to scores of challenges in other states.

The full impact of *Ring* has yet to be determined. Some death row inmates in the affected states could be retried, resentenced, or have their death penalties commuted to life in prison. The *Ring* decision appears to be one in a line of recent cases where the Supreme Court has restricted the death penalty. See *Atkins v. Virginia* (2002)—the Court struck down the death penalty for the mentally retarded—and *Roper v. Simmons* (2005), where the Court invalidated the death sentence of a 17-year-old. The *Atkins* and *Roper* decisions were based on the cruel and unusual proscription in the Eighth Amendment.

For more information: Banner, Stuart. *The Death Penalty: An American History.* Boston: Harvard University Press, 2002; N.A. "The Death Penalty and International Law," *William and Mary Bill of Rights Journal* 13 (2005): 305 (introduction to symposium issue).

—Richard J. Hardy

ripeness

The doctrine of ripeness has been derived from a particular understanding of the limited constitutional authority of the judiciary.

Under ARTICLE III, Section 2 of the United States Constitution the judicial power extends to certain "cases" and "controversies." The Supreme Court has construed this "case" and "controversy" language in ARTICLE III OF THE U.S. CONSTITUTION as limiting the judicial power to adjudication of those lawsuits that raise live disputes in which the parties have a present interest.

The doctrine of ripeness precludes adjudication by the federal courts of abstract controversies in the absence of present and concrete hardship. If the harm that a plaintiff claims he or she will suffer remains contingent on future events that are far from certain to occur, or the government has not yet rendered a final decision on the matter at issue, the case is not yet ripe for judicial consideration. In *Abbott Laboratories v. Gardner*, 387 U.S. 136 (1967), the Supreme Court explained that the basic rationale of the ripeness doctrine is to prevent the courts, through avoidance of premature adjudication, from entangling themselves in abstract disagreements over administrative policies, and also to protect the agencies from judicial interference until an administrative decision has been formalized and its effects felt in a concrete way by the challenging parties.

The Supreme Court has set out a two-part test for determining ripeness, requiring evaluation of both (1) "the fitness of the issues for judicial decision" at this time and (2) "the hardship to the parties of withholding court consideration" (*Ohio Forestry Ass'n*, 523 U.S. at 733; *Abbott Laboratories*, 387 U.S. at 149).

First, in terms of the *fitness* of the issue for adjudication, the courts look to whether the issue is fully developed in the context of a concrete and present dispute. The Court is reluctant to hear a facial challenge to a regulation or rule that has not yet been applied, because "judicial appraisal . . . is likely to stand on a much surer footing in the context of a specific application of [the] regulation" (*Toilet Goods Ass'n v. Gardner*, 387 U.S. 158, 164 [1967]). However, preenforcement relief is not always barred, if the party challenging the government rule can make a compelling showing on the second prong of the test, for example, that the party will endure high costs in complying with the rule or risks substantial civil or criminal penalties if the rule is violated (see, e.g., *Abbott Laboratories, supra*).

Second, with respect to the showing of *hardship* by delaying adjudication, the courts consider "the degree and nature of the [government rule's] present effect on those seeking relief." Thus, "[a] case may lack ripeness . . . even when it involves a final agency action presenting a purely legal question," where the action has no "sufficiently direct and immediate" impact on the parties (*Alascom, Inc. v. Federal Communications Comm'n*, 727 F.2d 1212, 1217 (D.C. Cir. [1984]).

For more information: Aman, Alfred C., Jr., and William T. Mayton. *Administrative Law.* 2d ed. St. Paul, Minn.: West Group, 2001; Nichol, Gene R., Jr. "Ripeness and the Constitution," *University of Chicago Law Review* 54, no. 153 (1987): 156–160; Pierce, Richard J., Jr., Sidney A. Shapiro, and Paul R. Verkuil. *Administrative Law and Process.* 4th ed. St. Paul, Minn.: West Group, 2004.

—Gregory C. Sisk

Roberts, John G., Jr. (1955–   ) *Supreme Court justice*

John G. Roberts, Jr., is the 17th chief justice of the Supreme Court of the United States. After nomination by President George W. Bush and confirmation by the U.S. SENATE, he was sworn in on September 29, 2005, at the age of 50, as the youngest chief justice in the last 200 years.

Roberts was born in Buffalo, New York, and grew up a Roman Catholic in Indiana. He lives in Bethesda, Maryland, and is married to Jane Marie Sullivan. They have two children. He received a bachelor's degree summa cum laude in 1976 after only three years at Harvard, entered Harvard Law School, and became managing editor of the *Harvard Law Review.* He graduated magna cum laude from law school in 1979.

During the 1980 term, he served as a law clerk for the then-associate Supreme Court justice (later chief justice and Roberts's predecessor) WIL-LIAM HUBBS REHNQUIST. From 1981 to 1982 he was special assistant to the U.S. attorney general, William French Smith. From 1982 until 1986 he served as associate counsel to President Ronald Reagan in the White House. From 1989 to 1993 he was principal deputy solicitor general of the U.S. Department of Justice. He argued 39 cases before United States Supreme Court and won 25, placing him among the most experienced litigators.

From 1986 to 1989 and from 1993 to 2003, Roberts entered private practice as an associate at the law firm of Hogan & Hartson in Washington, D.C., where he developed a civil litigation practice and ran the appellate division. As an attorney and member of the D.C. Bar, he was widely involved in bar activities. Roberts's arguments within the Supreme Court's jurisdiction extend over a wide range of issues, including antitrust, arbitration, admiralty, administration, free speech, Indian affairs, taxation, labor, CIVIL RIGHTS, and criminal law. He represented at different times a number of states, defending diverse state, health, and welfare policies before the United State Supreme Court. He also represented 18 states pursuing antitrust claims in the *United States v. Microsoft* case.

In 2003, when the U.S. Senate confirmed his nomination by unanimous consent, he was appointed to the United States Court of Appeals for the DISTRICT OF COLUMBIA Circuit, widely considered as the country's most important inter-mediate appellate court. At that time Roberts wrote 49 opinions; only two were not unanimous. He dissented only three times.

During Senate Judiciary Committee hearings on his nomination, Roberts testified about his views on jurisprudence. Roberts was thought to be conservative by temperament but not essentially by ideology. He supports limited government and believes in a narrow interpretation of the U.S. Constitution. In October 2005, when the Court began its 2005–06 session, he presided over his first oral arguments, and in January 2006, the ROBERTS COURT decided the first case argued before it.

For more information: McElroy, Lisa Tucker. *John G. Roberts, Jr.: Chief Justice.* Minneapolis, Minn.: Lerner Publications, 2007.

—Jurij Toplak

Roberts Court (2005–   )

The Roberts Court began on September 29, 2005, when JOHN GLOVER ROBERTS, JR., became chief justice of the United States Supreme Court. Originally, President George W. Bush had nominated him to the position held by retiring associate justice SANDRA DAY O'CONNOR (July 19, 2005); however, following the death of Chief Justice WIL-LIAM HUBBS REHNQUIST (September 3, 2005), President Bush withdrew the nomination and resubmitted it for the chief justice seat (September 6, 2005), asking Congress to confirm the nomination in time for the beginning of the fall term in October. Despite opposition from liberal Democrats, the Senate Judicial Committee approved his nomination. The full SENATE approved the nomination on September 29, 2005. He was sworn in a short time later by Associate Justice JOHN PAUL STEVENS in the East Room of the White House.

The members of the Roberts Court at the beginning, in order of their accession to the Court, were John Paul Stevens (appointed by President Gerald Ford, 1975), Sandra Day O'Connor (appointed by

President Ronald Reagan, 1981), ANTONIN GREG-ORY SCALIA (appointed by President Reagan, 1986), ANTHONY MCLEOD KENNEDY (appointed by President Reagan, 1988), DAVID HACKETT SOUTER (appointed by President George H. W. Bush, 1990), CLARENCE THOMAS (appointed by President G. H. W. Bush, 1991), Ruth Bader Ginsburg (appointed by President William Jefferson Clinton, 1993), and STEPHEN G. BREYER (appointed by President Clinton, 1994). On February 1, 2006, SAMUEL ALITO, JR., joined the court to replace the retiring O'Connor.

The retirement of O'Connor and the accession of Alito in the Court's mid-term meant that several decisions were subsequently decided without the full participation of either. The cases of *Garcetti v. Ceballos* (547 U.S. 410 [2006]), *Hudson v. Michigan* (547 U.S. 586 [2006]), and *Kansas v. Marsh* (547 U.S. 1,037 [2006]) were decided by 4-4 votes, allowing the ruling in the lower court to stand.

Chief Justice Roberts presided over the first case before the Roberts Court on October 3, 2005, as the Court began the fall term of its 2005–06 session. On November 8, 2005, the opinion of the first case decided by the Roberts Court was delivered by Associate Justice Stevens. *IBP, Inc. v. Alvarez,* unanimously decided, was viewed by observers as upholding a tradition that the first case in a new chief justice's court is decided unanimously. This "honeymoon" period of the Roberts Court ended with the decision in *GONZALES V. OREGON,* 546 U.S. 243 (2006). The chief justice joined the dissent of Antonin Scalia and Clarence Thomas in opposing physician-assisted suicide allowed by the state of Oregon for the terminally ill.

The new chief justice's first opinion came on March 6, 2006, when Roberts wrote the unanimous decision in *Rumsfeld v. Forum for Academic and Institutional Rights,* 547 U.S. 47 (2006). The opinion required colleges and universities taking federal funds to allow military recruiters on their campuses. The decision agreed with a number of earlier precedents.

The first written dissenting opinion of Chief Justice Roberts came in the case of *Georgia v. Randolph* (March 22, 2006). The majority opinion said that the police may not search a home if one spouse says that it is permissible and the other spouse objects. The thrust of Roberts's disagreement was his view that the decision was not consistent with prior case law.

Observers claim the Roberts Court is more conservative; however, Roberts joined the liberals in *Jones v. Flowers,* a case that seemed to protect property rights by ensuring adequate DUE PROCESS in tax-forfeiture cases. The Roberts Court moved to allow legislative action that restricts ABORTION when the Partial-Birth Abortion Ban Act was upheld in *GONZALES V. CARHART, ATTORNEY GENERAL* (127 S. Ct. 1610 [2007]). It also upheld school authority over student claims to freedom of speech ("bong hits for Jesus") in *MORSE V. FREDERICK,* 551 U.S. ___ (2007).

Observers of the Court believe there has been a change in tone in the way oral arguments are conducted. This may reflect the Roberts experience after arguing 39 cases before the Court.

For more information: Hutchinson, Dennis J., et al., eds. *Supreme Court Review 2006.* Chicago: University of Chicago Press Journals, 2007; Moller, Mark K., Timothy Lynch, and Robert A. Levy, eds. *Cato Supreme Court Review 2006–2007.* Washington, D.C.: Cato Institute, 2007; Moller, Mark K., Timothy Lynch, and Robert A. Levy, eds. *Cato Supreme Court Review 2005–2006.* Washington, D.C.: Cato Institute, 2006; Neubauer, David W. W., and Stephen S. Meinhold. *Battle Supreme: The Confirmation of Chief Justice John Roberts and the Future of the Supreme Court.* Belmont, Calif.: Wadsworth Publishing Company, 2005.

—Andrew J. Waskey

Roe v. Wade 410 U.S. 113 (1973)

Roe v. Wade, a landmark U.S. Supreme Court case, gave women access to ABORTIONS based on an implied right to PRIVACY in the FIRST, FOURTH, Fifth, NINTH, and FOURTEENTH AMENDMENTS of the U.S. Constitution. The right to privacy originated in *GRISWOLD V. CONNECTICUT,* 381 U.S. 479 (1965), and *EISENSTADT V. BAIRD,* 405 U.S. 438 (1972), which struck down laws making it illegal to use or distribute CONTRACEPTIVES and contraceptive devices. Under *Roe,* abortion restrictions were subjected to the STRICT SCRUTINY test, which meant that the abortion right was accorded the highest level of constitutional protection.

Highly controversial, *Roe v. Wade* specifically addressed the constitutionality of the 1857 Texas statute that banned abortion except to save the mother's life. The U.S. Supreme Court declared the Texas law unconstitutional. Building on the logic in the *Griswold* and *Eisenstadt* rulings, the Court used the privacy zone to protect a woman's right to terminate a pregnancy but also recognized the state's interest to intervene at some point in the pregnancy to protect potential human life.

Justice Harry Blackmun, writing for the majority, devised a trimester formula that would balance the rights of women, physicians, and states and established guidelines on whose rights would prevail across the nine months of pregnancy. In the first trimester (or first three months) of pregnancy, the abortion decision is left to the medical judgment of the woman and her assisting physician. In the second trimester, the state may regulate the abortion procedure in the interest of the mother's health. During the third trimester, the state may regulate or even prohibit abortions to protect the life of a fetus, thus allowing late-term abortions only when necessary to protect the life or health of the mother.

One major challenge to *Roe* came in *Planned Parenthood of Southeastern Pennsylvania v. Casey,* 505 U.S. 833 (1992). In *Casey,* a series of Pennsylvania abortion restrictions (parental consent, informed consent, a 24-hour waiting period, and spousal notification prior to obtaining an abortion) were challenged. Although the Court did not overturn *Roe,* it abandoned the strict scrutiny standard and the trimester formula and moved to the UNDUE BURDEN STANDARD. An "undue burden" consists of placing a substantial obstacle in the path of a woman who seeks to abort a nonviable fetus. The Court held that state restrictions on abortion access that carried an undue burden would be declared unconstitutional. In *Casey,* only the spousal notification requirement was struck down as unconstitutional under the undue

burden standard. A woman's right to an abortion still remains intact, but *Casey* allows states to enact laws that protect fetal rights and restrict access to abortions as long as restrictions do not unduly burden a woman's abortion rights.

Jane Roe, the plaintiff in this landmark case, is actually Norma L. McCorvey. Because the case took three years to get to the Court, McCorvey never actually obtained an abortion and instead put her child up for adoption. In 2005, she petitioned the Supreme Court to reopen *Roe* and overturn it based on changes in law and technology since 1973 and her personal conversion to Christianity. The Supreme Court did not rule in McCorvey's favor but has signaled a willingness to revisit some of *Roe*'s basic tenets.

McCorvey's change of heart personifies the abortion controversy in American politics. Generally, Americans believe abortion should be legal under certain, but not all, circumstances. President George W. Bush and Congress, acting on the ambivalence of public opinion toward abortion, have endorsed and passed laws to restrict abortion and protect the unborn. Despite the divisions caused by the *Roe* ruling, most Americans oppose efforts to overturn the decision and return to the pre-*Roe* era. Public opinion polls taken since 1989 indicate approximately 60 percent of Americans wish to maintain the *Roe* precedent.

Since the 1973 *Roe* ruling, all nine of the original *Roe* justices have died or retired. Many scholars question whether *Roe* will remain the law of the land. *Roe* leaves behind many unanswered questions such as: When does life begin? At what point during the pregnancy is the fetus viable? When should the state intervene to make sure the fetus will be given a chance to develop and thrive? Before her appointment to the U.S. Supreme Court, Ruth Bader Ginsburg argued that *Roe* stymied the political process that already was moving in a reformist direction and significantly prolonged the abortion controversy by making grounds for consensus less fertile.

Others argue that Roe has become irrelevant. Congress and states have erected financial barriers (laws barring public funding of abortions) and legal obstacles (various state restrictions such as waiting periods, parental consent, and mandatory counseling). In addition, abortion providers are scarce. Eighty percent of American women live in counties without abortion providers or must travel across state lines to obtain an abortion because many physicians refuse to provide abortions. If women lack access to abortion, *Roe* indeed may be moot. Whether *Roe* retains any relevance and whether any of its basic tenets will survive will be determined by battles in the political arena.

Since *Roe* was decided, its central holding that women have a right to terminate their pregnancies in the first trimester was upheld in *Planned Parenthood v. Casey*, 505 U.S. 833 (1992). However, in GONZALES V. CARHART, 550 U.S. ___ (2007), the Supreme Court in a 5-4 decision upheld a federal law banning certain late-term abortions commonly referred to as "partial birth abortions." This decision is the only abortion procedure the Court has upheld since it issued its *Roe* opinion.

For more information: Balkin, Jack M. "*Roe v. Wade:* An Engine of Controversy." In *What* Roe v. Wade *Should Have Said: The Nation's Top Legal Experts Rewrite America's Most Controversial Decision.* New York: New York University Press, 2005; Jones, Jeffrey M. "President Bush and *Roe v. Wade:* Public Favors Restrictive View of Abortion Rights, but Not *Roe v. Wade* Reversal." *Gallup News Service* (November 30, 2004); Nossif, Rosemary. *Before Roe: Abortion Policy in the States.* Philadelphia: Temple University Press, 2001; Strickland, Ruth Ann. "Abortion: Pro-Choice versus Pro-Life." In *Moral Controversies in American Politics.* 3d ed. Armonk, N.Y.: M.E. Sharpe, 2005.

—Ruth Ann Strickland

Romer v. Evans 116 S.Ct. 1620 (1996)

In *Romer v. Evans,* in a 6-3 decision, the Supreme Court upheld a lower court's ruling against Colorado's Amendment Two and found that it violated the federal EQUAL PROTECTION clause in classifying homosexual citizens of Colorado not to further a legitimate legislative end, but to make them unequal to other residents of Colorado. This amendment struck down any law or executive order in the state that indicated sexual orientation as a classification to be protected alongside other common antidiscrimination classifications such as religion and national origin.

The decision in *Romer* rebuffed the dissent's contentions that Amendment Two, a popular referendum, did not reflect animus toward gay persons, given that the advertisements used to gain support for it relied on anti-gay stereotype and bias. Indeed, the Court found that no reason existed for support of this law other than bias, an impermissible purpose, and hence it failed the RATIONAL BASIS TEST. *Romer* affirmed the very basic principle of equal citizenship through its use of the rational basis test, and set a minimum standard that has to be met when contemplating legislation against gay persons.

The opinion of the Court, given by Justice ANTHONY M. KENNEDY, held that the means employed by Amendment Two—the classification used—did not fit the ends, as it was both too narrow and too broad in its identification of a group of persons by a single trait and by denying them protections across the board. Kennedy's opinion also addressed the hot-button issue of "special rights," the notion that when gay persons are added to existing nondiscrimination or other legislation they are winning for themselves protections unavailable for the ordinary, non-gay citizen. The rights at issue, such as access to the public library and emergency medical treatment, were deemed quite ordinary and in the realm of what any American rightfully can expect; in addition, the various provisions of Colorado state law that protect gay persons were all duly enacted and so can be assumed to reflect popular and legislative will.

Romer was the first significant case for GAY AND LESBIAN RIGHTS after the disastrous BOWERS V. HARDWICK (478 U.S. 186 [1986]), and called into question the earlier case's holding that the morality of a majority in a state can by itself legitimate a law, a point of view defended by dissenting Justice ANTONIN GREGORY SCALIA, who argued that a behavior or practice that is regarded as against good morals by a citizenry may be legally proscribed on that basis alone. Scalia couched the dissent in terms of a broader *Kulturkampf* that has affected the nation's legal establishment, and he suggested that the decision in *Romer* would lead to striking down as constitutionally suspect laws against polygamy, incest, and cockfighting. Earlier, the Colorado Supreme Court struck down Amendment Two, finding not only that it forbade anyone from advocating on behalf of gay rights, whether or not gay him- or herself, but also that it required gay rights supporters to meet a higher bar—only a constitutional amendment could overturn it—than needed by anyone advocating on any other issue. It fenced a politically unpopular minority out of the political process, but this issue was not taken up in the Supreme Court.

For more information: Murdoch, Joyce, and Deb Price. *Courting Justice: Gay Men and Lesbians v. the Supreme Court.* New York: Basic Books, 2001.

—Gordon A. Babst

Rosenberger v. University of Virginia 515 U.S. 819 (1995)

In *Rosenberger v. University of Virginia*, the Supreme Court held that the university (UVA) could not discriminate against a student group's freedom of expression in order to avoid violating the ESTABLISHMENT CLAUSE of the First Amendment. In a case where a number of elements of the FIRST AMENDMENT intersected—freedom of speech, FREEDOM OF RELIGION, and religious establishment—the Court sided with *Wide Awake*, a student-run publication of which Rosenberger was a member, and its freedom of religious expression.

Wide Awake was a Christian student publication that requested monies from the Student Activities Fund (SAF) at UVA. The SAF exacted a mandatory $14 fee that each student had to pay every semester. Qualified student groups could request monies from the SAF for eligible expenditures related to these groups providing activities, publications, or other support to the student body at large. *Wide Awake* requested monies to pay a printer for the publication of its magazine, but the

student council, which managed the SAF, denied the request on the grounds that *Wide Awake* was a religious activity; funding of religious activities was prohibited under the SAF. After the UVA administration denied a challenge to the Student Council's ruling, *Wide Awake* filed an appeal in district court. Both the district and appellate courts denied the appeal, holding in the latter that UVA, as an agency of the state of Virginia, could engage in viewpoint discrimination, as the establishment clause of the First Amendment prohibited it from providing any assistance to a specific religion.

The Supreme Court, in a divided (5-4) decision, ruled in favor of *Wide Awake*. In his majority opinion, Justice ANTHONY M. KENNEDY distinguished between content discrimination (government discrimination of speech based on the subject of the speech) versus viewpoint discrimination (government discrimination based on the views or thoughts of the speaker). The Court has historically allowed content discrimination to afford government the opportunity to preserve the purposes of the forum it has created. However, as seen in the Court's ruling in *LAMB'S CHAPEL V. CENTER MORICHES UNION FREE SCHOOL DISTRICT*, 508 U.S. 384 (1993), the Court has been quite skeptical about government excluding speech based on its message. Applied to the *Rosenberger* case facts, Kennedy wrote that UVA was engaged in viewpoint discrimination, as it was the Christian nature of *Wide Awake*'s message that led the student group to seek money from the SAF.

Justice Kennedy was, much like Justice SANDRA DAY O'CONNOR in her concurrence, also dismissive of UVA's claim that it had the constitutional duty to discriminate against *Wide Awake*'s Christian message because the establishment clause of the First Amendment does not allow the government to favor one religion over others. Here, Kennedy demonstrated how UVA had taken steps in how it recognized and funded student organizations to show a clear separation between it and student groups. As such, UVA could not be seen to be establishing religion by funding *Wide Awake*.

Justice DAVID H. SOUTER, writing for the four dissenters on the Court, did not agree with Kennedy that there was a clear separation between *Wide Awake* and UVA. As UVA required each student to pay the mandatory activity fee, collected the monies, and then distributed the monies per rules it created, one could easily make the claim that public monies were being spent to fund religion. For Souter, then, the Court seemed to be approving for the first time "direct funding of core religious activities" in violation of the establishment clause of the First Amendment.

In a case context that blurred the lines between various parts of the First Amendment, the Court had to weigh which part of the amendment was more important in *Rosenberger*. Though empathetic toward the government's desire to avoid being seen as violating the establishment clause, the Court made clear that this desire could not result in viewpoint discrimination in a forum the government created.

For more information: O'Brien, David M. *Constitutional Law and Politics: Civil Rights and Liberties.* 5th ed. New York: W.W. Norton, 2003.

—John M. Aughenbaugh

Rostker v. Goldberg 453 U.S. 57 (1981)

In *Rostker v. Goldberg*, the United States Supreme Court rejected a challenge to the law that required males to register for the military. The case arose when President Jimmy Carter reactivated a military draft registration following the Russian invasion of Afghanistan in 1979. Although Carter recommended that Congress amend the Military Selective Service Act to allow women to register, Congress authorized funds to register men only. Several young men, subject to the new registration policy, brought suit against Bernard Rostker, director of the Selective Service System.

The lower court held that the law violated the DUE PROCESS clause of the Fifth Amendment and ordered the registration stopped. The court made it clear that it was expressing no opinion on the role of women in combat, but was limiting its ruling to the registration only. The circuit court stayed the order and the registration proceeded.

In a 6-3 vote, the Supreme Court reversed the lower court, with Chief Justice WILLIAM HUBBS REHNQUIST delivering the opinion of the Court. Noting that the Court's customary deference to congressional authority is heightened when considering a law governing military affairs, the Court approved the male-only registration scheme.

Rehnquist pointed out that the purpose of the registration was to prepare for a draft of combat troops. Acknowledging that the government could have required both sexes to register, he stressed the Court's only task was to determine if the decision to require only men to register was inconsistent with the EQUAL PROTECTION guarantee of the due process clause of the Fifth Amendment. He differentiated this situation from others in which government actions simply reflect stereotypical views of men's and women's roles. In enacting this law, Congress clearly indicated that the registration process was linked to a future draft of potential combat troops. With women ineligible for combat by statute and policy, he said, it was reasonable for Congress to exempt women from the registration process. Under these circumstances, the sexes were not similarly situated, and Congress could legitimately distinguish between them. Although the Court recognized that registration could have been extended to women, since they might fill a role in noncombat positions, it nevertheless accepted Congress's judgment that noncombat roles would be filled by volunteers, making registration unnecessary.

The dissenting justices argued that the Court had not been asked to decide whether women should be drafted into the military nor what role they should play in the service. They criticized the majority for concluding that women need not register because they would not be needed in a draft. They pointed out that if there were a mobilization, the military would require the service of thousands of people in noncombat positions, far beyond the numbers that could be satisfied by volunteers. Since women could serve in those roles, it would be sensible to require them to register so that they could be drafted into those positions as needed.

For more information: Stiehm, Judith Hicks. *Arms and the Enlisted Woman.* Philadelphia: Temple University Press, 1989.

—Susan Gluck Mezey

Roth v. United States 354 U.S. 476 (1957)

In *Roth v. United States,* the U.S. Supreme Court ruled for the first time that speech legally defined as obscene is not protected by the guarantee of freedom of speech in the FIRST AMENDMENT.

The ruling started the Court on a 15-year struggle, not to alter the basic principle of *Roth,* but to find a workable definition of OBSCENITY. In numerous subsequent cases, the Court found it difficult to decide whether material fell within the definition of obscenity, and the justices tinkered repeatedly with the definition.

In Roth, Justice WILLIAM J. BRENNAN, JR., wrote for the majority that material is obscene if it deals with sex in a manner that appeals to the "prurient" interest, meaning in a way that fosters lascivious or lustful thoughts. In the 6-3 ruling, Brennan stressed that many depictions of sex in art, science, and literature would not fall within the obscenity definition.

Brennan contrasted the definition he adopted to an historic approach much more restrictive of freedom of speech. The older standard, from English common law, determined whether something was obscene based on the effect a particularly provocative passage might have on an individual who was susceptible to be affected by it. Brennan said many U.S. courts had correctly repudiated this approach from the British ruling in *Regina v. Hicklin,* (1868) L.R. 3 Q.B. 360. In its place, Brennan said the correct approach is "whether to the average person, applying contemporary community standards, the dominant theme of the material taken as a whole appeals to prurient interest." This substituted standard focuses on the entire work, not on an explicit passage, making overall context relevant. This standard also focuses on an average person's reaction using community standards, not on the actions of a susceptible individual.

The decision upheld two criminal convictions. Samuel Roth had been convicted of violating fed-eral law for running a New York business that mailed obscene circulars and advertising to pro-mote the sale of books, photographs, and maga-zines. His conviction was upheld by the U.S. Court of Appeals for the 2nd Circuit. David Alberts had been convicted under state law in California for having obscene material for sale and for creating an obscene advertisement. His conviction was affirmed by a state appeals court. The Supreme Court decided the two cases together.

The ruling produced three other separate opinions. Chief Justice Earl Warren agreed with the convictions but expressed concern that the principles announced by the Court would cause problems. Warren wrote, "The line dividing the salacious or pornographic from literature or sci-ence is not straight and unwavering."

Justice JOHN MARSHALL HARLAN agreed with the conviction of Alberts under California law, but he said the interests of Congress in a nationwide, uniform obscenity law were too "attenuated" to justify the broad scope of federal law used to con-vict Roth.

Justice WILLIAM O. DOUGLAS dissented, joined by Justice Hugo L. Black. Douglas warned that the Court's new standard was not workable. He wrote, ". . . the test that suppresses a cheap tract today can suppress a literary gem tomorrow."

For more information: De Grazia, Edward. *Girls Lean Back Everywhere: The Law of Obscenity and the Assault on Genius.* New York: Random House, 1992; Hixson, Richard F. *Pornog-raphy and the Justices: The Supreme Court and the Intractable Obscenity Problem.* Carbondale: Southern Illinois University Press, 1996.

—Stephen Wermiel

Rummel v. Estelle 445 U.S. 263 (1980)

In *Rummel v. Estelle,* a divided Supreme Court held that the Eighth and FOURTEENTH AMEND-MENTS are not violated when a state imposes a mandatory life sentence for someone convicted of three nonviolent felonies.

In separate prosecutions over 15 years, Rum-mel had been convicted of the fraudulent use of a credit card, forging a check, and obtaining money under false pretenses. The total monetary value of these crimes was less than $230.00. Under Texas law, Rummel was considered a habitual offender and he was sentenced to life in prison. The lower courts rejected Rummel's claim that his sentence was so disproportionate to the crimes that his punishment was cruel and unusual.

Justice WILLIAM HUBBS REHNQUIST, joined by Chief Justice WARREN BURGER and Justices Stewart, White, and Blackmun, voted to affirm. Rehnquist's majority opinion acknowledged that proportionality analysis applies to the death penalty because of the unique nature of the punishment, and he recognized that previous decisions held that the CRUEL AND UNUSUAL PUNISHMENT clause of the Eighth Amendment "prohibits imposition of a sentence that is grossly disproportionate to the severity of the crime." Rehnquist argued, however, that the length of punishments for recidivists are "matters largely within the discretion of the punishing jurisdiction," and that Texas had a significant interest in dealing "in a harsher manner with those who by repeated criminal acts have shown that they are simply incapable of conforming to the norms of society." The Court also noted that, with good time credits and parole, there was a possibility that Rummel would not be imprisoned for the rest of his life.

Justice LEWIS POWELL's dissenting opinion, joined by Justices WILLIAM J. BRENNAN, JR., Marshall, and JOHN PAUL STEVENS, criticized the majority for suggesting that the proportionality principle may be less applicable to noncapital sentences, and he argued that such a "limitation finds no support in the history of Eighth Amendment jurisprudence." He stated that a few basic principles emerge from that history. Barbarous forms of punishment are cruel and unusual, and a sentence may be excessive if it serves no acceptable social purpose or is grossly disproportionate to the seriousness of the crime.

Powell identified several objective factors that courts should consider when assessing the proportionality of a sentence: (1) the nature of the offense; (2) the sentence imposed for the same crime in other jurisdictions; and (3) the sentence imposed upon other criminals in the same jurisdiction. Applying these factors, Powell concluded that Rummel's punishment was cruel and unusual. Rummel was guilty of nonviolent property crimes, and his sentence was harsher than those given first-time or second-time offenders convicted of more serious crimes. Finally, the Texas criminal justice system assumed that all three-time offenders deserve the same punishment, regardless of whether they committed three murders or cashed three fraudulent checks.

The majority opinion in *Rummel* weakened the proportionality principle under the Eighth Amendment by enhancing state authority to determine punishments for recidivists. The *Rummel* precedent was used by the Court in *EWING V. CALIFORNIA*, 538 U.S. 11 (2003), to uphold California's "Three-Strikes" law.

For more information: Fliter, John. *Prisoners' Rights: The Supreme Court and Evolving Standards of Decency.* Westport, Conn.: Greenwood Press, 2000.

—John Fliter

Rumsfeld v. Padilla 542 U.S. 426 (2004)

In *Rumsfeld v. Padilla* the Supreme Court refused to hear a suspected al-Qaeda terrorist's HABEAS CORPUS petition because it was filed improperly in the U.S. District Court for the Southern District of New York. The petition should have been filed in the U.S. District Court for the District of South Carolina, where the prisoner was being physically detained. Furthermore, the petition should have named Padilla's immediate custodian, Commander Melanie Marr, not Secretary of Defense Donald Rumsfeld, as the respondent.

Jose Padilla was accused of approaching Abu Zubaydah, the operational coordinator for al-Qaeda in Afghanistan, to propose a plan to steal radioactive material in order to construct and detonate a dirty bomb in the United States. Padilla was arrested at O'Hare International Airport in Chicago in May 2002. Originally held as a material witness, on June 9 President Bush directed the secretary of defense, Donald Rumsfeld, to detain

Padilla as an enemy combatant for conspiracy to commit warlike acts, including international terrorism. Padilla was placed in military custody at the U.S. Navy brig in Charleston, South Carolina. His lawyer filed a habeas corpus petition two days later in the U.S. District Court for the Southern District of New York.

The Supreme Court did not rule on the merits of the case but decided the case by a 5-4 split on jurisdictional grounds. Chief Justice WILLIAM HUBBS REHNQUIST, joined by Justices SANDRA DAY O'CONNOR, ANTONIN GREGORY SCALIA, ANTHONY M. KENNEDY, and CLARENCE THOMAS, stated that the habeas corpus petition was filed in the wrong court and that the proper respondent was not the secretary of defense but rather the individual who had direct custody of Padilla. The Court stated that Congress, in 1867, added the provision to the habeas statute that petitions could be filed only by the person with custody in their respective jurisdiction. This would avoid the problem of judges hearing habeas claims from petitioners in other jurisdictions. As such, Padilla's lawyers would have to file the petition for habeas corpus again, naming Marr as respondent in the case.

Justice Kennedy, in a concurrence joined by Justice O'Connor, noted that while there are exceptions to the two rules requiring the habeas corpus action to be brought against the person who was the immediate custodian of the prisoner and also in the district court that had territorial jurisdiction over the custodian, none of the exceptions were met in this case.

Justice JOHN PAUL STEVENS, joined by Justices STEPHEN G. BREYER, DAVID H. SOUTER, and Ginsburg, dissented, arguing that, special circumstances existed that justified the exception of the immediate-custodian rule and that the Supreme Court therefore had the jurisdiction to decide the case because it raised important national questions. Furthermore, the dissent suggests that the petition was filed properly in the Southern District of New York against the secretary of defense because he was given direct control over Padilla. Finally, the dissent also notes that at the very least Padilla should have received a hearing about the executive's justification for his detention.

The case was reheard by the district court and a decision in favor of Padilla was delivered. At the circuit court level, on September 9, 2005, the 4th U.S. Circuit Court of Appeals reversed the district court decision holding that the Bush administration had the authority to detain Padilla without pressing charges, as Congress necessarily authorized such detentions with the authorization for use of military force (AUMF). On November 25, 2005, however, Padilla was charged with three counts of conspiracy to murder U.S. nationals, conspiracy to provide material support to terrorists, and providing material support to terrorists. The charges did not include conspiracy to conduct terrorist acts in the United States. Padilla was tried in a civilian court in Miami, Florida, after he pled not guilty to all charges, and in August 2007 was convicted of all charges in a jury trial.

For more information: Leone, Richard, and Greg Anrig, Jr. *War on Our Freedoms: Civil Liberties in an Age of Terrorism.* New York: Century Foundation, 2003; Moeckli, Daniel. "The U.S. Supreme Court's 'Enemy Combatant' Decisions: A Major Victory for the Rule of Law." *Journal of Conflict and Security Law* 10, no. 1 (2005): 75–99.

—Amanda DiPaolo

Rust v. Sullivan 500 U.S. 173 (1991)

In *Rust v. Sullivan,* the U.S. Supreme Court upheld the federal government's authority to condition receipt of its funds to private organizations on those organizations refraining from espousing certain viewpoints. In this case, the Court upheld a regulation enacted during the Reagan administration that placed a "gag order" on family planning organizations, threatening to withdraw funding from any program that provided abortion-related services to its clients.

The lawsuit stemmed from Title X of the Public Health Service Act, which Congress originally passed in 1970 to prohibit federal funds from going to any program that used ABORTION as a means of family planning. In 1988, Health and Human Services secretary Otis R. Bowen extended this ban to any organization that counseled, referred, or otherwise promoted abortion as a means of family planning.

Dr. Irving Rust, representing a group of doctors and patients, sued, seeking an INJUNCTION to block these new regulations before they took effect. Dr. Louis Sullivan, then-secretary under President George H. W. Bush, was named as the defendant.

The HHS regulation was challenged under the FIRST, FOURTH and Fifth AMENDMENTS and on the grounds that the secretary had overstepped his discretion under the statute. However, the main significance of this case was whether it violated the free speech rights of health practitioners.

Ordinarily, government is not allowed to suppress the viewpoint of private individuals in PUBLIC FORUMS such as parks or streets. Even when government opens up a "limited" forum for a stated purpose, it cannot engage in viewpoint discrimination. For example, a town meeting that is convened to discuss the building of a highway can restrict the discussion of the meeting to that subject matter, but it cannot censor speakers because they either support or oppose the building of the new highway.

In a 5-4 opinion for the Court, Chief Justice WILLIAM HUBBS REHNQUIST held that when government subsidizes speech the issue of viewpoint discrimination does not arise. Government may not only express its own views, but also promote those views by granting funds to those organizations that agree with its perspective, to the exclusion of those who don't. For example, just because government promotes democracy and funds those organizations that espouse that view does not mean

it is required to subsidize those organizations that promote other political systems. Similarly, government is free to promote childbirth as a form of family planning and not subsidize those who espouse abortion. Censorship is not at issue, the Court said, because family planning organizations are still free to advise their patients about abortion. They just have to forgo federal funding if they do.

In dissent, Justice Harry Blackmun claimed that this was the first time the Court had allowed government to condition funds upon recipients having to relinquish a constitutional right. He stated that the Court's ruling not only condoned viewpoint suppression, but also it compelled medical practitioners to espouse antiabortion views against their will.

Two other dissenting opinions claimed that the secretary's regulation did not comport with Title X, which was enacted to prohibit funding of abortion *procedures* themselves, not *speech* about abortion. Rehnquist conceded that, though the statute did not explicitly call for a "gag-order," it was within the scope of the statute.

The Court also held that the regulation did not violate the Fifth Amendment right to abortion. Failing to subsidize a right, such as abortion, does not represent a denial of that right.

One of the lawyers arguing for the government was future chief justice, JOHN G. ROBERTS, JR.

For more information: Craig, Barbara Hinkson, and David O'Brien. *Abortion and American Politics*. Chatham, N.J.: Chatham House, 1993; Guittan, Stephanie, and Peter Irons, eds. *May It Please the Court*. New York: New Press, 1995.

—Tim Gordinier

S

Saenz v. Roe 526 U.S. 489 (1999)

Saenz v. Roe marked only the second time that the Supreme Court struck down a law as a violation of the PRIVILEGES AND IMMUNITIES clause of the FOURTEENTH AMENDMENT, enacted in 1868.

The federal welfare reform bill of 1996 authorized states to make lower welfare payments to first-year residents of the state by paying them only the lower monthly amount they would have received in their previous state of residence. California and about 15 other states instituted such two-tier systems. The ACLU challenged the California practice on behalf of two welfare recipients who had recently moved to California and received the lower benefits.

Writing for a majority of seven, Justice JOHN PAUL STEVENS struck down the two-tier system, holding that the privileges and immunities clause of the Fourteenth Amendment protects the right of citizens to move from state to state and to achieve equal citizenship, and equal eligibility for welfare benefits, in their new states. Chief Justice WILLIAM HUBBS REHNQUIST and Justice CLARENCE THOMAS dissented, viewing the one-year residency requirement for full benefits as an ordinary, bona fide residency requirement, and claiming that the majority had misinterpreted the intent and meaning of the privileges and immunities clause.

Both liberal and conservative constitutional theorists welcomed the Supreme Court's apparent revival of the long-dormant clause, which the Court had almost read out of the Constitution in the *Slaughterhouse Cases* of 1873. Conservatives had hoped the Court would view the clause as the source of "natural" economic rights such as freedom of contract and property ownership. Liberals had hoped the Court would see the clause as protecting fundamental personal liberties such as PRIVACY and autonomy. But the Court has made no further subsequent use of the privileges and immunities clause as of this writing.

For more information: Pilon, Roger, and Kimberly C. Shankman. "Reviving the Privileges or Immunities Clause to Redress the Balance among States, Individuals, and the Federal Government." *Texas Review of Law & Politics* 3 (Fall 1998): 1–48; Tribe, Laurence H. "Comment: *Saenz* sans Prophecy: Does the Privileges or Immunities Revival Portend the Future or Reveal the Structure of the Present?" *Harvard Law Review* 113 (November 1999): 110–198.

—Michael Comiskey

same-sex marriage

Same-sex marriage refers to a marriage between two persons who are of the same gender—two men or two women—who are both presumed to be homosexual, though modern technology that effects a change in sex assignment has enlarged the possibilities regarding who is encompassed in any marriage. While the highly contentious political debate over whether to recognize same-sex marriage in the law is relatively recent, the phenomenon of two persons, both or one of whom are not heterosexual, antedates the issue, as it was not uncommon for a gay man and a lesbian to marry each other so as to pass as "normal" for family, work, or other social purposes, especially during the McCarthy era of the 1950s, when homosexual persons were sought out and dismissed from government service.

That legal marriage, then, has been possible for opposite-sex couples, regardless of the sexual orientation of either person, may indicate the priority of the form of marriage (requires one man and one woman) over its substance (expectation of love and commitment between two lifelong partners, for example). Hence, the term "same-sex marriage" rather than "gay marriage" is the better one to refer to what's at issue today. Discussions over same-sex marriage have taken place in the nation's courts and legislatures, and have involved a variety of legal terms and concepts, but especially the EQUAL PROTECTION doctrine.

The idea of same-sex marriage received its first widespread introduction during the court proceedings surrounding *Baehr v. Lewin* (852 P.2d 44 [Haw. 1993]), a case within the state of Hawaii that turned on that state's equal rights provision whereby denial of legal marriage to a woman who wanted to marry her female partner was viewed as impermissible gender discrimination, given that, were she a man, she could legally marry her female partner. This case was followed by *Baker v. Vermont* (744 A.2d 864 [Vt. 1999]), which turned on that state constitution's robust equality provisions in its "common benefits clause," ultimately forcing that state's legislature to craft a regime of civil unions parallel to marriage and offering equal state benefits. These and other actions in the states prompted the Congress to pass the Defense of Marriage Act (DOMA) in 1996, which was itself followed by a host of similar acts enacted by state legislatures, via popular referenda, or through amendments to state constitutions. These acts clarify that marriage is defined as between one man and one woman for all legal purposes.

The primary instigators of vigorous definitions of marriage to the exclusion of same-sex couples have tended to be religious conservatives, whose traditional views of marriage continue to resonate with a lot of Americans, though not with people in several other Western countries, or with relevant professional organizations such as the American Psychiatric Association, which supports same-sex marriage on empirical grounds. The nature of the arguments against same-sex union has been predominantly sectarian or pseudo-religious, such as

in NATURAL LAW arguments that purport to prove that same-sex marriage, like homosexuality itself, is contrary to nature. The lack of verifiable empirical bases for the ban on same-sex marriage, and the support of it through what empirical evidence there is related to this issue, has led some commentators to suggest that the deeper issue here really is particular religious preferences ensconced in American law and politics.

Proponents of same-sex marriage will point to equality and the nature of marriage as a fundamental right or liberty interest established in a long line of cases, including *LOVING v. VIRGINIA* (388 U.S. 1 [1967]) and *Zablocki v. Redhail* (434 U.S. 374 [1978]), which together state that adults have a constitutional right to marry. Nonetheless, detractors point out that even today marriage is restricted to two adult persons, and so will argue that specifying a further restriction as to the different genders of each person is but to clarify the historical understanding and commonplace definition of marriage. Their opponents will counter that legal definitions change over time and are subject to constitutional filters, while historical understandings may reflect prejudice, rather than principle.

Hence, the issue has become a battlefield of various constituencies, each attempting a knockdown argument or legislative or legal maneuver to cement popular understanding and to foreclose any revisiting of the issue. Such moves are always suspect in the liberal-democratic political regime with a republican form of government operating under a written constitution. For example, DOMA raised the issue of the full faith and credit clause of the federal constitution, having taken an issue not mentioned in the U.S. Constitution, and so historically left to the states, and providing a rationale not to accept other states' laws when they diverge from one another. Ballot initiatives at the state level, and the still-anticipated move to amend the federal Constitution, raise the specter of majoritarianism directed against an unpopular minority. The religious element in the debates triggers FIRST AMENDMENT concerns even as a few recognized religious denominations have revised their understanding of marriage to include same-sex couples. In addition, the equal citizenship status of individual American citizens who happen to be gay or lesbian is called into question given the considerable federal- and state-level economic and other benefits triggered by legal marriage from which they are formally excluded.

For more information: Babst, Gordon A. *Liberal Constitutionlism, Marriage, and Sexual Orientation: A Contemporary Case for Dis-Establishment.* New York: Peter Lang, 2002; Gerstmann, Evan. *Same-Sex Marriage and the Constitution.* Cambridge, Mass.: Cambridge University Press, 2004.

—Gordon A. Babst

San Antonio v. Rodriguez 411 U.S. 1 (1973)

In *San Antonio v. Rodriguez,* the Supreme Court ruled that there was no federal right to education and that the classification of individuals based upon wealth was not suspect.

In this case, a class action lawsuit was brought on behalf of Demetrio Rodriguez and other school-aged children throughout the state of Texas by a Mexican-American family alleging that the Texas system of financing public education was unconstitutional. Initially, the federal district court found the Texas manner of financing and the scheme used to determine financing allocation in violation of the EQUAL PROTECTION clause of the U.S. Constitution. The United States Supreme Court disagreed.

The decision in the case at the U.S. Supreme Court level in 1973 ended the attempts by the public to use the federal court system to equalize the public education system, thereby forcing the plaintiffs to utilize other social pressures and more political vehicles to motivate and create equality within the schools. The basis of the suit was that the minorities in Texas were in urban schools funded mostly from local property taxes and were at a disadvantage due to the demise of urban community property values. The allegations made in the court proceedings evolved into a comparative analysis of taxation amounts in the poorer and more urban areas such as the Edgewood District, relationally speaking, against those taxed in the wealthier Alamo Heights District. Thus the facts showed that there was a disparity in the two districts comparatively and that the amount of financing available to the better areas was higher. In simpler terms, it was argued that the lack of a strong economy in these areas would generate less income to be taxed, and thus less money would be available for schools, and the effects of lower pay for teachers would be lesser quality instructors, fewer resources for children, and fewer activities to keep the children positively engaged—also challenging the maintenance of the schools themselves and potentially creating dangerous and inadequately maintained environments for children to learn.

San Antonio v. Rodriguez was the first federal case to challenge the manner in which schools were funded and the financing that goes into running a school. Another issue put to rest in this case was that the wealth of the denizens of an area was not to be considered a suspect classification, albeit relevant; that the Texas school financing laws were not and should not be considered a racial classification; and that the education available to the students of the areas was a "fundamental right," but that this right had not been violated. So the rational basis for the financing laws stood and the funding of schools continues in similar fashion to this day, although recent attempts at reclassifying the way in which funds are distributed is under review in several sections of the country.

Overall, as a result of this decision, litigation of state educational claims was moved to state courts to be litigated under state laws and constitutions.

For more information: Kozol, Jonathan. *Savage Inequalities: Children in America's Schools.* New York: HarperPerennial, 1992.

—Ernest Gomez

Santa Clara County v. Southern Pacific Railroad 118 U.S. 394 (1886)

The Supreme Court in *Santa Clara County v. Southern Pacific Railroad* ruled that corporations have the same rights as individual people do under the U.S. Constitution.

The ruling extended the FOURTEENTH AMENDMENT'S EQUAL PROTECTION clause to corporations. That clause says that no state shall "deprive any person of life, liberty, or property, without DUE PROCESS of law; nor deny to any person within its jurisdiction the equal protection of the laws." The Fourteenth Amendment was passed to ensure equal rights for former slaves after the Civil War.

Corporations have successfully used the *Santa Clara* case to claim many further rights, including freedom of speech in the CAMPAIGN FINANCE arena, freedom of PRIVACY in battling corporate disclosure, and other equal protection claims.

The case itself dealt with the fairly mundane topic of the proper taxation of fence posts on land held by the Southern Pacific Railroad. The Court upheld a lower court's ruling that the state had incorrectly included the value of the fence posts in its property tax assessment of land owned by the railroad.

The opinion never actually stated that corporations deserved the same constitutional protections as people do. In fact, the opinion explicitly says that the lower court should have ruled on the tax issues without reaching the question of corporate personhood:

[the] court below might have given judgment in each case for the defendant upon the ground that the assessment, which was the foundation of the action, included property of material value which the state board was without jurisdiction to assess, and the tax levied upon which cannot, from the record, be separated from that imposed upon other property embraced in the same assessment. As the judgment can be sustained upon this ground, it is not necessary to consider any other questions raised by the pleadings and the facts found by the court.

However, prior to oral arguments (or, by some accounts, prior to the reading of the opinion), Chief Justice Waithe is reported to have said, "The Court does not wish to hear argument on the question whether the provision of the Fourteenth Amendment to the Constitution, which forbids a State to deny any person in its jurisdic-

tion the equal protection of the law, applies to corporations. We are all of the opinion that it does" (Hartmann, p. 104).

The clerk who wrote the headnotes, J. C. Bancroft Davis, wrote Waithe prior to publishing the opinion to confirm if this quote accurately captured what Waithe said. Waithe replied that "I think your mem. in the California Rail Road tax cases expresses with sufficient accuracy what was said before the arguments began. I leave it with you to determine whether anything need be said about it in the report inasmuch as we avoided meeting the Constitutional question in the decision" (Hartmann, p. 112).

Davis then published the headnotes to say, "The defendant Corporations are persons within the intent of the clause in section 1 of the Fourteenth Amendment to the Constitution of the United States, which forbids a State to deny to any person within its jurisdiction the equal protection of the laws" (Hartmann, p. 105).

The *Santa Clara* ruling capped a decades-long effort by corporate America to win such protection. Corporations were not mentioned in the Constitution and were originally not considered to be persons. Rather, they were thought of as artificial persons—creations of the government and subject to strict charters outlining their authorities and to strict regulation in ways that individuals were not.

Four similar cases where corporations had asserted Fourteenth Amendment rights (94 U.S. 155, 94 U.S. 164, 94 U.S. 179, and 94 U.S. 180 [1877]) had previously been rebuffed by the Supreme Court. In these cases, the Court ruled without ever reaching the question of whether the corporation was a person.

It was highly unusual for the Court to issue a ruling with such monumental implications without any explanation for the ruling in the written opinion. If, indeed, the Court did mean to declare that corporations did have the rights of persons, why would Chief Justice Waithe leave it up to the discretion of a clerk to decide whether or not to include this in the headnotes?

These odd circumstances have led some to speculate that railroad interests used long-cultivated connections to spin this decision to their desired effect. J. C. Bancroft Davis, the clerk who wrote the headnotes, had been president of the Newburgh and New York Railroad. It is possible that he was influenced in how he wrote the headnotes by Justice Field, a longtime supporter of the railroads who wrote a concurring opinion that the Court should have reached the Fourteenth Amendment arguments.

For more information: Hartmann, Thom. *Unequal Protection: The Rise of Corporate Dominance and the Theft of Human Rights.* Emmaus, Pa.: Rodale Press, 2002.

—Derek Cressman

Sante Fe Independent School District v. Doe
530 U.S. 290 (2000)

In *Sante Fe Independent School District v. Doe,* the Supreme Court decided 6-3 that a school district policy allowing student-led prayer at public high school football games violated the ESTABLISHMENT CLAUSE of the FIRST AMENDMENT. The Supreme Court let stand the ruling of the U.S. Court of Appeals for the Fifth Circuit. The case generated a strong dissent from Chief Justice WILLIAM HUBBS REHNQUIST.

The Sante Fe Independent School District in Texas had been allowing student-initiated and student-led prayer before public high school football games for many years. An elected student chaplain was designated to provide the prayer. However, two students objected to the prayers and, through their mothers, filed suit in federal court to have the practice abandoned by the school district. The school district refined its procedures for allowing the prayer while the litigation moved forward by holding two separate student elections related to the issue. The first election allowed the students to choose whether or not to pray before a football game. When the results of this election showed that the majority of students wanted there to be prayer, a second election was held to pick a student representative to deliver the prayer. This prompted the district court to use the U.S. Court of Appeals for the

Fifth Circuit precedent in *Jones v. Clear Creek Independent School District* (1992) and issue an order stating that the prayers were constitutional as long as they were nonsectarian and nonproselytizing. Both sides to the case appealed to the U.S. Court of Appeals for the Fifth Circuit. In its ruling, the court upheld its decision in *Jones,* but did so by ruling that its decision applied specifically to graduation ceremonies in *Jones* and not high school football games. Therefore, the decision disallowed prayer at high school football games as instituted by the Santa Fe Independent School District.

The Supreme Court took the case on appeal. Writing for the majority, Associate Justice JOHN PAUL STEVENS said, "The delivery of such a message—over the school's public address system, by a speaker representing the student body, under the supervision of school faculty, and pursuant to a school policy that explicitly and implicitly encourages public prayer—is not properly characterized as 'private' speech." The majority was unconvinced that the student speech was private in nature, given the school district's control over the process and the content of the speech being delivered by the student. Stevens also pointed out toward the end of the decision that "nothing in the Constitution as interpreted by this Court prohibits any public school student from voluntarily praying at any time before, during, or after the schoolday."

In a stinging dissent, Chief Justice William Hubbs Rehnquist wrote that the majority opinion "bristles with hostility to all things religious in public life." Rehnquist continued, "Neither the holding nor the tone of the opinion is faithful to the meaning of the Establishment Clause, when it is recalled that George Washington himself, at the request of the very Congress which passed the BILL OF RIGHTS, proclaimed a day of 'public thanksgiving and prayer, to be observed by acknowledging with grateful hearts the many and signal favors of Almighty God.'"

The gist of this decision is that prayer before a public high school football game, as the school district had set it up, was deemed to be an endorsement of religion by the government.

For more information: Choper, Jesse H., Richard H. Fallon, Jr., Yale Kamisar, and Steven H. Shiffrin. *Constitutional Law: Cases & Comments.* 10th ed. St. Paul, Minn.: West Group, 2006; Hankins, Barry. "Is the Supreme Court Hostile to Religion?: *Good News Club et al. v. Milford Central School* (2001) and *Santa Fe v. Doe* (2000)." *Journal of Church and State* 43, no. 4 (Autumn 2001): 681–687.

—Jane Rainey and William Lester

Scales v. United States 367 U.S. 203 (1961)
In a 5-4 decision, Justice JOHN HARLAN upheld against four dissents (HUGO BLACK, WILLIAM J. BRENNAN, JR., WILLIAM O. DOUGLAS, and Earl Warren) the conviction of Junius Irving Scales for his membership in the North Carolina Communist Party under the membership section of the Smith Act.

Between 1951 and 1957 there were 145 indictments leading to 108 convictions as a result of *Dennis v. U.S.*, 391 U.S. 494 (1951), which upheld arrests for membership in the Communist Party. The Supreme Court contrasted its *Dennis* decision in *Yates v. U.S.*, 354 U.S. 298 (1957), resulting in numerous communists being released from jail or never being tried. However, for those in jail already (like Scales), the case did not mean freedom. Scales's 1955 decision was dismissed on appeal in 1957, but then he was again recharged and found guilty in a 1958 trial, which was upheld again by the court of appeals. The case reached the Supreme Court in 1961.

Justice Harlan reasoned that Section 4f of the Internal Security Act did not repeal the membership section of the Smith Act (18 U.S.C. §2385) if the person actively participated in the organization. Scales was not denied his Fifth Amendment DUE PROCESS rights because he belonged to an organization that was engaged in criminal advocacy. Nor were his FIRST AMENDMENT rights of political expression violated, since witnesses showed he had made statements favoring criminal advocacy. According to the Supreme Court: "We can discern no reason why membership, when it constitutes a purposeful form of complicity in a group engaging in this same forbidden advocacy, should receive any greater degree of protection from the guarantees of that Amendment" (p. 229). Reviewing the evidence standard found in the *Yates* case, Harlan found that there was sufficient evidence to show through two witnesses' accounts that Scales had gone beyond mere membership and had advocated criminal actions.

In the dissents, Justice Black claimed that the First Amendment forbade trying anyone for belonging to a political organization or association: "He has therefore been deprived of his right to be tried under a clearly defined, pre-existing 'law of the land' as guaranteed by the Due Process Clause and I think his conviction should be reversed on that ground" (p. 260–261). Douglas strongly objected to imprisonment of Scales because of guilt by association only and with no specific criminal acts charged against him. Brennan, with Warren and Douglas joining, found Section 4f of the Internal Security Act legislated immunity from the membership clause of the Smith Act.

In conclusion, the *Scales* case was offset by Justice Harlan's opinion in *Noto v. U.S.*, 392 U.S. 290 (1961), on the same day, which reversed the lower court on the basis that evidence did not reflect membership and set down guidelines for future membership cases that could not be sustained. These cases marked the end of Smith Act prosecutions in the courts. On December 25, 1962, President Kennedy commuted Scales's imprisonment.

For more information: Caute, David. *The Great Fear: The Anti-Communist Purge under Truman and Eisenhower.* New York: Simon & Schuster, 1978; Belknap, Michael R. *Cold War Political Justice: The Smith Act, the Communist Party, and American Civil Liberties.* Westport, Conn.: Greenwood Press, 1977; Frickey, Philip. "Getting from Joe to Gene (McCarthy): The Avoidance Canon, Legal Process Theory, and Narrowing Statutory Interpretation in the Early Warren Court." *California Law Review* 93 (2005): 397–464; Rohr, Marc. "Communists and the First Amendment: The Shaping of Freedom of Advocacy in the Cold War." *San Diego Law Review* 28 (1991): 1–106.

—Joel Fishman and Dan Krejci

Scalia, Antonin Gregory (1936–   ) *Supreme Court justice*

Antonin Gregory Scalia presently serves as a U.S. Supreme Court justice; his appointment was in 1986. Scalia was born March 11, 1936, in Trenton, New Jersey, the only child of S. Eugene Scalia and Catherine Scalia. Scalia's father was born in Sicily and immigrated to the United States as a young man. He was a professor of Romance languages. His mother, born to immigrant Italian parents, was a schoolteacher.

Scalia's family moved to Elmhurst, a section of Queens, New York. He attended public school in Queens and later at St. Francis Xavier, a military prep school in Manhattan, where he graduated first in his class. He received his B.A. summa cum laude in history in 1957 from Georgetown University and was the valedictorian of his class. He attended Harvard Law School, where he received his LL.B. magna cum laude. Following graduation, he spent a year traveling in Europe as a Sheldon Fellow of Harvard.

Scalia began his legal career in 1961 as an associate at the law firm of Jones, Day, Cockley, and Reavis in Cleveland, Ohio. He worked in a number of practice areas, including real estate, corporate financing, labor, and antitrust. In 1967 he decided to teach law and became a professor at the University of Virginia Law School.

Four years later, Scalia took leave from Virginia to begin a career in government service. Various positions included: general counsel, Office of Telecommunications Policy; chairman of the Administrative Conference of the United States; and assistant attorney general for the Office of Legal Counsel at the Justice Department.

After he left government service, Scalia returned to teaching law, briefly at Georgetown University Law Center and then at the University of Chicago from 1977 to 1982. In 1982 President Ronald Reagan appointed Scalia to the U.S. Court of Appeals for the DISTRICT OF COLUMBIA Circuit. He served on this court, considered second in importance only to the Supreme Court, for four years.

On June 17, 1986, President Reagan nominated Scalia to the Supreme Court, to fill the seat left vacant by the elevation of WILLIAM HUBBS REHNQUIST to chief justice. In his testimony before the Senate Judiciary Committee, Scalia said he considered the most important part of the Constitution to be the system of "CHECKS AND BALANCES among the three branches, . . . so that not one of them is able to run roughshod over the liberties of the people." Scalia was confirmed unanimously (98-0) by the SENATE on September 17.

An important case during his early years demonstrated his conviction concerning the "checks and balances" necessary among the three branches. *Morrison v. Olson,* 487 U.S. 654 (1988), was a suit challenging the constitutionality of the independent counsel, an individual selected by the judiciary to investigate senior officials of the executive branch. The Court upheld the legislation creating the post, but Scalia wrote a forceful dissent, arguing that Congress had impermissibly vested some of the traditional power to prosecute in the hands of someone not fully within the supervision and control of the president—an arrangement that had no support in the Constitution. Scalia asked, "Once we depart from the text of the Constitution, just where short of that do we stop?" (id. at 711).

Scalia is considered a formalist, following a "textualist" and/or "originalist" approach when interpreting the Constitution. He is unwilling to find constitutional rights that are not plainly set forth in the language of the Constitution or firmly grounded in American tradition. Both approaches emphasize careful adherence to the text of both the Constitution of the United States and federal statutes, as their meaning would have been understood when adopted. Some applaud Scalia's view; others believe the Constitution is a "living document" that entails more than the mere words with which it is written.

Scalia's strict adherence to originalism has led him to support many rights associated with a liberal viewpoint. One example is his support for the Court's holding in *TEXAS v. JOHNSON,* 491 U.S. 397 (1989), that flag burning is a form of political expression protected under the FIRST AMENDMENT, despite his personal contempt for flag burners. By contrast, Scalia's decisions on ABORTION or

GAY AND LESBIAN RIGHTS issues could be characterized as opposing a libertarian viewpoint; e.g., in *LAWRENCE V. TEXAS*, 539 U.S. 558 (2003), Scalia denied that the Constitution protected the right to engage in sodomy.

Although Scalia's views are not endorsed by a majority of the Court, he is well respected for his strong intellect, analytical ability, and obvious passion for the law.

For more information: Schultz, David, and Christopher Smith. *The Jurisprudential Vision of Justice Antonin Scalia.* Lanham, Md.: Rowman & Littlefield, 1996.

—Randy W. Hagedorn

Schechter Poultry Corporation v. United States 295 U.S. 495 (1935)

In *Schechter Poultry Corporation v. United States* the Supreme Court held that rules drafted under the National Industrial Act to regulate competition were an unconstitutional delegation of power. The importance of this case was that it struck down some of the first sets of laws drafted during the New Deal.

In *Schechter Poultry*, the Supreme Court was asked to determine the constitutionality of a section of the National Industrial Recovery Act of 1933. In the act, Congress gave the National Recovery Administration (NRA) the authority to establish fair codes for competition—including wages, hours, and working conditions—in various industries nationwide. By establishing these codes, the hope was that conditions in a host of industries would stabilize, thus ameliorating the ongoing economic depression affecting the country at the time.

In this case, the Schechter brothers operated a number of slaughterhouses in New York City. They imported chickens from out of state, slaughtered them, and then sold the chickens locally. At the federal district court level, the Schechters were found in violation of various codes established by the NRA, with the conviction being upheld by the appellate court. The Schechters challenged their conviction to the Supreme Court, claiming that

the act surpassed congressional powers per the COMMERCE CLAUSE and that the authority delegated to the NRA was unconstitutional due to the lack of specific standards to guide the NRA.

A unanimous Court, in an opinion written by Chief Justice Hughes, first held that the Schechter's business activities, particularly after receiving the chickens, were intrastate, and thus had little direct impact upon INTERSTATE COMMERCE. As such, the Court concluded Congress did not have the authority to regulate the Schechter brothers' enterprises under its commerce clause authority.

Next, the Court addressed the claim that the authority Congress granted the NRA was unconstitutional. Specifically, the Schechters contended that the authority given the NRA to establish fair competition codes was done so without giving the executive branch standards on which to base the codes. The Court, after an extensive review of the law, agreed with the Schechters, determining that Congress had not defined what it meant by fair competition, had not established a standard to guide executive branch action, and had not required any finding of fact by the executive branch before it exercised the authority found in the law. In the end, the Court concluded that Congress left to the executive branch's discretion the determination of what was or was not fair competition for a number of industries. As Justice Cardozo wrote in a concurring opinion, "(T)his was delegation running riot."

A broader issue surrounding this case was the question of what the Constitution demanded from the executive and legislative branches as expectations placed upon the federal government grew in the aftermath of the Great Depression in the late 1920s and throughout the 1930s. The Court in *Schechter*, like in *PANAMA REFINING COMPANY V. RYAN*, 293 U.S. 388 (1935), recognized that Congress had authority in the Constitution to pass legislation that gave the government an opportunity to adapt to complex situations that the legislative branch could not foresee. However, the Court also stressed how the Constitution firmly rests legislative authority in Congress and not the executive branch.

Nevertheless, the Court's rulings in *Panama Refining* and *Schechter Poultry* were the last two cases in which it limited the delegation of authority from Congress to the executive branch. The nondelegation doctrine, as these rulings came to be known, gave way to the Court typically ratifying broad congressional delegations of authority to the executive branch throughout the 20th century and into the next century.

Finally, by the late 1930s and early 1940s, the Court began to allow congressional efforts to regulate activities that had an indirect, albeit substantial, effect on the national economy (see UNITED STATES V. DARBY, 312 U.S. 100 [1941], and WICKARD V. FILBURN, 317 U.S. 111 [1941]). Whereas the Court was quite reluctant in the first years of the New Deal to read the Constitution as giving the political branches the authority to regulate areas of the economy that had previously been the purview of state governments (if at all), the Court changed course in 1937 (see NATIONAL LABOR RELATIONS BOARD V. JONES & LAUGHLIN STEEL CORP., 301 U.S. 1 [1937]) and began to deem such legislation as constitutional.

For more information: Leuchtenburg, William E. *The Supreme Court Reborn: The Constitutional Revolution in the Age of Roosevelt.* New York: Oxford University Press, 1995.

—John M. Aughenbaugh

Scheidler v. National Organization for Women, Inc. 547 U.S. 9, 126 S.Ct. 1264 (2006)

In *Scheidler v. National Organization for Women, Inc.*, the Supreme Court considered limits on antiabortion protests under the 1970 Racketeer Influenced and Corrupt Organizations Act (RICO). It ruled that, to win a civil RICO case, plaintiffs must prove that defendants committed at least two or more specified criminal acts within 10 years.

In 1986, the National Organization for Women (NOW) filed a civil RICO action against antiabortion protestors, charging that they were part of a nationwide conspiracy to close abortion clinics by engaging in racketeering activities that included blocking clinic entrances, arson, harassing clinic personnel and clients, destruction of property, physical injuries, bombings, extortion, threats, and intimidation. They claimed that the defendants violated the 1948 Hobbs Act, a federal anti-extortion law that forbids anyone from interfering with INTERSTATE COMMERCE "by robbery or extortion or . . . commits or threatens physical violence to any person or property in furtherance of a plan or purpose" to violate the act.

The circuit court dismissed the case, ruling that the plaintiffs had not shown that the defendants were economically motivated. The Supreme Court unanimously reversed, holding that RICO was not restricted to conspiracies that furthered economic interests.

Four years later, a federal court jury in Chicago found the defendants guilty of violating numerous counts of the Hobbs Act; the judge also issued a nationwide order barring protestors from blocking access to clinics, trespassing, damaging clinic property, and threatening or using violence against clinic personnel or patients. The defendants appealed, arguing that they had not violated the Hobbs Act because they had not "obtained" clinic property and were not guilty of extortion. The circuit court rejected their argument, ruling that they may be found guilty under the Hobbs Act for disrupting or interfering with the victim's business even if they had not physically "obtained" the victim's property.

In 2003, the Supreme Court reversed the appellate court. Chief Justice WILLIAM HUBBS REHNQUIST found that the defendants had not committed extortion because they did not "obtain" the abortion providers' property. Interfering with property is not extortion, he said, even if it succeeds in closing down clinics. Rehnquist concluded that because the defendants were not guilty of extortion, they had not violated the Hobbs Act.

Although the Supreme Court absolved the defendants of the extortion charge, NOW argued that they had still violated RICO by committing acts or threats of violence to persons or property associated with abortion clinics. Because NOW had not raised this issue before the Supreme Court, the appellate court remanded the case to the district court to allow it to determine whether threats or acts of violence constituted crimes under the Hobbs Act.

On appeal once again, the High Court ruled against NOW. Speaking for a unanimous Court, Justice STEPHEN G. BREYER stated that threatening or committing acts of physical violence that were unrelated to extortion or robbery did not violate the Hobbs Act. He said that the "plan or purpose" specified in the statute must affect interstate commerce through robbery or extortion.

After more than a decade, NOW ultimately failed in its attempt to use civil RICO to halt the actions of the antiabortion protestors who tried to disrupt the work of abortion clinics.

For more information: Nero, Autumn. "Where Are We Now?: Clinic Protection in the Wake of *Scheidler v. National Organization for Women, Inc.*" *Wisconsin Women's Law Journal* 21 (2006): 73–109; Schriver, Steven. "Applying Civil Rico to Antiabortion Demonstrators: *National Organization for Women v. Scheidler*," *Maryland Journal of Contemporary Legal Issues* 6 (1994–95): 179–204; Wentzel, Suzanne. "*National Organization for Women v. Scheidler:* RICO a Valuable Tool for Controlling Violent Protest," *Akron Law Review* 28 (1995): 391–408.

—Susan Gluck Mezey

Schenck v. United States 249 U.S. 247 (1919)

In *Schenck v. United States,* Justice OLIVER WENDELL HOLMES, writing for a unanimous Supreme Court, held that the prosecution of two Socialist Party organizers under the World War I–era Espionage Act for distributing leaflets opposing conscription did not violate the FIRST AMENDMENT. *Schenck* is notable as the first case in which Justice Holmes set forth the CLEAR AND PRESENT DANGER TEST.

The case grew out of opposition to U.S. entry into World War I. A number of Socialist Party officials, including Eugene Debs, made speeches opposing the war and military conscription. Charles T. Schenck, general secretary of the Socialist Party, was charged with a conspiracy to violate the Espionage Act by mailing leaflets opposing conscription to men who had been called up for military service. He was sentenced to six months imprisonment.

The leaflets called conscription "despotic" and likened it to involuntary servitude, banned by the THIRTEENTH AMENDMENT. They said that conscription served the interests of Wall Street's chosen few and told the reader to "Assert Your Rights" and not "submit to intimidation." But the leaflets stopped short of calling for violence—or even for draftees to resist induction. Instead, the leaflets called for peaceful measures such as repealing the Selective Draft Act by petition.

In upholding the convictions, Justice Holmes, conceding that "in many places and in ordinary times" the First Amendment would have protected the defendant's speech, observed that "the character of every act depends upon the circumstances in which it is done." Then, in a famous analogy, Justice Holmes said that "even the most stringent protection would not protect a man in falsely shouting fire in a theatre and causing panic." Nor, he continued, did the First Amendment allow someone to utter "words that may well have the effect of force."

Instead, the key question was whether the words, and the surrounding circumstances, created "a clear and present danger that they will bring about the substantive evils that Congress has a right to prevent." Justice Holmes emphasized that in wartime a nation cannot endure acts that hinder the war effort. Nor did it matter whether the leaflets persuaded anyone to obstruct recruitment—if the intent, tendency, and act are the same, Justice Holmes saw "no ground for saying that success alone warrants making the act a crime."

The week after *Schenck,* the Court upheld the Espionage Act conviction of Eugene Debs. However, in *Abrams v. United States,* 250 U.S. 616 (1919), Justice Holmes changed course and dissented against a majority opinion upholding a conviction under the Espionage Act. Significantly, he used the "clear and present danger" test developed in *Schenck* to protect speech—the beginning of a long career for this test.

The phrase "fire in a crowed theater" has entered the lexicon as a stock example of speech that can be restricted. Finally, Justice Holmes's concerns about the limits of political speech in wartime remain with us today.

For more information: Bobertz, Bradley C. "The Brandeis Gambit: The Making of America's 'First Freedom,' 1909–1931." *William and Mary Law Review* 40 (February 1999): 557–651; Kalven, Harry, Jr. *A Worthy Tradition: Freedom of Speech in America.* New York: Harper & Row, 1974.

—Robert A. Kahn

Schmerber v. California 384 U.S. 757 (1966) Just five years after its decision in *Mapp v. Ohio,* 367 U.S. 643 (1961), extending the application of the EXCLUSIONARY RULE to all state criminal court proceedings, the U.S. Supreme Court in *Schmerber v. California* significantly limited the rule's reach in the context of drunk driving investigations and rejected constitutional challenges to an involuntary blood-alcohol test.

The petitioner in *Schmerber v. California* was taken to a hospital after sustaining injuries when the car he was driving struck a tree. At the hospital, he was placed under arrest and subjected to a blood test over his objection. He was convicted of driving under the influence based largely on the fact that his blood-alcohol level exceeded the legally permissible level.

In a 5-4 decision, Justice WILLIAM J. BRENNAN, JR., writing for the majority, held that Schmerber's involuntary blood test did not violate the FOURTH, Fifth, or FOURTEENTH AMENDMENTS. Turning to the SUBSTANTIVE DUE PROCESS issue, he found that the blood extraction, made by a physician in a hygienic hospital environment, did not offend that "sense of justice" underlying a Fourteenth Amendment claim. With regard to Schmerber's contention that his Fifth Amendment privilege against self-incrimination had been violated, the Court held that the withdrawal of blood did not involve "evidence of a testimonial or communicative nature," and, as with the taking of finger-prints, the Fifth Amendment does not exclude the use of the accused's physical person when it is the source of evidence.

The Fourth Amendment claim, however, proved more troublesome for the Court. Brennan acknowledged that the warrantless invasion of Schmerber's body implicated the proscription against "unreasonable" searches and seizures. Although the police officer had probable cause to arrest the suspect in light of Schmerber's conduct at the scene of the accident and later at the hospital, the "search incident to arrest" exception to the warrant requirement was inapplicable. The exception is based on the need for officers to protect themselves and to prevent the imminent destruction of evidence; however, such concerns are unlikely to be relevant to searches below the body surface.

Nevertheless, the Court found the search was reasonable under the circumstances. First, because of the evanescent nature of alcohol in the bloodstream, the officer did not have time to take the accused to the hospital, investigate the scene of the accident, and then seek out a judicial officer and secure a warrant. Second, citing the commonplace nature of blood tests and the medically acceptable circumstances under which the extraction was performed, Brennan held that this minor intrusion into the suspect's body did not constitute an unreasonable search and seizure.

Legal commentators widely considered *Schmerber* to be the death knell for self-incrimination claims involving physical evidence obtained from the suspect's person and a major retreat in exclusionary rule application. However, subsequent case law indicated that the Court's emphasis on the "minimally intrusive" nature of the physical invasion was to be taken seriously; in *Winston v. Lee,* 470 U.S. 753 (1985), the Supreme Court refused to allow nonconsensual surgery under general anesthesia to remove a bullet for forensic purposes.

For more information: LaFave, Wayne R. *Criminal Law.* 4th ed. St. Paul, Minn.: Thomson/West, 2003; LaFave, Wayne R., Jerold H. Israel, and Nancy J. King. *Criminal Procedure.* 2d ed. St. Paul, Minn.: West Group, 1999.

—Virginia Mellema

school busing

School busing refers to the use of school buses to transport children to schools outside their neighborhood in order to promote racial and ethnic integration. It was most common during the 1970s, and its use declined thereafter. School busing, also sometimes called "forced busing" or "mandatory reassignment," is a development of the DESEGREGATION cases and is extremely controversial and politically contentious.

In BROWN V. BOARD OF EDUCATION OF TOPEKA, KANSAS, 347 U.S. 483 (1954), the United States Supreme Court ruled that segregated schools were a violation of the FOURTEENTH AMENDMENT's EQUAL PROTECTION clause. The case originally applied only to areas where schoolchildren were required to attend racially separate schools. In SWANN V. CHARLOTTE-MECKLENBURG BOARD OF EDUCATION, 402 U.S. 1 (1971), the Supreme Court ruled that busing was a legitimate method for integrating students, if assigning students to their neighborhood schools did not provide integration.

The desegregation debate moved outside the South with the Supreme Court's decision in *Keyes v. School District No. 1, Denver, Colorado*, 413 U.S. 189 (1973). The Denver case was an example of segregation that existed due to the drawing of district lines, placement of new schools, and other official actions that were less obvious than the traditional dual school systems of *Brown* and other cases. After *Keyes*, other federal judges began to require school desegregation within their own boundaries. Perhaps the most noted instance of school busing occurred in Boston, when Judge Garrity ruled in *Morgan v. Hennigan*, 379 F. Supp. 410 (1974), that Boston schools were segregated. With the requirement that Boston schools undergo segregation, the city saw school boycotts and riots.

Federal courts, however, were not the only institution to require school busing. In 1963, the California State Supreme Court ruled in *Jackson v. Pasadena City School District*, 59 Cal 2d. 876 (1963), that the state constitution required all public schools to be integrated. This was a step further than the federal courts had ever gone, as they had required desegregation only in cases of de jure (by law) segregation, not in cases of de facto (by fact) segregation.

The *Jackson* case was followed by *Crawford v. Board of Education of the City of Los Angeles*, 130 Cal. Rptr. 724 (1976), also a California State Supreme Court case. In this case, the court applied the *Jackson* doctrine to the city of Los Angeles and required that the district integrate the city's schools. Although Los Angeles did not experience the violence that occurred in Boston, there were school boycotts and protests throughout the city. Los Angeles had a school busing plan in place only for a brief time in the late 1970s; in 1979, voters of the state of California overwhelmingly passed (70 percent) Proposition 1, which forbade the use of busing to remedy de facto segregation. Proposition 1 was upheld and went into effect in 1981, marking the end of the Los Angeles busing program.

Although school busing was used in many communities, the Supreme Court ruled in *Milliken v. Bradley*, 418 U.S. 717 (1974), that cross-district busing was not required. The decision came from a case based in Detroit, where students were bused across district lines between Detroit and several suburbs. This plan was used because the Detroit schools were predominantly black and the suburban schools were predominantly white; interdistrict busing was seen as the only way to integrate either area. The Supreme Court, however, ruled that this was not required unless the suburbs had contributed to de jure segregation.

Some people argue that school busing was successful because it ended, in many communities, the continuance of segregated schools. Others, however, point to the development of "white flight." Under this phenomenon, white families left public school systems in high numbers, either by enrolling their children in private schools or by moving to the suburbs.

Although "school busing" generally refers to mandatory programs, more recent policies tend to be based on voluntary actions. In Boston, students may participate in a voluntary transfer program from the inner city to the suburbs. Los Angeles maintains a popular magnet school program (which also arose during the desegregation debate), and students who attend magnet schools are offered transportation by school bus.

For more information: Orfield, Gary. *Must We Bus?: Segregated Schools and National Policy.* Washington, D.C.: Brookings Institution, 1978; Orfield, Gary, and Susan E. Eaton. *Dismantling Desegregation: The Quiet Reversal of* Brown v. Board of Education. New York: Free Press, 1996.

—Ryane McAuliffe Straus

school prayer

"School prayer" has become the common phrase for referring to government-sponsored prayer, whether recited or silent, in public school settings that include classrooms, graduations, sports events, or other parts of school life. As addressed by the courts, it does not include the freedom of a student to pray silently in school in a nondisruptive manner, nor does it apply to sectarian or private schools.

Many proponents of school prayer argue that this practice dates back to the founding of the United States. While there is some truth to this, today's public school system and compulsory education laws did not begin to take shape until the 19th century. Therefore it is impossible to say with certainty what the Founders would have approved of in such settings, and it is likely that they would not have all agreed.

As public schools developed into a standard part of American life, they tended to carry forward the goal of a moral upbringing of children intertwined with educational instruction in the manner of the schools that had existed since colonial times. This was likely to include prayer and Bible reading with a distinctly Protestant flavor.

The Supreme Court did not begin to address school prayer until after the ESTABLISHMENT CLAUSE had been "incorporated" in 1947 to apply to the states. The Court's first school prayer case was *ENGEL V. VITALE*, 370 U.S. 421 (1962), disallowing a government-composed prayer to be recited by schoolchildren, followed one year later by *ABINGTON TOWNSHIP V. SCHEMPP*, 374 U.S. 203

(1963), which struck down devotional prayer and Bible reading in public schools.

Since the *Schempp* and *Engel* decisions, advocates of school prayer have continued to seek ways in which to include official prayers at various school functions, and in response there has been a series of cases further delineating the limits to state-sponsored school prayer. In *WALLACE V. JAFFREE*, 472 U.S. 38 (1985), the Court held that Alabama's "moment of silence for meditation or voluntary prayer" violated the establishment clause, while strongly suggesting that a legislatively mandated "moment of silence" with no mention of prayer might pass constitutional muster. In *LEE V. WEISMAN*, 505 U.S. 577 (1992), the Court invalidated clergy-led prayer at a middle school graduation, and in *Santa Fe v. Doe,* 530 U.S. 290 (2000), the Court struck down officially sponsored student-led prayers at high school football games.

The rulings in these cases suggest a consistent stance by the Court from 1962 to 2000; however, the votes tell a more complex story. While only one justice dissented in the two early landmark prayer cases, recent cases reflect a much more divided Court. The separationist rulings on "school prayer" have also differed from (a) the accomodationist positions of the Court on prayer in legislatures and (b) the Court's more permissive role toward a presence of religion in higher education. The Court's explanation for this is that public K–12 education is compulsory, and that children are more impressionable than college students or legislators. Children are also sensitive to social pressure and ostracism for being perceived as different, and psychological pressure can be a form of indirect coercion to conform.

The Court's refusal to back down on this issue has also led to various attempts in Congress and by groups supporting religious content in public schools to try other routes, such as posting the TEN COMMANDMENTS, to achieve their goals.

In 1984, Congress passed the Equal Access law, requiring schools receiving federal funds to allow religious organizations to meet for prayer and other religious activities when they also allow similar noncurricular clubs to form. Unlike the types of prayers at issue in *Engel, Schempp,* and

Football players at Odessa High School in Odessa, Texas, pray in their locker room, September 1, 2000, in an unsanctioned prayer session. On June 19, 2000, the Supreme Court handed down a ruling banning school-sanctioned pregame prayer. *(Joe Raedle/Newsmakers)*

the other school prayer cases, these activities are meant to involve student-led prayers and other religious activities with teachers present only in a nonparticipatory role. This was upheld by the Court in *West Side Community School v. Mergens,* 496 U.S. 226 (1990).

Detractors of the Court's rulings in school prayer cases have labeled the justices as hostile to religion. However, a careful reading of the majority opinions suggests otherwise. In fact, the justices have tried to address the sensitive nature of the issue by patiently explaining how their decisions are consistent with America's religious traditions, by discussing the risks of trivializing prayer, and by reminding the public of all the activities in schools and elsewhere that they were not striking down in these decisions.

The topic, along with other similar controversies about religion in schools, has also spawned considerable misunderstanding about what is and is not allowed in public schools, leading to publications in the mid-1990s by liberal and conservative advocacy groups: "Religion in the Public Schools: A Joint Statement of Current Law" was followed by a similar document by the Clinton administration to be disseminated to public schools. The latter was revised in 2003 by the Bush administration in a document entitled "Guidance on Constitutionally Protected Prayer in Public Elementary and Secondary Schools." It provides a much more accommodationist interpretation of what is allowed in schools than did its predecessor, and it has been criticized by separationists for making assertions about legally allowable prayer in school situations that remain unresolved in the courts.

Several advocacy groups exist on both the separationist and accommodationist side of the school prayer issue. The most visible and vocal separationist groups include Americans United for Separation of Church and State and the AMERICAN CIVIL LIBERTIES UNION. Accommodationist groups have included the Christian Coalition and the Eagle Forum, among others. Among religious denominations, "mainline" Protestant groups, Jews, Unitarians, and many Roman Catholics oppose school prayer, while fundamentalists and evangelicals would prefer some type of formal prayer or prayer time. While many Baptists, particularly in the South, fall in the latter group, others—in the Roger Williams tradition—have endorsed the Court's school prayer decisions.

School prayer cases keep coming into the Court because, with changing personnel, it is impossible to know what the Court will allow, and because accommodationists keep seeking ways to circumvent or defy previous rulings. For example, there has not yet been a definitive Supreme Court ruling on voluntary prayers by students at graduation (analogous to what the Court struck down in *Santa Fe*), and this continues to cause conflict in schools. Recent high school graduations have seen students "spontaneously" begin reciting the Lord's Prayer at a prearranged point in the ceremony.

School prayer is an issue that resonates emotionally with large segments of the population. Polls have consistently shown that a majority of the public wants some type of formal school prayer; thus the topic has provided a handy "political football" for politicians. Many members of Congress, presidential candidates, and other elected officials have touted school prayer as a "quick fix" to the problems of youth, have resurrected it in election campaigns, and have proposed legislation. In so doing, they have been accused of distracting voters from more serious public policy issues. Local officials, sometimes against the advice of their own attorneys, have risked costly litigation by either ignoring or seeking to circumvent Court rulings. A series of constitutional amendments have been proposed ever since the 1960s, but none received the necessary two-thirds vote in each House of Congress that would bring them before the states for ratification. One reason is that even some supporters of "school prayer" shy away from tampering in this way with the FIRST AMENDMENT, something that has never been done.

The establishment clause in general is in a period of transition along with changing Court personnel, and it is possible that future "school prayer" rulings will lower the "wall of separation" in public schools. However, with an increasingly diverse population, including not only the nonreligious but also many non-Christians with their own prayer traditions, a lowering of the "wall" is likely to meet with some resistance.

For more information: Alley, Robert S. *Without a Prayer: Religious Expression in Public Schools.* Amherst, N.Y.: Prometheus Books, 1996; Fenwick, Lynda Beck. *Should the Children Pray?: A Historical, Judicial, and Political Examination of Public School Prayer.* Waco, Tex.: Markham Press Fund of Baylor University Press, 1989; Ravitch, Frank S. *School Prayer and Discrimination: The Civil Rights of Religious Minorities and Dissenters.* Boston: Northeastern University Press, 2001.

—Jane G. Rainey and Rick A. Swanson

school vouchers

Government financial aid provided to parents to partially or completely defray the cost of educating their children at a public or non-public school of their choice.

Supporters argue that voucher programs give individuals the ability to seek out superior schools and escape inferior ones. From this view, vouchers fuel a healthy competition among public and religious and nonreligious private schools, promoting educational diversity while gradually weeding out poorly performing institutions. It is also argued that low-income families, who might not otherwise be able to afford private school tuition, would particularly benefit. In the face of a global and fiercely competitive job marketplace, vouchers level the playing field by providing more educational options to every child.

School voucher opponents attack the programs on two broad fronts. First, vouchers divert funds from an already beleaguered public school system, making their poor performances relative to private schools a self-fulfilling prophecy. Public schools are put at another disadvantage because they legally have to accept all students who apply, while private schools can "cherry pick" the better students. Vouchers therefore unnecessarily hobble public education and give private schools unfair advantages.

Supporters decry the current system as unfair because it imposes a "double tax" on those parents who pay tuition to private schools as well as school taxes to support the public school system. Voucher opponents justify this burden by claiming that the benefits of a common education rebound to the community as a whole. All property owners pay school taxes, whether they have children in the school system—or even have children—but the product of a public education is a more law-abiding, employable citizenry. If government is willing to provide an education to all, it should not feel compelled to compensate those who choose go outside the system. From this perspective, the state should not have to put its own school system at a disadvantage by providing monetary incentives to its competition.

A second criticism leveled against vouchers is not directed at all private schools, but only at vouchers that are given to religious schools. Many separationists argue that the ESTABLISHMENT CLAUSE of the FIRST AMENDMENT forbids state support of religion. Even if aid first goes to parents, religious schools are the ultimate beneficiaries. Even more egregious, many voucher programs favor only a few religious schools or even a single religious denomination, or provide aid to a few private secular schools.

An attempt by government to be evenhanded among religious schools may be even more problematic. Because of this nation's considerable religious diversity, efforts to equitably fund all religious schools might lead to bitter sectarian quarrels and administrative headaches. Also, vouchers may require greater regulation of religious schools as a condition for participating in

such programs, something voucher supporters might find objectionable.

Supporters argue that denying religious schools funding is discrimination, not government neutrality. Denying vouchers to religious schools would also threaten the survival of some of the best schools in the community.

This debate over the constitutionality and appropriateness of government financial support for religious schools has a long history.

Prominent men from the founding era such as THOMAS JEFFERSON were opposed to government money going to any religious institution—even if a taxpayer ended up supporting her own house of worship. Others, like Patrick Henry, believed that government should support religious bodies and even restrict such largesse to Protestant institutions. Language in the Northwest Ordinance of 1789 also seemed to indicate that government support for religious schools was important for promoting morality.

Prior to the First Amendment's incorporation to the states in the middle of the 20th century, they were free to subsidize religious schools, and even houses of worship, and many did so until the middle of the 19th century.

Arguments that the establishment clause foreclosed subsidization were seemingly belied by a campaign in the early 1800s to pass a constitutional amendment that would explicitly prohibit all funding of religious schools—whether through parental choice or direct subsidization of religious schools. This fear grew up in response to the enormous influx of Catholic immigration at that time and the immigrants' desire to educate their children in their own parochial schools. Many Catholics felt, with some justification, that the public school system was biased toward Protestantism.

The effort to amend the U.S. Constitution ultimately fell short of votes. However, 37 states eventually passed amendments to their own constitutions, prohibiting the funding of religious schools. Most of these "Blaine Amendments," named after James Blaine, the man who spearheaded the campaign, are still in force today.

The first Supreme Court case to deal with funding of religious schools did not occur until 1947 in

EVERSON V. BOARD OF EDUCATION, 330 U.S. 1 (1947). In a series of cases that followed, the Supreme Court adopted the church/state separation principle, but because of changing Court membership, seemed to apply the principle inconsistently. In *Everson,* the Court upheld reimbursing all parents—even those who send their children to religious schools—for the costs of bus transportation. But in LEMON V. KURTZMAN, 403 U.S. 602 (1971), the Court invalidated laws that supplemented the salaries of teachers who taught secular subjects in parochial schools.

In MUELLER V. ALLEN, 463 U.S. 388 (1983), a case that came closest to touching on the voucher question, the Court upheld a state law that allowed parents to deduct the costs of school tuition, textbooks, and transportation from their taxes. Though the language of the statute appeared to be religiously neutral, dissenting justices argued that its real purpose was to favor religious schools: Public schools do not charge tuition and religious schools make up the largest percentage of all private school beneficiaries.

These cases finally led up to ZELMAN V. SIMMONS-HARRIS, 536 U.S. 639 (2002). In a narrow 5-4 decision the Court upheld a Cleveland, Ohio, voucher program and ruled that similar programs would be constitutional as long as government aid was neutral and provided a "genuine and independent private choice" among many different kinds of schools.

After *Zelman,* the constitutional status of Blaine Amendments at the state level appeared to be in question. However, the U.S. Supreme Court left undisturbed a 2003 Florida ruling that interpreted that state's constitution to limit all educational funding to public schools. This seems to suggest that, while the establishment clause permits voucher programs, other constitutional provisions do not require them.

For more information: Doerr, Edd, et al. *The Case against School Vouchers.* Amherst, N.Y.: Prometheus Books, 1996; Good, Thomas L., and Jennifer S. Braden. *The Great School Debate: Choice, Vouchers and Charters.* Mahwah, N.J.: Lawrence Erlbaum Associates, 2000.

—Tim Gordinier

Scottsboro cases

The Scottsboro cases refer to the conviction of nine young African-American men for the alleged rape of two white girls in 1931. This incident led to two decisions by the United States Supreme Court, *Powell v. Alabama,* 287 U.S. 45 (1932), and *Norris v. Alabama,* 294 U.S. 587 (1935), both of which were important cases for criminal DUE PROCESS rights.

The youths, who ranged in age from 15 to 19 years old, were "riding the rails" in the Depression-era South, hoping to find work in Alabama. Several of them apparently got into a scuffle with some white youths. The white boys jumped from the train and reported the fight (which they described as an assault) to the local sheriff. By the time the train arrived in Paint Rock, the young black men were greeted by a white mob, ready for a lynching. When the posse boarded the train, they found two young white women dressed in men's clothes. It is not clear whether the lynch mob or the girls first cried "rape," but the young female stowaways seemed to conclude it was in their interest to appear as victims rather than as tramps who sneaked rides on trains. Although a lynching was avoided, Ozie Powell, Willie Roberson, Olen Montgomery, Clarence Norris, Haywood Patterson, Eugene Williams, Roy and Andy Wright, and Charlie Weems were tied together with a plow line, taken to the local jail, and charged with rape—a capital crime.

Surrounded by over 100 National Guard troops, the nine young men were brought to trial in Scottsboro on April 6, 12 days after the incident. A crowd of about 10,000 people milled about the courthouse, apparently enticed by the lurid accounts provided by the two alleged victims, Victoria Price and Ruby Bates. Judge Alfred Hawkins, in a gesture that provided a veneer of legality for the proceedings, appointed all the members of the local bar to represent the defendants. By appointing everyone as counsel, he effectively appointed no one. Ultimately, the only attorneys defending the "Scottsboro Boys" were a local, 70-year-old drunk named Milo Moody and a Tennessee lawyer unfamiliar with Alabama criminal law, who appeared inebriated when the trial began. The young men were convicted in four separate trials over a total of four days. All were found guilty and all but Roy Wright, who was only 13 years old, were sentenced to death. The men were convicted in the first and subsequent trials despite contradictory testimony by the "victims," conflicting stories by the accused men, and the local doctor's conclusion that the girls could not have suffered multiple rapes.

Coincidentally and fortunately, the International Labor Defense (ILD), a communist organization, had launched a campaign to exploit racial injustices in the United States and to recruit black members. They took an interest in the Scottsboro case and provided legal support for the young men to appeal their cases. After the Alabama Supreme Court affirmed the convictions, the U.S. Supreme Court reversed that decision by a vote of 7 to 2 in *Powell v. Alabama*. The Court held that the young men's due process rights under the FOURTEENTH AMENDMENT had been violated because the RIGHT TO COUNSEL in a capital case is a necessary component of a fair trial. As the defendants were indigent, young, uneducated, far from home, and in fear of their lives, due process demanded that the state provide adequate counsel. The *Powell* Court did not rule that the SIXTH AMENDMENT right to counsel was applicable to the states, as it would later in *GIDEON V. WAINWRIGHT* (1963).

The state of Alabama retried the cases several times. In December 1933 a jury again found Haywood Patterson and Clarence Norris guilty. Their ILD attorney, Samuel Leibowitz, appealed on the grounds that African Americans had been systematically excluded from the jury in violation of *Neal v. Delaware* (1880). In an unusual procedure, the members of the Supreme Court examined the pages of the Jackson County jury selection manual where the names of a few black citizens had obviously been added *after* the Scottsboro boys' trial. In *Norris v. Alabama,* the Court ruled 8 to 0 that the systematic exclusion of African Americans from Alabama juries denied the EQUAL PROTECTION of the law provided by the Fourteenth Amendment, and reversed Norris's conviction.

Patterson, Norris, Weems, and Andy Wright were convicted again. Charges were dropped against Roy Wright, Eugene Williams, Willie Rob-

ertson, and Olen Montgomery. Ozie Powell was found guilty of assaulting a deputy sheriff and was shot in the head while allegedly trying to escape. The Supreme Court's decisions prevented the men's executions, but altogether they spent close to one hundred years in prison for a crime that did not take place.

For more information: Goodman, James. *Stories of Scottsboro.* New York: Vintage Books, 1994; Weiner, Mark S. *Black Trials: Citizenship from the Beginnings of Slavery to the End of Caste.* New York: Vintage Books, 2006.

—Mary Welek Atwell

search and seizure

See EXCLUSIONARY RULE; FOURTH AMENDMENT.

search warrant exceptions

Search warrant exceptions are those circumstances when law enforcement officials do not need a warrant in order to search an individual or a place. These searches stand in contrast to the policy that the FOURTH AMENDMENT generally requires a search warrant for searches.

A search warrant is not required if one consents to a search (*Schneckloth v. Bustamonte*, 412 U.S. 218 [1972]); if the search is incident to an arrest (*CHIMEL V. CALIFORNIA*, 395 U.S. 752 [1969]); if the search is limited to looking for weapons (*TERRY V. OHIO*, 392 U.S. 1, 19 [1968] [STOP AND FRISK]); if necessary due to exigent circumstances, (*United States v. Watson*, 423 U.S. 411 [1976]) or due to public safety (*New York v. Quarles*, 467 U.S. 649 [1984]); if there is a risk of evidence being destroyed (*U.S. v. MacDonald*, 335 U.S. 451 [1948]); or if the police are in hot pursuit of a suspect (*Warden v. Hayden*, 387 U.S. 294 [1967]).

In addition, no warrant is required if items are in plain view of the police (*Arizona v. Hicks* 480 U.S. 321 [1987]), or if the items will inevitably be discovered (*Nix v. Williams*, 467 U.S. 431 [1984]). Finally, warrants are not required for searches of automobiles (*Carroll v. United States*, 267 U.S. 132 [1925]); border searches (*Almeida-Sanchez v.*

United States, 413 U.S. 266 [1973]); or for administrative inventory searches (*Camera v. Municipal Court,* 387 U.S. 523 [1967]).

Conversely, the Supreme Court has stated that warrants are presumptively always required for the search of a private home or apartment (KYLLO V. UNITED STATES, 533 U.S. 27 [2001]).

The Court has also ruled that there are exceptions to the warrant requirement. These exceptions would be departures from the EXCLUSIONARY RULE as articulated in *Mapp v. Ohio,* 367 U.S. 643 (1961). While some would defend the exceptions as commonsense applications of the Fourth Amendment, others counter that the exceptions are so numerous that they have effectively gutted the exclusionary rule and the Fourth Amendment warrant requirements.

For more information: LaFave, Wayne R., Jerold H. Israel, and Nancy J. King. *Criminal Procedure.* St. Paul, Minn.: Thomson/West, 2004.

—Ernest Gomez and David Schultz

Second Amendment
See RIGHT TO BEAR ARMS.

Section 1983
When government officials commit federal constitutional wrongs against individual citizens, these citizens can sue the government for relief. Such relief is embodied in 42 U.S.C. § 1983, a statute that gives citizens the tools to seek redress for constitutional violations. Section 1983 states that every person who, under color of any law, subjects, or causes to be subjected, any citizen of the United States to the deprivation of any rights, privileges, or immunities secured by the Constitution and laws shall be liable to the party injury in an action at law.

Section 1983 suits are most notably against police officers who have violated an individual's FOURTH AMENDMENT rights (*Tennessee v. Garner,* 471 U.S. 1 [1985]). Such violations can occur in the form of false arrests and excessive force. When a citizen believes that a municipality was also liable in a constitutional violation, he or she can sue that entity as well. The landmark case on this subject is MONELL V. DEPARTMENT OF SOCIAL SERVICES, 436 U.S. 658 (1978). In *Monell,* the Supreme Court held that a municipality should be treated as a person for the purpose of Section 1983 claims. As such, claims against a municipality for constitutional violations are commonly called *Monell* claims.

Over the years, the courts have defined what actions a city can be held liable for. A municipality is liable for a policy in place (*Pembaur v. City of Cincinnati,* 475 U.S. 469 [1986]) or deliberate indifference to a common situation (*City of Canton v. Harris,* 489 U.S. 378 [1989]). Additionally, an entity can be liable when a supervisor with final decision-making authority authorizes an agent to act (*City of St. Louis v. Praprotnik,* 485 U.S. 112 [1988]).

Complicating Section 1983 lawsuits for plaintiffs is the affirmative defense of qualified immunity. Qualified immunity can shield individual officers or officials from any constitutional liability. Municipalities are not able to use the qualified immunity defense, however (*Owen v. City of Independence,* 445 U.S. 622, 657 [1980]). Typically, courts deciding Section 1983 lawsuits deal with the issue of qualified immunity first. After a period of discovery into the defendant official's actions, the defendant will most likely move for summary judgment, claiming that, as a matter of law, he or she is not liable and is shielded from the relief requested by the plaintiff. The basis of this summary judgment claim would be qualified immunity.

The court will then begin a two-step inquiry into the defendant's claims. First, viewing the facts in the light most favorable to the plaintiff, the court will ask whether there is a constitutional violation (*Saucier v. Katz,* 533 U.S. 194, 201 [2001]). Note that the constitutional right must be established at the time of the act. If there was a violation, the court will next proceed to the question of whether the official deserves immunity from such a violation. The standard is whether it would have been clear to a reasonable officer that his conduct was unlawful in the situation he confronted (*id.* at 202).

How the court decides the claim against the officer or official is determinative—in some part—of how the court will rule on the *Monell* claims against the city. If the court finds no constitutional violation (the first part of the inquiry), then the court will dismiss the *Monell* claim against the locality (*City of Los Angeles v. Heller,* 475 U.S. 796 [1986] [per curiam]). However, if the court finds a constitutional violation, but rules that the officers are deserving of qualified immunity, then the *Monell* claim against the city may proceed and is not barred.

Typically, along with Fourth Amendment violations, plaintiffs may also allege other violations. For instance, it is common to see allegations of EQUAL PROTECTION clause violations. For example, after a police officer shoots and kills an unarmed individual, the plaintiff (normally a family member of the decedent) will sue the officer for the shooting (the Fourth Amendment violation, as the officer has seized the individual by shooting), sue the city for a policy—or lack thereof—in place that relates to the officer's actions (the *Monell* claim), and then allege that there was discriminatory motive behind the shooting (i.e., a racial discrimination claim under the equal protection clause).

While the Fourth Amendment and related qualified immunity inquiry is purely objective, the equal protection claim is subjective, meaning that the Court must look into the thoughts and mindset of the officials at the time of the alleged constitutional violation.

For more information: Chemerinsky, Erwin. *Federal Jurisdiction.* New York: Aspen Publishers, 2003; Lewis, Harold S., Jr., and Elizabeth J. Norman. *Civil Rights Law and Practice.* St. Paul, Minn.: West Group, 2001.

—Jason A. Abel

seditious libel

Seditious libel is a legal term that describes the crime of criticizing the government and public officials.

The concept was firmly a part of English common law in the 17th century and earlier, but its status in the United States has been the subject of great debate and much commentary. Under English common law, the aim of the law of seditious libel was to prevent criticism that would bring ridicule and thereby undermine the authority of the Crown. Under the English approach, the truer the libelous statement, the more harm it might do; as a result, truth was not a valid defense.

The American colonies confronted the status of seditious libel early on. The New York printer, John Peter Zenger, was charged with seditious libel and tried by a jury in 1735; he was accused of printing articles written by others in the *New York Weekly Journal* that were critical of New York governor William Cosby. Zenger's lawyer argued to the jury that truth should be a defense, that Zenger couldn't be punished because the printed information about Governor Cosby was true. The jury acquitted Zenger, effectively establishing the principle that truth should be recognized as a defense to libel.

When the new constitution was drafted in 1787 and modified by the BILL OF RIGHTS in 1791, the guarantees of freedom of speech and FREEDOM OF THE PRESS became important considerations in determining the status of seditious libel. However, the existence of FIRST AMENDMENT protections did not deter the Congress from passing the Sedition Act of 1798. The law made it a crime, punishable by fines and imprisonment, to engage in "false, scandalous and malicious" writing about the president or Congress or to write or utter statements that would bring them into "contempt or disrepute." Although ostensibly aimed at curtailing the actions of French immigrants to the United States, the law was largely politically driven, a means for the Federalists in power at the time to undercut their Republican opposition.

Some 25 citizens were prosecuted and many of them convicted under the law. Most of them were Republican newspaper editors. When THOMAS JEFFERSON was elected president in 1800, ending the Federalist control, he pardoned all those who had been convicted and persuaded Congress to repay their fines. There was no test, however, of whether the Sedition Act could pass muster under the First Amendment, and the act expired.

It would take more than 160 years for the Supreme Court in NEW YORK TIMES V. SULLIVAN, 376 U.S. 254 (1964), to make clear that the Sedition Act could not satisfy First Amendment standards. Justice WILLIAM J. BRENNAN, JR., writing for the majority, described "a broad consensus" of modern commentators who found that the Sedition Act violated the First Amendment.

Before the Supreme Court's repudiation, the issue of seditious libel had appeared again in U.S. history. Congress passed the Sedition Act of 1918 during World War I, again making it a crime to write or profess views that would foster disloyalty or opposition to the military. Many prosecutions ensued.

While there have been no new laws specifically punishing seditious libel in the United States since World War I, laws like the Smith Act of 1940, punishing advocacy of or teaching about the overthrow of the U.S. government, bear some resemblance and have remained the subject of controversy for decades.

For more information: Mayton, William T. "Seditious Libel and the Lost Guarantee of a Freedom of Expression." *Columbia Law Review* 84, no. 1 (January 1984): 91–142; Smolla, Rodney A., and Melville B. Nimmer. *Smolla and Nimmer on Freedom of Speech.* New York: Clark Boardman Callaghan, 1996.

—Stephen Wermiel

Selective Service System v. Minnesota Public Interest Research Group 468 U.S. 841 (1984)

In *Selective Service System v. Minnesota Public Interest Research Group* the Supreme Court upheld a law requiring male students aged 18 to 26 to register for the draft.

The act, under Title IV of the Higher Education Act of 1965, required that male students, ages 18–26, who failed to register for the draft be denied federal financial aid for school. In addition, the act required applicants for financial aid to submit a statement denoting compliance with the act. In addition, a presidential proclamation made it a criminal act if a male did not register for the draft within 30 days of his 18th birthday. Students who had not registered for the draft filed suit, asking the federal district court to prohibit the enforcement of Section 12 (f). The district court agreed on the grounds that the regulations set forth by Section 12 (f) of the act are unconstitutional because they serve as a BILL OF ATTAINDER (a legislative act that prescribes a form of punishment without the DUE PROCESS of a trial; see *Black's Law Dictionary*) and that the act violated the right against Fifth Amendment self-incrimination.

In a 6-2 decision, delivered by Chief Justice WARREN BURGER, the Court found the law constitutional because a student was not actually required to accept financial aid, thereby relieving an applicant of being in a position to sign a statement attesting to having or not having registered for the draft and consequently avoiding self-incrimination. Since a student who has not registered for the draft is bound to know that he will be denied Title IV aid, he is in no sense under any "compulsion" to seek that aid and has no reason to make any statement to anyone as to whether or not he has registered. As to a late registrant, since the law does not require him to disclose to his educational institution whether or not he registered late, he is not required to disclose any incriminating information in order to become eligible for aid.

For more information: Schwartz, Bernard. *A History of the Supreme Court.* New York: Oxford University Press, 1993.

—Dan Krejci

semi-suspect class

Semi-suspect class refers to a classification of sex or gender that is examined by the courts with analysis greater than a rational basis but less than STRICT SCRUTINY. The classification of gender as a semi-suspect class means that not all usages of sex will be invalidated by the Supreme Court.

Although government distinctions based on race have been held to be suspect and, in the absence of a compelling state interest, unconstitutional, sex is only a semi-suspect classification. Until 1974, sex-based distinctions received even less protection under the FOURTEENTH AMENDMENT.

That amendment forbids a state from denying "any person within its jurisdiction the EQUAL PROTECTION of the laws." However, because laws generally make distinctions, the courts have held that, most of the time, such distinctions merely have to be rational attempts to achieve legitimate governmental interests. For example, DWI laws will not be declared unconstitutional even though they discriminate against heavy drinkers who drive, nor will income taxes be thrown out because the rich pay more than the poor. On the other hand, since the Fourteenth Amendment was passed to give full rights to the newly freed slaves, race-based distinctions would be considered suspect and treated with strict scrutiny. In *Strauder v. West Virginia,* 100 U.S. 303 (1880), the Supreme Court ruled in favor of a challenge to a law limiting juries to whites but also declared, without giving any reasons, that states could bar women, non–citizens, or the less educated from jury service. From the passage of the post–Civil War constitutional amendments until the mid-20th century, the Supreme Court upheld numerous state laws that claimed to protect women from the dangers of jobs varying from lawyer to bartender by banning them from such occupations.

In the 1960s, as support for women's equality led to both federal and state laws against sex discrimination, the time seemed ripe to reconsider whether sex should be considered a suspect classification. Led by Ruth Bader Ginsburg, the AMERICAN CIVIL LIBERTIES UNION Women's Rights Project brought a series of cases for that purpose. In the breakthrough case of *Reed v. Reed,* 404 U.S. 71 (1971), the Supreme Court for the first time used the equal protection clause to overturn a law. However, because it found this statute, giving preference to men over women as executors of their children's estates, to be irrational, the Court did not reach the issue of whether sex should be inherently suspect. *Frontiero v. Richardson,* 411 U.S. 677 (1973), presented the issue more directly. Advocates argued that sex should be suspect because it is an immutable characteristic, there is a long history of sex discrimination, and sex generally bears no relation to ability. Opponents noted that, unlike people of color, women were not a minority and could therefore use the political process to accomplish their goals. Although the Court declared the law unconstitutional, only four of the nine justices believed that sex-based classifications should be suspect. Another four found the law irrational but preferred to leave the issue of declaring gender-based classifications subject to the political process, pointing to the equal rights amendment that had passed Congress and was pending state approval. That proposed constitutional amendment would eventually fall short of the required approval by 38 states.

However, the Court would ultimately find a compromise that has been termed semi-suspect classifications. *CRAIG V. BOREN,* 429 U.S. 190 (1976), created a middle tier in which "classifications based on gender must serve important governmental objectives and must be substantially related" to their achievement. Even under this test, later cases upheld draft registration for males but not females and statutory rape laws that punished only males who had sexual relations with underaged females. By 1996, although Ruth Bader Ginsburg had become a Supreme Court justice, she was still unable to require a compelling state interest to justify sex-based distinctions. However, in *United States v. VA,* 518 U.S. 515 (1996), she further tightened the middle-tier test, writing for the Court that an "exceedingly persuasive justification" was required. Thus despite moving most of the way toward becoming a suspect class, sex remains semi-suspect.

For more information: Rierson, Sandra L. "Race and Gender Discrimination: A Historical Case for Equal Treatment Under the Fourteenth Amendment." *Duke Journal of Gender Law and Policy* 1 (1994): 89–117; Sullivan, Kathleen. "Symposium on Constitutional Law: Constitutionalizing Women's Equality." *California Law Review* 90 (May 2002): 735–764.

—Bruce E. Altschuler

Senate

Along with the HOUSE OF REPRESENTATIVES, the United States Senate makes up the Congress and the legislative, or lawmaking, branch of the United States. The founders considered the legislative branch to be critical to republican freedoms. It would give the people a voice in controlling the government, yet also check the whims of a capricious populace through its structure. The Senate is the more aristocratic branch of the two. It is more stable due to the six-year terms of its members who, until 1913, were appointed by the various state legislatures. The structure of the Senate is laid out in ARTICLE I OF THE U.S. CONSTITUTION.

For the Senate, Article I states that it will share legislative power with the House, and the two together will have all legislative power for the federal government. Senators are to be elected every six years, and one must be 30 years old to serve in the Senate, which is midway between the age requirements for the House (25) and the president (35). A potential senator must have been a citizen of the United States for nine years and be a resident of the state from which he or she is elected from as well.

Each state in the United States has two senators, as laid out in Article I, Section 3. Originally these senators were appointed by the state legislatures. However, the SEVENTEENTH AMENDMENT changed the selection process for senators to a direct election, making the body somewhat more democratic. Elections are held every two years, and one-third of the body is up for reelection in each cycle. The VICE PRESIDENT is the presiding officer of the body; however, in modern practice it is rare for vice presidents to actively preside. According to the Constitution, the vice president votes only in the case of a tie. Though the president pro tempore is the presiding officer in the vice president's absence, the real power lies with the leadership of each party, who occupy positions that are not specified in the Constitution.

The formal powers of the Senate are quite numerous. Many of the formal powers are checked by powers of other branches or by the House of Representatives. The primary formal power of the Senate is the ability to make laws. Lawmaking is not a simple process. Passing a law requires much more than just a simple majority assent of the Senate. Both houses must pass a bill with identical language, and the president must sign the bill. If the president vetoes the bill, a two-thirds majority of both houses must vote to override the bill.

While the House has the power to impeach the president or other executive or judicial officials according to Article I, the Senate may then vote by two-thirds majority to convict or acquit the subject of the IMPEACHMENT. This is a strong check on the other branches, and on the House as well. There are a number of other powers granted to the House and the Senate jointly, such as the establishment of the post office, the regulation of commerce (which leads to an important implied power), and the ability to raise armies and declare war. The Senate also advises and consents on both treaties and executive appointments. This function provides a check on the executive branch and the judicial branch as well, since federal judges and justices are appointed. Finally, in the event that no presidential ticket receives enough electoral votes to win, the Senate selects the vice president of the United States. To do that, a candidate must receive a majority vote of the senators.

Both bodies also have a number of restrictions placed on them. They are forbidden from granting patents of nobility, for example, or from passing bills of attainder, making ex post facto laws, or suspending the writ of HABEAS CORPUS, which demands that the state produce a prisoner and show cause as to why he or she is being held.

The Senate has a number of implied powers. These are powers not expressly mentioned in the Constitution, but which later courts have found are in some way necessary or appropriate to support a constitutional function of the Senate. The classic example of an implied power is the creation of a national bank. In *McCulloch v. Maryland*, 17 U.S. 316 (1819), the Court ruled that the creation of a bank was appropriate to support the powers of the Congress to appropriate and to maintain an army. Due to the reserved powers clause, Congress may not interfere in state matters where it is not explicitly granted jurisdiction by the Constitution.

However, in *GIBBONS V. OGDEN,* 17 U.S. (4 Wheat) 316 (1819), the Court ruled that the COMMERCE CLAUSE allowed the regulation of almost all business transactions, since practically all trade had an effect on INTERSTATE COMMERCE. This power was confirmed and expanded in *WICKARD V. FILBURN,* 317 U.S. 111 (1942), and in *KATZENBACH V. MCCLUNG,* 379 U.S. 294 (1964). At present, the commerce clause allows the Congress to intervene in a wide variety of issues, including CIVIL RIGHTS, the environment, and bureaucratic regulation.

Though originally an aristocratic body of sorts, the Senate is an integral part of the republican system of the United States. Along with the House, it funnels the desires of the people into workable legislation, and provides a check on the other branches of the government.

For more information: Dodd, Lawrence C., and Bruce Oppenheimer. *Congress Reconsidered.* 8th ed. Washington, D.C.: CQ Press, 2005; Mason, Alpheus Thomas, and Donald Grier Stephenson, Jr. *American Constitutional Law.* 12th ed. Upper Saddle River, N.J.: Prentice Hall, 1999.

—Matthew W. Barber

Seneca Falls Resolution

The Seneca Falls Resolution of 1848 was one of the first major documents in the United States advocating for the equal rights of women. The resolution had a major constitutional impact.

Seneca Falls, New York, was chosen to hold the first women's rights convention in the United States on July 18–19, 1848. This convention has generally been considered the birthplace of the American feminist movement and the inauguration of women's struggle to cast their ballot in the United States.

The Seneca Falls Convention was conceived during the World Anti-Slavery Convention in London in 1840. In the course of the congress, there was a fierce debate on whether women should be allowed to attend. Finally, it was decided that women would be excluded from the convention as official delegates. It was at this time that Lucretia Mott, a veteran campaigner for both the abo-

litionist and women's cause, met Elizabeth Cady Stanton, a woman who was 22 years Mott's junior but had already shown her determination by participating in women's rights events and by marrying a fiery abolitionist. The two women started to lay plans to organize a convention in the United States to debate the issue of women's rights and women's liberation.

The women's rights conference was postponed until 1848 when the two women met again and outlined the details of the convention, which was to be the first of its kind in the United States. Stanton designed an invitation that was published in the *Seneca County Courier,* presenting the conference as a place "to discuss . . . the social, civil and religious condition and rights of women." The convention was planned only for women, but men were allowed to stay. In fact, several men, among them the former slave Frederick Douglass, attended the convention at Seneca Falls. Stanton designed and presented the *Declaration of Sentiments and Resolutions.* Following the style of the DECLARATION OF INDEPENDENCE, Stanton paraphrased some of the most famous passages of that foundational American document and rewrote them according to women's vindications. As a result, the *Declaration of Sentiments* contained assertions such as "we hold these truths to be self-evident; that all men and women are created equal" and "the history of mankind is a history of repeated injuries and usurpations on the part of man toward woman." The list of grievances included the deprivation of vote, the civil death of married women, the lack of educational opportunities, and the taxation of unrepresented single women. This document was followed by 11 resolutions, among them the radical proclamation that it was the duty of women to obtain for themselves the RIGHT TO VOTE. Although only about 100 people signed the resolution on women's suffrage, the suffrage resolution was passed, inaugurating a struggle that would culminate 72 years later in the NINETEENTH AMENDMENT to the United States Constitution. The Seneca Falls Convention encouraged other women such as Susan B. Anthony and Lucy Stone to follow Mott and Stanton's example and organize other women's conferences, among them one in New York State, where former slave Sojourner Truth would deliver her famous speech *Ain't I a Woman?*

From 1850 until the Civil War, American women's rights leaders and activists organized several other meetings and designed a program of lectures, petitions, and public acts. The women's rights movement gained supporters among prominent men such as Walt Whitman, Ralph Waldo Emerson, and William Lloyd Garrison. Slowly, women started to gain some legal rights, for instance the right of married women to control their own property.

The culmination of the activist women's rights struggle came with the Nineteenth Amendment, proposed on June 4, 1919, and eventually ratified on August 18, 1920. The Nineteenth Amendment to the U.S. Constitution reads: "The rights of citizens of the United States shall not be denied or abridged by the United States or by any state on account of sex." When American women were allowed to vote, only one of the signers of the Seneca Falls Declaration in 1848, Charlotte Woodson, had lived long enough to vote for the first time.

For more information: Cohen, Philip N. "Nationalism and Suffrage: Gender Struggle in Nation-Building America." *Signs* 21, no. 3 (1996): 707–727; Lander, Meta. "The Woman Movement." *The Ladies' Repository* 5, no. 5 (1870): 383–386; Stanton, Elizabeth Cady. *Eighty Years and More: Reminiscences 1815–1897.* New York: T. Fisher Unwin, 1898. Available online. URL: http://www.gutenberg.org/etext/11982. Accessed 14 May 2008.

—Laura Gimeno-Pahissa

sentencing and proportionality

A primary objective of modern criminal sentencing is to ensure that sentences imposed on convicted criminals be proportionate to the type and severity of offense that they have committed. The concept of proportionality finds some theoretical support in the retributivist theory of punishment, which has as an object the imposition of criminal sentences that are directly proportionate to the seriousness of the offense and the "blameworthi-

ness" of the defendant. This theory, also known as "just deserts," attempts to impose punishments that offenders deserve—nothing more and nothing less.

Proportionality has found its way into constitutional scrutiny of criminal sentences. Two aspects of the Eighth Amendment to the United States Constitution are linked to proportionality. The excessive fines clause of the Constitution precludes courts from imposing excessive fines in conjunction with a criminal sentence. The Supreme Court has viewed this clause as a form of proportionality review. In *United States v. Bajakajian*, 524 U.S. 321 (1998), the Supreme Court held that proportionality is the "touchstone" of the excessive fines clause and that criminal fines or forfeitures must be proportionate to the gravity of the offense in question. The difficulty lies in determining when a particular fine or forfeiture is "excessive" and thus disproportionate. In *Bajakajian*, the Court declined to provide a precise test for disproportionality, but did indicate that for a fine or forfeiture to be unconstitutional it must be "grossly" disproportional to the gravity of the offense.

The second aspect of the Eighth Amendment that is linked to proportionality review is the CRUEL AND UNUSUAL PUNISHMENT clause. The Supreme Court has, over time, come to believe that a criminal sentence of incarceration (or death) may be so disproportionate to the gravity of the offense as to be cruel and/or unusual. An early articulation of this position was in *Weems v. United States*, 217 U.S. 349 (1910), in which the Supreme Court adopted the notion that an especially lengthy prison sentence can be cruel because of its excessive length. The Supreme Court proceeded to exercise proportionality review in the context of CAPITAL PUNISHMENT in the 1970s and originally utilized the notion of proportionality to invalidate the death penalty in all circumstances. Later, the Court utilized a proportionality review to invalidate the death penalty for rape (*COKER V. GEORGIA*, 433 U.S. 584 [1977]) and for felony murder in circumstances in which the defendant did not actually kill the victim nor intend for him to be killed (*Enmund v. Florida*, 458 U.S. 782 [1982]). In addition, the Court has found the death penalty disproportionate for the mentally retarded offender (*ATKINS V. VIRGINIA*, 536 U.S. 304 [2002]) and the offender under the age of 18 (*Roper v. Simmons*, 543 U.S. 551 [2005]).

The Court has found it more difficult to apply a proportionality review to modern noncapital offenses. While the Court has tended to consistently accept the notion that a disproportionate sentence does violate the cruel and unusual punishment clause, it has not reached a consensus as to an objective standard by which to define disproportionality. In *RUMMEL V. ESTELLE*, 445 U.S. 263 (1980), the Court did not find disproportionate a Texas sentence of life imprisonment for a fairly minor offense by a repeat offender. In 1983, however, the Court found a sentence of life imprisonment without parole disproportionate for writing a bad check, even if the defendant was a repeat offender (*Solem v. Helm*, 463 U.S. 277 [1983]). Later, the Court refused to find life imprisonment without parole as disproportionate for possessing more than 650 grams of cocaine (*Harmelin v. Michigan*, 501 U.S. 957 [1991]). It was in *Harmelin* that Justice ANTONIN GREGORY SCALIA articulated a different view of the cruel and unusual punishment clause as it relates to the concept of proportionality. Scalia contended, after an extensive review of history, that the Eighth Amendment contains no proportionality guarantee. In *EWING V. CALIFORNIA*, 538 U.S. 11 (2003), the Court chose not to follow Scalia's strict position, but did back away from a broad notion of proportionality by asserting that the Eighth Amendment doesn't require strict proportionality but prohibits only "grossly disproportionate" sentences.

Ultimately, the Constitution does demand some degree of proportionality between the sentence imposed and the crime committed, but it is extremely difficult to ascertain in the abstract when a disproportionality of constitutional dimensions would arise. Rather, the Supreme Court seems content to engage in a "case by case" analysis with the aim of invalidating only those criminal sentences that are "grossly" disproportionate.

For more information: Berkson, Larry Charles. *The Concept of Cruel and Unusual Punishment.*

Lexington, Mass.: Lexington Books, 1975; Hirsch, A. Von. *Censure and Sanctions.* New York: Oxford University Press, 1993.

—Bryan H. Ward

sentencing guidelines

More than 35 years ago, judges made sentencing decisions on a case-by-case basis. This discretionary system of punishment often could lead to discrimination. Legislatures, therefore, called for reforms to sentencing policies. Sentencing reforms were developed to reduce discretion, which, arguably, led to reduced discrimination.

In order to provide a fairer system of justice, Judge Frankel called for more control over discretionary decisions of judges. In the mid-1970s, Judge Frankel suggested that a separate administrative agency be created to develop new sentencing rules to realize this goal—the sentencing commission.

Minnesota answered the call by developing the first sentencing commission, which was created in 1978 and followed by the first set of sentencing guidelines in 1980. Judges Frankel's suggestion was realized at the federal level with the advent of the Sentencing Reform Act of 1984. Sentencing guidelines are defined by a matrix of sentence lengths. The particular sentence is determined by the cross-section of prior criminal history and severity of the current offense. A particular defendant's sentence can vary depending on the combination of the prior criminal history and the severity of the current offense.

It has been well documented that sentencing reforms have created a system that is more determinate and more punitive. The objective behind these sentencing reforms was to limit judicial discretion and provide uniformity in sentencing decisions to avoid potential discrimination.

The United States Supreme Court first addressed the constitutionality of sentencing guidelines in *MISTRETTA V. UNITED STATES*, 488 U.S. 361 (1989). *Mistretta* addressed whether Congress violated the SEPARATION OF POWERS clause in the United States Constitution by creating the United States Sentencing Commission, which oversees judicial sentencing. The Court decided that Congress's delegation of its law-making power to an independent agency did not violate the separation of powers clause of the U.S. Constitution.

More recent cases—*Blakely v. Washington,* 124 S. Ct. 2531 (2004), UNITED STATES V. BOOKER, 125 S. Ct. 738 (2005), and *United States v. Fanfan,* 125 S. Ct. 738 (2005)—have addressed individual rights concerns in upward departure decisions within sentencing guidelines. An upward departure allows a judge to increase the sentence above the particular guideline range maximum. Guideline departures offer the most probable opportunity for the exercise of discretion and the existence of disparity because the restrictions on such decisions are loosely defined.

In *Blakely v. Washington* (2004), the sentence was raised above the maximum of the prescribed sentencing guideline range by a preponderance of the evidence. Relying on precedents set by *Apprendi v. New Jersey,* 530 U.S. 466 (2000), the Supreme Court found that this upward departure decided by a judge by a preponderance of the evidence violated the defendant's SIXTH AMEND-MENT right to a jury trial and the right to have facts against him be proven beyond a reasonable doubt.

In *United States v. Booker* (2005), a mandatory enhancement was applied by the judge in a federal case. The Supreme Court in *United States v. Booker* (2005) considered whether the federal sentencing guidelines' mandatory enhancements, which were based on facts not proven by a jury beyond a reasonable doubt, violated the Sixth Amendment right to a jury. A case consolidated with *Booker, United States v. Fanfan* (2005), considered the possible remedy if the Court in *Booker* were to find that the Sixth Amendment was violated.

The Court examined Congress's language and the intent of that language. The federal sentencing guidelines were mandatory and binding on all judges and, thereby, operated as a statute because they "have the force and effect of laws" (*United States v. Booker,* 2005, p. 742). The Supreme Court, therefore, found that these enhancements *did* violate the right to jury trial protected by the Sixth Amendment. The Supreme Court in *United States v. Fanfan* (2005) suggested that the remedy for this

error was to eliminate the mandatory nature of the federal sentencing guidelines; the Court ruled that the guidelines are now simply advisory.

In the first part of the 21st century, the United States Supreme Court drastically changed the face of sentencing guidelines. Although the Court in *Mistretta v. United States* ruled that the sentencing guidelines did not violate the separation of powers clause of the United States Constitution, the Supreme Court later decided that a judge could not depart above the prescribed guideline range maximum in state jurisdictions (*Blakely v. Washington,* 124 S. Ct. 2531 [2004]) or in the federal jurisdiction (*United States v. Booker,* 125 S. Ct. 738 [2005], and *United States v. Fanfan,* 125 S. Ct. 738 [2005]).

For more information: Spohn, C. *How Do Judges Decide?: The Quest for Fairness and Justice in Sentencing.* Thousand Oaks, Calif.: Pine Forge Press, 2002; Stith, K., and J. A. Cabranes, *Fear of Judging: Sentencing Guidelines in the Federal Courts.* Chicago: University of Chicago Press, 1998; Tonry, M. *Sentencing Matters.* New York: Oxford University Press, 1996; Ulmer, J. T. *Social Worlds of Sentencing: Court Communities under Sentencing Guidelines.* Albany: State University of New York Press, 1997.

—Jeremy D. Ball

separation of powers

The phrase *separation of powers* is generally representative of the idea that the framers of the Constitution created three coequal branches of government. ARTICLE I OF THE U.S. CONSTITUTION defines the legislative branch and creates two houses of Congress: the HOUSE OF REPRESENTATIVES and the SENATE, charging them with specific responsibilities. ARTICLE II OF THE U.S. CONSTITUTION identifies the executive branch, naming the president as its leader, while identifying the VICE PRESIDENT and executive departments as members of the branch responsible in some way for administering the laws. ARTICLE III OF THE U.S. CONSTITUTION identifies the judicial branch as the Supreme Court and inferior federal courts having charge over deciding individual cases and controversies in law or equity.

However, the phrase "separation of powers" is not enumerated in the seven articles of the Constitution. So where does the phrase come from? While proponents look to the writings of the framers in the *Federalist Papers,* such as those of JAMES MADISON or ALEXANDER HAMILTON, separation of powers is an idea that emerged centuries before the Convention of 1787 and has many variations. The common theme is that governmental functions are not concentrated in a single authority but those responsibilities, along with the political power associated with them, are dispersed among branches of government. By so doing, this encourages individual liberty—freedom from government oppression (commentators refer to this as ancient or ordered liberty) and freedom to enjoy the benefits of and participate in an organized society (modern liberty). Philosophers such as Aristotle, Montesquieu, Locke, and Constant are often quoted when discussing these ideas. While there are many permutations of separation of powers, commentators tend to fall into two basic schools of thought about what the phrase means: formalists and functionalists.

Generally, formalists view the fact that the framers drafted three distinct articles with enumerated duties as an implicit signal that the three branches are to behave in "watertight compartments." Justice Southerland represented this view in 1928 when he said, "It may be stated then, as a general rule inherent in the American constitutional system, that, unless otherwise expressly provided or incidental to the powers conferred, the Legislature cannot exercise either executive or judicial power; the judiciary cannot exercise either executive or legislative power. The existence in the various Constitutions of occasional provisions expressly giving to one of the departments powers which by their nature otherwise would fall within the general scope of the authority of another department emphasizes, rather than casts doubt upon, the generally inviolate character of this basic rule." A simplified characterization of this view is: The legislature makes, the executive executes, and the judiciary construes the law.

On the other side of the understanding of separation of powers are the functionalists. Functionalists suggest that the framers must have rejected the idea of "watertight compartments" because of the lack of the phrase "separation of powers" in the Constitution. Instead, as articulated by Justice OLIVER WENDELL HOLMES's dissent in that same 1928 case: "The great ordinances of the Constitution do not establish and divide fields of black and white. Even the more specific of them are found to terminate in a penumbra shading gradually from one extreme to the other. . . . To make the rule of conduct applicable to an individual who but for such action would be free from it is to legislate—yet it is what judges do whenever they determine which of two competing principles of policy shall prevail. . . . It does not seem to need argument to show that however we may disguise it by veiling words we do not and cannot carry out the distinction between legislative and executive action with mathematical precision and divide the branches into watertight compartments. . . ."

Instead, as Justice JOSEPH STORY suggests of functionalists: "When we speak of a separation of the three great departments of government, and maintain that that separation is indispensable to public liberty, we are to understand this maxim in a limited sense. It is not meant to affirm that they must be kept wholly and entirely distinct, and have no common link of connection or dependence, the one upon the other, in the slightest degree. The true meaning is, that the whole power of one of these departments should not be exercised by the same hands which possess the whole power of either of the other departments; and that such exercise of the whole would subvert the principles of a free Constitution. Indeed, there is not a single constitution of any state in the Union, which does not practically embrace some acknowledgement of the maxim, and at the same time some admixture of powers constituting an exception to it."

One of the primary examples of the functionalist theory at work is the advent of the administrative agency. While housed in the executive branch to administer the day-to-day activities of those who are regulated, as well as to create rules that govern their behavior, Congress provides the funds and the legislative authority for these bodies to execute those duties. The courts ensure that the administration of the law neither unduly encroaches upon nor curtails the liberties of those being regulated.

This then gives rise to the argument that the framers embraced the principle of CHECKS AND BALANCES rather than an exclusive separation of powers. Support for this position is found in the framers' enumeration of many specific methods by which one of the branches can curtail the activities of another branch. For example, the executive can VETO legislation, while the veto can be overridden by the Congress; the Supreme Court can declare a particular act unconstitutional, while Congress can regulate the manner in which cases come before federal courts.

One can conclude that, so long as government is focused on providing for only as much government as is appropriate (a political question) and on ensuring to the most practical degree the overall public's health, safety, and welfare by using its enumerated powers, then individual liberty can be maximized by each separate branch discharging its respective responsibilities concomitant with the checks and balances put in place by the framers.

For more information: Breyer, Stephen. *Active Liberty: Interpreting Our Democratic Constitution.* New York: Knopf, 2005; Brown, Rebecca. "Separated Powers and Ordered Liberty." *University of Pennsylvania Law Review* 139, no. 1513 (1991): 315–320; Elliott, E. Donald. "Why Our Separation of Powers Jurisprudence Is So Abysmal." *George Washington Law Review* 57, no. 506 (1989): 515–518.

—Cleveland Ferguson III

September 11 attacks and the Constitution

The terrorist attacks of September 11, 2001, forever changed the United States. Within weeks of these attacks, Congress passed the Authorization for the Use of Military Force (Public Law 107–40)—directing the president to "use all necessary and proper force against those nations, organizations, or persons he determines planned, authorized, committed, or aided the terrorist attacks"—and the PATRIOT ACT (Public Law 107–56) designed to "deter and punish terrorist acts in the United States and around the world." With these pieces of legislation from Congress, combined with the presidential authority as COMMANDER IN CHIEF listed in ARTICLE II OF THE U.S. CONSTITUTION, the federal government enacted new programs and initiatives to combat global terrorism. At the outset, many of these initiatives were viewed as necessary to protect the national security of the United States. However, as time progressed, these same programs and initiatives received additional scrutiny, and questions arose pertaining to the nature of constitutional authority and the protection of CIVIL LIBERTIES.

In the several months immediately following the September 11 attacks, the federal government detained thousands of individuals in the United States who might have been linked to, or might have possessed information about, the terrorists' plot. One such individual was Rabih Haddad, accused of operating an Islamic charity and funneling contributions to suspected terrorist organizations. Haddad's family, friends, and the media sought to attend his hearing, but were informed that the proceedings were closed to the public and the press. This procedure raised constitutional questions about whether Haddad could receive a fair, impartial, and unbiased hearing without public scrutiny. Writing for a unanimous panel, Sixth District Court of Appeals Judge Keith stated, "The public's interests are best served by open proceedings. A true democracy is one that operates on faith—faith that government officials are forthcoming and honest, and faith that informed citizens will arrive at logical conclusions. This is a vital reciprocity that America should not discard in these troubling times. Without question, the events of September 11, 2001, left an indelible mark on our nation, but we as a people are united in the wake of the destruction to demonstrate to the world that we are a country deeply committed to preserving the rights and freedoms guaranteed by our democracy" (*Detroit Free Press v. Ashcroft,* 303 F. 3d 681 [2002]). Following these statements, the panel affirmed the lower court decision and supported the civil liberties challenge to the government.

In contrast to this decision is a ruling by the Third Circuit. The case was a response by New Jersey newspapers to repeated denials by the immigration courts of docket information and access to deportation hearings. According to the majority opinion, written by Judge Becker, "This case arises in the wake of September 11, 2001, a day on which American life changed drastically and dramatically. The era that dawned on September 11, and the war against terrorism that has pervaded the sinews of our national life since that day, are reflected in thousands of ways in legislative and national policy, the habits of daily living, and our collective psyches. Since the primary national policy must be self-preservation, it seems elementary that, to the extent open deportation hearings might impair national security, that security is implicated in the logic test" (*North Jersey Media Group, Inc. v. Ashcroft*, U.S. App. LEXIS 21032 [2002]). The Third Circuit ruled against civil liberties, concluding that the federal government had justified its request for secret deportation hearings, given the importance of preserving national security.

These two cases demonstrate the confusion facing federal judges as they attempt to resolve immigration and deportation disputes. On the one hand, judges are ordering public trials consistent with the practice before September 11. However, some other judges acknowledge that the terrorist attacks changed many aspects of the law and, consequently, in the name of national security, some trials must be closed to public scrutiny.

While the cases involving secret deportation hearings received a fair amount of media coverage, the vast share of public attention focused on the war on terror and, in particular, on the detainment of individuals labeled "enemy combatants." The first of these cases, RASUL V. BUSH, 542 U.S. 466 (2004), focused on complaints brought on behalf of individuals detained in Guantánamo Bay, Cuba. As the record indicates, the petitioners were citizens of Australia and Kuwait and were captured by the U.S. military

Smoke billows from the World Trade Center's twin towers after they are struck by commercial airliners that had been hijacked by terrorists. *(Shaw/Getty)*

during its armed confrontation with the Taliban regime in Afghanistan. They brought HABEAS CORPUS suits against the United States in protest of an executive order authorizing the indefinite detention of individuals suspected of terrorist actions. Writing for the majority, Justice JOHN PAUL STEVENS ruled in favor of the detainees at Guantánamo Bay. He stated that the individuals "have never been afforded access to any tribunal, much less charged and convicted of wrongdoing; and for more than two years they have been imprisoned in territory over which the United States exercises exclusive jurisdiction." Justice Stevens concluded that these individuals therefore were entitled to bring their disputes before U.S. courts to challenge the "enemy combatant" label.

A second case involved allegations by the federal government against Jose Padilla, a U.S. citizen apprehended at Chicago's O'Hare airport for potentially conspiring with the al-Qaeda terrorist network. During the course of a grand jury investigation in New York, President Bush signed an executive order directing Secretary of Defense Rumsfeld to designate Padilla an "enemy combatant." Rumsfeld complied and Padilla was sent to a military detention facility in South Carolina. His attorney brought a habeas corpus suit against Rumsfeld to challenge the president's authority to designate U.S. citizens as "enemy combatants." Chief Justice WILLIAM HUBBS REHNQUIST's opinion overturned an appeals court decision that had invalidated the executive order (RUMSFELD V. PADILLA, 542 U.S. 426 [2004]). However, this was accomplished by claiming that Padilla filed his lawsuit against the wrong party. Rehnquist indicated that the habeas corpus statute, passed by Congress over 100 years earlier, specifically indicated that lawsuits should proceed against the individual in immediate custody. As such, Commander Marr of the South Carolina military detention facility, not Secretary Rumsfeld, was Padilla's custodian and the proper respondent to the habeas petition.

The third case decided that same year by the Supreme Court involved the detention of a U.S. citizen, taken from the field of combat in Afghanistan. Yaser Hamdi was seized by Northern Alliance forces and turned over to the U.S. military shortly after Congress adopted a resolution entitled the Authorization for the Use of Military Force to the president. Writing on behalf of the majority in the case of HAMDI V. RUMSFELD, 542 U.S. 507 (2004), Justice SANDRA DAY O'CONNOR rejected the government's claim that federal courts had no authority to review the status of American citizens labeled "enemy combatants." She stated, "we have long made clear that a state of war is not a blank check for the President when it comes to the rights of the Nation's citizens."

Another "enemy combatant" case involved another detainee at Guantánamo Bay, Cuba. Following the Supreme Court's decision in *Rasul v. Bush*, the federal government established a series of military tribunals where detainees could challenge the "enemy combatant" status. Yet, because these tribunals were established under military regulations, many of the constitutional safeguards that would otherwise operate in civilian courts did not exist. Salim Ahmed Hamdan was captured in Afghanistan and transported to Guantánamo Bay. Because of his close affiliation to Osama bin Laden, President Bush announced that Hamdan was an "enemy combatant." In challenging this classification, Hamdan and his military-appointed attorney encountered several significant obstacles placed by the military tribunal. Consequently, he filed a habeas corpus petition in federal court for a determination of his status. In writing for the majority, Justice Stevens announced that these military tribunals violated both the Uniform Code of Military Justice and aspects of international law that are codified in the Geneva Conventions (*Hamdan v. Rumsfeld*, 126 S. Ct. 2749 [2006]). He noted that, "even assuming that Hamden is a dangerous individual who would cause great harm or death to innocent civilians given the opportunity, the Executive nevertheless must comply with the prevailing rule of law in undertaking to try him and subject him to criminal punishment."

These cases indicate that the status of "enemy combatant" places individuals in a constitutional limbo, and the Supreme Court has had difficulty announcing clear definitions of the rights and privileges afforded to these individuals. The justices seem to state that the federal government cannot bypass the fundamental protections afforded by the Constitution, but they also allow the government tremendous leeway in the handling of "enemy combatants."

The terrorist attacks of September 11, 2001, may have profoundly altered certain aspects of the Constitution. At this point in time, it is extremely difficult to determine precisely which aspects have changed. Since we rely on judges to interpret the Constitution, their opinions are essential to help clarify its meaning. In the two areas of secret deportation hearings and "enemy combatants," the courts have issued mixed, and sometimes contradictory, opinions. And more constitutional questions keep emerging. For example, the news media recently announced a program from the National Security Agency to eavesdrop on communications in the United States without a search warrant or judicial oversight. Advocates of civil liberties claim this program is a violation of the FOURTH AMENDMENT, while the other side of the debate claims the program is essential to protect the national security of the United States by preventing future terrorist attacks. Which side is correct? Only federal judges (and ultimately Supreme Court justices) can decide, from a constitutional standpoint.

For more information: Cohen, David B., and John W. Wells, eds. *American National Security and Civil Liberties in an Era of Terrorism.* New York: Palgrave Macmillan, 2004; Whitehead, John W., and Steven H. Aden. "Forfeiting 'Enduring Freedom' for 'Homeland Security': A Constitutional Analysis of the USA PATRIOT Act and the Justice Department's Anti-Terrorism Initiatives." *American University Law Review* 51 (August 2002): 1,081–1,133.

—Kirk A. Randazzo

Serrano v. Priest 487 P.2d 1241 (1971)

In *Serrano v. Priest,* in a 6 to 1 decision, the California Supreme Court held that the state's school finance system violated the FOURTEENTH AMENDMENT to the U.S. Constitution.

Like school finance systems in virtually all states in the late 1960s, California's system relied heavily on local property taxes to fund education. Thus, property-rich districts could tax at low rates and spend at high levels, while property-poor districts had to tax at high rates and spend at low levels. The *Serrano* reform lawyers attacked this system as discriminatory. Following the logic of the U.S. Supreme Court's EQUAL PROTECTION clause jurisprudence, they argued that district wealth was a "suspect classification" (just like race), and that education was a "fundamental right" (just like the RIGHT TO VOTE). The California high court agreed. The state bore a heavy burden of justification for its finance policies, which the high court found that it could not meet.

Serrano was a landmark case, for it was the first time that a court had invalidated a state's school finance policies as unconstitutional. While the California court's interpretation of the federal equal protection clause would not survive the U.S. Supreme Court's decision in *San Antonio v. Rodriguez* (1973), *Serrano* itself survived as a central part of a national trend that saw reformers challenging school finance policies in state courts on state constitutional grounds.

In *Serrano II,* 557 P.2d 929 (1976), in a 4 to 3 decision, the California Supreme Court reaffirmed its earlier ruling, this time by relying on its own constitution's equal protection provisions. The high court also affirmed a trial court ruling requiring that "wealth-related disparities" (that is, differences in local spending attributable to unequal property tax bases) in per pupil expenditures for basic education across school districts be reduced to "less than $100.00" within six years (557 P.2d 929, at 940, nt. 21). The dissenters in *Serrano II* argued that relying less on local property taxes and making the state pick up more of the tab might well undermine overall public support for education (557 P.2d 929, at 964, Clark, J., dissenting).

In June 1978, less than a year after the legislature had passed a new finance law, California voters endorsed Proposition 13, a state constitutional amendment adopted through the initiative process. Proposition 13 placed strict limits on the ability of local governments and school districts to raise local revenues by rolling back assessments to 1 percent of value. Over the next several years, the state came to finance about 80 percent of the total costs for public education. In 1986, a state appellate court found that the state had complied with *Serrano*. It determined that wealth-related revenue differences had been reduced to "insignificant amounts" for 93 percent of all school districts (*Serrano III,* 226 Cal. Rept. 584, at 614 [Ct. of App., 2nd App. Dist., Div. Two] [1986]).

Current observers generally agree that much more equality in tax rates and spending across districts was achieved. However, there was much more leveling down than leveling up. *Serrano,* in conjunction with Proposition 13, also produced a precipitous decline in overall public support for education spending. Although California had ranked among the top 10 states in per pupil spending in the late 1960s, it placed among the bottom 10 states in that late 1990s.

For more information: Elmore, Richard F., and Milbrey W. McLaughlin. *Reform and Retrenchment: The Politics of California School Finance.* Cambridge, Mass.: Ballanger Publishing, 1982; Martin, Isaac. "Does School Finance Litigation Cause Taxpayer Revolt?" *Law and Society Review* 40, no. 4 (September 2006): 525–558; Schrag, Peter. *Final Test: The Battle for Adequacy in America's Schools.* New York: New Press, 2003; Sonstelie, Jon, Eric Brunner, and Kenneth Ardon. *For Better or For Worse?: School Finance Reform in California.* Public Policy Institute of California, 2000. Available online. URL: http://www.ppic.org/main/publication.asp?i=65. Accessed 15 May 2008.

—Michael Paris

Seventeenth Amendment

The Seventeenth Amendment, adopted on May 31, 1913, provides for popular election of United States senators. Prior to this, senators had been selected by action of their respective state legislatures, not by direct voter participation. With this amendment, the Constitution's original ARTICLE II, Section 3 language of "chosen by the legislatures thereof" was replaced with the more democratic "elected by the people thereof."

The successful passage and adoption of the Seventeenth Amendment is attributable as much to Progressive Era attitudes toward greater democratization and public participation, as to less well-known but just as significant changes: the increased importance of the SENATE and the growing power of political parties.

In the early days of the republic, the HOUSE OF REPRESENTATIVES was popularly viewed and functioned as the more important chamber. It was not uncommon for sitting senators to resign their posts, sometimes with several years remaining in their terms, to run for House seats. In the run-up to the Civil War, and even more dramatically following it, the Senate emerged on a parity with the House or, arguably, as the more important, visible, and influential chamber.

Recognizing the growing influence that senators (and senatorial candidates alike) had within their states, state party organizations learned that their senators could further their objectives and rally local organizations like no other official. Taking advantage of this situation, parties began to select, promote, and organize around particular senatorial candidates prior to their official election by the legislature. Initially known as "endorsements" and "canvassing the public," these tactics short-circuited the framers' original selection process and presaged the modern direct primary. Among early canvasses, and certainly the best known, was the 1858 Lincoln-Douglas contest wherein ABRAHAM LINCOLN reshaped the Republican Party and won the popular vote, but lost the Senate seat because the Illinois legislature remained Democratic and sent Douglas to Washington.

As the Senate became a body where critical issues affecting the nation and its future were shaped, and state political party machines became more pronounced, the very process of choosing senators grew more contentious and protracted. Deadlocks wherein legislatures were completely unable to agree on a senatorial candidate became commonplace. Deadlocks had become enough of a problem by 1866 that Congress passed a law designed to remedy the situation. The well-intentioned statute, proscribing daily balloting, common sessions, and concurrent majorities only made matters worse.

Between 1891 and 1905, 45 deadlocks were recorded. They lasted from a week to a record of 114 days, in 20 different states, with states accepting vacancies in the U.S. Senate as a consequence of their inability to decide. Delaware's experience is the most extreme: Between 1899 and 1901 it had only one senator in Washington, and between 1901 and 1903 it had none. Acrimonious charges of bribery, corruption, backroom dealing, and senators beholden to narrow financial interests clouded these proceedings even further. Modern journalists and students seeking historical examples of legislatures acting badly need look no further than this pre-Seventeenth Amendment era to find wonderfully colorful stories of pandemonium and bizarre behavior as state legislatures squabbled over choosing their U.S. senators.

Throughout the country, multiple strategies were implemented to respond in one way or another to these crises. Deadlocks were addressed through state-by-state reforms. Beginning with Illinois in 1890, several forms of direct senatorial primaries (advisory in nature and not legally binding upon the legislature) were approved so that, by 1910, 28 states had them. In 1901, Oregon added a "pledge" to its primary regimen, one that required state legislative candidates to indicate their support for the senatorial candidate who won the popular vote. Other states followed suit. In 1900, the national Democratic Party initiated quadrennial presidential platform advocacy of a constitutional amendment for direct election of senators. The GOP joined the chorus in 1908. By 1910, more than 30 states (at that time, more than the sufficient three-fourths necessary to approve a constitutional amendment) had asked Congress to call a national convention on the subject or to pass an amendment to that effect. Responding to these local pressures, the House of Representatives had, between 1893 and 1902, considered such an amendment five times and had twice passed them with the necessary two-thirds majority, only to have them ignored in the Senate.

A decade later, in a Senate changed by the attitude of members who had themselves been selected by these reformed and more popular forms of elections, the House for the third time sent a direct election amendment to the Senate; following a difficult Senate resolution of yet another fraudulent senatorial election, the Senate quickly ratified the new amendment. The states that had long been "ahead" of the Congress on this issue promptly gave their approval and the amendment became law.

For more information: Haynes, George H. *The Senate of the United States*. New York: Russell & Russell, 1960; Hoebeke, C. H. *The Road to Mass Democracy: Original Intent and the Seventeenth Amendment*. New Brunswick, N.J.: Transaction Publishers, 1995.

—George Peery

Seventh Amendment

The Seventh Amendment to the Constitution guarantees individuals a right to a trial by jury when the value in dispute is in excess of $20. This amendment is one of the original 10 in the BILL OF RIGHTS, which amended the Constitution in 1791; it was originally proposed by JAMES MADISON.

Both the Sixth and Seventh Amendments were adopted to provide for jury trials for defendants facing accusations. However, while the SIXTH AMENDMENT right to a jury trial applies to criminal trials, the Seventh Amendment involves civil cases or issues. Additionally, while the Sixth Amendment has been incorporated in its entirety to apply to the states, the Supreme Court has declined to do the same for the Seventh Amendment. This puts it, along with the Second and THIRD AMENDMENTs, among the only ones that do not in whole or in part limit state action.

The Supreme Court in *Baltimore & Carolina Line v. Redman*, 295 U.S. 654 (1935), declared that the general purpose of the Seventh Amendment is to preserve the common law right to a jury trial. Yet in *Colegrove v. Battin*, 413 U.S. 149 (1973), the Court ruled that this federal right did not mandate a 12-person jury and that instead a six-person jury would be acceptable. Finally, even though the Seventh Amendment does not apply to state proceedings, state law matters adjudicated in federal court, such as under DIVERSITY JURISDICTION, would be required to follow the requirements of this amendment.

For more information: Stone, Geoffrey R., Richard A. Epstein, and Cass R. Sunstein. *The Bill of Rights in the Modern State*. Chicago: University of Chicago Press, 1992.

—David Schultz

Shapiro v. Thompson 394 U.S. 618 (1969)

In *Shapiro v. Thompson*, the Supreme Court ruled that a state's imposition of a one-year waiting period for eligibility for welfare benefits discriminated against individuals on the basis of length of residency and interfered with the fundamental right to travel from one state to another.

The 6-3 ruling, written by Justice WILLIAM J. BRENNAN, JR., was a major first step in the Supreme Court's rethinking of the status of government benefits under the Constitution. The process continued two years later in *GOLDBERG v. KELLY*, 397 U.S. 254 (1970), when the Supreme Court ruled that cutting off or denying welfare benefits required the protection of DUE PROCESS notice and a chance to be heard.

The ruling also marked a significant step in constitutional analysis, as Justice Brennan for the first time held that government discrimination in the exercise of a fundamental right required a "compelling" justification. Brennan imported this tough standard from free speech analysis and gave new bite to the EQUAL PROTECTION clause.

Shapiro involved the consolidation of cases from Connecticut, Pennsylvania, and the DISTRICT OF COLUMBIA. Each jurisdiction had a one-year waiting period for eligibility for welfare benefits, with the Aid for Families with Dependent Children (AFDC) program involved in the cases. Lower federal courts held the waiting period unconstitutional, and state officials appealed to the Supreme Court.

Justice Brennan set the tone for the opinion by noting that the line between residence in a state for more than a year and less than a year could determine arbitrarily which families were able "to obtain the very means to subsist—food, shelter, and other necessities of life."

The Court said the main purpose of the restriction was to keep poor people from moving into a state and becoming a burden on the fiscal resources of the state. Justice Brennan said that was not a constitutionally valid goal because the Constitution protects the FUNDAMENTAL RIGHTS of people to travel from one state to another. He also rejected the argument by states that they were trying to prevent individuals from relocating in order to seek higher welfare benefits; he said such a goal was no more valid than would be a ban on persons moving to a state to take advantage of a good school system.

The Court also rejected the argument that Congress specifically encouraged the states to adopt waiting periods. This portion of the decision prompted a dissent by Chief Justice Earl Warren, usually a close ally of Justice Brennan. Warren argued that Congress specifically authorized and encouraged states to adopt residency periods. He also warned that the Court's rejection of welfare residency waiting periods would have ramifications for voting, in-state tuition, and the practice of some professions. Justice Hugo L. Black joined Warren's dissent.

Justice JOHN M. HARLAN also dissented and warned that the Court was interfering too much with state and federal legislative processes. In a strong critique of what he deemed to be the liberal excesses of the Court, he criticized what he described as "the current notion that this Court possesses a peculiar wisdom all its own whose capacity to lead this Nation out of its present troubles is contained only by the limits of judicial ingenuity in contriving new constitutional principles to meet each problem as it arises."

For more information: Michelman, Frank I. "Forward: On Protecting the Poor through the Fourteenth Amendment." *Harvard Law Review* 83, no. 7 (1969): 14–15; Schwartz, Bernard. "How Justice Brennan Changed America." In *Reason and Passion: Justice Brennan's Enduring Influence.* New York: W.W. Norton, 1997.

—Stephen Wermiel

Shaw v. Reno 509 U.S. 630 (1993)

In *Shaw v. Reno* the Supreme Court invalidated a redistricting plan developed under the VOTING RIGHTS ACT to enhance minority representation, arguing that it violated the FOURTEENTH AMENDMENT's EQUAL PROTECTION clause. The decision was important because it represented a REHNQUIST COURT criticism of the use of race to remedy discrimination in reapportionment issues.

North Carolina is a state where the bulk of the black population is found in counties covered by Section 5 of the Voting Right Act of 1965. In 1990, the state had no black congressional districts, and the last black member elected to Congress was during the Reconstruction era. Following the 1990 census, North Carolina acquired its 12th congressional seat. In 1991, a congressional plan enacted by the North Carolina state legislature created one majority-black district to comply with Section 5 of the Voting Rights Act, which prohibits a covered jurisdiction from implementing changes in a "standard, practice, or procedure with respect to voting" without federal authorization. This plan was rejected by the Department of Justice, first on the grounds that the state failed to demonstrate that it did not have the purpose or effect of diluting minority voting strength. This was followed by suggestions that a second majority black district be drawn in the southeastern portion of the state.

In response to the Department of Justice's order, the state instead produced a new plan with a second majority-black congressional district elsewhere in the state. The lines of the new district stretched for approximately 160 miles along Interstate 85, with much of its length no wider than the highway's corridor. Five white residents from North Carolina filed suit against the state and the Department of Justice on the grounds that the plan unconstitutionally distinguished between voters according to their race. The two majority-black districts created by the state legislature constituted, they claimed, an unconstitutional racial gerrymander in violation of the Fourteenth Amendment. Furthermore, they said that the two districts concentrated the majority of black voters arbitrarily without regard to contiguity, compactness, geographical boundaries, or respect for political subdivisions for the sole purpose of creating congressional districts along racial lines to guarantee the election of two black representatives. A three-judge district court dismissed the complaint by a 2-1 vote for the following reasons: (1) lack of subject matter jurisdiction over the federal government and the state, (2) failure to state an equal protection claim, since favoring minority voters is not an invidious discrimination in the constitutional sense, and (3) the redistricting plan did not lead to proportional underrepresentation of white voters statewide.

On certiorari, the Supreme Court was presented with variations of the same issues. The first was whether the revised plan, which contains district boundary lines of dramatically irregular shape, constituted an unconstitutional gerrymandering and therefore presented a cognizable claim for resolution. The second question was whether redistricting legislation that is so bizarre on its face that it is unexplainable on grounds other than race demands the same close scrutiny given to other state actions that classify citizens by race. Summarily, do claims that the North Carolina legislature created a racially gerrymandered district raise a valid constitutional issue under the equal protection clause, and if so are the stated objectives narrowly tailored to further a COMPELLING GOVERNMENTAL INTEREST? Justice SANDRA DAY O'CONNOR delivered the 5-4 opinion of the Court. Chief Justice WILLIAM HUBBS REHNQUIST and Justices ANTONIN GREGORY SCALIA, ANTHONY M. KENNEDY, and CLARENCE THOMAS joined, while Justice White filed a dissenting opinion in which Justices Blackmun and JOHN PAUL STEVENS joined, with Blackmun, Stevens, and DAVID H. SOUTER also posting separate dissenting opinions.

Writing for the majority in a decision that reversed and remanded the case to the district court, Justice O'Connor ruled as follows: First, that the district court properly dismissed the claim against the Department of Justice. Second, while the lack of compactness, per se, is not a constitutional violation, equal protection is violated when and if a redistricting legislation, though race-neutral on its face, is so extremely irregular that it cannot rationally be understood as anything other than an effort by the legislature to segregate voters into separates districts on the basis of race and for purposes of voting. This, O'Connor reasoned, is especially acute when such redistricting is done without regard for traditional districting principles, and more importantly, without a sufficiently compelling state justification. If, on remand, the allegations of a racial gerrymander are not contradicted, the Court observed, the district court must determine whether the plan is narrowly tailored to further a compelling governmental interest. Addressing compliance under Section 5 of the Voting Right Act of 1965, the Court observed further that "a covered jurisdiction's interest in creating majority-minority districts in order to comply with the Act does not give States carte blanche to engage in racial gerrymandering." Third, that the North Carolina redistricting plan at issue did not violate the rights of white voters because it did not lead to unfairly diluting or canceling out votes.

To Justice O'Connor, the question of the meaning of the RIGHT TO VOTE and the propriety of race-based state legislation designed to benefit members of a historically disadvantaged racial minority group, in this case, involve two of the most complex and sensitive issues the Court has faced in recent years. Appearances, she argues, matter in reapportionment. She sees as suspect reapportionment plans that include, in one district, individuals belonging to the same race, who otherwise are widely separated by geographical and political boundaries and who may have little in common with one another but the color of their skin. She sees such plans as bearing an uncomfortable resemblance to political apartheid. While it is obvious that Justice O'Connor's opinion in this case is tough on race-based classification, she finds plenty of merit in the use of race-conscious districting if properly validated with a compelling state interest. Indeed, she carefully observes that "this Court has never held that race-conscious decision-making is impermissible in all circumstances." Classifications of citizens based solely on race, she argues, are by their nature odious to a free people whose institutions are founded upon the doctrine of equality. Such classifications threaten to stigmatize persons by reason of their membership in a racial group and to incite racial hostility. Even in the pursuit of genuine remedial objectives, O'Connor continues, "an explicit policy of assignment by race may serve to stimulate our society's latent race-consciousness, suggesting the utility and propriety of basing decisions on a factor that ideally bears no relationship to an individual's worth or needs." Thus, state legislation that expressly distinguishes among citizens on account of race, she argues, whether it contains an explicit distinction or is "unexplainable on grounds other than race, must be narrowly tailored to further a compelling governmental interest."

Citing the Court's 1960 opinion in *GOMIL-LION ET AL. V. LIGHTFOOT,* 364 U.S. 339 (1960), she observed further that "redistricting legislation that is alleged to be so bizarre on its face that it is unexplainable on grounds other than race demands the same close scrutiny regardless of the motivations underlying its adoption." Thus, although it may be difficult to determine from the face of a single-member districting plan that it makes such a distinction, this does not mean that a racial gerrymander, once established, should receive less scrutiny than other legislation distinguishing citizens by race. Speaking of the inherent effect of racial gerrymandering, O'Connor noted that "by perpetuating stereotypical notions about members of the same racial group—that they think alike, share the same political interests, and prefer the same candidates,—a racial gerrymander, may indeed, exacerbate the very patterns of racial bloc voting that majority-minority districting is sometimes said to counteract." Accordingly, Justice O'Connor continued, it sends to elected representatives the message that their primary obligation is to represent only that group's members, rather than their constituency as a whole. Limiting its ruling to the current case, she observed in summary that the Court "expresses no view as to whether the intentional creation of majority-minority districts, without more, always gives rise to an equal protection challenge."

The four dissenting justices took not only drastically different positions but also did so with vigor. Common to their arguments is the vagueness of the new equal protection test announced by the majority decision. Specifically, they questioned the soundness of the test relative to equal protection given that no claim of white voting dilution was made or could be sustained in the case. For example, Justice White, in a dissent joined by Blackmun and Stevens, wondered how "given two districts drawn on similar, race based grounds," one became more injurious than the other simply by virtue of being snakelike, so far as the Constitution is concerned absent of any evidence of differential racial impact. According to Justice Souter, "the majority offered no adequate justification for treating the narrow category of bizarrely shaped district claims differently from other districting claims." Until today, he argued, "the Court has analyzed equal protection claims involving racial electoral redistricting differently from equal protection claims involving other forms of government conduct." In light of the history of the Voting Rights Act and redistricting, Souter asserts, "the mere placement of an individual in one district instead of another denies no one a right or benefit provided to others." In his view, therefore, the higher test of STRICT SCRUTINY is unnecessary.

The overall effect of *Shaw* on the Voting Rights Act of 1965 is worth noting. As designed, the act requires that jurisdictions consider issues of race when designing reapportionment plans. That is, to determine if a standard, practice, or procedure affecting voting discriminates on the basis of race, it is necessary to look at the issue in terms of race. This assumes that when states adopt redistricting plans, they almost always will be making decisions with some consideration of race. While most post-*Shaw* case decisions adopt the *Shaw* doctrine, it is quite clear that the Voting Rights Act and *Shaw* decision are contradictory and, if not, are in tension. The act holds that race should be considered when drawing district lines, while *Shaw* holds that decisions should not be based upon race. Supreme Court rulings since 1990 attempt to resolve this contradiction. While some rulings argue that "race should not be the predominant factor in the redistricting process to the subordination of traditional districting principles," others argue that districts are not necessarily unconstitutional because they have odd shapes, however bizarre they may be. If race is the predominant consideration in a districting decision, the now-prevailing view holds that such a plan is subject to a strict scrutiny analysis where it must be demonstrated that it is narrowly tailored to address a compelling state interest. This leaves open the question of how to address a compelling interest or what exactly constitutes an acceptable compelling state interest. On the basis of these opinions, the current applicable standards appear to be that, if race is the predominant consideration in the districting decision, the districts must be subject to strict scrutiny analysis where the state must demonstrate that its plan is narrowly tailored to address a compelling state interest.

For more information: Peacock, Anthony A. *Affirmative Action and Representation: Shaw v. Reno and the Future of Voting Rights.* Durham, N.C.: Carolina Academic Press, 1997.

—Marc G. Pufong

Shays's Rebellion

Shays's Rebellion (1786–87) was an armed insurrection against the government of the United States and the state government of Massachusetts. It was this rebellion that prompted many of the framers to argue for revisions to the Articles of Confederation when it appeared that the national government lacked the authority to keep the peace and order in the country.

The leader of the rebellion was Daniel P. Shays, who had served as a decorated officer in the Revolutionary War. The war debt was being borne disproportionately by small farmers and landowners located in the largely barter-based economy of western and central Massachusetts. These farmers and landowners were being taxed by the state in order to pay off war bonds. Faced with mounting debt and taxes, they had little paper money to use for payment. Many had to sell their farms and land at a fraction of their value in order to pay their debts and/or taxes. Those who could not pay often had their farms and lands confiscated by the state and were placed in debtor's prisons.

Under the leadership of Shays and other local leaders, groups were organized that initially freed people from debtor's prisons. Soon, Shays began to call for an open rebellion. The "Regulators," as they came to be known, took up arms and shut down debtor's courts throughout western and central Massachusetts. Massachusetts militia forces that were called out to deal with the rebellion often refused to confront their friends and neighbors. Hence, the state force, which would normally deal with such a situation, was ineffective. Also, the Continental Army had largely disbanded due to the predisposition against a standing military force. Therefore, the U.S. government under the Articles of Confederation could not deal with the rebellion.

The Congress of the Confederation was virtually powerless in the situation without a standing army and without the power to intervene in state affairs. This left Massachusetts to deal with the rebellion. With the state militia largely useless and with large elements of the population sympathetic to the rebellion, Massachusetts governor James Bowdoin approved the raising of private funds in December 1786 to hire 4,400 mercenaries under General Benjamin Lincoln to deal with the Regulators. Shays responded by ordering his forces to take the federal arsenal in Springfield. On January 25, 1787, two of three rebel regiments advanced on Springfield, with the other regiment planning to attack on January 26. The leader of the missing regiment had sent a message to the other two regiments stating that he would postpone his attack. However, the note was intercepted, thus ensuring that the rebel force was below strength. At Springfield, they were faced by General William Sheppard and 1,200 members of the Massachusetts militia who had not defected to the rebellion. Once the fighting began, many of the inexperienced and poorly trained troops of the rebellion fled under fire. Four rebels were killed and many were wounded. The rebel force broke apart, seeing that they were outnumbered. With the additional 4,400 soldiers from the mercenary force (earlier legitimized as a part of the Massachusetts militia by the state government) arriving the next day, the rebel cause was lost. Lincoln's force pursued the rebels and defeated them on February 3, 1787. Ultimately, Shays and most of his allies were pardoned by John Hancock, the new governor of Massachusetts.

Shays's Rebellion helped to expose the weakness of the U.S. government under the Articles of Confederation. With the rebellion fresh on everyone's mind, George Washington came back to the national stage, and he and others began to plan for a new nation with a stronger central government, which ultimately resulted in the adoption of the U.S. Constitution.

For more information: Gross, Robert A., ed. *In Debt to Shays: The Bicentennial of an Agrarian Rebellion.* Charlottesville: University of Virginia Press, 1993; Richards, Leonard. *Shays's Rebellion:*

The American Revolution's Final Battle. Philadelphia: University of Pennsylvania Press, 2002.
—William Lester

Shelley v. Kraemer 334 U.S. 1 (1948)

In *Shelley v. Kraemer,* the U.S. Supreme Court unanimously (6-0) declared state court enforcement of private, racially restrictive covenants unconstitutional under the FOURTEENTH AMENDMENT'S EQUAL PROTECTION clause.

The restrictive covenants reviewed by the Supreme Court were private agreements among property owners that identified particular racial groups to which property owners or occupants must belong. The covenant reviewed in the Missouri case excluded "people of the Negro or Mongolian Race," while, in the Michigan case, the covenant allowed only "those of the Caucasian race."

In the Missouri case, Shelley (who was African American) was sued by Kraemer (who was Caucasian) for purchasing property in Kraemer's St. Louis neighborhood. Kraemer sought to nullify the sale on the grounds that it violated the area's racially restrictive covenant. The trial court ruled for Shelley, declaring that the racially restrictive covenant was not in effect at the time Shelley purchased the property, since it covered only 47 of the 57 properties in the designated area. The Supreme Court of Missouri reversed the trial court's decision. In the Michigan case, the trial court had upheld and enforced the racially restrictive covenant against the African-American property purchaser, and the Supreme Court of Michigan affirmed the trial court's decision.

In *Shelley v. Kraemer,* the U.S. Supreme Court confronted for the first time the constitutionality of private restrictive covenants, as well as state judicial enforcement of such contracts. The opinion of the Court relied on its earlier nullifications of state and local legislative acts that sought to limit the fundamental property rights of racial minorities. It held that the acts of the state judiciary, as a branch of state government, were subject to the Fourteenth Amendment's prohibitions against discriminatory state action with regard to property rights. Thus, the enforcement of racially restrictive private agreements, through the state's judicial process, violated the Fourteenth Amendment's guarantee of equal protection of the laws. Given its disposition of the state judicial enforcement question, the Court explicitly declined to decide the constitutionality of the covenants themselves. Yet, by eliminating the possibility of judicial enforcement, the Court's decision in *Shelley* effectively nullified such private covenants.

Seventeen amicus curiae briefs were filed in support of the petitioners, including those by the solicitor general of the United States, the AMERICAN CIVIL LIBERTIES UNION, and the National Bar Association; three amicus curiae briefs were filed in support of the respondents. Future Supreme Court justice Thurgood Marshall, then legal director for the National Association for the Advancement of Colored People (NAACP), represented the petitioners. *Shelley* was the culmination of the NAACP's decades-long campaign to dismantle the legal framework that enforced housing discrimination. The NAACP's legal strategy in the *Shelley* case—the development of ideal test cases, coordination of amicus curiae briefs, and use of social science data—would be duplicated in subsequent CIVIL RIGHTS litigation campaigns.

For more information: Vose, Clement. *Caucasians Only.* Berkeley: University of California Press, 1959.

—Jinney S. Smith

Sheppard v. Maxwell 384 U.S. 333 (1966)

Sheppard v. Maxwell is the 8-1 decision wherein the Supreme Court reversed and remanded the conviction of Dr. Sam Sheppard for the second-degree murder of his wife. Justice Tom Clark wrote the opinion, holding that the massive, pervasive, and prejudicial publicity surrounding Sheppard's case prevented him from having the fair trial assured by the DUE PROCESS clause of the FOURTEENTH AMENDMENT. The *Sheppard* case is famous as the basis for the television series and the movie *The Fugitive.*

The brutal murder of Marilyn Sheppard on July 4, 1954, in a suburb of Cleveland, Ohio, had led to an avalanche of media attention. From the outset, newspapers and broadcast stations focused on the husband, osteopathic surgeon Sam Sheppard, as the prime suspect. Between the crime and Sheppard's conviction, the local papers ran stories that filled five volumes. The coverage included many front-page editorials asserting Sheppard's guilt. Potential jurors had been subjected to an incessant message that a lying, cheating Sheppard had killed his wife and that his privileged family were using their influence to protect him. The trial, conducted by a judge running for reelection, began two weeks before he faced the voters.

In addition to the pretrial publicity, the Court cited a number of errors in the trial itself. The names and addresses of potential jurors were released to the press, which published them. All veniremen received letters and phone calls about the case before jury selection began. During the trial, jurors' photographs and personal information were continuously shown in the news media. Although the judge suggested that the jurors not read or listen to comments on the case, he made no effort to enforce such rules. The jury was sequestered only during deliberations, but even then they were allowed to make phone calls.

The justices found that "bedlam reigned in the courthouse" during Sheppard's trial. Although the bar is intended to provide clients and counsel some PRIVACY to confer and to keep papers, 20 reporters were allowed to set up cameras and to take notes inside the bar, crowding the counsel tables and the jury box. Almost every available seat in the courtroom was assigned to newsmen, leaving only two rows for the defendant's and the victim's families. Reporters moved in and out of the room at will, causing distraction and confusion. By giving the press "absolute free reign," the judge "lost his ability to supervise the environment."

In addition, police officers, attorneys, and witnesses made frequent statements to the newspapers and radio reporters alleging evidence and repeating gossip against Sheppard. Although witnesses were barred from the courtroom before they testified, the papers printed verbatim accounts of each day's proceedings, allowing witnesses to know exactly what had been said.

The Supreme Court found that the judge could have avoided such a "carnival atmosphere." He had the option of granting a change of venue or a continuance. He might have set stricter rules for the media in the courtroom, limiting their numbers and their access to the principals in the case. He should have insulated the witnesses and controlled the gossip, information, and speculation issued by officials. He could have prohibited extrajudicial statements by lawyers and sequestered the jury. Ultimately, because the trial court did not protect Sheppard from prejudicial publicity and did not control disruptive influences in the courtroom, the justices granted his habeas petition and released him from custody. Sheppard was retried and acquitted.

Sheppard v. Maxwell set some ground rules for courts' responsibility for decorum in a high-profile case. They held that defendants need not demonstrate specific prejudice if, as in this instance, the totality of the circumstances raised the probability of prejudice. The case is also famous as the inspiration for a 1960s television series, *The Fugitive,* as well as a 1990s movie of the same name.

For more information: Schuetz, Janice E., and Kathryn Holmes Snedaker. *Communication and Litigation: Studies of Famous Trials.* Carbondale: Southern Illinois University Press, 1988.

—Mary Welek Atwell

Sherman, Roger (1721–1793) *Legislator and jurist*

Roger Sherman is one of the most significant Founding Fathers because of his political career, which included serving as U.S. senator from Connecticut as well as a signer of the DECLARATION OF INDEPENDENCE, and his political thought, including his authorship of the CONNECTICUT COMPROMISE (or Great Compromise) at the CONSTITUTIONAL CONVENTION in Philadelphia.

Roger Sherman was born on April 19, 1721, in Newton, Massachusetts, near Boston. The family moved to Stoughton, Massachusetts, while Roger was very young, and it was in Stoughton that Roger was influenced during his formative educational years by his Harvard-educated church minister, the Reverend Samuel Danbar. Sherman married Elizabeth Hartwell and had seven children. He was by trade a cobbler and merchant, and later an attorney, being admitted to the bar of Litchfield, Connecticut, in 1754.

Roger Sherman's political career included service as a justice of the peace; election to the General Assembly, representing New Milford, Connecticut, 1755–58, 1760–61; commissary for the Connecticut Troops, 1759; election to represent New Haven in the Connecticut legislature, 1760–80; judge of the Superior Court of Connecticut, 1766–89; election to Continental Congress, 1774–75; and election to represent Connecticut in Congress 1776–81, 1783–84. He was a distinguished member of the Constitutional Convention, 1787, and was elected U.S. senator for Connecticut, 1791–93. Roger Sherman was on the Committee of Five that drafted the Declaration of Independence, and he served in the Continental Army and held several distinguished posts of political leadership that established him among the Founding Fathers' generation as a man of character, trust, and steady, pragmatic leadership.

Roger Sherman is significant because he was the author of the Connecticut Compromise that served as a foundation for the original FEDERALISM in the Constitution of 1787. After the convention, Roger Sherman joined other Federalists in advocating for ratification of the new constitution, and his leadership led Connecticut to be one of the early states to ratify. In fact, as Donald Lutz has noted, "Roger Sherman . . . was one of the most highly regarded men in Connecticut."

Sherman not only authored the critical compromise that brought forth a new constitution and defined a new American form of government the federalists termed "federalism," but he also gave his political support to ratification in Connecticut and New England. As M. E. Bradford remarked, "It was as much Sherman's constitution as MADISON's or Wilson's." Otherwise, Connecticut would have voted a resounding "no." Sherman understood and articulated a state-centered federalism as a guarantor of the rights of the people and, unlike fellow Federalist ALEXANDER HAMILTON, Sherman held that the states protections under the Connecticut Compromise were a continuation of states' rights under the Articles of Confederation. Thus, Sherman was a limited-government, small-state Federalist who played a crucial role in defining the new constitutions and governments of the United States.

For more information: Bradford, M. E. *A Worthy Company.* Marlborogh, N.H.: Plymouth Rock Foundation, 1982; Collier, Christopher. *Roger Sherman's Connecticut.* Middletown, Conn.: Wesleyan University Press, 1971; Lutz, Donald S. "Connecticut." In *Ratifying the Constitution.* Lawrence: University Press of Kansas, 1989; Walker, David B. *The Rebirth of American Federalism.* Chatham, N.J.: Chatham House, 1995; Wood, Gordon. *The Creation of the American Republic.* New York: W.W. Norton, 1969.

—Michael W. Hail

shopping malls and the First Amendment

Protests and political activities at shopping malls oftentimes raise FIRST AMENDMENT issues, asking whether these commercial places are public squares or private property.

As commercial and social activity has moved from public property (such as town squares) to private property, speakers' need to reach audiences for their political, religious, or social messages has come into increasing conflict with the property rights of the owners of shopping malls, along with company-owned towns, grocery stores, and the like.

The United States Supreme Court began considering the issue with *Marsh v. State of Alabama*, 326 U.S. 501 (1946). *Marsh* concerned not a shopping mall, but a company-owned town. Objecting to the speech of a protestor, the town owners attempted to have the speaker convicted of criminal trespass. After considering the injury to the public sphere from the replacement of traditional public fora for free speech with private property, the Court held that the criminal trespass law could not be applied to bar this speech. In *Amalgamated Food Employees Union Local 590 v. Logan Valley Plaza, Inc.,* 391 U.S. 308 (1968), the Court extended the *Marsh* doctrine to cover shopping malls as the "functional equivalent" of a historical town square. However, in *Lloyd Corp. v. Tanner,* 407 U.S. 551 (1972), the Court de facto overruled *Logan.*

Most of the action today is centered in state courts. After *Lloyd,* the federal courts became unreceptive to the First Amendment claims of most speakers seeking to enter private property in order to reach an audience for their political messages. In response, state courts, starting with California, began extending protection under the free speech and petition clauses of their state constitutions. A significant minority of states have followed California's lead and adopted rules protecting some political speakers or petitioners, in some private property, from eviction or civil and criminal penalties for trespass. In PRUNEYARD SHOPPING CENTER V. ROBINS, 447 U.S. 74 (1980), the U.S. Supreme Court ruled that these state protections do not violate the TAKINGS CLAUSE of the Fifth Amendment to the United States Constitution. The Supreme Court ruling in *Pruneyard* is very significant in the Fifth Amendment context: It permitted the state of California to undermine the right to exclude, traditionally one of the most significant property rights, for the benefit of the public in general and without any compensation under the takings clause. Consequently, this body of jurisprudence has continuing relevance to the very active law of REGULATORY TAKING, the hotly contested notion that state regulation that significantly impairs a private property owner's use of his or her property has suffered a Fifth Amendment "taking," for which she or he is owed compensation.

At the state level, several state courts have ruled under their own constitutions that shopping malls are public and that free speech rights apply.

For more information: Epstein, Richard. "Takings, Exclusivity, and Speech: The Legacy of *Pruneyard v. Robins.*" *University of Chicago Law*

Review 64 (1997): 21–56; Michelman, Frank. "The Common Law Baseline and Restitution for the Lost Commons: A Reply to Professor Epstein." *University of Chicago Law Review* 64 (1997): 57–69.

—Paul Gowder

Sixteenth Amendment

Often referred to as the "income tax amendment," the Sixteenth Amendment went into effect in 1913.

The amendment was a deliberate overturning of the U.S. Supreme Court's 1895 decision in POL-LOCK V. FARMERS' LOAN & TRUST CO., 157 U.S. 409 (1895). In *Pollock,* the Court ruled that taxes upon rents and profits of real estate and upon returns from investments of personal property were in effect direct taxes upon the property from which such income arose, imposed by reason of ownership; and that Congress could not impose such taxes without apportioning them among the states according to population, as required by ARTICLE I, Section 2, Clause 3 and by Section 9, Clause 4 of the original Constitution.

While some have argued that this amendment was never properly adopted, these ideas have largely been dismissed, and the constitutionality of federal income taxes is not seriously in doubt.

For more information: Kelly, Alfred H., Winfred A. Harbison, and Herman Belz. *The American Constitution: Its Origins and Development.* New York: W.W. Norton, 1991.

—David Schultz

Sixth Amendment

The Sixth Amendment is among the original 10 in the BILL OF RIGHTS that amended the Constitution in 1791. This amendment, as proposed originally by JAMES MADISON and subsequently modified in Congress prior to its adoption, provides several protections to individuals who are accused of crimes. These rights include the RIGHT TO A SPEEDY AND PUBLIC TRIAL by jury the right to be informed of the crimes one is accused of committing, the right to confront witnesses and compel individuals to testify for you, and the right to have legal assistance in the preparation and conduct of the trial. While originally the Bill of Rights did not apply to the states, the United States Supreme Court has selectively incorporated all of the Sixth Amendment protections through the FOURTEENTH AMENDMENT to the individual states.

The right to jury trial dates back to English common law. This right also extends to defendants facing criminal charges at the state level, according to the Supreme Court in DUNCAN V. LOUISIANA, 391 U.S. 145 (1968). However, that right appears to apply only to serious offenses, and not petty ones, according to *Williams v. Florida,* 399 U.S. 23 (1968), with "petty" defined as those punishable by six or less months of incarceration. Similarly, in *Williams,* the Court also ruled that a jury need not always consist of 12 individuals and that in some cases, according to *Taylor v. Louisiana,* 419 U.S. 522 (1975), less than a unanimous verdict would be sufficient for a conviction so long as large segments of the population are not excluded from participation in the jury. In BATSON V. KENTUCKY, 476 U.S. 79 (1986), the Court ruled that excluding individuals from serving on juries simply on account of their race was a violation of a defendant's Sixth Amendment rights. Subsequently, this rule was applied to the exclusion of women from juries.

Determinations of when and whether one has had a speedy trial are often difficult. Many if not most defendants want a quick trial to resolve their innocence, but in some cases time may be needed to secure witnesses or prepare a case. In *Barker v. Wingo,* 407 U.S. 514 (1972), the Court was asked to determine what constituted a speedy trial for Sixth Amendment purposes. Here the Court refused to impose a flat fixed-time period, instead offering a balancing test. The Court said that, if a trial did not occur within six to eight months, it would assume the delay was prejudicial unless one could show that it was occurring due to factors such as overcrowded courts, the needs of the defense to prepare, or other reasons such as looking for witnesses. All these factors would be balanced and weighed to determine if a speedy trial had occurred.

The Sixth Amendment also guarantees to defendants public trials. In some cases, defendants may wish the trial closed to avert publicity that could result in a mistrial. Pretrial or trial publicity can often prejudice a case, making it impossible to have a fair deliberation. Balancing the right of a defendant to have a fair and open trial versus the right of the press to cover it often creates problems. In *Sheppard v. Maxwell*, 384 U.S. 333 (1966), the case that inspired the 1960s television series and the 1990s movie *The Fugitive*, the Supreme Court ruled that extensive media coverage of the murder trial of Sam Sheppard violated his Sixth Amendment rights. Similarly, in *Gannett v. DePasquale*, 443 U.S. 368 (1979), the Supreme Court ruled that the closing of a pretrial hearing to the media, at the request of the defendant, to prevent excessive publicity, was not a violation of the Sixth Amendment. This decision raised such a cry that one year later, in *Richmond Newspapers, Inc. v. Virginia*, 448 U.S. 555 (1980), the Court effectively overturned *Gannett*, ruling that the media has a FIRST AMENDMENT right to cover criminal trials.

The rights to receive notice of the accusations one is facing as well as to confront witnesses also date back to English common law. In *United States v. Cruikshank*, 92 U.S. 542 (1876), the Court stated that accusations cannot be vague and must be stated with enough detail and particularity that defendants know the reasons why they are facing criminal charges. The Sixth Amendment right to question witnesses implicates what is known as the CONFRONTATION CLAUSE. This clause prevents the government from using anonymous sources to convict someone of a crime. It makes it possible for the defense to cross-examine and question witnesses to ensure the truth or relevancy of their testimony. However, does that right to confrontation require a direct face-to-face cross-examination? In the case of defendants charged with sexually molesting or committing other crimes against children, this direct confrontation might intimidate witnesses who are minors. In response, states in the 1980s passed laws allowing

for minors to testify through closed-circuit television or from behind screens. In *Coy v. Iowa*, 487 U.S. 1012 (1988), and again in *Maryland v. Craig*, 497 U.S. 836 (1990), the Court upheld these trial procedures, with Justice SANDRA DAY O'CONNOR declaring in the latter case that the Sixth Amendment does not require a direct face-to-face confrontation. Justice ANTONIN GREGORY SCALIA, joined by WILLIAM J. BRENNAN, JR., Marshall, and JOHN PAUL STEVENS, dissented, with Scalia taking a literal view of the confrontation clause and arguing that the intent of it was to permit exactly this type of cross-examination.

Finally, the last major right protected by the Sixth Amendment is the RIGHT TO COUNSEL. In *Powell v. Alabama*, 287 U.S. 45 (1932), the Court ruled that the right to counsel applied in special circumstances to individuals facing criminal trials at the state level. However, it was not until *GIDEON V. WAINWRIGHT*, 372 U.S. 335 (1963), that the Court ruled that defendants were entitled to free, court-appointed attorneys if they could not afford their own. This right to counsel under the Sixth Amendment is one of the rights that individuals accused of a crime must be informed of under the Fifth Amendment, when they receive their *Miranda* warnings.

Overall, the Sixth Amendment contains numerous protections for defendants facing criminal charges. The purpose of these protections is both to protect the innocent and to ensure that every individual charged with a crime is given a fair trial to determine guilt or innocence.

For more information: Schwartz, Bernard. *A History of the Supreme Court*. New York: Oxford University Press, 1993.

—David Schultz

Skinner v. Oklahoma 316 U.S. 535 (1942)

In *Skinner v. Oklahoma*, the Supreme Court found that Oklahoma's Habitual Criminal Sterilization Act (1935) violated the EQUAL PROTECTION clause of the FOURTEENTH AMENDMENT to the United States Constitution. The law provided that those convicted for the third time of a "felony involving moral turpitude" may be subject to sterilization as part of their punishment. This case is important as part of the politics of eugenics and in the development of PRIVACY rights.

The Oklahoma statute (Okl.St.Ann. Tit. 57, 171, et seq.; L.1935, p. 94 et seq.) was part of the eugenics movement, which peaked in the 1930s. This movement misapplied Mendel's work on genetics and Darwin's theories in an attempt to improve the race. Sterilization of those defined as undesirable was one of the most common policy approaches. In a case decided just 15 years before *Skinner, BUCK V. BELL,* 274 U.S. 200 (1927), the Court upheld a Virginia eugenics law providing for the sterilization of people with mental deficiencies.

The *Skinner* Court rejected the Oklahoma law without attacking eugenics directly. Writing for the Court, Justice WILLIAM O. DOUGLAS found that the Oklahoma law made distinctions among definitions of crimes that did not reflect intrinsic differences among the criminal acts. For example, one of Skinner's convictions involved stealing chickens. The law defined this as a "felony involving moral turpitude." If he had worked on the farm, however, the crime would have been embezzlement, which is not a "felony involving moral turpitude" and thus would not have counted toward the three convictions leading toward sterilization.

The problem with punishing one group in one way and another group in a different way was the punishment itself: sterilization. This denies the sterilized group what Justice Douglas called "one of the basic CIVIL RIGHTS of man." He suggested that procreation and marriage are FUNDAMENTAL RIGHTS and then concluded that the failure to be consistent among "intrinsically similar" acts caused an unfair denial of rights. It was an "invidious discrimination." Because fundamental rights are involved, the Court applied the STRICT SCRUTINY test to the law. This was the first application of it in an equal protection of the laws case.

This case moved the law one step further in the process of establishing marriage as a fundamental right, a process that reached fruition in the 1960s and 1970s. Although some people do not read this case as establishing a right to procreate, many Supreme Court justices, when listing constitutional rights in their opinions, have cited *Skinner* as doing exactly that. This makes *Skinner* an important case in the evolution of the right to privacy and in the creation of fundamental rights.

Although the decision was unanimous, Chief Justice Stone and Justice Jackson wrote concurring opinions. Chief Justice Stone found the law violated the DUE PROCESS clause because the statute did not offer the defendant an opportunity to show that he or she did not fit into the class eligible for sterilization. Justice Jackson found both the due process and equal protection clauses relevant.

For more information: Kevles, Daniel. *In the Name of Eugenics.* Cambridge, Mass.: Harvard University Press, 1998; Murphy, Walter, James Fleming, and Sotirios Fleming. *American Constitutional Interpretation.* 2d ed. Westbury, N.Y.: Foundation Press, 1995.

—Douglas C. Telling

Skinner v. Railway Labor Executives' Association 489 U.S. 602 (1989)

In *Skinner v. Railway Labor Executives' Association,* the Supreme Court upheld the practice of mandatory drug tests after an accident, ruling that they did not violate the FOURTH AMENDMENT.

In the case of *Skinner* (a case that was decided at the same time as *National Treasury Employees Union v. Raab,* 489 U.S. 656 [1989], since they involved related issues), the Court focused on the Fourth Amendment issues of search and seizure. The FRA (Federal Railroad Administration), in order to improve the safety standards by which the railroads in the United States operated, instituted regulations that required the mandatory testing of an employee who is involved in certain types of train accidents. The Railway Labor Executives' Association sued, and the federal district court concluded that the regulations did not violate Fourth Amendment rights against unreasonable search. The case was appealed to the U.S. Court of Appeals for the Ninth Circuit. The court of appeals reversed the lower court's ruling, noting that for the search to be valid, some particular suspicion is essential to validate the search.

The case was appealed to the Supreme Court. The Court, in a 7–2 decision with Justice ANTHONY M. KENNEDY delivering the opinion of the Court, concluded that the government had a valid interest in protecting the safety of U.S. railways, which provides a valid exception to the need for probable cause in searches. According to the Court:

> In most criminal cases, we strike this balance in favor of the procedures described by the Warrant Clause of the Fourth Amendment . . . Except in certain well-defined circumstances, a search or seizure in such a case is not reasonable unless it is accomplished pursuant to a judicial warrant issued upon probable cause . . . We have recognized exceptions to this rule, however, "when special needs, beyond the normal need for law enforcement, make the warrant and probable-cause requirement impracticable." . . . When faced with such special needs, we have not hesitated to balance the governmental and PRIVACY interests to assess the practicality of the warrant and probable-cause requirements in the particular context . . . The Government's interest in regulating the conduct of railroad employees to ensure safety, like its supervision of probationers or regulated industries, or its operation of a government office, school, or prison, "likewise presents special needs beyond normal law enforcement that may justify departures from the usual warrant and probable-cause requirements.

In effect, because railroads were a historically regulated industry and the government had an interest in promoting safety, workers in this industry had already forfeited some of their expectations of privacy. Thus, the mandatory drug tests were not a violation of the Fourth Amendment.

Skinner was an important Fourth Amendment decision that set a precedent for subsequent court rulings that permitted mandatory drug tests, for example, for students in schools.

For more information: Cann, Steven J. *Administrative Law.* 4th ed. Thousand Oaks, Calif.: Sage Publications, 2006.

—Dan Krejci

slavery and the Constitution

Chattel slavery is the extension of market relations to the human person as a marketable property and human commodity (*res commerciabilis*) or legal tender, outside the domain of mutual obligation. Slavery was a difficult and vexing constitutional question from the time of the writing of the Constitution in 1787, and its aftereffects continue to raise problems for the United States well into the 21st century.

In 1550, the Spanish king and Holy Roman Emperor, Charles V, called a halt to military operations in the New World until the status of Native Americans, together with the morality and legality of the Spanish conquest, had been thoroughly debated. A group of theologians and jurists was convoked in Valladolid to listen to the arguments of Bartolomé de Las Casas and Juan Ginés de Sepúlveda and settle this question once and for all.

The papal bull "Sublimis Deus," issued in 1537 by Pope Paul III, had already clarified the Holy See's official position on the subject. The pope condemned slavery and the portrayal of Indians as "dumb brutes created for our service" and incapable of exercising self-government, free will, and rational thinking, and therefore incapable of receiving the message of Christ. Las Casas, elaborating on this bull and on the writings of Francisco de Victoria, a Dominican professor at the prestigious university of Salamanca, decried the barbarity of Spaniards by contrasting it with the meekness, humbleness, and good-heartedness of the Indians. Sustained by an unswerving faith in the essential unity of humankind and by his conviction that a commitment to global justice was a moral imperative, he argued that Indians were fully capable of governing themselves and were entitled to certain basic rights, regardless of the nature of their practices and beliefs, which should anyhow be understood from an indigenous point of view.

Sepúlveda, who knew very little of the Spanish colonial subjects, drew on the doctrine of NATURAL LAW and on pragmatic realism to marshal most of the arguments that would later be deployed by American anti-abolitionists. He explained that, given their innate physical and intellectual

A 1780s broadside advertising a slave auction
(Library of Congress)

inferiority, Indians should be considered similar to Aristotle's "natural slaves." In consequence of their being ruled by passions rather than reason, Indians were born to be slaves. As men ruled over women, and adults ruled over children, so inferior races should be subordinated to the will of superior races. This allowed for the enslavement of indigenous peoples and Africans.

Puritan settlers in North America took the same stance as Sepúlveda, and resorted to natural law to validate the claim that religious conversion could not change the legal status of African slaves or Indians. Their status would instead be anchored to biological, and thus inalterable, attributes, which justified hereditary slavery and perpetual bondage for African Americans and Native Americans. Because their status was equivalent to that of a domestic animal or an infant, slaves enjoyed no legal protection: Only their commercial value shielded them from the structural violence of a society that regarded them as less than human. Slavery was described as a necessary evil, not the result of greed, callousness, or "human parasitism."

In 1700, Indians accounted for one-fourth of all South Carolina's slaves, and in 1790, when the Naturalization Act was introduced, which restricted American citizenship to "free white persons," nearly one-third of the people living in the American South were black slaves. The paradox of a society fighting for freedom and for individual rights and granting juridical personality to corporations, ships, and states, but at the same time tolerant that 20 percent of the population was subject to chattel slavery, is epitomized by JOHN ADAMS's protest against the English yoke in 1765: "We won't be their Negroes."

Even though they may have expressed doubts about the morality of slave ownership, George Washington, JAMES MADISON, and THOMAS JEFFERSON profited from it and were evidently prepared to live with it. When Southern delegates refused to support a government and a Constitution hostile to their economic and political interests, Northern delegates sought all sorts of compromises to avoid conflict. Abolitionist William Lloyd Garrison called the final draft of the Constitution "a covenant with death, and an agreement with hell." Indeed, consensus was bought at the highest price: the constitutional sanctioning of slavery, an institution irreconcilable with the libertarian spirit of the Constitution, but comfortable with its protection and promotion of private property and enterprise. These compromises included passage of the three-fifths law in ARTICLE I, Section 2, Clause 3, which determined how slaves would be counted for the purpose of states being awarded representatives in Congress. This clause counted five slaves as the equivalent of three free individuals. This greatly augmented the political power of the Southern states. As a result, 12 out of the first 16 American presidents were Southern slaveholders, even though, by 1804, slavery had been substantially abolished in the Northern states, where an inclusive civic nationalism had taken root.

In addition, the "fugitive slave clause" of Article IV of the Constitution prevented slaves who had escaped and reached an abolitionist state from being freed. Thus, for all intents and purposes, it may be said that the American Constitution protected the peculiar institution and the Southern caste society until the outbreak of the Civil War.

In *Dred Scott v. Sandford,* 60 U.S. (19 How.) 393 (1857), ROGER BROOKE TANEY (1777–1864), chief justice from 1836 until his death in 1864, a Catholic and a former slave-owner, played a significant role in furthering the sectional interests of those who interpreted the meaning of the Constitution as precluding the federal government from applying restrictions to the citizens' right to property. This would include the property of slaves, which was protected by the DUE PROCESS clause of the Fifth Amendment. Echoing Sepúlveda's arguments, he maintained that, in 1787, at the time of the writing of the Constitution, blacks were not expected to become citizens and to exercise the associated rights, for they were considered as "a subordinate and inferior class of beings, who had been subjugated by the dominant race, and, whether emancipated or not, yet remained subject to their authority, and had no rights or privileges but such as those who held the power and the government might choose to grant them."

This infamous, though formally and historically not incongruous, decision, which foreshadowed a future Supreme Court ruling nullifying the abolition of slavery in the North, strengthened the resolve of abolitionists. Eight years and over 600,000 casualties afterward, institutional racial slavery and involuntary servitude officially ended with the passage of the THIRTEENTH AMENDMENT.

Even though slavery was abolished after the Civil War, freed African Americans faced a variety of restrictions on employment, housing, and in politics for another century. It was not until the Civil Rights movement of the 1950s and 1960s that many of these laws were abolished or declared unconstitutional. Since the 1960s, African Americans continue to deal with discrimination, and remedies, such as AFFIRMATIVE ACTION, remain constitutionally controversial.

For more information: Bush, Michael L. *Serfdom and Slavery: Studies in Legal Bondage.* London and New York: Longman, 1996; Graber, Mark A. *Dred Scott and the Problem of Constitutional Evil.* New York: Cambridge University Press, 2006.

—Stefano Fait

Smith v. Allwright 321 U.S. 649 (1944)

In *Smith v. Allwright*, the Supreme Court ruled that a political party could not exclude African Americans. This was an important decision affirming the political rights of African Americans over the FIRST AMENDMENT rights of parties. *Smith v. Allwright* is part of what is known as the "White Primary" cases.

In one-party states, the result of a primary election amounts to a win in the general election. Although the FIFTEENTH AMENDMENT (1870) protects the RIGHT TO VOTE for African Americans, most Southern states restricted and limited that right of black voters only to general elections. They did so by using different tactics, chief amongst which was the so-called white primaries. Thus, since African Americans were denied suffrage in primary elections by law, their participation in general elections was reduced to ratifying white-approved candidates in the general elections. For over 30 years, civil rights groups labored unsuccessfully to strike down white primary election laws, but initial litigation seemed to be ineffective in reforming an electoral system fraught with deep and egregious racial discrimination. The white-only primaries system would collapse only over a 17-year period—1927 to 1944—during which the Supreme Court considered four Texas cases involving statutes that barred blacks from voting. Among those key cases was *Smith v. Allwright,* decided in 1944.

The issue in *Smith v. Allwright* was whether a state statute that provided for a private third-party organization of primary elections by convention constituted a "state action" and therefore a violation of the Fifteenth Amendment. Writing for the Court's 8-1 majority and reversing *Grovey v. Townsend* (1935), Justice Reed held that state statutes providing for a private third-party organization of primary election for U.S. senators, congressmen, and state officers constitutes a state action and therefore a violation of the Fifteenth Amendment of the U.S. Constitution. Lonnie E. Smith, an African American, had sued S. E. Allwright, a county election official, challenging a Texas state statute that provided for a primary election for senators, congressmen, and state officers to be administered by a private organization.

In Texas, the Democratic Party, which the Texas Supreme Court called a "voluntary association," had adopted in a state convention a resolution permitting white citizens only to participate in Democratic primary elections. After a failed attempt to mount a challenge at the district and Fifth Circuit Court of Appeals, Lonnie Smith appealed to the Supreme Court. His suit raised the issue of whether the Texas resolution constituted a state action and, if so, whether it violated the Fifth Amendment. Thus, Mr. Smith asked the Court to consider whether such an indirect exclusion of the right to vote in primary elections by a voluntary association violates the Fifteenth Amendment.

Speaking for the Court's majority, Justice Reed reasoned that, even though the Democratic Party was a voluntary organization, the facts—that Texas statutes governed the selection of county-level party leaders, to include Mr. Allwright; that the party conducted primary elections under state statutory authority; and that state courts were given exclusive ORIGINAL JURISDICTION over contested elections—meant that the state had to guarantee blacks the right to vote in primaries. Thus Allwright, according to the Court, had engaged in a state action abridging Smith's right to vote because of his race. A state, Justice Reed summed, cannot permit a private organization to practice racial discrimination in elections.

Setting aside *Grovey v. Townsend,* 295 U.S. 45 (1941), which had made legal the practice of "white primary," the Supreme Court held that the restrictions against blacks in primary elections are unconstitutional. The Court observed that the right of a citizen of the United States to vote for the nomination of candidates for the United States SENATE and HOUSE OF REPRESENTATIVES in a primary, which is an integral part of the elective process, is a right secured by the federal Constitution. This right, the majority argued, "may not be abridged by the State on account of his race or color." With specific reference to the scheme instituted in Texas, the Supreme Court noted that "whether the exclusion of citizens from voting on account of their race or color has been effected by action of the State rather than of individuals or of a political party is a question upon which the decision of the courts of the State is not binding on the federal courts, but which the latter must determine for themselves."

Dissenting in *Smith,* Justice Robert, quoting *Mahnich v. Southern Steamship* (1944), disagreed with respect to what he termed "the Court's policy to freely disregard and to overrule considered decisions and rules of law announced in those decisions." This tendency, he noted "seems to . . . indicate an intolerance for what those who have composed this court in the past have conscientiously and deliberately concluded, and involves an assumption that knowledge and wisdom reside in us which was denied to our predecessors. I shall not repeat what I there said, for I consider it fully applicable to the instant decision, which but points the moral anew."

In summary, *Smith v. Allwright* stands for the proposition that, where a state convention of Democrats establishes a rule that only whites can vote in a primary election, such a racial restriction violates the Fifteenth Amendment prohibition against denial of right to vote on account of race. Although the precise rationale for the *Smith* case was then unclear, the Court held that (1) under Texas law, the primary is an integral part of the election scheme; (2) the running of elections is a governmental function; and (3) therefore, the running of primaries is a governmental function, even where the task of doing so is delegated by the state to a private party.

These private parties, according to the Supreme Court, are an agency of the state and are therefore prevented from excluding blacks from voting in the primary. Nine years later, in *Terry v. Adams,* 345 U.S. 461 (1953), extending the *Smith* prohibition to "pre-primary elections," the Supreme Court held that a state action is racially restrictive where a "pre-primary" election is held by the Jay-bird Democratic Association, a group whose candidate almost always won the ensuing Democratic primary, especially when running unopposed. While there was no majority opinion in *Terry*, the prevailing rationale appeared to be that the state, by inaction, had permitted this unofficial preelection to usurp the role of the official primary election, which, under *Smith*, was itself an integral part of the election process. Several of the justices seemed to rely on the fact that the state tolerance of private discrimination reflected a purposeful decision to maintain a racially discriminatory system of elections.

Lastly, conceptually it is not clear how broadly applicable the rationale of the white primary cases should be understood, since it does not seem likely that all or most other conduct by political parties will be deemed to be state actions. For instance, the selection of party chairmen would probably not be held to be a public function. Nor is it clear that discrimination based on grounds other than race, even in the primary process, would necessarily be held to be state action, since the white primary cases were founded on the Fifteenth Amendment, which applies only to racial discrimination. Thus, it is possible that a party that limits its membership solely to men, or solely to Protestants, might well be found not to be engaged in state action. In the end, the Supreme Court, in articulating a "public function" doctrine in *Smith v. Allwright*, holds that when a private individual (or group) is entrusted by the state with the performance of functions that are governmental in nature, that group or person becomes an agent of the state and its acts constitute a state action. The *Smith v. Allwright* case on white-only primaries, and those cases before, stand for the view that the exclusion of African Americans from voting in primary elections violates the Fifteenth Amendment.

For more information: Ryden, David K. *The U.S. Supreme Court and the Electoral Process.* Washington, D.C.: Georgetown University Press, 2002.

—Mark Pufong

Smith v. City of Jackson 544 U.S. 228 (2005)
In *Smith v. City of Jackson*, the Supreme Court upheld a "disparate-impact claim"—a lawsuit claiming there was unintentional discrimination—under the Age Discrimination in Employment Act of 1967 (ADEA). The significance of *Smith v. City of Jackson* is that it allows persons adversely affected by age discrimination at work to sue their employer under this federal statute, even when age discrimination was not intended. However, the Court also ruled that the employees in *Smith* failed to prove an adverse affect on older workers, or that the city's plan was impermissibly based on age.

Azel P. Smith and other older municipal police officers brought this suit against the city of Jackson, Mississippi, claiming that a city pay plan discriminated by age. The city had adopted a pay plan for all city employees in 1998 to "attract and retain qualified people." In 1999, the city revised the plan to bring up starting salaries of police officers to the regional average. Officers with less than five years' service received proportionately greater raises than those with more seniority. Most officers over age 40 had more than five years' service. Thus, salary increases were less generous to police officers over age 40 than to younger officers. Smith and other older officers sued the city under the ADEA in two claims: deliberate age discrimination by the city against them (a "disparate-treatment" claim) and adverse affect of unintentional age discrimination by the city's actions (a "disparate-impact" claim).

The district court ruled by summary judgment in favor of the city on both claims. The court of appeals sent back the "disparate-treatment" case for more hearings on allegations of deliberate discrimination. However, it dismissed the unintentional discrimination claim, ruling that "disparate-impact claims are categorically unavailable under the ADEA." The Supreme Court affirmed the court of appeals, because the older officers did not set forth a valid disparate-impact claim. However, the Court ruled that disparate-impact claims were available under the ADEA.

In an 8-0 decision, Justice JOHN PAUL STEVENS wrote for a four-person plurality, joined by Justices

DAVID H. SOUTER, Ginsburg, and STEPHEN G. BREYER. First, Stevens relied on *GRIGGS V. DUKE POWER,* 401 U.S. 424 (1971), where the Court first authorized a disparate-impact claim of unintentional EMPLOYMENT DISCRIMINATION under Title VII of the CIVIL RIGHTS ACT of 1964. Justice Stevens found that the language of the ADEA was virtually identical to Title VII, except that the ADEA allowed some types of employment discrimination based on reasonable factors other than age. Thus, the ADEA did authorize disparate-impact claims of unintentional age discrimination like the *Griggs* case. Second, however, Justice Stevens's plurality opinion found that the older officers did not state a valid disparate-impact claim in this case. Unlike the unintentional race discrimination in *Griggs,* unintentional discrimination by age may be allowed when it is based on reasonable factors other than age. ADEA protections against age discrimination are more narrow than prohibitions against race discrimination. The record showed that the city's pay plan was based on other reasonable factors. Finally, for the above reasons, and by Equal Employment Opportunity Commission (EEOC) authority and regulation, disparate-impact claims are available under the ADEA.

In a separate concurring opinion, Justice ANTONIN GREGORY SCALIA agreed with the decision of the plurality, but reasoned the Court should simply defer to the reasonable view of the EEOC that disparate-impact claims were available under the ADEA.

In a separate concurring opinion, Justice SANDRA DAY O'CONNOR (joined by Justices ANTHONY M. KENNEDY and CLARENCE THOMAS) agreed with the decision of the plurality, but reasoned that disparate-impact claims were not available under the ADEA.

For more information: Langran, Robert W. *The Supreme Court: A Concise History.* New York: Peter Lang, 2004; MacNichol, John. *Age Discrimination: An Historical and Contemporary Analysis.* New York: Cambridge University Press, 2006.

—Bradley Chilton

Smith v. Doe 538 U.S. 84 (2003)
In *Smith v. Doe,* the Supreme Court ruled that a state law that required individuals to register with a sexual offender list after their conviction for a sex crime did not violate the Constitution's EX POST FACTO CLAUSE.

This case, originating from Alaska, dealt with one of the ex post facto clauses of the U.S. Constitution, which contains two such clauses: ARTICLE I, Section 9, Clause 3, and Article I, Section 10, Clause 1. Article I, Section 9, Clause 3 makes it illegal for Congress to pass an ex post facto law, whereas Article I, Section 10, Clause 1 notes that states shall pass no ex post facto law. This case focused on the latter clause. Provisions of the Alaska Sex Offender Registration Act focused on sex offenders and child kidnappers incarcerated in the states. The issue in *Smith* was whether the registration law for sex offenders was an ex post facto law.

Two convicted sex offenders in this case, John Doe I and John Doe II, were convicted prior to the passage of the Alaska Sex Offender Registration Act and, by the law, were covered by the act. They brought suit claiming the act was unconstitutional because it violated Article I, Section 10, Clause 1 (ex post facto). The district court ruled against the plaintiffs, and they appealed to the Court of Appeals for the Ninth Circuit. The court of appeals reversed the lower court decision, citing that the act was punitive and therefore violated the ex post facto clause.

The Court heard oral arguments on November 12, 2002, and announced its decision on March 5, 2003. In a 6-3 decision, which Justice ANTHONY M. KENNEDY delivered, the Court ruled that the act was not punitive and did not violate the ex post facto clause of the Constitution.

The Court reversed and remanded the case. The three dissenting justices noted the ex post facto nature of the law. Justice JOHN PAUL STEVENS posited that the act could apply only to those individuals who committed an offense after the effective date of the act or it would violate the ex post facto clause. The other two dissenting justices—Ginsburg and STEPHEN G. BREYER—added that the act was punitive in nature and its retroactive aspect violated the ex post facto clause.

For more information: Cann, Steven J. *Administrative Law.* 4th ed. Thousand Oaks, Calif.: Sage Publications, 2006.

—Dan Krejci

Souter, David H. (1939–   ) *Supreme Court justice*

David H. Souter became an associate justice of the U.S. Supreme Court on October 9, 1990, after a career in the state attorney general's office and in the state courts of New Hampshire. He replaced WILLIAM J. BRENNAN, JR., on the Supreme Court.

He was born in Melrose, Massachusetts, on September 17, 1939, but he spent much of his youth in the small New Hampshire town of Weare, where his grandparents lived. He graduated from Harvard University, earned a degree at Oxford University as a Rhodes scholar, and then received his law degree at Harvard Law school. After two years in private practice, he joined the state attorney general's office headed by Warren B. Rudman, who would later become a U.S. senator and Souter's chief advocate for a Supreme Court seat. In 1976, Souter succeeded Rudman as New Hampshire attorney general. In 1978 he became a state court judge and in 1983 a justice of the state supreme court. Just eight weeks after taking a seat on the U.S. Court of Appeals for the First Circuit in May 1990, Souter was nominated by President George H. W. Bush to succeed Justice Brennan on the Supreme Court.

Souter's nomination was intended by the first president Bush to add to a growing conservative majority under the leadership of Chief Justice WILLIAM H. REHNQUIST. But Souter disappointed conservatives and proved to be the moderate, independent thinker that his friends, like Rudman, expected him to be. He became a consistent member of the Court's moderate-to-liberal wing, which included Justices JOHN PAUL STEVENS, Ruth Bader Ginsburg, and STEPHEN G. BREYER, and which from time to time attained a Supreme Court majority with the support of Justice SANDRA DAY O'CONNOR or Justice ANTHONY M. KENNEDY.

Souter's views came through most strongly when he felt that the Supreme Court majority was manipulating history to achieve incorrect results. Thus, he dissented strongly from a number of decisions curtailing the ability of Congress to regulate INTERSTATE COMMERCE or finding that Congress was encroaching on the power of state governments. In one such dissent, he relied on the intent of the CONSTITUTIONAL CONVENTION to argue forcefully that the Court was wrong to restrict the ability of Congress to open up the states to citizen lawsuits for damages. The case, *Seminole Tribe of Florida v. Florida,* 517 U.S. 44 (1996), ruled that Congress could not use its commerce power to waive the ELEVENTH AMENDMENT, sovereign immunity of the states. Citizens should be able to "enforce federal rights in a way that Congress provides," Souter wrote.

He objected to a number of rulings that he said were breaking down the separation of church and state under the FIRST AMENDMENT. Writing for the majority in *MCCREARY COUNTY V. AMERICAN CIVIL LIBERTIES UNION,* 545 U.S. 844 (2005), Souter held unconstitutional the display of the TEN COMMANDMENTS in two Kentucky courthouses. He used the occasion to defend the Court's decades-old test for church-state separation in *LEMON V. KURTZMAN,* 403 U.S. 602 (1971).

He was highly critical of the limitations placed by the Court on the use of race to draw legislative districts to try to increase minority representation. He played a lead role in preserving women's access to ABORTION in *Planned Parenthood v. Casey,* 505 U.S. 833 (1992), and then voted to retain that access in subsequent cases.

Throughout his tenure on the Court, Souter has remained an enigma. He rarely makes public appearances or gives interviews and prefers to lead a cloistered life that he believes is most appropriate for a Supreme Court justice. While by all accounts he interacts well with his fellow justices and is well liked and respected, he has no interest in being a visible figure in Washington and believes that the views of justices should be voiced through their written opinions.

For more information: Yarbrough, Tinsley E. *David Hackett Souter: Traditional Republican on the Rehnquist Court.* New York: Oxford University Press, 2005.

—Stephen Wermiel

South Carolina v. Katzenbach 383 U.S. 301 (1966)

In *South Carolina v. Katzenbach,* the Supreme Court upheld Congress's authority to enforce the FIFTEENTH AMENDMENT's ban on racial discrimination in voting. This broadening of congressional powers occurred largely within the framework of voting-rights measures adopted during the 1960s, for which the amendment's historical context is worth appreciating to understand the Court's ruling in *South Carolina v. Katzenbach.*

Historically, Reconstruction-era efforts by Congress to eradicate racial discrimination in voting in the South were only marginally successful, and most enacted statutory provisions were repealed in 1894. Meanwhile, many Southern states enacted literacy tests and other tests that were often used to deny blacks the franchise. The Fifteenth Amendment was theoretically available for relief in these situations, but litigation under it was generally time consuming and difficult. Even when states or counties were ordered by the courts to eliminate one discriminatory practice or another, they were often able to devise some new scheme by which to perpetuate racial discrimination in voting. Initial statutory efforts by Congress in 1957, 1960, and 1964 proved largely ineffective. Thusly, Congress enacted the VOTING RIGHTS ACT OF 1965 for the express purpose of eradicating racial discrimination in voting by dealing with it prophylactically rather than on a case-by-case basis. The most important aspect of the act, from the perspective of Congress's power to enforce the Fifteenth Amendment, was its treatment of literacy tests and other voter eligibility standards.

Briefly, the act suspended, for a period of five years, literacy and similar voting tests in any state or political subdivision from which the following administrative findings were made as of November 1964: (a) the jurisdiction maintained or had used a "test or device" for voter eligibility (including not only literacy tests, but also requirements of good moral character or knowledge of particular subject matter); and (b) less than 50 percent voting-age residents were registered to vote. Accordingly, these findings were not judicially reviewable. The only way a jurisdiction found to fall within the act's prohibitions could escape coverage was by obtaining a declaratory judgment from the federal district court for the DISTRICT OF COLUMBIA confirming that it had not used tests or devices for the purpose of racial discrimination in the previous five years. Thus, the statutory scheme provided was one of administrative fact finding, with no requirement that those findings include discriminatory intent. Only thereafter did the jurisdiction have the right to seek JUDICIAL REVIEW in Washington, in a proceeding in which it, not the federal government, bore the burden of proof.

Thus, in *South Carolina v. Katzenbach* (1966), the state of South Carolina invoked the Supreme Court's ORIGINAL JURISDICTION under ARTICLE III, Section 2 and sought to have the Court rule on the constitutionality of the various provisions of the Voting Rights Act of 1965, which prohibits the use of "tests" as a qualification for voting. South Carolina contended that this act was a violation of the Tenth Amendment that prohibits Congress from passing legislation that violates states' rights to implement and control elections. Rejecting South Carolina's claim that the Voting Rights Act of 1965 prohibitions violated the state's Tenth Amendment rights and writing for an 8-1 court, Chief Justice Warren broadly construed the power of Congress to enforce the Fifteenth Amendment and ruled that any "rational means" could be used to enforce the act's ban on racial discrimination in voting. In doing so, the Court upheld the lower courts' decisions and rejected South Carolina's argument that Congress may do no more than to forbid violations of the Fifteenth Amendment in general terms.

The task of fashioning specific remedies or of applying them to particular localities, the chief justice reasoned, must necessarily be left to the courts. The decision observed that difficulties previously encountered with the case-by-case judicial enforcement of the amendment amply justified the remedies chosen by Congress. Thus, according to Chief Justice Warren, where there is evidence of racial discrimination in voting, the particular scheme chosen by Congress to ban *tests* or *devices* (coinciding with less-than-50 percent registration) satisfies the rationality standard. The use of tests or devices therefore furnishes a clear means of carrying out racial discrimination, and low registration figures were, indeed, an obvious symptom of such discrimination. In the end, *South Carolina v. Katzenbach* demonstrated that Congress's enforcement power under Section 2 of the Fifteenth Amendment permits it to outlaw practices that the Court would not on its own find to violate Section 1 of that amendment. Congress, the Court reasoned, is authorized to enforce the prohibitions of the Fifth Amendment by appropriate legislation. Congress therefore has full remedial powers to effectuate the constitutional prohibition against racial discrimination in voting. Citing Chief Justice JOHN MARSHALL in yet another specific legislative authorization in the Constitution, Chief Justice Warren noted that "this power, like all others vested in Congress, is complete in itself, may be exercised to its utmost extent, and acknowledges no limitations, other than are prescribed in the Constitution."

In a more decisive concurring opinion, Justice Fortas reiterated the view that the Fifth Amendment is an unequivocal command to the states and the federal government that no citizen shall have his RIGHT TO VOTE denied or abridged because of race or color. This amendment, Justice HUGO BLACK argued, unmistakably gives Congress specific powers to go further and pass appropriate legislation to protect the right to vote against any method of abridgment, no matter how subtle. Departing from the ruling and dissenting from the majority opinion of the Court, Justice Black observed that one of the most basic premises upon which our structure of government was founded was that the federal government was to have certain specific and limited powers and no others, and all other power was to be reserved either "to the States respectively, or to the people."

In the end, and by an 8-1 margin, the Supreme Court swept aside all arguments questioning the validity of the Voting Rights Act of 1965 in *South Carolina v. Katzenbach*. It upheld the lower court's decision and rejected South Carolina's argument that Congress may do no more than to forbid violations of the 15th Amendment, a decision that allowed Congress to adopt enforcement legislation. While the Voting Rights Act is best known for attacking racial discrimination against blacks in the South, another facet of the act dealt with Puerto Ricans disenfranchised in New York City. In *Katzenbach v. Morgan*, 384 U.S. 641 (1966), the Supreme Court reaffirmed Section 4(e) of the Voting Rights Act. Relying instead on congressional authority to enforce the EQUAL PROTECTION clause of the FOURTEENTH AMENDMENT against New York, Justice WILLIAM J. BRENNAN, JR., speaking for the Court, in a sentence that evoked stunning possibilities, wrote, "More specifically, 4(e) may be viewed as a measure to secure for the Puerto Rican community residing in New York City nondiscriminatory treatment by government—both in the imposition of voting qualifications and the provision or administration of governmental service, such as public schools, housing and law enforcement."

For more information: Finkelman, Paul. *African Americans and the Right to Vote.* New York: Garland, 1992; Hasen, Richard. *The Supreme Court and Election Law: Judging Equality from Baker v. Carr to Bush v. Gore.* New York: New York University Books, 2003.

—Marc G. Pufong and Sean Evans

South Dakota v. Dole 483 U.S. 203 (1987)

In *South Dakota v. Dole,* the Supreme Court ruled that the National Minimum Drinking Age Amendment (23 U.S.C. § 158) is a valid use of Congress's spending power under ARTICLE I, Section 8, Clause 1 of the U.S. Constitution. The *Dole* decision is significant because it details a four-part test defining when Congress can put conditions on federal funding for state projects.

Conditions are strings attached to a state's receipt of federal money. They are very different from directives on how to spend the money. Conditions extend the reach of the federal government into states' rights by indirectly legislating what a state can or cannot do in order to receive funding. The National Minimum Drinking Age Amendment put a condition on the receipt of federal highway money. Every state receiving federal highway funds had to have a minimum drinking age of 21 before it could receive 100 percent of its allocation.

In the *Dole* decision, South Dakota fought the conditions. The state did not want to change its drinking age from 19 to 21, but it also did not want to lose 10 percent of its highway funding. In the lawsuit, South Dakota asserted that Section 2 of the TWENTY-FIRST AMENDMENT of the U.S. Constitution grants states the power to set minimum drinking ages, and it is unconstitutional for the federal government to usurp this power with a condition on its funding.

Chief Justice WILLIAM HUBBS REHNQUIST wrote the seven-person majority opinion favoring the federal government. Rehnquist focused on four criteria that a condition must meet to be constitutionally valid. First, the federal funds must be spent on the general welfare of the public. Second, the condition must be unambiguous. Third, the condition should relate to the federal interest. Fourth, the condition cannot ask states to engage in unconstitutional activities. This is referred to in the opinion as the "independent constitutional bar." It is a key issue the Court focused on.

The Court declared that states cannot be induced to act unconstitutionally, but the Court agreed that Congress can indirectly induce state action. Congress can achieve its objectives through use of its spending power, even if the Twenty-first Amendment bars it from directly achieving the same objectives. Congress is barred by the Twenty-first Amendment from directly telling a state it must have a minimum drinking age of 21. Congress is not barred by the Twenty-first

Amendment from telling a state it must have a minimum drinking age of 21 before it can receive 100 percent of its federal highway funding.

The Court also stated that Congress cannot be coercive with its conditions on federal funds. This is a check on Congress's ability to set conditions as part of its spending power. But it is not a strong check because coercion is not defined. *Dole* clarifies only that withholding 10 percent of federal highway funds is not coercive.

Justices WILLIAM J. BRENNAN, JR., and SANDRA DAY O'CONNOR dissented. In Justice O'Connor's dissenting opinion, she did not agree that a state's drinking age was sufficiently related to the federal government's interest in highway construction, which is what the funds were going to be spent on in South Dakota. She agreed that Congress can attach conditions to its money, but the conditions have to be reasonably related to the money's purpose. Otherwise, "Congress could effectively regulate almost any area of a State's social, political, or economic life." Her dissent is important because the Court since *Dole* has tended to rule in favor of states' rights.

Dole is an important case for its four-part test regarding Congress's ability to attach conditions to its funding. It is also important for the dissent's discussion of relatedness. The issue could easily come before the Court again, and it might just go in favor of the states next time.

For more information: Beer, Samuel H. *To Make a Nation: The Rediscovery of American Federalism.* Cambridge, Mass.: Belknap Press of Harvard University Press, 1993.

　　　　　　　　　　　　　　　—R. Reid LeBeau

Southern Pacific Company v. Arizona 325 U.S. 761 (1945)

In *Southern Pacific Company v. Arizona,* the Supreme Court ruled that a state law regulating the length of trains violated ARTICLE I, Section 8, Clause 3 of the COMMERCE CLAUSE.

The case addressed the question: Does a law enacted by the state of Arizona (the Arizona Train Limit Law of May 15, 1912, Arizona Code Ann.,

1039, §69–119) place a burden on INTERSTATE COMMERCE, therefore making the law unconstitutional? The Arizona law made it unlawful for any entity to operate "within the state a railroad train of more than fourteen passenger cars or seventy freight cars, and authorizes the state to recover a money penalty for each violation of the Act."

The state of Arizona, in 1940, brought suit in Arizona Superior Court against the Southern Pacific Company in order to recover penalties for operating a train of more than 14 cars and a freight train of more than 70 cars. The Southern Pacific Company admitted to the facts in the case, yet offered the defense that the Arizona law "offends against the commerce clause (Article I, Section 8, Clause 3) and the DUE PROCESS of the FOURTEENTH AMENDMENT, and conflicts with federal legislation." The Arizona Superior Court found for the defendant (Southern Pacific Company) and the state of Arizona appealed the case to the Supreme Court of Arizona, which reversed the decision of the lower court. Southern Pacific Company appealed the case to the Supreme Court. Chief Justice Stone delivered the opinion of the Court, Justice Rutledge concurred, and Justice HUGO BLACK dissented.

The Court determined that the law created a burden on interstate commerce and imposed a stiff economic burden on the railroad. Based on the Arizona law, Southern Pacific had to operate more trains in the state and at a cost of several million more dollars a year. The Court noted that

> The findings show that the operation of long trains . . . trains of more than fourteen passenger and more than seventy freight cars, is standard practice over the main lines of the railroads of the United States, and that, if the length of trains is to be regulated at all, national uniformity in the regulation adopted, such as only Congress can prescribe, is practically indispensable to the operation of an efficient and economical national railway system.

The Court reversed the decision of the Supreme Court of Arizona.

Southern Pacific Company v. Arizona is an important case that found that even though states may occasionally claim that they are adopting laws to protect the health, safety, or welfare of their citizens, these laws may nonetheless violate the commerce clause.

For more information: Farber, Daniel A., William N. Eskridge, Jr., and Philip P. Frickey. *Cases and Materials on Constitutional Law: Themes for the Constitution's Third Century.* St. Paul, Minn.: West Publishing, 1993.

—Dan Krejci

speech and government funding

At least since the expansion of the grant-in-aid programs of the New Deal and Great Society eras, there has been a persistent question of the proper role of government in regulating speech through federal administrative action. As government policy and funding expanded in the 20th century to almost every area of society, the constitutional balance between questions of free speech rights for individuals have been increasingly weighed against government interest in properly regulating speech.

The Administrative Procedures Act (APA), 5 U.S.C. § 500, of 1946 formally established legislative limits on federal regulatory agencies. The APA's primary purpose was to ensure DUE PROCESS for citizens affected by the agency regulations. Due process was protected by requiring publication of rules (552) and providing standards and procedures (553), uniform hearing processes (556–557), and JUDICIAL REVIEW of final decisions where applicable (702). The individual states also followed the federal government and passed APAs of their own. It is through these legislative delegations of power that the administrative agencies developed standards for rule making, hearing procedures, and judicial review; through judicial challenges to either legislative or executive action, the courts have adjudicated the meaning of "speech" and addressed its protection from government regulation. However, the courts have also recognized the substantive rights of individuals or organizations to have access to government funding or of governments to utilize a diversity of "subjective" criteria as another perspective on "free speech" and government funding.

In 1990, Congress included a "decency standard," 20 U.S.C. §954(d) (1), in the reauthorization bill for the National Endowment for the Arts. Senator Jesse Helms, a Republican from North Carolina, led the fight for this standard in response to the endowment's funding of controversial art, such as Robert Mapplethorpe's homoerotic photographs and Andres Serrano's urine-soaked crucifix called "Piss Christ." Senator Helms described these NEA-funded projects as "homosexual pornography" and "blasphemy." The subsequent COMMUNICATIONS DECENCY ACT and other federal legislation have been enacted and proposed to provide for the establishment of a "decency standard" and extend the regulatory power of Congress.

In NATIONAL ENDOWMENT FOR THE ARTS V. FINLEY, 524 U.S. 569 (1998), Justice SANDRA DAY O'CONNOR wrote the 8-1 majority opinion, which interpreted the 20 U.S.C. §954(d) (1) decency standard as merely advisory because it provided one more "consideration" to a host of subjective factors already utilized by the NEA when it awards grant funds to artists. "It does not preclude awards to projects that might be deemed indecent or disrespectful," O'Connor said in the majority opinion. As a result, "the court does not perceive a realistic danger that it will be utilized to preclude or punish the expression of particular views." O'Connor also noted that the grant-in-aid process is inherently subjective and that artists are probably already molding their art to comply with their perceptions of the agency's criteria, and therefore adding additional subjective considerations would not be affected due to the decency requirement. "When the government is acting as patron rather than as sovereign, the consequences of imprecision are not constitutionally severe," O'Connor said in the majority opinion.

Justice ANTONIN GREGORY SCALIA's concurring opinion offered a very different understanding that would have substantively changed FIRST AMENDMENT jurisprudence and, thereby, the delicate balance between speech rights and government responsibilities. "The operation was a success, but the patient died," Scalia said. "What such a procedure is to medicine, the court's opinion in this case is to law. It sustains the constitutionality of [the law] by gutting it. . . . The nub of the difference between me and the court is that I regard the distinction between abridging speech and funding as a fundamental divide, on this side of which the First Amendment is inapplicable." He summarizes the complicated issue by separating his opinion from the majority's as well as that of Congress. "Instead of banning the funding of such productions absolutely, which I think would have been entirely constitutional, Congress took the lesser step of requiring them to be disfavored in the evaluation of grant applications. The Court's opinion today renders even that lesser step a nullity."

For more information: Marbach, Joseph R., Ellis Katz, and Troy E. Smith, eds. *Federalism in America*. Westport, Conn.: Greenwood Publishing, 2005; Solove, Daniel J. *The Digital Person*. New York: New York University Press, 2004.

— Michael W. Hail and Robert Drew Grey

speech or debate clause

The speech or debate clause of the U.S. Constitution, found in ARTICLE I, Section 6, Clause 1, protects the independence of members of Congress by allowing them to perform their constitutional duties without fear of intimidation, reprisal, or inappropriate intrusions by the executive or judicial branches of government. Often, the clause is described as creating a legislative "privilege," because it spares legislators from the burdens of being required to testify about their legislative work, or alternatively creates a legislative "immunity," because it also spares legislators from legal liability for this work.

The speech or debate clause has its origins in British common law and Parliament's skirmishes with the Crown concerning freedom of speech and legislative independence. These skirmishes, including King Charles's seizure of the legislative papers of several members of Parliament in 1642, and the 1686 prosecution of another member for republishing a committee report critical of King James II, culminated in the inclusion of a legislative privilege provision in the ENGLISH BILL OF RIGHTS in 1689. This privilege was justified not on the grounds of protecting the representatives themselves, but on the basis of serving the public at large by protecting the independence of Parliament.

In postcolonial America, analogous legislative privilege provisions appeared in the constitutions of many of the original thirteen states, beginning with Maryland in 1776, as well as in the Articles of Confederation, which the text of Article I, Section 6, Clause 1 of the Constitution closely followed. Although the speech or debate clause was included in the Constitution in 1789 without significant discussion, THOMAS JEFFERSON explained a decade later that the clause existed "in order to give to the will of the people the influence it ought to have," by freeing the people's representatives "from the cognizance or coercion" of the other branches.

The first recorded application of the legislative privilege in America occurred in Massachusetts in 1808, in the case of *Coffin v. Coffin*, 4 Mass. 1 (1808). This case, which the U.S. Supreme Court once called "perhaps the most authoritative case in this country" concerning the legislative privilege, stands for the proposition that the privilege should be construed liberally to protect not just speeches and debates on the floor of the legislature, but "every thing said or done" by a representative acting in a legislative capacity, whether in or out of the legislative chamber.

The U.S. Supreme Court has interpreted the scope and application of the speech or debate clause about a dozen times, most of them between 1966 and 1979. These cases also established that the protections of the clause extend well beyond its literal language, and that it should be construed broadly to foster legislative independence. For instance, in *GRAVEL V. UNITED STATES*, 408 U.S. 606 (1972), the Court explained that the clause applies to all activities that are "an integral part of the deliberative and communicative processes by which Members participate in committee and House proceedings with respect to the consideration and passage or rejection of proposed legislation or with respect to other matters which the Constitution places within the jurisdiction of either House." Thus, as many subsequent lower court cases have confirmed, the clause applies not only to floor debates and votes, but also to meetings, committee hearings, and other congressional efforts to collect and analyze information relevant to potential legislation.

In addition, in *Gravel* the Court held that the protections of the clause apply not just to the members of Congress themselves, but also to congressional staff when they are engaged in activities that would be protected if performed directly by the members. The Court observed that, in the modern legislative process, elected representatives depend upon the assistance of a number of aides who perform acts that would be privileged if performed by the members. The key question therefore is whether the activities themselves are an integral part of the legislative process.

Where the clause applies, its protections are absolute (meaning they cannot be outweighed by competing concerns, in the way that many common law privileges can). However, limits do exist on the protections that the clause affords. The Supreme Court has concluded that the clause does not extend to congressional press releases or to republications of otherwise protected material outside of Congress, to cajoling the executive branch, or to providing constituent services. The Court also has held that the clause does not bar prosecuting members of Congress for bribery or other unlawful conduct, provided the misconduct can be proven without inquiring into protected legislative acts. Thus, if a member is alleged to have received a bribe to vote in a particular way, the crime must be proven not by showing how the member voted or even the motive for an actual vote, both of which are absolutely privileged, but by showing that the member agreed to vote in a particular way in exchange for payment.

In recent years, a variety of lower court decisions have addressed other interpretive problems under the clause. One of the thorniest issues to arise involves the extent to which the clause bars congressional employees from bringing suits against their employers over the terms and conditions of their employment. Lower courts have raised questions concerning the extent to which the clause limits the executive branch's ability to execute a search warrant of a congressional office. But regardless of the particular outcomes of these cases, the clause will remain a crucial bulwark in Congress's defense against judicial and executive branch encroachments.

For more information: Reinstein, Robert J., and Harvey A. Silverglate. "Legislative Privilege and the Separation of Powers." *Harvard Law Review* 86, no. 1,113 (1973): 1,135–1,140; Huefner, Steven F. "The Neglected Value of the Legislative Privilege in State Legislatures." *William & Mary Law Review* 45, no. 221 (2003): 213–309.

—Steven F. Huefner

Standard Oil Co. of New Jersey v. United States 221 U.S. 1 (1911)

Standard Oil Co. of New Jersey v. United States was an important antitrust case under the Sherman Act that resulted in the breakup of John D. Rockefeller's company. Constitutionally, the case affirmed the power of the federal government under the COMMERCE CLAUSE to regulate monopolies.

Standard Oil Company rose to power from the vertical and horizontal integration of both technological innovation and market manipulation. The monopoly of the Cleveland-area oil refineries and subordinate chemical products manufacturing led to a leverage of the transportation of those chemicals and oil products against the railroads. The success of these actions, resulting in favorable conditions for Standard Oil, caused a ripple effect in the markets, thereby driving down the number of companies able to compete with Rockefeller.

By the mid-1880s, Rockefeller had manipulated the overall refinery markets and controlled what was considered to be the majority of refinery production within the United States and, relationally, the world. Rockefeller continued his push into both vertical/horizontal markets until he controlled the majority of production, distribution, and retail markets. The facts of the case derived from the power of John D. Rockefeller and the belief that his large company consisted of an unnecessary and illegal restraint of trade. The arguments for Rockefeller failed in 1909 when he lost a court case when his company, Standard Oil, was found in violation of the Sherman Anti-trust Act. The dissolution of the company into smaller companies was challenged on the grounds that Rockefeller did not in fact violate the act, but rather used superior business tactics and technology to drive Standard Oil's market penetrations through legal market procedures. Challenged was the right of Congress even to impose such restrictions upon American business.

Writing for the Court, Chief Justice Edward White affirmed the power of Congress under the Sherman Act to regulate monopolies, finding that restraint of trade did interfere with commerce. Congress, under the commerce clause, could thus regulate commerce. However, Justice White also redefined the meaning of the Sherman Act, arguing that it did not ban all combinations of business, but only those that were unreasonable and that restrained trade. The *Standard Oil* case thus became famous for its development of what has become known as the "rule of reason" when it comes to enforcing antitrust laws.

For more information: Fligstein, Neil. *The Transformation of Corporate Control.* Cambridge, Mass.: Harvard University Press, 1990; Tarbell, Ida. *The History of the Standard Oil Company.* Dover Publication, 2003.

—Ernest Gomez

standing

Under ARTICLE III, Section 2 of the United States Constitution, the judicial power extends to certain "cases" and "controversies." Thus, the federal courts may not offer advisory opinions on issues that are of only theoretical or abstract interest to the parties in a lawsuit. Rather, the courts may take jurisdiction only of concrete disputes in which the complaining party has suffered an actual and present injury and will realize a practical and significant consequence from resolution of the lawsuit. The doctrine of "standing" has been derived from this understanding of the limited constitutional authority of the judiciary.

In the context of public law questions, the Supreme Court holds that "[o]ne element of the 'bedrock' case-or-controversy requirement is that plaintiffs must establish that they have standing to sue," that is, standing to invoke the power of a federal court to review the conduct of government. See McCONNELL V. FEDERAL ELECTION COMMISSION, 540 U.S. 93, 225 (2003); see also *Whitmore v. Arkansas,* 495 U.S. 149, 155 (1990). ("[T]he doctrine of standing serves to identify those disputes which are appropriately resolved through the judicial process.") Standing thus requires the plaintiff to have "such a personal stake in the outcome of the controversy as to assure the concrete adverseness which sharpens the presentation of issues" (BAKER V. CARR, 369 U.S. 186, 204 [1962]).

To satisfy the constitutional requirements for standing, a plaintiff must allege a personal stake in the outcome of the litigation (*Sierra Club v. Morton,* 405 U.S. 727 [1972]) in the form of "some direct injury" that is "real and immediate" (*City of Los Angeles v. Lyons,* 461 U.S. 95, 102 [1983]). The injury alleged must be "distinct and palpable" and not "abstract," "conjectural," or "hypothetical" (*Allen v. Wright,* 468 U.S. 737, 751 [1984]). Moreover, this "injury in fact" suffered by the plaintiff must be "fairly traceable to the defendant's allegedly unlawful conduct and likely to be addressed by the requested relief" (*Allen v. Wright,* 468 U.S. at 751; see also LUJAN V. DEFENDERS OF WILDLIFE, 504 U.S. 555, 560–61 [1992]). In sum, there are three interrelated constitutional components of standing—injury in fact, causation, and redressability by the courts (*Lujan,* 504 U.S. at 560–61).

As a prudential matter of judicial self-restraint, the Supreme Court has further restricted standing to those cases in which the plaintiff can show that the interest sought to be protected in the lawsuit is arguably within the zone of interests to be pro-tected by the statutory or constitutional provision upon which the plaintiff depends (*National Credit Union Admin. v. First Nat'l Bank & Trust Co.,* 522 U.S. 479, 488 [1998]; *Association of Data Processing Service Organizations, Inc. v. Camp,* 397 U.S. 150 [1970]). However, Congress by legislation may expressly negate the zone-of-interests test or expand the zone of interests to more generously authorize suits against the federal government (*Bennett v. Spear,* 520 U.S. 154, 163–65 [1997]; see also *Raines v. Byrd,* 521 U.S. 811, 820 n. 3 [1997], holding that an explicit grant of authority by Congress to bring suit "eliminates any prudential standing limitations and significantly lessens the risk of unwanted conflict with the Legislative Branch").

Under these standing restrictions, generalized and abstract grievances about the conduct of the government are insufficient to establish the personal injury required for standing (*United States v. Richardson,* 418 U.S. 166, 173–74 [1974]). Thus, an asserted right to have the government act in accordance with law is not sufficient, standing alone, to confer federal court jurisdiction (*Allen v. Wright,* 468 U.S. at 754). Nor will the mere assertion of a right "to a particular kind of government conduct, which the Government has violated by acting differently," satisfy the Article III requirements for standing (*Id.,* quoting VALLEY FORGE CHRISTIAN COLLEGE V. AMERICANS UNITED FOR SEPARATION OF CHURCH AND STATE, INC., 454 U.S. 464, 483 [1982]).

The Supreme Court has long held that "standing to sue may not be predicated upon an interest of the kind . . . which is held in common by all members of the public" (*Schlesinger v. Reservists Comm. to Stop the War,* 418 U.S. 208, 220 [1974]). However, the Court has clarified that, where a harm is sufficiently concrete and specific—especially if it implicates FUNDAMENTAL RIGHTS, such as voting—standing may be found, even if the asserted harm is widely shared by other citizens (*Federal Election Comm'n v. Akins,* 524 U.S. 11, 22–24 [1998]). Nonetheless, abstract or indefinite harm, such as a common concern that the government obey the law, remains insufficient for standing.

For more information: Aman, Alfred C., Jr., and William T. Mayton. *Administrative Law.* 2d ed. St. Paul, Minn.: West Group, 2001; Pierce, Richard J., Jr., Sidney A. Shapiro, and Paul R. Verkuil. *Administrative Law and Process.* 4th ed. St. Paul, Minn.: West Group, 2004.

—Gregory C. Sisk

Stanford v. Kentucky 492 U.S. 361 (1989)

In *Stanford v. Kentucky,* a divided Supreme Court clarified the minimum age of defendants eligible for CAPITAL PUNISHMENT by deciding that offenders could be sentenced to death for murders that they committed after their 16th birthday. The Court previously ruled against applying capital punishment to offenders aged 15 and younger. The *Stanford* decision set the constitutional standard for capital punishment until it was overruled by the Court's 2005 decision in *Roper v. Simmons* (543 U.S. 441), which forbade executions for offenders whose capital crimes were committed before they reached the age of 18.

In the course of robbing a gas station of 300 cartons of cigarettes and a small amount of cash, 17-year-old Kevin Stanford abducted, raped, and murdered the young woman who worked at the gas station. Because of the seriousness of his crime and his record of previous offenses, Stanford was sent from juvenile court to regular court to be tried as an adult. After a trial, he was convicted of murder and sentenced to death. Stanford's attorney appealed his sentence by claiming that the execution of a juvenile would violate the U.S. Constitution's Eighth Amendment prohibition on CRUEL AND UNUSUAL PUNISHMENTs.

Stanford's attorneys argued that American society's standards no longer regarded the death penalty as a permissible punishment for juveniles. However, Justice ANTONIN GREGORY SCALIA's opinion on behalf of a five-member majority of the Supreme Court disagreed. In Justice Scalia's view, the varying minimum ages in states' death penalty statutes did not establish the existence of a national consensus against the execution of offenders for murders committed when under the age of 18. In a dissenting opinion on behalf of four of the Court's nine justices, Justice WILLIAM J. BRENNAN, JR. argued that the application of the death penalty to anyone under the age of 18 should be considered as cruel and unusual punishment and prohibited by the Eighth Amendment.

The decision by the deeply divided Supreme Court permitted the application of capital punishment to 16- and 17-year-old murderers in those states whose death penalty laws did not set a higher minimum age. The *Stanford* decision spurred opponents of capital punishment to file additional legal challenges. They sought to remove the United States from the short list of countries that executed juvenile offenders—Iran, Pakistan, Saudi Arabia, Yemen, Nigeria, Democratic Republic of Congo, and China—none of which at that time were rights-protecting democracies that are typically aligned with American values and policies. When the Supreme Court revisited the issue in *Roper v. Simmons* (2005), Justice ANTHONY M. KENNEDY, a member of Justice Scalia's *Stanford* majority, changed his position and provided the fifth vote for a new majority that ruled against capital punishment for juveniles.

For more information: Haines, Herbert G. *Against Capital Punishment: The Anti-Death Penalty Movement in America, 1972–1994.* New York: Oxford University Press, 1996; Savage, David G. *Turning Right: The Making of the Rehnquist Supreme Court.* New York: John Wiley & Sons, 1992.

—Christopher E. Smith

Stanley v. Georgia 394 U.S. 557 (1969)

In *Stanley v. Georgia,* the Supreme Court ruled that individuals have a FIRST AMENDMENT right to possess and view pornographic materials in their homes.

Federal and state agents, armed with a warrant to search Robert Stanley's home for evidence of illegal bookmaking, seized and viewed three films that they deemed "obscene." Stanley was then charged and convicted of violating a Georgia law that made it a crime to "knowingly have possession of . . . obscene matter."

The U.S. Supreme Court overturned Stanley's conviction unanimously. Writing for five justices, Justice Thurgood Marshall held that "[w]hatever may be the justifications for other statutes regulating OBSCENITY, we do not think they reach into the PRIVACY of one's own home. If the First Amendment means anything, it means that a State has no business telling a man, sitting alone in his own house, what books he may read or what films he may watch. Our whole constitutional heritage rebels at the thought of giving government the power to control men's minds." The majority emphasized that its holding protected only the possession of reading materials and films, and not items such as narcotics and stolen goods. Justice HUGO BLACK agreed with the result, but concurred separately because his absolutist interpretation of the First Amendment did not accord government any power to prohibit allegedly "obscene" materials. The remaining three justices (Stewart, WILLIAM J. BRENNAN, JR., and White) voted to overturn Stanley's conviction on the FOURTH AMENDMENT ground that the search warrant for evidence of bookmaking did not authorize the seizure of pornographic films.

The Court has generally continued to follow *Stanley*'s rule protecting the private possession of obscene materials. In 2002, for instance, six justices struck down a federal law criminalizing the possession of "virtual" CHILD PORNOGRAPHY generated with computers; seven justices struck a similar provision banning sexually explicit films using youthful-looking adult actors (*Ashcroft v. Free Speech Coalition*, 535 U.S. 234 [2002]). In 1990, however, six justices created an exception to the *Stanley* doctrine by upholding an Ohio law that banned the possession of pornographic photographs of actual children (*Osborne v. Ohio*, 496 U.S. 913 [1990]).

For more information: Nowak, John E., and Ronald D. Rotunda. *Principles of Constitutional Law*. St. Paul, Minn.: Thomson/West, 2005.

Stanton, Elizabeth Cady (1815–1902) *activist*

Elizabeth Cady Stanton was a 19th-century political activist who worked hard for equal rights for women, including the constitutional RIGHT TO VOTE.

Stanton was born in Johnstown, New York, on November 12, 1815. Through political activism, writing, and lecturing she would become one of the best-known advocates for woman suffrage and women's rights in the United States. Stanton would not only emerge as a major influence in shaping the movement toward the eventual ratification of the NINETEENTH AMENDMENT (1920) providing federal protection for women's right to vote, but also, in the years following the Civil War, she would participate in critical national debates surrounding the Fourteenth (1868) and Fifteenth (1870) Amendments. When Stanton died in New York on October 26, 1902, she left behind a letter she was preparing to send to President Theodore Roosevelt in an effort to persuade him to support the right of women to vote.

Stanton proved herself to be one of the boldest and most independent of the suffragists of her generation. Eschewing the more moderate stances of women's rights advocates who were uncomfortable with critiques of the institution of marriage and with questioning organized religion's relationship to gender inequality, Stanton embraced controversial dress reforms, shocked her colleagues by demanding less restrictive divorce laws, and published *The Woman's Bible* to refute what she regarded as mainstream uses of Christian doctrine to perpetuate women's subordination to men.

Though she died before the Nineteenth Amendment was ratified, Stanton's contribution to the cause of woman suffrage would be hard to exaggerate. She was a primary organizer of the Seneca Falls Convention (July 19–20, 1848), the first formally organized women's rights convention in the United States. She also wrote the Declaration of Sentiments adopted at Seneca Falls. In composing the Declaration of Sentiments, Stanton modeled her language upon the U.S. DECLARATION OF INDEPENDENCE (1776) and, like many 19th-century American thinkers, she grounded her political principles in her interpretation of the logical implications of the work of English legal theorist WILLIAM BLACKSTONE (1723–1780). After pronouncing that "all men and women are created equal" and possess the "inalienable rights" of "life, liberty, and the pursuit of happiness," Stanton's declaration proceeded to identify a number of ways in which "absolute tyranny" had been exercised by men over women. Specifically, the Declaration of Sentiments outlined discrimination in economic fields, education, marriage and divorce laws, and in political rights. The declaration concluded with resolutions calling for a reform of laws that placed women in "inferior" positions relative to men and for the "sacred right to the elective franchise." Including an explicit demand for the actual right to vote was so controversial in 1848—even among women's rights advocates—that the suffrage resolution was the only section of the Declaration of Sentiments to fail to win unanimous support among Seneca Falls Convention delegates. Stanton would later become a leader in the National Woman Suffrage Association, an organization that worked for the proposal and ratification of a federal amendment—rather than merely state and local laws—guaranteeing women the right to vote.

Like many 19th-century women's rights advocates, Stanton was also an abolitionist. After the Civil War, Stanton and her friend and colleague Susan B.Anthony (1820–1906) worked unsuccessfully for the inclusion of woman suffrage provisions in the FOURTEENTH and FIFTEENTH AMENDMENTS. When Republican leaders resisted Stanton's efforts as injurious to what they regarded as the more pressing cause of African-American CIVIL RIGHTS and suffrage, Stanton publicly opposed the Fourteenth and Fifteenth Amendments. Stanton's quandary—the choice between supporting deeply flawed amendments as the best that could be hoped for in post–Civil War America or insisting that woman suffrage was not subject to negotiation and was no longer to be delayed—illustrates the tensions between movements to expand constitutional protections during the Reconstruction period.

For more information: Gurko, Miriam. *The Ladies of Seneca Falls: The Birth of the Woman's Rights Movement.* New York: Schocken Books, 1974; Ryan, Barbara. *Feminism and the Women's*

Movement: Dynamics of Change in Social Movement Ideology and Activism. New York: Routledge, 1992; Stanton, Elizabeth Cady. *Eighty Years and More: Reminiscences 1815–1897.* Boston: Northeastern University Press, 1993.

—Ellen Grigsby

state tax incentives and interstate commerce

State governments frequently offer tax reductions to businesses as an incentive to locate or to remain within the state. Some scholars warn that states are engaged in a "race to the bottom" as each one offers greater incentives, thereby reducing the tax revenues that fund government services. Certain state tax incentive programs have been found to violate the COMMERCE CLAUSE of the U.S. Constitution, which is intended to create a free trade area between and among the states. A tax incentive violates the commerce clause when it has the effect of providing lower tax rates to in-state businesses than those imposed on out-of-state ventures. Because such tax incentives do not directly conflict with congressional legislation under the commerce clause, they are said to violate the "dormant" or "negative" commerce clause.

In *COMPLETE AUTO TRANSIT, INC. V. BRADY,* 430 U.S. 274 (1977), the Supreme Court articulated a four-part standard for taxes challenged under the commerce clause. A tax provision will survive commerce clause scrutiny when it "is applied to an activity with a substantial nexus to the taxing State, is fairly apportioned, does not discriminate against INTERSTATE COMMERCE, and is fairly related to the services provided by the State." In the decades since this decision, the Court has frequently revisited the issue of state tax incentives.

The Supreme Court struck down a New York tax incentive in *Westinghouse Electric Corp. v. Tully,* 466 U.S. 388 (1984). The challenged law provided credits against the corporate franchise tax for exports shipped from a regular place of business within the state. The Court found that the law had a discriminatory effect on interstate commerce and violated the commerce clause because it was designed to coerce businesses to locate in New York. In *Bacchus Imports, Ltd. v. Dias*, 468 U.S. 263 (1984), the Court struck down a similar Hawaii law, providing tax exemptions from the state liquor tax for certain locally produced beverages. The Supreme Court ruled that the exemption discriminated against interstate commerce by providing a direct commercial advantage to in-state businesses.

Four years later in *New Energy Co. of Ind. v. Limbach*, 486 U.S. 269 (1988), the Court considered an Ohio fuel sales tax law that provided offsetting credits for ethanol sales. Out-of-state ethanol producers were eligible for the credit if their home state granted reciprocal treatment to Ohio ethanol producers. A unanimous majority of the Court held that this provision clearly discriminated against interstate commerce. The majority opinion, authored by Justice ANTONIN GREGORY SCALIA, observed that while discriminatory tax provisions violate the DORMANT COMMERCE CLAUSE, direct government subsidies to in-state businesses do not, because they are not based on the state's regulatory powers.

The most recent commerce clause challenge to a state tax incentive program arose in *DAIMLERCHRYSLER V. CUNO*, 126 S. Ct. 1854 (2006). Although the Sixth Circuit Court of Appeals found that portions of the challenged tax incentives discriminated against interstate commerce, the Supreme Court rejected the case because the plaintiffs did not have proper STANDING to challenge the tax incentive law. The issue is almost certain to appear on the Court's docket again, however, as state and local governments continue to offer new tax incentives in response to the pressure to recruit and retain more businesses.

For more information: Enrich, Peter D. "Saving the States from Themselves: Commerce Clause Restraints on State Tax Incentives for Business." *Harvard Law Review* 110, no. 377 (1996): 390–393; Gillette, Clayton P. "Business Incentives, Interstate Competition, and the Commerce Clause." *Minnesota Law Review* 82, no. 447 (1997): 478–492; Hellerstein, Walter, and Dan T. Coenen. "Commerce Clause Restraints on State Business Development Incentives." *Cornell Law Review* 81, no. 4 (1996): 789–878.

—Joshua A. Kimsey

Stevens, John Paul (1920–) *Supreme Court justice*

John Paul Stevens was nominated to the Supreme Court by President Gerald Ford, and began his tenure on the nation's highest court on December 19, 1975. He replaced WILLIAM O. DOUGLAS on the Court.

Justice Stevens was born on April 20, 1920, in Chicago, Illinois. He earned a B.A. from the University of Chicago and his D.J. from Northwestern University School of Law. He served his country in the navy during World War II. His first professional exposure to the United States Supreme Court was as a law clerk to Justice Wiley Rutledge during the 1947 term. He served in various capacities in the U.S. government before becoming a member of the federal judiciary. These prior employments include: associate counsel to the HOUSE OF REPRESENTATIVES Judiciary Committee and as a member of the attorney general's National Committee to Study Antitrust Law. He served as a judge on the Seventh Circuit Court of Appeals from 1970 to 1975 before he took his place on the Supreme Court.

Following his appointment to the High Court, Stevens was widely perceived as a moderate or a pragmatist in the same vein as LEWIS POWELL or Harry Blackmun. However, as the Court has shifted further away from the liberal WARREN COURT to the less liberal Burger Court to the extremely conservative REHNQUIST and ROBERTS COURTs, Stevens has increasingly moved to the left of the Supreme Court ideological spectrum. As a liberal member of the Court he tends to vote against the conservative majority and often dissents in non-unanimous decisions.

For much of his time on the Supreme Court, Justice Stevens has been the most senior associate justice. Due to his opposition to the "core" group of conservative justices on the Rehnquist Court (Chief Justice WILLIAM HUBBS REHNQUIST and Associate Justices CLARENCE THOMAS and

ANTONIN GREGORY SCALIA), he has been able to assign most of the opinions of the Supreme Court in which the core conservatives were not joined by the swing justices ANTHONY M. KENNEDY and SANDRA DAY O'CONNOR. Indeed, from 1994 to 1999, Stevens was the only associate justice on the Court to assign a majority opinion. In the 2000 and 2001 terms, associate justices also assigned opinions, but Stevens still assigned 25 of 28 opinions that Chief Justice Rehnquist did not. In other words, while Justice Stevens was the most liberal justice on the 1994–2005 Supreme Court, he was able to influence its opinions due to his role as senior-most associate justice. Given the recent appointment of two conservative members to the Supreme Court, Chief Justice JOHN G. ROBERTS, JR., and Associate Justice SAMUEL ALITO, it is likely that Stevens will continue to assign opinions, when he is in the majority and the Chief Justice is not, on a regular basis. He will also dissent in many cases in which a group of justices more conservative decide cases he disagrees with. This will allow him to influence the Supreme Court decisions and the understanding of the U.S. Constitution in a similar fashion as he did during his time on the Rehnquist Court.

Stevens's opinions have contributed to the current understanding of the Constitution in various areas, as in two recent developments in his jurisprudence: his role in the death penalty question and in questions of standing with "enemy combatants." Justice Stevens has long been concerned about the application of the death penalty. In ATKINS V. VIRGINIA (2002), he penned the opinion for a 5-4 decision in which the death penalty for mentally retarded murderers amounted to CRUEL AND UNUSUAL PUNISHMENT, prohibited by the Eighth Amendment. He also used that opinion to note that he believed that the death penalty for juvenile offenders was also unconstitutional. The first subsequent juvenile death penalty cases coming to the Court failed to convince a majority to side with Stevens's belief, despite his best efforts. However, in 2005, Justice Anthony M. Kennedy sided with Stevens and four other justices, and in *Roper v. Simmons* (2004), the death penalty for juveniles was deemed unconstitutional. While it was Kennedy who altered his opinion, and ultimately wrote the Court's opinion, it was Stevens who put the issue on the national screen again and who worked to sway his brethren's view of the issue.

Stevens has also affected the understanding of the rights of enemy combatants in the current war on terror. In RASUL V. BUSH (2003), Stevens, writing for the Court, found that courts in the United States have the power to hear cases brought by foreign nationals captured abroad and held in Guantánamo Bay, Cuba. Stevens and the Supreme Court dismissed the government's claim that enemy combatants, who were not captured in the United States and were not held in place where the United States is considered sovereign, had no right to relief in U.S. courts. *Rasul*, along with some other cases rooted in the war on terror, such as *HAMDI V. RUMSFELD* (2003) and *Hamdan v. Rumsfeld* (2005), the latter of which was also written by Stevens, forms the basis for the understanding of questions in CIVIL LIBERTIES and separations of power in the still new, post-9/11 constitutional landscape.

For more information: Amann, Diane Marie. "John Paul Stevens, Human Rights Judge," *Fordham Law Review* 74 (2006): 1,569–1,606; Jacobi, Tonja. "The Judicial Signaling Game: How Judges Shape Their Dockets." *Supreme Court Economic Review.* Paper presented at the annual meeting of the American Political Science Association, Philadelphia Marriott Hotel, Philadelphia, Pa., Aug. 27, 2003. Available online. URL: http://www.all-academic.com/meta/p61999_index.html. Downloaded May 15, 2008; Sickels, Robert Judd. *John Paul Stevens and the Constitution.* University Park: Pennsylvania State University Press, 1988; Thai, Joseph T. "The Law Clerk Who Wrote *Rasul v. Bush:* John Paul Stevens's Influence from World War II to the War on Terror." *Virginia Law Review* 92 (2006): 501–553.

—Tobias T. Gibson

Stone, Harlan Fiske (1872–1946) *Supreme Court justice*

Harlan Fiske Stone is one of only three individuals to serve as both an associate justice and as chief justice. He was born on October 11, 1872, in Chesterfield, New Hampshire. In 1890 he entered Amherst College, where he studied science and philosophy. As a student he demonstrated a developing command of public speaking and debate. After graduating from Amherst, Stone moved to New York City to attend Columbia Law School in 1895, from which he graduated in 1898.

Between 1905 and 1916, Stone worked as a practicing attorney and as a teacher at Columbia Law School. With brief interludes of private practice, he continued teaching until February 21, 1923, when he resigned. On April 1, 1924, President Calvin Coolidge, a classmate at Amherst with Stone, appointed him attorney general in order to restore confidence in the Justice Department after the scandals of Harding's administration. Nominated to the Supreme Court to replace Justice Joseph McKenna, he was sworn in on March 2, 1925.

In the area of economic regulation, Stone was usually in the minority when Justice Roberts and the "four horsemen" (Butler, McReynolds, Sutherland, and Van Devanter) opposed the New Deal legislation of Roosevelt's first administration. He believed that it was not the role of the Court to pronounce upon the wisdom of legislation, only its constitutionality.

In 1937, Stone included a footnote (footnote 4) in the opinion in *United States v. Carolene Products Co.* (1938) that has been hailed as an early expression of the "preferred freedoms doctrine." The doctrine gives greater protection to CIVIL LIBERTIES than to economic freedoms. He was sole dissenter in the first Jehovah's Witnesses flag saluting case. On June 12, 1941, Stone was nominated by President Franklin D. Roosevelt to the office of chief justice of the Supreme Court, to replace Charles Evans Hughes. He took the oath of office as chief justice on July 3, 1941.

During World War II, Stone was in the majority in the Japanese removal cases (*Hirabayshi* [1943] and *Korematusu* [1944]) as well as the German saboteurs case (*Ex parte Quirin,* et al., 1942).

Stone's tenure as chief justice was probably the most divisive in the Court's history. He favored open debate in a battle of ideas; this leadership style too often produced clashing egos between those seeking to protect civil liberties and those seeking to give the government power to deal with the problems of a wartime era. Stone died April 22, 1946, in Washington, D.C. He suffered a massive cerebral hemorrhage while reading in open court his dissenting opinion in *Girouard v. United States* and died later that day.

For more information: Mason, Alpheus. *Harlan Fiske Stone: Pillar of the Law.* New York: Viking Press, 1956; Renstrom, Peter G. *The Stone Court: Justices, Rulings, and Legacy.* Santa Barbara, Calif.: ABC-CLIO, 2001; Unofsky, Melvin I., and Herbert A. Johnson. *Division and Discord: The Supreme Court under Stone and Vinson, 1941–1953.* Charleston: University of South Carolina Press, 1997.

—Andrew J. Waskey

Stone Court (1941–1946)

The Stone Court began on July 3, 1941, when Harlan Fiske Stone (1872–1946) was sworn in as the 12th chief justice of the Supreme Court to succeed Charles Evans Hughes, who had retired. It ended with Stone's unexpected death from a cerebral hemorrhage on April 22, 1946, while he was reading an opinion from the bench.

Serving on the Stone Court when it was formed were Justices Owen J. Roberts (appointed by President Warren G. Harding, 1930), Hugo L. Black (appointed by President Franklin D. Roosevelt, 1937), Stanley F. Reed (appointed by Roosevelt, 1938), Felix Frankfurter (appointed by Roosevelt, January 1939), WILLIAM O. DOUGLAS (appointed by Roosevelt, April 1939), Frank Murphy (appointed by Roosevelt, 1940), and James F. Burns (appointed by Roosevelt, 1940). Because Stone was serving as an associate justice at the time of his accession to chief justice, his seat came open. It was filled on July 11, 1941, by Robert H. Jackson.

The first addition to the Stone Court was Wiley B. Rutledge (February 1943), who replaced James F. Byrnes (resigned October 1942). The only other addition was Harold H. Burton, who was appointed by President Harry S. Truman in

October 1945 as a replacement for Owen J. Roberts (resigned July 1945).

Stone's appointment came shortly before the entry of the United States into World War II. The Stone Court's decision overturning California's "anti-Okie" law enforced the constitutional right of people to move from state to state. *Edwards v. People of State of California,* 314 U.S. 160 (1941), thus allowed Edwards to bring his unemployed brother-in-law to California from Texas.

With the entry of the United States into World War II, the Stone Court would be forced to deal with cases involving spies, Japanese detention, martial law, CIVIL LIBERTIES, and other issues. The spy and TREASON cases arose in *Ex parte Quirin,* 317 U.S. 1 (1942). Eight German spies, who had lived for years in the United States before returning to Nazi Germany, had been captured trying to conduct Operation Pastorius, which if successful would have demolished a number of installations in the United States. They were tried as unlawful enemy combatants, the status given to spies, and were all condemned to death by a military commission, authorized by President Roosevelt, that met in secret. Six were executed (August 8, 1942), and the death sentence was commuted to life in prison for the other two.

Arising out of *Ex parte Quirin* was a review of the treason conviction of Anthony Cramer, who had previously known and had brief contact with two of the executed Nazi spies. His conviction was overturned in the first review in history of a treason conviction by the Supreme Court, *Cramer v. United States,* 325 U.S. 1 (1945).

Criminal CIVIL RIGHTS for indigent defendants in noncapital cases were limited in *Betts v. Brady,* 316 U.S. 455 (1942). That year the Court also decided that sterilization could not be used by the states as a form of punishment (*Skinner v. Oklahoma,* 316 U.S. 535 [1942]).

In 1943 and 1944, the Stone Court upheld the removal of Japanese-American citizens in *Hirabayashi v. United States,* 320 U.S. 81 (1943), and their internment in *Korematsu v. United States,* 323 U.S. 214 (1944), although the latter decision was issued by a divided court. The same day *Korematsu* was issued, the Court allowed Mitsuye Endo, a Japanese American deemed to be a loyal citizen, to return to California in *Ex parte Mitsuye Endo,* 323 U.S. 283 (1944), thereby signaling that the Court was changing its views.

The scope of martial law and military tribunals was also clarified in *Duncan v. Kahanamoku,* 327 U.S. 304 (1946). It added clarity to the ruling in *Ex parte Milligan,* 71 U.S. 2 (1866), which had sought to limit the executive authority of President ABRAHAM LINCOLN.

Other wartime decisions regarding civil liberties included several Jehovah's Witnesses. In *Chaplinsky v. State of New Hampshire,* 315 U.S. 586 (1942), the Stone Court ruled that "fighting words" used by a Jehovah's Witness street preacher could be a justification for limiting freedom of speech. However, in the Jehovah's Witness flag saluting case of *West Virginia State Board of Education v. Barnette,* 319 U.S. 642 (1943), the ruling issued on June 14, Flag Day, rejected the claim that compelling the saluting of the American flag promoted national unity.

The next year the Stone Court outlawed white primaries in *Smith v. Allwright,* 321 U.S. 649 (1944). The case was a harbinger of the DESEGREGATION decisions to come after the war as well as voting rights cases.

The COMMERCE CLAUSE of the Constitution was the subject of many cases. Of landmark significance was *Wickard v. Filburn,* 317 U.S. 111 (1942). The decision allowed the broadest application of the commerce clause when it ruled that the Agricultural Adjustment Act of 1938 could be used to order a farmer to plow under and not to consume wheat in excess of his allotment, even if the wheat were only for the personal consumption of his family.

On May 10, 1943, the Court ruled in *National Broadcasting Co. v. United States,* 319 U.S. 190 (1943), that the Federal Communications Commission could issue regulations that governed radio stations that formed into broadcasting networks. The case was an important interpretation of the constitutional authority of Congress to set up regulatory agencies and for the agencies to develop administrative law.

For more information: Douglas, William O. *Harlan Fiske Stone: Chief Justice of the United States.* New York: Columbia University Press, 1946; Konefsky, Samuel Joseph. *Chief Justice Stone and the Supreme Court.* New York: Macmillan, 1946; Renstrom, Peter. *The Stone Court: Justices, Rulings, and Legacy.* Santa Barbara, Calif.: ABC-CLIO, 2001; Urofsky, Melvin L. *Division and Discord: The Supreme Court under Stone and Vinson, 1941–1953.* Columbia: University of South Carolina Press, 1999.

—Andrew J. Waskey

Stone v. Powell 428 U.S. 465 (1976)

In a 6-3 decision, the Supreme Court in *Stone v. Powell* reversed a ruling from the Ninth Circuit Court of Appeals and rejected HABEAS CORPUS petitions from prisoners Lloyd Powell and David Rice, who had claimed FOURTH AMENDMENT violations. The case is important for its ruling on when the federal courts will review a state conviction.

Powell alleged that he had been arrested on the basis of an unconstitutional California vagrancy statute and that the evidence used to convict him of murder, a revolver, was seized incident to an unlawful arrest. In a companion case from Nevada, Rice argued that materials used in making explosive devices, cited in the case against him, were found as the result of an illegal search based on a defective warrant. The Court held that if a state provides full and fair litigation of a Fourth Amendment claim, a prisoner may not be granted federal habeas corpus relief when evidence from an unconstitutional search and seizure was introduced at his trial. The decision created almost insurmountable limitations on the ability of defendants to cite breaches of the EXCLUSIONARY RULE as grounds for a federal writ of habeas corpus.

In previous cases, including *Kaufman v. United States,* 394 U.S. 217 (1969), the Court had implied that if a prisoner was convicted in state court on the basis of an illegal search or seizure, such a violation of the Fourth Amendment was grounds for federal habeas corpus relief. But in *Stone v. Powell,* the justices retreated from that position. The majority, Justices LEWIS POWELL, Stewart, Blackmun, WILLIAM HUBBS REHNQUIST, JOHN PAUL STEVENS, and Chief Justice WARREN BURGER, stated that the principal purpose of the exclusionary rule was to prevent improper conduct by the police. Law enforcement officers would presumably refrain from unlawful conduct if they knew that evidence improperly obtained would be tossed out at trial. However, the attenuated process of waiting until a federal court granted a habeas petition would have little or no deterrent on police behavior.

The Court expressed further reservations about the exclusionary rule when it stated that its application often diverted courts from their major task, an accurate determination of guilt or innocence. They warned that "indiscriminate application" of the rule would undermine the public's respect for the law by allowing too many guilty people to go free. In a concurring opinion, Chief Justice Burger went further by arguing that the exclusionary rule was used to prohibit reliable evidence and led to "bizarre miscarriages of justice." He would see its use drastically reduced to exclude only "egregious, bad-faith conduct."

Two dissenters, Justices WILLIAM J. BRENNAN, JR., and Marshall, feared that the decision would eviscerate Fourth Amendment protections. They argued that the guarantees against unreasonable searches and seizures were not second-class constitutional rights, but that any constitutional error by the state courts could be grounds for federal habeas corpus. The dissent prophesied that a major result of *Stone v. Powell* would be that denials of Fourth Amendment rights in state courts would go unreviewed, and that the potential ramifications of the case for federal habeas jurisdiction, when other constitutional rights were concerned, were "ominous."

For more information: LaFave, Wayne R., Jerold H. Israel, and Nancy J. King. *Criminal Procedure.* St. Paul, Minn.: Thomson/West, 2004.

—Mary Welek Atwell

stop and frisk

"Stop and frisk" refers to a procedure employed by law enforcement officers when they have reason to believe that an investigation is needed, which has been recognized by the United States Supreme Court as an exception to the FOURTH AMENDMENT's search warrant requirement. This procedure is also referred to as a "protective pat-down search," a "pat down for weapons," or a *Terry* stop and frisk," based on the Supreme Court decision in *TERRY V. OHIO*, 392 U.S. 1, 19 (1968).

A law enforcement officer who has a reasonable suspicion that a person is involved in criminal activity may briefly detain that person in order to investigate his suspicion. If the officer has reason to believe that the person is armed or dangerous, or poses a threat to the safety of the officer or bystanders, the officer is permitted to pat down the outside of the person's clothing to search for concealed weapons. Under these circumstances, the officer is not required to get a search warrant before conducting the stop and frisk. However, the search must be conducted in a reasonable manner. If the officer detects a weapon while frisking the person, the officer may disarm the person. If the officer detects contraband during the pat-down search, the officer may seize the contraband.

In *Terry v. Ohio*, 392 U.S. 1 (1968), the United States Supreme Court approved this procedure and established a test for evaluating future stop and frisk procedures on a case-by-case basis. *Terry* involved an undercover police officer who observed two men alternately walk by a store window, peer inside, and then confer with each other. They repeated this behavior five or six times, and then they conferred with a third man. Convinced that the men were "casing" the store in preparation for a robbery, the officer suspected they were armed with concealed weapons and decided to investigate. He approached the three men, identified himself, and asked for their names. After receiving mumbled responses, the officer grabbed one of the men, Mr. Terry, spun him around, and patted down the outside of his clothes. He felt a handgun and reached into Mr. Terry's pocket to remove it. Mr. Terry was charged with carrying a concealed weapon, and the pistol was used as evidence against him at trial.

The Fourth Amendment to the Constitution of the United States provides that "[t]he right of the people to be secure in their persons, houses, papers, and effects, against unreasonable searches and seizures, shall not be violated, and no Warrants shall issue, but upon probable cause." The United States Supreme Court granted review of Mr. Terry's case to answer the question of whether the stop and frisk procedure violated the Fourth Amendment's prohibition of unreasonable searches and seizures. To answer that question, the Court decided that the reasonableness of the search was best determined by balancing the police officer's interest in conducting the search against the degree of invasion inflicted by the search. The Court also stated that the frisk must be justified under the circumstances before being conducted and that the frisk could be no more intrusive than justified. Accordingly, the Court balanced the reasonableness of the officer's reasons for frisking the suspect and the manner in which the frisk was carried out. Ultimately, the Supreme Court approved of the frisk of Mr. Terry because the officer was reasonable in his belief that Mr. Terry and his associates were about to commit a crime, that they were likely to be armed with concealed weapons, and that they posed a threat to the safety of others. The Court also approved of the frisk because it was conducted in a very limited fashion, was performed only to discover weapons, and was not performed as a general search for evidence of criminal activity.

After the *Terry* decision, a stop and frisk is permissible under the Fourth Amendment so long as the officer has reasonable grounds for frisking the suspect and the officer limits the frisk to a search for weapons. In 1993, the Supreme Court further clarified the constitutionality of the stop and frisk in the case of *MINNESOTA V. DICKERSON*, 508 U.S. 366 (1993). Under the "plain feel" doctrine, a law enforcement officer may seize any other contraband—usually illegal drugs or drug paraphernalia—detected during a legitimate pat-down search for weapons. However, for the seizure of the contraband to be valid under the Fourth Amendment, its illegal character must be immediately apparent to the officer based upon its contour or mass. Thus, an officer is not allowed to manipulate the object with his fingers in order to determine whether the object is contraband. If the object is obviously not a weapon and is not obviously contraband of another sort, the officer is not permitted to investigate further. If the officer goes beyond a superficial pat-down of the suspect's outer clothing, the frisk is constitutionally unreasonable, and the object will not be allowed to be used as evidence at the suspect's trial.

For more information: Bloom, Robert M. *Searches, Seizures, and Warrants: A Reference Guide to the United States Constitution.* Westport, Conn.: Praeger, 2003; Hubbart, Phillip A. *Making Sense of Search and Seizure Law: A Fourth Amendment Handbook.* Durham, N.C.: Carolina Academic Press, 2005.

—Mark A. Fulks

Story, Joseph (1779–1845) *Supreme Court justice*

Joseph Story was nominated to sit as an associate justice on the Supreme Court of the United States in 1811. He was 32 years old, and to this day remains the youngest person ever appointed and one of its longest-serving justices. While he was not President JAMES MADISON's first choice to fill that particular vacancy on the Court, he nonetheless went on to become one of its most preeminent judges and one of the most famous scholars of the Constitution. His opinions and scholarly writings are still carefully studied and debated, and continue to contribute to the rich fabric of American jurisprudence.

Born in Massachusetts in 1779, Story attended Harvard College and then studied law. Prior to his appointment to the Court, he served in both the Massachusetts legislature and the U.S. HOUSE OF REPRESENTATIVES. While serving on the Supreme Court, he was also appointed Dane Professor at the Harvard Law School in 1829. He held both positions until his death in 1845, and was held to be a great teacher, scholar, and jurist.

Story was a conservative New Englander who believed in the need for a strong national government. He was a steadfast supporter and ally of Chief Justice JOHN MARSHALL and an opponent of slavery. Agreeing with Marshall's federalist view of the founding, Story's interpretation of the Constitution emphatically rejected the "states' rights" view that the United States was a compact of sovereign states. His legal scholarship was extensive, and he is often referred to as "the Blackstone of the American Constitution." His various commentaries on the Constitution remain to this day as one of the authoritative sources of American constitutionalism and the conceiving of the original INTENT OF THE FRAMERS of the Constitution.

Story was the author of three of the Supreme Court's most famous decisions: MARTIN V. HUNTER'S LESSEE, *The Amistad*, and *Prigg v. Pennsylvania*. In the first case, Story successfully asserted the power of the Supreme Court to decide on appeal cases decided by a state supreme court, and to overturn their decisions. Such a decision was necessary if the United States was to have a uniform interpretation of state laws under the Constitution. In the *Amistad* and *Prigg* cases, the Court was forced to deal with the issue of slavery and the interpretation of the Constitution with respect to the legality of slavery. In the *Amistad* case, Story successfully argued that the law of the United States prohibited the importation of slaves, and hence the Africans being transported on the captured slave ship *Amistad* were free persons. In the latter case, Story upheld the right of slave owners to have fugitive slaves returned to them even if the slave had escaped to a state in which slavery had been outlawed. While Story was opposed to slavery, he also reluctantly conceded that the Constitution recognized its existence and it thus fell under the jurisdiction of state law. Story unfortunately did not live long enough to see the passage of the THIRTEENTH AMENDMENT in 1865, which outlawed slavery from the entire United States.

For more information: McClellan, James. *Joseph Story and the American Constitution: A Study in Political and Legal Thought.* Norman: University of Oklahoma Press, 1990; Newmeyer, R. Kent. *Supreme Court Justice Joseph Story: Statesman of the Old Republic.* Chapel Hill: University of North Carolina Press, 1985; Schotten, Peter. "Joseph Story." In *American Political*

Thought. 2d ed. Itasca, Ill.: Peacock Publishers, 1983; Story, Joseph. *A Familiar Exposition of The Constitution of the United States.* Lake Bluff, Ill.: Regnery Press, 1986.

—Patrick Malcolmson

strict constructivism

Strict constructivism is a theory of CONSTITUTIONAL INTERPRETATION according to which provisions of the U.S. Constitution are construed in accordance with their meaning at the time the Constitution was drafted. This theory of interpretation focuses on the words of the Constitution in order to determine what its clauses and amendments mean. In essence, strict constructivism calls for a narrow and measured interpretation of the Constitution.

Generally, the debate over constitutional interpretation is between two theories: strict constructivism and interpretivism. Strict constructivism, which is also called originalism and textualism, looks primarily to the text of the Constitution to define the rights of the people and the role of the government. When the text alone is insufficient, strict constructivism may consider the context in which the Constitution was drafted and the history and traditions that preceded and followed it. Nevertheless, the history and traditions are allowed only to guide the interpretation to clearly implicit principles and protections. Under this theory, constitutional rights are not inferred or derived from the text to address modern issues. Rather, modern issues are viewed as being either within the scope of the original protections afforded by the Constitution or outside of them. If an issue falls outside the text of the Constitution, it is left to the people to amend the Constitution to conform to modern society or to enact legislative remedies when permissible. According to strict constructivism, it is not within the province of judges to fill in the gaps based upon their own creative sense of justice and democracy. Instead, this theory posits that the only reliable understanding of the Constitution comes from the expressed intentions of the Founding Fathers, which are found in the text of the Constitution and can be understood through consideration of the history and traditions that guided them and those who followed.

The primary goal of strict constructivism is a consistent theoretical framework for constitutional interpretation. However, it is also focused on eliminating bias, activism, and vigilance from the legal system by requiring judicial restraint instead. The Constitution is the written embodiment of the rule of law that governs society and, according to strict constructivism, the rule of law is undermined when judges stray from the original meaning of the text.

On the other side of the debate, interpretivism views the Constitution as a living document that establishes general principles rather than specific rules. From this view, the Constitution should be interpreted as needed to achieve justice and to resolve social problems and political issues. Judges are not constrained by the text of the Constitution or the history and traditions of the country. Moreover, interpretivism rejects the view that the Constitution has one meaning. Instead, judges are empowered to be creative in making constitutional law, guided by the spirit of the Constitution and the values it expresses. For example, the interpretivist views the Constitution as protecting human dignity and personal freedom in a broad sense and seeks to advance those values through constitutional interpretation. Accordingly, the Constitution is seen as adaptable to modern times, rather than being fixed in time.

The clash between these two theories of constitutional interpretation most often plays itself out in debate over the scope of individual autonomy protected by the Constitution. A judge adhering to the theory of strict constructivism may look at claims of a right to PRIVACY with some skepticism because the text of the Constitution does not expressly grant such a right. Instead, such a judge would look to the explicit rights and protections granted to citizens as well as the scope of authority granted to the federal government in order to resolve issues of privacy. If the text of the Constitution does not resolve the matter, a judge abiding by strict constructivism may view the issue as one more amenable to resolution in the U.S. Congress or at the state level.

In contrast, a judge of an interpretivist mindset may look at the protections specifically granted by the Constitution and glean a general principle of privacy that extends beyond the explicit rights set forth in the Constitution. Then, when applying that general principle to a specific case, the interpretivist judge may extend constitutional rights that are not explicitly stated in the Constitution and had not been recognized previously. Thus, the outcome of the case depends upon the interpretive creativity of the judge as well as the judge's personal sense of justice. Although interpretivism will have resolved the case, strict constructivism will decry the uncertainty injected into the justice system as a result.

In the final analysis, interpretivism favors a more creative approach that emphasizes general constitutional principles and case-by-case pragmatic results. On the other hand, strict constructivism emphasizes specifically defined constitutional rights and consistent results in similar cases.

For more information: Breyer, Stephen. *Active Liberty: Interpreting our Democratic Constitution.* New York: Alfred A. Knopf, 2005; Scalia, Antonin. *A Matter of Interpretation: Federal Courts and the Law.* Princeton, N.J.: Princeton University Press, 1997.

—Mark A. Fulks

strict scrutiny

Strict scrutiny is the most intense standard of JUDICIAL REVIEW for a challenged policy or law. The strict scrutiny standard is based on the EQUAL PROTECTION clause of the FOURTEENTH AMENDMENT and is applied based on the constitutional conflict at issue, regardless of whether a law or action of the federal government, a state government, or a local municipality is at issue.

Federal courts use strict scrutiny to determine whether certain types of government policies are constitutional. The United States Supreme Court has applied this standard to laws or policies that impinge on a right explicitly protected by the Constitution, such as the RIGHT TO VOTE. The Court

has also identified certain rights that it deems to be FUNDAMENTAL RIGHTS worthy of protection, including the right to travel and the right to PRIVACY, even though they are not enumerated in the Constitution.

The strict scrutiny standard is one of three employed by the courts in reviewing laws and government policies. The other standards are: the RATIONAL BASIS TEST, which is the lowest form of judicial scrutiny, with great deference given to the legislative branch; and the heightened scrutiny test, which is used in cases involving matters of discrimination based on sex.

Under the strict scrutiny standard, the courts presume the policy to be invalid unless the government can demonstrate a compelling interest to justify the policy. In other words, to withstand strict scrutiny, the government must show that its policy is necessary to achieve a compelling state interest. While the courts have never defined how to determine whether an interest is compelling, the concept generally refers to something necessary or crucial, as opposed to something merely preferred. This requires proof that the law is the least restrictive or least discriminatory alternative. If the law is not the least restrictive alternative, then it is not "necessary" to accomplish the end. Examples include national security, preserving the lives of multiple individuals, and not violating explicit constitutional protections.

Second, the law or policy must be "narrowly tailored" to achieve that goal or interest. If the government action encompasses too much or fails to address essential aspects of the compelling interest, then the rule is not considered narrowly tailored.

Finally, the law or policy must be the least restrictive means for achieving that interest. More accurately, there cannot be a less restrictive way to effectively achieve the compelling government interest; however, the test will not fail just because there is another way that is equally the least restrictive.

The impetus for the strict scrutiny standard came from Supreme Court Justice HARLAN FISKE STONE's famous FOOTNOTE FOUR in the case *United States v. Carolene Products Co.,* 304 U.S.

144 (1938). Justice Stone identified legislation that might not merit deference toward constitutional validity and under which a more exacting judicial scrutiny might be warranted. He wrote: "prejudice against DISCRETE AND INSULAR MINORITIES may be a special condition . . . which may call for a correspondingly more searching judicial inquiry."

Since *Carolene Products,* laws or practices that draw distinctions on the basis of race or national origin are inherently suspect and subject to strict scrutiny. In *CITY OF RICHMOND V. J.A. CROSON CO.,* 488 U.S. 469 (1989), the Supreme Court held that all laws that discriminate on the basis of race are subject to strict scrutiny under the equal protection clause of the Fourteenth Amendment, including laws that discriminate against whites. While the Court applies strict scrutiny to test all racial classifications, it was noted in *GRUTTER V. BOLLINGER,* 123 S. Ct. 2325 (2003), that such "scrutiny is not 'strict in theory, but fatal in fact.' . . . When race-based action is necessary to further a COMPELLING GOVERNMENTAL INTEREST, such action does not violate the constitutional guarantee of equal protection so long as the narrow-tailoring requirement is also satisfied." One example is the Supreme Court's widely criticized opinion in *KOREMATSU V. UNITED STATES,* 323 U.S. 214 (1944), upholding as constitutional the internment of Japanese Americans during World War II.

The strict scrutiny standard is also applied to many classifications drawn on the basis of alienage and to classifications that bear on the exercise of a fundamental right. While the mode of analysis is the same in all these areas, the strict scrutiny standard is applied with special rigor in cases that involve race or national origin.

For more information: Nowak, John E., and Ronald D. Rotunda. *Principles of Constitutional Law.* St. Paul, Minn.: Thomson/West, 2005.
—Randy W. Hagedorn

student activity fees

The collection and allocation of student activity fees raises several important constitutional questions involving the free speech, freedom of association, and establishment provisions of the FIRST AMENDMENT.

More than 70 percent of public colleges and universities impose mandatory student fees to help fund programs and activities that benefit the students. A portion of the money generated from these fees is distributed to various student groups on campus, usually by a committee within student government.

The Supreme Court first addressed the issue of mandatory student activity fees in the case of *ROSENBERGER V. RECTOR AND VISITORS OF THE UNIVERSITY OF VIRGINIA,* 515 U.S. 819 (1995). Rosenberger, a student at the university, sought funding from the Student Activity Fund (SAF) for publication of a Christian magazine by Wide Awake Productions. The university argued that the magazine was a religious activity and that it had a compelling interest to deny funding in order to comply with the ESTABLISHMENT CLAUSE.

In *Rosenberger,* a divided Supreme Court held that the denial of funds for the religious publication was unconstitutional viewpoint discrimination. Justice ANTHONY M. KENNEDY's majority opinion emphasized free speech over the establishment clause concerns. He concluded that the SAF constituted a limited PUBLIC FORUM and that the student publication was denied funding because of its religious viewpoint. Kennedy said that funding the publication would not advance religion and that the government program was neutral toward religion. In a concurring opinion, Justice SANDRA DAY O'CONNOR noted that numerous student groups received funding, and she suggested that no reasonable person would perceive that the university endorsed or supported the message of the magazine. In a dissenting opinion, Justice DAVID H. SOUTER, joined by Justices JOHN PAUL STEVENS, STEPHEN G. BREYER, and Ginsburg, argued that the magazine was a sectarian religious publication and the university's refusal to fund the publication was compelled by the establishment clause. Souter believed that funding the magazine violated the INTENT OF THE FRAMERS with regard to government support of religion, and he was concerned that the decision would open the door to greater government entanglement with religion.

In 1996, three students attending the University of Wisconsin Law School sued the Board of Regents and the University of Wisconsin. The students, self-described religious conservatives, claimed that the allocable student fee system violated their rights against "compelled" speech. In *West Virginia State Board of Education v. Barnette,* 319 U.S. 624 (1943), the Supreme Court recognized a right against compelled speech by holding that the First Amendment prohibits government from requiring a citizen to support ideas that the citizen finds objectionable. Some of the organizations whose advocacy the students strongly opposed included the Lesbian, Gay, Bisexual Campus Center, Amnesty International, and a socialist student group.

The funds were distributed in three ways: (1) the student senate appropriated funds for registered student groups for general operations, travel, and special events; (2) funds were distributed by a committee of the student government; and (3) any registered student group could seek funding through a student-body referendum vote. In defending the fee distribution system, the university argued that no student was required to join an organization, nor were they required to attend programs or events that are offensive to them. Moreover, objecting students may form their own organizations and seek funding.

After examining the university's fee program under the three-part test outlined in *Lehnert v. Ferris Faculty Association,* 500 U.S. 507 (1991), the lower federal courts concluded that the program was not germane to the university's mission, did not further a vital policy of the university, and imposed too much of a burden on the free speech rights of objecting students. A unanimous Supreme Court, however, upheld the student fee system in *University of Wisconsin v. Southworth,* 529 U.S. 217 (2000). The Court rejected the *Lehnert* germaneness test as applied to student activity fees. Writing for the Court, Justice Kennedy argued that it was inappropriate for courts to determine what is germane to the mission of a university because such a determination is "contrary to the very goal the University seeks to pursue." The university had a legitimate educational

policy of encouraging a marketplace of ideas among students. A mandatory fee was a reasonable way to promote this goal. The Court emphasized that such programs had to be administered in a viewpoint-neutral fashion, and the Wisconsin program, except for the voting procedure, satisfied this requirement.

The *Rosenberger* holding expanded the protection for student religious speech, and the *Southworth* decision rejected a compelled speech challenge to a mandatory student activity fee system. As long as funds are distributed in a viewpoint-neutral fashion, public universities and colleges may use student activity fees to promote a diverse marketplace of ideas.

For more information: Calvert, Clay. "Where the Right Went Wrong in *Southworth*: Underestimating the Power of the Marketplace." *University of Maine Law Review* 53 (2001).

—John Fliter

student rights

The U.S. Constitution makes no mention of student rights. Nonetheless, it shapes student rights in several ways. Students are protected by basic constitutional guarantees of CIVIL LIBERTIES. Congress, using its constitutional power to legislate, has carved out areas of student rights and created administrative bodies to oversee them. The courts, particularly the Supreme Court, have played a key role in determining how the Constitution, written in an era before compulsory education, public school systems, or public universities existed, applies to these institutions. The federal system established by the Constitution allows state variation in defining some student rights. States, for example, differ in the type of punishment teachers may administer or the qualifications for in-state tuition in public universities.

Two definitive Supreme Court cases in the 20th century set forth the principle that students do not surrender their fundamental civil liberties at the schoolhouse door. In 1944, in *West Virginia v. Barnette,* 319 U.S. 624 (1943), a case involving laws requiring students to recite the Pledge of

Allegiance to the flag, the Supreme Court broadened the issue, ruling that students could not be compelled to recite the pledge whether for religious or other reasons of conscience.

The second case, TINKER V. DES MOINES, 393 U.S. 503 (1969), grew out of the wearing of black armbands by students to protest the Vietnam War. The Court, in earlier cases, had extended FIRST AMENDMENT protection to nonverbal or SYMBOLIC SPEECH; in *Tinker,* they determined that students did not automatically surrender this right when in school. Schools must tolerate differences, even at the risk of unpleasantness, and students have the right to express controversial viewpoints not just in class but throughout the school. The Court recognized the need to balance this right against schools' needs to control disruptive behavior and carry out their educational functions, but found neither to be threatened by the *Tinker* scenario. The challenge for subsequent courts has been to determine where lines should be drawn in allowable symbolic speech and in other forms of student expression. Issues have ranged from dress codes, hair length, and display of Confederate flags, to controversial student publications, drug-related speech, and suggestive student speech at school assemblies.

The latter was the focus of *Bethel School District v. Fraser,* 478 U.S. 675 (1986), in which the Court appeared to take a giant step away from the expansive tone of *Tinker* by arguing that society expected schools to teach socially appropriate behavior and that school administrators had the power to determine when speech was inappropriate. In MORSE V. FREDERICK, 551 U.S. ___ (2007), the Court was very divided as to the future and precedential application of *Tinker* but ruled that, because of the critical need to combat drug abuse, the *Tinker* standard did not confer on students the right to engage in speech that might be interpreted as advocating illegal drug use. *Tinker* rights have not generally helped students who wish to wear controversial clothing or violate prevailing standards of decency. However, while *Bethel v. Fraser, Morse v. Frederick,* and other cases have undercut *Tinker*'s broad guarantees, the Court has not repudiated the *Tinker* principle that students do not forfeit their constitutional rights while in school.

Student publications receiving official school support are more restricted than individual student speech because they are viewed as representing the school. The Court has held that FREEDOM OF THE PRESS does not offer the same degree of protection to school-sponsored student publications as it does to the broader mass media, and that school authorities may censor student writing deemed inappropriate for such publications (*Hazelwood School District v. Kuhlmeier,* 484 U.S. 260 [1988]).

Students' religious rights have long been controversial. The Supreme Court has interpreted the ESTABLISHMENT CLAUSE to mean that students have the right to be free from state-imposed religious exercises, such as teacher-led prayer or state endorsement of religion, such as posting of the TEN COMMANDMENTS in classrooms. At the same time, the free exercise clause guarantees students the right to discuss their beliefs about religion and to organize and participate in religious organizations in their schools on the same basis as other noncurricular organizations.

Students have the right to be free from unreasonable searches, but courts have granted considerable latitude to school officials to determine what is unreasonable. School officials do not need to get a search warrant or to show probable cause, but the Court has ruled that they must have "reasonable suspicion" of wrongdoing and must limit the search to relevant objects. Where drug testing of students in sports and extracurricular activities is the issue, however, the courts have upheld broader discretion for school authorities.

Congress has granted students in schools receiving federal funds the right to confidentiality of certain records, accessed only by the child's parents, under the Family Educational Rights and Privacy Act (FERPA). This right to PRIVACY does not, however, extend to such in-class activities as letting students grade each other's quizzes and announce the scores (*Owasso v. Falvo,* 534 U.S. 426 [2002]).

Students are entitled to procedural DUE PROCESS in cases involving disciplinary actions against them by school authorities. Courts have left much discretion to the school administrators while developing the principle that more serious cases require a more rigorous attention to due process. Generally, students should know the charges against them, be given the evidence, and have the chance to contest the charges.

Although the Constitution contains no explicitly stated right to an education, the courts have treated public schools as more than just another social welfare benefit because of the importance of education to the country and the individual child. Thus the EQUAL PROTECTION clause of the FOURTEENTH AMENDMENT has been used to mandate an equal right to public education for disadvantaged and minority groups, ranging from African Americans in the segregated south to the children of illegal immigrants (BROWN V. BOARD OF EDUCATION, 347 U.S. 483 [1954]; *Plyler v. Doe*, 457 U.S. 202 [1982]). In 2007, in *Parents Involved in Community Schools v. Seattle School District No. 1*, 551 U.S. ___(2007), Supreme Court justices disagreed among themselves as to whether the legacy of *Brown* was best served by color-blind policies or by policies that consciously created racial balance in assigning students to schools, ruling 5-4 that school systems could not use race as the predominant criterion in assigning students to schools for the purpose of achieving diversity.

The Court makes a distinction between K–12 students and college students. The latter have more protected rights because higher education is not compulsory; it is meant to expose students to controversial ideas, and its students are more mature. For example, the Court has never extended to universities the limits it allows on expression in high schools, and universities must be viewpoint-neutral in dealing with student organizations and activities. Prior restraint of student publications in higher education is considered a violation of First Amendment rights, and *Hazelwood* does not apply to universities.

Universities must accord more procedural protections to their students, who legally are adults and are considered to have both "liberty" and "property" interests invested in higher education. Disciplinary proceedings do not have to acquire

the nature of a criminal court, but more protections are expected as the gravity of the offense increases. In cases of suspension or expulsion for academic reasons, procedural safeguards are fewer because courts tend to defer to educators where academic judgments are involved. Confidentiality of records under FERPA applies to the university level; here, however, control over access to records rests with students, not parents. Congressional legislation, particularly the Americans with Disabilities Act, protects the educational rights of students with disabilities in both schools and colleges receiving federal funding.

Awareness of and respect for student rights has grown since the student activism of the 1960s; yet the topic continues to evoke controversy because of the potentially adversarial nature of the student-school relationship and because of conflicts between presumed student rights and the academic and social goals of public education. At the K–12 level, for example, educators continue to debate methods for combating de facto racial segregation and promoting diversity while respecting a student's right to be treated in a color-blind manner. AFFIRMATIVE ACTION in admissions based on race and gender to achieve diversity on college campuses as an educationally relevant goal of academia also remains controversial, despite several major Supreme Court cases seeking to set guidelines. The right to free speech and academic freedom has come into conflict with campus speech codes and directives that attempt to create harmonious academic environments by broadly defining offensive language and sexual and racial harassment, but in so doing tread a fine line between providing a comfortable learning atmosphere for all and infringing on free expression.

Private schools and universities are not covered by constitutional protections and thus have more leeway in placing restrictions on students. However, courts have protected students' rights to attend private or parochial schools, to be home-schooled subject to state regulations, or in certain instances even to drop out of school early for religious reasons. Some voucher programs allowing students to receive public funds for use at private or parochial schools have been upheld. Private schools and universities may be legally bound by what they promise students in their advertising or student handbooks that may be seen as contractual promises. Finally, federal funding for private universities may come with congressional stipulations protecting student rights.

For more information: Foundation for Individual Rights in Education. FIRE's *Guides* to Student Rights on Campus. Available online. URL: http://www.thefire.org. Downloaded May 15, 2008; Johnson, John W. *The Struggle for Student Rights.* Lawrence: University of Kansas Press, 1997; Raskin, Jamin B. *We the Students: Supreme Court Cases for and about Students.* 2d ed. Washington, D.C.: CQ Press, 2003.

—Jane G. Rainey

substantive due process

Substantive DUE PROCESS is a constitutional doctrine that extends the Supreme Court's role beyond that of providing due process protection as a procedural guarantee, to enabling the Court to review the substance of legislation to determine whether the law itself, and not just the procedures followed in its enactment and enforcement, are constitutional. The significance of extending the concept of due process protection to the substance of enacted legislation is that it enables the Supreme Court to become a virtually equal partner with the legislative and executive branches in public policy making.

The Fifth Amendment to the United States Constitution protects the right of individuals not to be deprived of life, liberty, or property without due process. For the first hundred years of the United States, the protection offered by the Supreme Court under the due process clause amounted to fair notice and hearing only. Challenges to government action as an infringement of due process that the Supreme Court was willing to entertain were limited to charges that proper legislative procedures had not been followed, enacted legislation had not been properly promulgated (made public), or those charged with a breach of the legislation had not been given a fair

hearing to plead their case. In 1868, the FOURTEENTH AMENDMENT was added to the Constitution, requiring the states to provide the same due process protections imposed on the federal government under the Fifth Amendment.

In the aftermath of the Civil War, populist (and later progressive) politics swept the country, challenging state and local governments to regulate business more aggressively. Out of this movement came state consumer and labor protective measures that made businesses chafe at the limits placed on their freedom to do business as they chose. Consequently, businesses felt the need for a constitutional conceptual framework through which they could get the courts to take on the role of examining the substance of legislation to determine its constitutionality as a check on regulation of business by elected legislatures. Substantive due process is the conceptual framework conceived by big business attorneys to further this end. This CONSTITUTIONAL INTERPRETATION of due process calls on courts to review the substance of legislation to determine if an act amounts to an unconstitutional invasion of businesses' liberty under the Fifth and Fourteenth Amendments and, thus, should be struck down.

Although originally resistant to this expanded conception of due process, by the 1880s the Supreme Court had embraced this interpretation and used it to strike down numerous state statutes regulating business. Giving credence to substantive due process as a legitimate interpretation of the Fifth and Fourteenth Amendments put the unelected courts in the position of second-guessing legislative action by elected representatives and called into question government's previous and broadly recognized authority to impose regulations on the private sector. With the institution of substantive due process as a constitutional norm, the Supreme Court no longer considered itself blind to the outcomes of the legislative process.

By the 1930s, with the election of Franklin D. Roosevelt and his "New Deal," the Supreme Court's almost exclusive protection of business interests against those of the worker and consumer came to be widely unpopular. Faced with threats to its authority from both the executive and legislative branches, in 1937 in the case of *West Coast Hotel v. Parrish* (300 U.S. 379, 57 S. Ct. 578 [1937]), the Supreme Court repudiated the use of substantive due process in behalf of powerful economic interests but reserved its use for the protection of the rights of DISCRETE AND INSULAR MINORITIES.

Substantive due process remains a powerful tool of the Supreme Court in its exercise of JUDICIAL REVIEW of legislation, securing the Court's continuing influence on American politics and public policy formation.

For more information: Corwin, Edwin S. *The Higher Law Background of American Constitutional Law.* Ithaca, N.Y.: Cornell University Press, 1955; O'Brien, David M. *Storm Center: The Supreme Court in American Politics.* 7th ed. New York: W.W. Norton, 2005.

—Phyllis Farley Rippey

supremacy clause

The supremacy clause is found in Article VI of the United States Constitution.

Under the supremacy clause, the Constitution, federal laws, and U.S. treaties are the "supreme law of the land," and state judges are bound to uphold the Constitution and laws made pursuant to it even if they conflict with state laws or the state constitution.

The supremacy clause was at the center of some of the most divisive debates in the early Republic. At issue was the question of who would have the final say as to whether a federal or state law was made in pursuance of the Constitution and, therefore, entitled to supremacy protection: the federal government or the states. During the ratification debates, critics of the Constitution feared that without a BILL OF RIGHTS, the supremacy clause would result in the destruction of the states. ARTICLE I, Section 8 of the Constitution gave Congress the power to "make all Laws which shall be necessary and proper for carrying into Execution" its powers, and the states feared that Congress would use the supremacy clause and the NECESSARY AND PROPER CLAUSE to justify any federal law as supreme over the states.

Another point of contention related to the supremacy clause was: Who would decide if a state or federal law, made in pursuance of the Constitution, would be afforded supremacy status? In *Marbury v. Madison,* 1 Cranch (5 U.S.) 137 (1803), Chief Justice JOHN MARSHALL placed this prerogative in the Supreme Court by invoking the clause to strike down Section 13 of the JUDICIARY ACT OF 1789 (a federal law), which ordered the Court to issue writs of mandamus. Marshall famously wrote, "it is emphatically the province and the duty of the judicial department to say what the law is." If a law violated the Constitution (the Supreme Law), the Court was obliged to strike it down.

The MARSHALL COURT also invoked the supremacy clause to enhance national supremacy with respect to the states. In *McCulloch v. Maryland,* 4 Wheaton 316 (1819), the Court ruled that a state tax on the Bank of the United States violated the supremacy clause. Writing for the Court, Chief Justice John Marshall argued that all laws made in pursuance of the Constitution—in this case, the Bank—were supreme, and therefore laws repugnant to the Constitution—Maryland's tax on non-state banks—violated the supremacy clause and as such were null and void. Similarly, in *Gibbons v. Ogden,* 9 Wheaton (U.S.) 1 (1824), the Court found that the New York state law giving a monopoly on steamship travel in New York was an interference with INTERSTATE COMMERCE. The Court invoked the supremacy clause and made it clear that a state law that was contrary to the Constitution, or laws of Congress made in pursuance of the Constitution, was void. In *Worcester v. Georgia,* 31 U.S. 515 (1832), Marshall struck down all Georgia laws governing the Cherokee Indians on the grounds that the laws violated the federal laws and treaties in place at the time.

The Supreme Court also clashed with state courts over the supremacy clause. At issue was the role, if any, of state judges in interpreting and enforcing the Constitution. In *Martin v. Hunter's Lessee,* 14 U.S. 304 (1816), and *Cohens v. Virginia,* 19 U.S. 264 (1821), the Court answered that question in the negative. Accordingly, the supremacy clause was, as Marshall noted in *Cohens,* the "authoritative language of the American people" and any attempt by state court jurists to interpret the Constitution or federal laws was subject to review by the federal judiciary.

As the nation edged toward civil war, the Court continued to clash with state courts over the Constitution. In a series of cases involving state-imposed taxes on state-chartered banks—cases that focused primarily on whether these taxes violated the Constitution's ban on the impairment of contracts (the CONTRACT CLAUSE)—the Court used the supremacy clause to its advantage. In *Dodge v. Woolsey,* 59 U.S. 331 (1855)—a case where the Court ruled that an Ohio tax on the state bank violated the contract clause—the Court argued that the supremacy of the Constitution could be maintained only if there was one final and authoritative interpreter of constitutional conflicts between the states and the federal government. Indeed, the supremacy clause would be "useless" if state court judges had the final say over the Constitution and laws enacted pursuant to it.

For more information: Bailyn, Bernard, ed. *The Debate on the Constitution: Federalist and Anti-federalist Speeches, Articles, and Letters during the Struggle over Ratification.* New York: Literary Classics of the United States, 1993; Rakove, Jack. *Original Meanings: Politics and Ideas in the Making of the Constitution.* New York: Alfred A. Knopf, 1997.

—Randa Issa

Swann v. Charlotte-Mecklenburg Board of Education 402 U.S. 1 (1971)

In *Swann v. Charlotte-Mecklenburg Board of Education,* the Supreme Court ruled that busing was a reasonable method of achieving racial integration in schools. *Swann* is significant because it signified that the Supreme Court would not allow school districts to put off integration any longer. It also permitted the use of a controversial remedy.

The *Swann* case is one of a long line of court cases about school DESEGREGATION. The first major case, BROWN V. BOARD OF EDUCATION OF TOPEKA, KANSAS, 347 U.S. 483 (1954), ruled that segregated schools violated the EQUAL PROTECTION clause of the FOURTEENTH AMENDMENT. The Supreme Court ruled in GREEN V. COUNTY SCHOOL BOARD OF NEW KENT COUNTY, VIRGINIA, 391 U.S. 430 (1968), that school districts must take AFFIRMATIVE ACTION to integrate their schools.

In *Swann,* the affirmative action taken by the district court that oversaw Charlotte-Mecklenburg's desegregation plan was to bus students to schools that would be racially integrated. The school district challenged this remedy, but the Supreme Court upheld it. In his opinion for the unanimous court, Chief Justice WARREN BURGER first established that the federal court system did have a right to oversee desegregation in schools.

The primary section of the opinion was broken into four parts. First, Burger argued that the Constitution does not permit a strict RACIAL QUOTA. However, he upheld the district court's use of quotas as a starting point, because the lower court had acknowledged that quotas must be flexible.

Second, Burger maintained that a district with a small number of one-race schools (or schools that were very near to being one-race) was not necessarily in violation of the Constitution. However, he also said that those schools should come under STRICT SCRUTINY to determine whether or not they were related to previous state-supported dual school systems.

Third, Burger argued that district courts may alter attendance zones as a means to achieve desegregation. He reiterated the *Green* argument that a simple race-neutral attendance policy, if it did not achieve integration, was not enough to comply with *Brown.* Instead, a district court may use grouping or pairing of noncontiguous attendance zones in order to achieve integration.

Finally, Burger addressed the use of busing for integration. Because assigning children to their neighborhood schools would not create integration, Burger argued that the district court had the power to approve a plan that assigned children farther away. He did acknowledge that there were limits to the use of busing; for example, he said there may be a legitimate objection when children were assigned to bus rides so long that their health and safety might be threatened, or when a long bus ride infringed upon the educational process.

Ultimately, *Swann* is most well known for the Supreme Court's approval of the use of busing to create integrated schools. *Swann* did not say that busing must be used, only that it may be used.

For more information: Hochschild, Jennifer. *The New American Dilemma: Liberal Democracy and School Desegregation.* New Haven, Conn.: Yale University Press. 1984; Orfield, Gary. *Must We Bus?: Segregated Schools and National Policy.* Washington, D.C.: The Brookings Institution, 1978.

—Ryane McAuliffe Straus

Swift & Co. v. United States 196 U.S. 375 (1905)

In *Swift & Co. v. United States,* the Supreme Court upheld an INJUNCTION against the so-called Beef Trust in a major federal prosecution under the Sherman Antitrust Act of 1890. The *Swift* Court distanced itself from earlier Court decisions that had severely limited the applicability of the act, and in so doing helped expand not only federal antitrust enforcement, but also Congress's power under the COMMERCE CLAUSE of the Constitution.

The massive expansion of American industry in the late 1800s was accompanied by the emergence of "trusts"—combinations of companies that attempted to gain monopolistic control of an industry, often through unscrupulous tactics. As trusts began to threaten vital sectors of the economy, Congress sought to intervene. But legislators were unsure whether they had constitutional authority to address the problem: Although ARTICLE I gives Congress the power to regulate INTERSTATE COMMERCE, lawmakers had never before attempted to use this authority to meddle with the national economy. In spite of this uncertainty, Congress in 1890 passed the Sherman Act, which purported to ban many forms of anticompetitive behavior. It would be up to the courts to decide how far the act could go toward breaking up the trusts.

In its first encounter with the Sherman Act, the Supreme Court gave it a restrictive scope. UNITED STATES V. E.C. KNIGHT CO., 156 U.S. 1 (1895), held that the act could not be used to prevent a merger between companies engaged in sugar refining because production and manufacturing activities were inherently local and not a part of interstate commerce. This ruling chilled federal antitrust efforts until President Theodore Roosevelt took office in 1901 and attacked the trusts with renewed vigor.

The *Swift* case itself dealt with the federal government's attempt to break up the Beef Trust, a cartel of meatpacking companies that together accounted for nearly 60 percent of the national market in fresh meat. The companies had agreed to fix their prices and to avoid bidding against each other, and had jointly negotiated for illegally low shipping rates with railroad companies. When the *New York Herald* and *Chicago Tribune* brought these arrangements to light in 1902, Roosevelt instructed the Justice Department to bring suit under the Sherman Act. The firms, relying in part on the *E.C. Knight* decision, argued that the business practices at issue were purely local and thus beyond the reach of federal prosecution.

Four new justices had joined the Supreme Court since *E.C. Knight,* however, and the Court ruled unanimously in favor of the federal government. Justice OLIVER WENDELL HOLMES's opinion declared that, although the specific transactions between the companies were indeed *intra*state, they were nonetheless a part of a "current" or "stream" of commerce that was irrefutably *inter*state in character. Moreover, their effect on interstate commerce was "direct" and "not accidental, secondary, remote, or merely probable." Holmes's stream-of-commerce theory would later be employed by the Court to permit expansion of both the U.S. enforcement power in antitrust cases specifically, and Congress's power under the commerce clause more generally.

For more information: Gordon, David. "*Swift & Co. v. United States:* The Beef Trust and the Stream of Commerce Doctrine," *American*

Journal of Legal History 28, no. 3 (July 1984): 244–279.

—Bruce Huber

symbolic speech

Symbolic speech is conduct or activity expressing an idea or emotion without the use of words or language. Some forms of speech are protected under the FIRST AMENDMENT to the U.S. Constitution.

Although the description of symbolic speech seems apparent, there is a difficulty that arises between speech and action. There is an inherent relationship between speech and nonspeech communication in certain contexts, and when these elements are simultaneous in occurrence, government regulation of the nonspeech component might be justified even if it infringed on speech to some extent. So, many forms of symbolic speech and expression are protected by the First Amendment and the free speech clause, while others are not protected. Over time, the Court has developed several rules that depend upon certain circumstances and factors to evaluate what symbolic speech is protected.

Examination of *Chaplinsky v. State of New Hampshire,* 315 U.S. 568 (1942), provides an explanation for a freedom of speech violation. This case discusses the First Amendment and asks what constitutes free speech. Justice Murphy, joined by unanimous consent, concluded that Chaplinsky's use of "fighting words . . . tend to incite an immediate breach of the peace." The Court held that Chaplinsky's conduct was not protected by the First Amendment under the free speech clause. In this case, Chaplinsky was arrested for verbally assaulting a police officer.

Later, in *UNITED STATES V. O'BRIEN,* 391 U.S. 267 (1968), the 7-1 vote was led by Justice Warren and concurred in by Justice JOHN HARLAN, who indicated that the mutilation of a Selective Service certificate was unconstitutional and subject to punishment because this system ensures the proper functioning of the United States military draft. Justice WILLIAM O. DOUGLAS dissented, and Justice Marshall did not participate in the decision of this case.

TEXAS V. JOHNSON, 491 U.S. 397 (1989), further examined the First Amendment's free speech clause by ruling on flag desecration. In a 5-4 decision, Justice WILLIAM J. BRENNAN, JR., joined by Justice ANTHONY M. KENNEDY's concurrence, ruled that Johnson's expressive conduct had a political nature and this category is protected under the First Amendment.

Resulting from these rulings, a series of tests have been established that provide for the categorization of conduct as protected expression or symbolic speech. These tests are known as the STRICT SCRUTINY test and the O'Brien (intermediate scrutiny) test.

These tests should be understood in the broader jurisprudence of the Court, and with respect to the REHNQUIST and ROBERTS COURTS, jurisprudence regarding symbolic speech has been conservatively expressed within the prior free speech regime and with general support for precedent.

For more information: Anastaplo, George. *Reflections on Constitutional Law.* Lexington: University Press of Kentucky, 2006; Shapiro, Martin, and Rocco Tresolini. *American Constitutional Law.* New York: Macmillan, 1983.

—Michael W. Hail and Erica Allen

Taft Court (1921–1930)

The Taft Court refers to the Supreme Court era under the chief justiceship of William Howard Taft. It was during this era that the Court confronted many constitutional issues arising out of the Progressive Era.

William Howard Taft, born September 15, 1857, in Cincinnati, Ohio, held a number of positions during his career and in service to his country prior to fulfilling his lifelong ambition to become chief justice of the Supreme Court. It was his upbringing as the son of a lawyer and judge (Alphonso Taft), who as a prominent Republican served as secretary of war under President Ulysses S. Grant, along with Taft's own career progression starting with his appointment as assistant prosecutor of Hamilton County in Ohio, that led him to his post as chief justice. In addition to his first appointment as assistant prosecutor, Taft was also appointed local collector of internal revenue in 1882. Five years later saw his further progression and appointment as a judge to the Ohio Superior Court, where he sat until 1890, when President Benjamin Harrison appointed Taft as solicitor general of the United States. Two years later President Harrison appointed Taft as an associate judge for the newly created U.S. Court of Appeals for the Sixth Circuit. He became chief judge and held a post within the Sixth Circuit until 1900. While serving in this post, Taft also earned a doctor of laws degree from Yale Law School.

It was perhaps through his work and association with various presidents that Taft rose to prominence with appointments such as chief civil administrator to the Philippines, by President McKinley, in 1900. Later he served as governor-general of the Philippines from 1901 to 1903, before himself serving as President Roosevelt's secretary of war in 1904. It was because of his strong beliefs and work ethic that Roosevelt began to plan for Taft to succeed him as the Republican presidential candidate in 1908. Taft ran and won the presidency in 1908, despite the fact that he would have preferred a post as Supreme Court chief justice instead.

As president, Taft's style of governing differed dramatically from that of his predecessor and mentor. Most significantly, Taft believed in the use of law and working within its confines, rather than stretching presidential powers as Roosevelt had.

During his presidency, Taft's accomplishments included: the establishment of a parcel post system, expansion of the civil service, strengthening of the INTERSTATE COMMERCE COMMISSION, the signing into law of *The Organic Act of the Department of Labor*—thereby creating the U.S. Department of Labor—and promoting the enactment of two constitutional amendments in the form of the SIXTEENTH AMENDMENT, regarding income tax, and the SEVENTEENTH AMENDMENT, mandating the direct election of senators by the people. In addition to these, he pursued what he termed "dollar diplomacy" to further economic development of less-developed nations, as well as using the opportunity to appoint six justices to the Supreme Court.

Following his reelection defeat in 1913, Taft went on to serve as Kent Professor of Constitutional Law at Yale Law School and as president of the American Bar Association. It was in 1921, with the death of Chief Justice Edward Douglas White, that President Harding presented Taft with his lifelong ambition, nominating Taft to the post of chief justice. Taft's nomination lacked any opposition and was unanimously confirmed by the SENATE. While chief justice of the U.S. Supreme Court, Taft wrote the opinion in over 250 cases—utilizing a strict constructivist approach to CONSTITUTIONAL INTERPRETATION that was historically and contextually based.

Of particular note during his time as chief justice, the Court examined the question of whether the FIRST AMENDMENT prosecution and protections extended to states, and not only to the federal government. In two particular cases, the Court decided that the First Amendment did in fact extend the rights of states to prosecute individuals inciting violence against the U.S. government and also extended the protection of individual rights by states, according to the BILL OF RIGHTS. Prior to these decisions, fewer rights were conferred by states to individuals than were protected under the Bill of Rights. Therefore, through their decisions, the Taft Court highlighted the states' obligations to ensure protection of individual rights under the First Amendment. The *GITLOW V. NEW YORK*, 268 U.S. 652 (1925), case provided the benchmark for future decisions that were to strike down state laws that violated individual rights protected under the First Amendment. Later cases, such as *Fiske v. Kansas*, 274 U.S. 380 (1927), solidified that position and upheld the INCORPORATION doctrine (which holds that selected provisions of the Bill of Rights are applicable to states through the DUE PROCESS clause of the FOURTEENTH AMENDMENT) as undertaken in *Gitlow*. Other opinions of note written by Taft during his tenure as chief justice include: *BAILEY V. DREXEL FURNITURE CO.*, 259 U.S. 20 (1922), whereby the 1919 Child Labor Tax Law was held unconstitutional; *MYERS V. UNITED STATES*, 272 U.S. 52 (1926), providing the president of the United States with the power to unilaterally dismiss executive appointees who had been confirmed by the Senate; and *OLMSTEAD V. UNITED STATES*, 277 U.S. 438 (1928), the majority ruling delivering the opinion that the Fourteenth Amendment's proscription on unreasonable search and seizures did not cover wiretaps.

Prior to his retirement in 1930, Taft successfully argued for the construction of the Supreme Court building on the basis that, as part of a separate branch of government, the Court needed to distance itself from Congress, and thereby needed its own facilities rather than chambers located within the basement of the Capitol building. Taft, however, was not to witness the building's completion in 1935.

Taft retired on February 3, 1930, as chief justice due to ill health. He was succeeded as chief justice by Charles Evans Hughes, whom Taft himself had appointed to the U.S. Supreme Court during his tenure as president. Taft died a little over a month after his retirement from the Court, on March 8, 1930, due to heart failure. As of 2006, he remains the only person to have held positions in both the executive and judicial branches of the United States government, as well as the honor of leading both branches during his tenure in each.

For more information: Pringle, Henry F. *The Life and Times of William Howard Taft.* New York: Farrar & Reinhart, 1939; The Supreme Court History. "Taft Court (1921–1930)." Available online. URL: http://www.supremecourthistory.org/02_history/subs_history/02_c10.html. Accessed May 15, 2008; Taft, William Howard. *The Collected Works of William Howard Taft.* Edited by David H. Burton. Athens, Ohio: Ohio University Press, 2001 (6 of 8 volumes have been published); "Biography of William Howard Taft." Available online. URL: www.whitehouse.gov/history/presidents/wt27.html. Accessed May 15, 2008.

—Dale Mineshima-Lowe

takings clause

The takings clause of the Fifth Amendment provides government—both national and state—with the power to take private property under the concept of EMINENT DOMAIN, even if the owner does not consent. The takings clause reads, "nor shall private property be taken for public use, without JUST COMPENSATION." This provision of the U.S. Constitution is intended both to empower government—by allowing government to take property—and to protect property owners from government abuse through the requirements that takings are limited to public uses and that the owner receive just compensation.

When drafted and ratified, the takings clause was a largely uncontroversial compromise between the conflicting values of protecting private property rights and the expressed need for a vigorous national government. During the Revolutionary period and beyond, Americans increasingly defined economic liberty as a central value. English common law, transferred to the American colonies, allowed government to take land as long as compensation was paid and government had a public purpose for the taking. But these concepts were ignored at times. In some colonies, unimproved land required no compensation at all. Similarly, the idea of public purpose could be defined broadly. It was not unusual for states to permit eminent domain proceedings that allowed land to be taken by private enterprises in order to encourage the growth of local industries as well as privately owned highways or other infrastructure improvements. By the time of the Revolution, these practices were in decline, and the constitutions of Vermont and Massachusetts included takings provisions that explicitly limited government power. Other states, including Virginia, wrote the common law limits on takings into state laws. Many leading Americans of the founding period saw the need for economic growth and believed that the power of eminent domain was a powerful tool to encourage such growth.

During the early history of the Republic, the takings clause of the Fifth Amendment applied only to the national government. This position was upheld by the Supreme Court in the 1833 decision, BARRON V. MAYOR AND CITY COUNCIL OF BALTIMORE (32 U.S. 243). Except for cases where the federal government was taking land, *Barron* left landowners subject to the various provisions of state law. The original states, as they revised their state constitutions, and new states, as they entered the Union, typically included takings provisions. But the states, wanting to encourage economic development while being short of funds, often took narrow interpretations of these provisions. In *Chicago, Burlington, and Quincy Railroad Company v. Chicago,* 166 U.S. 226 (1897), the Court changed its mind on the application of the takings clause to the states. The Court reasoned that the DUE PROCESS clause of the FOURTEENTH AMENDMENT, ratified in 1868, included a protection against uncompensated takings.

With the power—and the protections—of eminent domain well established, the interpretation of the takings clause has centered on three questions in the 20th and 21st centuries: What is a taking? What is public use? What is just compensation? The last question is the most easily explained. Generally, when government wishes to acquire property from a private owner, government officials negotiate a price with the property owner. If a price is not agreed upon, government officials can assert the power of eminent domain and make what it believes is a fair market value offer. Property owners may go to court and challenge the government's offer. A judge will decide on what compensation—price—is due the property owner. However, the property owner cannot challenge the taking of the property.

The answers to the two remaining questions were clear for much of the 20th century, but have been the subject of controversy over the last quarter-century. In answer to the question of what is a taking, the courts have ruled that physical invasions of property are a taking whether government wishes to acquire the private property for a valid purpose, such as land to build a new school, or invades it in some other way, such as flooding the property as part of a flood control project. Invasions need not be total, nor physical, to be a taking. For example, in *United States v. Causby,* 328 U.S. 256 (1946), the Supreme Court found that when a new military air base had created so much noise that it made an adjacent and existing chicken farm worthless, the federal government was required to pay compensation in the same way that would be required were the invasion physical.

The Supreme Court has also recognized that there are limits to government's power to regulate property, while giving government wide discretion to regulate. Federal, state, and local governments widely regulate land use for a variety of reasons, including zoning, historic preservation, and environmental protection. As Justice OLIVER

WENDELL HOLMES stated in the rule still followed today, in *Pennsylvania v. Mahon,* 260 U.S. 393 (1922), "while property may be regulated to a certain extent, if regulation goes too far it will be recognized as a taking." Since 1987, the Supreme Court has been more sympathetic to claims of landowners who argue that government regulation has gone "too far." In one leading case, *Lucas v. South Carolina Coastal Council,* 505 U.S. 1003 (1992), the Supreme Court held that regulations that precluded a beachfront property owner from building a home on the property because of concerns about beach erosion were a taking. The opinion by Justice ANTONIN GREGORY SCALIA was limited to situations where regulation eliminates the total value of the property. In other recent decisions, the Court has found that even temporary total takings require compensation, as do total takings of portions of property. While the Court has been asked on numerous occasions to find that the taking that diminishes only part of the value of property is a taking, it has not done so.

With the 2005 Supreme Court's decision in *KELO V. CITY OF NEW LONDON,* 545 U.S. 469 (2005), the question of what is public use has been in the news. In *Kelo,* the Court found that state and local governments may use their eminent domain power to transfer property from one private owner to another. The decision, built on a 1954 case, *Berman v. Parker,* 346 U.S. 26 (1954), authorized the federal government to do the same. Susette Kelo was one of many homeowners whose land was taken to clear the way for a large-scale development intended to buoy the economy of depressed New London, Connecticut. The public outcry at this decision was unusual in size and scope. Editorial pages criticized the decision, and polling showed widespread opposition to the ruling. In his opinion of the Court, Justice JOHN PAUL STEVENS noted that "nothing in our opinion precludes any State from placing further restrictions on its exercise of the takings power." Since the decision in June 2005, 34 states have enacted laws limiting the use of eminent domain power. In addition, President George W. Bush signed an executive order, on the one-year anniversary of the *Kelo* decision, limiting the federal use of the eminent domain power.

For more information: Schultz, David. *Property, Power, and American Democracy.* New Brunswick, N.J.: Transaction, 1992.
—William R. Wilkerson

Taney, Roger (1777–1864) *Supreme Court justice*

Roger Brooke Taney was the chief justice of the United States Supreme Court for the 28-year period between 1836 and 1864. He was the 25th justice and the fifth chief justice to serve on the Court.

Taney was born in Calvert County, Maryland, where his parents owned a tobacco plantation. Taney was educated at Dickinson College in Pennsylvania. After graduating in 1795, Taney then read law for approximately two years under the supervision of Jeremiah Chase, a Maryland lawyer. Taney's political career began in state politics. In 1816 he was elected as a Federalist to the Maryland state senate. He would serve as state attorney general before moving to national politics during the presidency of Andrew Jackson. Between 1831 and 1834, Taney held positions as attorney general, acting secretary of war, and, finally, as secretary of the treasury.

Taney was first nominated to the Supreme Court in 1835, as a replacement to Justice Duvall. The SENATE, in opposition to Taney's nomination, indefinitely postponed the confirmation vote. Just one year later, President Jackson again nominated Taney, this time to fill the position of chief justice, which had been vacated by JOHN MARSHALL. In March 1836, the Senate confirmed Taney by a vote of 29 to 15.

Once on the Court, Taney's efforts were directed primarily toward refining the expansive legal policy of his predecessor, Chief Justice John Marshall. Marshall's legal legacy had left a series of opinions that vastly expanded the power of the federal government. *MARBURY V. MADISON,* 5 U.S. 137 (1803), for example, created JUDICIAL REVIEW, which is the power of the judiciary to assess the constitutionality of laws passed by Congress. Taney sought not to dismantle national power, but rather to strike a crucial balance between state and federal power.

One example of Taney's effort to find this balance is a series of decisions known collectively as the *License Cases*, 46 U.S. 504 (1847). At issue in these cases was whether anti-liquor regulations passed by Massachusetts, New Hampshire, and Rhode Island violated the Constitution. Merchants and others against the regulations argued that only Congress could regulate commerce. Taney's opinion rebuked that position, arguing that the states may regulate their own internal affairs. So long as the states did not ban the importation of liquor, the regulation of it through taxes was permissible.

Regardless of his contribution to the continually developing state–federal power debate, Taney's greatest historical legacy will be his involvement in the Court's 1857 decision in *Dred Scott v. Sandford* (60 U.S. 393), which is generally acknowledged as the most infamous and ill-regarded decision in the history of the Supreme Court. In *Dred Scott,* Chief Justice Taney wrote a broad opinion holding that the prohibition of slavery in a U.S. territory violated the DUE PROCESS rights of slaveholders. Most notoriously, Taney went on to argue that no one who was an African descendant could ever obtain citizenship in the United States.

The impact of *Dred Scott* was wide and severe. The Court decision was one of the reasons for the resignation of Justice Curtis later that same year. While Taney had hoped the decision would prevent conflict between North and South, it served only to embolden the opponents of slavery. At the same time, the decision brought on tremendous criticism of the Court for delving into so-called political questions.

In 1864, after nearly 29 years as chief justice, Taney died in Washington, D.C. His length of time served makes him the second-longest serving chief justice in the history of the Supreme Court (second only to John Marshall). Taney's position was filled by Chief Justice Salmon P. Chase.

For more information: Freedman, Suzanne. *Roger Taney: The Dred Scott Legacy.* Springfield, N.J.: Enslow Publishers, 1995; Siegel, Martin. *The Supreme Court in American Life.* Vol. 3, *The Taney Court: 1836–1864.* Millwood, N.Y.: Associated Faculty Press, 1987.

—Ryan C. Black

Taney Court (1836–1864)

The Taney Court refers to the period when the U.S. Supreme Court was under the leadership of Chief Justice ROGER TANEY. Under Taney, the Supreme Court refined and developed many of the legal doctrines first articulated under his predecessor, Chief Justice JOHN MARSHALL, especially in the direction of moving away from some of the nationalistic ideas that had supported federal over state power. Instead of thinking of the Taney Court as reversing MARSHALL COURT doctrines, it is more accurate to see it as having rethought them to accommodate states' rights. Yet, whatever legal legacy the Taney Court left on the Constitution, the issue of slavery and the Civil War overshadowed everything it did.

Most accounts or assessments of the Taney Court are made in terms of its comparison to the Supreme Court under Chief Justice John Marshall. The Marshall Court generally represented a judicial and political philosophy of the Federalist political party. It was a philosophy that supported a strong national government in comparison to states, and it generally favored property rights over government power. In cases such as *GIBBONS v. OGDEN*, 22 U.S. 1 (1824), involving the COMMERCE CLAUSE; *DARTMOUTH COLLEGE v. WOODWARD*, 17 U.S. 518 (1819), with the CONTRACT CLAUSE; and *McCulloch v. Maryland*, 17 U.S. 316 (1819), upholding the power of the national government to create a national bank immune from state taxation, the Marshall Court demonstrated its commitment to this nationalistic philosophy.

But if the Marshall Court represented the views of the Federalists, the Taney Court reflected the views of President Andrew Jackson and his populist Democratic Party values. This would be a judicial philosophy more supportive of state interests, property rights, and the interests of corporations than the Marshall Court.

Serving originally in Andrew Jackson's cabinet as secretary of the treasury and attorney general,

Roger Taney was appointed by the president in 1836 to replace John Marshall upon Marshall's death. While Federalists had hoped that President Jackson would elevate JOSEPH STORY from the Marshall Court to become the chief, there was little chance that this would occur. Story, one of the staunch Federalists from the Marshall era, would increasingly find himself in dissent on the Taney Court. As President Jackson and subsequent presidents had the opportunity to replace the Marshall Court justices, the composition turned from Federalists to Democrats, who dominated the Taney Court and brought with them a different approach to interpreting the Constitution. At Taney's arrival on the Court, several Federalist and traditionalist justices from the Marshall Court, such as Joseph Story and Smith Thompson, remained on the bench, with the former serving as chief rival to Taney for influence in the early years of the chief justice's tenure.

However, prior to President Jackson appointing Taney, he had the opportunity to replace several of the Marshall Court justices. In 1829 he nominated John McLean to replace Justice Robert Timble, and in 1830 Jackson replaced the deceased Bushrod Washington with Henry Baldwin. Five years later, in 1835, James Wayne was picked by President Jackson to replace Wayne Johnson, who had died in 1834, and when Gabriel Duval died in 1835, Philip Barbour was picked to replace him. Thus, by the time Taney actually began work as chief justice in 1837, Jackson had been able to nominate four associate justices. Add these four to Taney, and the president had placed a total of five of his people on a Supreme Court that at the time was composed of seven justices. Thus, Jackson was able to use his appointment power effectively to place five individuals on the bench who would presumably be more sympathetic to his views than those on the Marshall Court. Specifically, President Jackson was no friend of the national bank, and it was Taney, while serving as treasury secretary, who withdrew the federal government's deposits from it.

After Jackson left office, Congress passed the Judiciary Act of 1837, which increased the number of justices on the Supreme Court from seven

to nine. This gave President Martin Van Buren—Jackson's former vice president—the chance to place more Democrats on the Court. His selections were John Catron and John McKinley. In 1841, Van Buren would nominate Peter Daniel to replace Justice Barbour, who had died. Other Democratic Party presidents had the opportunity to leave their imprint on the Court with their appointments. Overall, except for Benjamin Curtis, a Whig who was selected by President Millard Fillmore in 1851, justices appointed by Democratic presidents dominated the Court until President ABRAHAM LINCOLN took office in 1861 and was able to pick three justices for the Court while Taney was still chief justice. Upon Taney's death in 1864, Lincoln selected Salmon Chase to replace him.

In looking at the major decisions dominating the Taney Court, it was states' rights, property rights, corporate power, slavery, and the Civil War that dominated the agenda. In *Charles River Bridge v. Warren Bridge*, 36 U.S. 420 (1837), the Taney Court began to narrow the use of the contract clause as a limit upon state power and as a tool to defend property rights. In this case, the Massachusetts legislature had granted a 40-year charter to the Charles River Bridge in 1785 to build a toll bridge in Boston. Later, the charter was extended for another 30 years. In 1828, the legislature chartered the Warren River Bridge to be built not far from the Charles River Bridge. Taking the Marshall-era *Dartmouth College* decision as its cue, the latter sued under the contract clause, claiming that the new charter had breached its contract. The Taney Court disagreed. It ruled that, since nothing in the original Charles River Bridge charter precluded the legislature from authorizing another bridge, there was no violation of the contract clause. *Charles River Bridge* served to signal that states' and property rights were about to change under the new chief justice.

Several other cases also signaled victories for states at the expense of private property and corporations. In *Briscoe v. Commonwealth Bank of Kentucky*, 36 U.S. 257 (1837), the Court ruled that the ARTICLE I, Section 10 prohibition against states coining money did not prohibit state-owned banks from issuing notes. This appeared to reverse the Marshall Court decision of *Craig v. Missouri*, 29 U.S. 410 (1830), which used this constitutional clause to bar states from issuing paper money. In *New York v. Miln*, 36 U.S. 102 (1837), the Court distinguished federal commerce power from the residual powers states retained under their inherent sovereignty. In *Miln*, the Court indicated that states retain the police authority to legislate for the health, safety, welfare, and morals of their citizens. Similar sentiments were expressed in the *License Cases*, 46 U.S. 504 (1847), three cases that put at issue the scope of state power to regulate alcohol. The Court upheld state regulations in all three cases. *Miln* and the *License Cases* tested the limits of *Gibbons v. Ogden* and whether the expansive scope of the federal commerce clause precluded the states from ever acting in areas that might affect INTERSTATE COMMERCE. These decisions suggested that the Taney Court might reverse *Gibbons*, or perhaps narrow its scope.

However, in COOLEY V. BOARD OF WARDENS OF THE PORT OF PHILADELPHIA, 53 U.S. 299 (1852), written by Justice Curtis, the Taney Court issued arguably one of its most important opinions. At issue here was whether a state could regulate the local navigable waters of one of its ports. Justice Curtis said yes in a strong affirmation of state authority. States would not run afoul of the commerce clause if they engaged in regulation of local matters of commerce that did not demand national uniformity. In describing what has become known as the doctrine of selective exclusiveness, the commerce clause grants the federal government authority to regulate national matters demanding uniform legislation, while at the same time reserving for states, under the POLICE POWER, authority to regulate so long as they address local needs that do not conflict with national priorities. In *Cooley*, the Court managed both to defend strong federal commerce power and have room open for state regulation.

While the Taney Court is known for its defense of state power, it also issued important decisions limiting property and corporate interests. *Charles River Bridge* limited the use of the contract clause as a tool to check state authority over property interests and corporations. In *West River Bridge*

v. Dix, 47 U.S. 507 (1848), the state use of EMINENT DOMAIN to condemn and take for public use a bridge and its franchise was upheld over claims that the action violated the contract clause. This decision was a defeat for property rights and private corporations. In *Ohio Life Insurance and Trust Company v. DeBoalt*, 57 U.S. 416 (1854), the Taney Court again rejected contract clause arguments that a state tax on chartered banks was unconstitutional.

In addition to cases that dealt with state versus federal power, the Taney Court issued important case decisions regarding federal judicial power. In LUTHER V. BORDEN, 48 U.S. 1 (1849), they ruled that the federal courts had no authority to hear disputes involving alleged violations of the GUARANTEE CLAUSE (Article IV, Section 4) of the Constitution. This clause guarantees to each state a "republican form of government." Here there was a dispute over which of two rival state governments in Rhode Island during the Dorr Rebellion was the legitimate government. Instead of addressing the question, the Court ruled that guarantee clause issues were "political questions" best handled by Congress. *Luther* thus enunciated what has come to be known as the political question doctrine, a theory of law that states that some constitutional matters are not for the Court to address. Besides *Luther*, in DRED SCOTT V. SANDFORD, 60 U.S. 393 (1857), the Supreme Court, for only the second time since MARBURY V. MADISON, 5 U.S. 137 (1803), used its power of JUDICIAL REVIEW to invalidate a federal law. In this case, it was the MISSOURI COMPROMISE.

While addressing the power of states, property, or corporations was important for the Taney Court, the issue of slavery and the Civil War would truly define its role in history. In *Prigg v. Pennsylvania*, 41 U.S. 539 (1842), the Court upheld the Fugitive Slave Act of 1783 and the use of the Fugitive Slave Clause of the Constitution (Article IV, Section 2) to strike down a state law that made it difficult for slave owners to recapture their runaway slaves. In *United States v. Amistad*, 40 U.S. 518 (1841), the Court upheld a lower court decision that returned a mutinous slave ship to Africa against the wishes of the slave owner. This decision, written by Justice Story, constituted one of the few victories for abolitionists.

However, there is no question that *Dred Scott v. Sandford* is the defining case for the Taney Court. Here, Dred Scott, a slave owned by his master, was taken north of the slave territory to Fort Snelling, Minnesota. This area was free according to the Missouri Compromise of 1820. Because he was now in free territory, Dred Scott sued for his freedom in federal court. In a contentious and split opinion, the Court refused to grant him his freedom. Writing for the Court, Taney indicated that it was clear from the original intent of the Constitution that African slaves could not be citizens, and therefore they did not have the right to sue for their freedom in federal court. Instead, they were the property of owners. Furthermore, because the Missouri Compromise appeared to take away a slave owners' property, it was a violation of the Fifth Amendment's TAKING CLAUSE. In effect, the Missouri Compromise was unconstitutional, and Congress lacked the power to prohibit slavery in the territories.

Dred Scott was a political bombshell. It upset a delicate compromise on slavery that Congress had effected, and it was a major setback to the abolitionist movement. Immediately, the decision was viewed as a political if not a legal disaster. Justice Curtis, who wrote a bitter dissent in the case, resigned soon after it was decided. Abraham Lincoln condemned it. *Dred Scott* was viewed then and now by historians as one of the final precipitating causes of the Civil War; once the North defeated the South, both the THIRTEENTH and FOURTEENTH AMENDMENTS were passed to overturn it.

Finally, once the Civil War began, the Taney Court was asked to decide several cases regarding the scope of presidential power. In the *Prize Cases*, 67 U.S. 635 (1863), the Court upheld Lincoln's order to blockade the South's ports, ruling that the president's power as COMMANDER IN CHIEF was broad enough to permit this action. However, the Taney Court came to an end before the Civil War ended. On October 12, 1864, Roger Taney died and was replaced by Chief Justice Chase two months later. Perhaps the best sign of how Taney was immediately viewed after his death came in 1865, when Congress refused to appropriate money for a bust of the former chief justice.

Roger Taney served nearly 28 years as chief justice, making it the second-longest term next to John Marshall. While many historians judge Taney as a great justice, *Dred Scott* will forever cast a shadow over him and his Court. It is perhaps appropriate to view the legacy of the Taney Court as one that transitioned the United States from the Federalist era of the 18th century to a country more reflective of the democratic and populist attitudes of the 19th century. It created many important legal doctrines regarding property rights, police power, judicial review, and state authority that remain good precedent and law even into the 21st century.

For more information: Huebner, Timothy S. *The Taney Court: Justices, Rulings and Legacy.* Santa Barbara, Calif.: ABC-CLIO, 2003; Rehnquist, William H. *The Supreme Court: How It Was, How It Is.* New York: Quill, 1987; Schwartz, Bernard. *A History of the Supreme Court.* New York: Oxford University Press, 1993.

—David Schultz

taxing and spending powers

ARTICLE I, Section 8 OF THE U.S. CONSTITUTION grants Congress the power to collect taxes and to spend money for the general welfare. Initially, the power to tax was controversial when Congress used it to impose a tax on incomes. In *POLLOCK V. FARMERS LOAN & TRUST CO.*, 158 U.S. 601 (1895), the Court found that a tax on income from property was an invalid direct tax, because it was not apportioned among the states. The SIXTEENTH AMENDMENT (1913) overruled *Pollock* by granting Congress the power to impose taxes on income from any source without having to comply with the apportionment requirement.

The taxing power was also controversial when Congress used it to regulate behavior, but the Court did uphold regulatory taxes, which had an independent source of constitutional authority. *McCray v. United States*, 195 U.S. 27 (1904), upheld a tax on oleomargarine, and *United States v. Doremus,* 249 U.S. 86 (1919), a federal tax on opium, because Congress had power to regulate INTERSTATE COMMERCE. In *BAILEY V. DREXEL FURNITURE CO.,* 259 U.S. 20 (1922), however, the Court struck down the Child Labor Tax Act of 1919, because the purpose of the tax was not to raise revenue but to penalize the employment of children, an exclusively state function under the Tenth Amendment, which the Court had used in *HAMMER V. DAGENHART,* 247 U.S. 251 (1918), to forbid congressional regulation of CHILD LABOR based on the COMMERCE CLAUSE.

The Court first addressed the spending clause in *United States v. Butler,* 297 U.S. 1 (1936), which involved the Agricultural Adjustment Act (AAA) of 1933. This major New Deal statute created a program to stabilize farm prices by imposing a processing tax on agricultural products and then spending the tax monies in the form of benefit payments to farmers who were required to take acreage out of production. The Court acknowledged that Congress could use its power to tax and spend for the general welfare, but it had no independent power to regulate agriculture, and the Tenth Amendment barred it from requiring farmers to enter into contracts to reduce acreage in exchange for benefit payments.

The Court abandoned its restrictive taxing and spending clause jurisprudence when its decisions striking down major New Deal programs provoked President Franklin Roosevelt's court-packing proposal. *Sonzinsky v. United States,* 300 U.S. 506 (1937), rejected the distinction between revenue and regulatory taxes and upheld a federal license tax on firearms dealers because the statute produced some income. Then two Social Security Act (1935) decisions substantially altered the meaning of the spending power.

Helvering v. Davis, 301 U.S. 619 (1937), upheld the expenditure of federal funds acquired from employer and employee taxes in order to provide retirement benefits, because it was a reasonable exercise of the power to spend for the general welfare. *Steward Machine v. Davis,* 301 U.S. 548 (1937), its companion case, went further by approving the statute's unemployment compensation provisions, which allowed employers to receive a federal unemployment tax credit for payments made to a state unemployment fund. The statute did not violate the spending power by requiring states to make payments to unemployed workers, nor did the Tenth Amendment bar the payments, because states had been unable or unwilling to provide unemployment relief for a nationwide problem.

Taxing and spending issues became even less important, because the Court abandoned its restrictive interpretation of the commerce clause in *NATIONAL LABOR RELATIONS BOARD V. JONES AND LAUGHLIN STEEL CORP.,* 301 U.S. 1 (1937), and in *UNITED STATES V. DARBY LUMBER CO.,* 312 U.S. 100 (1941), the Court overruled *Hammer* and its reliance on the Tenth Amendment as a limitation on the commerce power. *United States v. Kahriger,* 345 U.S. 22 (1953), confirmed this development by upholding a federal occupation tax on persons engaged in accepting bets or wagers, because the tax was reasonably related to the production of substantial revenue and Congress could use its taxing power to suppress gambling, just as it had done to regulate the sale of oleomargarine, drugs, or firearms. Then, in *SOUTH DAKOTA V. DOLE,* 483 U.S. 203 (1987), the Court provided its current interpretation of the spending power by approving a conditional expenditure of federal highway funds directly related to safe interstate travel. The TWENTY-FIRST AMENDMENT would bar Congress from directly establishing a nationwide minimum drinking age, but it could indirectly achieve that objective by using its spending power to deny states their federal highway funds, if they did not enact a statute prohibiting persons under 21 years of age from purchasing or possessing alcoholic beverages.

For more information: McCloskey, Robert G. *The American Supreme Court.* 4th ed. Chicago: University of Chicago Press, 2004; Sullivan, Kathleen, and Gerald Gunther. *Constitutional Law.* 15th ed. New York: Foundation Press, 2004.

—William Crawford Green

temporary restraining order

A temporary restraining order is an INJUNCTION, signed by a judge, preventing a person or entity from acting to change the status quo until a full hearing can be held. Under certain circumstances, a temporary restraining order may be issued without notice to the adverse party.

Although temporary restraining orders may be warranted in certain situations, this extraordinary remedy may have drastic consequences for the adverse party by depriving that party of the use of his property or the exercise of his rights.

The DUE PROCESS clause generally guarantees notice to the adverse party and a hearing prior to the deprivation of rights or property. However, in *Carroll v. President & Commissioners of Princess Anne*, 393 U.S. 175 (1968), the Court stated that "there is a place in our jurisprudence for the *ex parte* issuance, without notice, of temporary restraining orders of short duration." And, in *Granny Goose Foods, Inc. v. Brotherhood of Teamsters & Auto Truck Drivers Local No. 70 of Alameda County*, 415 U.S. 423 (1974), the Court held that temporary restraining orders could be issued if restricted to the purposes of preserving the status quo and preventing irreparable harm and if they were in effect only as long as necessary to hold a hearing.

Rule 65 of the Federal Rules of Civil Procedure, which governs temporary restraining orders in federal courts, attempts to satisfy the requirements of the due process clause by requiring temporary restraining orders to be (1) clearly supported, (2) brief in duration, and (3) secured by a bond.

1. *Support.* A temporary restraining order may be granted without notice to the adverse party only if the applicant clearly shows by sworn statement that immediate and irreparable injury will result before the adverse party can be heard in opposition. Courts often require the applicant also to show that the threatened injury to the applicant outweighs the harm the injunction may cause to the adverse party, third parties, or society in general. Imminent violations of constitutional rights, such as violations of the FIRST AMENDMENT, usually constitute irreparable injury, even where the violation exists only for a minimal period of time.

2. *Duration.* A temporary restraining order must expire not more than 10 days after it is issued. The expiration date may be extended if either the court finds good cause for an additional 10-day extension or the adverse party agrees to an extension. Temporary restraining orders continued without the consent of the adverse party beyond 20 days may be treated as preliminary injunctions.

3. *Bond.* Rule 65 also requires the applicant to post a bond or other security whenever a temporary restraining order is issued.

The Supreme Court implicitly approved Rule 65 by adopting the rule in its present form under its powers under the Rules Enabling Act.

Rule 65 does not confer either subject-matter jurisdiction or personal jurisdiction on a federal court. Also, because temporary restraining orders often are issued after a summary and ex parte hearing, a temporary restraining order is not a decision on the merits of the underlying dispute and has neither preclusive effect nor precedential effect. Finally, state rules governing temporary restraining orders vary, though most are modeled after Rule 65.

For more information: Kane, Mary Kay. *Civil Procedure in a Nutshell.* St. Paul, Minn.: West Group, 2007.

—Scott Dodson

Ten Commandments (display of)

Government display of the Ten Commandments is constitutionally controversial. Advocates of Ten Commandments displays and monuments argue that it is a historical document reflecting the foundation of the American legal system. Opponents see it as religious in nature, and argue that posting the Commandments on public property violates the ESTABLISHMENT CLAUSE of the FIRST AMENDMENT and trivializes the sacred.

While evidence may be found for government endorsement of the Ten Commandments in colonial America, the document was even then not above controversy. It was one of the topics over which Roger Williams clashed with governing officials in Massachusetts. Williams's view was that the first half of the Commandments setting forth man's relation to God were not the business of the state, while the second half, involving man's relation to man, could be.

In the records of the CONSTITUTIONAL CONVENTION, there is no evidence that the Ten Commandments were discussed as a basis for the new government, while the DECLARATION OF INDEPENDENCE, despite references to a Creator, suggests that governing power comes from the consent of the governed, not from laws handed down by God.

When the Supreme Court Building was constructed, a frieze including a figure of Moses holding the tablets was included along with the figures of other lawgivers. This has become a rallying point for those who want the Commandments posted in other public buildings. However, as noted in Court opinions on this topic, the emphasis in that setting is on Moses the man; what is visible of the Commandments is written in Hebrew.

In the mid-20th century, accompanying the film *The Ten Commandments,* many Ten Commandments monuments were distributed to local governments, where in some cases they remained largely unnoticed until recent challenges.

Modern interest in the Ten Commandments as the legal and moral cornerstone of the United States emerged in the 1970s with the rise of religious conservatism in American politics. The catalyst was a Supreme Court case, *Stone v. Graham,* 449 U.S. 39 (1980). This case challenged a Kentucky law mandating the posting of a framed copy of the Ten Commandments in every public school classroom. Although no public money was involved, it was challenged as a state endorsement of a religious document. Five members of the Court in a *per curiam* opinion largely summarized their arguments from previous public school establishment clause cases and found that the law failed the purpose prong of the *Lemon* test. They said this ruling did not mean that the Commandments could never be used in the school curriculum, but that merely posting them served only to make them objects of religious veneration.

This ruling, like the SCHOOL PRAYER cases, brought a flurry of objections from conservative religious groups and public officials, who began to search for ways to get the Commandments into the public arena. Various advocacy groups formed and began efforts such as the "Hang Ten" campaign to put the Commandments on public property. (Meanwhile, a small industry of yard signs, bumper stickers, t-shirts, and other items sprang up to display the Ten Commandments—perfectly legal, as these involved personal freedom of expression, protected under the First Amendment.)

While advocates of Ten Commandments postings present their cause as harmless and inoffensive to all except the hardened antireligious, the issue is not so simple, as it involves a choice by public governments as to which version of the Commandments to post. Catholic, Protestant, and Jewish versions differ in their numbering and their wording. While some of the differences appear insignificant, others, such as whether to say "kill" or "murder," may have profound implications for those who would make them a basis for public policy. When a government chooses from among them, it fails the third part of the *Lemon* test by entangling itself in religion and promoting religious divisiveness.

A self-styled Ten Commandments advocate, Judge Roy Moore of Alabama precipitated a showdown with fellow judges and other authorities when he personally put a 5,000-pound granite Ten Commandments monument in his courthouse. After being removed from office, he sent his monument on a nationwide tour and has used it to try, thus far unsuccessfully, to promote his political future.

Recent efforts to post the Commandments have centered on making them part of larger displays about Western civilization or American law and government. In 2005, a divided Supreme Court struck down such a display in Kentucky in MCCREARY COUNTY, KENTUCKY V. AMERICAN CIVIL LIBERTIES UNION, 545 U.S. 844 (2005), while allowing a Ten Commandments monument as part of a larger array of monuments and historical markers on the Texas capitol grounds in VAN ORDEN v. PERRY, 545 U.S. 677 (2005). Posting advocates continue to seek the right "mix" for a legal display, and religious conservatives keep the issue alive by offering "gifts" of displays and monuments to public officials to force them to take a position.

For more information: Hester, Joseph P. *The Ten Commandments: A Handbook of Religious, Legal, and Social Issues.* Jefferson, N.C.: McFarland, 2003.

—Jane G. Rainey

Tennessee v. Lane 541 U.S. 509, 1978 (2004)

In *Tennessee v. Lane,* the Supreme Court ruled that states may be sued if they deny disabled individuals access to the courts. *Lane* was an important victory for individuals with disabilities, and it also was a significant limit on the ability of states to insulate themselves from both federal regulation and suits against them by private individuals.

Tennessee v. Lane was one of several cases testing the convergence of two trends in American law. The first trend was federal efforts to protect the rights of the disabled; the second was the Rehnquist Court's federalism rulings that limited federal control over states.

In 1990, President George H. W. Bush signed the Americans with Disabilities Act (ADA). The ADA was a federal law that prohibited discrimination in employment, public accommodations, commercial facilities, and state and local government based on disability. The act generally requires employers and other parties covered by the ADA to provide reasonable accommodation for individuals with disabilities. The ADA covers all disabled individuals, and it specifically states in Title II that state and local governments are to ensure that these individuals have access to all public programs and services.

Since the ADA went into effect, there have been several suits directed against state governments, seeking to compel them to comply with the law. However, in many cases, the Rehnquist Court has limited the application of the ADA to the states, ruling either that the Tenth Amendment and the principles of federalism, or the Elev-enth Amendment and the concept of sovereign immunity that limits the ability of individuals to sue states, prevents the federal government from permitting individuals to sue states for violation of this law. For example, in *Alden v. Maine,* 527 U.S. 706 (1999), the Court held that state sovereignty immunity bars state employees from suing a state to comply with the federal Fair Labor Standards Act. In *Board of Trustees of the University of Alabama v. Garrett,* 531 U.S. 356 (2001), the Court held that state sovereignty prohibited state employees from being able to sue under Title I of the ADA. Thus, in cases like these and others, the Supreme Court seemed prepared to defend the rights of the states over disabled individuals.

In reaching these decisions, the Supreme Court has constructed a series of tests to determine when Congress may constitutionally limit a state's Eleventh Amendment sovereign immunity. In *City of Boerne v. Flores,* 521 U.S. 507 (1997), and *Kimel v. Florida Board of Regents,* 528 U.S. 62 (1998), the Court said that one needs to ask: (1) whether Congress unequivocally expressed its intent to abrogate this immunity, and (2), if so, whether it acted pursuant to a valid grant of constitutional authority. With regard to the second question, Congress can abrogate state sovereign immunity pursuant to a valid exercise of its power under Section 5 of the Fourteenth Amendment. Section 5 gives Congress the authority to enforce the amendment.

In *Lane v. Tennessee,* George Lane was a paraplegic using a wheelchair when he was required to appear in court. Because the courthouse lacked a ramp or elevator, Lane had to crawl up two flights of stairs to reach the courtroom. When he was again required to return to court, he refused to crawl up the stairs and he was arrested for his failure to appear in court. Lane sued the state under the ADA, and Tennessee sought to dismiss the suit, claiming that it was barred under the Eleventh Amendment. The district court refused to dismiss the case and the state appealed to the Sixth Circuit Court of Appeals. The court initially delayed its decision until *Garrett* was decided. It then decided to let the case proceed, claiming that the *Garrett* decision had barred cases based upon EQUAL PROTECTION but not DUE PROCESS. The case was then appealed to the Supreme Court by Tennessee.

In a divided 5-4 opinion, Justice JOHN PAUL STEVENS ruled that the Eleventh Amendment does not bar an ADA suit based upon a Title II claim. According to Stevens, Section II of the ADA was a valid exercise of Congress's Fourteenth Amendment power in that it sought to protect the rights of the disabled from irrational discrimination. Second, it was clear that the law had meant to limit state sovereign immunity in that, in its fact finding and hearing leading up to passage of the ADA, Congress had documented the many problems individuals had in securing services from state and local governments, including securing access to the courts.

In dissent, Chief Justice WILLIAM HUBBS REHNQUIST, joined by Justices ANTHONY M. KENNEDY and CLARENCE THOMAS, contended that *Garrett* controlled and that therefore even ADA Title II claims were barred by the Eleventh Amendment. Justice ANTONIN GREGORY SCALIA also dissented, claiming that Congress had exceeded its Section 5 power under the Fourteenth Amendment.

Overall, as a result of *Tennessee v. Lane*, states are still required to follow the mandates of the ADA, at least in terms of Title II. The decision represented a major victory for those with disabilities, as well as a limit upon the ability of states to use sovereign immunity to avoid compliance with federal mandates to prevent discrimination.

For more information: Freilich, Robert H., Adrienne H. Wyker, and Leslie Eriksen Harris. "Federalism at the Millennium: A Review of U.S. Supreme Court Cases Affecting State and Local Government." *Urban Lawyer* 31, no. 4 (Fall 1999): 683–775; Krieger, Linda Hamilton, ed. *Backlash against the ADA: Reinterpreting Disability Rights.* Ann Arbor: University of Michigan Press, 2003; Scotch, Richard K. *From Good Will to Civil Rights: Transforming Federal Disability Policy.* Philadelphia, Penn.: Temple University Press, 1984.

—David Schultz

Tenure of Office Act (1867)

After the Civil War, President Andrew Johnson and Congress, led by the Radical Republicans, battled over the nature of Reconstruction in the South. In an effort to consolidate its position, the Thirty-Ninth Congress passed several pieces of legislation limiting Johnson's power, including the Tenure of Office Act (14 Stat. 430). Under this act, officials nominated by the president and confirmed by the SENATE were subject to removal by the chief executive only with the consent of the Senate. The act also specified that cabinet officers would hold office for the full term of the president who appointed them (plus one added month) and that any removal of those officials required Senate approval. If the Senate was not in session, the president could temporarily suspend, but not remove, the cabinet member. The final decision would remain with the Senate when it returned.

Supported by a unanimous vote of his cabinet (which included Secretary of War Edwin Stanton), Johnson vetoed the bill, arguing that its provisions limiting the chief executive were in conflict with the Constitution and with historical precedent going back to the First Congress in 1789. On March 2, 1867, Congress voted to override the VETO, and the Tenure of Office Act became law. When Congress adjourned, Johnson decided to remove his secretary of war, whom he viewed as an ally of the Radical Republicans. Stanton refused the offer to resign, and Johnson suspended him, transferring authority to an interim appointee, General Ulysses S. Grant. In January 1868, Congress reconvened and the Senate, by a vote of 35-16, refused to approve the removal. Grant then turned the office back to Stanton.

Again stating that the law was unconstitutional (limiting, as it did, the president's constitutional power to "faithfully" execute the laws), Johnson named General Lorenzo Thomas as his new secretary of war. Stanton, in response, barricaded himself in his office, refusing to relinquish his position. Motivated by this conflict, the HOUSE OF REPRESENTATIVES voted to impeach the president, with almost all of the charges focusing on Johnson's willful violation of the Tenure of Office Act. On May 16, 1868, the Senate declined to remove Johnson—just one vote shy of the two-thirds majority required—and, following that, Stanton resigned.

In 1869, the Tenure of Office Act was modified at the beginning of the Grant administration and was finally repealed in 1887. Ironically, in 1926, 59 years after the act was passed and 39 years after its repeal, the United States Supreme Court, in a 6-3 decision, supported the constitutional position taken by Johnson in his struggle with Congress. In MYERS v. UNITED STATES, 272 U.S. 52 (1926) Chief Justice (and former president) William Howard Taft authored the opinion striking down an 1876 statute that required Senate approval for the removal of postmasters before their term expired. In that opinion, Taft also noted that, insofar as the Tenure of Office Act had unconstitutionally limited presidential power, the law, previously untested in the courts, was invalid.

For more information: Pious, Richard. "Tenure of Office Act." In *Encyclopedia of the American Presidency.* Vol. 4. New York: Simon & Schuster, 1994; Rehnquist, William Hubbs. *Grand Inquests: The Historic Impeachments of Justice Samuel Chase and President Andrew Johnson.* New York: William Morrow, 1992.

—Norman Provizer

Terminiello v. City of Chicago 337 U.S. 1 (1949)

In *Terminiello v. City of Chicago,* the Supreme Court ruled that the FIRST AMENDMENT precludes punishing a speaker as a result of violence, led by the speaker's opponents, that erupts at a rally. The Supreme Court's answer stands for the conclusion that the government must go to considerable lengths to defend free speech against hostile opponents rather than restrict the speech.

Father Arthur Terminiello, a conservative priest, was invited to speak at a rally, but before he even got there the police were struggling to control large, hostile crowds outside the auditorium. Terminiello delivered a controversial speech, attacking a broad conspiracy of Zionists, communists, and Eleanor Roosevelt, and he included some epithets to describe the rioters. During and after the rally, crowds threw bricks and engaged in a battle with police. Many arrests were made. Later, Terminiello was charged with causing a breach of the peace and fined $100.

By a 5-4 decision, the Supreme Court threw out the conviction. Justice WILLIAM O. DOUGLAS, who in conference first voted to uphold the conviction, switched his vote and wrote the majority opinion. Rather than clearly addressing the Court's established doctrines of whether the speech presented a "clear and present danger" or so-called "fighting words," Douglas focused on the charge given to the jury by the judge, which had invited a conviction for a "breach of the peace" if some misbehavior "stirs the public to anger, invites dispute, brings about a condition of unrest, or creates a disturbance." Douglas's opinion is frequently quoted for an elegant passage about the importance of the protection of free speech, including his observation that "a function of free speech under our system of government is to invite dispute. It may indeed best serve its high purpose when it induces a condition of unrest, creates dissatisfaction with conditions as they are, or even stirs people to anger."

The four dissenters disagreed but were not of a single mind. Procedurally, they objected to the majority's use of the charge, since the issue was not raised in Terminiello's appeal. Justice Robert Jackson's lengthy dissent is notable, arguing the view that the police needed the discretion to control the situation by restraining Terminiello's incendiary speech.

Terminiello is sometimes compared with *Feiner v. United States,* 340 U.S. 315 (1951), as an example of the Supreme Court's approach to so-called "fighting words" amid hostile audiences. Most importantly, the case stands as a classic example of the "hecklers' VETO" problem. When a speech generates a perceived threat to public safety, the easiest police response may be to remove a speaker; yet, in such a case, opponents would have the incentive to become violent if their actions would justify police action against a speaker, with serious consequences for the First Amendment freedom.

For more information: Kalven, Harry. *A Worthy Tradition: Freedom of Speech in America.* New York: Harper & Row, 1988; Schmidt, Patrick. "The Dilemma to a Free People: Justice Robert Jackson, Walter Bagehot, and the Creation of a Conservative Jurisprudence." *Law and History Review* 20, no. 3 (2002): 517–539.

—Patrick Schmidt

term limits

Term limits are constitutional or statutory restrictions on how long one single individual may remain in any one office. They are grounded in the idea that elected officials should not exercise political power for an indefinite or undetermined amount of time. Term limits are different than the tenure set for any given office. For example, a U.S. senator is elected to serve a tenure of six years when he or she is elected, a congressional tenure is two years, and a city mayor may serve four years. Term limits add additional conditions for individuals who serve in these offices beyond their periodic reelection to it. Term limits specify how many times an individual may be elected, or the number of years a person may serve, either continually or cumulatively, before being forced to stand down.

Term limits are not a new idea. The Articles of Confederation included restrictions that limited officials to serve no longer than "three years in six." It is significant that the framers of the Constitution, who sought to establish a more robust and powerful central government than had been evident under the Articles, unanimously decided *not* to include them in the document they wrote. JAMES MADISON's championing of "energy in the executive" (in *Federalist* 70) reflects these concerns.

It was not until 1951, when the TWENTY-SECOND AMENDMENT limiting presidential terms was approved by the requisite number of states, that the U.S. Constitution imposed any term limits on any federal official's time in office. This amendment prohibits anyone being elected president more than twice; and, in the case of a VICE PRESIDENT ascending to the higher office, only once if more than two years of the former president's tenure is served.

This "two term" idea began when George Washington voluntarily retired from the presidency after being elected twice and serving eight years. THOMAS JEFFERSON seized on Washington's action and, in a public letter, elevated it to a tradition that prevailed until Franklin D. Roosevelt ran for a third term in 1940.

Attempts at making the "two term" tradition permanent through a constitutional amendment had regularly cropped up in congressional proposals and on occasional party platforms, but it was not until 1947—with FDR's four election victories fresh on their minds, and with Republicans regaining majorities in the HOUSE OF REPRESENTATIVES and SENATE for the first time since the New Deal realignment (making the issue a very partisan affair)—that a presidential term-limit amendment was passed by the Congress.

In their fixation about preventing another FDR-like long-term presidency, the authors of the amendment gave very little thought to how this proposal would change the nature of the executive that the framers had so carefully fashioned. Today, immediately upon the election of a president to a second term, the president becomes a "lame duck" and the vice president becomes a "likely candidate" for the nomination four years later. The result is that, in a second administration, a vice president's activity and visibility today is much greater than enjoyed by any pre-Twenty-second Amendment vice president. This is a very significant constitutional shift in the role and power of the vice presidency.

Similar proposals AMENDING THE CONSTITUTION to limit congressional terms have also been proposed but have not yet been adopted.

In *UNITED STATES TERM LIMITS V. THORNTON*, 514 U.S. 779 (1995), the Supreme Court ruled that state laws seeking to impose term limits upon members of Congress were unconstitutional because they violated the qualifications set for the House of Representatives and the Senate in ARTICLE I OF THE U.S. CONSTITUTION. However, many states have imposed term limits upon members of their own state legislatures, and the courts have not found them to be violations of the United States Constitution.

For more information: Peabody, Bruce G. "Presidential Term Limits, and the Problem of Reluctant Political Leadership." *Presidential Studies Quarterly* 31, no. 3 (September 2001): 439; Rossiter, Clinton L. *The American Presidency.* Baltimore, Md.: Johns Hopkins University, 1987.

—George Peery

Terry v. Ohio 392 U.S. 1 (1968)

In *Terry v. Ohio*, the Supreme Court ruled that the FOURTH AMENDMENT does not prevent a police officer from approaching individuals suspected of a crime and lightly patting them down for weapons. The decision in this case allows for police to undertake what has come to be known as a "*Terry* stop," or a "STOP AND FRISK," without having to first obtain a search warrant.

This case was a landmark United States Supreme Court case that altered the FUNDAMENTAL RIGHTS related to the manner in which police officers and law enforcement personnel could approach potential criminal scenarios. The underlying facts related to the case involved a police detective by the name of McFadden. McFadden had been employed as a police officer for a total of 39 years and had served 35 of those years as a detective and 30 as a beat officer within the Cleveland municipal district. On October 31, 1963, at about 2 P.M. in the afternoon, Officer McFadden was patrolling in plain clothes. He observed two men, one named Chilton, who would become the defendant within the underlying case, standing on a corner. He had never observed the men before, and he was unable to say precisely what first drew his attention to them. With interest aroused, McFadden studied the two men. McFadden saw one man leave the other and walk past stores.

The suspect under McFadden's surveillance paused and looked into a store window, then resumed walking a short distance, whereupon he turned around and walked back toward the corner, pausing once again to look in the same store window. Following this, the second suspect repeated movements, and the two suspects repeated the process approximately a dozen times. At one point, a third man approached the suspects, engaged them in a brief conversation, and then left the immediate area. Chilton and the other defendant resumed this operationally routine strategy for approximately 10 minutes before leaving to meet with the third man again, McFadden reported.

Officer McFadden testified in his own words that his belief was that he suspected these three men were "casing a job, a stick-up," and that he feared "they may have a gun." McFadden then acted to approach the three men, identified himself as an officer, and then asked for their names. McFadden reported that the suspects "mumbled something" in response to his inquiry. Officer McFadden then grabbed the defendant, spun him around, and patted down the outside of his clothing. Officer McFadden felt a pistol in the left upper chest pocket of the man's overcoat and retrieved the weapon. With tension rising again, he then patted down Chilton. He felt and retrieved another handgun. McFadden patted down the third man, Katz, but found no weapon. Taking these persons into custody, the state of Ohio charged Chilton and the other defendant with carrying concealed weapons.

The major issue within the case that ensued was whether the detective's actions amounted to a seizure. In addition, the challenge for the Court was to decide whether the detective's actions amounted to a search that needed to be in compliance with the Fourth Amendment warrant requirements. It was decided that McFadden had in fact "seized" the defendant when he grabbed him, and had committed a "search" or had "searched" the defendant when he put his hands on the defendant's person.

The Court stated that the Constitution does not forbid all searches and seizures, nor does the Constitution forbid searches and seizures if probable cause exists. The Constitution forbids only unreasonable searches and seizures. The Court, in *Terry,* permitted police to conduct limited intrusions of stopping the suspects based on articulable (reasonable) suspicion that criminal activity was present. The Court also found that Detective McFadden had demonstrated reasonable suspicion that the men were armed and dangerous. Therefore, the Court allowed his limited intrusion onto their persons in search of weapons. While both standards are considered less than probable cause, the Court acknowledged that limited intrusions, based on articulated, reasonable suspicion, can be reasonable.

Overall, *Terry* stop and frisks are one of the general exceptions to the Fourth Amendment requirements that a warrant is required before a search is undertaken.

For more information: *"Terry v. Ohio* at Thirty: A Revisionist View." *Mississippi Law Journal* 74 (Special Edition 2004): 424.

—Ernest Gomez

Texas v. Johnson 491 U.S. 397 (1989)

In *Texas v. Johnson,* the Supreme Court ruled in a 5-4 decision that flag burning was a form of SYMBOLIC SPEECH that merited full protection under the FIRST AMENDMENT. Its immediate effect was to overturn laws banning flag desecration. The decision received a great deal of popular attention and sparked a movement for a constitutional amendment to ban flag desecration.

Gregory Lee Johnson, a member of the Revolutionary Communist Youth Brigade, was arrested on August 22, 1984, after a demonstration against the Republican National Convention. In a two-hour, mile-long march, demonstrators engaged in numerous acts of vandalism and stole at least one flag from outside a bank. The march culminated in the burning of an American flag outside Dallas City Hall. Johnson was initially charged with disorderly conduct, but the charge was later changed to desecration of a venerated object, a misdemeanor under Texas law. Johnson's defense was two-pronged, as his lawyers argued that (1) he had not personally burned the flag, and (2) even if he did, the statute he was charged under was an unconstitutional violation of his free-speech rights. Johnson was found guilty and sentenced to a year in prison and a $2,000 fine. His conviction was upheld by the Dallas Court of Appeals, but was overturned on First Amendment grounds by the Texas Court of Criminal Appeals. Prosecutors then appealed the decision to the U.S. Supreme Court.

Justice WILLIAM J. BRENNAN, JR., wrote for the majority and was joined by Justices Marshall, Blackmun, ANTONIN GREGORY SCALIA, and ANTHONY M. KENNEDY, concluding that Johnson's burning of the flag was expressive conduct, making it appropriate to invoke First Amendment protections. Texas had asserted that there existed compelling state interests in preventing flag desecration in order to preserve public order and to protect the flag's status as a symbol of national unity. The Court opinion rejected both of those claims, noting that the state did not present evidence of an actual threat to public order caused by Johnson's actions. As for the interest in preserving the flag as a symbol, the Court found that interest to be directly related to the expressive nature of flag burning and thus insufficient to outweigh Johnson's First Amendment rights.

Congress responded to the decision in *Texas v. Johnson* by passing the Flag Protection Act (18 U.S.C.A. § 700 [Supp. 1990]), which supporters characterized as a way to reverse the Court's ruling without resorting to a constitutional amendment. This statute was struck down in *United States v. Eichmann* 496 U.S. 310 (1990). Since 1990, there have been numerous attempts to amend the Constitution to ban flag desecration. Supporters of a constitutional argument typically argue that *Texas v. Johnson* was decided wrongly; that flag desecration involves conduct, not speech; and that the American flag is unique and thus merits special protection.

For more information: Goldstein, Robert Justin. *Flag Burning and Free Speech: The Case of Texas v. Johnson.* Lawrence: University Press of Kansas, 2000.

—Thomas C. Ellington

Third Amendment

The Third Amendment is perhaps one of the least known of all in the BILL OF RIGHTS. The Third Amendment to the United States Constitution reads: "No Soldier shall, in time of peace be quartered in any house, without the consent of the Owner, nor in time of war, but in a manner to be prescribed by law."

This amendment traces its origins back to early Anglo-Saxon law. Beginning sometime around the 12th century, due to soldiers making use of English homes, many charters of English towns began to declare a right of citizens against the involuntary quartering of soldiers in their homes. This right eventually spread throughout England, Ireland, and Scotland, but never took root outside Britain. Despite this right, English citizens frequently were forced to quarter soldiers in their homes, from the 13th through the 17th centuries. Because of their anger at this, English citizens frequently declared they possessed a right against such a practice, such as in the 1689 ENGLISH BILL OF RIGHTS.

English colonization of North America continued the practice of quartering, and there were continued public objections to the practice. Quartering became a major problem in the colonies during the French and Indian War (1754–63). In 1765, the British Parliament passed the Quartering Act, which required the colonists to provide barracks, food, and other supplies to British soldiers. If enough barracks were not available, citizens were required to provide shelter to the troops in private buildings, such as barns. Under the act, limited compensation was supposed to be provided to private citizens for the food, supplies, and shelter given to the troops. However, the citizens were often paid less than what they were owed or were not paid at all.

As tensions between England and the American colonies increased, the British Parliament passed a second Quartering Act in 1774. This new act additionally authorized the quartering of troops in private homes, not just private buildings. This practice of quartering soldiers in private homes without the consent of citizens was listed in the U.S. DECLARATION OF INDEPENDENCE as one of the abuses committed by King George against the colonies. Upon independence, most states included in their state constitutions a right against involuntary quartering of soldiers. After the U.S. Constitution's ratification in 1789, JAMES MADISON submitted a proposed list of rights to the first Congress, one of which was a right against the involuntary quartering of soldiers. Congress passed this proposal and the states ratified it, and

it became the Third Amendment to the Constitution. The wording of the amendment essentially means that government cannot house soldiers in private homes at any time during peace without the homeowners' consent. In time of war, however, the government may house soldiers in private homes, but only subject to express preexisting guidelines written in law. This wartime exception was probably enacted so as to allow the government to engage in this practice in a crisis or emergency.

Despite the Third Amendment's protection, the U.S. government has disregarded it on more than one occasion. American troops were quartered in private residences during the War of 1812. During the Civil War, the Union army quartered Union troops in residences, mostly in Southern states. Congress eventually paid out several hundred thousand dollars in claims based on quartering during the Civil War, but this was only a fraction of the potential claim totals, and Congress did not provide any further compensation.

The third amendment is often called the "forgotten" amendment because not a single case in U.S. history has ever resolved a Third Amendment claim. The most direct discussion of the Third Amendment came in the case of *Engblom v. Carey*, 677 F. 2d 1957 (2d Cir. 1982). The case involved a claim by striking prison workers against the state of New York. The workers had been provided apartments on the prison site, but were locked out of their residences by the prison superintendent when the workers went on strike. In response to the strike, the governor called out National Guard troops and housed the troops in the workers' apartments. The workers filed a lawsuit claiming their Third Amendment rights had been violated. Eventually the case was decided on other grounds, but both the district court and the court of appeals noted the workers arguably had presented a legitimate Third Amendment claim.

The U.S. Supreme Court has rarely cited the Third Amendment. Probably the most significant citation was in the case of GRISWOLD V. CONNECTICUT, 381 U.S 479 (1965). In *Griswold*, the Court declared that the Third Amendment was one of several amendments in the Bill of Rights that together demonstrated the existence of a right of PRIVACY in the Constitution. However, the Court later declared that the right of privacy was instead contained in the word "liberty," found in the DUE PROCESS clause of the FOURTEENTH AMENDMENT. In short, absent a direct violation of the Third Amendment in the future, it has little legal relevance today. Although the Third Amendment may seem obsolete, it nevertheless stands as part of the important and enduring principle of limited military power, particularly the foundational principle of ultimate civilian control over the military, in our U.S. democracy.

The Third Amendment is one of the very few parts of the Bill of Rights that have not been incorporated to apply to the states through the due process clause of the Fourteenth Amendment.

For more information: Bell, Tom W. "The Third Amendment: Forgotten but not Gone." *William and Mary Bill of Rights Journal* 2 (1993): 117–150; Fields, Thomas S., and David T. Hardy. "The Third Amendment and the Issue of the Maintenance of Standing Armies: A Legal History." *Journal of American Legal History* 35 (1991): 393–431.

—Rick A. Swanson

Thirteenth Amendment

The Thirteenth Amendment was adopted in 1865, and it outlawed slavery and involuntary servitude (except as punishment for a crime). Its passage ended the bitter struggle over slavery's existence in the United States. The Thirteenth Amendment also became an important tool for advancing the CIVIL RIGHTS of black Americans in the years after the Civil War.

The immediate origin of the amendment can be traced to the Emancipation Proclamation of 1863. Invoking his war powers, President ABRAHAM LINCOLN freed all persons held as slaves in areas controlled by the Confederacy. He did not emancipate slaves in states loyal to the Union, however, because he did not believe that the Constitution gave him the power to do so. There was, in fact, some question as to whether Lincoln had exceeded the authority of his office by emancipating slaves even in the rebel states. Because the U.S. Constitution permitted states to practice slavery (see Art. I, Sec. 2; Art. I, Sec. 10; and Art. IV, Sec. 3), only a constitutional amendment could end the practice.

Congress took up the issue in 1864. Only representatives from the Union states were present, because the Civil War was still ongoing. The SENATE was quick to pass the Thirteenth Amendment, but the House initially rejected it. President Lincoln threw his weight behind the measure, insisting that the Republican Party support the amendment in the upcoming election. His effort succeeded: The newly elected HOUSE OF REPRESENTATIVES passed the Thirteenth Amendment on January 31, 1865, during the final months of the Civil War. It became part of the U.S. Constitution on December 6, 1865, when Georgia provided the crucial 27th vote for ratification. (The amendment was eventually ratified by all 36 states, although a few dragged their heels: Kentucky waited until 1876 and Mississippi until 1895!)

Congress quickly moved to use the power granted to it by the Thirteenth Amendment to pass the Civil Rights Act of 1866 (42 U.S.C. 1982), which gave black citizens "the same right in every state . . . to make and enforce contracts, to sue, be parties, . . . to inherit, purchase, sell, and convey real and personal property; and to the full and equal benefit of all laws and proceedings for the security of person and property as is enjoyed by white citizens." This law was seen as necessary to enforce the right of black citizens to be free from the burdens of slavery.

The Thirteenth Amendment is unusual in that it is one of the few provisions of the U.S. Constitution that regulates the power and conduct of private individuals. Because of this, Congress has been able to use the Thirteenth Amendment to prevent private individuals from discriminating on the basis of race. For example, in *Jones v. Alfred H. Mayer Co.*, 392 U.S. 409 (1968), the Supreme Court ruled that Congress had the authority to ban private discrimination in housing. Said the Court, "At the very least, the freedom that Congress is empowered to secure under the Thirteenth Amendment includes the freedom to buy whatever a white man can buy, the right to live wherever a white man can live. If Congress cannot say that being a free man means at least this much, then the Thirteenth Amendment made a promise the Nation cannot keep" (392 U.S. 409, 433).

For more information: Vorenberg, Michael, and Christopher Tomlins. *Final Freedom: The Civil War, the Abolition of Slavery, and the Thirteenth Amendment.* Cambridge, Mass.: Cambridge University Press, 2001.

—Ellen Ann Andersen

Thomas, Clarence (1948–   ) *Supreme Court justice*

Clarence Thomas was the second African American appointed to the Supreme Court of the United States. He replaced Thurgood Marshall, the first African American to sit on the Court and one of the most significant CIVIL RIGHTS lawyers in U.S. history.

Thomas was born in 1948 in the dirt-poor town of Pin Point, Georgia. Abandoned by his father and then given up by his mother, he was raised by his maternal grandparents in a segregated society. Through hard work, sacrifice, and sheer force of will—both his own and that of his grandfather—he graduated with honors from the College of the Holy Cross in Worcester, Massachusetts, and then from Yale Law School in New Haven, Connecticut. Seven years later, Thomas, who had become active in the black conservative movement after arriving in Washington, D.C., in 1979 to work for Senator John C. Danforth (R-Mo.), was named assistant secretary for civil rights in the U.S. Department of Education by President Ronald Reagan. Ten months after that, he was appointed chairman of the EEOC—the federal agency charged with enforcing the nation's equal employment opportunity laws.

It was during Thomas's tenure that the EEOC shifted away from a group-based approach to civil rights enforcement to an individual-based approach. And it was Thomas's rejection of group-based relief in civil rights cases—most notably, AFFIRMATIVE ACTION—that led civil rights groups to oppose his confirmation to the Supreme Court.

Thomas's Supreme Court confirmation process was arguably the most dramatic and divisive ever conducted. The NAACP, the nation's preeminent civil rights organization, took the highly unusual step of opposing an African-American nominee to the federal bench when it sought to block Thomas's nomination on the grounds that his record on civil rights was "reactionary." Others objected as well, most notably to Thomas's apparent willingness to invoke NATURAL LAW in CONSTITUTIONAL INTERPRETATION and to his seeming opposition to *ROE V. WADE*, the 1973 Supreme Court decision that legalized ABORTION. However, the issue that made all others pale in comparison was the allegation by law professor Anita Hill that Thomas had sexually harassed her during their tenure together at the Department of Education and at the EEOC.

Thomas was confirmed to the Supreme Court, albeit by the narrowest margin in modern history. He fascinates the American people as few justices ever have. Although much of that interest can be traced to the controversy surrounding his confirmation process, his performance on the Court has received increasing attention over the years. Commentators initially tried to label Thomas as little more than Justice ANTONIN GREGORY SCALIA's loyal apprentice, but that label has been rejected by most serious students of the Court.

Thomas has written many provocative opinions—separate opinions, primarily. In his civil rights opinions, he appeals to the principle of inherent equality at the heart of the DECLARATION OF INDEPENDENCE. In CIVIL LIBERTIES and FEDERALISM cases, in contrast, he does what ROBERT BORK would have done had he been confirmed to the Supreme Court: He asks how JAMES MADISON would have decided the question.

Thomas has been a member of the nation's highest court since 1991. However, he is still a relatively young man, and he has stated publicly that he intends to serve on the Court for "decades to come."

For more information: Gerber, Scott Douglas. *First Principles: The Jurisprudence of Clarence*

Thomas. Expanded ed. New York: New York University Press, 2002.

—Scott D. Gerber

Timmons v. Twin Cities Area New Party
520 U.S. 351 (1997)

In *Timmons v. Twin Cities Area New Party,* the Supreme Court upheld Minnesota's ban on an individual appearing on the state ballot as the candidate of more than one party, sometimes called a fusion candidacy. The Twin Cities Area New Party, a minor party, challenged the law on FIRST AMENDMENT freedom of association grounds, alleging the ban unlawfully prohibited a party from associating with the nominee of its choice.

In 1994, local election officials rejected the Twin Cities Area New Party's attempt to nominate State Representative Andy Dawkins because he was first nominated by the Democratic Farmer Labor Party. The New Party filed suit in federal district court alleging that Minnesota's ban on fusion candidacies violated the party's First and FOURTEENTH AMENDMENT right to freedom of association. The district court sided with Minnesota, but the Eighth Circuit Court of Appeals reversed, holding that the state's interest in banning fusion candidacies was not sufficient and did not outweigh minor parties' rights to freedom of association. The Supreme Court accepted the case for review.

Writing for the six-member majority, Chief Justice WILLIAM HUBBS REHNQUIST saw the case as one balancing parties' First Amendment associational freedoms against the state's interest in reasonable regulations of the political process. In its reasoning, the Court balanced the "character and magnitude" of the burdens placed by the state's regulations against the political party's First Amendment claims. Because Minnesota's election law did not "restrict the ability of the New Party and its members to endorse, support, or vote for anyone they like," nor did it infringe upon the party's "internal structure, governance, [or] policy making," Chief Justice Rehnquist maintained that Minnesota had to demonstrate only "impor-

tant regulatory interests" for its ban on fusion candidacies.

The Court majority found Minnesota's stated interests in the fusion ban sufficient. Chief Justice Rehnquist argued that the ban was justified in avoiding voter confusion, promoting candidate competition, discouraging party splintering, and ensuring political stability. For the majority, allowing fusion candidacies would allow minor parties to nominate a major party candidate, gain popularity as a party and, therefore, gain electoral success on the backs of the major parties.

Most controversial in the majority opinion was Chief Justice Rehnquist's contention that the fusion ban would protect the two major parties and political stability by minimizing the "destabilizing effects of party splintering and excessive factionalism." This argument caused much concern for supporters of minor parties and scholars, since Minnesota made no such argument either in its briefs or at oral argument.

Writing for himself and Justice Ginsburg in dissent, Justice JOHN PAUL STEVENS argued that the burdens placed on minor parties by the fusion ban were severe, the state's interests were not sufficiently weighty, and preserving the two-party system is not a valid interest of the state. The fusion ban placed a monumental restriction on parties, considering that parties best communicate their ideas to voters through the nominee. Therefore, prohibiting parties from nominating a candidate of their choice places a fundamental burden on their First Amendment speech and association rights. Writing separately in dissent, Justice DAVID H. SOUTER noted that an abundance of political science literature supported the "two parties produce political stability" argument, but he declared that he was unable to join the majority, since that argument was never presented to the Court in the litigation record.

For more information: Cain, Bruce E. "Party Autonomy and Two-Party Electoral Competition," *University of Pennsylvania Law Review* 149 (2001): 793–814.

—Kyle L. Kreider

Tinker v. Des Moines Independent Community School District 393 U.S. 503 (1969)

In *Tinker v. Des Moines,* the U.S. Supreme Court upheld on First Amendment grounds the right of students in the Des Moines public schools to wear black armbands as a means of protesting the Vietnam War. Referring to the act of wearing the armbands as a type of expression, and thus of speech, the Court noted that previous Supreme Court rulings had established the fact that the First Amendment's protection of freedom of speech applies to the states and the public schools through the Fourteenth Amendment's due process clause. The Court concluded that, in the Des Moines controversy, wearing the armbands was a form of symbolic speech and that students were "persons" whose constitutional rights were to be acknowledged by school authorities.

The controversy that culminated in the *Tinker* decision began in Des Moines in December 1965 when a group of individuals initiated plans for a special holiday protest against the Vietnam War and in support of a truce. Specifically, the group decided to hold holiday fasts and to wear black armbands throughout the holiday season. When word of the planned protests reached Des Moines school authorities, a group of principals quickly enacted a policy against wearing black armbands on school grounds. Mary Beth Tinker (age 13), John Tinker (age 15), and Christopher Eckhardt (age 16) wore their armbands to school and were suspended.

After failing to win a reversal of the school policy in U.S. District Court and in the Court of Appeals for the Eighth Circuit, the students looked to the U.S. Supreme Court. The Supreme Court agreed to hear the case, and arguments were presented on November 12, 1968. The Court decided the case on February 24, 1969, and, in a 7-2 decision, ruled in favor of the students. Justice Abe Fortas wrote the Court's opinion. In speaking for the Court, Fortas emphasized that the "symbolic speech" of wearing the armbands at school had neither disrupted the school's routines nor interfered with the rights of other students. Indeed, the symbolic speech of the students was "akin to 'pure speech'" in its utter unobtrusiveness, Fortas wrote. Not only were no students put at risk for harm, but the larger student population's right "to be let alone" was never violated by the Tinkers or Eckhardt. Moreover, Fortas continued, evidence such as official school documents indicated that the school authorities had been motivated by a desire to avoid controversy, not by a concern for student safety. Also problematic was the fact that school authorities had "singled out" the black armbands for exclusion while routinely allowing other students to wear political buttons and emblems at school. Fortas summed up by acknowledging that public schools have the authority to restrict the freedom of students when such is necessary to maintain order, but public schools cannot regulate speech so excessively that schools come to resemble "totalitarian" systems.

While *Tinker* was a victory for advocates of free speech and student rights, in subsequent cases the Supreme Court has upheld public school policies limiting freedom of expression in cases involving offensive speech and in cases of speech determined to be disruptive of educational processes. Most notably, in *Morse v. Frederick,* 551 U.S. 127 S. Ct. 2618 (2007), the Supreme Court, by a 5-4 vote, held that public school officials were not barred by the First Amendment from restricting students' drug-related speech when a student displayed his 14-foot banner reading "BONG HiTS 4 JESUS" during a school-sponsored outing to watch the Olympic torch parade.

For more information: Burt, Robert A. "Developing Constitutional Rights of, in, and for Children." *Law and Contemporary Problems* 39 (Summer 1975): 118–143; Irons, Peter. *The Courage of Their Convictions: Sixteen Americans Who Fought Their Way to the Supreme Court.* New York: Penguin Books, 1979; N.A. "Prior Restraints in Public High Schools." *The Yale Law Journal* 82 (May 1973): 1,325–1,336.

—Ellen Grigsby

titles of nobility

Both the Articles of Confederation and the United States Constitution specifically prohibited either the states or the federal government from granting titles of nobility. This may be a result of concern following the American Revolution for the possibility of the establishment of an American peerage, seen as a grievous threat to the Republic.

The United States Constitution, ARTICLE I, Section 9, Clause 8, provides that "[n]o Title of Nobility shall be granted by the United States: And no Person holding any Office of Profit or Trust under them, shall, without the Consent of the Congress accept of any present, Emolument, Office, or Title, of any kind whatever, from any King, Prince or foreign State." This language is similar to that contained in Article VI of the Articles of Confederation, which provided that "nor shall any person holding any office of profit or trust under the united states, or any of them, accept of any present, emolument, office or title of any kind whatever from any king, prince or foreign state; nor shall the united states in congress assembled, or any of them, grant any title of nobility." In 1871, the U.S. attorney general ruled that "[a] minister of the United States abroad is not prohibited by the Constitution from rendering a friendly service to a foreign power, even that of negotiating a TREATY for it, provided he does not become an officer of that power" (13 Ops. Atty. Gen. 538).

JAMES MADISON, in *Federalist* 39, wrote that "[c]ould any further proof be required of the republican complexion of this system, the most decisive one might be found in its absolute prohibition of titles of nobility, both under the federal and the State governments; and in its express guaranty of the republican form to each of the latter." ALEXANDER HAMILTON, in *Federalist* 84, described the prohibition of titles of nobility as being "the cornerstone of republican government," noting that "so long as they are excluded there can never be serious danger that the government will be any other than that of the people." In *Federalist* 85, Hamilton listed the prohibition as being among "[t]he additional securities to republican government, to liberty, and to property."

In 1810, a proposed constitutional amendment strengthening the prohibition of titles of nobility was submitted to the states for ratification. The proposed amendment provides that "[i]f any citizen of the United States shall accept, claim, receive or retain, any title of nobility or honour, or shall, without the consent of Congress, accept and retain any present, pension, office or emolument of any kind whatever, from any emperor, king, prince or foreign power, such person shall cease to be a citizen of the United States, and shall be incapable of holding any office of trust or profit under them, or either of them."

The proposed amendment was approved by 12 states, falling short of the number then needed for ratification. Because it was submitted without an expiration clause, the proposed amendment is still technically subject to approval. There are continuing rumors that it was actually ratified because it was included as a thirteenth amendment in some printed copies of the Constitution published prior to the Civil War.

U.S. Public Law 103–150 (1993) includes an apology "to Native Hawaiians on behalf of the people of the United States for the overthrow of the Kingdom of Hawaii" and urges reconciliation efforts. Whether those efforts could include some recognition of the Hawaiian monarchy, and whether that would be permitted under the Constitution, remains to be seen.

For more information: Hamilton, Alexander, and Clinton Lawrence Rossiter. *The Federalist Papers; Alexander Hamilton, James Madison, John Jay.* New York: New American Library, 1961; Silversmith, Jol A. "The 'Missing Thirteenth Amendment': Constitutional Nonsense and Titles of Nobility." *Southern California Interdisciplinary Law Journal* 8 (1999): 577–611.

—Mark W. Podvia

torture and the Constitution

The Constitution prevents the use of torture either as a punishment or as a technique of interrogation.

Images of torture in the Abu Ghraib prison, Iraq, and Guantánamo Bay, Cuba, in the post-9/11 United States have brought a focus on torture in recent times. In contemporary popular discourse as well as mainstream literature, torture is often considered as a feature primarily of ancient regimes and medieval times, which gradually disappeared with the advent of modern societies. Historically, from the 13th to the 18th century, following Greek and Roman traditions, torture was a part of the "ordinary criminal procedure of the Latin Church and most of the states of Europe" (Peters, 1995, p. 54).

Torture was institutionalized as a practice, with confession becoming the "queen of proofs" while torture became the "queen of torments" (Peters, 1995). The subsequent decline of torture in the 18th and 19th centuries has often been associated with a demand for reform by Enlightenment philosophers such as Beccaria and Voltaire, which ostensibly led to the removal of many "barbaric" forms of punishment in favor of those that respect the human body and dignity. In contrast to this standard narrative about the decline of torture (the "fairy tale" of abolition, Langbein, 1997, pp. 10–11) as a story of progress in modern societies, historians state that the decline of torture was linked to a change in the requirements of the legal system.

The rejection of torture was due mainly to two juridical forces: first, the development of "new criminal sanctions" that gave discretionary power to judges for handing out a range of punishments, not just death and disfigurement, and second, "revolution in the law of proof" such as forensic and fingerprinting techniques that provided more circumstantial and physical evidence (Langbein, 1997). Therefore, the disappearance of the "legal and technical underpinnings of torture" allowed it to be the "subject" of "moral criticisms" (Peters, 1996, p. 85). This revisiting of the legal history of torture by historians illustrates why, in modern democracies such as the United States, Israel, and India, the question of torture constantly pushes the boundaries of law.

In the United States, there are both constitutional and statutory provisions that serve as a protection against torture. Based on the UN Convention against Torture, ratified by the United States in 1994, the Federal Torture Statute was instituted to address the issue of torture outside the United States. However, the applicability of this act in many contexts has been a point of contention, particularly in the "war on terror" and apart from debates regarding the very definition of torture. Torture is defined by the United Nations as the intentional infliction of "severe pain or suffering, whether physical or mental" by state officials directly or indirectly for purposes of confession, punishment, intimidation, or discrimination. The United States, however, adopted this definition with certain qualifications.

First, the United States clarified that an act had to be *specifically* intended to inflict severe pain and suffering" to constitute torture. In addition, the United States added the meaning of mental torture, which occurs when certain acts lead to "prolonged mental harm" due to intentional infliction (or threat) of physical pain and suffering, administering (or threatening to administer) mind-altering substances, threatening imminent death, and threatening to do all the above acts to a third person. While the specific reservations of the United States were meant to distinguish torture from other forms of violence, this has led to acrimonious debates on the characterization of many acts of violence, particularly highlighted at Abu Ghraib and Guantánamo.

Furthermore, the distinction between torture and inhuman and degrading treatment often leads to contentious debate on whether certain forms of interrogation are one or the other (Parry, 2004). Over the years, acts such as "piercing eye balls, needle under the finger nail, and application of electrical shock on the genital area" have been consensually defined as physical torture, but certain other forms such as "exploitation of phobias, or adjustment in daily routines regarding sleep and diet" may not be considered torture, inhuman and degrading treatment, or even too coercive given the less visible impact of the acts and their necessity in contemporary times. Certain scholars, however, have suggested that torture can be understood as any form of violence that "destroys the capacity to communicate," as Robert Cover and Elaine Scarry point out, or represent a form of "complete domination" as John Parry argues, thereby creating a broader definition of torture than the present ones (Lokaneeta, 2006).

In the United States, there are also significant cases that illustrate the constitutional protections against torture in domestic interrogations—particularly related to the Fifth Amendment right against self-incrimination and the DUE PROCESS clause of the FOURTEENTH AMENDMENT. In addition, the Eighth Amendment ban on CRUEL AND UNUSUAL PUNISHMENT serves as a protection against torture in the context of punishment.

The Wickersham Commission Report in 1931 illustrated the widespread use of the "third degree" throughout the United States, ranging from whipping and beating to "softening up" methods such as sleep and food deprivation during illegal detention and protracted questioning. The *Brown v. Mississippi* (297 U.S. 278 [1936]) case is considered as firmly upholding the constitutional protection against torture. In this case, three African-American defendants were subject to physical torture, including whipping and hanging, to procure confessions and were subsequently made to repeat the confessions "freely" and "voluntarily."

Shocked at the intensity of the torture, the U.S. Supreme Court used the due process clause to write that "the rack and torture chamber may not be substituted for the witness stand." This case is often cited as outlawing torture of any kind in the United States, though the racist attitude of the sheriff during the trial has led scholars to argue that torture actually continued after the *Brown* case.

While physical torture was the subject of *Brown,* later efforts to outlaw mental torture were not unanimously successful. For example, in *Ashcroft v. Tennessee* (327 U.S. 274 [1946]), there was no consensus on whether persistent and prolonged questioning for 36 hours constituted mental torture. Thus, *MIRANDA V. ARIZONA*'s attempt to disallow physical, mental, and inherent coercion using the warnings as protecting the Fifth Amendment right against self-incrimination seemed to be a definitive way to deal with violence of any kind, including torture during interrogations.

Recent debates on torture in the post-9/11 context, however, have led to a discussion on whether the *Miranda* regime is adequate to disallow torture or inhuman and degrading treatment and punishment. In 2002 Alan Dershowitz, for instance, suggested that if torture is used primarily to gain information, but not used as evidence in a trial, Fifth Amendment rights are protected. Thereby, he proposed "torture warrants" as a way of ensuring the more regulated use of some forms of torture in the "war on terror."

In the domestic context, the *Chavez v. Martinez,* 538 U.S. 760 (2003), case has also raised the issue of whether the due process clause or the right against self-incrimination should be applied to a case of torture. In the *Chavez* case, Martinez was apprehended by the police in a place of narcotics investigation, shot several times, and questioned while he was being treated. In a civil suit against Chavez, the Supreme Court determined that the Fifth Amendment was not applicable, since no criminal case was filed against Martinez. Further, certain opinions of the Court suggested that persistent questioning of a person while he was in agony was not torture. Scholars such as Jerome Skolnick (2004) do consider the *Chavez* case as torture, but as an atypical case, and state that the issue in interrogations is primarily of bypassing *Miranda* or the use of deception and trickery. Others such as Parry see a weakening in the protections against torture in two ways, one by not invoking the Fifth Amendment in the *Chavez* case, and two by the use of the Fourteenth Amendment due process clause that assesses the nature of the act with the "shock the conscience" test, a concept that historically has not been easily definable. Above all, the focus on the necessity of an act or on an identifiable government interest is also taken as a factor in determining whether a particular act is coercive or not.

The combination of statutory and constitutional provisions reiterates the fact that torture as a category is prohibited in the United States. The debates on the very definition of torture and the difficulty in distinguishing between different forms of violence suggest that the prohibition particularly of mental torture may not be as clearly carved out as assumed in the United States.

For more information: Darmer, M. K. B. "Beyond Bin Laden and Lindh: Confessions Law in an Age of Terrorism." *Cornell Journal of Law and Public Policy* 12 (2003): 319–372; Dershowitz, Alan. *Why Terrorism Works.* New Haven, Conn.: Yale University Press, 2002; Klarman, Michael J. "The Racial Origins of Modern Criminal Procedure." *Michigan Law Review* 99 (2000): 48–97; Langbein, John. *Torture and the Law of Proof: Europe and England in the Ancien Regime.* Chicago and London: University of Chicago Press, 1997; Lokaneeta, Jinee. *Legal Discourses on Torture in Contemporary Liberal Democracies: The United States and India.* Ph.D. dissertation, University of Southern California, Los Angeles, 2006; Parry, John T. "Escalation and Necessity: Defining Torture at Home and Abroad." In *Torture: A Collection,* edited by Sanford Levinson, 145–165. New York: Oxford University Press, 2004; Peters, Edward. *Torture.* New York: B. Blackwell, 1985; Skolnick, Jerome H. "American Interrogation: From Torture to Trickery." In *Torture: A Collection,* edited by Sanford Levinson, 105–129. New York: Oxford University Press, 2004; Chafee Zechariah, Jr., Walter H. Pollak, and Carl Stern. *The Third Degree: Report to the National Commission on Law Observance and Enforcement (June 1931).* New York: Arno Press and New York Times, 1969.

—Jinee Lokaneeta

treason

Treason is the only crime that is specifically defined, in ARTICLE III, Section 3 of the Constitution.

Article III, Section 3 of the Constitution defines treason as "levying war against the United States or giving aid and comfort to an enemy of the United States." It also requires that in a trial for treason the accused must either confess in open court or the prosecution must produce two witnesses to an overt act. Since treason is a breach of the loyalty owed to a country, it can be committed only by one who owes such loyalty, a citizen or legal resident of the country. The constitutional framers chose to place grave restrictions on its use. In the words of Benjamin Franklin during the constitutional debates, "Prosecutions for treason were too virulent and perjury too easily made use of against the innocent." The Constitution also gives Congress the power to set the punishment for treason but restricts the punishment to the accused. For example, the family of the accused shall not be "attainted" (lose their CIVIL RIGHTS) as had been the practice in England.

Throughout American history, several notable individuals have been placed on trial for treason. For example, in 1807 former vice president Aaron Burr was acquitted on charges of conspiracy arising out of allegations that he wanted to form an independent nation in the middle of what was then the Louisiana territory. In 1859, John Brown, an abolitionist, was convicted of treason by the state of Virginia as a result of his raid at Harpers Ferry, Virginia, where he had seized a federal arsenal as part of an effort to help free slaves. During the Civil War the Congress, citing its war powers, passed the Confiscation Act of 1862 to "punish treason and rebellion." While several lower courts found activities in support of the Confederacy treasonous, a general amnesty in 1868 pardoned all Confederates.

After World War II and during the cold war, fear of communist spying and infiltration led to the prosecution of numerous individuals for espionage under the Smith Act or other laws. Espionage laws refer to what is commonly known as spying, and individuals, whether they are American citizens or foreigners, can be convicted on these laws, whereas noncitizens cannot be tried for treason, since they do not have the required loyalty to the United States. Finally, it is easier to convict for espionage than it is for treason. Among notable convictions for espionage rather than treason were Julius and Ethel Rosenberg. In 2002, John Walker Lindh, an American citizen who fought for the Taliban, pled guilty to conspiracy to murder Americans.

The term *treason* appears in three other places in the Constitution: Legislator's Privilege from Arrest (ARTICLE I, Section 6), IMPEACHMENT clause (ARTICLE II, Section 4), and the interstate comity clause (Article IV, Section 2), in each case beginning a list of offenses, e.g., in the impeachment clause, "treason, bribery or other HIGH CRIMES AND MISDEMEANORS."

For more information: Hurst, James Willard. *The Law of Treason in the United States: Collected Essays.* Westport, Conn.: Greenwood, 1978; Klement, Frank L. *Dark Lanterns: Secret Political Societies, Conspiracy and Treason Trials in the Civil War.* Baton Rouge: Louisiana State University Press, 1984; Melton, Buckner F. *Aaron Burr: Conspiracy to Treason.* New York: Wiley, 2002.

—James R. Fox

treaty

A treaty is a formal, solemn, binding agreement between nations. The U.S. Constitution refers to treaties in several places, making them part of the law. The term "convention" is often used when the treaty involves several nations—a multilateral treaty. Nations also conclude agreements that fall short of the status of treaty, agreements that do not have the formal status that comes from the process of ratification. Generally, according to the Vienna Convention on the Law of Treaties, all international agreements are, more or less, binding on the parties to the agreement, *pacta sunt servanda* (agreements must be served).

Treaties have been a part of statecraft at least since biblical times and were common among the Greek city-states. The United States, under the Articles of Confederation, had negotiated treaties that were viewed as critical to sustaining independence from England and to avoiding involvement in European wars that would be detriment to the new nation. The delegates to the CONSTITUTIONAL CONVENTION agreed that keeping the commitments made in treaties was important to the new country's standing in the world, while some delegates worried that treaties might be used as a tool to disadvantage certain of the states, particularly in matters of trade.

The Constitution in ARTICLE II, Section 2, Clause 2 divides the power to make treaties between the president, who negotiates, and the SENATE, which gives its "advice and consent" and must "concur" in the treaty by a two-thirds majority. Consent and two-thirds concurrence authorizes the president to ratify a treaty, though the term *ratification* does not appear in the Constitution. The Senate's advice was sought by President Washington, but it became clear that involving the Senate in the initial development of treaties was cumbersome, and the practice was dropped. Even so, presidents often consult with members of the Senate about treaty negotiations. Congress may urge the president to a certain course through resolutions. Senate concurrence in a treaty may come with conditions or reservations, forcing the president to inform the other parties of such conditions and, in some cases, renegotiate the agreement. To avoid this in the conclusion of trade agreements, several presidents have been given a "fast track" authority wherein the Congress promises a timely up or down vote on agreements with no conditions or changes.

The United States enters into several other kinds of international agreements that do not follow the Senate ratification process. The Congress, by simple majority of both houses, may authorize the president to conclude an international agreement in areas where Congress has power to legislate (congressional-executive agreements). Trade agreements often take this form. The president is also competent to enter into international agreements that are within the sphere of executive power (sole executive agreements), such as an agreement to base U.S. troops in a foreign country (a Status of Forces Agreement), within his power as COMMANDER IN CHIEF. For purposes of international law, all these agreements produce binding international obligations.

Article VI, Clause 2 of the Constitution declares that treaties made by the United States (along with the Constitution and laws made by Congress) are the "supreme Law of the Land." This provision grew out of the conflict between state law and the Jay Treaty that ended the Revolutionary War. State laws in direct conflict with commitments made by the United States threatened to undermine the peace (*WARE V. HYLTON*, 3 U.S. 199 [1796]). By making treaties part of the law of the land, the Founders introduced the idea of the self-executing treaty, i.e., treaties would have domestic legal application just like any other legislative act. But not all provisions of all treaties are self-executing. Often treaties require additional legislation. The Jay Treaty contained self-executing provisions (state laws in conflict with the obligation under the treaty to honor debts were void), but provisions requiring the United States to make certain payments required congressional authorization of the funds.

The judicial power created by ARTICLE III OF THE U.S. CONSTITUTION includes cases arising under treaties made by the United States. Because treaties are equivalent in status to other laws made by Congress, conflicts inevitably arise. Courts will go to great lengths to interpret a treaty to make it consistent with other laws. In cases where it is impossible to reconcile a treaty with another law, the newer provision will prevail. In many instances the Supreme Court has refused to answer questions that flow from treaties by invoking the political question doctrine, i.e., the question presented is not a legal question but a matter for the executive or legislature to decide. Such questions include whether a foreign government has the authority to enter into a particular agreement (*Doe v. Braden,* 57 U.S. 635 [1853]) or whether a treaty has lapsed because a foreign party has lost its sovereign independence (*Clark v. Allen,* 331 U.S. 503 [1947]).

The Constitution is silent on the question of termination of treaties. Treaties often contain provisions for their termination by notice to the other party. The Senate's power to concur in the making of treaties might imply a role in termination, but the practice has varied considerably. In one instance Congress passed an act terminating a treaty, the treaty with France of 1778 (*Bas v. Tingy,* 4 U.S. 37 [1800]). Congress has also authorized the president to terminate treaties, and presidents have acted on their own. An example of the latter was President George W. Bush's withdrawal of the United States from the Anti-Ballistic Missile Treaty. Originally made with the Soviet Union by President RICHARD NIXON in 1972 with Senate concurrence, four former states of the Soviet Union, including Russia, succeeded to the treaty at the Union's breakup. The succession was confirmed by a memorandum of understanding negotiated by the Clinton administration but never submitted to the Senate. In 2001 President Bush notified Russia that the United States would withdraw from the treaty in six months as required by the treaty's termination clause.

The United States government made treaties with various of the Native American tribes, though they were not sovereign nations possessing territory. Chief Justice JOHN MARSHALL confirmed the practice in *Cherokee Nation v. Georgia,* 30 U.S. 1 (1831). Concluding treaties with Indian tribes ended with the Indian Appropriation Act of 1871, which reaffirmed existing treaties, though over the years these treaties have been more honored in the breach.

For more information: Aust, Anthony. *Modern Treaty Law and Practice.* New York: Cambridge University Press, 2000; Johnson, Loch K. *The Making of International Agreements: Congress Confronts the Executive.* New York: New York University Press, 1984; United States Senate, Committee on Foreign Relations. *Treaties and Other International Agreements: the Role of the United States Senate.* Washington, D.C.: U.S. Government Printing Office, 2001.

—James R. Fox

Turner Broadcasting System v. Federal Communications Commission 520 U.S. 180 (Turner II) (1997)

In *Turner Broadcasting System, Inc. v. Federal Communication Commission* (Turner II), the Court affirmed the must-carry provisions of the Consumer Protection and Competition Act of 1992, mandating that cable television operators give free carriage to all local television broadcast stations. The Court found that the law did not impermissibly infringe upon cable system operators' free speech rights. Deferring to Congress's fact-finding between Turner I and Turner II, the Court held that the regulations were content-neutral and deserved only intermediate scrutiny under the FIRST AMENDMENT.

In *Turner Broadcasting System v. Federal Communications Commission* (Turner I), 512 U.S. 622 (1994), Congress argued that the rationale for the must-carry rules was: (1) preserving the benefits of local television service, (2) promoting the widespread dissemination of information from diverse sources, and (3) promoting fair competition in the video marketplace. Thus Congress believed that the provisions were content-neutral. The Court agreed, finding no attempt by the provisions to distinguish between favored and disfavored speech. Thus the Court held that the appropriate constitutional standard for the act was intermediate scrutiny.

Using the framework set forth in *UNITED STATES v. O'BRIEN,* 391 U.S. 367 (1968), the Court reiterated that "[a] content neutral regulation will be sustained under the First Amendment if it advances important governmental interests unrelated to the suppression of free speech and does not burden substantially more speech than necessary to further those interests." Nevertheless, the Court remanded the case to allow Congress to provide factual evidence as to whether the provisions would survive the O'Brien test. After approximately 18 months of fact-finding, the lower court again granted summary judgment in favor of the government.

In Turner II, the Court's 5-4 majority affirmed summary judgment for the government, holding that the record was sufficiently developed to apply O'Brien and meet the intermediate scrutiny standard. For four members of the majority (ANTHONY M. KENNEDY, DAVID H. SOUTER, JOHN PAUL STEVENS, and WILLIAM HUBBS REHNQUIST), the fact that cable operators used their market power to exclude local broadcast stations from carriage, thus limiting broadcasters' ability to compete for local advertising revenues, was a key factor in their reasoning given that 40 percent of U.S. households depended on off-air broadcasting. The cable operators had a strong economic incentive in opposing these provisions.

Justice STEPHEN G. BREYER, concurring in part, provided the fifth vote under a different rationale. He held that under the O'Brien test it was sufficient that the must-carry provisions were intended "to assure over-the-air 'access to a multiplicity of information sources.'"

The dissent, led by Justice SANDRA DAY O'CONNOR, believed in both cases that Congress's rationale for the must-carry rules required using STRICT SCRUTINY because the law was not content neutral. Citing the same facts, Justice O'Connor found that Congress made value judgments about a diversity of viewpoints which, in her argument, went directly to content and thus the must-carry provisions needed to be invalidated. These issues will reemerge if there is an attempt to apply the must-carry provisions to digital signals in 2009.

For more information: Aaron, Harris J. "I Want My MTV: The Debate over Digital Must-Carry." *Boston University Law Review* 80, no. 885 (2000); Hazlett, Thomas W. "Digitizing 'Must-Carry' under *Turner Broadcasting v. FCC* (1997)," *Supreme Court Economic Review* 8, no. 141 (2000); Winder, Laurence H. "The Red Lion of Cable and Beyond: *Turner Broadcasting v. FCC.*" *Cardozo Arts and Entertainment Law Journal* 15, no. 1 (1997).

—Cleveland Ferguson III

Twelfth Amendment

The Twelfth Amendment was ratified in 1804; it provides that members of the ELECTORAL COLLEGE shall cast separate votes for president and vice president of the United States. The purpose of the amendment grew out of the disputed election of 1800.

In 1800 THOMAS JEFFERSON ran for president of the United States as a member of the Democratic-Republican Party against JOHN ADAMS, a member of the Federalist Party. Jefferson had selected Aaron Burr as his vice presidential running mate. When the members of the electoral college voted, they followed the procedures of ARTICLE II, Section 1, which required them to vote for two persons; presumably one person would become president, the other the vice president. In the first three presidential elections this did not appear to create too much of a problem.

However, under strong political party and partisan voting, the electors of 1800 cast an equal number of votes for both Jefferson and Burr, thereby producing a tie. Since no candidate had a clear majority of the electoral votes, Article II required the HOUSE OF REPRESENTATIVES to select the president. After 35 ballots, the deadlock between Jefferson and Burr was broken, and the former became the third president of the United States while the latter became his vice president. To prevent this problem in the future, Congress adopted the Twelfth Amendment in 1803 and it was ratified in 1804.

The presidential election of 1824 is the only one since the passage of the Twelfth Amendment where Congress has selected the president. Here, while Andrew Jackson had the plurality of popular and electoral votes, he did not win the presidency. Instead, the House of Representatives selected John Quincy Adams to be president.

The Twelfth Amendment's real purpose is limited to presidential elections. Its need was a result of the emergence of political parties in the United States, something the original framers of the Constitution did not either anticipate or desire.

For more information: Kelly, Alfred, Winfred Harbinson, and Herman Belz. *The American Constitution: Its Origins and Development.* New York: W.W. Norton, 1991.

—David Schultz

Twentieth Amendment

The Twentieth Amendment was ratified in 1933, and it changed the dates for both the inauguration of the president and the vice president of the United States and the beginning of the new Congress following an election. The purpose of the amendment was to eliminate the long gap in time between elections and the swearing in of new officials.

Prior to the Twentieth Amendment, Congress did not begin its new session after an election until the following March, and a new presidential term, according to the Twelfth Amendment, did not commence until March 4. The reason for this long gap between the election and taking office was due in part to the long time once necessary to travel to Washington, D.C. However, with improved transportation, this traveling time became a matter of hours, resulting instead in a lame duck Congress unable to act from November to March. This gap especially became a problem following the election of Franklin D. Roosevelt during the Great Depression. After his victory in 1932, the solutions he proposed to address the problems facing the national economy, such as the banking crisis, had to wait until he was president in March, nearly four months after the election. To prevent this gap in the future Senator George Norris from Nebraska proposed the Twentieth Amendment.

The Twentieth Amendment moved the inauguration of the president from March 4 to January 20, and it moved the date for the start of the new Congress to January 3.

For more information: Kelly, Alfred, Winfred Harbinson, and Herman Belz. *The American Constitution: Its Origins and Development.* New York: W.W. Norton, 1991.

—David Schultz

Twenty-fifth Amendment

The Twenty-fifth Amendment provides for a process of presidential succession in the event of the death, incapacity, or resignation of the president or vice president. The amendment was proposed in 1965 and ratified in 1967.

ARTICLE II OF THE U.S. CONSTITUTION provides for the vice president to assume the duties of the president if the latter is unable to perform them. Throughout American history the death or illness of the president has resulted in the vice president taking over. When William Henry Harrison died after serving as president for little more than a month in 1841, his vice president, John Tyler, became president. When ABRAHAM LINCOLN was assassinated in 1865, his vice president, Andrew Johnson, took over. However, when James Garfield was shot in 1881, he lingered in a coma for two months before he died, leaving open the question of who was in charge as president. Similarly, after President Woodrow Wilson had a stroke in 1919, questions about who was in control were also raised. The Twenty-fifth Amendment is meant to address these concerns.

Section 1 of the Twenty-fifth Amendment makes it clear that when the president dies or is removed from office, the vice president becomes president. Section 2 allows for the president to nominate, subject to confirmation by majority votes in both houses of Congress, a person to become vice president if there is a vacancy in that office. Sections 3 and 4 set up procedures to allow the president to transfer power temporarily to the vice president if health or other reasons preclude the president from performing these duties.

The Twenty-fifth Amendment was used almost immediately upon its ratification. In 1973, when Vice President Spiro Agnew resigned, President RICHARD NIXON named HOUSE OF REPRESEN-TATIVES member Gerald Ford to become vice president. After Nixon resigned in 1974 and Ford became president, he selected former New York governor Nelson Rockefeller to become vice president. In both cases, Congress voted to support the nominations.

Finally, Presidents Ronald Reagan and George W. Bush temporarily transferred power to their vice presidents during medical emergencies.

For more information: Kelly, Alfred, Winfred Harbinson, and Herman Belz. *The American Constitution: Its Origins and Development.* New York: W.W. Norton, 1991.

—David Schultz

Twenty-first Amendment

In 1933, the American people, by congressional vote and state ratification in special conventions, repealed the EIGHTEENTH AMENDMENT. Like the Eighteenth Amendment, the Twenty-first Amendment was passed with great rapidity, much more quickly than its supporters expected or its opponents feared. Repeal of the Eighteenth Amendment had been considered an impossibility, as likely as a sparrow carrying a rocket ship to the moon, according to Senator Sheppard of Texas. The American people did not remove any reference to intoxicating liquor from the Constitution. Instead they included a second section to the Twenty-first Amendment, which read: "The trans-portation or importation into any State, Territory, or possession of the United States for delivering or use therein of intoxicating liquors, in violation of the laws thereof, is hereby prohibited."

National prohibition was considered to have failed because it did not provide for effective regulation of alcoholic beverages. Americans rejected what was in effect a regulatory vacuum from 1920 to 1933, during which time alcoholic beverages were distributed and sold illicitly. Almost everyone wanted the repeal of national prohibition to lead not to alcoholic beverage deregulation but to better, more effective regulation under the leadership of the states, which would encourage and foster what was called at the time, by Franklin Roosevelt, among others, "true temperance." National prohibition was rejected as ineffective because it was too extreme. Moderation, more limited expectations, and more nuanced demands would, it was expected, serve to better effect.

The Democratic platform of 1932 called for repeal. The Republican platform was equivocal, advocating, much like many members of Congress when submitting Prohibition to the states in 1919, only that the people have the opportunity to reconsider the matter. It also called for continued federal authority to prevent the return of the saloon. While many writers criticized Prohibition for replacing, for the worse, the saloon with the speakeasy, it was yet commonly asserted that the disappearance of the saloon was an unequivocal achievement of national Prohibition. While definitions of a "saloon" were varied, the general consensus described an institution that, for the profit motive, pursued the sale of alcoholic beverages and had been largely immune from regulation, or at least effective regulation, and had been active politically in opposition to the implementation of such regulation.

Why was Section 2 added to the Twenty-first Amendment? It is sometimes asserted that its drafters meant Section 2 only to protect dry states from DORMANT COMMERCE CLAUSE invalidation of laws establishing restrictions on importation of alcoholic beverages. The Supreme Court has always rejected this view. Even when it has found that particular state statutes were not saved by the Twenty-first Amendment, it has always interpreted the amendment as intended to protect state laws other than Prohibition. In addition, state laws arguably in conflict with federal statutes are not summarily dismissed, but are evaluated with the recognition that both the Twenty-first Amendment and the commerce clause are in the Constitution. Certainly there was specific mention in the congressional discussions of 1932 about the need to protect dry states. There was also discussion on the importance of protecting state law in general and letting states take the lead in regulatory efforts. The particular example should not negate the general concern. Moreover, even a desire to protect dry states is somewhat broader in scope than one might suppose. As Charles Merz observed of the state of law in 1917, before passage of the Eighteenth Amendment: "Thirteen of the twenty-six 'dry' states pre-Prohibition permitted some receipt and delivery of out-of-state intoxicating liquors." What they did not permit was sales within the states, instead implementing what Merz described as a "system of regulation." In his Proclamation of the Adoption of the Twenty-first Amendment, President Roosevelt called "specific attention to the authority given by the Twenty-first Amendment to the government to prohibit transportation or importation of intoxicating liquors into any state in violation of the laws of such state." He did not limit such state laws to prohibitory statutes.

In 1917, Congress had passed the Reed Amendment, prohibiting importation of alcoholic products into a state that prohibited manufacture and sale within it. This was an attempt to deny states the regulatory flexibility to permit purchases from out of state but not from within the state. In 1935, Congress abandoned this rule as antithetical to its desire to let states create their own systems and to support them in this effort.

The initial draft of what became the Twenty-first Amendment included a third section. This reflected the 1932 platform of the Republican Party and would have prohibited the saloon and given the federal government concurrent enforcement authority. This paragraph was deleted following comments from many, Senator Wagner of New York in particular, that the lesson of the failure of Prohibition was that the national government should not be taking the lead in alcoholic beverage policy. Parenthetically, the Twenty-first Amendment, along with the Webb-Kenyon Act of 1913, and the Federal Alcohol Act of 1935, which stated that one of its purposes was to help states enforce the Twenty-first Amendment, all suggest that there was no intent by either Congress or the American people to have Congress either explicitly, through actions such as the Reed Amendment, or implicitly, through prior regulations such as the Sherman Act, assert primacy in the regulation of alcoholic beverages and limit the scope of state regulation.

Almost immediately following passage of the Twenty-first Amendment, some states began enacting laws that gave special benefits to in-state producers. These laws were similar to other efforts by states during the Great Depression to support local agriculture. From the outset, these laws were controversial, being rejected by some lower courts and criticized by some commentators. The Supreme Court, in several decisions written by Justice Brandeis, upheld such laws, maintaining that the Twenty-first Amendment permitted discrimination under the EQUAL PROTECTION clause (although as Justice JOHN PAUL STEVENS has pointed out, Brandeis was talking only about economic classifications) and that burdens on INTERSTATE COMMERCE that would otherwise have been prohibited by the dormant commerce clause were now saved by the Twenty-first Amendment. No one thought that these opinions meant that states, for instance, could ban importation by only blacks or by Jews. Thus a case like CRAIG V. BOREN, 429 U.S. 190 (1976), using equal protection analysis to reject a state law permitting women to purchase alcohol at a younger age than men, did not mark an end to general judicial deference toward state alcoholic beverage regulation. A similar rule had been upheld by Justice Frankfurter, not on the grounds that the state could do whatever it wanted, but on the grounds that what it had done was reasonable.

In GRANHOLM V. HEALD, 540 U.S. 460 (2005), the Supreme Court rejected the Brandeis decisions and held that facial discrimination between in-state and out-of-state wine producers was not saved by the Twenty-first Amendment and that, under ordinary first-tier dormant commerce clause analysis, the states of New York and Michigan had failed to meet their burden of justifying the differential rules. In and of itself, this marks only a small restriction of state alcoholic beverage powers, particularly when the Supreme Court majority in its 5-4 decision had several times asserted that the three-tier system was unquestionably valid and that states' alcoholic beverage powers under the Twenty-first Amendment remained. Justice Brandeis had not been in favor of discrimination. He and the Court probably had been concerned that individual judges' notions of unjustified protectionist activity would be the thin edge of the wedge to crippling nascent state regulation. Brandeis believed strongly both in state regulation and in regulation of alcoholic beverages, with the consumption of which he had little sympathy. The Supreme Court's recent decision could be explained as a reflection of the abandonment of any need to have a kind of infant regulatory structure doctrine in which even questionable state laws were upheld to give state lawmaking a chance. State alcoholic beverage regulation now has existed for almost 75 years, and state regulation presumably is less vulnerable to judicial nullification than it was at its outset. On the other hand, the case could be described as one expressing a certain judicial impatience with the Twenty-first Amendment. Such an impatience is expressed by those who do not believe in regulation as a general proposition, by those who think that alcoholic beverages should not be treated differently from other products, either by regulators or by judges, or by those who believe that, just as it was unwise to bring intoxicating liquors into the Constitution through the Prohibition amendment, it was unwise to repeal that amendment without completely excising any constitutional reference to intoxicating liquors.

The Constitution mentions only two products: human beings as slaves and intoxicating liquors. We regret that slavery was ever permitted in the Constitution, but clearly do not regret that it is now prohibited. Moreover, this is simply a part of our history. We may regret that alcoholic beverages were once prohibited by the federal Constitution, but the majority of us do not regret that this prohibition has been lifted. Some may think that it was unwise that repeal did more than end national prohibition and that Section 2 was included, but it was. The Constitution, although a living document, is not written in invisible ink.

For more information: Nowak, John E., and Ronald D. Rotunda. *Principles of Constitutional Law.* St. Paul, Minn.: Thomson/West, 2005.

—Steve Diamond

Twenty-fourth Amendment

The Twenty-fourth Amendment prohibits the paying of poll taxes or the paying of any other fees in order to vote in a federal election. The amendment was passed in Congress in 1962 and ratified by the states in 1964.

Poll taxes have a long history in the United States. When the Constitution was first adopted, many states limited the franchise to property owners. The idea often offered for this stipulation was that property ownership ensured that voters had a sufficient stake or interest in the community to vote. Others argued that the purpose of property ownership was to disenfranchise the poor.

During the Jacksonian era of the 19th century, many states abandoned property ownership as a criterion for voting and instead substituted a poll tax in its place. Advocates of the poll tax argued that it was more democratic than property ownership because it allowed more individuals to vote. Critics of the poll tax again contended that it discriminated against the poor.

After the Civil War and the passage of the FIFTEENTH AMENDMENT Southern states sought various means to deny former slaves the RIGHT TO VOTE. They enacted numerous rules, including poll taxes, literacy tests, and "grandfather laws" (allowing one to vote only if your grandfather also voted) as ways to discourage African Americans from voting. These requirements, adopted mostly after Reconstruction ended in 1877, were often called Jim Crow laws. They were effective in discouraging African Americans from voting.

Poll taxes were increasingly under attack during the Civil Rights movement of the 1950s and 1960s. The Twenty-fourth Amendment was adopted by Congress shortly before it passed the CIVIL RIGHTS ACT OF 1964, and it was ratified just before the VOTING RIGHTS ACT OF 1965 was adopted.

While the Twenty-fourth Amendment banned poll taxes only in federal elections, the Supreme Court in *Harper v. Virginia Board of Elections,* 383 U.S. 663 (1966), declared the use of poll taxes in state elections to be unconstitutional under the FIRST and FOURTEENTH AMENDMENTS.

As a result of concerns or beliefs that voter fraud was a problem, states such as Michigan, Indiana, Georgia, and Missouri adopted laws starting in 2004 requiring individuals to produce a photo identification when voting in person at the polls. Critics charged that these photo ID laws were a form of poll tax. As of 2007, only one court, the Missouri Supreme Court, had ruled that these laws were an unconstitutional poll tax.

For more information: Keyssar, Alexander. *The Right to Vote: The Contested History of Democracy in the United States.* New York: Basic Books, 2001.

—David Schultz

Twenty-second Amendment

The Twenty-second Amendment limits individuals to being elected to no more than two terms as president of the United States. The amendment was proposed by Congress in 1947 and ratified in 1951.

Beginning with George Washington's decision in 1796 not to seek a third time as president of the United States, no individual sought to run for a third term until Franklin D. Roosevelt in 1940. Not only did he decide to run, and then get elected, but also he ran for a fourth term and was elected in 1944. Because of both the long-standing two-term tradition and concern that a president would get too much power if serving for more than two terms, the Twenty-second Amendment was adopted.

Section 1 of the Amendment prevents a person from being elected president more than two times. However, the amendment does permit vice presidents who succeed to the presidency to run for two additional terms if they have served as president for less than two years. This means that, if a president dies after serving more than two years, the vice president who replaces him or her can run and get elected to two additional terms. This means that one can be president for up to 10 years. However, if the president dies before serving two years, the vice president would be allowed to finish this term and get elected to one more four-year term.

An example of how the Twenty-second Amendment applies dates from the 1960s. In November 1963, when President Kennedy was assassinated, he had already served for about two-and-one-half years as president. Lyndon Johnson was his vice president and he became president. He ran again and was elected to his own term in 1964, and he was eligible and planned to run for president again in 1968 but decided to leave the race after a poor showing in the New Hampshire primary.

For more information: Kelly, Alfred, Winfred Harbinson, and Herman Belz. *The American Constitution: Its Origins and Development.* New York: W.W. Norton, 1991.

—David Schultz

Twenty-seventh Amendment

The Twenty-seventh Amendment provides that pay increases for Congress may not go into effect until after the next election for members of the HOUSE OF REPRESENTATIVES. This amendment was passed by Congress in 1789 but was not ratified until 1992.

When JAMES MADISON offered the 10 amendments to the Constitution that came to be known as the BILL OF RIGHTS, Congress also adopted two other amendments. The Bill of Rights Amendments passed in 1791. One of them would have stated that there would be one member in the House of Representatives for every 50,000 people. That amendment never was ratified. The other amendment, which is the Twenty-seventh, did not immediately pass. However, there was no time limit on its passage. While there was no action on the amendment by states for many years, for almost 200 years states continued to adopt this amendment. In 1978 Wyoming ratified it and Michigan did the same in 1992, giving it the three-quarters vote it needed to become an official amendment.

Some may contend that because it took nearly 200 years to adopt this amendment it is not valid, as it was not adopted in a timely fashion. For example, the Equal Rights Amendment, which Congress proposed in 1972, failed because it did not get the required three-fourths of states to adopt within the initial seven years and not in the extension of three more years, as required by Congress. However, in *Coleman v. Miller*, 307 U.S. 433 (1939), the Supreme Court ruled that it is a prerogative of Congress to place a time limit on ratification by the states. If no time limit is placed on its adoption, an amendment remains available for states to adopt. The *Coleman* ruling made the 1992 adoption of the Twenty-seventh Amendment possible.

For more information: Bernstein, Richard. "The Sleeper Wakes: The History and Legacy of the Twenty-Seventh Amendment." *Columbia Law Review* 61 (1992): 497–557.

—David Schultz

Twenty-sixth Amendment

The Twenty-sixth Amendment lowered to 18 the age of individuals eligible to vote in federal and state elections. The amendment was proposed by Congress in 1971 and was ratified by the required three-quarters of the states in less than four months.

Student protest during the 1960s demanded that Congress lower the voting age from the traditional 21 to 18. In part, these demands were fueled by arguments during the Vietnam War that 18-year-olds who were old enough to be drafted could not vote. In response to these demands, Congress passed the Voting Rights Act of 1970, which lowered the voting age to 18 in federal, state, and local elections.

However, in *Oregon v. Mitchell*, 400 U.S. 112 (1970), the Supreme Court declared the law unconstitutional, holding that Congress lacked the power to do this since it violated both the Tenth Amendment and ARTICLE I, Section 2 of the Constitution. Four justices ruled that Congress could change the voting age for all races, four justices said for none. Justice HUGO BLACK, the swing vote, ruled that Congress could lower the voting age in federal but not state elections. Had this ruling stayed in effect, individuals from 18 to 20 could have voted in federal but not state and local elections. In order to remedy this confusion and to overturn *Mitchell*, Congress adopted the Twenty-sixth Amendment.

For more information: Keyssar, Alexander. *The Right to Vote: The Contested History of Democracy in the United States.* New York: Basic Books, 2001.

—David Schultz

Twenty-third Amendment

The Twenty-third Amendment grants to the DISTRICT OF COLUMBIA the right to select electors to vote for president and vice president of the United States.

ARTICLE I, Section 8 of the Constitution called for the creation of the area that would become the national capital, Washington, D.C. Yet from 1787 until the second half of the 20th century, residents of the District of Columbia had no say in who was elected president of the United states because Washington, D.C., was not entitled to any presidential electors. Many thought this was unfair. In 1960 Congress adopted the Twenty-third Amendment, which sought to change that. It gave the District of Columbia the same number of electoral votes in presidential/vice presidential elections as the area would be entitled to receive if it were a state, subject to the stipulation that it could not have more electoral votes than the smallest state (three votes). In 1961 the Twenty-third Amendment was ratified, and residents were able to select their electors for the first time in the 1964 presidential election between Lyndon Johnson and Barry Goldwater.

While the District of Columbia now has three electoral votes, it still lacks representation in Congress; there have been efforts to change the Constitution to allow for this too.

For more information: Kelly, Alfred, Winfred Harbinson, and Herman Belz. *The American Constitution: Its Origins and Development.* New York: W.W. Norton, 1991.

—David Schultz

Twining v. State of New Jersey 211 U.S. 78 (1908)

In *Twining v. State of New Jersey*, the Supreme Court decided that Fifth Amendment protections do not apply in state courts.

The case involved Twining and Cornell, directors of a bank in New Jersey, who were indicted for having knowingly exhibited a false paper to a state bank examiner with the intent to deceive him as to the condition of the bank. At the trial, the defendants called no witnesses and did not testify in their own behalf. The trial judge commented to the jury that their refusal to testify should not be held against them, although the jury could consider the fact that they did not take the stand in response to a direct accusation. New Jersey, at the time of this trial, was one of two states that did not have a provision in its state constitution protecting individuals from being forced to give self-incriminating testimony. The defendants were convicted and sentenced to imprisonment for six and four years, respectively. The sentence was affirmed by the court of errors and appeals.

The case then went to the U.S. Supreme Court. Until the adoption of the FOURTEENTH AMEND-MENT, the BILL OF RIGHTS did not apply to state courts. The attorneys for the defendants argued that the charge to the jury constituted a form of self-incrimination that abridged the defendants' PRIVILEGES AND IMMUNITIES as American citizens. They also argued that protection from self-incrimination is so fundamental that a refusal of the right is a denial of DUE PROCESS as promised in the Fourteenth Amendment.

The Supreme Court, in an 8 to 1 ruling, decided against Twining. Justice William H. Moody delivered the opinion while JOHN MARSHALL HARLAN dissented. As expected, the Court rejected the proposition that the Fourteenth Amendment required states to honor every right in the Bill of Rights. The Court also rejected the claim that protection from self-incrimination is necessary for due process. It did, however, make the important concession that the Fourteenth Amendment might safeguard some of the presumed rights in the Bill of Rights in state action, not because they are enumerated in the Bill Rights, but because a denial of them would be a denial of due process of law. Harlan argued that protection against self-incrimination is a right that states should uphold. The Supreme Court overruled the *Twining* decision in 1964 when deciding the case of *Malloy v. Hogan*, 378 U.S. 1 (1964).

For more information: Abernathy, M. Glenn. *Civil Liberties under the Constitution.* Columbia: University of South Carolina Press, 1989; Banaszak, Ronald, Sr. *Fair Trial Rights of the Accused: A Documentary History.* Westport, Conn.: Greenwood Press, 2002.

—Caryn E. Neumann

U

ultra vires

Ultra vires is a constitutional and statutory concept stating that a specific body lacks the authority to do something.

The central principle of administrative law has long been that the right of the judicial branch to review the acts and decisions of public authorities rests upon the ultra vires rule. This rule holds that a public body that has been granted powers must not exceed the powers so granted. The application of ultra vires consists of nothing other than the application of the law itself. The courts police those boundaries that Congress intended should apply to the discretionary power created by enabling legislation. The rule of ultra vires reconciles JUDICIAL REVIEW with constitutional framework, but it does not protect the Constitution against external forces of constitutional change.

The ultra vires rule is an old legal principle that has its roots in English parliamentary law. The traditional theory of ultra vires holds that judicial review of the exercise of statutory power involves nothing more than the enforcement of parliamentary intention. Review lies on the sole ground that administrative action is ultra vires, or beyond the powers granted by Parliament.

Under the U.S. Constitution, the principle of ultra vires is essentially the same as it is under English law. An authority will be regarded as acting ultra vires if in the course of doing or deciding to do something that is *intra vires,* in the strict or narrow sense, it acts improperly or unreasonably in various ways. These ways include disregard of the rules of natural justice; unfairness; taking into account irrelevant considerations; ignoring relevant considerations; bad faith; attempting to raise taxation; or interfering with the free exercise of individual liberties. Essentially, a governmental body may not do something that it does not have the legal capacity to do.

The court's broad review jurisdiction that applies the principles of good administration to the decision-making process poses severe problems for the ultra vires doctrine. It is extremely difficult to maintain that the broad grounds of review derive straightforwardly from the will of Congress, particularly in light of the detached and complex nature of certain grounds, such as the rules of natural justice. The doctrine has nothing to say as to what the court will count as a want of power in the deciding body, and so of itself it illuminates nothing. It amounts to no more than a tautology that the court will strike down what it chooses to strike down. Additionally, ultra vires is faulted for its inability to legitimize the extension of the supervisory jurisdiction beyond the realm of statutory power.

For more information: Forsyth, Christopher. *Judicial Review and the Constitution.* Portland, Ore.: Hart Publishing, 2000.

—Caryn E. Neumann

undue burden standard

The undue burden standard is a rule to determine the constitutionality of ABORTION regulations.

In *Planned Parenthood of Southeastern Pennsylvania v. Casey,* 505 U.S. 833 (1992), the Supreme Court adopted a new test to determine the constitutionality of abortion regulations. The case revolved around the constitutionality of the 1982 Pennsylvania Abortion Control Act, which included several limitations on abortions, the most significant requiring a doctor to obtain a woman's informed consent by telling her the risks of abortion and childbirth and then waiting at least 24 hours before performing the abortion; a married woman needed to present a signed statement that she notified her husband of the planned abortion.

In a joint opinion for herself and Justices DAVID H. SOUTER and ANTHONY M. KENNEDY, Justice SANDRA DAY O'CONNOR reaffirmed the Court's commitment to upholding its 1973 ruling in ROE v. WADE, 410 U.S. 113 (1973), and outlined three essential factors of *Roe*. First, women have a right to have an abortion before a fetus is viable, that is, before it can live outside the mother's womb, without "undue interference" from the state. Second, a state can restrict abortions after the fetus has become viable as long as it allows exceptions to protect the mother's life or health. Third, a state's interest in maternal and fetal life commences at the start of the pregnancy.

The Court explained that because of its legitimate interest in protecting "potential human life," a state was not entirely precluded from involving itself in the abortion decision throughout the pregnancy, but was forbidden to enact abortion regulations, which imposed an "undue burden" on the woman's choice, only during the pre-viability stage. It defined "undue burden" as a state regulation that places a substantial obstacle in the path of a woman seeking an abortion during the stage before the fetus is viable.

The Court explained that it was adopting the "undue burden" standard to balance its commitment to *Roe* with the state's interest in "potential life." Under this standard, the Court concluded that the 24-hour waiting period and the physician's lecture to obtain informed consent were permissible regulations because they were not "unduly" burdensome. However, the Court held that the provision requiring women to notify their husbands of their intention to have an abortion was unconstitutional, since it placed an undue burden on the right of women to choose to have an abortion. The opinion concluded that most women inform their husbands of a pregnancy, and those who do not are likely to have a legitimate reason for refusing to do so; thus the Court believed the

regulation created a "substantial obstacle" for many women.

Following *Casey*, the Court relied on the "undue burden" standard in *Stenberg v. Carhart*, 530 U.S. 914 (2000), when it struck a Nebraska abortion law. Speaking for the majority, Justice STEPHEN G. BREYER reiterated the "undue burden" standard: that a state may not place an undue burden on a woman's right to terminate her pregnancy before viability. Based on this standard, the Court held that the law prohibiting doctors from performing certain kinds of abortion procedures was unconstitutional because it unduly restricted a woman's ability to receive the most commonly used method for performing pre-viability abortions, and therefore placed an "undue burden" on her right of abortion itself.

For more information: Guenther, Hilary. "The Development of the Undue Burden Standard in *Stenberg v. Carhart:* Will Proposed RU-486 Legislation Survive?" *Indiana Law Review* 35 (2001/2002): 1,021–1,044; Mezey, Susan Gluck. *Elusive Equality: Women's Rights, Public Policy, and the Law.* Boulder, Colo.: Lynne Rienner Publishers, 2003.

—Susan Gluck Mezey

union dues and political activity

The FIRST AMENDMENT and federal labor laws limit the use to which unions can put fees collected from objecting nonmembers. In general, unions can not use fees from objecting nonmembers for political or other purposes unrelated to collective bargaining (*Air Line Pilots v. Miller*, 523 U.S. 866 [1998]).

When a union is elected to represent a unit of employees, the union is permitted, under various federal and state labor laws, to reach an agreement with the employer establishing an "agency shop." In an agency shop, employees who are union members must pay union dues, and employees who are not union members must pay equivalent fees to the union, in both cases as a condition of continued employment. Fees from nonmembers are known as "agency fees" or "fair share" fees.

Agency fees cannot be greater than the dues the union receives from union members. The agency shop is found both in the public sector (government employment) and in the private sector. In the private sector, in industries governed by the National Labor Relations Act (NLRA) and the Railway Labor Act (RLA), employers and unions can also agree to a "union shop." In a union shop, employees must theoretically be members of the union. However, the only aspect of union membership that can be enforced, in a union shop, is the obligation to pay dues; membership as a condition of employment "is whittled down to its financial core" (*NLRB v. General Motors*, 373 U.S. 734, 742 [1963]). Therefore, the union shop is in practice almost the same as the agency shop: Despite the term "union shop," employees do not really have to become union members, but can instead pay what are in effect agency fees (*Marquez v. Screen Actors Guild*, 525 U.S. 33 [1998]). The union shop and the agency shop are both known as "union security" arrangements.

The Supreme Court has upheld union security arrangements against constitutional challenges, in *Abood v. Detroit Board of Education*, 431 U.S. 209 (1977), upholding agency shop for public-sector employees and in *Railway Employees v. Hanson*, 351 U.S. 225 (1956), upholding union shop under RLA. But the Court has also limited the use to which unions can put agency fees. If a public-sector union uses agency fees to "contribute to political candidates" or to "express political views unrelated to its duties as exclusive bargaining representative," there is a First Amendment violation of the right of objecting nonmembers to be free of compelled speech and association (*Abood*, at 234). In *Air Line Pilots v. Miller*, 523 U.S. 866 (1998), the Court summarized the rules for permissible agency fees in the public sector: "[A]gency fees assessed by public-employee unions must (1) be 'germane' to collective-bargaining activity; (2) be justified by the government's vital policy interest in labor peace and avoiding 'free riders'; and (3) not significantly add to the burdening of free speech that is inherent in the allowance of an agency or union shop" (*Miller*, quoting *Lehnert v. Ferris Faculty Assn.*, 500 U.S. 507, 519 [1991]).

Similar or identical rules apply to private-sector employment governed by the NLRA and the RLA (*Communications Workers v. Beck*, 487 U.S. 735 [1988]; *Miller*, 523 U.S. at 872–74). There is some question whether union security arrangements in the private sector involve governmental action, i.e., whether they are subject to constitutional challenge by reason of labor laws that permit them. The Supreme Court has more readily found governmental action under the RLA than the NLRA (*Hanson*, 351 U.S. at 231–232), since the RLA preempts any state law barring union security arrangements, while the NLRA allows states to prohibit union security arrangements through so-called "right to work" laws. In any event, the Supreme Court has interpreted the RLA's union security provisions to conform to the First Amendment (*Machinists v. Street*, 367 U.S. 740, 749 [1961]), and it has interpreted the NLRA's union security provisions to conform to its interpretation of the RLA (*Beck*, 487 U.S. 735).

To some extent, public-sector unions actually have greater leeway than private-sector unions in using the fees of objecting nonmembers for political purposes. The line between prohibited political activities and permitted bargaining-related activities is "somewhat hazier" in the public sector (*Abood*, 431 U.S. at 236), because public-sector unions "often expend considerable resources in securing ratification of negotiated agreements by the proper state or local legislative body" (*Lehnert*, 500 U.S. at 520). Even in the public sector, however, unions may not use agency fees for "legislative lobbying or other political union activities outside the limited context of contract ratification or implementation" (*Lehnert*, 500 U.S. at 522).

If a union spends dues money for purposes that cannot be charged to objecting nonmembers, it must reduce the agency fees paid by objecting nonmembers below the level of dues. For example, if 80 percent of a union's expenditures are for purposes that are germane to collective bargaining and 20 percent are for purposes that are not germane, the agency fee the union charges to nonmembers can be only 80 percent of dues. "[T]he union bears the burden of proving the proportion of chargeable expenses to total expenses" (*Lehnert*, 500 U.S. at 524).

The agency-fee regime imposed by the Court under the First Amendment is an opt-out regime. A public-sector union must provide certain information to nonmembers explaining the agency fee (*Teachers v. Hudson*, 475 U.S. 292 [1986]), but having provided the required information, the union need not reduce any nonmember's agency fee below the level of union dues unless the nonmember objects to the use of his fee for nonbargaining purposes. As this encyclopedia goes to press, the Supreme Court is considering whether states that permit the agency shop, for state and local employees, may impose on public-sector unions a considerably more onerous method of administering agency fees. In *Davenport v. Washington Education Assn.*, 551 U.S. ___ (2007), the Supreme Court of Washington struck down, as violative of the First Amendment, a state law that required unions to obtain the affirmative consent of nonmembers before using their agency fees for political purposes. The Supreme Court reversed this decision, holding that it does not violate a union's First Amendment rights to receive non-union members' consent before spending their money on election activities.

For more information: Higgins, John E. *The Developing Labor Law.* Washington, D.C.: BNA Books, 2006.

—Mark S. Stein

United Jewish Organization v. Carey 430 U.S. 144 (1977)

The Supreme Court, in *United Jewish Organization v. Carey*, held that the use of racial criteria in drawing voting district lines to comply with Section 5 of the VOTING RIGHTS ACT (VRA) was permissible under the FOURTEENTH and FIFTEENTH AMENDMENTS. The holding in *UJO* made all race-conscious redistricting to advantage minority voters constitutionally permissible for over a decade and a half.

Under Section 5 of the Voting Rights Act, states or political subdivisions with a history of discrimination must obtain preapproval for any voting changes from the attorney general of the United States. The attorney general approves only changes that do "not have the purpose and [would] not have the effect of denying or abridging the RIGHT TO VOTE on account of race or color." The attorney general's determination that New York's 1972 redistricting plan resulted in certain districts in Brooklyn that failed to meet the burden of Section 5 led to the litigation in *UJO*. In particular, the attorney general objected to the lack of state senate and state assembly districts with substantial nonwhite majorities of at least 65 percent, the percentage deemed necessary to secure an opportunity for minorities to elect their candidates of choice. In response to these objections, in 1974 the state of New York revised the redistricting plan and created additional districts with substantial nonwhite majorities. The revised plan split a community of Hasidic Jews, previously located entirely in one district, into two separate state senate and assembly districts in which they constituted a smaller minority of the population.

Members of the Hasidic Jewish community in Brooklyn challenged the 1974 redistricting plan, arguing that: (a) it diluted the value of each plaintiff's franchise for the sole purpose of achieving a RACIAL QUOTA in violation of the Fourteenth Amendment, and (b) assigned them to districts solely on the basis of race, which diluted their voting power in violation of the Fifteenth Amendment. Justice White, writing for a majority of the Court, held that the deliberate use of race in this case was permissible under the Constitution because its use did not represent a "racial slur or stigma with regards to whites or any other race." Hasidic Jews, who were grouped into the category of whites by the Court, were not deprived of access to the political process by the plan, and their voting strength was not diluted as demonstrated by the fact that 70 percent of the districts continued to be majority white in a county that was 65 percent white. The Court concluded that in light of the unfortunate reality of racial bloc voting, the plan was necessary "to achieve a fair allocation of political power between white and non-white voters in [Brooklyn]."

Chief Justice WARREN BURGER dissented, contending that the redistricting in this case was analogous to that in *GOMILLION V. LIGHTFOOT*, 364 U.S. 339 (1960), in which the Court found the drawing of district lines solely on the basis of race (i.e., "racial gerrymandering") unconstitutional under the Fifteenth Amendment. He argued that the way to address past race-based reapportionment in favor of whites was not to require more race-based reapportionment in favor of minority groups, but instead to require race-neutral redistricting. Allowing for continued racial gerrymandering, Chief Justice Burger concluded, "puts the imprimatur of the State on the concept that race is a proper consideration in the electoral process."

After *UJO*, the Justice Department aggressively pursued a policy under Section 5 of ensuring that minorities, and primarily blacks, had the opportunity to elect candidates of their choice by requiring that states or subdivisions with a history of discrimination draw districts with substantial nonwhite populations. As a result of the policy, blacks and other minorities were elected to state and federal offices at a rate greater than at any point in American history. In 1993, the Supreme Court in *SHAW V. RENO*, 509 U.S. 630 (1993), implicitly repudiated part of the holding in *UJO* and placed constitutional limits on the ability of states to draw majority-minority districts.

For more information: Guinier, Lani. "Groups, Representation, and Race Conscious Redistricting: A Case of Emperor's Clothes." *Texas Law Review* 71, no. 7 (1993): 1589–1642; Issacharoff, Samuel. "Groups and the Right to Vote." *Emory Law Journal* 44, no. 869 (1995): 882–884; Sherry, Suzanne. "Selective Judicial Activism in the Equal Protection Context: Democracy, Distrust and Deconstruction." *Georgetown Law Journal* 73, no. 89 (1984): 103–105.

—Jonathan Cooper and Bertrall Ross

United States Term Limits, Inc. v. Thornton
514 U.S. 779 (1995)

In *United States Term Limits, Inc. v. Thornton,* the Supreme Court struck down an Arkansas law that limited the number of times a person could be elected to the U.S. SENATE as well as the number of times a person could be elected to the U.S. HOUSE OF REPRESENTATIVES. A closely divided court (5-4) concluded that Arkansas's term limits *added* qualifications for office to those expressed in the U.S. Constitution, and were therefore unconstitutional and could not be enforced. The majority expressed no objections to limitations on congressional terms per se, saying only that such restrictions, like the TWENTY-SECOND AMENDMENT limiting presidential terms, would have to be incorporated with an amendment to the Constitution that enforced uniform and similar standards throughout the entire nation.

By the 1980s the notion of legislative term limits—a given candidate should not serve an indefinite amount of time in a particular office—had gained national political credibility and significant organizational support. (See the Twenty-second Amendment, approved in 1951, which limited presidential terms.) Groups who were frustrated with ever increasing reelection rates of members of both houses of the U.S. Congress, as well as with what they saw as greater "professionalization" in state legislatures, began advocating term limits for all of these offices. The movement was jump-started in 1990 when three states, Colorado, California, and Oklahoma, were the first to approve term limits for their respective state legislators. Other states quickly followed suit and set term limits for their state and U.S. congressional legislators. By 1994 21 states had passed some form of term limitation on their state or federal legislators.

Arkansas was among these states. This case grew out of a challenge to its 1992 referendum approving term limits for state legislators and U.S. House and Senate candidates. Specifically at issue was Amendment 73, which denied ballot access to candidates for the U.S. House of Representatives who had served three or more terms (6+ years) and to candidates for the U.S. Senate who had served two or more terms (12+ years). The Arkansas ban stipulated that candidates who had served longer than those specified periods would not be eligible to have their names placed on ballots for reelection to those offices.

Almost immediately after its passage, this amendment was challenged by an Arkansas citizen, Bobbie Hill, who made the general argument that these congressional term limits took away her right to return to office a candidate of whom she approved and wanted to continue serving in office. Specifically claiming that these new restrictions were unconstitutional, she was joined in her suit by the Arkansas League of Women Voters. Various state officials, party organizations, and U.S. Term Limits, Inc., a think tank and advocacy group that had been actively involved in the Arkansas referendum, defended the state's limits. They argued that these limits were nothing more than a regulatory decision that was consistent with the Constitution's "Times, Places and Manner" provisions (the elections clause of ARTICLE I, Section 4) which mandated state administration of elections for federal officials.

The Supreme Court was faced with a judgment as to whether these term limits were additional qualifications to those specified in the Constitution or merely an appropriate procedural activity.

In a detailed and historically revealing opinion that reviewed previous and unsuccessful attempts to exclude members from House and Senate offices, Justice JOHN PAUL STEVENS said, "Amendment 73 is an indirect attempt to accomplish what the Constitution prohibits Arkansas from accomplishing directly. . . . [an] effort to dress eligibility to stand for Congress in ballot access clothing."

The Court's decision in this case terminated the state-by-state strategy of limiting congressional terms, one that had piggy-backed on initiatives limiting state legislators. The Court said an amendment would be required to do that. The legacy of *Thornton* and the Court's subsequent decisions to allow state term limits to stand when applied to state legislatures has left 18 states with various limits on members of their legislatures and the U.S. Constitution silent about congressional ones. For the U.S. House and U.S. Senate, the qualifications specified by the framers are still in place.

For more information: Peery, George. "A Time Line of Term Limits." In *State and Local Government, 2000–2001,* edited by Thad L. Beyle, 88–92. Washington, D.C.: Congressional Quarterly, 2000; Will, George. *Restoration: Congress, Term Limits, and the Recovery of Deliberative Democracy.* New York: Free Press, 1992.

—George Peery

United States Trust Company v. New Jersey
431 U.S. 1 (1977)

In *United States Trust Company v. New Jersey,* the Supreme Court ruled that the CONTRACT CLAUSE prohibited the repeal of a covenant between New York and New Jersey. The significance of the case is that it is one of the few cases in recent times to use this clause of the Constitution to invalidate a law.

In 1962, the states of New Jersey and New York agreed to limit the Port Authority of New York and New Jersey's ability to use revenues and reserves pledged as security for consolidated bonds in order to subsidize rail passenger service. This was good for the bondholders, yet in 1974 both New York and New Jersey passed statutes effectively repealing the 1962 agreement.

The appellant in this case sued in New Jersey Superior Court under the claim that "the 1974 New Jersey statute impaired the obligation of the States' contract with the bondholders in violation of the Contract Clause of the United States Constitution." The contract clause in this case involved ARTICLE I, Section 10, Clause 1, which prohibits the states from passing a law "impairing the Obligation of Contracts." The New Jersey Superior Court dismissed the complaint, concluding that repeal of the 1962 statute was within the purview of New Jersey's POLICE POWER and therefore not in violation of the contract clause of Article I, Section 10. The New Jersey Supreme Court affirmed the lower court's decision.

The constitutional question before the Supreme Court when the case came up on appeal was: Did the states violate the contract clause? In a 4-3 decision—opinion delivered by Justice Blackmun—the Court narrowly concluded that the contract clause of the Constitution prohibits the repeal of the 1962 covenant between New York and New Jersey. Justice Blackmun noted:

> The more specific justification offered for the repeal of the 1962 covenant was the States' plan for encouraging users of private automobiles to shift to public transportation. The States intended to discourage private automobile use by raising bridge and tunnel tolls and to use the extra revenue from those tolls to subsidize improved commuter railroad service. Appellees contend that repeal of the 1962 covenant was necessary to implement this plan because the new mass transit facilities could not possibly be self-supporting and the covenant's "permitted deficits" level had already been exceeded. We reject this justification because the repeal was neither necessary to achievement of the plan nor reasonable in light of the circumstances.

> The determination of necessity can be considered on two levels. First, it cannot be said that total repeal of the covenant . . . was essential; a less drastic modification would have permitted the contemplated plan without entirely removing the covenant's limitations on the use of Port Authority revenues and reserves to subsidize commuter railroads . . . Second, without modifying the covenant at all, the States could have adopted alternative means of achieving their twin goals of discouraging automobile use and improving mass transit . . . Appellees contend, however, that choosing among these alternatives is a matter for legislative discretion. But a State is not completely free to consider impairing the obligations . . . of its own contracts on a par with other policy alternatives

Overall, *United States Trust Company v. New Jersey* seemed to demonstrate that the contract clause was not dead and that it might still affect actions of the government.

For more information: Farber, Daniel A., William N. Eskridge, Jr., and Philip P. Frickey. *Cases and Materials on Constitutional Law: Themes for the Constitution's Third Century.* St. Paul, Minn.: West Publishing, 1993.

—Dan Krejci

United States v. American Library Association 539 U.S. 194 (2003)

In *United States v. American Library Association,* 539 U.S. 194 (2003), the U.S. Supreme Court found the Children's Internet Protection Act (CIPA) constitutional. CIPA prohibited public libraries that did not install filtering software, designed to prevent library patrons from accessing obscene or pornographic material, from receiving federal funds. A plurality of the Court, Chief Justice WILLIAM HUBBS REHNQUIST, joined by Justices SANDRA DAY O'CONNOR, ANTONIN GREGORY SCALIA, and CLARENCE THOMAS, held that CIPA was a valid exercise of congressional spending that did not raise FIRST AMENDMENT problems; Justices ANTHONY M. KENNEDY and STEPHEN G. BREYER each concurred, finding that CIPA's restrictions would withstand STRICT SCRUTINY or heightened scrutiny, respectively. The three dissenters in the case, Justices JOHN PAUL STEVENS, DAVID H. SOUTER, and Ginsburg, objected that the filtering technology would, in practice, "overblock" or filter "nonobscene material harmful to children but lawful for adult examination, and a substantial quantity of text and pictures harmful to no one."

The Children's Internet Protection Act followed a series of congressional efforts designed to regulate pornography on the Internet, including the COMMUNICATIONS DECENCY ACT of 1996 (struck down as unconstitutional in *Reno v. ACLU,* 521 U.S. 844 [1997]), the Child Pornography Prevention Act of 1996 (struck down as unconstitutional in *Ashcroft v. The Free Speech Coalition,* 535 U.S. 234 [2002]), and the Child Online Protection Act (struck down as unconstitutional in *Ashcroft v. ACLU,* 542 U.S. 656 [2004]). The contents of this particular legislation were the result of several factors. First, the First Amendment, in general, prohibits limitations on "pornography," but instead allows governments in some circumstances to restrict "OBSCENITY" (*MILLER V.*

CALIFORNIA, 413 U.S. 15 [1973]). Second, case law has upheld restrictions against CHILD PORNOGRAPHY depicting actual children who are exploited by the production process (*New York v. Ferber,* 458 U.S. 747 [1982]). And third, the Supreme Court has upheld congressional spending provisions that would not have been upheld as outright regulations (*SOUTH DAKOTA V. DOLE,* 483 U.S. 203 [1987]; *RUST V. SULLIVAN,* 500 U.S. 173 [1991]; *NEA v. FINLEY,* 524 U.S. 569 [1998]). Given these three factors, Congress opted not to regulate pornography directly, but instead to condition federal funds to libraries on using filtering software to block obscenity or child pornography, and to block minors from reviewing harmful material.

The plurality found that libraries may consider the content of material in deciding what to include in their collections, including whether to include pornography, noting that such filtering is not fundamentally different from the selection that libraries undertake with their physical book collections. As such, congressional spending provisions tied to the blocking of such material did raise First Amendment problems. Further, the plurality argued that the constitutional concerns voiced by the dissents about the tendency of filtering software to "overblock," are eliminated by the ability of library patrons to request that Web sites be unblocked, even if such requests would be embarrassing. Justices Kennedy and Breyer, both of whom voted to uphold the constitutionality of CIPA, voiced reasons different from the plurality. These opinions both balanced the interests of the government served by the legislation and the burden foisted upon library patrons in favor of the government, either one of which provided the government with the winning fifth vote—albeit for reasons different from the plurality.

—Martin J. Sweet and Jensen Grant

United States v. Belmont 301 U.S. 324
(1937)

In *United States v. Belmont,* the Supreme Court upheld a presidential executive agreement reached to settle debts with the Soviet Union. This case is important because it gave wide constitutional authority to the president to use executive agreements in foreign affairs.

Executive agreements are international compacts negotiated by the president of the United States with other heads of state. Although the U.S. Constitution (ARTICLE II, Section 2) requires that treaties—formal agreements between nations—be approved by a two-thirds vote of the U.S. SENATE, the Constitution does not specifically mention executive agreements. In *United States v. Belmont,* the U.S. Supreme Court recognized for the first time the constitutionality of executive agreements, thus placing them on a par with U.S. treaties. Additionally, the Court reinforced that the president alone has power to recognize foreign governments and establish diplomatic relations with foreign states. This case significantly expanded the power of the presidency, not only in the field of international diplomacy, but also in the area of domestic affairs.

Prior to the Bolshevik Revolution in October 1917, the Petrograd Metal Works, a Russian corporation, deposited investments in a New York City bank owned by August Belmont. In 1917, the Bolshevik (Communist) party led a bloody revolution, established the Soviet Union, nationalized corporations, confiscated their property, and claimed all corporate assets—including funds deposited in American banks. President Woodrow Wilson refused to recognize the legitimacy of the newly created Soviet Union, and in 1918 cut off diplomatic relations with the Soviet state. It was not until 1933 that President Franklin Roosevelt officially recognized the Soviet Union and reopened diplomatic channels. Under the Litvinov Assignments, President Roosevelt entered into an executive agreement whereby the United States government would serve as the agent to release Soviet assets held in American banks before the October Revolution of 1917. When the U.S. government ordered the Belmont bank to relinquish the Petrograd Metal Works assets, the bank refused, and the government filed suit in U.S. district court to recover the funds for the Soviet Union.

The federal district court, however, ruled in favor of Belmont, noting that: (a) the U.S. government had no authority to supersede the New

York law that specifically forbade the confiscation of bank assets; (b) the confiscation of such funds violated the Fifth Amendment's command that private property shall not be taken without JUST COMPENSATION; and (c) the president was acting pursuant to an executive agreement and not a TREATY, which required the advice and consent of the U.S. Senate. The U.S. Court of Appeals affirmed the lower court decision, and the federal government appealed to the U.S. Supreme Court.

Writing for the majority, Justice George Sutherland ruled that the lower courts erred in dismissing the suit. According to Sutherland: (a) the president had the sole constitutional authority to recognized foreign governments and exchange diplomatic personnel; (b) the executive agreement entered into by the president had the same effect as a treaty; (c) the Constitution's SUPREMACY CLAUSE (Article VI, Section 2) makes treaties and executive agreements superior to any conflicting state laws; and (d) the Fifth Amendment's TAKINGS CLAUSE applies only to U.S. citizens and not Soviet subjects. Justice Sutherland was joined by Justices Pierce Butler, Charles Evans Hughes, Owen Roberts, James McReynolds, and Willis Van Devanter. Delivering a concurring opinion was Justice HARLAN FISKE STONE, joined by Justices Benjamin Cardozo and Louis Brandeis. There was no dissenting opinion.

The implications of *Belmont* are far-reaching. Over the years, presidents have increasingly relied upon executive agreements to accomplish foreign-policy goals that might not otherwise be ratified as treaties by skeptical senators. Critics charge that executive agreements are more secretive than treaties and have shifted too much power to the president in the field of international affairs. Moreover, critics maintain that, because of the supremacy clause, it is possible for a president to alter domestic policy through executive agreements that otherwise might be unconstitutional. The *Belmont* decision was reaffirmed in *UNITED STATES V. PINK* (1942), when the Court ruled that state insurance companies also had no authority to prevent the restoration of Soviet assets under the terms of an executive agreement.

For more information: Margolis, Lawrence. *Executive Agreements and Presidential Power in Foreign Policy.* New York: Praeger, 1985; Mayer, Kenneth R. *With the Stroke of a Pen: Executive Orders and Presidential Power.* Princeton, N.J.: Princeton University Press, 2001.

—Richard J. Hardy

United States v. Booker 543 U.S. 220 (2005)
In *United States v. Booker* (2005), the Supreme Court ruled that a judge could not set a sentence above the federal SENTENCING GUIDELINE maximum without a jury determination of the facts beyond a reasonable doubt supporting such a decision. The importance of the decision is that more discretionary power has been taken away from the judge to ensure that the guarantee of the right to jury trial and the right to DUE PROCESS of the defendant is retained.

Freddie Booker was found guilty by a federal jury of the possession to distribute 50 grams of crack. The Federal Sentencing Guideline Commission mandated a "base" sentence range from a minimum of 210 months to a maximum of 262 months. The statutory maximum at the federal level for this offense is life imprisonment. During sentencing, the judge found, by a preponderance of the evidence, that Booker had possessed an additional 566 grams of crack—an additional fact not found by the jury. Based on this "relevant conduct" mandatory enhancement, the judge imposed a sentence of a minimum of 360 months, with the maximum of life imprisonment. "Relevant conduct" is evidence substantiated during sentencing but not found in the facts at trial. In conjunction with *United States v. Fanfan*, 543 U.S. 220 (2005), the Supreme Court considered two issues: (1) Did the federal sentencing guidelines' mandatory enhancement, which were based on facts not proven by a jury beyond a reasonable doubt, violate the SIXTH AMENDMENT right to jury, and (2) if this provision did violate the right to jury, what was the remedy for such violation? The Supreme Court found that the trial court did violate the right to jury trial with these relevant-conduct mandatory enhancements.

The United States Supreme Court found that the federal sentencing guidelines were mandatory and binding on all judges and, thereby, should be treated more like a statute because they "have the force and effect of laws." The Court mirrored its own decision in *Blakely v. Washington* (2004) by devoting its legal analysis to the effect of this enhancement departure rather than its form.

The most decisive rule made by the Supreme Court in *Booker* was its suggestion for remedy. The Court considered two possible remedies: (1) Insert statutory protection of the constitutional right to a jury trial within the articulated sentencing guidelines, or (2) rule that the federal sentencing guidelines are advisory. The Court concluded that the remedy for this error was to eliminate the mandatory nature of the federal sentencing guidelines—that is, they are now simply advisory. The Supreme Court saw value in retaining a strong connection between the use of "relevant conduct" or "real offense" factors for purposes of increased uniformity of sentencing. "Real conduct" is often not proved beyond a reasonable doubt and is often inadmissible in the trial court (see Spohn, 2000). Sentences based on real conduct were often decided on a case-by-case basis, which is now the official stance of the Court.

In the first part of the 21st century, the United States Supreme Court drastically changed the face of sentencing reforms. Although the Court, in *Mistretta v. United States*, 488 U.S. 361 (1989), ruled that sentencing guidelines did not violate the separation of powers doctrine and were constitutional, the Court has now ruled that a judge can not increase the sentence with facts not determined by a jury beyond a reasonable doubt (*Apprendi v. New Jersey*, 530 U.S. 466 [2000]). Judges also can not depart above the prescribed guideline range under the same principle whether they increase the sentence over the statutory maximum or not (*Blakely v. Washington*, 542 U.S. 296 [2004], and *United States v. Booker*, 543 U.S. 220 [2005]). Therefore, the face of the sentencing guidelines has drastically changed, and sentencing guidelines, at the federal level, have been all but eliminated.

For more information: Barrueco, A. L. "Fast-tracking *United States v. Booker:* Why Judges Should Not Fix Fast-track Disparities." *Connecticut Public Interest Law Journal* 6 (2006): 65–109; Spohn, C. *How Do Judges Decide?: The Quest for Fairness and Justice in Sentencing.* Thousand Oaks, Calif.: Pine Forge Press, 2002; United States Sentencing Commission. *Final Report on the Impact of* United States v. Booker *on Federal Sentencing.* Washington, D.C.: United States Sentencing Commission, March 2006; Yellen, D. "Saving Federal Sentencing Reform after Apprendi, Blakely and Booker." *Villanova Law Review* 50 (2005): 163–187.

—Jeremy D. Ball and Barbara J. Hayler

United States v. Classic 313 U.S. 299 (1941)

In *United States v. Classic,* the Supreme Court upheld the power of Congress under ARTICLE I, Section 4 to regulate political primaries when they are part of the process of choosing candidates for federal office. *Classic* is part of a group of decisions known as the "White Primary" cases that sought to ban discrimination against African Americans in politics.

In *Newberry v. United States,* 256 U.S. 232 (1921), the Supreme Court ruled that Article I, Section 4 of the U.S. Constitution did not provide Congress the power to regulate the states' primary elections. In other words, Congress did not have the authority to dictate how political parties conducted their primaries, which are used to select party candidates who will run in the general election in November. For the one-party (Democrats) South, this essentially alienated black voters from the selection process. States dominated by one political party chose their representatives in the primary elections (known as White Primaries)—the general election was only a formality. In other words, the candidates from these one-party states who would become the members of Congress were actually elected in the primary election, not the general election, because these candidates usually ran unopposed or faced weak challengers. *United States v. Classic* changed precedent, to some degree, which was established in the *Newberry* case.

In *United States v. Classic,* the Supreme Court reversed itself from the decision it reached in *Newberry.* In this case, two counts of an indictment were brought against the commissioners of elections, who conducted a primary election in Louisiana to nominate a Democratic candidate for Congress. The case centered on whether or not "the right of qualified voters to vote in the Louisiana primary and to have their ballots counted is a right 'secured by the Constitution' within the meaning of 19 and 20 of the Criminal Code, and whether the acts of appellees charged in the indictment violated those sections." The Court held that Article I, Section 4 provides Congress with the power to regulate elections, including primary elections, when state law incorporates the primary as an essential part of the process used for choosing candidates who will be national representatives. In addition, the Court ruled that Article I, Section 2 provides citizens with a guaranteed RIGHT TO VOTE in congressional primaries, and these citizens have a right to have their votes counted, and the state cannot interfere with this right.

For more information: Bixby, David M. "The Roosevelt Court, Democratic Ideology, and Minority Rights: Another Look at *United States v. Classic.*" *Yale Law Journal* 90, no. 4 (March 1981): 741–815.

—Dan Krejci

United States v. Curtiss-Wright Export Corp.
299 U.S. 304 (1936)

In *United States v. Curtiss-Wright Export Corp.,* the Supreme Court held that Congress was not in violation of the nondelegation doctrine when it gave authority to the executive to declare an arms embargo in South America in an effort to reestablish peace in the region.

On May 28, 1934, Congress passed a joint resolution that gave the president the authority to prohibit the sale of weapons and munitions to countries that were engaged in the Gran Chaco War, if the president believed that such a course of action would help to reestablish peace in the region. The next day, President Roosevelt issued a proclamation making it illegal for American companies to sell such products to countries engaged in the armed hostilities. The proclamation was revoked by a second executive-issued proclamation allowing for the sale of weapons and munitions at the end of 1935. In 1936, the Curtiss-Wright Export Corporation was charged with conspiring to illegally sell 15 machine guns to Bolivia before the second proclamation was issued. Since Bolivia was engaged in the Chaco conflict, the corporation was in violation of the joint resolution of Congress as well as the first proclamation issued by President Roosevelt.

The issue before the Supreme Court was whether or not Congress was within its authority to delegate to the executive broad authority to execute the joint resolution, granting to the office lawmaking power. The Court did not find a constitutional violation, though in the year prior to this decision, the Court had struck down congressional grants of power to the president in the domestic sphere (*PANAMA REFINING CO. V. RYAN,* 293 U.S. 388 [1935], and *Schechter Corp. v. United States,* 295 U.S. 495 [1935]).

Justice Sutherland, joined by Chief Justice Hughes and Justices Devanter, Brandeis, Butler, STONE, Roberts, and Cardozo, wrote for the Court, holding that if the joint resolution had related solely to internal affairs, it could be challenged whether or not it constituted an unlawful delegation of legislative power to the executive, as had been the case in the cases the year before. However, the stated purpose of the resolution was to control a situation external to the United States, thus falling within the category of foreign affairs. The Court held that the limitation on the federal government exercising only powers specifically enumerated in the Constitution is true in respect to domestic affairs alone. The Court found that, while the Constitution does not specifically grant to the president authority to conduct foreign relations alone, it is implicitly granted and therefore the "broad discretion" that Congress conferred upon the executive should be vested in the president to decide whether or not the enforcement of the congressional joint resolution would aid in the reestablishment of peace in the affected countries. Sutherland makes it clear that it is important to note that this case does not take into consideration only the authority vested in the president by Congress, but also the power of the president "as the sole organ of the federal government in the field of international relations." Justice McReynolds dissented in a very short sentence, stating simply that he did not agree and was of the opinion that the circuit court had reached the right opinion and its judgment should have been affirmed.

While the ruling in this case concerns the powers of the federal government in general, and in particular how far the powers of delegation from Congress to the president reach, it is remembered and often cited for Sutherland's suggestion, quoting a speech of former chief justice JOHN MARSHALL, made in 1800 when he was a member of the HOUSE OF REPRESENTATIVES and one year before being appointed chief justice of the Supreme Court, that the president is the "sole organ" of the nation in the area of foreign affairs. This ruling is significant not only because it upheld export limitations on the grounds of national security but also, more important, because it established the broad principle of executive supremacy in matters relating to both national security and foreign affairs. Since the decision, presidents on both sides of the aisle have been known to quote the decision in letters to Congress, suggesting the executive's power in the area of foreign affairs is broad. It should be noted that Marshall's concept of the executive as the "sole organ" in foreign affairs actually was in regard to the president's authority to communicate with other nations, not to make policy concerning other nations without consultation from Congress.

Proponents of expanded executive authority in the area of international relations draw upon the *Curtiss-Wright* decision as authoritative. For example, as assistant attorney general, future chief justice of the Supreme Court WILLIAM HUBBS REHNQUIST would argue the constitutionality of the Vietnam War's Tonkin Gulf Resolution on the basis of the *Curtiss-Wright* decision. As a justice, Rehnquist would again rely on *Curtiss-Wright* affirming the power of the president to terminate

treaties without the consent of the SENATE (*GOLDWATER V. CARTER*, 444 U.S. 996 [1979]). Yet members of the Court have also tried to curtail such reasoning. Justice Jackson argued that *Curtiss-Wright* actually suggests that that, while the president may act in foreign affairs without explicit congressional authority to do so, he cannot act contrary to an act of Congress and has the most leniency from the federal courts when the executive acts pursuant to a congressional statute (*YOUNGSTOWN SHEET & TUBE V. SAWYER*, 343 U.S. 579, 636 n. 2 [1952]), showing the prominence of Congress even in the area of foreign affairs. A federal circuit court also criticized the opinion, stating that the dicta in which Sutherland claims the president is the sole organ in foreign affairs is a "blanket endorsement" of the executive having control over all policy that extends beyond the borders of the country. That court rejected this view (*American Intern. Group v. Islamic Republic of Iran,* 657 F.2nd 430, 438 n. 6 [D.C. Cir. 1981]).

For more information: Fisher, Louis. *Presidential War Power.* Lawrence: University Press of Kansas, 2004; Silverstein, Gordon. *Imbalance of Powers.* Oxford: Oxford University Press, 1997; Wormuth, Francis, and Edwin Firmage. *To Chain the Dog of War: The War Powers of Congress in History and Law.* 2d ed. Chicago: University of Illinois Press, 1989; Yoo, John. *The Powers of War and Peace: The Constitution and Foreign Affairs after 9/11.* Chicago: Chicago University Press, 2005.

—Amanda DiPaolo

United States v. Darby Lumber Co. 312 U.S. 100 (1941)

In *United States v. Darby*, the U.S. Supreme Court upheld federal minimum wage laws as a valid power of Congress under the COMMERCE CLAUSE.

In 1938 Congress passed the Fair Labor Standards Act (FLSA). This law prevented the shipping in INTERSTATE COMMERCE of goods that are produced by companies whose employees are paid less than the minimum wage or who work more than 40 hours a week without overtime pay.

Fred Darby was an owner of a lumber business who was indicted for violating the provisions of the FSLA, and he challenged the constitutionality of the law on the grounds that it exceeded Congress's commerce clause authority in the Constitution. At issue in this case was whether Congress could regulate the conditions of manufacturing. If manufacturing conditions were considered solely intrastate (no matter whether they were eventually distributed across state lines), then it would appear that Congress had violated its authority under the commerce clause, and the matter would be left to individual state governments for regulation, if at all.

A unanimous Court held the FLSA was a constitutional exercise of congressional authority under the commerce clause. The Court conceded that the manufacturing that occurred at the Darby Lumber Company was intrastate; however, once the goods were shipped and crossed state lines, then the goods became interstate and could be regulated by the federal government. Relying upon GIBBONS V. OGDEN (1824), the Court concluded that the Congress's commerce clause authority is complete concerning goods that are or could become commerce, even if congressional intent was to regulate the conditions of manufacturing (and not necessarily just the distribution of goods across state lines).

A roadblock for the Court in *Darby* was its ruling in HAMMER V. DAGENHART (1918). In that case, the Court held that Congress did not have the authority under the commerce clause to pass a law that excluded products of CHILD LABOR from becoming interstate commerce. The Court's vote in *Hammer* was 5-4, and it contained a classic dissent authored by Justice OLIVER WENDELL HOLMES. The Court in *Darby* proclaimed that the *Hammer* decision was wrongly decided and was a departure from its body of rulings concerning the commerce clause.

Moreover, addressing the claim that the power to regulate manufacturing conditions was a right reserved to the states per the Tenth Amendment, the Court stated that its ruling in this case was unaffected by the Tenth Amendment. Indicating quite clearly a jurisprudential philosophy that would be controlling on the Court for next 50+ years, Justice STONE's opinion for the Court stated that the Tenth Amendment was nothing more than a declaration of the general relationship between the national and state governments. As far as Congress's commerce clause authority was concerned, Congress could regulate interstate commerce and the conditions related to the production of goods that were eventually transported interstate without being hampered by the Tenth Amendment.

The ruling in *Darby* represented a fine example of how the Court in the late 1930s and early 1940s began to show great deference to the elected branches of the federal government to regulate the economy per various New Deal legislation and programs. In the early years of the New Deal, the Court was quite skeptical of the idea that the Constitution gave the national government the authority to enact legislation that would create economic policy for the entire nation (see *United States v. Butler*, 1936, wherein the Court struck down a farm subsidies program). However, in a few short years, the Court changed its philosophy and began to uphold the constitutionality of numerous New Deal programs, like the one questioned in *Darby*.

For more information: Leuchtenburg, William E. *The Supreme Court Reborn: The Constitutional Revolution in the Age of Roosevelt.* New York: Oxford University Press, 1995; Schwartz, Bernard. *A History of the Supreme Court.* New York: Oxford University Press, 1993.

—John M. Aughenbaugh

United States v. E.C. Knight Co. 156 U.S. 1 (1895)

In *United States v. E.C. Knight Company*, the Supreme Court ruled that sugar manufacturing was not part of INTERSTATE COMMERCE and therefore was beyond the scope of federal regulation. The Court's narrow definition of interstate commerce severely weakened the national government's efforts to eradicate monopolies under the Sherman Antitrust Act of 1890.

ARTICLE I, Section 8 of the Constitution delegates to Congress the authority to regulate interstate commerce. Under the aegis of this COMMERCE CLAUSE, Congress enacted the Sherman Antitrust Act of 1890. This landmark act banned trusts and combinations that restrain trade in interstate or foreign commerce. The law authorized the Justice Department to seek INJUNCTIONS, seize property, and file criminal and civil suits against violators.

One target of the federal prosecutors under the Sherman Antitrust Act was the sugar monopoly involving the E.C. Knight Company. By the early 1890s, just six companies controlled the American sugar industry. The largest company, the American Sugar Refining Company, dominated approximately 65 percent of the market. Four Pennsylvania-based refiners, including the E.C. Knight Company, collectively controlled about 33 percent of the market, and one Massachusetts-based company did a mere 2 percent of the nation's sugar refining. In 1892, the American Sugar Refining Company acquired the four Pennsylvania companies, giving it control over 98 percent of the sugar refining market. The U.S. government filed suit under the Sherman Antitrust Act to prevent the merger. The E.C. Knight Company, which favored the merger, argued that sugar refining constituted "manufacturing"—not "commerce"—and was therefore beyond the scope of federal regulation. The lower court ruled in favor of Knight, and the federal government appealed.

Is the manufacturing of refined sugar part of interstate commerce and therefore subject to congressional regulation? In *United States v. E.C. Knight,* the Supreme Court affirmed the lower court decision holding that sugar production did not constitute commerce. Delivering the majority opinion, Chief Justice Melville Fuller observed, "Commerce succeeds to manufacturing, and is not a part of it. . . . The fact that an article is manufactured for export to another State does not of itself make it an article of interstate commerce, and the intent of the manufacturer does not determine the time when the article or product passes from the control of a State and belongs to commerce." Fuller concluded that any regulation would have to come

from the states under their POLICE POWERS. Justices Stephen Field, Horace Gray, David Brewer, Henry Brown, Rufus Peckham, Edward White, and George Shiras, Jr., joined in the decision.

The lone dissenter was JOHN MARSHALL HARLAN. Harlan recognized the threat monopolies posed and argued that collusion in manufacturing had a direct impact on the price of goods in interstate commerce. Moreover, Harlan believed that the magnitude of the problem was beyond the scope of individual states to remedy. According to Harlan, "The general government is not placed by the Constitution in such a condition of helplessness that it must fold its arms and remain inactive while capital combines, under the name of a corporation, to destroy competition. . . . The doctrine of the autonomy of the states cannot properly be invoked to justify a denial of power in the national government to meet such an emergency, involving, as it does, that freedom of commercial intercourse among the states which the Constitution sought to attain."

The Court's ruling in this case weakened the enforcement of the Sherman Antitrust Act. However, in *Addystone Pipe and Steel Company v. United States* (1899) the Court upheld portions of the Sherman Antitrust Act in restricting the collusive sale and distribution of pipes in interstate commerce. Significant federal antitrust action did not occur until 1914, when Congress enacted the Clayton Antitrust Act and established the Federal Trade Commission. And it was generally not until the New Deal that the Supreme Court began to consistently uphold federal antitrust regulations under the commerce clause.

For more information: Bork, Robert. *The Anti-Trust Paradox: A Policy at War with Itself.* New York: Basic Books, 1978; Hovenkamp, Herbert. *Enterprise and American Law, 1836–1937.* Cambridge, Mass.: Harvard University Press, 1991.

—Richard J. Hardy

United States v. Lopez 514 U.S. 549 (1995)

In *United States v. Lopez,* the U.S. Supreme Court held that, in enacting the provision of the federal Gun-Free School Zones Act of 1990 that makes carrying a firearm within 1,000 feet of a public school a federal crime, Congress exceeded its authority under the Constitution's INTERSTATE COMMERCE power.

Alfonso Lopez had been convicted under the federal act for carrying a weapon within a school zone. In an attempt to have his federal indictment dismissed, he challenged the act as an unconstitutional exercise of Congress's interstate commerce power. To understand the significance of this case, it is necessary to examine its historical and constitutional context. One of the enumerated powers granted to Congress in the Constitution is the interstate commerce power. It was not until the end of the 19th century that Congress began to use this power as the basis of federal laws. At that same time, however, the Court began to see the commerce power less as a source of federal power and more as a prohibition on federal interference in a state's local or internal commerce. From the 1870s until 1937, the Court progressively restricted Congress's use of the commerce power in most areas of regulation.

Beginning abruptly in 1937, the Court dramatically shifted its position on the scope of federal commerce power, moving to a position of great deference to Congress's judgment on the link between the regulated activities and interstate commerce. The Court gave Congress virtually complete discretion to regulate the channels of interstate commerce with respect to the movement of any people or goods as well as activities within a state, if such activities are a part of or affect interstate commerce. Under this view, even if the commercial impact of the activity of a single individual is minute, the aggregate of such activities was seen as having a sufficient impact on interstate commerce to satisfy the constitutional threshold. During the years following 1937, Congress acted pursuant to this broad interpretation and greatly expanded the use of this power well beyond economic regulation into other areas such as CIVIL RIGHTS and social welfare, making it the most significant source of federal regulatory power. This approach, extending over a 60-year period, came to an end in 1995 with the decision in *United States v. Lopez*.

In this landmark decision, the Supreme Court, for the first time since 1937, declared a federal statute to be beyond Congress's interstate commerce power. The Court found that: (1) The statute at issue had "nothing to do with 'commerce' or any sort of economic enterprise"; (2) it lacked a provision that would require a judicial examination of whether the defendant's firearm possession affected interstate commerce; and (3) there were no congressional findings that might assist the Court in evaluating the legislature's judgment on that question. The Court rejected the government's argument that, even if Lopez's possession of a gun in a school zone did not impact interstate commerce, the aggregate effect of guns in public schools had a substantial effect on interstate commerce.

Given the widespread use of the commerce power as a basis for federal regulation, the potential impact of this decision is enormous. The decision casts doubt on a tremendous amount of federal legislation based on the commerce power. The dissenting opinions in *Lopez* expressed some alarm over this matter. During the decade since the *Lopez* decision, the Court has decided two more cases that rest on a similarly narrow view of the interstate commerce power. This reinforces the suggestion that a majority of the Court has embraced a new interpretation of that power. The exact contours of this power and its consequences for American life remain to be seen.

For more information: Merritt, Deborah Jones. "Reflections on *United States v. Lopez:* Commerce!" *Michigan Law Review* 94 (1995): 674–751; Tribe, Lawrence H. *American Constitutional Law.* 3d ed. New York: Foundation Press, 2000.

—Steven B. Dow

United States v. Morrison 529 U.S. 598 (2000)

In a 5 to 4 decision, the Supreme Court in *United States v. Morrison* found Section 13981 of the 1994 Violence Against Women Act (VAWA) unconstitutional. The disallowed provision permitted victims of gender-motivated violence to sue their assailants in federal court.

In 1994, as a freshman at Virginia Polytechnic Institute and State University (Virginia Tech), Christy Brzonkala claimed she was raped by Antonio Morrison and James Crawford, members of the school's football team. When Brzonkala brought charges through the university's judicial system, the results seemed unsatisfactory. Crawford was acquitted and Morrison was given only a nominal penalty to be served after he graduated. Brzonkala then sued her alleged assailants under Section 13981 of the newly passed Violence Against Women Act. Based on the premise that citizens have the civil right to be free from violence based on gender just as they should be free of violence based on race, VAWA provided that victims of rape and domestic violence could bring suit in federal court. The federal district court and the Fourth Circuit found the relevant section of VAWA unconstitutional. The Supreme Court affirmed.

Congress had cited two constitutional provisions, the COMMERCE CLAUSE and the FOURTEENTH AMENDMENT, as authority for VAWA. The legislators heard hours of testimony about the effects of violence against women on the economy. Rape, domestic violence, and the fear engendered by those crimes limited women's career choices and job opportunities, curtailed their freedom to travel, and had a negative impact on their educational choices. Without a doubt, gender-based violence cost millions of dollars each year in health care and mental health costs. Based on such information, Congress determined that violence against women had a significant economic impact and could be addressed under its power to regulate INTERSTATE COMMERCE.

The Court disagreed with that analysis. They held that only economic activities or noneconomic activities with a substantial effect on the economy could be regulated under the commerce power. It took exception to Congress's judgment about the connection between violence against women and its economic impact. The Court drew a distinction between what was truly national and what was truly local. Violent crime and its repercussions were considered local matters for state law and state courts.

With respect to the Fourteenth Amendment, lawmakers heard substantial testimony that the states had failed to respond adequately to violence directed at women, especially in affording protection against rape and domestic violence. Forty-four state attorneys general agreed that the ability to sue an assailant in federal court would provide a valuable remedy for victims. If the states were failing to provide those who suffered from gender-motivated violence with EQUAL PROTECTION, Congress had the authority under the Fourteenth Amendment to enforce the equal protection guarantee.

Again, five members of the Court disagreed. They did not concede that, if women have a right to be free from gender-based violence and if the states fail to safeguard that right, the ability to sue assailants in federal court is an appropriate remedy. The justices found that the Fourteenth Amendment did not apply, as the remedy was not congruent with the offense. They believed that if the states were not protecting victims, a federal suit against an individual rapist or abuser was aimed at the wrong target.

Many supporters of VAWA draw a parallel with racism and racial violence. They argue that violence against women is a systemic problem, reflecting deep gender inequities in American society. If this is true and if gender-based violence violates a civil right to be free from attacks that grow out of bias, then the federal courts are an appropriate forum in which to address such pervasive expressions of inequality. If, however, as the Court seemed to believe, violence against women consists of isolated, individual crimes, then state and local remedies should be sufficient.

For more information: Atwell, Mary Welek. *Equal Protection of the Law?: Gender and Justice in the United States.* New York: Peter Lang, 2002; Schneider, Elizabeth M. *Battered Women and Feminist Lawmaking.* New Haven, Conn.: Yale University Press, 2000.

—Mary Welek Atwell

United States v. Nixon 418 U.S. 683 (1974)

In *United States v. Nixon,* the Supreme Court ruled against President RICHARD M. NIXON and his lawyers in favor of the United States, ordering the president to turn over tapes of White House conversations to a special prosecutor investigating the Watergate break-ins. The significance of the case was to establish not only that the president has a limited constitutional power of executive privilege, but also that a sitting president is not exempt from being subpoenaed and held legally accountable for his actions.

The case arose out of investigations into the involvement of Nixon in the break-in at the Democratic Party's national headquarters in the Watergate complex in Washington, D.C., in 1972. During congressional investigations into the break-in, one witness indicated that Nixon had tape-recorded conversations in his office. After it was revealed that the tapes existed, Archibald Cox, a special prosecutor appointed to investigate the matter, was fired in October 1973 in what has come to be known as the Saturday Night Massacre. A subsequent special prosecutor, Leon Jaworski, subpoenaed the tapes. Nixon refused to turn them over. The president's position, as defined by his lawyers, offered a claim that the president of the United States had an absolute right of executive privilege not to turn the tapes over. This concept of executive privilege was supposedly rooted in the idea of a separation of powers. The case was litigated in the federal courts until it reached the Supreme Court, which in an 8-0 decision disagreed with Nixon.

Writing for the Court, Chief Justice WARREN BURGER stated that, while executive privilege does exist within the Constitution under the concept of separation of powers and protects the office of the president from having to reveal some private conversations, this privilege is not absolute and has to give way to the needs of a pending criminal investigation. As a result of this decision, Nixon was forced to turn over the taped conversations, and this led to his eventual resignation.

United States v. Nixon is considered a watershed case in American constitutional law. It stood for the principle that presidents are not above the law and that they too have to comply with orders of the court. This case thus became a major precedent for cases such as *CLINTON V. JONES*, 520 U.S. 681 (1997), where the Court ruled that

President Richard Nixon reads a farewell speech to his staff on August 9, 1974, at the White House, Washington, D.C., following his resignation. *(George Tames/New York Times Co./Getty)*

President Clinton was not excepted from having to face a sexual harassment lawsuit brought by Paula Jones while he was still president. However, *Nixon* also has created some constitutional confusion. While the Court stated that executive privilege did exist, it did not say how extensive it was or what it protected. As a result, subsequent presidents such as George Bush, and his vice president Dick Cheney, have invoked executive privilege to prevent individuals in their administration from testifying about activities such as the firing of federal attorneys or allegations of illegal WIRETAPPING and electronic surveillance of individuals.

For more information: Kurland, Phillip. *Watergate and the Constitution.* Chicago: University of Chicago Press, 1978; Small, Melvin. *The Presidency of Richard Nixon.* Lawrence: University Press of Kansas, 2003.

—Ernest Gomez and David Schultz

United States v. O'Brien 391 U.S. 367 (1968)

In *United States v. O'Brien*, the Supreme Court decided that the FIRST AMENDMENT did not protect all "expressive conduct"—in this case, burning a draft card. The Court held that a legitimate and important government interest in the regulation of conduct could justify incidental limitations on freedom of speech.

On March 31, 1966, David Paul O'Brien and three compatriots burned their draft cards on the steps of a Boston courthouse. O'Brien was promptly arrested and charged with violating federal law. In 1965, in response to emerging protests against the Vietnam War and the draft, Congress had amended the Uniform Military Training and Service Act (UMTSA) of 1948 to proscribe the knowing destruction of any Selective Service document.

Before trial, O'Brien argued that he was engaged in protected speech and that the 1965 amendment to the UMTSA abridged his rights under the First Amendment. After the trial court rejected that argument, O'Brien was tried, convicted, and sentenced to six years in federal custody. On appeal, the court of appeals reversed. It held that Congress had indeed targeted the protesters' message for suppression when it passed the 1965 amendment. The government then appealed to the U.S. Supreme Court.

O'Brien was a hard case. On its face, the 1965 amendment banned conduct, not speech. Could the first amendment protect any conduct through which a speaker sought to convey a message? If it protected DRAFT CARD BURNING, then why not urinating on the Washington Monument? Yet, both the social context and statements by legislators backing the 1965 amendment indicated that Congress was bothered much more by what the draft card burners were saying than by what they were doing.

Confronted with this dilemma in the year 1968, the Supreme Court split the difference between two polar positions. The Court could have viewed O'Brien's action as "conduct," not "speech," and therefore as not entitled to any protection. Alternatively, it could have treated his action as just like the written or spoken word, and therefore as entitled to maximum protection.

Chief Justice Warren's opinion for the Court took neither of these approaches. Rather, he began with the proposition that O'Brien's action involved a combination of "speech" and "nonspeech" elements. When this was the case, War-

ren continued, a particular logic should apply. This logic would become known as the *O'Brien* test: ". . . a government regulation is sufficiently justified [1] if it is within the constitutional power of government; [2] if it furthers an important or substantial government interest; [3] if the governmental interest is unrelated to the suppression of free expression; and [4] if the incidental restriction on alleged First Amendment freedoms is no greater than is essential to the furtherance of that interest" (391 U.S. 367, at 377). Warren then went on to uphold the constitutionality of the 1965 amendment, both on its face and as applied to O'Brien. Warren accepted the government's claim that it had a "substantial interest"—namely, the smooth functioning of the draft—and that this interest was "unrelated to expression." The incidental burden on O'Brien's speech could not be avoided.

The Court's decision was 7 to 1, with Justice Marshall not participating. Only Justice WILLIAM O. DOUGLAS dissented, and he did so not on the merits of the First Amendment claim, but rather on the basis of his view that the Court should decide "whether conscription is permissible in the absence of a declaration of war."

The Court's opinion has come in for sharp criticism. One kind of objection goes to the nature of the *O'Brien* test itself. The Court's general approach, some have argued, severely discounts the vital importance of allowing citizens to control the form, and therefore, potentially, the power and effectiveness, of their speech. The crucial question in the *O'Brien* test is what the government is up to, and not what the citizen is up to—what the government's "interest" is, and not what the government in fact or in effect limits. The Court's use of balancing language, moreover, gives future judges wide latitude to call it as they want to see it.

Another kind of objection grants the desirability or plausibility of the *O'Brien* test, but goes on to criticize the Court for how it applied it in this case. In this view, the Court's conclusions—that the government's interest was both "unrelated to the suppression of free expression" and "substantial"—simply "blinked reality" (Stone, p. 477). The Court discounted the substantial evidence of an actual legislative motive and purpose to suppress speech. Indeed, it wrote that it was always reluctant to examine legislative motives in constitutional cases. This claim was transparently false, for it had often done just that in EQUAL PROTECTION and ESTABLISHMENT CLAUSE cases. Finally, the Court's discussion of the government's "substantial interest" reads very much like a discussion of mere bureaucratic convenience.

But *O'Brien* had implications reaching beyond its peculiar facts and context. The Court recognized SYMBOLIC SPEECH as potentially protected, and offered a new set of authoritative terms under which many future cases would be evaluated (*TEXAS V. JOHNSON*, 491 U.S. 397 [1989] [flag burning protected], and *Barnes v. Glenn Theatre, Inc.*, 501 U.S. 560 [1991] [ban on totally NUDE DANCING upheld via an application of the *O'Brien* test]).

For more information: Gunther, Gerald, and Kathleen M. Sullivan. *Constitutional Law: Cases and Materials.* 13th ed. Westbury, N.Y.: Foundation Press, 1997; Powe, Lucas A. *The Warren Court and American Politics.* Cambridge, Mass.: Harvard University Press, 2000; Stone, Geoffrey. *Perilous Times: Free Speech during Wartime.* New York: W.W. Norton, 2005.

—Michael Paris

United States v. Pink 315 U.S. 203 (1942)

In *United States v. Pink*, the Supreme Court expanded the president's foreign affairs authority. The Court reaffirmed presidential power to enter into executive agreements with foreign nations without the consent of the SENATE; and it held again that such agreements were a form of federal law, thus overriding conflicting state laws.

The case arose from President Franklin Roosevelt's 1933 recognition of the Communist regime as the lawful government of the Soviet Union. As part of that recognition, the president had entered into an agreement (the Litvinov agreement) with the Soviet government, transferring all property of the Soviet Union within the United States to the government of the United States to settle American claims against the Soviet Union. Americans owed money by a Russian corporation sued to obtain that corporation's funds held by the New York state insurance commissioner. The United States government also claimed those funds under the Litvinov agreement, arguing that the funds belonged to the Soviet government, which had nationalized the Russian corporation. The New York courts rejected the government's claim because of state law prohibiting the confiscation of property.

Five justices, in an opinion by Justice WILLIAM O. DOUGLAS, upheld the government's position. Drawing on broad language in *UNITED STATES V. CURTISS-WRIGHT EXPORT CORPORATION*, 299 U.S. 304 (1936), and *UNITED STATES V. BELMONT*, 301 U.S. 324 (1937), the Court held: (1) that the president is the "sole organ" of the United States for the recognition of foreign governments, (2) that the president has authority to make executive agreements that set the conditions for recognition of foreign governments, (3) that executive agreements do not require the consent of the Senate, as do treaties, and (4) that executive agreements override state laws because, like treaties, they are the "supreme law of the land" under the Constitution. The five justices in the majority in the *Pink* case had all been appointed since the decision in *Belmont*, therefore giving additional credibility to this strong statement of presidential power in foreign affairs. Chief Justice HARLAN FISKE STONE and Justice Owen Roberts dissented; two others did not participate.

Presidents have made thousands of executive agreements. Some have been authorized by Congress or approved afterward. But most have been made by the president alone—often called "sole agreements"—on the authority of the *Belmont* and *Pink* cases. Sole executive agreements have been criticized as presidential lawmaking without the approval of Congress and as bypassing the Senate's constitutional power to ratify treaties under ARTICLE I, Section 2 of the Constitution. Critics also argue that the Constitution does not give the president a power to "recognize" foreign governments, as stated in the *Pink* case. ARTICLE II, Section 3 gives him only the power to "receive" foreign ambassadors, which the Constitution's framers apparently intended only as a routine ceremonial function.

Despite the critics, the Supreme Court has repeatedly affirmed presidential power to enter into executive agreements that become the law of the land as established in the *Belmont* and *Pink* cases. Recently, in *American Insurance Association v. Garamendi,* 539 U.S. 396 (2003), the Court not only affirmed presidential power to enter into sole executive agreements, but also held that state laws on a related subject were invalid if those laws might interfere with an executive agreement.

For more information: Adler, David Gray. "Court, Constitution, and Foreign Affairs." In *The Constitution and the Conduct of American Foreign Policy.* Lawrence: University of Kansas Press, 1996; Adler, David Gray. "The President's Recognition Power." In *The Constitution and the Conduct of American Foreign Policy.* Lawrence: University of Kansas Press, 1996; Henkin, Louis. *Foreign Affairs and the United States Constitution.* 2d ed. New York: Oxford University Press, 1996.

—David Adamany

United States v. Wong Kim Ark 169 U.S. 649 (1898)

In *United States v. Wong Kim Ark,* the Supreme Court ruled that mere birth on the soil (jus soli) of the United States made a baby a citizen, unless the parents were enemy aliens or diplomatic personnel.

United States v. Wong Kim Ark was the center of a landmark case interpreting the definition of citizenship in the FOURTEENTH AMENDMENT. Wong Kim Ark was born in San Francisco in 1873 to Chinese parents who were legally the subjects of the emperor of China. They were living and working in the United States as private persons and were not in any way employed by the government of China.

In 1888 the Scott Act barred the return to the United States of Chinese laborers who had exited the United States. In 1892 Congress adopted the Chinese Exclusion Act, which prohibited the immigration of Chinese persons to the United States.

In 1890 Wong traveled to China and returned the same year without incident. In 1894 Wong, now age 21, traveled again to China from San Francisco, where he maintained a residence. When he tried to reenter the United States, the collector of the port of San Francisco barred his entry. He then sued to be allowed to reenter the United States.

Justice Horace Gray delivered the opinion of the Court. He observed that all of Wong's life, except for his brief journeys to China, had been spent in California at the same San Francisco residence. Nor was there any proof that he had ever renounced his allegiance the United States nor committed any act that would exclude him. He further noted that Wong had been a native-born citizen since his birth and that the Chinese exclusion acts therefore could not apply to him.

Justice Gray also noted that the Constitution nowhere defines the meaning of the word "citizen" or "natural-born citizen," by way of either inclusion or exclusion. The meaning of the phrase, he argued, must therefore be interpreted in the light of the common law.

The fundamental principle of the common law was birth "within the allegiance of the king." Children of aliens born in England were natural-born subjects, as were children of ambassadors representing England, although born on foreign soil. Children of foreign ambassadors or diplomats or of alien enemies were not natural-born subjects, since they were born outside of the obedience of the king. This was the rule in all English colonies up to the DECLARATION OF INDEPENDENCE.

For more information: Furer, Howard B. *The Fuller Court, 1888–1910.* Danbury, Conn.: Grolier Educational, 1995.

—Andrew J. Waskey

United Steelworkers of America v. Weber 443 U.S. 193 (1979)

The Supreme Court ruled in *United Steelworkers of America v. Weber* that a voluntary race-conscious affirmation action plan did not violate Title VII of the CIVIL RIGHTS ACT OF 1964. This was the first employment AFFIRMATIVE ACTION case to reach the Supreme Court.

Until 1974, Kaiser Aluminum had hired only trained craft workers, but since craft unions had long excluded blacks from membership, very few black craft workers were available. At its plant in Gramercy, Louisiana, for example, only 1.83 percent of the craftsmen were black, even though they constituted 39 percent of the local workforce.

To redress this clear racial imbalance, the corporation and the steelworkers union developed an affirmative action plan that included on-the-job training programs to teach craft skills to unskilled production workers. While admission to the training program was based on seniority, half of the training positions were set aside for blacks and half for whites, until the percentage of black craftsmen reflected the percentage of blacks in the local labor pool.

In the first year, the training program at the Gramercy plant admitted black workers with less seniority than white workers, who were rejected. Brian Weber, one of the white workers, filed a class action lawsuit alleging discrimination against him and other similarly situated white employees in violation of Title VII, which bars EMPLOYMENT DISCRIMINATION on the basis of race, color, sex, religion, and national origin.

The federal district court agreed with Weber, and the court of appeals affirmed, holding that all race-based employment preferences violated Title VII.

The Supreme Court ruled only on this narrow question: Does Title VII forbid private employers and unions from voluntarily setting up affirmative action plans to eliminate traditional patterns of racial segregation? By a 5-2 vote, the Court answered no. For the majority, Justice WILLIAM J. BRENNAN, JR., wrote that ruling otherwise would contradict Congress's purpose in passing the Civil Rights Act to open up economic opportunities for blacks.

Brennan pointed out that "the plan does not unnecessarily trammel the interests of white employees," because it does not require that they be fired and replaced by black employees; nor does it deny white employees access to the training programs. Instead, the plan is limited and temporary, "not intended to maintain racial balance, but simply to eliminate a manifest racial imbalance" (pp. 208–209).

Finally, as a private—not government—plan, it did not violate the Fourteenth Amendment of the U.S. Constitution, which requires EQUAL PROTECTION of the law. This distinguished *Weber* from the Court's ruling the previous year in REGENTS OF THE UNIVERSITY OF CALIFORNIA V. BAKKE, 438 U.S. 265 (1978), where a similar plan established by a public university was struck down. It also distinguishes the case from later affirmative action rulings, such as CITY OF RICHMOND V. J. A. CROSON COMPANY, 488 U.S. 469 (1989), ADARAND CONSTRUCTORS, INC. V. PENA, 515 U.S. 200 (1995), and GRATZ V. BOLLINGER, 539 U.S. 244 (2003).

For more information: Kluger, R. *Simple Justice: The History of* Brown v. Board of Education *and Black America's Struggle for Equality.* New York: Knopf, 1975; Nowak, John E., and Ronald D. Rotunda. *Principles of Constitutional Law.* St. Paul, Minn.: Thomson/West, 2005.

—Nancy V. Baker

V

Valley Forge Christian College v. Americans United for the Separation of Church and State, Inc. 454 U.S. 464 (1981)

In *Valley Forge Christian College v. Americans United for Separation of Church and State, Inc.*, the Supreme Court ruled that the respondents did not have the required STANDING to challenge the free conveyance of government property into the hands of Valley Forge Christian College. The Court ruled that the respondents could not satisfy the ARTICLE III requirements of "injury in fact" and "case or controversy." This case set an important precedent concerning separation of church and state in reference to the ESTABLISHMENT CLAUSE of the FIRST AMENDMENT.

The U.S. Department of the Army acquired the property in question in 1942 to construct the Valley Forge General Hospital to care for U.S. Army members. In 1973 it was declared "surplus property" by the U.S. government, and the Department of Health, Education, and Welfare (HEW) assumed the task of its disposal. Although the land in question was appraised for $577,500, HEW permitted a 100 percent benefit allowance to the "buyer," in essence selling the land for free with the condition that the land would be used for 30 years solely for educational purposes.

Americans United filed a complaint soon after the transaction, challenging the conveyance on the ground that it violated the establishment clause of the First Amendment. They argued that the sale of Valley Forge General Hospital to a religious institution violated constitutional provisions concerning the separation of church and state, and this unconstitutional transaction deprived its members of the constitutional use of their tax dollars. The U.S. District Court dis-

missed their case because of Americans United's failure to show actual injury beyond a generalized grievance common to all taxpayers. The U.S. Court of Appeals for the Third Circuit reversed, allowing Americans United standing merely as "citizens claiming 'injury in fact'" to their rights under the establishment clause of the First Amendment.

The Supreme Court reversed. In a 5-4 decision, Justice WILLIAM HUBBS REHNQUIST gave the majority decision of the Court, which included Justices WARREN BURGER, White, LEWIS POWELL, and SANDRA DAY O'CONNOR. They ruled that the respondents did not have standing, either as taxpayers or citizens, to challenge the conveyance in question. Because the establishment clause does not create exceptions to this "standing" requirement, no personal injury to the respondents occurred as a result of the alleged constitutional violation. Precedential cases such as *Warth v. Seldin* solidified this requirement of "distinct and palpable injury," and the abstract nature of the respondents' "psychological injury" was insufficient to build a satisfactory "case or controversy" under the establishment clause.

Dissenting, Justices WILLIAM J. BRENNAN, JR., Marshall, Blackmun, and JOHN PAUL STEVENS claimed that the case was decided on logistical rather than substantive issues. Justice Brennan argued that the decision of the Court to base its ruling on Article III standing deprived the respondents of the opportunity to "prove that [their] rights [had] been violated" under the establishment clause. Justice Brennan also claimed that, if the case was reduced to a question of standing, the precedent of cases such as *Frothingham v. Mellon* reveals the Court's authorization of taxpayer standing as "sufficiently direct and immediate to warrant injunctive relief."

In conclusion, the significance of *Valley Forge Christian College v. Americans United* is rooted in the Article III requirements that delineate the standards for bringing a lawsuit in federal court. The Supreme Court exercised Article III prudence when choosing which cases to address, especially in controversial issues such as the separation of church and state.

For more information: Hamburger, Philip. *Separation of Church and State*. Cambridge, Mass.: Harvard University Press, 2002; Levy, Leonard. *The Establishment Clause*. 2d ed. Chapel Hill: University of North Carolina Press, 1994.

—Mary J. Piper

Van Orden v. Perry 545 U.S. 677 (2005)

In *Van Orden v. Perry*, the Supreme Court ruled 5-4 that a TEN COMMANDMENTS monument on the Texas state capitol grounds was not unconstitutional. The complexity of the issue is reflected in the seven different written opinions accompanying the case, and its relation to *McCREARY COUNTY, KENTUCKY v. ACLU*, 545 U.S. 844 (2005), announced on the same day but with an opposite outcome. The monument, one of 17 adorning the 22-acre lawn, was presented to Texas in 1961 by the Fraternal Order of Eagles. Thomas Van Orden challenged it as a violation of the ESTABLISH-MENT CLAUSE. The lower courts found the monument served a valid secular purpose—recognizing the work of the Eagles among youth—and said it would not indicate state endorsement of religion to a "reasonable observer." Representing a plurality of four, Chief Justice WILLIAM HUBBS REHNQUIST dismissed the test for determining violations of the establishment clause found in *Lemon v. Kurtzman*, 403 U.S. 602 (1971), as of no value in this case. He focused on the monument's setting and context. He characterized the establishment clause as both protecting against government intervention in religion and protecting America's religious traditions. He accepted the *Stone v. Graham*, 449 U.S. 39 (1980), ruling that Ten Commandments

displays were inappropriate in public classrooms, but saw nothing in *Stone* to mandate a similar ruling in *Van Orden,* since the Texas display, viewed occasionally by passers-by, was "more passive" than the *Stone* displays seen daily by schoolchildren.

Justice ANTONIN GREGORY SCALIA concurred, but would have gone further to sculpt an establishment clause standard under which "there is nothing unconstitutional in a state's favoring religion generally, honoring God through public prayer and acknowledgment, or, in a non-proselytizing manner, venerating the Ten Commandments." Justice CLARENCE THOMAS agreed: "This case would be easy if the Court were willing to abandon the inconsistent guideposts it has adopted for addressing Establishment challenges."

Justice STEPHEN G. BREYER, who was also part of the majority in *McCreary,* explained his reason for switching sides in this case by defining *Van Orden* as "borderline." The physical setting suggested predominantly nonreligious messages such as "civic morality." Time was also a factor. For the previous 40 years there had been no legal challenges, unlike McCreary's "short (and stormy) history of the courthouse Commandments' displays." Breyer thought the Texas monument might pass the *Lemon* test, but based his judgment on his sense that to rule otherwise would suggest "a hostility toward religion that has no place in our Establishment Clause traditions."

Justice JOHN PAUL STEVENS, dissenting, found nothing to offset a predominantly religious message. He recounted the monument's past. Not part of Texas history, it was one of thousands distributed across America with the help of Cecil B. DeMille, producer of the popular 1956 film, *The Ten Commandments*. The text's religious nature was highlighted by inclusion of the prologue, "I AM the LORD thy God." Though passive, the monument's permanency conveyed government endorsement. Finally, Stevens catalogued his disagreements with Rehnquist's version of history.

Justice DAVID H. SOUTER also found the monument religious, and explained how it differed from depictions of Moses in the Supreme Court building. He found no "common denominators" in the 17 monuments to qualify them as a "museum" and no contextual factors to detract from the religious character. That the monument had gone unchallenged for 40 years was not surprising: "Suing a State over religion puts nothing in a plaintiff's pocket and can take a great deal out, and . . . the risk of social ostracism can be powerfully deterrent."

For more information: Boston, Rob. "Decalogue Divide," *Church and State* (July/August 2005): 7–9; Hester, Joseph P. *The Ten Commandments: A Handbook of Religious, Legal, and Social Issues.* Jefferson, N.C.: McFarland, 2003.

—Jane G. Rainey

veto

A presidential veto is formal action by the president that stops and prevents a legislative bill from being enacted into law. As a source of many other governmental powers, the United States Constitution (ARTICLE I, Section 7) explicitly and clearly gives the president the veto power. According to the Constitution, bills passed by Congress shall be presented to the president for his approval and signature before the law can take effect. Procedurally, if the president decides that he does not like or approve of the bill's contents, the president returns the bill to Congress within 10 days stating his particular objections to it. The bill is not dead, though, for Congress then has the opportunity to override the veto or repass the bill by considering it again. However, the reconsidered bill cannot become law over the president's veto unless a super-majority of two-thirds of both the HOUSE OF REPRESENTATIVES and SENATE votes for the bill.

In addition to the veto, the president also has what is called a pocket veto. A pocket veto is one way a president can veto a bill without taking any action when Congress is not in session. The pocket veto gives the president a third option other than signing or vetoing the bill. He can take no action and do nothing, that is, he neither signs nor returns the bill. If the president does not sign or veto the bill within 10 days after receiving it from Congress, the bill becomes law automatically if Congress is

in session. However, if Congress is not in session, then the bill does not become law—that is, if Congress adjourns before the president's 10-day bill return period ends (excluding Sundays), the bill dies and cannot be enacted into law. This is called a pocket veto, implying that the president can just simply put the bill in his pocket as a means to veto a bill and stop it from becoming law.

The reason for giving the president a pocket veto was to prevent Congress from having too much power. The drafters of the Constitution were concerned that Congress might pass a bill and then adjourn quickly, thereby preventing the president from having the opportunity to return or veto the bill. Although the Constitution grants Congress the principal responsibility for making laws, the president's veto power shows that the Founding Fathers wanted the president to play a role in lawmaking. The writers of the Constitution were worried that even an assembly of popularly elected representatives might intrude on the rights, liberties, and interests of the citizenry. The presidential veto power is an example of one of the U.S. Constitution's principles, commonly referred to as check-and-balance.

Congress cannot override a bill that has been stopped through a pocket veto, unlike a bill subjected to a regular veto. Under a regular veto, Congress can reconsider the bill, if it so chooses, and override the president's decision with at least a two-thirds majority in both the House and the Senate. However, since Congress is no longer in session in the case of a pocket veto, Congress cannot override a pocket veto. This institutional rule gives the president a very powerful tool in affecting legislative outcomes. However, Congress may reintroduce the same bill in the next session of Congress, but subject again to the presidential veto. The average number of pocket vetoes is about five per year, which is only about 2–3 percent of the bills that Congress passes.

Scholars often consider the effects of the constitutional rules and powers, like the veto, on the policy-making process and good governance. One criticism of the veto power is that it gives too much power to one person—the president—who can mute the voice of the 535 senators and representative comprising Congress. Another criticism is that the veto power may add to political stalemate or policy gridlock because the veto creates one more obstacle to be overcome in passing legislation. Conversely, the Founding Fathers intentionally created an institutional system that made it difficult to pass laws because they wanted to protect personal liberty by limiting government.

For more information: Diclerico, Robert D. *The American Presidency.* 5th ed. Upper Saddle River, N.J.: Prentice Hall, 2000; Gregg, Gary L. *Thinking about the Presidency: Documents and Essays from the Founding to the Present.* Lanham, Md.: Rowman & Littlefield, 2005.

—Miles A. Cooper

vice president

The vice president holds an executive office position in the national government, serving as the head of the SENATE, and is first in line to succeed the president were the latter incapacitated.

ARTICLE I, Section 3, Clause 4 makes the vice president the presiding officer of the Senate, with voting power only if the body is deadlocked.

For much of its history, the American vice presidency has been the subject of satire and political humor. Vice presidents themselves have made fun of their office. Woodrow Wilson's vice president, Thomas Marshall, joked that serving as vice president was like "a man in a cataleptic fit; he cannot speak; he cannot move; he suffers no pain; he is perfectly conscious of all that goes on, but has no part in it." The office of the vice president was created as a weak office and has not grown much in power since that time. The main function of the vice president is as successor to the American presidency in the event that the president can no longer function in that role, possibly as a result of illness, death, resignation, or IMPEACHMENT. It has also become a launch pad for a run for the presidency. More recently, vice presidents have increasingly become regarded as advisers to the president.

The idea for a vice presidency was largely an afterthought during the CONSTITUTIONAL CONVENTION. However, this office was not well specified. It was unclear as to whether or not the vice president would become president or simply perform the duties of the president if the president was no longer able to fulfill the duties of the office. It was also left unclear as to whether the vice president would carry out the remainder of the president's term or would simply fill in until a special election could be called. JOHN ADAMS was the first person to be elected to the office of the vice presidency.

During the 19th century, it was the political parties rather than presidential candidates who chose the vice presidential nominees. This created tension within the government, largely due to the fact that parties would actively seek out a nomination from a particular party or region that had been adversely affected by the presidential nomination. This did not allow for much respect and camaraderie between the president and the vice president. However, some presidents during the 19th century sought and respected the advice of their vice presidents. It was also during this time, in 1841, that the first opportunity was presented for a vice president, John Tyler, to assume the role and responsibility of the president, when William Henry Harrison became the first president to die while still in office. When Tyler became president he resisted efforts to refer to him as an acting president, preferring that he be considered a regular president with all the formal duties of the presidency.

In more modern times, the vice presidential candidate is selected as a running mate by the presidential nominees. It is often the case today that presidential nominees choose running mates who were their losing opponents in the primary election. They care more about competence, loyalty, and the ability to succeed the president rather than geographic region. Today, vice presidents are encouraged to be more active. They are kept up to date on issues and receive security briefings as well. They often sit in on cabinet meetings and have sometimes served as a liaison between Congress and the White House.

Constitutionally, the vice presidency has caused some problems. Initially, when George

Washington and then John Adams ran for president in 1788, 1792, and 1796, there were no political parties. The individual who received the most electoral votes became president and the runner-up became vice president. However, in 1800, with the emergence of party slates, THOMAS JEFFERSON ran as president and he picked Aaron Burr to be his vice president. When the electors cast their ballots, both Jefferson and Burr tied, forcing the HOUSE OF REPRESENTATIVES to select the president. As a result of this problem, the TWELFTH AMENDMENT was adopted in 1804. It allowed for the president and vice president to run as a team, with separate ballots for president and vice president. As a result of this amendment, while the House of Representatives would select the president, the Senate would pick the vice president.

Over the course of American history, presidents have faced incapacities that eventually led to their vice presidents taking over. For example, in 1865 ABRAHAM LINCOLN's vice president, Andrew Johnson, became president when Lincoln was assassinated. In 1881 James Garfield was assassinated but laid in a coma for two months before dying and being succeeded by his vice president, Chester A. Arthur. Lyndon Johnson replaced John Kennedy in 1963 when Kennedy was assassinated. In 1974 RICHARD NIXON's vice president, Gerald Ford, became president when Nixon resigned to avoid impeachment charges growing out of Watergate.

The TWENTY-FIFTH AMENDMENT, ratified in 1967, sought to formally describe the role of the vice presidency in the case of a presidential vacancy. The vice president is to take over the office of the presidency for the remainder of the term. The amendment also set out the procedures for when presidents experience disabilities, allowing for the president to temporarily turn power over to the vice president.

For more information: Milkis, Sidney M., and Michael Nelson. *The American Presidency: Origins and Development, 1776–2002.* 4th ed. Washington, D.C.: CQ Press, 2003.

—Jacqueline M. Loubet

Village of Euclid, Ohio v. Ambler Realty Co.
272 U.S. 365 (1926)

In *Village of Euclid v. Ambler Realty,* the Supreme Court decided that the village of Euclid acted constitutionally and within its POLICE POWER by establishing zones for varying intensities of land use. The significance of the *Euclid* decision is that it established a test to determine the constitutionality of zoning ordinances. The Court found that a zoning ordinance is constitutional provided it reasonably relates to the public health, safety, and welfare.

Ambler Realty possessed 68 acres of land in the village of Euclid, a suburb of Cleveland, Ohio. The village, in fear that the growth of industry in the surrounding area might change the character of the village, established a zoning ordinance based on three classes of height, four classes of area, and six classes of use. The property in question was divided into three use classes, as well as various height and area classes. Ambler Realty sued the village, arguing that the zoning ordinance had substantially reduced the value of their property by limiting its use, amounting to deprivation of Ambler's liberty and property without DUE PROCESS. At the district court level, the village of Euclid moved to dismiss the complaint entirely, arguing that Ambler Realty had no right to sue in the first place without taking the issue before the Euclid Zoning Board, as required by the zoning ordinance. The district court denied this motion and ruled in favor of Ambler Realty, stating that the ordinance was an improper use of the village's police powers and therefore unconstitutional.

The Supreme Court agreed with the lower court's denial of the dismissal motion, but overturned the outcome of the case and sided with the village of Euclid. On behalf of a six-member majority, with Justices McReynolds, Van Devanter, and Butler dissenting, Justice Sutherland argued that "the exclusion of buildings devoted to business, trade, etc., from residential districts, bears a rational relation to the health and safety of the community." In other words, the zoning ordinance was not an unreasonable extension of the village's police power and did not have the character of arbitrary fiat, and thus it was not unconstitutional.

Further, the Court found that Ambler Realty had offered no evidence that the ordinance had any effect on the value of the property in question, but based its assertions of depreciation on speculation only. This speculation, the Court ruled, was not a valid basis for a claim of takings.

The Supreme Court, in finding that there was valid government interest in maintaining the character of a neighborhood and in regulating where certain land uses should occur, cleared the way for the subsequent explosion in zoning ordinances across the country. To date, the power of government to address land use issues via zoning ordinances is almost universally accepted.

For more information: Fischel, William A. *Regulatory Takings: Law, Economics, and Politics.* Cambridge, Mass.: Harvard University Press, 1995.

—Erika N. Cornelius

Vinson Court (1946–1953)

The Vinson Court refers to the Supreme Court under Chief Justice Fred Vinson. The Vinson Court is often labeled as a Court in transition from the New Deal Court of Stone to the progressive court of Earl Warren. It is also a Court seen as one that was conservative, struggling with the issues of the Cold War and racism. For many, Vinson's leadership is seen as one of the weakest in history.

Fred Vinson was a devoted New Dealer and supporter of President Franklin Roosevelt. In 1937, after a career in politics and law, he was appointed to the Court of Appeals for the DISTRICT OF COLUMBIA circuit. In 1943 he resigned, taking the job as director of price stabilization in the FDR administration. He moved on to other jobs within the executive branch until his ascent to the Supreme Court in 1946, replacing HARLAN FISKE STONE as chief justice.

When Stone had died there was significant controversy surrounding his replacement. President Harry Truman debated moving an associate justice into the chief's position, with rumors circulating that perhaps it would be Robert Jackson. Yet some justices threatened to resign if that occurred.

Instead, Truman decided to appoint Vinson—a lifelong friend—to be chief justice.

Vinson presided over a Court in ideological transition from a liberal New Deal bench to a more conservative one, which in turn would be transformed when Earl Warren replaced him in 1953. The liberals on the Court included WILLIAM O. DOUGLAS, HUGO BLACK, Frank Murphy, and Wiley Rutledge, and the conservatives were Robert Jackson, Felix Frankfurter, Stanley Reed, and Harold Burton. In 1949, Rutledge left the Court along with another FDR appointee, Frank Williams, paving the way for Truman to appoint Sherman Minton and Tom Clark as their replacements. These appointments further pushed the Court into a more ideologically polarized body, with Vinson often providing the critical fifth vote for the conservatives.

Race, CIVIL RIGHTS, and the cold war dominated the agenda of the brief Vinson Court. In *Dennis v. United States,* 341 U.S. 494 (1951), the Court, with Vinson writing for a split majority, upheld the conviction of a member of the Communist Party for a violation of the Smith Act. The Smith Act had made it illegal to "knowingly or willfully advocate, abet, advise or teach the duty, necessity, desirability or propriety of overthrowing the Government of the United States or of any State by force or violence, or for anyone to organize any association which teaches, advises or encourages such an overthrow, or for anyone to become a member of or to affiliate with any such association." In effect, the act criminalized membership in the Communist Party, and Dennis, a leader in it, was convicted under this law. Justices Black and Douglas, in dissent, viewed this as a FIRST AMENDMENT free speech issue.

In *Sweatt v. Painter,* 339 U.S. 629 (1950), the Court pushed the segregationist doctrine of separate but equal to its extreme, holding that the University of Texas at Austin law school had to admit an African-American student because the school reserved for blacks was not comparable. Noting that the school for African Americans lacked books and faculty, the Court said it was not a separate and equal facility and therefore Herman Sweatt was entitled to admission to the

University of Texas law school. *Sweatt*, along with SHELLEY V. KRAEMER, 334 U.S. 1 (1948), where the Court ruled that courts could not enforce racially restrictive covenants, were important civil rights victories for African Americans that paved the way for BROWN V. BOARD OF EDUCATION OF TOPEKA, 347 U.S. 483 (1954), and the future WARREN COURT decisions that struck down many other discriminatory laws.

Finally, in YOUNGSTOWN SHEET AND TUBE V. SAWYER, 343 U.S. 579 (1952), better known as the steel seizure case, the Court rejected President Truman's contention that under ARTICLE II OF THE U.S. CONSTITUTION he had the authority to seize or nationalize the steel mills during the Korean War in order to avert a strike. Writing for the Court, Justice Black rejected claims that the president as COMMANDER IN CHIEF had this authority to take control of the mills. Black took a literalist reading of the Constitution, stating there was no explicit language authorizing this action. Douglas also rejected the claims of presidential power with equally absolute language. However, in separate concurrences, other justices were more conciliatory. Of special note, Justice Jackson's concurrence, describing how presidential power might change depending on whether Congress enabled or opposed it, is often cited by presidents as a defense of executive authority. President Bush, in defending many of his actions following the terrorist attacks of 9/11, invoked Jackson's concurrence to support his authority. Only Vinson and Minton voted to uphold Truman's actions.

Scholars and Supreme Court historians have not been kind to the Vinson Court. They rate Vinson as a justice as one of the worst and see him as a weak and ineffectual chief. In his defense, the Court and American society were divided by many issues, forcing the Court to confront some very difficult matters. However, at least in the area of civil rights, some of the Vinson Court precedents may have opened up American society.

For more information: Frank, John P. *The Justices of the United States Supreme Court: Their Lives and Major Opinions.* New York: Chelsea House, 1995; Schwartz, Bernard. *A History of the Supreme Court.* New York: Oxford University Press, 1993.

—David Schultz

Virginia Declaration of Rights (1776)

The Virginia Declaration of Rights was an important document that influenced THOMAS JEFFERSON in writing the DECLARATION OF INDEPENDENCE and later JAMES MADISON in drafting the U.S. BILL OF RIGHTS.

Adopted on June 12, 1776, by the colonial Virginia Constitutional Convention meeting in Williamsburg, Virginia, the declaration consists of 16 provisions outlining measures for limiting the power of government for the purpose of protecting the rights of citizens. George Mason (1725–1792), a successful Virginia plantation owner, civic leader, and neighbor of George Washington, was the primary author of the Virginia Declaration of Rights. Mason would later oppose the ratification of the U.S. Constitution on the grounds that the U.S. Constitution lacked a national Bill of Rights.

The Virginia Declaration of Rights opens with a philosophical discussion of human nature and the nature of legitimate political authority. By virtue of their very humanity, the declaration asserts, "all men are by nature equally free and independent" and equally hold claim to various natural rights. These rights include the right to life, liberty, and the ability to seek property, "happiness and safety." Governments exist to enhance the enjoyment of such rights and—in the event of governments' failure to protect natural rights—are subject to reform or abolition when the majority considers such action necessary for the public good.

However, while affirming the people's right to abolish "inadequate" or oppressive government, the declaration's most extensive analysis is oriented toward an elaboration of what a well-managed and liberty-promoting government would look like. Government will foster "the greatest degree of happiness and safety" when the following conditions are met: free elections occur often and at known, predictable times; legislative, executive, and judicial powers are separate; the military is under civilian control; religious liberty is recognized; FREEDOM OF THE PRESS is ensured; and both criminal rights and property rights are guaranteed. With respect to the former, the declaration upholds the RIGHT TO TRIAL BY JURY, the RIGHT AGAINST SELF-INCRIMINATION, the right to know any accuser and witnesses summoned, the right to trial without inordinate delay, the right against capricious searches and seizures, and the right to be free from both "excessive BAIL" and "CRUEL AND UNUSUAL PUNISHMENT," and, with respect to the latter, the document calls for prohibitions on taxation or removal of one's property without consent.

In addition to outlining the procedural and administrative components of good government, as discussed above, the Virginia Declaration also addresses the cultural foundations of a free people. The declaration proclaims the need for virtues such as "moderation, temperance, [and] frugality," and claims that all citizens have "the mutual duty . . . to practice Christian forbearance, love, and charity, towards each other." That is, while the Virginia Declaration promotes individual rights, it embodies a concept of rights linked with obligations, namely, obligations that would limit the exercise of individual rights in any manner injurious to that which the community regards as virtuous. Thus, while George Mason and his fellow Virginians, in adopting the Virginia Declaration of Rights, advocated FREEDOM OF RELIGION as a necessary component of living in a free society, their concepts of freedom and religion were culturally informed by an 18th-century worldview in which religious meaning and individual liberty were thought to be mutually sustaining.

For more information: Bowling, Kenneth R. "'A Tub to the Whale': The Founding Fathers and Adoption of the Federal Bill of Rights," *Journal of the Early Republic* 8 (Autumn 1988): 223–251; Scott, James Brown. "George Mason," *The Virginia Law Register* 12 (January 1927): 556–561.

—Ellen Grigsby

Virginia Plan, the

The Virginia Plan, presented at the Philadelphia (Constitutional) Convention by the Virginia delegate, Edmund J. Randolph, governor of Virginia, on May 29, 1787, was the first of three alternatives presented. Randolph's Resolutions were titled "The Virginia Plan" and became informally known as the "large states" plan because of the advantages the resolutions would provide states with larger populations. Federalist in theme, the 15 resolutions affirmed the necessity of correcting deficiencies in the Articles of Confederation, strengthening and centralizing the national government, and creating three separate branches: legislative, executive, and judicial.

Following a general resolution expressing the need to address the weaknesses in the Articles, Resolutions 2–6 concerned the national legislature, suggesting a BICAMERAL LEGISLATURE having a "lower house" elected by the people of each state and an "upper house" with members chosen by the lower house. How the representation in each house would be selected presented the most contention. Resolution 5 suggested two alternatives: representation in the lower house based on the proportion of free citizens or based upon the amount of taxes rendered by each state; this was debated over eight days!

The 10 small states were concerned that Virginia, Massachusetts, and Pennsylvania could conspire to dictate their will on the rest by virtue of their larger delegations if representation was based upon the proportion of citizens in each state. The alternative of equality would not solve the problem either, as the smaller states outnumbered the larger ones as described by BENJAMIN FRANKLIN. The issue of slaves complicated matters further. Were they to be considered property or citizens? As William Paterson, the attorney general of New Jersey and author of the NEW JERSEY PLAN, argued, ". . . if Negroes are not represented in the States to which they belong, why should they be represented in the General Government?" The proposal that wealth provide the means by which representation would be allocated offered no better solution; as William Samuel Johnson, a supporter of the CONNECTICUT

COMPROMISE, stated, "Population was the best measure of wealth." Ultimately, as was suggested by William Richardson Davie, North Carolina's delegate, slaves would be counted as three-fifths of each state's population for the purpose of determining apportionment in the House.

Resolutions 7 and 8 called for the selection of a single executive by the national legislature, which, in tandem with a "Council of revision," would be allowed to review all laws before they take effect. Resolution 9 proposed a national judiciary and the circumstances under which it would hear cases of dispute. Resolutions 10 through 15 concerned the admission of new states, assurances of a republican form of government, the necessity for a provision for amendments, a mandate of supremacy for the new constitution, and finally, the means by which the new constitution would be ratified.

For more information: Rakove, Jack N. *Original Meanings: Politics and Ideas in the Making of the Constitution.* Vintage Series. New York: Knopf Publishing, 1997; United States, James Madison, Gaillard Hunt, and James Brown Scott. *The Debates in the Federal Convention of 1787: Which Framed the Constitution of the United States of America.* New York: Oxford University Press, 1920; Wood, Gordon S. *The Creation of the American Republic 1776–1787.* Chapel Hill: University of North Carolina Press, 1998.

—Christy Woodward Kaupert

Virginia State Board of Pharmacy v. Virginia Citizens Consumer Council
425 U.S. 748 (1976)

In *Virginia State Board of Pharmacy v. Virginia Citizens Consumer Council,* the U.S. Supreme Court held that the state of Virginia violated the free speech clause by prohibiting pharmacists from advertising prescription-drug prices. The case is important in that it is one of several decisions recognizing the FIRST AMENDMENT protection for COMMERCIAL SPEECH.

Writing for the majority, Justice Blackmun acknowledged that the advertising of prices is "commercial speech," that is, speech that does no more than propose a commercial transaction. This was significant because *Valentine v. Christensen,* 316 U.S. 52 (1942), had held that commercial speech was not central to political discourse and therefore was not constitutionally protected. Disagreeing with this precedent, Justice Blackmun explained that, though commercial speech might not have the same constitutional status as core political speech, the free flow of commercial information is nonetheless important to the marketplace of ideas because it is essential to a free market economy. For this reason, Justice Blackmun concluded that, while states may regulate false or deceptive advertisements, states may not suppress truthful information about a lawful economic activity. Here, Virginia's price-advertising restriction did not regulate false or deceptive information, but rather suppressed truthful information that consumers might find important in choosing prescription-drug suppliers. Thus, the Court held the restriction unconstitutional.

Chief Justice WARREN BURGER concurred and explained that the decision did not extend to professional services, such as medicine and law, which involve personal judgment. Similarly, Justice Stewart wrote a concurrence clarifying that the holding recognized constitutional distinctions between commercial and political speech, and that, accordingly, states may restrict deceptive or false advertising.

Dissenting alone, Justice WILLIAM HUBBS REHNQUIST declared that the free speech clause does not protect commercial speech at all. As a practical matter, Justice Rehnquist questioned how much of a burden Virginia's price restriction imposed on consumers, since consumers could compare prices without pharmacists providing this information in the form of advertisements. Justice Rehnquist also warned that by protecting the speech at issue in this case, the Court had prohibited states from restricting the advertising of liquor and cigarettes, subjects that the states had traditionally regulated. *Virginia State Board of Pharmacy* has generated strict limitations on how government may regulate commercial transactions. Just one year later, in *Bates v. State Bar of Arizona,* 433 U.S. 350 (1977), the Court interpreted

Virginia State Board of Pharmacy as limiting how states may regulate ATTORNEY ADVERTISING. Then, in *Central Hudson Gas & Elec. Co. v. Public Serv. Comm'n*, 447 U.S. 557 (1980), the Court announced a commercial-speech test, which the Court has since applied on numerous occasions to invalidate commercial regulation. This has aroused concern in some justices, who have claimed that, in the guise of commercial-speech doctrine, the Court has revived the *Lochner* era's laissez-faire jurisprudence. There is also some confusion as to the doctrine's applicability, as the Court has questioned whether it applies with the same rigor to prior restraints and to restrictions on electronic broadcasting. Despite this controversy and uncertainty, however, the legacy of *Virginia State Board of Pharmacy,* giving commercial speech a constitutional status, seems secure.

For more information: Baker, C. Edwin. "Commercial Speech: A Problem in the Theory of Freedom." *Iowa Law Review* 62, no. 1 (1976): 1–56; Post, Robert. "The Constitutional Status of Commercial Speech." *UCLA Law Review* 48, no. 1 (2000): 1–57.

—Jesse R. Merriam

void for vagueness doctrine

The void for vagueness doctrine requires that criminal laws and statutes be written such that the language is clear and straightforward enough that a person of average intelligence is able to understand.

The void for vagueness doctrine results from the DUE PROCESS clause of the Fifth Amendment to the United States Constitution. Simply, if a person of average intelligence cannot determine from the law or statute behavior that is prohibited, and the corresponding punishment to such behavior, then the law is considered vague, and therefore unconstitutional. Vague statutes are considered unconstitutional based on the notion that a person who does not understand what constitutes a crime cannot defend himself against criminal accusation or indictment and consequently would be deprived "due process." In essence, a person of average intelligence should not be made to "guess" at the meaning of a law or statute (*Winters v. New York*, 333 U.S. 507, 515–516 [1948]).

A noted example of the Court voiding a statute for vagueness is found in the Supreme Court case CITY OF CHICAGO V. MORALES, 527 U.S. 41 (1999). In this case, Chicago's Gang Congregation Ordinance prohibited "criminal street gang members" from loitering in public places. Under the ordinance, if law enforcement observed a person whom they reasonably believed to be a gang member loitering in a public place with one or more persons, they could order them to disperse. Any person who did not comply with the order was considered to have violated the ordinance and could be arrested. Specifically, the ordinance required that in any public place in Chicago, persons in the company of a gang member would be ordered to disperse if their purpose was not apparent to law enforcement.

The difficulty with the ordinance was that it included both protected (harmless) and prohibited (criminal) behavior. The ordinance's definition of loitering—"to remain in any one place with no apparent purpose"—was inherently subjective and thus could have been construed differently by different individuals. For example, a law-abiding citizen holding a conversation with friends on a street corner under the law could unwittingly be turned into a criminal. The application of this definition by law enforcement depended on whether some purpose was apparent to the officer, who could subsequently arrest individuals at his own discretion. Simply, it is difficult for anyone, including law enforcement, to discern if any Chicagoan standing in a public place with a group of people would or would not have an "apparent purpose." As a result, the Supreme Court ruled that the ordinance was vague and thus unconstitutional. Justice SANDRA DAY O'CONNOR found that the Chicago ordinance was "unconstitutionally vague because it lacked sufficient minimal standards to govern law enforcement officers; in particular, it failed to provide any standard by which police can judge whether an individual has an *apparent* purpose."

For more information: Fellman, David. *The Defendant's Rights Today.* Madison: University of Wisconsin Press, 1976; Gardner, Thomas, and Terry Anderson. *Criminal Law: Principles and Cases.* St. Paul, Minn.: West Publishing, 1996.

—Brigette J. Bush

Voting Rights Act of 1965

The Voting Rights Act (VRA) adopted in 1965 and extended in 1970, 1975, 1982, and 2006 is an act that implements the Fifteenth Amendment provision that voting rights cannot be denied on account of race. Congress designed this law to give the executive and judicial branches of government the ability to implement the achievements guaranteed in the Fourteenth and Fifteenth Amendments.

The Fifteenth Amendment provides that "the right of citizens of the United States to vote shall not be denied or abridged by the United States or by any State on account of race, color or previous condition of servitude." Thus, Section 2 of the Fifteenth Amendment, like Section 2 of the Thirteenth Amendment and Section 5 of the Fourteenth Amendment, gives Congress the power to enforce these amendments by appropriate legislation. Beside the ban on the infringement of franchise rights on the listed accounts, the VRA also contains several special but temporary provisions that impose stringent requirements on certain jurisdictions. Yet, the VRA and the long line of amendments and judicial intervention that form its lineage today can be properly understood only within the context of its evolution and the historical struggle to establish a secure basis of black suffrage in the United States.

Before the Civil War, neither the U.S. Constitution nor federal laws provided for a specific protection of voting rights. Voting qualifications were established by states, a practice that led to a political franchise exercised only by white males. Historical records reveal that black men could register and vote only in six northern states, and black women were denied franchise rights in all states. By adopting the Military Reconstruction Act of 1867 after the Civil War, Congress took measures to extend the RIGHT TO VOTE to most adult males in the secessionist southern states.

This act imposed on these states, as conditions for readmission to the Union, requirements that they adopt new constitutions that granted universal male suffrage regardless of race. Three years later in 1870, Congress enshrined the black right to vote in the Fifteenth Amendment. This amendment followed the Thirteenth and Fourteenth Amendments, both of which guaranteed freedom from slavery and citizenship to all persons born or naturalized in the United States. Together, all three amendments were designed to eradicate the vestiges of slavery.

By granting the right of franchise to blacks and forbidding its abridgment on account of race or previous condition of servitude, the Fifteenth Amendment superseded existing state laws to the contrary. Following its enactment, Congress exercised its powers under Section 2 of that amendment by enacting two measures, notably, the Enforcement Act of 1870 and the Force Act of 1871. Together both acts prohibited state officials from applying election laws in a racially discriminatory manner and outlawed physical threats and economic intimidation against voters. They also made it illegal for individuals to conspire to interfere with the right to cast a ballot. To implement the Force Act, Congress authorized the appointment of officials to observe registrations and election proceedings. The net result was that, between 1871 and 1887, the sudden influx in black registration and voting facilitated the election of black candidates to local, state, and federal offices.

While northern states came to accept black voting, in the 1880s southern states resisted the enforcement of the Fifteenth Amendment. They did so by adopting laws that imposed poll taxes and literacy test requirements as well as measures that disqualified those deemed to have committed crimes of "moral turpitude." The so-called white primary was a practice designed to evade the Fifteenth Amendment by using private political parties to conduct elections and establish membership qualifications. Tactics of the overall effort to reverse post-Reconstruction political advances were: violence, fraud, structural discrimination, statutory suffrage restriction, and constitutional disenfranchisement. Each of these became more effective as they allowed others to be employed. Violence and intimidation for example, enabled southern Democrats to take over the polls, after which election returns were compromised. Similarly, fraudulently elected officials gerrymandered election districts and imposed other structurally discriminatory devices. In the end, a decreasing number of Republicans and third-party members in legislatures meant that legislative and constitutional measures that imposed franchise restrictions on blacks were hardly contested. In many ways these efforts paid off in disenfranchising blacks in all southern states.

In 1876 two Supreme Court decisions abruptly ended any prospect of using the Enforcement and Forces Acts to enforce the Fifteenth Amendment. In both *United States v. Reese* (1876) and *United States v. Cruiksank* (1876), the Court threw out indictments based on various provisions of both acts. It held that in order to secure convictions under both acts, a showing had to be made establishing intent to discriminate for reasons of race and with the approval of the state. Thus, absent tacit state action or authority, neither legislation could be enforced. While the Court's ruling was effective in crippling any effort by Congress to protect the right of franchise for African Americans, it coincided with a growing shift in national attitude toward noninterference. The culmination of this attitude was the Hayes-Tilden Compromise Act passed by Congress in 1877, which marked the end of Southern Reconstruction. The overall effect of this legislation was immediate. It removed federal troops from the South and precipitated a climate where violence was used to suppress black voter turnout and fraud was used to undo lawfully cast black votes. Thus, in virtually all southern states between 1890 and 1910, constitutional rewrites with explicit provisions that excluded blacks from the electoral process became the means of replacing previous statutes. In the end, efforts to break the grip of black disenfranchisement and to restore rights to the franchise took many decades to crystallize. The enactment of civil right acts in the late 1950s and early 1960s, or specifically in 1957, 1960, and 1964 and the Voting Rights Act of 1965, were integral to these efforts.

As enacted, the Voting Rights Act represented an entirely different tack compared to previous CIVIL RIGHTS acts. For 1965, it was at best revolutionary and yet unique in that it went beyond reliance on litigation, to prescription of concrete measures to aid in the enforcement of promises in the Fourteenth and Fifteenth Amendments. It suspended most voting qualifications for five years and gave the attorney general and the courts broad powers to grant relief whenever violations of the Fifteenth Amendment occurred. Generally divided into 14 sections, the VRA did three things: first, it defined the enforcement mechanisms to ensure the administration of a discrimination-free electoral process; second, it established extraordinary mechanisms to monitor certain states and counties; and third, it created a triggering mechanism to bring most of the South under federal monitoring and instituted special provisions to enforce compliance.

A general outline of the VRA recapitulates pertinent aspects of the act from Sections 2–14. The permanent Sections 2 and 3, the most significant aspect of the act, codified the Fifteenth Amendment. Both sections provided for penalties as well as empowered the attorney general to litigate for (a) the suspension of literacy tests, (b) the appointment of federal examiners to oversee voter registration, and (c) the retention of court jurisdiction to review proposed changes in voting procedures before local governments could enforce them. The special provisions of the act (Sections 4 through 9) placed the burden of litigation and administrative appeals on the states and local jurisdictions rather than on the aggrieved individuals. To bypass southern courts that, for the most part, were a captive of local politics, the Justice Department was authorized by the VRA to take direct administrative action at the D.C. District Court on behalf of the disenfranchised blacks.

Unlike the permanent provisions, the special provisions under Sections 4–9 were intended to be temporary for five years—between 1965 and 1970—and applicable only to certain jurisdictions with specified criteria. For example, Section 4 banned "literacy tests" for five years in any subdivision where such tests were then in force. The targets were states that historically used literacy tests as an instrument to discriminate in the electoral process. While the trigger provisions of the act successfully captured offenders, they could avoid this by filing for a declaratory judgment at the D.C. District Court and demonstrating that such tests had not been used in the five years prescribed by the act. Since historically state courts and local officials hindered efforts to ensure black franchise rights by passing bogus legislation, Section 5 of the VRA sought to prevent such by requesting preclearance of all electoral laws with the attorney general or the court before implementation. In this view, all pre- and post-November 1964 voting regulations or proposals were part of the preclearance to the Justice Department except where specific showing was made establishing that such regulations did not in purpose or effect deny the right to vote on the basis of race or color. Thus, under the VRA the decision whether a state could change its voting procedure was a matter for the Justice Department or the District of Columbia Court of Appeals to decide.

To counter the corrupt conduct of local registrars who often made biased decisions favoring local laws, Sections 6–8 provided for federal registration examiners and election observers. Appointed by the Federal Civil Service Commission, their duties were distinct. While election registration examiners were to ensure that people who actually registered could vote, election observers served as poll watchers to ensure that all eligible persons were indeed allowed to vote and the ballot accurately counted. Sections 9 and 10 provided procedures where target states could challenge federally compiled registration lists and also made applicable the poll tax prohibition to states. Also, Section 11 provided criminal penalties for false registrations, false votes, and the destruction of voting records as well as giving the attorney general wide latitude to intervene where necessary to prosecute offending parties. Lastly, Section 14 defined voting to include all actions necessary to make a vote effective. To sum, any jurisdiction could be subject to the special provisions of the VRA under the statistical automatic trigger of Section 4(b), or found guilty for outright violation of the Fifteenth Amendment.

In January 1969, former attorney general Ramsey Clark submitted a piece of legislation to Congress to extend "all provisions" of the Voting Rights Act of 1965 for an additional five years. While the justifications for renewal were debatable, the effect of nonrenewal was obvious. At the core of the debates was whether the underlying objectives of the special provisions of the act had been accomplished. Originally, the "special provisions" were conceived as temporary measures to be discontinued once blacks were successfully integrated into the political system. That did not happen. Congressional hearings held to extend the act established that, between 1965 and 1970, voting electorates were manipulated through gerrymandering, annexations, packing, switching to at-large elections, and the adoption of various structural changes to prevent the newly registered blacks from effectively using the ballot. Similarly, the U.S. Commission on Civil Rights also noted the emergence of new techniques to dissuade blacks, including increases in CANDIDATE FILING FEES when black candidates ran for office, abolishing or making positions appointive, extending terms of office for white incumbents, and withholding job-opening information from blacks. Based on these reports it is therefore possible that, without further extension of the VRA in 1970, jurisdiction that fell within the automatic trigger provision would have simply bailed out and perhaps reinstated the literacy test requirements again.

Surely southern states would have liked the special provisions of the Voting Rights Act to lapse. However, their objections revolved around the preclearance requirements and the regional attention of the act directed their way. Specifically, they decried the stigma it placed on the South and southerners as a whole. However, after considerable debate in 1970, Congress imposed a temporary ban on the use of all literacy tests and extended the "temporary provision" of VRA for another five years, until 1975. Also attached to these amendments was a provision extending to 18 years of age the right to the franchise; to ensure its constitutionality, a proposal to that effect was sent to the states for ratification and led to passage of the TWENTY-SIXTH AMENDMENT. The 1970 revisions also provided an allowance to recapture new black voters if it were shown that literacy tests had in fact been used in a jurisdiction where registration and voting rates fell below 50 percent in the 1968 presidential elections. Lastly, a nationwide uniform standard for absentee balloting was initiated to give citizens denied the right to vote, the ability to take action in a U.S. district court on behalf of the United States.

When the special provision of the VRA was again close to expiration in 1975, the Civil Rights Commission issued a report evaluating the overall impact of the act since 1970. The conclusions reached were mixed. While the commission cited progress, it also argued that it was not enough and that relaxing or nonrenewal could hamper forward movement by reversing previous achievements in voting rights. While proponents called for another 10-year renewal, in the end Congress extended the "special provisions" of VRA for only seven years (1975 to 1982), and made permanent the temporary ban on literacy tests introduced in 1970. Also, responding to widespread discrimination against Hispanics, Asians, and Native Americans, Congress made the protection of "language minorities" part of the 1975 revisions, to be in effect until 1985. The source of congressional power for this addition, unlike those of "racial minority" provided under the Fifteenth Amendment, was Congress's power to secure guarantees of EQUAL PROTECTION by appropriate legislation under the Fourteenth Amendment. Using the assumption that the lack of foreign-language voting material was itself a discriminatory test, the new language provision required the production and use of voting material in both English and the language minority at issue in any given jurisdiction. This provision was made compulsory in political subdivisions where members of a single language minority were at least 5 percent of the voting population.

In 1982, after much debate for and against, Congress again renewed the "special provisions" of the Voting Rights Act for 25 years. Support for renewal this time was predicated on the general notion that progress heretofore achieved could vanish if the special provisions were not renewed. Clearly non-renewal could have engendered

ramifications on two fronts. The first was that the special provisions renewed and the language requirements included for the first time in 1975 could have expired. The second was that Congress had to provide clarity in light of the Supreme Court's decision in *Mobile v. Bolden,* 446 U.S. 55 (1980), which ruled that plaintiffs had to show "discriminatory intent along with discriminatory effect" to prevail in a voting rights violation claim. However, the *Bolden* decision was in sharp contrast to an earlier ruling in *White v. Regester,* 412 U.S. 755 (1973), in which the Court held certain multimember districts incompatible with the equal protection clause of the Fourteenth Amendment. To reconcile *Bolden* and *White,* Congress in 1982 amended Section 2 of the VRA to provide that plaintiffs could indeed establish violation under the subsection without having to show a "discriminatory purpose." Predictably, had Congress not acted in 1982, it could have seriously undermined the important gains made in minority rights to the franchise since 1965.

In the end, proponents in Congress not only got the special provisions of the Voting Rights Act extended for 25 years, but also the language assistance provision included in 1975 was extended to include 1985 to 1992. In many ways, the language provision agreed upon in 1982 was somewhat restrictive in that it made it more difficult for language communities to qualify and therefore be properly protected under the Voting Rights Act. By changing how to determine a community's language proficiency requirement, the added provision also cut to nearly half the number of counties that qualified for language assistance under the act in 1975.

With the growth of language minorities both in population and political power in the United States, it was obvious by 1992 that Congress could not afford to drop what to that point had become an essential component of political participation for those whose major, first language was other than English. Thus, the 1992 extension of the the language provision to 15 more years with the addition of new language minorities to the coverage was indeed a victory for the language minority communities. The 15-year extension also brought the language provision into parallel timing with other special provisions of the Voting Rights Act. In so doing, the legislation changed the previous 5 percent rule for mandatory coverage to an absolute numerical count of 10,000 people. That is, for any jurisdiction with a minority language population of 10,000, voting instruments and information must be made available to voters in English and in the minority language.

Recently, on July 13 and 20, 2006, both the HOUSE OF REPRESENTATIVES and the SENATE voted to renew the expiring provisions of the VRA. By 390 to 33 and 98 to 0 votes, both houses overwhelmingly agreed to extend the act for another 25 years. The consensus view was that federal supervision was still necessary to protect the ability of minorities and the disadvantaged to cast ballots in some regions of the country. In urging the adoption of the act and recalling the Selma Alabama 1965 Bloody Sunday civil rights demonstration march, Rep. John Lewis, Democrat of Georgia, said "Yes, we've made some progress; . . . but the sad truth is, discrimination still exists." That's why we still need the Voting Rights Act, and we must not go back to the dark past." Senator Barack Obama, Democrat of Illinois, added a similar reference as he stated that "despite the progress . . . made so far in upholding the right to vote, it is clear the problems still exist."

The Voting Rights Act of 1965 was enacted during a period when, in parts of the South, blacks were forbidden to vote. Those who attempted to register to vote or to organize or assist others to register risked losing their jobs, homes, or their lives. Today's America is a world different from 1965, when President Lyndon B. Johnson signed the act into law after the violent attacks on civil rights marchers who demanded the right to vote. Yet, it remains in some respects the same. While the purpose of the act then was to ensure that blacks were afforded full rights to vote, along the way Congress adjusted this purpose to include other minorities, who either avoided or simply could not partake in the electoral process because they could not read, write, or understand English.

As demonstrated here, along the way the act did more than establish a nationwide prohibition against voting discrimination based on race. It banned poll taxes and literacy tests and impanelled the federal government to play a more active role than it had before. In regions where discrimination was egregious, the Justice Department was given the authority to review progress made in electoral processes such as redistricting to determine if they were discriminatory. While critics charge that the core requirements of the act are outdated and also that Congress has moved beyond primary questions of access, supporters stake different positions. They maintain that the long history of deliberate and calculated voting discrimination justifies the act's continued relevance and importance as an instrument that fosters meaningful black and other minority representation. They point, for example, to the overwhelming 2006 approval in Congress for extending the VRA to retain the original preclearance requirements, the temporary provisions, and language provisions as evidence of its continued relevance.

In the end, Congress's willingness to extend the act as demonstrated thus far means that, while it has produced historic results, it is indeed still necessary. Arguably, it is necessary for the advancement of political equality beyond access to the ballot box and on to meaningful representation and meaningful political membership in our democracy.

For more information: Ball, Howard, Dale Krane, and Thomas P. Lauth, *Compromised Compliance: Implementation of the 1965 Voting Rights Act.* Westport, Conn.: Greenwood Press, 1982; Grofman, Bernard, Lisa Handley, and Richard Niemi. *Minority Representation and the Quest for Voting Equality.* New York: Cambridge University Press, 1992; Hudson, David Michael. *Along Racial Lines: Consequences of the 1965 Voting Rights Act.* New York: Peter Lang, 1998; Kousser, J. Morgan. *Colorblind Injustice: Minority Voting Rights and the Undoing of the Second Reconstruction.* Chapel Hill: University of North Carolina Press, 1999; Morgan, Ruth P. *Governance by Decree: The Impact of the Voting Rights Act in Dallas.* Lawrence: University of Kansas Press, 2004.

—Marc G. Pufong

Wagner Act (National Labor Relations Act)

The Wagner Act (National Labor Relations Act) is the main New Deal–era law that regulates collective bargaining and union activity in the private sector in the United States.

In May 1935, in SCHECHTER POULTRY CORPORATION V. UNITED STATES, 295 U.S. 495 (1935), the Supreme Court struck down as unconstitutional the National Industrial Recovery Act. Less than two months later, to fill the void left by this decision, Congress, at the urging of President Franklin D. Roosevelt, passed the National Labor Relations Act—better known as the Wagner Act. The act, one of the key pieces of legislation in American labor history, awarded workers the right to unionize and to collectively bargain through a union of their choice and placed the authority of the federal government behind the idea of unionization. The right to unionize and collectively bargain guaranteed by the Wagner Act repeated the assurance to do such in Section 7a of the National Industrial Recovery Act.

Robert Wagner (D-New York), the author of the legislation, was elected to the SENATE in 1926 and became chairman of the Senate Banking and Currency Committee during the New Deal era. Two of his most notable accomplishments were enacted into law in 1935: the Social Security Act, providing old-age pensions to Americans, and the Wagner Labor Act.

The National Labor Relations Board (NLRB) established by the Wagner Act was charged with investigating and ruling on charges of unfair labor practices, and conducting elections on union representation. It was given more across-the-board powers than the weaker entity of the same name established under the National Industrial Recovery Act.

Because the courts had been so antilabor and to a lesser degree anti–New Deal up to this point, many companies and unions operated for the first year or two after passage as though the Wagner Act did not exist, presuming Congress lacked authority to enact such legislation under the COMMERCE CLAUSE. Unions often followed traditional tactics such as sit-down strikes rather than appeal to the NLRB for a ruling.

One of the largest steel producers in the country was Jones and Laughlin, a company that operated in many states and was involved in every facet of steel production from extraction through distribution of the finished product. Charges of unfair labor practices, including discriminating against workers who wanted to join a labor union, were filed against the company for actions at a plant in Pennsylvania. The NLRB ruled against the company and ordered it to reinstate workers who had been dismissed consequent to participating in union activities. The lower courts ruled in favor of the company, and the NLRB appealed to the Supreme Court.

In National Labor Relations Board v. Jones & Laughlin Steel Corporation, 301 U.S. 1 (1937), the Court upheld the Wagner Act. Jones and Laughlin argued that Congress had no power to regulate the steel industry. The issue before the Court was whether Congress could regulate a manufacturer if the manufacturer's activity significantly affects INTERSTATE COMMERCE. Chief Justice Charles Evans Hughes's majority opinion held that Congress has the constitutional authority to safeguard the right of the respondent's employees to self-organization and freedom in the choice of representatives for collective bargaining. Justice James McReynolds wrote the dissent, which was joined by Justices Pierce Butler, George Sutherland, and Willis Van Devanter, holding that the right to contract was fundamental and included the privilege of selecting those with whom one wished to contract.

Following *Jones & Laughlin*, the Supreme Court and the NLRB were in general agreement with the Court ruling in favor of the NLRB, with a few exceptions. In *NLRB v. Mackay Radio & Telephone Co.*, 304 U.S. 333 (1938), with Justice Owen Roberts writing for a 7-0 majority, the Court held that while a company could not fire workers for going on strike, it could permanently replace them. Five years later, in *Virginia Electric & Power Co. v. NLRB*, 319 U.S. 533 (1943), a 6-3 Court, with Justice Frank Murphy writing the opinion, held that the FIRST AMENDMENT barred the NLRB from making it illegal for employers to express opposition to unions, provided they did not try to intimidate or threaten workers with retaliation for exercising their rights under the Wagner Act.

Originally the Wagner Act banned unjust labor practices by management; it was amended in 1947 with the Taft-Hartley Act, which imposed limitations on unions such as forbidding secondary boycotts. Congress has altered the original provisions since, but the National Labor Relations Act, or Wagner Act, remains the primary law governing relations between unions and employers in the private sector.

Some union advocates and supporters now criticize the Wagner Act as being outdated and urge that it be modernized to reflect the new realities of the workplace.

For more information: Cletus, Daniel. *The ACLU and the Wagner Act: An Inquiry into the Depression-Era Crisis of American Liberalism.* Ithaca: New York State School of Industrial and Labor Relations, Cornell University, 1980; Millis, Harry A. *From the Wagner Act to Taft-Hartley.* Chicago: University of Chicago Press, 1950; St. Antoine, Theodore J. "How the Wagner Act Came to Be: A Prospectus." *Michigan Law Review* 96, no. 8 (August 1998): 2,201–2,211.

—Mark Alcorn

Waite Court (1873–1888)

In 1873, President Ulysses S. Grant chose little-known Ohio attorney Morrison R. Waite to replace the deceased Salmon P. Chase as chief justice of the U.S. Supreme Court. The SENATE quickly approved Waite. None of his contemporaries regarded Waite as the possessor of a first-rate legal mind, but most recognized that Grant could have done far worse. The Waite Court holds a minor place in constitutional history.

Iowa attorney Samuel Freeman Miller, flamboyant former California Supreme Court justice Stephen J. Field, and New Jersey railroad attorney Joseph P. Bradley assumed intellectual leadership of the Waite Court. The remaining justices were holdovers from the CHASE COURT. Former chief judge of the New York Court of Appeals Ward Hunt, former attorney general Nathan Clifford of Maine, former attorney general Noah H. Swayne of Ohio, and former Illinois judge David Davis had all been on the bench for a number of years. In 1877, JOHN MARSHALL HARLAN, former attorney general of Kentucky, replaced Davis. Harlan became one of the great dissenters in Supreme Court history with his rejection of a narrow view of CIVIL RIGHTS, generally acclaimed by recent scholars.

Hunt suffered a stroke in 1878 but held on until 1882, when Congress approved a special pension bill. Circuit Judge Samuel Blatchford of New York replaced Hunt and, although a good worker, never proved to be an outstanding jurist. Horace Gray, chief justice of the Supreme Judicial Court of Massachusetts, replaced the deceased Clifford in 1881. Upon Strong's resignation in 1880, President Rutherford B. Hayes appointed Circuit Judge William B. Woods of Georgia. Woods became the first judge from the south since the appointment of John A. Campbell of Alabama in 1852. On Swayne's retirement in 1881, Ohio railroad lawyer and U.S. senator Stanley Mathews replaced him. In 1888, upon the death of Woods, Lucius Quintus Cincinnatus Lamar of Mississippi joined the Court. Lamar was the first justice who had served in the Confederate army, and his appointment symbolized post-Reconstruction reconciliation.

The most important Waite opinion came in the *Granger Cases*, 94 U.S. 113–187 (1877). During Waite's term, the Supreme Court was asked for the first time to respond to social legislation. This marked the beginning of the epoch when DUE PROCESS served as the most fertile source of constitutional lawmaking. The *Granger Cases* ruling upheld the power of the states to regulate the rates of railroads and other businesses. It came in response to abuses that accompanied the post–Civil War growth of railroads. Angry midwestern farmers, who flocked to the Granger movement in the early 1870s, sought to correct these abuses through state regulation. The *Granger Cases* decision has served as the basis upon which government regulation has generally rested.

The Reconstruction era witnessed the enactment of significant civil rights statutes by the U.S. Congress. The Civil Rights Act of 1875 is the most important of these laws. It contained a prohibition against racial discrimination in inns, public conveyances, and places of amusement. In the 1883 CIVIL RIGHTS CASES, 109 U.S. 3 (1883), the Waite Court ruled this provision invalid on the ground that it sought to reach discriminatory action that was purely private in nature and consequently not within the state scope of the EQUAL PROTECTION clause. Harlan, a former slaveowner, dissented from this narrow construction of the FOURTEENTH AMENDMENT by declaring that the majority's narrow concept of state action reduced the amendment to baubles thrown to those who deserved fair treatment. Nevertheless, the Court has continued to follow the rule set down in the *Civil Rights Cases*.

The Waite Court's narrow construction of the Fourteenth Amendment in the *Civil Rights Cases* can be contrasted with its extension of constitutional protection to corporations. In 1886, in SANTA CLARA COUNTY V. SOUTHERN PACIFIC RAILROAD, 118 U.S. 394, 396 (1886), the Court decided that corporations were persons within the meaning of the Fourteenth Amendment. Chief Justice Waite refused to hear arguments on the question, and the Court wrote no opinion. Nevertheless, Waite pronouncement definitively settled the law on the matter.

The Supreme Court became involved in the contested presidential election of 1876 through the appointment of five justices to the commission set up by Congress to resolve the dispute. The justices, with the exception of one, were reluctant to serve. Bradley, viewed as the least partisan of the justices, cast the decisive vote that put Hayes in the White House in 1877. Bradley's vote created a storm of controversy and tarnished his career. The episode served as another example of a judicial involvement in the political arena that reflected unfavorably on the Supreme Court. However, the involvement of the justices persuaded the nation to accept the decision and may have averted another national crisis.

The Supreme Court's reputation had been tarnished during the turbulence of *Dred Scott*, the Civil War, Reconstruction, and the political maneuverings of Chase. Waite restored its reputation. At his death in 1888, the Supreme Court had resumed its position as a fully coordinate department of government.

For more information: Currie, David P. *The Constitution in the Supreme Court: The First Hundred Years, 1789–1888.* Chicago: University of Chicago Press, 1986; Frankfurter, Felix. *The Commerce Clause under Marshall, Taney, and Waite.* Chapel Hill: University of North Carolina Press, 1960; Schwartz, Bernard. *The History of the Supreme Court.* New York: Oxford University Press, 1992.

—Caryn E. Neumann

Wallace v. Jaffree 472 U.S. 38 (1985)

In *Wallace v. Jaffree* the Supreme Court invalidated as a violation of the ESTABLISHMENT CLAUSE an Alabama law allowing students to engage in one minute of silent meditation. This case contains a classic exposition of originalist interpretation of the FIRST AMENDMENT's establishment clause.

While the majority opinion by Justice JOHN PAUL STEVENS applied the *LEMON V. KURTZMAN*, 403 U.S. 602 (1971), test in workaday fashion, Justice WILLIAM HUBBS REHNQUIST's dissent forever exploded the historical argument laid out by Justice HUGO BLACK in cases such as *EVERSON V. BOARD OF EDUCATION,* 330 U.S. 1 (1947), and *ENGEL V. VITALE,* 370 U.S. 421 (1962). As Rehnquist put it, "It is impossible to build sound constitutional doctrine upon a mistaken understanding of constitutional history," and he demonstrated irrefutably that the *Everson* line of cases was an attempt to do precisely that. Since 1985, no one can be said to have applied the Court majority's mistaken reading of the establishment clause out of ignorance.

The *Wallace* case arose out of Alabama's response to the Court's decision in *Engel* that the establishment clause forbade teacher-led prayer in public schools. Alabama legislators undertook in 1978 to enact a statute providing for a one-minute moment of silence "for meditation," in 1981 to enact a statute providing a minute for meditation "or voluntary prayer," and in 1982 to allow teachers to lead "willing students" in a prayer to "Almighty God . . . the Creator and Supreme Judge of the world."

Surprisingly, U.S. District Court Judge Brevard Hand at trial interpreted the establishment clause, as originally understood, to apply only to limit Congress and the federal government, and allowed Alabama to establish a state church if it wanted to. Inexplicably, he ruled the 1978 law constitutional and the other two unconstitutional, under the establishment clause; however, he dismissed the plaintiffs' claims concerning all three because they had failed to state a claim for which relief could be granted. The circuit court of appeals reversed Hand's decision (Stevens said "not surprisingly") on the basis of an unfounded assertion that the Supreme Court had considered and rejected the historical arguments Hand found persuasive. Stevens found no difficulty in upholding the circuit court's decision under *Lemon v. Kurtzman.*

In a solitary dissent, Rehnquist eviscerated the Court's entire 1947–85 line of establishment clause precedent. Rehnquist did not address the fatuous INCORPORATION doctrine, as he might have done. He did show, however, that the *Everson* Court's elevation of THOMAS JEFFERSON's "wall of separation" metaphor to the status of constitutional dogma made no sense, as Jefferson had neither helped draft nor participated in ratifying the First Amendment. Rehnquist also demonstrated in great detail that the authors and ratifiers of the establishment clause had not understood that provision as banning government encouragement of nonsectarian prayer, and had taken care to avoid any such implication.

For more information: Curry, Thomas J. *The First Freedoms: Church and State in America to the Passage of the First Amendment.* New York: Oxford University Press, 1986; Hutson, James H., ed. *Religion and the New Republic: Faith in the Founding of America.* Lanham, Md.: Rowman & Littlefield, 2000; Sheldon, Garrett Ward, and Daniel L. Dreisbach. *Religion and Political Culture in Jefferson's Virginia.* Lanham, Md.: Rowman & Littlefield, 2000.

—Kevin R. C. Gutzman

War Powers Act

Passed on November 7, 1973, over President RICHARD M. NIXON's veto, the War Powers Act (WPA) was a congressional effort to limit the president's perceived powers as COMMANDER IN CHIEF. The act came in response to what many in Congress viewed as the exercise of "imperial" powers by presidents during the Vietnam War.

The WPA attempted to place a number of limitations on the commander in chief. The act required the president to "consult" with Congress in "every possible circumstance" when military action was being considered and eventually used abroad. If there had not been a formal declaration of war, specific statutory authorization for military action, or a direct attack on the United States, its possessions, or territories abroad—and the president had used force—the act required that the commander in chief notify congressional leaders within 48 hours of the military action. Upon this notification, the president then has 60 days to gain congressional approval to continue the military action. If approval is not gained, the act requires that the military action shall be terminated. For reasons of military necessity, and in order to produce a more expeditious end to the military action, the president may determine that a 30-day extension beyond the original 60-day requirement may be needed. It should be noted that Congress clearly intended the act to have broad application, which included all situations in which U.S. troops would be involved in hostilities abroad.

Most analysts treat the events surrounding the WPA's passage as an era of congressional assertiveness in foreign policy, which came after a deep distrust of the president had developed over the conduct of the Vietnam War. Yet at the same time, there is wide concurrence that the WPA has failed miserably in limiting the president in military affairs. There are multiple reasons for its failure.

One of the most important reasons for its failure is that all presidents since 1973 have argued that the act is an unconstitutional infringement of the president's powers as commander in chief. While presidents have chosen to comply with the clause's requirement to notify Congress of military actions conducted, they simultaneously note that they are not acting under a specific constitutional obligation to do so.

Other critics of the WPA point to the act's imprecise language, which allows for broad interpretations of the word "consult." For example, when President Ronald Reagan launched air strikes on Libyan leader Muammar Qaddafi in 1986, congressional leaders were told of the forthcoming missile strikes three hours prior to the military action. Similarly, in 1989, President George H. W. Bush gave congressional leaders five hours' notice before the American military invasion of Panama. In both cases, each administration maintained that it had consulted Congress prior to the military action. In contrast, some in Congress felt that they had been merely notified of the ensuing military action and were not privy to any aspect of the decision-making process.

Just as presidents have chosen to ignore the WPA's intent, Congress has simultaneously chosen to avoid strict applications of the act. Rather, Congress has been especially deferential to presidents' unilateral military actions, and has treated military actions in a political manner, waiting to see how the public responds to the commander in chief's decision. For example, in 1993 and 1996, when President Bill Clinton conducted major military strikes on Iraq, no member of Congress was consulted in advance. With strong public approval for the strikes, the voices of criticism from Congress on the constitutionality of Clinton's strikes were insignificant. Most members of Congress applauded the actions and remained silent on the WPA. President Clinton, however, did go to considerable lengths to consult with Congress prior to the 1999 military strikes on Yugoslavian president Slobodan Milošević. Once the bombings ensued, Congress again chose against a specific application of the WPA.

President George W. Bush's first term in office followed the same practice as his predecessor. Barely a month into his presidency, more than two years prior to Operation Iraqi Freedom, Bush launched an extensive, one-day air strike on Iraq on February 16, 2001. Like President Clinton, Bush did not consult with or even notify any member of Congress prior to the military action. Congress applauded the military action, despite the clear violation of the act. Since the terrorist strikes on the United States on September 11, 2001, Congress has rarely raised concern over the WPA, in large part due to the wide authorizations that Congress granted Bush in the global war on terrorism and for the war in Iraq.

The War Powers Act has never been examined by the U.S. Supreme Court, but in *Immigration and Naturalization Service v. Chadha*, 462 U.S. 919 (1983), the Court determined that a one-house LEGISLATIVE VETO was unconstitutional. The Court's decision suggests that Congress's requirement in the WPA that the president terminate military action abroad if both houses vote to require this is unconstitutional. However, others contend that, unlike the one-house legislative veto, the two-house one is not unconstitutional. In addition, others assert that the WPA is unconstitutional in that it encroaches either upon the executive power of the president or upon his role as commander in chief, or that it limits some of the powers that Congress has in military affairs under ARTICLE I OF THE U.S. CONSTITUTION.

For more information: Fisher, Louis, and David Gray Adler. "The War Powers Resolution: Time to Say Goodbye." *Political Science Quarterly* 113, no. 1 (1998): 1–20; Hendrickson, Ryan C. *The Clinton Wars: The Constitution, Congress and War Powers.* Nashville, Tenn.: Vanderbilt University Press, 2002; Katzman, Robert A. "War Powers: Toward a New Accommodation." In *A Question of Balance: The President, Congress, and Foreign Policy.* Washington, D.C.: Brookings Institution, 1990.

—Ryan C. Hendrickson

Ware v. Hylton 3 U.S. [Dallas] 199 (1796)

Ware v. Hylton is an important precursor to the monumental case, *MARBURY V. MADISON* (1 Cranch 137 [1803]) in the development of the concept of JUDICIAL REVIEW.

The facts of this case are rather straightforward. In 1777, before the conclusion of the Revolutionary War, Virginia, passed a law preventing the collection of debts by British creditors. However, the Treaty of Paris of 1783, which officially ended the war, stated clearly that preexisting debts must be honored. Thus, by the terms of the TREATY, debts against Americans by British citizens would be collectable. A British citizen began an action against a Virginian debtor. The state law was cited by the Virginian as a reason for immunity from the claim. This was the basis of the legal action. The Virginia court agreed that the debt could not be collected. The case was appealed to the Supreme Court; the argument before the Court lasted several days.

This was the era of the Supreme Court in which seriatim decisions were the norm. That is, each justice would normally author a separate opinion; the majority would carry the day. Justice Chase's opinion put the matter most clearly in his conclusion. He went through the facts and the arguments made by the various parties to the case. In a very lengthy opinion, he concluded that

the Constitution is retrospective and its terms are applicable to actions taken before the Treaty of 1783 (note the terms of Article VI, Section 1);

the Constitution and laws of states, if they come into conflict with the Constitution or national laws or treaties "are by force of the said article [Article VI], prostrated before the treaty";

the Treaty of 1783 is supreme over any state law or constitution, ". . . because no legislature of any State has any kind of power over the Constitution. . . .";

state and federal judges have the duty to determine that state laws and constitutions are "null and void" if they violate the United State Constitution, federal laws, and federal treaties.

Other justices' opinions, such as Paterson's, concur and provide the basis for the rejection of the Virginia statute.

The importance of this case is that it was one early case, along with others such as *HYLTON V. UNITED STATES*, *Hayburn's Case* (1792), and *Yale Todd's Case* (1794) (presented in *United States v. Ferreira*, 54 U.S. 40 [1851]), that explicitly or implicitly explored the concept of judicial review.

For more information: Frankel, Robert P., Jr. "Before *Marbury: Hylton v. United States* and the Origins of Judicial Review." *Journal of Supreme Court History* 28, no. 1 (2003).

—Steven A. Peterson

Warren Court (1953–1969)

The Warren Court began on September 30, 1953, when President Dwight D. Eisenhower appointed Earl Warren (March 19, 1891–July 9, 1974), governor of California, as the 14th chief justice of the Supreme Court—a recess appointment because Congress was not in session. The appointment was to replace Chief Justice Frederick Vinson who had died on September 8, 1953, and was made quickly because leadership was needed for the fall term of the Supreme Court, about to begin in a few days. The appointment was not confirmed until March 1, 1954.

The Warren Court ended on June 23, 1969, a year after Warren had announced his plans to retire. In June of 1968, Warren sent a letter to President Lyndon B. Johnson announcing his

Supreme Court justices (left to right) William O. Douglas, Stanley Reed, Chief Justice Earl Warren, Justices Hugo Black, Felix Frankfurter, and others stand with President Eisenhower on the White House steps, 1953. *(Library of Congress)*

coming retirement, with the intention of influencing Johnson's decision for his replacement or preventing RICHARD M. NIXON, who was the likely next president, from appointing his successor. The letter did not work.

Serving on the Warren Court at the time of the chief justice's appointment were five appointees made by President Franklin D. Roosevelt: Hugo L. Black (August 1937), Stanley F. Reed (January 1938), Felix Frankfurter (January 1939), WILLIAM O. DOUGLAS (April 1939), and Robert H. Jackson (July 1941). In addition there were three who had been appointed by President Harry Truman: Harold H. Burton (October 1945), Tom C. Clark (August 1949), and Milton Sherman (October 1949).

Added to the Warren Court as Eisenhower appointees were JOHN MARSHALL HARLAN II (March 1955) to replace Justice Roberts (died October 1954), WILLIAM J. BRENNAN, JR. (October 1956), to replace Sherman Minton (retired October 1956), Charles E. Whittaker (March 1957) to replace Stanley F. Reed (retired February 1957), and Potter Stewart (October 1958) to replace Harold H. Burton (retired October 1958).

Appointees made to the Warren Court by President John F. Kennedy were Byron R. White (April 1962) to replace Charles E. Whittaker (retired March 1962) and Arthur J. Goldberg (October 1962) to replace Felix Frankfurter (retired August 1962).

Goldberg resigned in July 1965 and President Lyndon B. Johnson appointed Abe Fortas (October 1965), who resigned in May of 1969. He was replaced by the first African American to serve on the Court, Thurgood Marshall (October 1967).

The short tenure of Justice Goldberg on the Court was due to President Johnson's strong urging that Goldberg become the American ambassador to the United Nations during the troubling time of the Vietnam War. Frustrated with the war, Goldberg resigned the position in 1968, wanting to become chief justice when Warren announced his pending retirement. Instead, Johnson nominated Abe Fortas as chief justice; however, the nomination was blocked by northern Republicans and southern Democrat conservatives. A few months later, ethical charges were brought against Fortas, forcing him to resign.

The appointment of Earl Warren as chief justice was a political payoff made by President Eisenhower to California supporters. Warren at the time was governor of California. He had previously been California attorney general and had participated in the World War II Japanese internments. Instead of judicial experience or legal scholarship, he brought to the Court political skills. These were to help the Court greatly during his tenure as chief justice because the Court was deeply divided when he arrived.

The split among the justices upon Warren's accession was between those favoring judicial restraint and those favoring judicial activism. Frankfurter was the leader of the faction in favor of judicial restraint, while Justices Black and Douglas were leaders of the activists. Tom Clark was often on the side of the activists, but could be expected to take an independent stance if he were so inclined.

The Warren Court in its first phase was split between the two factions. In its second phase, it was firmly engaged in judicial activism, especially in the area of CIVIL LIBERTIES and CIVIL RIGHTS. The first major case faced by the Warren Court was BROWN V. BOARD OF EDUCATION OF TOPEKA (1954), a case that had been held over from the Vinson Court, which had been unable to reach a decision. It was heard again in December of 1953. Warren used his political skills to achieve complete consensus. Warren wrote the opinion, which was delivered on May 17, 1954. The Court then adjourned and left town. The case marked the beginning of a shift from focusing on property rights to focusing on personal rights. It also put the Court into the center of enormous controversy and sparked the Civil Rights movement. A flood of antisegregation cases followed, which were eventually matched by federal legislation. The decisions were divisive and engendered calls for Warren's IMPEACHMENT.

In 1956 the Warren Court took the first of its many cases involving criminal rights with *Griffin v. Illinois*, 351 U.S. 12. It ruled that publicly financed trial transcripts be supplied to criminal indigents in order to support their appeals. This was followed by GIDEON V. WAINWRIGHT, 372 U.S. 335 (1963), giving a court-appointed attorney paid for by the state as representation for an indigent defendant. In subsequent cases the right was extended to defendants in misdemeanors.

The *Gideon* case, described in the book *Gideon's Trumpet*, overturned the rule established in BETTS V. BRADY, 316 U.S. 455 (1942). The RIGHT TO COUNSEL was expanded in ESCOBEDO V. ILLINOIS, 378 U.S. 478 (1964), and MIRANDA V. ARIZONA, 384 U.S. 436 (1966), moved law enforcement away from confessions to having to develop scientific evidence in criminal cases. The *Miranda* decision meant that defendants were to be informed of their constitutional rights as soon as the finger of suspicion pointed at them.

Cases protecting the rights of the accused from unreasonable searches and seizures were decided in *Mapp v. Ohio*, 367 U.S. 643 (1963), and *Katz v. United States*, 389 U.S. 347 (1967). These and other similar cases were landmark cases that interpreted many clauses in the first 10 amendments (BILL OF RIGHTS) and applied them to the states through the Court doctrine of selective INCORPORATION.

Other momentous decisions of the Warren Court included the decisions to ban prayer (*Engle v. Vitale*, 370 U.S. 421 [1962]) and Bible reading (ABINGTON TOWNSHIP V. SCHEMPP [with *Murray v. Curlett*], (374 U.S. 203 [1963]) in the schools; Sunday closing laws (blue laws), *McGowan v. Maryland*, 366 U.S. 420 (1961); and other cases seeking to remove religious influence from the public square—adding to the controversy surrounding the Court.

In *BAKER V. CARR*, 369 U.S. 186 (1962), the Warren Court reversed precedent and ruled that apportionment of voting districts and voting rights in general were no longer political questions, but instead were judicable disputes. Numerous other voting rights cases followed, adding fuel to the fires of controversy surrounding the era of the Warren Court.

For more information: Belknap, Michal R. *The Supreme Court under Earl Warren, 1953–1969.* Columbia: University of South Carolina Press, 2004; Cox, Archibald. *The Warren Court: Constitutional Decisions as an Instrument of Reform.* Cambridge, Mass.: Harvard University Press, 1968; Newton, Jim. *Justice for All: Earl Warren and the Nation He Made.* New York: Penguin Group, 2006; Scheiber, Harry N., ed. *Earl Warren and the Warren Court: The Legacy in American and Foreign Law.* Lanham, Md.: Rowman & Littlefield, 2007; Schwartz, Bernard, ed. *Warren Court: A Retrospective.* New York: Oxford University Press, 1996; Urofsky, Melvin. *The Warren Court: Justices, Rulings, and Legacy.* Santa Barbara, Calif.: ABC-CLIO, 2001.

—Andrew J. Waskey

Washington v. Davis 426 U.S. 229 (1976)

In *Washington v. Davis*, the Supreme Court held that the discriminatory impact of a law is not sufficient, by itself, to establish a racial classification in violation of the Fifth Amendment's DUE PROCESS clause, which guarantees EQUAL PROTECTION of the laws.

Davis concerned whether the DISTRICT OF COLUMBIA Police Department's recruiting procedures discriminated against blacks in violation of the due process clause of the Fifth Amendment. To join the police department, the District of Columbia required applicants to pass a written test "designed to test verbal ability, vocabulary, reading and comprehension." Statistics revealed that blacks failed the entrance examination far more often than whites. The Court held that proof that a law is administered in a manner that disproportionately impacts minorities is insufficient, by itself, to establish a racial classification in violation of the constitutional guarantee of equal protection.

Writing for the Court, Justice White explained that evidence of discriminatory impact "[s]tanding alone . . . does not trigger the rule that racial classifications are to be subjected to the strictest scrutiny and are justifiable only by the weightiest considerations." A law that, on its face, is racially neutral will be upheld if it is rationally related to a legitimate government purpose, even if there is evidence of discriminatory impact. But if, in addition to evidence of a discriminatory impact, a person challenging a law as violating equal protection presents evidence of a law's discriminatory purpose—meaning that a law was enacted with the purpose of discriminating against persons of a certain race or national origin—then the challenger will have made a prima facie case that the law violates equal protection.

The Supreme Court offered two justifications for its conclusion that discriminatory impact, standing alone, is insufficient to establish an equal protection violation. First, the Court reasoned that the purpose of equal protection "is the prevention of official conduct discriminating on the basis of race." Second, the Court noted that "a whole range of tax, welfare, public service, regulatory, and licensing statutes that may be more burdensome to the poor and to the average black than to the more affluent white" might be threatened were the Court to permit a racial classification to be proved based solely on proof of discriminatory impact.

The Court has subsequently reaffirmed the rule articulated in *Washington v. Davis* in *Mobile v. Bolden*, 446 U.S. 55 (1980), and *McClesky v. Kemp*, 481 U.S. 279 (1987).

For more information: Lawrence, Charles R., III. "The Id, the Ego, and Equal Protection: Reckoning with Unconscious Racism." *Stanford Law Review* 39, no. 317 (1987): 323; Selmi, Michael.

"Was the Disparate Impact Theory a Mistake?" *UCLA Law Review* 53, no. 701 (2006).

—Andre Mura

wealth and the Constitution

Wealth or financial status is often problematic for the Supreme Court in that their use may deny some rights and liberties.

The U.S. Constitution is widely viewed as the legal foundation of America's wealth-building system. Most of the 55 delegates to the convention that created the American constitution were of some financial substance, raising speculation that the document was designed to benefit the mercantile or landed class. A version of this argument was first articulated by anti-Federalists and small agrarian interests opposed to the Constitution's ratification.

In the early 20th century the allegation of the Constitution's embedded economic bias was expounded by CHARLES A. BEARD (1874–1948), a noted American historian who founded New York's New School for Social Research, in his 1925 *An Economic Interpretation of the Constitution of the United States.* For a time, Beard's thesis was influential among cosmopolitan academics. His theory began to lose luster, however, when challenged by traditionalist scholars, most notably Forrest McDonald. Professor McDonald's book *We the People: The Economic Origins of the Constitution* (1958) claimed a much more pluralistic landscape of financial interests than did Beard. More recently, Beard's thesis has received criticism for failing to account for the Constitution's contribution to the general welfare.

The connection between governmental foundations and wealth building was highlighted under the Articles of Confederation, as Congress was dependent upon the states to enforce its laws and collect its taxes. With some states shirking their duties, the early Congress had to borrow from wealthy individuals to sustain government operations, yet without adequate means to repay the debts. The chaos of the era was heightened by states issuing their own currencies and monetizing debts.

In response to the problems, merchants gathered first in Alexandria, Virginia, and then in Annapolis, Maryland. The Annapolis Convention produced a request for a constitutional convention to address the country's growing crisis. Congress responded on February 21, 1787, by calling for a convention of the states to revise the Articles of Confederation and render them adequate to the exigencies of government and the preservation of the Union. Thus, the American constitution resulted, in part, from a commercial interest in reordering the system. The goal was to engender national economic prosperity—an idea that Whig senator Henry Clay popularized in the 1820s as the "American System."

Working from this perspective it is possible to conceive of the U.S. Constitution as an engine of commerce and wealth generation. This contrasts with the popularized view that the overriding purpose of the Constitution was to secure individual rights and liberties. Certain particulars of the U.S. Constitution lend support to this interpretation. In ARTICLE I, Section 8, Clause 1 the Congress is granted power to lay and collect taxes, pay debts, provide for the common welfare of the states, borrow money on the nation's credit, regulate commerce, coin money and regulate its value, and other things essential to a prosperous commercial state. Elsewhere there are prohibitions against feudalism and nonappropriated government spending as well as protections for interstate free trade, DUE PROCESS, and private property—protections that facilitate the spread of wealth in a society. Even the Madisonian aim of constituting a geographically far-flung republic helps stimulate competition among factions so as to pluralistically disperse wealth. But none of these observations answer the question as to why the voting public has kept their Constitution unengaged regarding wealth concentration. This void is increasingly consequential now that the top 1 percent of American wealth holders control well over one-third of all U.S. private wealth, with foreign elites holding large shares as well.

Since the Founders created CHECKS AND BALANCES for most hazards they identified, it is worth considering what they might have done had they foreseen a financial system capable of concentrating immense wealth for some individuals. Indeed, THOMAS JEFFERSON bemoaned the convention's failure to add a constitutional clause prohibiting long-term national debt. This hazard, he feared, could benefit the upper capital class at the expense of the working man, even endangering republican institutions at some point.

Some political observers believe that a cultural reformation could produce constitutional amendments limiting wealth concentration. This is unlikely, however, as illustrated by billionaire Donald Trump's aborted bid for the U.S. presidency in 1999–2000. Trump built his political platform around the idea of a one-time asset tax of 14.25 percent on American fortunes over $10 million, arguing that the tax would pay off the national debt (then about $5.7 trillion), among other things. Predictably, the American public and both major political parties barely took notice. Yet, in 1992 the public ratified our TWENTY-SEVENTH AMENDMENT to provide a bit more control over modest congressional salaries. These observations suggest that American culture is not yet ready to use the Constitution to address wealth distribution challenges.

Nevertheless, constitutional battles have made it conceivable for the American electorate to someday challenge the evolving mediated democratic plutocracy—a system where large capital holders engineer much of the political process by using wealth to influence primary races, especially for the presidency and the U.S. SENATE. This so-called "wealth primary" reflects the advantages that accrue to those who garner exceptional media attention by early domination of a campaign fund-raising cycle. Yet, the plutocratic primary is not constitutionally predestined; notable U.S. Supreme Court decisions have found scant constitutional grounds for privileging wealth in elections.

In *Harper v. Virginia Board of Elections*, 383 U.S. 663 (1966), the U.S. Supreme Court found (by a 6-3 margin) that "a state violates the EQUAL PROTECTION clause of the FOURTEENTH AMENDMENT . . . whenever it makes the affluence of the voter or payment of any fee an electoral standard." This decision finalized the de-linkage of monetary means to voter qualifications, shutting the door on the poll tax in state elections two years after the TWENTY-FOURTH AMENDMENT accomplished the same in federal elections. Likewise, in *Bullock v. Carter,* 405 U.S. 134 (1972), the Court's majority opinion stated that a sound primary system should "spread the cost among all the voters in an attempt to distribute the influence without regard to wealth." This decision came in response to a system in Texas where candidates seeking placement on primary ballots had to pay CANDIDATE FILING FEES to their political parties ranging from $150 to $8,900. The Court majority stated, "We would ignore reality were we not to find that this system falls with unequal weight on voters, as well as candidates, according to their economic status."

While the aforementioned Court decisions follow a semi-egalitarian track in electoral matters, other decisions have taken a different path. In *BUCKLEY V. VALEO,* 424 U.S. 1 (1976), the Court equated a candidate's personal campaign expenditures with FIRST AMENDMENT rights of free speech, effectively limiting the range of CAMPAIGN FINANCE reform as it affects wealthy candidates. In a somewhat related matter, the High Court overturned a federal district court decision that found wealth to be a suspect classification in the funding of public education through local real estate taxes, since tax revenue for school districts varies widely based upon housing values. Thus, *San Antonio School District v. Rodriquez,* 411 U.S. 1 (1973), acts as a limitation on the reach of the equal protection clause as it regards the impact of disparate wealth.

The nation's judicial system faces daunting challenges in protecting property and associated benefits of capital holding while simultaneously preventing the wealth privilege from distorting representative democracy toward modernized plutocracy. If history is any guide, solutions to current constitutional impasses are most likely to arise from major economic dislocations that shift electoral alignments or engage passive voters.

For more information: Kelly, Marjorie. *The Divine Right of Capital: Dethroning the Corporate Aristocracy.* San Francisco: Berrett-Koehler,

2001; Skousen, W. Cleon. *The Making of America: The Substance and Meaning of the Constitution.* Washington, D.C.: National Center for Constitutional Studies, 1985.

—Timothy J. Barnett

Webster v. Reproductive Health Services
492 U.S. 490 (1989)

In *Webster v. Reproductive Health Services,* the U.S. Supreme Court ruled on the constitutionality of a Missouri law. Speaking for himself and Justices ANTHONY M. KENNEDY and Byron White, Chief Justice WILLIAM HUBBS REHNQUIST announced the judgment of the Court.

The first issue was a preamble in the Missouri law declaring that human life "begins at conception." The Court held that, because this was merely an abstract statement favoring childbirth over ABORTION, it need not decide on its constitutionality. The second part of the law barred abortions not necessary to save a woman's life in public facilities such as the Truman Medical Center in Kansas City, Missouri. Although Truman was a private hospital, it was built on state-leased land and therefore considered "public," even though no state funds were spent on abortions performed there. Rehnquist explained that states may show they prefer childbirth to abortion by restricting the performance of abortions at public hospitals.

As with the preamble, the Court also found it unnecessary to rule on the provision of the law forbidding the use of public funds, employees, and facilities to encourage or counsel women to have abortions not necessary to save their lives. Accepting the state's argument that it was intended only to prevent hospital administrators from allocating funds for abortion counseling, the Court never addressed the question of whether the law restricted physicians' freedom of speech by barring them from discussing abortion with their patients.

The last, and most important, provision of the law involved the requirement to determine fetal viability by measuring its age, weight, and lungs when a physician believes it is at least 20 weeks of age. In upholding this provision, Rehnquist interpreted the law as requiring doctors to perform these tests only when they believed them useful in determining viability. He rejected the lower court's interpretation that the law required these tests to be performed on any woman a physician believes is at least 20 weeks pregnant.

Rehnquist acknowledged that the Missouri law was inconsistent with *ROE V. WADE,* 410 U.S. 113 (1973), because it required these tests to be performed during the second trimester of the pregnancy. He believed that the best way to resolve the inconsistency was to change the requirements of *Roe.* Although he insisted that the Court was not overruling *Roe,* he seemed to encourage legislation that would require the Court to revisit and overrule *Roe* in the future.

Justice SANDRA DAY O'CONNOR agreed with the three justices, but wrote separately to state her view that the viability tests were consistent with *Roe* and the Court did not have to examine its constitutionality. Justice ANTONIN GREGORY SCALIA agreed as well, but expressed disappointment in the Court's refusal to explicitly overrule *Roe,* which in his view was wrongly decided.

Speaking for Justices WILLIAM J. BRENNAN, JR., and Thurgood Marshall, Justice Harry Blackmun charged that the law plainly stated that doctors must determine the age, weight, and lung maturity of every 20-week fetus. This provision, he argued, risked the lives of the woman and the fetus and did not further the state's interest in protecting their health. In his view, the Court was inviting states to adopt restrictive abortion regulations in the hopes that *Roe* would be overruled. If this occurred, he warned, women's lives would be endangered by being forced into dangerous illegal abortions.

For more information: Mezey, Susan Gluck. *Elusive Equality: Women's Rights, Public Policy, and the Law.* Boulder, Colo.: Lynne Rienner, 2003; Tribe, Laurence. *Abortion: The Clash of Absolutes.* New York: Norton, 1990.

—Susan Gluck Mezey

Weeks v. United States 232 U.S. 383 (1914)

In *Weeks v. United States,* the U.S. Supreme Court held that criminal evidence must be excluded from use in court when it is obtained by federal law enforcement officers through an improper search. The decision provided the Supreme Court's first endorsement of the EXCLUSIONARY RULE, a controversial remedy for improper searches. The rule was later expanded for application to state and local law enforcement officers in *Mapp v. Ohio*, 367 U.S. 643 (1961). The *Weeks* decision led to debates that continue into the 21st century about whether evidence of a criminal suspect's guilt should be excluded from use in court.

Fremont Weeks was arrested on December 21, 1911, in Kansas City, Missouri, at his place of employment. A U.S. marshal accompanied by Kansas City police officers went to Weeks's boarding house where another resident admitted them. They entered Weeks's room without a search warrant and seized various papers. These items were used to convict Weeks for violating federal laws against using the mail to transport lottery tickets.

According to the words of the FOURTH AMENDMENT to the U.S. Constitution, the amendment is to protect "[t]he right of the people to be secure in their persons, houses, papers, and effects, against unreasonable searches and seizures." The U.S. marshal violated Weeks's Fourth Amendment rights by failing to obtain a search warrant from a judge before conducting the search. In nonemergency situations, the Fourth Amendment requires that the police obtain a warrant from a judge before searching a home. In writing on behalf of a unanimous Supreme Court, Justice William Day emphasized the justices' view that the use of improperly obtained evidence would effectively nullify people's rights. In Day's words, "If letters and private documents can thus be seized and held and used in evidence against a citizen accused of an offense, the protection of the [Fourth] Amendment, declaring his right to be secure against such searches and seizures, is of no value, and, so far as those thus placed are concerned, might as well be stricken from the Constitution" (*Weeks v. United States*, 232 U.S. at 393).

The exclusionary rule from *Weeks* remains controversial because it creates situations in which a guilty person may escape punishment because the evidence of guilt was excluded from use in court.

During the 20th century, the Supreme Court identified specific kinds of searches for which the exclusionary rule will not apply. However, despite the adjustments to the exclusionary rule, the 21st-century Supreme Court continues to endorse the fundamental rule of *Weeks v. United States* requiring the exclusion of evidence when police officers who had an opportunity to obtain a search warrant failed to do so.

For more information: Abraham, Henry J. *Freedom and the Court: Civil Rights and Liberties in the United States.* 5th ed. New York: Oxford University Press, 1988; Smith, Christopher E. *Criminal Procedure.* Belmont, Calif.: Wadsworth Publishing, 2003.

—Christopher E. Smith

welfare and the Constitution

Welfare and welfare rights implicate constitutional issues regarding the power of the national government.

Among the powers granted to Congress in ARTICLE I, Section 8 of the U.S. Constitution are the powers to "lay and collect Taxes, Duties, Imposts, and Excises, to pay the Debts and provide for the common defense and general Welfare of the United States." There is no elaboration on the meaning of "general welfare," and the placement of this phrase in the clause authorizing Congress to tax and spend has caused confusion over how or whether these powers fit together. Over time, conflict over the meaning of the general welfare clause has given way to debate over the proper application of the FOURTEENTH AMENDMENT to protect the welfare of disadvantaged populations, and most recently to the use of statutory interpretation to shape the implementation of welfare policies.

Disagreements over the general welfare clause date back to the Founding period. Although both JAMES MADISON and ALEXANDER HAMILTON supported the establishment of a strong national government, they clashed over how to interpret Congress's power to tax and spend to "provide for the general welfare." Madison believed that

Congress could tax and spend only for things enumerated in the Constitution. To him, the phrase "general welfare" was a preface to the powers listed in the remainder of Article I, Section 8, not a separate grant of power. Hamilton, however, interpreted the general welfare clause as an independent power that was not limited by other powers granted in the Constitution. Under his logic, Congress could levy taxes and spend the revenue on new programs provided they advanced the general welfare in a broad sense and as long as the benefits were appropriated on a national, rather than local, scale.

It is reasonable to say that, in general, Hamilton's reading of the general welfare clause has dominated American political history. In the 19th century, federal initiatives, such as a national banking system, and internal improvements, such as lighthouses and roads, were justified, in part, by the general welfare power. Initiatives aimed at poverty relief, though, remained the province of the states and private organizations. This scheme changed during the New Deal. In the case *United States v. Butler*, 297 U.S. 1 (1936), the U.S. Supreme Court explicitly supported Hamilton's interpretation, saying that "the power of Congress to authorize expenditure of public moneys for public purposes is not limited by the direct grants of legislative power found in the Constitution." The decision did, however, specify that Congress's spending power was limited by the Tenth Amendment. Subsequent Supreme Court decisions on other New Deal initiatives chipped away at the qualifying power of the Tenth Amendment in favor of promoting the general welfare, specifically in federal policy areas that aimed to help disadvantaged populations, such as the elderly and widows and their children.

The implementation of New Deal policies to promote the general welfare signaled the beginning of the federal government's involvement in programs to relieve poverty and other social inequalities. Concomitantly, the Supreme Court increasingly decided cases that required an evaluation of the impact of various inequalities. Beginning in the 1940s, however, the constitutional basis for the broadening spectrum of federal welfare policies moved away from taxing and spending for the "general welfare" toward a greater reliance on the Fourteenth Amendment's EQUAL PROTECTION clause to promote not only legal, but also social, equality.

Use of the equal protection clause to promote social welfare and equality is commonly traced to legal reasoning found in FOOTNOTE FOUR of *U.S. v. Carolene Products Co.*, 304 U.S. 144 (1938), which suggested that the courts are obligated to heavily scrutinize any law that affects, among others, "insular minorities" to ensure that it does not impinge on their FUNDAMENTAL RIGHTS. In *BROWN V. BOARD OF EDUCATION*, 347 U.S. 483 (1954), the Court activated this reasoning to find racially segregated schools unconstitutional. Many observers suggest that *Brown* initiated an "Equal Protection Revolution" that led the Court to "strictly scrutinize" new areas of legislation in order to protect the welfare of disadvantaged "classifications" or groups. Since then, classifications based on race have received STRICT SCRUTINY; other classifications such as ethnicity, gender, mental capacity, and wealth have received various levels of scrutiny over time.

From the New Deal through the 1960s, the courts generally deferred to agency discretion in the implementation of welfare policies, which amounted to a rather low level of scrutiny. Beginning in the late 1960s, however, JUDICIAL REVIEW of welfare programs took a new direction; welfare entitlements were more broadly defined, and welfare beneficiaries enjoyed a new kind of right. While the U.S. Supreme Court found that there is no fundamental right to welfare entitlements, these entitlements came to be viewed as a kind of property. In other words, beneficiaries of entitlements were understood to have statutorily conferred programmatic rights that could not be reasonably denied. Two seminal Supreme Court decisions helped shape this new conception of welfare. In *GOLDBERG V. KELLY*, 397 U.S. 254 (1970), the Court determined that a welfare recipient's continued interest in receiving benefits is a statutory entitlement that is equivalent to property under the DUE PROCESS clause. In *SHAPIRO V. THOMPSON*, 394 U.S. 618 (1969), the Court held that state residency requirements or waiting periods for welfare benefits violate both the implied constitutional right to travel and the equal protection clause because they discriminate against the poor. Although, in the modern era, the federal courts have relied on statutory interpretation of welfare laws to shape and protect this area of rights, the constitutional analyses in *Goldberg* and *Shapiro* are often referenced as the sources of the new welfare rights.

For more information: Gunther, Gerald. *Individual Rights in Constitutional Law.* 5th ed. Westbury, N.Y.: Foundation Press, 1990; Melnick, R. Shep. *Between the Lines: Interpreting Welfare Rights.* Washington, D.C.: Brookings, 1994; Post, Russell L. "The Constitutionality of Government Spending for the General Welfare." *Virginia Law Review* 22 (1935): 1–38.

—Margaret Tullai

West Coast Hotel v. Parrish 300 U.S. 379 (1937)

In *West Coast Hotel v. Parrish*, the Supreme Court upheld a state minimum wage law for women. *West Coast Hotel* formally overruled an earlier Supreme Court case, ADKINS V. CHILDREN'S HOSPITAL, 261 U.S. 525 (1923), which held that a minimum-wage law for women violated the DUE PROCESS clause of the FOURTEENTH AMENDMENT. This case was an important decision that eventually led the Court to uphold New Deal legislation and give the government more authority to regulate the economy.

In 1913, the Washington state legislature passed a law fixing a minimum wage for women to combat the "sweating system" of long hours and little pay, which the state found to be hazardous to a woman's health and safety. The plaintiff in this case brought suit against her employer for back wages, which should have been paid at a rate of $14.50 per 48-hour week.

The hotel alleged that the due process clause of the Fourteenth Amendment protected its freedom of contract with employees. Justice Hughes, who wrote on behalf of the majority, disagreed. He argued that the Constitution contains no free-

dom of contract, and that any liberties protected by the Fourteenth Amendment can be deprived if due process of law is satisfied. He found the state's interest in keeping women healthy was justified because they were typically paid less and were in a weaker bargaining position than men. He noted that the physical structure of women places them at a disadvantage in the struggle for subsistence and that their maternal functions must be preserved to ensure the "strength and vigor of the race." Because of these factors, the Court ruled that a state can pass legislation to protect the health and safety of women that might not be constitutional if also applied to men.

West Coast Hotel was an expansion of *Muller v. Oregon*, 208 U.S. 412 (1908), in which the Court upheld a law limiting the number of hours women could work. The Court distinguished both of these cases from LOCHNER V. NEW YORK, 198 U.S. 45 (1905), which invalidated a law limiting the number of hours a baker could work, because the law applied only to women. Eventually, the Court would use the same reasoning to uphold laws protecting men as well as women. See *Williamson v. Lee Optical Co.,* 348 U.S. 483 (1955).

For more information: Cushman, Barry. *Rethinking the New Deal Court: The Structure of a Constitutional Revolution.* New York: Oxford University Press, 1998.

—Dylan R. Kytola

West Lynn Creamery, Inc., v. Healy 512 U.S. 186 (1994)

In *West Lynn Creamery, Inc. v. Healy,* the Supreme Court struck down a pricing statute that related to in-state and out-of-state milk producers violating the DORMANT COMMERCE CLAUSE of the Constitution.

In this case, the state of Massachusetts subjected all fluid milk sold by dealers in the state to a social assessment via a pricing order. It imposed this assessment in order to help preserve Massachusetts dairy farms. Most milk sold in Massachusetts was produced outside of the state, yet funds collected from this assessment were, in effect, distributed to Massachusetts dairy farmers. West

Lynn Creamery sued in a Massachusetts court, claiming that the assessment violated the federal commerce clause. The Massachusetts court denied relief to West Lynn Creamery, and the case was appealed to the Massachusetts Supreme Court, which affirmed the lower court's decision, "concluding that the order was not facially discriminatory, applied evenhandedly, and only incidentally burdened INTERSTATE COMMERCE, and that such a burden was outweighed by the 'local benefits' to the dairy industry."

The case was appealed to the Supreme Court and, in a 7-2 decision delivered by Justice JOHN PAUL STEVENS, the Court concluded that the pricing order was unconstitutional. According to the Court:

> Neither the power to tax nor the POLICE POWER may be used by the state of destination with the aim and effect of establishing an economic barrier against competition with the products of another state or the labor of its residents. Restrictions so contrived are an unreasonable clog upon the mobility of commerce. They set up what is equivalent to a rampart of customs duties designed to neutralize advantages belonging to the place of origin.

Thus, because the minimum price regulation had the same effect as a tariff or customs duty—neutralizing the advantage possessed by lower-cost out-of-state producers—it was held unconstitutional as a violation of the commerce clause. Similarly, in *Bacchus Imports, Ltd. v. Dias*, 468 U.S. 263 (1984), this Court invalidated a law that advantaged local production by granting a tax exemption to certain liquors produced in Hawaii.

West Lynn Creamery, Inc. v. Healy is one of several recent commerce clause cases that demonstrate that there are limits on state taxing and police power authority, even absent explicit congressional action.

For more information: Nowak, John E., and Ronald D. Rotunda. *Principles of Constitutional Law.* St. Paul, Minn.: Thomson/West, 2005.

—Dan Krejci

West River Bridge Company v. Dix 47 U.S. 507 (1848)

This case marked the first time the Supreme Court dealt with the power of EMINENT DOMAIN, holding that the taking of a bridge for public use was not a violation of the CONTRACT CLAUSE in the United States Constitution.

In 1795, Vermont passed an act of legislation entitled "An act granting to John W. Blake, Calvin Knowlton, and their associates, the privilege of building a toll-bridge over West River, in Brattleboro." The act authorized Blake and his associates to incorporate and run a toll bridge for 100 years. In May of 1843, local commissioners, on petition from some of the populace to take charge of the bridge operation, recommended the use of eminent domain to take the bridge and make it a public way. The bridge was taken by eminent domain. The case was tried in a Vermont court in November 1843, and the report filed by the commissioners was accepted; the West River Bridge Company was to be compensated with $4,000 for their bridge, which was to be taken for public use.

The case was appealed to the Supreme Court, which was asked to decide if the taking of the bridge for public use was a violation of the contract clause. Justice Daniel delivered the opinion of the Court, concluding that the taking of the bridge and land for public use was not a violation of the contract clause of ARTICLE I OF THE CONSTITUTION. The Court stated that eminent domain was a fundamental power of the states, and as long as fair and JUST COMPENSATION was paid to the West River Bridge Company, then Vermont had the power to take the land for public use.

Overall, while viewed as a contract clause case, *West River Bridge Company v. Dix* is an important case supporting the use of eminent domain for a wide variety of public uses, including the taking of different types of property, such as contracts.

For more information: Nowak, John E., and Ronald D. Rotunda. *Principles of Constitutional Law.* St. Paul, Minn.: Thomson/West, 2005.

—Dan Krejci

White Court (1910–1921)

The White Court began on Monday, December 19, 1910, when Edward Douglass White, Jr. (born November 3, 1845), became the ninth chief justice of the Supreme Court, replacing Chief Justice Melville Weston Fuller. It ended with White's death in office on May 19, 1921.

The members of the Court when Chief Justice White was elevated from a Supreme Court associate justice position to chief justice were justices JOHN MARSHALL HARLAN (appointed in 1877), Joseph McKenna (appointed 1898), OLIVER WENDELL HOLMES, JR. (appointed in 1902), William R. Day (appointed 1903), Horace H. Lurton (appointed January 1910), and Charles E. Hughes (appointed October 1910). Added to the Court almost immediately in January of 1911 were Willis Van Devanter and Joseph R. Lamar.

In March of 1912, Mahlon Pitney took the seat of John Marshall Harlan, who died in October of 1911. James C. McReynolds replaced Horace H. Lurton, who died in July of 1914. Louis D. Brandeis was added to the court (June 5, 1916), and John H. Clarke was added in October of 1916. They replaced Joseph Rucker Lamar (appointed 1911), who died in January of 1916, and Charles Evans Hughes, who resigned on June 10, 1916.

White's appointment by President William Howard Taft upon the death of Melville Fuller was a surprise to many because White was a Democrat and President Taft was a Republican. His appointment as chief justice was the first time an associate justice had been elevated to the office since John Rutledge in 1795.

The new chief justice had a new majority to deal with political outrage over decisions of the FULLER COURT. Cases coming before the White Court reflected the politico-economic battles then raging between the Progressive Movement and the laissez-faire industrial capitalism that had developed in late-19th-century America. The Court was to achieve a reputation as a "progressive" court because of its decision in STANDARD OIL CO. OF NEW JERSEY V. UNITED STATES, 221 U.S. 1 (1911).

The *Standard Oil* case had been argued March 14, 15, and 16, 1910, and then reargued in January of 1911. It was decided on May 15, 1911. In a unanimous decision written by Chief Justice White (with Justice Harlan issuing a concurring opinion), the Court declared that the prosecution of Standard Oil for monopoly practices under the Sherman Antitrust Act was constitutional. It recognized the authority of Congress derived from the COMMERCE CLAUSE to prevent practices that were otherwise acceptable under common law. However, in the American Tobacco case (1920), the Court followed the rule of reason in common law that mere bigness is not unreasonable and that there are reasonable and unreasonable "trusts."

Other commerce cases included the upholding of the constitutionality of the Pure Food and Drug Act of 1906 in *Hipolite Egg Co. v. United States* (1911), the MANN ACT of 1910 in *Hoke v. United States* (1913), and *HAMMER V. DAGENHART* (1918), supporting regulation of the Keating-Owen Child Labor Act of 1916. However, a Kansas law forbidding the use of "yellow dog contracts" was overturned in *COPPAGE V. KANSAS* (1915).

Two other commerce clause cases were the *Minnesota Rate Cases* (1913) and the *Shreveport Rate Case* (1914). These upheld the power of the federal government to limit individual state actions in the area of commerce.

Income tax legislation based upon the SIXTEENTH AMENDMENT was upheld in *Brushaber v. Union Pacific Railroad* (1916) and extended in *Stanton v. Baltic Mining Co.* (1916).

Race relations arose in *McCabe v. Atchison, Topeka & Santa Fe Railway Company* (1914). In the strongest day of Jim Crow legislation, the Court decided that separate-but-equal meant equal. However, in *BUCHANAN V. WARLEY* (1917), it struck down racial segregation laws in housing as restraints on the equal rights of property for all. And in *Guinn v. Oklahoma* (1915) it struck down "grandfather clauses" used to disenfranchise blacks from exercising the RIGHT TO VOTE.

Conservation and the use of public lands was addressed in *United States v. Grimaud* (1911). The Court found that Congress could legislate to regulate the control of forest reserves. It also upheld the right of the federal government to legislate on conservation matters involving migratory birds, upon the basis of treaties in Missouri v. Holland (1920).

Dowdell v. United States (1911) and Ocampo v. United States (1914) were the latest in a number of Insular Cases that argued the question, "Do Constitutional rights follow the flag?" The White Court accepted the case from the Philippines Supreme Court (in what was then an American-governed territory) but refused to fully apply the Constitution to the facts of the case, observing that DUE PROCESS had been followed.

American involvement in World War I generated cases involving the government's war powers, which were upheld in Northern Pacific Railway Co., v. North Dakota (1919). It upheld as well the virtual nationalization of the economy during the war.

The Espionage Act of 1916 (adopted in response to German sabotage in the Black Tom munitions explosion) and the Sedition Act of 1917 brought freedom of speech cases to the Court. Justice Holmes in Schenck v. United States (1919) issued the unanimous decision of the Court that freedom of speech was limited when there was a "clear and present danger" of substantive evils that Congress could seek to prevent. However, in Abrams v. United States (1919) Brandeis and Holmes sought to restrain the limiting of freedom of speech.

The White Court's decision in Muskrat v. United States (1911) defined the jurisdiction of the federal courts as limited to "real" cases and controversies. As Justice Day warned petitioners, the Court does not issue advisory opinions.

For more information: Bindler, Norman. *The Conservative Court, 1910–1930.* Danbury, Conn.: Grolier Educational Corp., 1995; Highsaw, Robert Baker. *Edward Douglass White: Defender of the Conservative Faith.* Baton Rouge: Louisiana State University Press, 1981; Pratt, Walter F. *Supreme Court under Chief Justice Edward Douglass White, 1910–1921.* Columbia: University of South Carolina Press, 1999; Shoemaker, Rebecca S. *White Court: Justices, Rulings and Legacy.* Santa Barbara, Calif.: ABC-CLIO, 2004.

—Andrew J. Waskey

Whitney v. California 247 U.S. 357 (1927)

In the case of *Whitney v. California,* the United States Supreme Court held that membership in an organization advocating criminal syndicalism was substantively dangerous, and therefore such membership must be given great weight in the analysis of the law. Although this case was overruled in Brandenburg v. Ohio, 395 U.S. 444 (1969), the "concurrence" of Justice Brandeis (voted as such because the defendant did not raise the correct constitutional issues in her appeal) is a classic dealing with First Amendment issues.

The defendant in this case, Miss Whitney, was a known member of the Socialist Party. She attended a convention of the Socialist Party in 1919, which split into two groups. She went with the more radical group and subsequently attended a second meeting to help organize a new California section of the Communist Labor Party. She encouraged workers to vote for Communist Labor Party candidates at future elections, but her resolution stating so was defeated and a more radical resolution adopted, although it was not her intention to violate any known law.

Miss Whitney was later convicted under the California Criminal Syndicalism Act. "Criminal syndicalism" was defined in the act challenged by Miss Whitney as "any doctrine or precept advocating, teaching, or aiding and abetting the commission of crime, sabotage, or unlawful acts of force and violence or unlawful methods of terrorism, as a means of accomplishing a change in industrial ownership or control or effecting any political change." Such act held it unlawful to organize a group that advocated acts of violence as a means of effecting change in industry and politics. Miss Whitney argued that neither her "mere membership" nor her presence at a convention could be defined as a "crime." She was convicted and appealed to the United States Supreme Court on the basis of DUE PROCESS violations and violations of her First Amendment and EQUAL PROTECTION rights.

The majority held that the Syndicalism Act was not repugnant to the due process clause for its vagueness or uncertainty of definition because the definition of "criminal syndicalism" was very specific. They went further and held that the act also did not violate the equal protection clause because its penalties were confined to people who were advocating a resort to violent and unlawful actions as a means of changing industrial and political conditions. The final holding of the Court stated that the act did not violate free speech because a state may, through the exercise of its POLICE POWER, punish people who utter speech inimical to the public welfare, tending to incite crime, disturbing the peace, or endangering the foundations of organized government and threatening its overthrow by unlawful means.

For more information: Kalven, Harry, Jr. *A Worthy Tradition: Freedom of Speech in America.* New York: Harper & Row, 1988.

—Kelli Styron

Whren v. United States 517 U.S. 806 (1996)

In *Whren v. United States,* the U.S. Supreme Court held that pretextual traffic stops are constitutional, so long as the officer that made the stop believes that either a traffic violation or some other offense has occurred.

Plainclothes officers in Washington, D.C., were patrolling, in an unmarked car, an area that had been known for drug activity and drug sales. They noticed a truck with temporary license plates and driven by youthful occupants, waiting at a stop sign for more than 20 seconds, which seemed to be an unusually long time, as there were no other vehicles in the vicinity. The police turned their car around to head back to the truck, but as they did so the vehicle drove away from the police car at "unreasonable" speed. The officers pulled the truck over on the grounds that the driver had been speeding and had remained too long in the intersection, a violation of the city traffic code. When the police officer approached the passenger's side window, he noticed two large bags containing crack cocaine in the passenger's (Whren) hands. The police arrested both Whren and the driver.

Whren was subsequently convicted of drug possession and appealed, arguing the search of his person was invalid because the officers lacked either probable cause or reasonable suspicion that the defendants were engaged in the dealing of illegal narcotics, and that the traffic stop was unconstitutional because it was conducted as a pretext, or excuse, to search the vehicle and its occupants for drugs.

The Supreme Court disagreed. A prior case, *Pennsylvania v. Mimms,* 434 U.S. 106, 109 (1977), held that the decision to stop an automobile is reasonable if the police believe a traffic violation occurred. Whren agreed with this but believed that probable cause that a traffic violation has occurred is not enough, because there are myriad reasons an officer can pull a car over. Whren argued that the subjective intent of the officer was relevant. In other words, did the officer pull over the vehicle Whren was riding in because he wanted to look for drugs, or because he really cared about the traffic violation? The Court determined that the subjective intent of the officer was irrelevant. So long as there was probable cause to make a traffic stop, the stop was reasonable under the FOURTH AMENDMENT.

This case is significance because it gives police the authority to make traffic stops as long as they have probable cause to believe any offense has been committed (Hemmens, Worrall, and Thompson, 2004). More specifically, it endorses a practice known as pretext stops, which is when an officer detains a motorist on a traffic violation, with the real motivation of looking for evidence of other criminal activity (Hemmens et al., 2004).

For more information: Hemmens, Craig, John Worrall, and Alan Thompson. *Criminal Justice Case Briefs: Significant Cases in Criminal Procedure.* Los Angeles: Roxbury, 2004.

—Brian Iannacchione

Wickard v. Filburn 317 U.S. 111 (1942)

Wickard v. Filburn is a U.S. Supreme Court decision that upheld a tax on the production of wheat for personal use under the Agricultural Adjustment Act. *Wickard* provides a window into debates over the COMMERCE CLAUSE (Article I, Section 8, Clause 3) vis-à-vis the Tenth Amend-

ment that date back to before the 1789 RATIFICA-
TION OF THE CONSTITUTION. Nominally about
wheat farming, fundamentally *Wickard* is about
FEDERALISM.

Wickard originated in a complaint filed by
Ohio farmer Roscoe C. Filburn. He sought to
enjoin collection of a fine imposed on him under
the terms of the 1938 Agricultural Adjustment
Act (AAA). The AAA established allotments limiting wheat planting. Filburn violated his quota
with his 1941 crop, only part of which he sold, the
remainder being fed to his animals and used for
cooking or as seed. For disregarding his quota,
Filburn was fined $117.11. Filburn argued that the
fine was uncollectible because the AAA exceeded
the authority of Congress under the commerce
clause.

Writing for a unanimous Court, Justice Robert H. Jackson upheld the AAA. Notable about
the Court's reasoning is its embrace of Congress's
expansive understanding of "commerce." Enacting
the AAA, Congress extended "federal regulation
to production not intended in any part for commerce but wholly for consumption on the farm."
In so doing, Congress rejected existing categori-
cal judicial distinctions between "production"
and "manufacture" versus "commerce," on the
one hand, and "direct" versus "indirect" effects
that had thwarted regulation. Saying that "the
mechanical application of legal formulas [is] no
longer feasible," Jackson validated the congressional approach: "even if [Filburn's] activity be local
and though it may not be regarded as commerce, it
may still, whatever its nature, be reached by Congress if it exerts a substantial economic effect on
INTERSTATE COMMERCE and this irrespective of
whether such effect is what might at some earlier
time have been defined as 'direct' or 'indirect.'"

For over half a century, the prevailing view
was that *Wickard* articulated the final constitutional word on congressional commerce power.
Along with two other landmark New Deal–era
cases (*NATIONAL LABOR RELATIONS BOARD V. JONES
AND LAUGHLIN STEEL CORP.*, 301 U.S. 1 [1937]) and
UNITED STATES V. DARBY LUMBER CO., 312 U.S. 100
[1941]), it came to symbolize the expansive regulatory power of the federal government, post–New

Deal. Nevertheless, as a counterpoint to the existing consensus, during the last 20 years of the 20th
century *Wickard* increasingly became the target
of a steady drumbeat of criticism as having cor-
rupted the role of states in the federal system. By
1995, Court appointments by successive Republican presidents had created a slim majority of justices who embraced this criticism. This majority
drew the line—some would say threw down the
gauntlet—in *UNITED STATES V. LOPEZ*, 514 U.S. 549.
Chief Justice Rehnquist wrote: "we [decline] . . .
to pile inference upon inference in a manner that
would bid fair to convert congressional authority
under the commerce clause to a general POLICE
POWER of the sort retained by the States. Admit-
tedly, some of our prior cases have taken long steps
down that road, giving great deference to congressional action. . . . This we are unwilling to do."

For more information: Brown, Judith Olans,
and Peter D. Enrich. "Nostalgic Federalism."
Hastings Constitutional Law Quarterly 28 (Fall
2000): 1; Chen, Jim. "Filburn's Legacy." *Emory
Law Journal* 52 (Fall 2003): 1,719; Merritt, Deborah Jones. "Reflections on *United States v. Lopez*:
Commerce!" *Michigan Law Review* 94 (December 1995): 674.

—James C. Foster

wiretapping

Wiretapping is electronic surveillance related to
message interception, with or without knowledge
of the parties who are having their communications intercepted. Wiretapping is generally recognized to be any interception of a telephone
transmission by accessing the telephone signal
itself, and electronic eavesdropping is the use of
an electronic transmitting or recording device to
monitor conversations without the consent of the
parties. Wiretapping or electronic surveillance
by the government raises constitutional concerns
under the FOURTH AMENDMENT.

In *OLMSTEAD V. UNITED STATES*, 277 U.S. 438
(1928), the Supreme Court ruled that electronic
surveillance without a warrant violated neither
the Fourth nor Fifth Amendments to the Consti-

tution, and the thing seized—conversation—was not protected by these amendments. However, in *Katz v. New York,* 389 U.S. 347 (1967), the Court overruled *Olmstead,* ruling that the Fourth Amendment did apply to wiretaps. In *Nardone v. United States,* 302 U.S. 379 (1937), the EXCLUSIONARY RULE was applied to illegal wiretapping in federal prosecutions. Eventually it was also applied to state criminal actions.

In the year 2006, several concerns emerged in relation to the constitutionality of the ability of the president to authorize warrantless wiretapping by the National Security Agency (NSA) for both domestic and foreign protection purposes. The president, George W. Bush, and his VICE PRESIDENT, Dick Cheney, have argued that the actions were necessary so as to continue protecting the country from enemies foreign and domestic and to thwart surprise attacks similar to the World Trade Center terrorist attacks on September 11, 2001. Many have argued that these warrantless wiretaps are contrary to the requirements of the FOREIGN INTELLIGENCE SURVEILLANCE ACT OF 1978. The AMERICAN CIVIL LIBERTIES UNION challenged this electric surveillance, but the federal courts ruled that it lacked STANDING. In 2007 Congress authorized much of the president's authority to order this surveillance. However, many still argue that this wiretapping violates the Fourth Amendment.

For more information: LaFave, Wayne R., Jerold H. Israel, and Nancy J. King. *Criminal Procedure.* St. Paul, Minn.: Thomson/West, 2004.
—Ernest Gomez

Wisconsin v. Yoder 406 U.S. 205 (1972)

In *Wisconsin v. Yoder,* the Supreme Court upheld the claim of Amish parents that the free exercise clause of the FIRST AMENDMENT gave them the right to remove their children from school after the eighth grade despite state compulsory education laws requiring high school attendance through age 16.

They argued that this law violated their religious freedom because they believe they must separate themselves from worldly influences to attain salvation. They maintained that an eighth-grade education taught children sufficient reading and math skills to function within the Amish community. Beyond that, youths would learn the practical skills of farming and homemaking simply by working with their elders.

Wisconsin v. Yoder maintained the expansive range of religious freedom staked out in *Sherbert v. Verner,* 374 U.S. 398 (1963). Even in situations where a law applied to the general public, exceptions must be made to protect religious liberty if the government cannot demonstrate a "compelling interest" to restrict a religious practice. In *Wisconsin v. Yoder,* the U.S. Supreme Court maintained in a 6-1 vote that the state had not adequately demonstrated that its educational concerns should override the Amish right to exercise their religion. (Two justices had retired, with replacements not yet confirmed.)

While the ruling emphasized the religious nature of the Amish demand, the majority opinion, written by Chief Justice WARREN BURGER, also addressed the need to protect the Amish "way of life," the psychological harm Amish youth might suffer from exposure to worldly values, and the fact that Amish high school dropouts typically developed into productive law-abiding citizens. The Court dismissed the state's argument that young people who might choose to leave the Amish community would be ill equipped to do so without a high school education. First, the education of Amish youths did not cease after the eighth grade but continued within their community. In fact, they were taught many virtues that THOMAS JEFFERSON had pronounced essential for a democratic society. Secondly, compulsory high school education laws, of relatively recent origin, were developed to prevent idleness among youth. Finally, Burger emphasized that the Court's ruling addressed the rights of parents as the parties traditionally in charge of their children's religious upbringing. Whether children had an independent right to a secondary education or to make their own religious choices was beyond the scope of the case.

It was on this point that Justice WILLIAM O. DOUGLAS dissented. With one exception, the views of the affected children were not part of the record; and Douglas, citing the Court's respect for the views of young people in such cases as *TINKER V. DES MOINES,* 393 U.S. 503 (1969), was unwilling to cede full control over children's educational futures to their parents. However, Douglas endorsed the Court's continued application of the "compelling interest" standard, and even argued that the Court's reliance on the favorable "law and order" record of the Amish was irrelevant: "A religion is a religion irrespective of what the misdemeanor or felony records of its members might be."

This case became a precedent for advocates of home schooling. However, the Court's opinion was so narrowly tailored to fit the specific situation that its applicability to other faiths or to non-educational Amish conflicts has been limited. Moreover, the "compelling interest" standard that shaped this decision was abandoned by the Court in 1990.

For more information: Peters, Shawn Francis. *The Yoder Case: Religious Freedom, Education, and Parental Rights.* Lawrence: University Press of Kansas, 2003.

—Jane G. Rainey

Wolf v. Colorado 338 U.S. 25 (1949)

In *Wolf v. Colorado,* the United States Supreme Court held that the FOURTEENTH AMENDMENT did not apply to the states when dealing with the use of illegally obtained evidence in a criminal proceeding, even though it did apply to the federal government. This case addressed the issue of whether or not the standards set by the DUE PROCESS clause should apply to the states in upholding the conviction of the defendant Wolf, who was prosecuted with the use of evidence illegally obtained by authorities in their investigation.

Julius Wolf was convicted of conspiring to perform abortions, with the aid of illegally obtained evidence. On appeal, the Supreme Court of Colorado upheld his conviction. Wolf then applied for

a writ of certiorari and the writ was granted by the Supreme Court in 1949. The Supreme Court upheld his conviction, stating that while the FOURTH AMENDMENT applied to the federal government, it did not apply to the states, which were instead governed by the due process clause of the Fourteenth Amendment.

Writing for the majority, Justice Felix Frankfurter addressed the issue of incorporating the BILL OF RIGHTS and stated that, while the Fourteenth Amendment prohibits unlawful use of illegally obtained evidence in a federal case, due to the application of the Bill of Rights, it does not apply to the states. This opinion was in accord with the decision in *PALKO V. CONNECTICUT,* 302 U.S. 319 (1937), in which the Supreme Court refused to apply the Fifth Amendment prohibition on DOUBLE JEOPARDY to the states through the use of the Fourteenth Amendment. In *Wolf,* the Court determined that no prohibition on the use of illegally obtained evidence in a court of law was stated anywhere in the Fourteenth Amendment.

While the precedent for this decision was established in the case of *WEEKS V. UNITED STATES,* 232 U.S. 383 (1914), where the Court ruled that the use of illegally obtained evidence was prohibited in federal, but not state, courts, Justice Frankfurter further stated that, while most of the modern world "does not regard as vital . . . the exclusion of evidence such obtained, [the Court must hesitate] to treat this remedy as an essential ingredient of the right." He reasoned that while such state-condoned police action would be unlawful, the states had an obligation unto themselves to protect society from ill uses of authority by the police, such as civil actions, and that they do not need the application of the due process clause of the Fourteenth Amendment to do this for them.

For more information: Hemmens, Craig, John Worrall, and Alan Thompson. *Criminal Justice Case Briefs: Significant Cases in Criminal Procedure.* Los Angeles: Roxbury, 2004.

—Marianne Hudson

Yick Wo v. Hopkins 118 U.S. 356 (1886)

In *Yick Wo v. Hopkins,* the U.S. Supreme Court held that a city ordinance was invalid if applied in a discriminatory manner to a particular class of persons, even if the ordinance appeared valid and impartial on its face. The *Yick Wo* decision was the first instance where the Court relied upon evidence of discriminatory application of a law to strike it down. This precedent became significant later when the WARREN COURT used similar logic to strike down laws discriminating against African Americans.

Throughout the 19th century there was a massive influx of Chinese immigrants into California. In response, the state of California and many of its municipalities began to pass anti-Chinese laws. *Yick Wo v. Hopkins* involved a San Francisco city ordinance prohibiting laundries in wooden buildings without the approval of the city's board of supervisors. While approximately two-thirds of the laundries affected by this ordinance were operated by Chinese, all of the Chinese applicants were denied the required permits to stay in business. In contrast, all but one of the Caucasians who operated laundries affected by the ordinance were granted the permit.

Yick Wo was one of the laundry operators denied a permit by the board of supervisors. Continuing to operate his business, he was arrested for violating the ordinance. Yick Wo petitioned the Supreme Court of California for a writ of HABEAS CORPUS, arguing that he had been deprived of liberty. The California court denied his petition and he appealed to the United States Supreme Court.

Justice Matthews wrote the decision for a unanimous Court. In his opinion, Justice Matthews stated that while it is necessary for the Court to defer to the California Supreme Court with regard to questions of state law, questions arising under the United States Constitution or federal law require an independent construction of the ordinance. Justice Matthews argued that the Supreme Court of California had erred in construing the ordinance as a reasonable exercise of the POLICE POWER of the state, designed to protect the public from the danger of fire. In place of this interpretation, he posited that the ordinance in question gave "naked and arbitrary power" to the board of supervisors.

In holding the San Francisco ordinance invalid, Justice Matthews relied on both the EQUAL PROTECTION clause of the FOURTEENTH AMENDMENT and a TREATY between the United States and China. In doing so, he found the ordinance to have been applied "with an evil eye and an unequal hand" to a particular class of persons. Thus, the ordinance created a system of discrimination that violated the principle of equal protection, regardless of the intent of the ordinance.

As the first Supreme Court decision to rely on evidence of applied discrimination to overturn an ordinance, *Yick Wo* laid down a foundation that would later be used to strike down laws discriminating against African Americans. At the time of the decision, however, its greatest significance was as a justification for striking down laws regulating business (for example LOCHNER V. NEW YORK, 198 U.S. 45 [1905]).

For more information: Hall, Kermit L. *The Magic Mirror: Law in American History.* New York: Oxford University Press, 1989; Saxton, Alexander. *The Indispensable Enemy: Labor and the*

Anti-Chinese Movement in California. Berkeley: University of California Press, 1975.

—Michael P. Fix

Youngstown Sheet & Tube v. Sawyer 343 U.S. 579 (1952)

In *Youngstown Sheet & Tube v. Sawyer,* the Supreme Court ruled that the president did not have emergency authority to seize steel mills during the Korean War in order to avert a strike. The case is important in that it described the scope of the powers of the presidency, especially during an emergency.

Youngstown went to the Supreme Court as a result of President Truman's executive order that nationalized the steel industry. Truman argued that this nationalization was necessary because the nation was at war in Korea and the industry faced a national walk-out. Although Congress had refused to allow governmental seizures of property to prevent work stoppages when deliberating the Taft-Hartley Act of 1947, Truman issued EO 10430 in an effort to ensure that the nation's munitions would not fall short. This executive order, based on broad constitutional grounds rather than specific statutory grounds, authorized the secretary of commerce to seize the steel mills. The Supreme Court disagreed with Truman's broad claims, and found that Truman had exceeded his constitutional powers by issuing the executive order.

This decision is noteworthy for two reasons. First, *Youngstown* is a rare example of the Supreme Court, or any court, hearing a case related to a president's issuing an executive order. It is all the more rare in that the executive order was overturned, as occurred in this case.

More importantly, however, is the finding of the decision. The Court found, in a 6-3 decision, that the president had overstepped his powers in issuing the executive order. However, multiple opinions were issued explaining the reasons why the Court made its decision as such. Without doubt, the most important of the opinions issued in *Youngstown* was not the opinion of the Court, written by Justice HUGO BLACK. Instead, in a con-currence, Justice Robert H. Jackson wrote what has become the most important doctrine to arise from this case. In his concurrence, Jackson issued a rough blueprint explaining when presidential action is most likely to be upheld as constitutional by the Supreme Court.

Jackson famously explains that the president enjoys three levels of judicial deference, *based on congressional support of his actions.* If Congress is supportive of his actions, then the Court will likely accept a given action; if Congress is ambivalent about an action, then the Court will accept reasonable action; if Congress has specifically forbidden an action, the Court is highly unlikely to support the actions of the president. The Supreme Court noted that Congress had specifically forbidden the actions of President Truman, and that is why the Court did not find in favor of the executive.

As Justice Jackson argued, "When the President acts pursuant to an express or implied authorization of Congress, his authority is at its maximum, for it includes all that he possesses in his own right plus all that Congress may delegate. In these circumstances, and in these only, may he be said (for what it may be worth) to personify the federal sovereignty."

Although only an outline of what the Supreme Court is likely to uphold, and there have been exceptions, the basis of Jackson's opinion has withstood the test of time. The president's legal advisers are acutely aware of the importance of Jackson's opinion, and may advise him of the likelihood that an action will be accepted. Perhaps more importantly, the Supreme Court itself has upheld the central argument in Jackson's concurrence. In *DAMES AND MOORE V. REGAN* (1981), the Supreme Court argued that because Congress had not acted specifically in an effort to prevent the president from suspending payments or transfers of Iranian assets during the Iran Hostage Crisis, and in fact the "relevant Senate Committee" had supported his action, President Carter was justified in his actions. The opinion of the Court in *Dames* was written by then-justice WILLIAM HUBBS REHNQUIST—a former clerk for Justice Jackson.

Since the attacks of September 11, 2001, *Youngstown* has remained important in understanding the separations of power in the Constitution. For the most part, federal courts have acted with restraint regarding presidential action, due in large part to the PATRIOT ACT and a congressional resolution allowing the president to act to limit future attacks on Americans and American soil. There have been a few exceptions to this general rule, however. Perhaps the most important have been related to President Bush's formation and use of a detainment center at Guantánamo Bay, Cuba. The detainees, called enemy combatants, have been held without trial. The Supreme Court ruled in *HAMDI V. RUMSFELD* that Hamdi, an American citizen, had a right to trial. Most recently, the Court ruled in *Hamdan v. Rumsfeld* (2006) that Congress, in its resolution, had in no way given the president the authority to alter military trials. Moreover, it is possible that other parts of the opinion may be interpreted as the Court's attempt to limit other actions taken by the Bush administration, including actions taken by the National Security Agency.

For more information: Marcus, Maeva. *Truman and the Steel Seizure Case: The Limits of Presidential Power.* Durham, N.C.: Duke University Press, 1994; Schubert, Glendon A. *The Presidency in the Courts.* Minneapolis: University of Minnesota Press, 1957.

—Tobias T. Gibson

youth curfew laws

Youth curfew laws are laws that place limits on when individuals under the age of 18 may be out in public. These laws raise FIRST AMENDMENT questions regarding freedom of association.

Historically, the establishment of youth curfew laws has stemmed from both society's discontent over juvenile crime and concern for the safety of juveniles in general. Common justifications for state intervention in juvenile affairs are: (1) protection of children from harm, (2) the reduction of juvenile delinquency, (3) community protection, and (4) strengthened parental authority.

Curfew laws established during the Progressive Era were motivated primarily by a belief that social decay in the community was the product of unruly, unsupervised juveniles; curfews were seen as a means to correct this problem. The mindset of society during this period was that children needed guidance and protection, and that the state should assume that role in the absence of adequate parental supervision. After the turn of the century, and as juveniles gained more rights, the states expanded their social welfare agendas to adopt the changes occurring as juvenile rights began to evolve.

Curfew laws are primarily local, municipal legislation and typically include restricting juveniles from being on public streets during late hours unaccompanied by an adult; the specifics vary. Generally, there are exceptions made for emergency situations or special circumstances such as traveling to and from one's place of employment and if accompanied by a parent or guardian.

At issue in *Ex parte McCarver,* 46 S.W. 936, 937 (1898), the first case to test the constitutionality of youth curfew laws, was a Texas curfew ordinance banning juveniles from being on the streets after 9 P.M. without special cause. The Court held the curfew to be unconstitutional, asserting that it was paternalistic and an intrusion on the personal liberties of the individual. In contrast, the Court in *Baker v. Borough of Steelton,* 443 U.S. 622 (1979), found that a curfew banning juveniles from being on the streets after 9 P.M. was lawful, under the state's POLICE POWER. These early cases set the foundation for future cases debating the constitutionality of such laws.

Constitutional challenges to youth curfew laws include alleged violations of the First, Fourth, and FOURTEENTH AMENDMENTs. Opponents of juvenile curfew laws argue that the laws place restrictions on a juvenile's First Amendment freedoms of association and assembly, the FOURTH AMENDMENT protection against unreasonable search and seizure, and the Fourteenth Amendment right to DUE PROCESS and EQUAL PROTECTION. However, the general consensus in state and lower federal court decisions has been that youth curfews are constitutional, as juveniles have limited freedom and are not afforded rights to the same extent as adults. In *Schall v. Martin,* 513 F.Supp. 691 (SDNY, 1981), a federal district court, in upholding a juvenile curfew, explained that juveniles, unlike adults, are always in some sort of custody and, therefore, restrictions placed on their activities may be more extensive than that of adults.

Bellotti v. Baird, 443 U.S. 622 (1979), was a significant Supreme Court case whose rationale can be applied when determining the constitutionality of juvenile curfew laws. The Supreme Court's decision included three reasons why the constitutional rights of juveniles are not equal to those of adults: "the peculiar vulnerability of children; their inability to make critical decisions in an informed, mature manner; and the importance of the parental role in child rearing."

At issue in *Qutb v. Strauss,* 11 F.3d 488 (5th Cir. 1993), was a Dallas curfew that made it a misdemeanor for juveniles, under the age of 17, to be on public streets or in public places after certain hours and without special cause. The ordinance did permit a number of exceptions to the curfew: If the juvenile was in the presence of an adult, on an errand for an emergency or an errand for a guardian, traveling to or from a place of employment, or on interstate travel, the ordinance did not apply. Qutb claimed that the ordinance violated both the United States and Texas constitutions. The Fifth Circuit Court of Appeals found that the curfew laws imposed by the city of Dallas were in the best interest of the city and that any burdens placed on the constitutional rights of minors were minimal.

While the effectiveness of youth curfew laws has been heavily debated, they have become increasingly popular and widely accepted forms of controlling juvenile delinquency. Studies on the effectiveness of the curfews on crime and delinquency reduction are mixed, but politicians and the public continue to support their imposition.

For more information: Hemmens, Craig, and Katherine Bennett. "Out in the Street: Juvenile Crime, Juvenile Curfews, and the Constitution." *Gonzaga Law Review* 34, no. 2 (1999): 267–327.

—Virginia Hatch

Zelman v. Simmons-Harris 536 U.S. 639 (2002)

In *Zelman v. Simmons-Harris*, the Court affirmed, against an ESTABLISHMENT CLAUSE challenge, the ability of state and local governments to establish a school voucher system that includes private religious schools.

Due to continuing poor performance, a federal district court in 1995 placed Cleveland's public school system under state control. Ohio then passed the Pilot Project Scholarship Program, granting two types of financial assistance to families in state-controlled school systems: funds to provide tutoring for students who remain in public schools; and up to $2,250 in tuition aid for low-income students in kindergarten through eighth grade to attend a participating public, private, or private religious school. Of the 3,700 Cleveland students during the 1999–2000 school year who chose tuition aid to private schools, 96.6 percent enrolled in religious (mainly Catholic) schools. Doris Simmons-Harris and other Ohio taxpayers sued Susan Zelman, superintendent of Ohio schools, claiming the funding for tuition to religious schools violated the FIRST AMENDMENT. A district court found the program unconstitutional under LEMON V. KURTZMAN, 403 U.S. 602 (1971), because it had the primary effect of advancing religion. A divided court of appeals affirmed.

The Supreme Court reversed, upholding the program by a 5-4 vote. Chief Justice WILLIAM HUBBS REHNQUIST's majority opinion stated the program's purpose was neutral and general: to improve education in a failing system. Recipients were chosen on a nonreligious basis, and parents had many choices—tutoring or tuition aid, public or private schools, religious or nonreligious

schools. The state did not coerce parents to send their children to religious schools, the program did not endorse religious schooling, and the 96.6 percent enrollment figure did not include those who chose tutoring or other public schools. Further, government funds were not given directly to schools but to parents. Individual decisions about the use of these monies thus constituted "genuine and independent private choice."

Justice SANDRA DAY O'CONNOR concurred, arguing that this ruling was consistent with past decisions and that the program was neutral because it provided parents many educational options. Justice CLARENCE THOMAS's concurrence—which opens and closes with quotes from Frederick Douglass on the importance of education—focused on the crisis in Cleveland public schools. He also questioned applying the establishment clause against the states instead of relying solely on free exercise.

In dissent, Justice JOHN PAUL STEVENS wrote that Cleveland's educational crisis, the wide range of choices under the program, and its voluntary nature were all irrelevant to the constitutional issue. The crucial fact was the "use of public funds to pay for the indoctrination of thousands of grammar school children." Justice DAVID H. SOUTER, writing for all four dissenters, found the majority opinion inconsistent with the Court's statement in *EVERSON V. BOARD OF EDUCATION*, 330 U.S. 1 (1947), that "no tax, in any amount, large or small, can be levied to support religious activities or institutions, whatever they may be called, or whatever form they may adopt to teach or practice religion." Souter described the choice in this program as "Hobsonian," because for most children "the only alternative" to a failing public school is attending a school of a religion not their own. Justice STE-PHEN G. BREYER, joined by Stevens and Souter, would have struck Cleveland's program because it would introduce religious divisiveness and social conflict.

For more information: Tushnet, Mark. "Vouchers after *Zelman*," *Supreme Court Review* (2002): 1–39.

—Frank J. Colucci

Zobrest v. Catalina Foothills School District
509 U.S. 1 (1993)

In *Zobrest v. Catalina Foothills School District*, the U.S. Supreme Court ruled that the ESTABLISHMENT CLAUSE of the FIRST AMENDMENT did not prevent a school system from providing a sign-language interpreter to a deaf student attending a Catholic high school.

The case involved a request by the Zobrest family in Tucson, Arizona, to have the school district pay for a sign-language interpreter for their deaf son, James, at a private Catholic high school. Under the federal Individuals with Disabilities Education Act (IDEA), James was disabled and was provided a sign-language interpreter when attending public school in earlier years.

However, when the student moved to a Catholic high school, the school district said it could not provide support to Zobrest because spending public funds at a religious school would violate the establishment clause principle of separation of church and state. The Zobrest family sued, but a federal district court and the U.S. Court of Appeals for the Ninth Circuit ruled in favor of the school district.

In a 5-4 decision, Chief Justice WILLIAM HUBBS REHNQUIST said that the presence of a government-paid interpreter in a religious school would be the result of the parents' choice, not the government's intervention, and therefore would not violate the establishment clause. Rehnquist said the federal law determined who was disabled and eligible for education assistance but left it to each family to select the school for their child.

He relied on two earlier rulings to reverse the lower court and rule in Zobrest's favor. In *Mueller v. Allen*, 463 U.S. 388 (1983), Rehnquist wrote the Court's decision upholding a Minnesota law that allowed parents to deduct education expenses from their taxes even though most of the deductions went for expenses at religious schools. In *Witters v. Washington Dept. of Services for Blind*, 474 U.S. 481 (1986), Justice Thurgood Marshall upheld state education assistance provided to a blind student studying at a Christian college to become a religious leader. In both cases the Court emphasized, as it did in *Zobrest*, that the flow of public funds to religious institutions was entirely the product of individual, private choice about where to spend funds that were part of a generally available aid program.

In dissents by Justices Harry A. Blackmun and Sandra Day O'Connor, four justices faulted Rehnquist for reaching out to decide the establishment clause issue when there were narrower grounds on which to resolve the case. They said the case could have been resolved by interpreting whether the requirements of the federal IDEA law were satisfied by making a sign-language interpreter available at a public school. Blackmun, joined by Justice DAVID H. SOUTER, also disputed Rehnquist's constitutional analysis, saying the case marked the first time the Court had permitted a public employee to participate in "religious indoctrination."

For more information: Bartlett, Larry. "Post-Zobrest: Where Are We on the Issue of Special Education Programs and Services to Parent-Placed Private School Students?" *Education Law Reporter* 108, no. 1,039 (1996).

—Stephen Wermiel

Zorach v. Clausen 343 U.S. 306 (1952)

In *Zorach v. Clausen*, the Supreme Court upheld a public school release program to allow students to attend religious education off of school grounds.

The issue before the Court in *Zorach* was whether the policy of the state of New York—to allow public school students to participate in a program whereby they, with written permission of their parents, may be released to leave school during the day and go to their religious institution to receive religious education or for religious observance—violated provisions of the FIRST AMENDMENT that prohibited religion establishment but guaranteed the free exercise of religion. Six justices upheld the validity of the program, citing the absence of coercion in addition to off-campus location and found that it did not violate the First Amendment.

Zorach followed *McCollum v. Board of Education* (333 U.S. 203 [1948]), which found that the Illinois "released time" program, permitting interested public school students to be released from their public school duties to attend a religious education program conducted by a "duly constituted religious body" in classrooms on campus, violated the Constitution. *McCollum* is often taken to have asserted a right to be free from religion in its suggestion that the government's official stance toward religion should be characterized by strict separation and indifference.

Zorach established that coercion is a necessary attribute of church-state entanglement that runs afoul of the religion clauses, and that, absent a showing of coercion, there is a range of permitted ACCOMMODATION of religion that does not implicate the separation principle. *Zorach* also established that separation need not be so complete that it renders the state and religion "aliens to each other, hostile, suspicious, and even unfriendly." Not to allow accommodation would be to express "callous indifference to religious groups," indicating an impermissible preference for nonbelievers over believers. *Zorach* gave weight to the nation's religious heritage in legal argument, albeit in a constitutionally circumscribed manner.

Justice HUGO BLACK's dissenting opinion noted that, as in *McCollum*, the Court indicated that where the religious instruction took place made no difference to the case; the result in *Zorach* combined church and state because the state's adjustments—here, of its public school schedules—had the effect of aiding the religious sects that benefited in gaining attendants, thus indicating an impermissible preference for believers over

nonbelievers. Justice Jackson's dissenting opinion echoed the same themes, but emphasized that equality between irreligion and religion should be the operating principle at work, a point that speaks to the nonpreferentialist argument that accommodations of religion in general are constitutionally permissible so long as no religion is given a preference over others or unavailable to others.

What *Zorach* is most known for is the following statement in the opinion by Justice WILLIAM O. DOUGLAS: "We are a religious people whose institutions presuppose a Supreme Being." This statement from *Zorach* has been frequently cited in later cases where a nonpreferentialist argument is being made, or by political activists concerned that the United States's Christian heritage be reflected in its law and public policy, and not impugned.

For more information: Hitchcock, James. *The Supreme Court and Religion in American Life.* Vol. 1, *The Odyssey of the Religion Clauses.* Princeton, N.J.: Princeton University Press, 2004.
—Gordon A. Babst

Zurcher v. Stanford Daily 436 U.S. 547 (1978)

In *Zurcher v. Stanford Daily*, the Supreme Court held that neither the First or FOURTH AMENDMENTs prohibited the police from searching the offices of a newspaper, even when the newspaper is not the subject of a criminal investigation. In this case, the Palo Alto, California, police confronted demonstrators at the Stanford University hospital, which eventually led to violence and various injuries. While the police were unable to identify most of the demonstrators, the *Stanford Daily*, a student newspaper, had a photographer on the scene, and on the following day published a photo from the confrontation. The police then secured a warrant to search the *Daily*'s offices for evidence that could help identify the demonstrators.

The *Stanford Daily* filed suit in federal district court under 42 U.S.C. 1983, alleging that its CIVIL RIGHTS had been violated by the search in that police searching its newsroom infringed upon the FREEDOM OF THE PRESS in the FIRST

AMENDMENT and conducted an unconstitutional search per the Fourth Amendment. The district court agreed with the *Stanford Daily*, holding that the Fourth Amendment did not allow for the issuance of a warrant to search for materials possessed by one not suspected of a crime, unless a subpoena would prove to be impracticable for the police. Additionally, the First Amendment had some bearing in this case because a warrant could be issued only when there was some showing that evidence would be destroyed or removed from a news office; otherwise, the First Amendment's freedom of the press would suggest caution in granting searches of newsrooms due to the impact said searches could have upon newsroom operations. The district court, affirmed by the appellate court, held that neither condition applied here—the *Stanford Daily* was not a suspect in this case, and there was no showing that the newspaper would destroy evidence.

On appeal, the Supreme Court reversed the appellate court by 5-3 vote (Justice WILLIAM J. BRENNAN, JR., not participating). Justice White, writing for the majority, took a dim view of the reasoning of the lower courts; in particular, White stated Court precedent made clear that search warrants per the Fourth Amendment are directed not at persons but at places where things may be seized that have a bearing upon on ongoing criminal investigation. As such, the search warrant was not directed at the *Stanford Daily*, but at the newsroom where there might be photographic evidence of who was at the demonstration.

Furthermore, White rejected the First Amendment concerns, especially those premised on the idea that warrant-based searches would hinder news organizations' abilities to gather, analyze, and disseminate news. White reminded how forc-

ing searches to be reasonable or warrants to be granted by neutral magistrates satisfied the Constitution's framers, who were quite alarmed at how British authorities intruded upon the colonial press without cause. Since the framers did not prohibit warrants when the press was involved, White was loath to agree with the reasoning of the lower courts on this issue.

In dissent, Justice Stewart was not as sanguine as White about the effect of searches in newsrooms. Stewart concluded that such searches were sure to physically disrupt press operations and possibly lead to the disclosure of confidential sources. Justice JOHN PAUL STEVENS also dissented on the grounds that, unlike the majority's reading of the Fourth Amendment, he believed that for a search to be reasonable, a newspaper would have to be under suspicion for committing a crime; in this case, there was no evidence of that.

The Court's ruling in *Zurcher* caused an outcry among the press corps. For example, James Reston wrote in *The New York Times,* on June 2, 1978, an op-ed piece that was addressed to Justice White, inviting him to visit his newspaper and explain how it should handle in practical terms the inevitable police searches his *Zurcher* opinion would encourage. Two years after the *Zurcher* ruling, Congress responded by passing the Privacy Protection Act of 1980; this law made it more difficult to obtain warrants for searches of press operations when a member of the press was not under suspicion for committing a crime.

For more information: Hutchinson, Dennis J. *The Man Who Once Was Whizzer White: A Portrait of Justice Byron R. White.* New York: Free Press, 1998.

—John M. Aughenbaugh

Appendixes

❧

Declaration of Independence

⟡

Action of Second Continental Congress, July 4, 1776.

The unanimous Declaration of the thirteen United States of America.

We hold these truths to be self-evident, that all men are created equal, that they are endowed by their Creator with certain unalienable Rights, that among these are Life, Liberty, and the pursuit of Happiness. That to secure these rights, Governments are instituted among Men, deriving their just powers from the consent of the governed. That whenever any Form of Government becomes destructive of these ends, it is the Right of the People to alter or to abolish it, and to institute new Government, laying its foundation on such principles and organizing its powers in such form, as to them shall seem most likely to effect their Safety and Happiness. Prudence, indeed, will dictate that Governments long established should not be changed for light and transient causes; and accordingly all experience hath shown, that mankind are more disposed to suffer, while evils are sufferable, than to right themselves by abolishing the forms to which they are accustomed. But when a long train of abuses and usurpations, pursuing invariably the same Object, evinces a design to reduce them under absolute Despotism, it is their right, it is their duty, to throw off such Government, and to provide new Guards for their future security. Such has been the patient sufferance of these Colonies; and such is now the necessity which constrains them to alter their former Systems of Government. The history of the present King of Great Britain is a history of repeated injuries and usurpations, all having in direct object the establishment of an absolute Tyranny over these States. To prove this, let Facts be submitted to a candid world.

HE has refused his Assent to Laws, the most wholesome and necessary for the public good.

HE has forbidden his Governors to pass Laws of immediate and pressing importance, unless suspended in their operation till his Assent should be obtained; and when so suspended, he has utterly neglected to attend to them.

HE has refused to pass other Laws for the accommodation of large districts of people, unless those people would relinquish the right of Representation in the Legislature, a right inestimable to them and formidable to tyrants only.

HE has called together legislative bodies at places unusual, uncomfortable, and distant from the depository of their public Records, for the sole purpose of fatiguing them into compliance with his measures.

HE has dissolved Representative Houses repeatedly, for opposing with manly firmness his invasions on the rights of the people.

HE has refused for a long time, after such dissolutions, to cause others to be elected; whereby the Legislative powers, incapable of Annihilation, have returned to the People at large for their exercise; the State remaining in the mean time exposed to all the dangers of invasion from without, and convulsion within.

HE has endeavoured to prevent the population of these States; for that purpose obstructing the Laws of Naturalization of Foreigners; refusing to pass others to encourage their migrations hither, and raising the conditions of new Appropriations of Lands.

HE has obstructed the Administration of Justice, by refusing his Assent to Laws for establishing Judiciary powers.

HE has made Judges dependent on his Will alone, for the tenure of their offices, and the amount and payment of their salaries.

HE has erected a multitude of New Offices, and sent hither swarms of Officers to harass our People, and eat out their substance.

HE has kept among us, in times of peace, Standing Armies without the Consent of our legislatures.

HE has affected to render the Military independent of and superior to the Civil power.

HE has combined with others to subject us to a jurisdiction foreign to our constitution, and unacknowledged by our laws; giving his Assent to their Acts of pretended Legislation:

FOR quartering large bodies of armed troops among us:

FOR protecting them, by a mock Trial, from Punishment for any Murders which they should commit on the Inhabitants of these States:

FOR cutting off our Trade with all parts of the world:

FOR imposing Taxes on us without our Consent:

FOR depriving us in many cases, of the benefits of Trial by Jury:

FOR transporting us beyond Seas to be tried for pretended offences:

FOR abolishing the free System of English Laws in a neighbouring Province, establishing therein an Arbitrary government, and enlarging its Boundaries so as to render it at once an example and fit instrument for introducing the same absolute rule into these Colonies:

FOR taking away our Charters, abolishing our most valuable Laws, and altering fundamentally the Forms of our Governments:

FOR suspending our own Legislatures, and declaring themselves invested with power to legislate for us in all cases whatsoever.

HE has abdicated Government here, by declaring us out of his Protection and waging War against us.

HE has plundered our seas, ravaged our Coasts, burnt our towns, and destroyed the Lives of our people.

HE is at this time transporting large armies of foreign mercenaries to compleat the works of death, desolation and tyranny, already begun with circumstances of Cruelty & perfidy scarcely paralleled in the most barbarous ages, and totally unworthy the Head of a civilized nation.

HE has constrained our fellow Citizens taken Captive on the high Seas to bear Arms against their Country, to become the executioners of their friends and Brethren, or to fall themselves by their Hands.

HE has excited domestic insurrections amongst us, and has endeavoured to bring on the inhabitants of our frontiers, the merciless Indian Savages, whose known rule of warfare, is an undistinguished destruction of all ages, sexes and conditions.

IN every stage of these Oppressions We have Petitioned for Redress in the most humble terms: Our repeated Petitions have been answered only by repeated injury. A Prince, whose character is thus marked by every act which may define a Tyrant, is unfit to be the ruler of a free people.

NOR have We been wanting in attention to our British brethren. We have warned them from time to time of attempts by their legislature to extend an unwarrantable jurisdiction over us. We have reminded them of the circumstances of our emigration and settlement here. We have appealed to their native justice and magnanimity, and we have conjured them by the ties of our common kindred to disavow these usurpations, which would inevitably interrupt our connections and correspondence. They too have been deaf to the voice of justice and of consanguinity. We must, therefore, acquiesce in the necessity, which denounces our Separation, and hold them, as we hold the rest of mankind, Enemies in War, in Peace Friends.

WE, therefore, the Representatives of the UNITED STATES OF AMERICA, in GEN-

ERAL CONGRESS, Assembled, appealing to the Supreme Judge of the world for the rectitude of our intentions, do, in the Name, and by Authority of the good People of these Colonies, solemnly publish and declare, That these United Colonies are, and of Right ought to be FREE AND INDEPENDENT STATES; that they are Absolved from all Allegiance to the British Crown, and that all political connection between them and the State of Great Britain, is and ought to be totally dissolved; and that as FREE AND INDEPENDENT STATES, they have full Power to levy War, conclude Peace, contract Alliances, establish Commerce, and to do all other Acts and Things which INDEPENDENT STATES may of right do. And for the support of this Declaration, with a firm reliance on the Protection of Divine Providence, we mutually pledge to each other our Lives, our Fortunes and our sacred Honor.

John Hancock.

Georgia
    Button Gwinnett
    Lyman Hall
    Geo. Walton
North Carolina
    William Hooper
    Joseph Hewes
    John Penn
South Carolina
    Edward Rutledge
    Thomas Heyward, Jr.
    Thomas Lynch, Jr.
    Arthur Middleton
Maryland
    Samuel Chase
    William Paca
    Thomas Stone
    Charles Carroll
        Of Carrollton
Virginia
    George Wythe
    Richard Henry Lee
    Thomas Jefferson
    Benjamin Harrison

Thomas Nelson, Jr.
Francis Lightfoot Lee
Carter Braxton
Pennsylvania
    Robert Morris
    Benjamin Rush
    Benjamin Franklin
    John Morton
    George Clymer
    James Smith
    George Taylor
    James Wilson
    George Ross
Delaware
    Caesar Rodney
    George Read
    Thomas M'kean
New York
    William Floyd
    Philip Livingston
    Francis Lewis
    Lewis Morris
New Jersey
    Richard Stockton
    John Witherspoon
    Francis Hopkins
    John Hart
    Abraham Clark
New Hampshire
    Josiah Bartlett
    William Whipple
    Matthew Thornton
Massachusetts-bay
    Samuel Adams
    John Adams
    Robert Treat Paine
    Elbridge Gerry
Rhode Island
    Stephen Hopkins
    William Ellery
Connecticut
    Roger Sherman
    Samuel Huntington
    William Williams
    Oliver Wolcott

IN CONGRESS, JANUARY 18, 1777.

Articles of
Confederation

Agreed to by Congress November 15, 1777 then ratified and in force, March 1, 1781.

Preamble

To all to whom these Presents shall come, we the undersigned Delegates of the States affixed to our Names send greeting.

Articles of Confederation and perpetual Union between the states of New Hampshire, Massachusetts-bay Rhode Island and Providence Plantations, Connecticut, New York, New Jersey, Pennsylvania, Delaware, Maryland, Virginia, North Carolina, South Carolina and Georgia.

Article I

The Stile of this Confederacy shall be "The United States of America".

Article II

Each state retains its sovereignty, freedom, and independence, and every power, jurisdiction, and right, which is not by this Confederation expressly delegated to the United States, in Congress assembled.

Article III

The said States hereby severally enter into a firm league of friendship with each other, for their common defense, the security of their liberties, and their mutual and general welfare, binding themselves to assist each other, against all force offered to, or attacks made upon them, or any of them, on account of religion, sovereignty, trade, or any other pretense whatever.

Article IV

The better to secure and perpetuate mutual friendship and intercourse among the people of the different States in this Union, the free inhabitants of each of these States, paupers, vagabonds, and fugitives from justice excepted, shall be entitled to all privileges and immunities of free citizens in the several States; and the people of each State shall free ingress and regress to and from any other State, and shall enjoy therein all the privileges of trade and commerce, subject to the same duties, impositions, and restrictions as the inhabitants thereof respectively, provided that such restrictions shall not extend so far as to prevent the removal of property imported into any State, to any other State, of which the owner is an inhabitant; provided also that no imposition, duties or restriction shall be laid by any State, on the property of the United States, or either of them.

If any person guilty of, or charged with, treason, felony, or other high misdemeanor in any State, shall flee from justice, and be found in any of the United States, he shall, upon demand of the Governor or executive power of the State from which he fled, be delivered up and removed to the State having jurisdiction of his offense.

Full faith and credit shall be given in each of these States to the records, acts, and judicial proceedings of the courts and magistrates of every other State.

Article V

For the most convenient management of the general interests of the United States, delegates shall be annually appointed in such manner as the legislatures of each State shall direct, to meet in Congress on the first Monday in November, in every year, with a power reserved to each State to recall its delegates, or any of them, at any time within the year, and to send others in their stead for the remainder of the year.

No State shall be represented in Congress by less than two, nor more than seven members; and no person shall be capable of being a delegate for more than three years in any term of six years; nor shall any person, being a delegate, be capable of holding any office under the United States, for which he, or another for his benefit, receives any salary, fees or emolument of any kind.

Each State shall maintain its own delegates in a meeting of the States, and while they act as members of the committee of the States.

In determining questions in the United States in Congress assembled, each State shall have one vote.

Freedom of speech and debate in Congress shall not be impeached or questioned in any court or place out of Congress, and the members of Congress shall be protected in their persons from arrests or imprisonments, during the time of their going to and from, and attendance on Congress, except for treason, felony, or breach of the peace.

Article VI

No State, without the consent of the United States in Congress assembled, shall send any embassy to, or receive any embassy from, or enter into any conference, agreement, alliance or treaty with any King, Prince or State; nor shall any person holding any office of profit or trust under the United States, or any of them, accept any present, emolument, office or title of any kind whatever from any King, Prince or foreign State; nor shall the United States in Congress assembled, or any of them, grant any title of nobility.

No two or more States shall enter into any treaty, confederation or alliance whatever between them, without the consent of the United States in Congress assembled, specifying accurately the purposes for which the same is to be entered into, and how long it shall continue.

No State shall lay any imposts or duties, which may interfere with any stipulations in treaties, entered into by the United States in Congress assembled, with any King, Prince or State, in pursuance of any treaties already proposed by Congress, to the courts of France and Spain.

No vessel of war shall be kept up in time of peace by any State, except such number only, as shall be deemed necessary by the United States in Congress assembled, for the defense of such State, or its trade; nor shall any body of forces be kept up by any State in time of peace, except such number only, as in the judgement of the United States in Congress assembled, shall be deemed requisite to garrison the forts necessary for the defense of such State; but every State shall always keep up a well-regulated and disciplined militia, sufficiently armed and accoutered, and shall provide and constantly have ready for use, in public stores, a due number of filed pieces and tents, and a proper quantity of arms, ammunition and camp equipage.

No State shall engage in any war without the consent of the United States in Congress assembled, unless such State be actually invaded by enemies, or shall have received certain advice of a resolution being formed by some nation of Indians to invade such State, and the danger is so imminent as not to admit of a delay till the United States in Congress assembled can be consulted; nor shall any State grant commissions to any ships or vessels of war, nor letters of marque or reprisal, except it be after a declaration of war by the United States in Congress assembled, and then only against the Kingdom or State and the subjects thereof, against which war has been so declared, and under such regulations as shall be established by the United States in Congress assembled, unless such State be infested by pirates, in which case vessels of war may be fitted out for that occasion, and kept so long as the danger shall continue, or until the United States in Congress assembled shall determine otherwise.

Article VII

When land forces are raised by any State for the common defense, all officers of or under the rank of colonel, shall be appointed by the legislature of each State respectively, by whom such forces shall be raised, or in such manner as such State shall direct, and all vacancies shall be filled up by the State which first made the appointment.

Article VIII

All charges of war, and all other expenses that shall be incurred for the common defense or general welfare, and allowed by the United States in Congress assembled, shall be defrayed out of a common treasury, which shall be supplied by the several States in proportion to the value of all land within each State, granted or surveyed for any person, as such land and the buildings and improvements thereon shall be estimated according to such mode as the United States in Congress assembled, shall from time to time direct and appoint.

The taxes for paying that proportion shall be laid and levied by the authority and direction of the legislatures of the several States within the time agreed upon by the United States in Congress assembled.

Article IX

The United States in Congress assembled, shall have the sole and exclusive right and power of determining on peace and war, except in the cases mentioned in the sixth article—of sending and receiving ambassadors—entering into treaties and alliances, provided that no treaty of commerce shall be made whereby the legislative power of the respective States shall be restrained from imposing such imposts and duties on foreigners, as their own people are subjected to, or from prohibiting the exportation or importation of any species of goods or commodities whatsoever—of establishing rules for deciding in all cases, what captures on land or water shall be legal, and in what manner prizes taken by land or naval forces in the service of the United States shall be divided or appropriated—of granting letters of marque and reprisal in times of peace—appointing courts for the trial of piracies and felonies committed on the high seas and establishing courts for receiving and determining finally appeals in all cases of captures, provided that no member of Congress shall be appointed a judge of any of the said courts.

The United States in Congress assembled shall also be the last resort on appeal in all disputes and differences now subsisting or that hereafter may arise between two or more States concerning boundary, jurisdiction or any other causes whatever; which authority shall always be exercised in the manner following.

Whenever the legislative or executive authority or lawful agent of any State in controversy with another shall present a petition to Congress stating the matter in question and praying for a hearing, notice thereof shall be given by order of Congress to the legislative or executive authority of the other State in controversy, and a day assigned for the appearance of the parties by their lawful agents, who shall then be directed to appoint by joint consent, commissioners or judges to constitute a court for hearing and determining the matter in question: but if they cannot agree, Congress shall name three persons out of each of the United States, and from the list of such persons each party shall alternately strike out one, the petitioners beginning, until the number shall be reduced to thirteen; and from that number not less than seven, nor more than nine names as Congress shall direct, shall in the presence of Congress be drawn out by lot, and the persons whose names shall be so drawn or any five of them, shall be commissioners or judges, to hear and finally determine the controversy, so always as a major part of the judges who shall hear the cause shall agree in the determination: and if either party shall neglect to attend at the day appointed, without showing reasons, which Congress shall judge sufficient, or being present shall refuse to strike, the Congress shall proceed to nominate three persons out of each State, and the secretary of Congress shall strike in behalf of such party absent or refusing; and the judgement and sentence of the court to be appointed, in the manner before prescribed, shall be final and conclusive; and if any of the parties shall refuse to submit to the authority of such court, or to appear or defend their claim or cause, the court shall nevertheless proceed to pronounce sentence, or judgement, which shall in like manner be final and decisive, the judgement or sentence and other proceedings being in either case transmitted to Congress, and lodged among the acts of Congress for the security of the parties concerned: provided that every commissioner, before he sits in judgement, shall take an oath to be administered by one of the judges of the supreme or superior court of the State, where the cause shall be tried, 'well and truly to hear and determine the matter in question, according to the best of his judgement, without favor, affection or hope of reward': provided also, that no State shall be deprived of territory for the benefit of the United States.

All controversies concerning the private right of soil claimed under different grants of two or more States, whose jurisdictions as they may respect such lands, and the States which passed such grants are adjusted, the said grants or either of them being at the same time claimed to have originated antecedent to such settlement of jurisdiction, shall on the petition of either party to the Congress of the United States, be finally determined as near as may be in the same manner as is before prescribed for deciding disputes respecting territorial jurisdiction between different States.

The United States in Congress assembled shall also have the sole and exclusive right and power of regulating the alloy and value of coin struck by their own authority, or by that of the respective States—fixing the standards of weights and measures throughout the United States—regulating the trade and managing all affairs with the Indians, not members of any of the States, provided that the legislative right of any State within its own limits be not infringed or violated—establishing or regulating post offices from one State to another, throughout all the United States, and exacting such postage on the papers passing through the same as

may be requisite to defray the expenses of the said office—appointing all officers of the land forces, in the service of the United States, excepting regimental officers—appointing all the officers of the naval forces, and commissioning all officers whatever in the service of the United States—making rules for the government and regulation of the said land and naval forces, and directing their operations.

The United States in Congress assembled shall have authority to appoint a committee, to sit in the recess of Congress, to be denominated 'A Committee of the States', and to consist of one delegate from each State; and to appoint such other committees and civil officers as may be necessary for managing the general affairs of the United States under their direction—to appoint one of their members to preside, provided that no person be allowed to serve in the office of president more than one year in any term of three years; to ascertain the necessary sums of money to be raised for the service of the United States, and to appropriate and apply the same for defraying the public expenses—to borrow money, or emit bills on the credit of the United States, transmitting every half-year to the respective States an account of the sums of money so borrowed or emitted—to build and equip a navy—to agree upon the number of land forces, and to make requisitions from each State for its quota, in proportion to the number of white inhabitants in such State; which requisition shall be binding, and thereupon the legislature of each State shall appoint the regimental officers, raise the men and cloath, arm and equip them in a solid-like manner, at the expense of the United States; and the officers and men so cloathed, armed and equipped shall march to the place appointed, and within the time agreed on by the United States in Congress assembled. But if the United States in Congress assembled shall, on consideration of circumstances judge proper that any State should not raise men, or should raise a smaller number of men than the quota thereof, such extra number shall be raised, officered, cloathed, armed and equipped in the same manner as the quota of each State, unless the legislature of such State shall judge that such extra number cannot be safely spread out in the same, in which case they shall raise, officer, cloath, arm and equip as many of such extra number as they judge can be safely spared. And the officers and men so cloathed, armed, and equipped, shall march to the place appointed, and within the time agreed on by the United States in Congress assembled.

The United States in Congress assembled shall never engage in a war, nor grant letters of marque or reprisal in time of peace, nor enter into any treaties or alliances, nor coin money, nor regulate the value thereof, nor ascertain the sums and expenses necessary for the defense and welfare of the United States, or any of them, nor emit bills, nor borrow money on the credit of the United States, nor appropriate money, nor agree upon the number of vessels of war, to be built or purchased, or the number of land or sea forces to be raised, nor appoint a commander in chief of the army or navy, unless nine States assent to the same: nor shall a question on any other point, except for adjourning from day to day be determined, unless by the votes of the majority of the United States in Congress assembled.

The Congress of the United States shall have power to adjourn to any time within the year, and to any place within the United States, so that no period of adjournment be for a longer duration than the space of six months, and shall publish the journal of their proceedings monthly, except such parts thereof relating to treaties, alliances or military operations, as in their judgement require secrecy; and the yeas and nays of the delegates of each State on any question shall be entered on the Journal, when it is desired by any delegates of a State, or any of them, at his or their request shall be furnished with a transcript of the said journal, except such parts as are above excepted, to lay before the legislatures of the several States.

Article X

The Committee of the States, or any nine of them, shall be authorized to execute, in the recess of Congress, such of the powers of Congress as the United States in Congress assembled, by the consent of the nine States, shall from time to time think expedient to vest them with; provided that no power be delegated to the said Committee, for the exercise of which, by the Articles of Confederation, the voice of nine States in the Congress of the United States assembled be requisite.

Article XI

Canada acceding to this confederation, and adjoining in the measures of the United States, shall be admitted into, and entitled to all the advantages of this Union; but no other colony shall be admitted into the same, unless such admission be agreed to by nine States.

Article XII

All bills of credit emitted, monies borrowed, and debts contracted by, or under the authority of Congress, before the assembling of the United States, in pursuance of the present confederation, shall be deemed and considered as a charge against the United States, for payment and satisfaction whereof the said United States, and the public faith are hereby solemnly pledged.

Article XIII

Every State shall abide by the determination of the United States in Congress assembled, on all questions which by this confederation are submitted to them. And the Articles of this Confederation shall be inviolably observed by every State, and the Union shall be perpetual; nor shall any alteration at any time hereafter be made in any of them; unless such alteration be agreed to in a Congress of the United States, and be afterwards confirmed by the legislatures of every State.

Conclusion

And Whereas it hath pleased the Great Governor of the World to incline the hearts of the legislatures we respectively represent in Congress, to approve of, and to authorize us to ratify the said Articles of Confederation and perpetual Union. Know Ye that we the undersigned delegates, by virtue of the power and authority to us given for that purpose, do by these presents, in the name and in behalf of our respective constituents, fully and entirely ratify and confirm each and every of the said Articles of Confederation and perpetual Union, and all and singular the matters and things therein contained: And we do further solemnly plight and engage the faith of our respective constituents, that they shall abide by the determinations of the United States in Congress assembled, on all questions, which by the said Confederation are submitted to them. And that the Articles thereof shall be inviolably observed by the States we respectively represent, and that the Union shall be perpetual.

Signatories

In Witness whereof we have hereunto set our hands in Congress. Done at Philadelphia in the State of Pennsylvania the ninth day of July in the Year of our Lord One Thousand Seven Hundred and Seventy-Eight, and in the Third Year of the independence of America.

On the part and behalf of the State of New Hampshire:

Josiah Bartlett
John Wentworth Junior

On the part and behalf of the State of Massachusetts Bay:

John Hancock
Francis Dana
Samuel Adams
James Lovell
Elbridge Gerry
Samuel Holten

On the part and behalf of the State of Rhode Island and Providence Plantations:

William Ellery
John Collins
Henry Marchant

On the part and behalf of the State of Connecticut:

Roger Sherman
Titus Hosmer
Samuel Huntington
Andrew Adams
Oliver Wolcott

On the Part and Behalf of the State of New York:

James Duane
William Duer
Francis Lewis
Gouverneur Morris

On the Part and in Behalf of the State of New Jersey:

Jonathan Witherspoon
Nathaniel Scudder

On the part and behalf of the State of Pennsylvania:

Robert Morris
William Clingan
Daniel Roberdeau
Joseph Reed
John Bayard Smith

On the part and behalf of the State of Delaware:

Thomas Mckean
John Dickinson
Nicholas Van Dyke

On the part and behalf of the State of Maryland:

John Hanson
Daniel Carroll

On the Part and Behalf of the State of Virginia:

Richard Henry Lee
Jonathan Harvie
John Banister
Francis Lightfoot Lee
Thomas Adams

On the part and Behalf of the State of No Carolina:

John Penn
Corns Harnett
Jonathan Williams

On the part and behalf of the State of South Carolina:

Henry Laurens
Richard Hutson
William Henry Drayton
Thomas Heyward Junior
Jonathan Matthews

On the part and behalf of the State of Georgia:

Jonathan Walton
Edward Telfair
Edward Langworthy

The Constitution of the United States of America

We the people of the United States, in order to form a more perfect union, establish justice, insure domestic tranquility, provide for the common defense, promote the general welfare, and secure the blessings of liberty to ourselves and our posterity, do ordain and establish this Constitution for the United States of America.

Article I

Section 1. All legislative powers herein granted shall be vested in a Congress of the United States, which shall consist of a Senate and House of Representatives.

Section 2. The House of Representatives shall be composed of members chosen every second year by the people of the several states, and the electors in each state shall have the qualifications requisite for electors of the most numerous branch of the state legislature.

No person shall be a Representative who shall not have attained to the age of twenty five years, and been seven years a citizen of the United States, and who shall not, when elected, be an inhabitant of that state in which he shall be chosen.

Representatives and direct taxes shall be apportioned among the several states which may be included within this union, according to their respective numbers, which shall be determined by adding to the whole number of free persons, including those bound to service for a term of years, and excluding Indians not taxed, three fifths of all other Persons. The actual Enumeration shall be made within three years after the first meeting of the Congress of the United States, and within every subsequent term of ten years, in such manner as they shall by law direct. The number of Representatives shall not exceed one for every thirty thousand, but each state shall have at least one Representative; and until such enumeration shall be made, the state of New Hampshire shall be entitled to choose three, Massachusetts eight, Rhode Island and Providence Plantations one, Connecticut five, New York six, New Jersey four, Pennsylvania eight, Delaware one, Maryland six, Virginia ten, North Carolina five, South Carolina five, and Georgia three.

When vacancies happen in the Representation from any state, the executive authority thereof shall issue writs of election to fill such vacancies.

The House of Representatives shall choose their speaker and other officers; and shall have the sole power of impeachment.

Section 3. The Senate of the United States shall be composed of two Senators from each state, chosen by the legislature thereof, for six years; and each Senator shall have one vote. Immediately after they shall be assembled in consequence of the first election, they shall be divided as equally as may be into three classes. The seats of the Senators of the first class shall be vacated at the expiration of the second year, of the second class at the expiration of the fourth year, and the third class at the expiration of the sixth year, so that one third may be chosen every second year; and if vacancies happen by resignation, or otherwise, during the recess of the legislature of any state, the executive thereof may make temporary appointments until the next meeting of the legislature, which shall then fill such vacancies.

No person shall be a Senator who shall not have attained to the age of thirty years, and been nine years a citizen of the United States and who shall not, when elected, be an inhabitant of that state for which he shall be chosen.

The Vice President of the United States shall be President of the Senate, but shall have no vote, unless they be equally divided.

The Senate shall choose their other officers, and also a President pro tempore, in the absence of the Vice President, or when he shall exercise the office of President of the United States.

The Senate shall have the sole power to try all impeachments. When sitting for that purpose, they shall be on oath or affirmation. When the President of the United States is tried, the Chief Justice shall preside: And no person shall be convicted without the concurrence of two thirds of the members present.

Judgment in cases of impeachment shall not extend further than to removal from office, and disqualification to hold and enjoy any office of honor, trust or profit under the United States: but the party convicted shall nevertheless be liable and subject to indictment, trial, judgment and punishment, according to law.

Section 4. The times, places and manner of holding elections for Senators and Representatives, shall be prescribed in each state by the legislature thereof; but the Congress may at any time by law make or alter such regulations, except as to the places of choosing Senators.

The Congress shall assemble at least once in every year, and such meeting shall be on the first Monday in December, unless they shall by law appoint a different day.

Section 5. Each House shall be the judge of the elections, returns and qualifications of its own members, and a majority of each shall constitute a quorum to do business; but a smaller number may adjourn from day to day, and may be authorized to compel the attendance of absent members, in such manner, and under such penalties as each House may provide.

Each House may determine the rules of its proceedings, punish its members for disorderly behavior, and, with the concurrence of two thirds, expel a member.

Each House shall keep a journal of its proceedings, and from time to time publish the same, excepting such parts as may in their judgment require secrecy; and the yeas and nays of the members of either House on any question shall, at the desire of one fifth of those present, be entered on the journal.

Neither House, during the session of Congress, shall, without the consent of the other, adjourn for more than three days, nor to any other place than that in which the two Houses shall be sitting.

Section 6. The Senators and Representatives shall receive a compensation for their services, to be ascertained by law, and paid out of the treasury of the United States. They shall in all cases, except treason, felony and breach of the peace, be privileged from arrest during their attendance at the session of their respective Houses, and in going to and returning from the same; and for any speech or debate in either House, they shall not be questioned in any other place. No Senator or Representative shall, during the time for which he was elected, be appointed to any civil office under the authority of the United States, which shall have been created, or the emoluments whereof shall have been increased during such time: and no person holding any office under the United States, shall be a member of either House during his continuance in office.

Section 7. All bills for raising revenue shall originate in the House of Representatives; but the Senate may propose or concur with amendments as on other Bills.

Every bill which shall have passed the House of Representatives and the Senate, shall, before it become a law, be presented to the President of the United States; if he approve he shall sign it, but if not he shall return it, with his objections to that House in which it shall have originated, who shall enter the objections at large on their journal, and proceed to reconsider it. If after such reconsideration two thirds of that House shall agree to pass the bill, it shall be sent, together with the objections, to the other House, by which it shall likewise be reconsidered, and if approved by two thirds of that House, it shall become a law. But in all such cases the votes of both Houses shall be determined by yeas and nays, and the names of the persons voting for and against the bill shall be entered on the journal of each House respectively. If any bill shall not be returned by the President within ten days (Sundays excepted) after it shall have been presented to him, the same shall be a law, in like manner as if he had signed it, unless the Congress by their adjournment prevent its return, in which case it shall not be a law.

Every order, resolution, or vote to which the concurrence of the Senate and House of Representatives may be necessary (except on a question of adjournment) shall be presented to the President of the United States; and be-fore the same shall take effect, shall be approved by him, or being disapproved by him, shall be repassed by two thirds of the Senate and House of Representatives, according to the rules and limitations prescribed in the case of a bill.

Section 8. The Congress shall have power to lay and collect taxes, duties, imposts and excises, to pay the debts and provide for the common defense and general welfare of the United States; but all duties, imposts and excises shall be uniform throughout the United States;

To borrow money on the credit of the United States;

To regulate commerce with foreign nations, and among the several states, and with the Indian tribes;

To establish a uniform rule of naturalization, and uniform laws on the subject of bankruptcies throughout the United States;

To coin money, regulate the value thereof, and of foreign coin, and fix the standard of weights and measures;

To provide for the punishment of counterfeiting the securities and current coin of the United States;

To establish post offices and post roads;

To promote the progress of science and useful arts, by securing for limited times to authors and inventors the exclusive right to their respective writings and discoveries;

To constitute tribunals inferior to the Supreme Court;

To define and punish piracies and felonies committed on the high seas, and offenses against the law of nations;

To declare war, grant letters of marque and reprisal, and make rules concerning captures on land and water;

To raise and support armies, but no appropriation of money to that use shall be for a longer term than two years;

To provide and maintain a navy;

To make rules for the government and regulation of the land and naval forces;

To provide for calling forth the militia to execute the laws of the union, suppress insurrections and repel invasions;

To provide for organizing, arming, and disciplining, the militia, and for governing such part of them as may be employed in the service of the United States, reserving to the states respectively, the appointment of the officers, and the authority of training the militia according to the discipline prescribed by Congress;

To exercise exclusive legislation in all cases whatsoever, over such District (not exceeding ten miles square) as may, by cession of particular states, and the acceptance of Congress, become the seat of the government of the United States, and to exercise like authority over all places purchased by the consent of the legislature of the state in which the same shall be, for the erection of forts, magazines, arsenals, dockyards, and other needful buildings;—And

To make all laws which shall be necessary and proper for carrying into execution the foregoing powers, and all other powers vested by this Constitution in the government of the United States, or in any department or officer thereof.

Section 9. The migration or importation of such persons as any of the states now existing shall think proper to admit, shall not be prohibited by the Congress prior to the year one thousand eight hundred and eight, but a tax or duty may be imposed on such importation, not exceeding ten dollars for each person.

The privilege of the writ of habeas corpus shall not be suspended, unless when in cases of rebellion or invasion the public safety may require it.

No bill of attainder or ex post facto Law shall be passed.

No capitation, or other direct, tax shall be laid, unless in proportion to the census or enumeration herein before directed to be taken.

No tax or duty shall be laid on articles exported from any state.

No preference shall be given by any regulation of commerce or revenue to the ports of one state over those of another: nor shall vessels bound to, or from, one state, be obliged to enter, clear or pay duties in another.

No money shall be drawn from the treasury, but in consequence of appropriations made by law; and a regular statement and account of receipts and expenditures of all public money shall be published from time to time.

No title of nobility shall be granted by the United States: and no person holding any office of profit or trust under them, shall, without the consent of the Congress, accept of any present, emolument, office, or title, of any kind whatever, from any king, prince, or foreign state.

Section 10. No state shall enter into any treaty, alliance, or confederation; grant letters of marque and reprisal; coin money; emit bills of credit; make anything but gold and silver coin a tender in payment of debts; pass any bill of attainder, ex post facto law, or law impairing the obligation of contracts, or grant any title of nobility.

No state shall, without the consent of the Congress, lay any imposts or duties on imports or exports, except what may be absolutely necessary for executing its inspection laws: and the net produce of all duties and imposts, laid by any state on imports or exports, shall be for the use of the treasury of the United States; and all such laws shall be subject to the revision and control of the Congress.

No state shall, without the consent of Congress, lay any duty of tonnage, keep troops, or ships of war in time of peace, enter into any agreement or compact with another state, or with a foreign power, or engage in war, unless actually invaded, or in such imminent danger as will not admit of delay.

Article II

Section 1. The executive power shall be vested in a President of the United States of America. He shall hold his office during the term of four years, and, together with the Vice President, chosen for the same term, be elected, as follows:

Each state shall appoint, in such manner as the Legislature thereof may direct, a number of electors, equal to the whole number of Senators and Representatives to which the State may be entitled in the Congress: but no Senator or Representative, or person holding an office of trust or profit under the United States, shall be appointed an elector.

The electors shall meet in their respective states, and vote by ballot for two persons, of whom one at least shall not be an inhabitant of the same state with themselves. And they shall make a list of all the persons voted for, and of the number of votes for each; which list they shall sign and certify, and transmit sealed to the seat of the government of the United States, directed to the President of the Senate. The President of the Senate shall, in the presence of the Senate and House of Representatives, open all the certificates, and the votes shall then be counted. The person having the greatest number of votes shall be the President, if such number be a majority of the whole number of electors appointed; and if there be more than one who have such majority, and have an equal number of votes, then the House of Representatives shall immediately choose by ballot one of them for President; and if no person have a majority, then from the five highest on the list the said House shall in like manner choose the President. But in choosing the President, the votes shall be taken by States, the representation from each state having one vote; A quorum for this purpose shall consist of a member or members from two thirds of the states, and a majority of all the states shall be necessary to a choice. In every case, after the choice of the President, the person having the greatest number of votes of the electors shall be the Vice President. But if there should remain two or more who have equal votes, the Senate shall choose from them by ballot the Vice President.

The Congress may determine the time of choosing the electors, and the day on which they shall give their votes; which day shall be the same throughout the United States.

No person except a natural born citizen, or a citizen of the United States, at the time of the adoption of this Constitution, shall be eligible to the office of President; neither shall any person be eligible to that office who shall not have attained to the age of thirty five years, and been fourteen Years a resident within the United States.

In case of the removal of the President from office, or of his death, resignation, or inability to discharge the powers and duties of the said office, the same shall devolve on the Vice President, and the Congress may by law provide for the case of removal, death, resignation or inability, both of the President and Vice President, declaring what officer shall then act as President, and such officer shall act accordingly, until the disability be removed, or a President shall be elected.

The President shall, at stated times, receive for his services, a compensation, which shall neither be increased nor diminished during the period for which he shall have been elected, and he shall not receive within that period any other emolument from the United States, or any of them.

Before he enter on the execution of his office, he shall take the following oath or affirmation:— "I do solemnly swear (or affirm) that I will faithfully execute the office of President of the United States, and will to the best of my ability, preserve, protect and defend the Constitution of the United States."

Section 2. The President shall be commander in chief of the Army and Navy of the United States, and of the militia of the several states, when called into the actual service of the United States; he may require the opinion, in writing, of the principal officer in each of the executive departments, on any subject relating to the duties of their respective offices, and he shall

have power to grant reprieves and pardons for offenses against the United States, except in cases of impeachment.

He shall have power, by and with the advice and consent of the Senate, to make treaties, provided two thirds of the Senators present concur; and he shall nominate, and by and with the advice and consent of the Senate, shall appoint ambassadors, other public ministers and consuls, judges of the Supreme Court, and all other officers of the United States, whose appointments are not herein otherwise provided for, and which shall be established by law: but the Congress may by law vest the appointment of such inferior officers, as they think proper, in the President alone, in the courts of law, or in the heads of departments.

The President shall have power to fill up all vacancies that may happen during the recess of the Senate, by granting commissions which shall expire at the end of their next session.

Section 3. He shall from time to time give to the Congress information of the state of the union, and recommend to their consideration such measures as he shall judge necessary and expedient; he may, on extraordinary occasions, convene both Houses, or either of them, and in case of disagreement between them, with respect to the time of adjournment, he may adjourn them to such time as he shall think proper; he shall receive ambassadors and other public ministers; he shall take care that the laws be faithfully executed, and shall commission all the officers of the United States.

Section 4. The President, Vice President and all civil officers of the United States, shall be removed from office on impeachment for, and conviction of, treason, bribery, or other high crimes and misdemeanors.

Article III

Section 1. The judicial power of the United States, shall be vested in one Supreme Court, and in such inferior courts as the Congress may from time to time ordain and establish. The judges, both of the supreme and inferior courts, shall hold their offices during good behavior, and shall, at stated times, receive for their services, a compensation, which shall not be diminished during their continuance in office.

Section 2. The judicial power shall extend to all cases, in law and equity, arising under this Constitution, the laws of the United States, and treaties made, or which shall be made, under their authority;—to all cases affecting ambassadors, other public ministers and consuls;—to all cases of admiralty and maritime jurisdiction;—to controversies to which the United States shall be a party;—to controversies between two or more states;—between a state and citizens of another state;—between citizens of different states;—between citizens of the same state claiming lands under grants of different states, and between a state, or the citizens thereof, and foreign states, citizens or subjects.

In all cases affecting ambassadors, other public ministers and consuls, and those in which a state shall be party, the Supreme Court shall have original jurisdiction. In all the other cases before mentioned, the Supreme Court shall have appellate jurisdiction, both as to law and fact, with such exceptions, and under such regulations as the Congress shall make.

The trial of all crimes, except in cases of impeachment, shall be by jury; and such trial shall be held in the state where the said crimes shall have been committed; but when not committed within any state, the trial shall be at such place or places as the Congress may by law have directed.

Section 3. Treason against the United States, shall consist only in levying war against them, or in adhering to their enemies, giving them aid and comfort. No person shall be convicted of treason unless on the testimony of two witnesses to the same overt act, or on confession in open court.

The Congress shall have power to declare the punishment of treason, but no attainder of treason shall work corruption of blood, or forfeiture except during the life of the person attainted.

Article IV

Section 1. Full faith and credit shall be given in each state to the public acts, records, and judicial proceedings of every other state. And the Congress may by general laws prescribe the manner in which such acts, records, and proceedings shall be proved, and the effect thereof.

Section 2. The citizens of each state shall be entitled to all privileges and immunities of citizens in the several states.

A person charged in any state with treason, felony, or other crime, who shall flee from justice, and be found in another state, shall on demand of the executive authority of the state from which he fled, be delivered up, to be removed to the state having jurisdiction of the crime.

No person held to service or labor in one state, under the laws thereof, escaping into another, shall, in consequence of any law or regulation therein, be discharged from such service or labor, but shall be delivered up on claim of the party to whom such service or labor may be due.

Section 3. New states may be admitted by the Congress into this union; but no new states shall be formed or erected within the jurisdiction of any other state; nor any state be formed by the junction of two or more states, or parts of states, without the consent of the legislatures of the states concerned as well as of the Congress.

The Congress shall have power to dispose of and make all needful rules and regulations respecting the territory or other property belonging to the United States; and nothing in this Constitution shall be so construed as to prejudice any claims of the United States, or of any particular state.

Section 4. The United States shall guarantee to every state in this union a republican form of government, and shall protect each of them against invasion; and on application of the legislature, or of the executive (when the legislature cannot be convened) against domestic violence.

Article V

The Congress, whenever two thirds of both houses shall deem it necessary, shall propose amendments to this Constitution, or, on the application of the legislatures of two thirds of the several states, shall call a convention for proposing amendments, which, in either case, shall be valid to all intents and purposes, as part of this Constitution, when ratified by the legislatures of three fourths of the several states, or by conventions in three fourths thereof, as the one or the other mode of ratification may be proposed by the Congress; provided that no amendment which may be made prior to the year one thousand eight hundred and eight shall in any manner affect the first and fourth clauses in the ninth section of the first article; and that no state, without its consent, shall be deprived of its equal suffrage in the Senate.

Article VI

All debts contracted and engagements entered into, before the adoption of this Constitution, shall be as valid against the United States under this Constitution, as under the Confederation.

This Constitution, and the laws of the United States which shall be made in pursuance thereof; and all treaties made, or which shall be made, under the authority of the United States, shall be the supreme law of the land; and the judges in every state shall be bound thereby, anything in the Constitution or laws of any State to the contrary notwithstanding.

The Senators and Representatives before mentioned, and the members of the several state legislatures, and all executive and judicial officers, both of the United States and of the several states, shall be bound by oath or affirmation, to support this Constitution; but no religious test shall ever be required as a qualification to any office or public trust under the United States.

Article VII

The ratification of the conventions of nine states, shall be sufficient for the establishment of this Constitution between the states so ratifying the same.

Done in convention by the unanimous consent of the states present the seventeenth day of September in the year of our Lord one thousand seven hundred and eighty seven and of the independence of the United States of America the twelfth. In witness whereof We have hereunto subscribed our Names,

G. Washington: Presidt. and Deputy from Virginia

New Hampshire: John Langdon, Nicholas Gilman

Massachusetts: Nathaniel Gorham, Rufus King

Connecticut: Wm: Saml. Johnson, Roger Sherman

New York: Alexander Hamilton

New Jersey: Wil Livingston, David Brearly, Wm. Paterson, Jona: Dayton

Pennsylvania: B. Franklin, Thomas Mifflin, Robt. Morris, Geo. Clymer, Thos. Fitzsimons, Jared Ingersoll, James Wilson, Gouv Morris

Delaware: Geo: Read, Gunning Bedford Jun, John Dickinson, Richard Bassett, Jaco: Broom

Maryland: James Mchenry, Dan of St Thos. Jenifer, Danl Carroll

Virginia: John Blair—, James Madison Jr.

North Carolina: Wm. Blount, Richd. Dobbs Spaight, Hu Williamson

South Carolina: J. Rutledge, Charles Cotesworth Pinckney, Charles Pinckney, Pierce Butler

Georgia: William Few, Abr Baldwin

The Conventions of a number of the States having, at the time of adopting the Constitution, expressed a desire, in order to prevent misconstruction or abuse of its powers, that further declaratory and restrictive clauses should be added, and as extending the ground of public confidence in the Government will best insure the beneficent ends of its institution;

Resolved, by the Senate and House of Representatives of the United States of America, in Congress assembled, two-thirds of both Houses concurring, that the following articles be proposed to the Legislatures of the several States, as amendments to the Constitution of the United States; all or any of which articles, when ratified by three-fourths of the said Legislatures, to be valid to all intents and purposes as part of the said Constitution, namely:

Amendment I

Congress shall make no law respecting an establishment of religion, or prohibiting the free exercise thereof; or abridging the freedom of speech, or of the press; or the right of the people peaceably to assemble, and to petition the government for a redress of grievances.

Amendment II

A well regulated militia, being necessary to the security of a free state, the right of the people to keep and bear arms, shall not be infringed.

Amendment III

No soldier shall, in time of peace be quartered in any house, without the consent of the owner, nor in time of war, but in a manner to be prescribed by law.

Amendment IV

The right of the people to be secure in their persons, houses, papers, and effects, against unreasonable searches and seizures, shall not be violated, and no warrants shall issue, but upon probable cause, supported by oath or affirmation, and par-

ticularly describing the place to be searched, and the persons or things to be seized.

Amendment V

No person shall be held to answer for a capital, or otherwise infamous crime, unless on a presentment or indictment of a grand jury, except in cases arising in the land or naval forces, or in the militia, when in actual service in time of war or public danger; nor shall any person be subject for the same offense to be twice put in jeopardy of life or limb; nor shall be compelled in any criminal case to be a witness against himself, nor be deprived of life, liberty, or property, without due process of law; nor shall private property be taken for public use, without just compensation.

Amendment VI

In all criminal prosecutions, the accused shall enjoy the right to a speedy and public trial, by an impartial jury of the state and district wherein the crime shall have been committed, which district shall have been previously ascertained by law, and to be informed of the nature and cause of the accusation; to be confronted with the witnesses against him; to have compulsory process for obtaining witnesses in his favor, and to have the assistance of counsel for his defense.

Amendment VII

In suits at common law, where the value in controversy shall exceed twenty dollars, the right of trial by jury shall be preserved, and no fact tried by a jury, shall be otherwise reexamined in any court of the United States, than according to the rules of the common law.

Amendment VIII

Excessive bail shall not be required, nor excessive fines imposed, nor cruel and unusual punishments inflicted.

Amendment IX

The enumeration in the Constitution, of certain rights, shall not be construed to deny or disparage others retained by the people.

Amendment X

The powers not delegated to the United States by the Constitution, nor prohibited by it to the states, are reserved to the states respectively, or to the people.

BILL OF RIGHTS

The Conventions of a number of the States having, at the time of adopting the Constitution, expressed a desire, in order to prevent misconstruction or abuse of its powers, that further declaratory and restrictive clauses should be added, and as extending the ground of public confidence in the Government will best insure the beneficent ends of its institution;

Resolved, by the Senate and House of Representatives of the United States of America, in Congress assembled, two-thirds of both Houses concurring, that the following articles be proposed to the Legislatures of the several States, as amendments to the Constitution of the United States; all or any of which articles, when ratified by three-fourths of the said Legislatures, to be valid to all intents and purposes as part of the said Constitution, namely:

Amendment I

Congress shall make no law respecting an establishment of religion, or prohibiting the free exercise thereof; or abridging the freedom of speech, or of the press; or the right of the people peaceably to assemble, and to petition the government for a redress of grievances.

Amendment II

A well regulated militia, being necessary to the security of a free state, the right of the people to keep and bear arms, shall not be infringed.

Amendment III

No soldier shall, in time of peace be quartered in any house, without the consent of the owner, nor in time of war, but in a manner to be prescribed by law.

Amendment IV

The right of the people to be secure in their persons, houses, papers, and effects, against unreasonable searches and seizures, shall not be violated, and no warrants shall issue, but upon probable cause, supported by oath or affirmation, and particularly describing the place to be searched, and the persons or things to be seized.

Amendment V

No person shall be held to answer for a capital, or otherwise infamous crime, unless on a presentment or indictment of a grand jury, except in cases arising in the land or naval forces, or in the militia, when in actual service in time of war or public danger; nor shall any person be subject for the same offense to be twice put in jeopardy of life or limb; nor shall be compelled in any criminal case to be a witness against himself, nor be deprived of life, liberty, or property, without due process of law; nor shall private property be taken for public use, without just compensation.

Amendment VI

In all criminal prosecutions, the accused shall enjoy the right to a speedy and public trial, by an impartial jury of the state and district wherein the crime shall have been committed, which district shall have been previously ascertained by law, and to be informed of the nature and cause of the accusation; to be confronted with the witnesses against him; to have compulsory process for obtaining witnesses in his favor, and to have the assistance of counsel for his defense.

Amendment VII

In suits at common law, where the value in controversy shall exceed twenty dollars, the right of trial by jury shall be preserved, and no fact tried by a jury, shall be otherwise reexamined in any court of the United States, than according to the rules of the common law.

Amendment VIII

Excessive bail shall not be required, nor excessive fines imposed, nor cruel and unusual punishments inflicted.

Amendment IX

The enumeration in the Constitution, of certain rights, shall not be construed to deny or disparage others retained by the people.

Amendment X

The powers not delegated to the United States by the Constitution, nor prohibited by it to the states, are reserved to the states respectively, or to the people.

OTHER AMENDMENTS TO THE CONSTITUTION

Amendment XI

(1798)

The judicial power of the United States shall not be construed to extend to any suit in law or equity, commenced or prosecuted against one of the United States by citizens of another state, or by citizens or subjects of any foreign state.

Amendment XII

(1804)

The electors shall meet in their respective states and vote by ballot for President and Vice-President, one of whom, at least, shall not be an inhabitant of the same state with themselves; they shall name in their ballots the person voted for as President, and in distinct ballots the person voted for as Vice-President, and they shall make distinct lists of all persons voted for as President, and of all persons voted for as Vice-President, and of the number of votes for each, which lists they shall sign and certify, and transmit sealed to the seat of the government of the United States, directed to the President of the Senate;—The President of the Senate shall, in the presence of the Senate and House of Representatives, open all the certificates and the votes shall then be counted;—the person having the greatest number of votes for President, shall be the President, if such number be a majority of the whole number of electors appointed; and if no person have such majority, then from the persons having the highest numbers not exceeding three on the list of those voted for as President, the House of Representatives shall choose immediately, by ballot, the President. But in choosing the President, the votes shall be taken by states, the representation from each state having one vote; a quorum for this purpose shall consist of a member or members from two-thirds of the states, and a majority of all the states shall be necessary to a choice. And if the House of Representatives shall not choose a President whenever the right of choice shall devolve upon them, before the fourth day of March next following, then the Vice-President shall act as President, as in the case of the death or other constitutional disability of the President. The person having the greatest number of votes as Vice-President, shall be the Vice-President, if such number be a majority of the whole number of electors appointed, and if no person have a majority, then from the two highest numbers on the list, the Senate shall choose the Vice-President; a quorum for the purpose shall consist of two-thirds of the whole number of Senators, and a majority of the whole number shall be necessary to a choice. But no person constitutionally ineligible to the office of President shall be eligible to that of Vice-President of the United States.

Amendment XIII

(1865)

Section 1. Neither slavery nor involuntary servitude, except as a punishment for crime whereof the party shall have been duly convicted, shall exist within the United States, or any place subject to their jurisdiction.

Section 2. Congress shall have power to enforce this article by appropriate legislation.

Amendment XIV

(1868)

Section 1. All persons born or naturalized in the United States, and subject to the jurisdiction thereof, are citizens of the United States and of the state wherein they reside. No state shall make or enforce any law which shall abridge the privileges or immunities of citizens of the United States; nor shall any state deprive any person of life, liberty, or property, without due process of law; nor deny to any person within its jurisdiction the equal protection of the laws.

Section 2. Representatives shall be apportioned among the several states according to their respective numbers, counting the whole number of persons in each state, excluding Indians not taxed. But when the right to vote at any election for the choice of electors for President and Vice President of the United States, Representatives in Congress, the executive and judicial officers of a state, or the members of the legislature thereof, is denied to any of the male inhabitants of such state, being twenty-one years of age, and citizens of the United States, or in any way abridged, except for participation in rebellion, or other crime, the basis of representation therein shall be reduced in the proportion which the number of such male citizens shall bear to the whole number of male citizens twenty-one years of age in such state.

Section 3. No person shall be a Senator or Representative in Congress, or elector of President and Vice President, or hold any office, civil or military, under the United States, or under any state, who, having previously taken an oath, as a member of Congress, or as an officer of the United States, or as a member of any state legislature, or as an executive or judicial officer of any state, to support the Constitution of the United States, shall have engaged in insurrection or rebellion against the same, or given aid or comfort to the enemies thereof. But Congress may by a vote of two-thirds of each House, remove such disability.

Section 4. The validity of the public debt of the United States, authorized by law, including debts incurred for payment of pensions and bounties for services in suppressing insurrection or rebellion, shall not be questioned. But neither the United States nor any state shall assume or pay any debt or obligation incurred in aid of insurrection or rebellion against the United States, or any claim for the loss or emancipation of any slave; but all such debts, obligations and claims shall be held illegal and void.

Section 5. The Congress shall have power to enforce, by appropriate legislation, the provisions of this article.

Amendment XV

(1870)

Section 1. The right of citizens of the United States to vote shall not be denied or abridged by the United States or by any state on account of race, color, or previous condition of servitude.

Section 2. The Congress shall have power to enforce this article by appropriate legislation.

Amendment XVI

(1913)

The Congress shall have power to lay and collect taxes on incomes, from whatever source derived, without apportionment among the several states, and without regard to any census of enumeration.

Amendment XVII

(1913)

The Senate of the United States shall be composed of two Senators from each state, elected by the people thereof, for six years; and each Senator shall have one vote. The electors in each state shall have the qualifications requisite for electors of the most numerous branch of the state legislatures.

When vacancies happen in the representation of any state in the Senate, the executive authority of such state shall issue writs of election to fill such vacancies: Provided, that the legislature of any state may empower the executive thereof to make temporary appointments until the people fill the vacancies by election as the legislature may direct.

This amendment shall not be so construed as to affect the election or term of any Senator chosen before it becomes valid as part of the Constitution.

Amendment XVIII

(1919)

Section 1. After one year from the ratification of this article the manufacture, sale, or transportation of intoxicating liquors within, the importation thereof into, or the exportation thereof from the United States and all territory subject to the jurisdiction thereof for beverage purposes is hereby prohibited.

Section 2. The Congress and the several states shall have concurrent power to enforce this article by appropriate legislation.

Section 3. This article shall be inoperative unless it shall have been ratified as an amendment to the Constitution by the legislatures of the several states, as provided in the Constitution, within seven years from the date of the submission hereof to the states by the Congress.

Amendment XIX

(1920)

The right of citizens of the United States to vote shall not be denied or abridged by the United States or by any state on account of sex.

Congress shall have power to enforce this article by appropriate legislation.

Amendment XX

(1933)

Section 1. The terms of the President and Vice President shall end at noon on the 20th day of January, and the terms of Senators and Representatives at noon on the 3d day of January, of the years in which such terms would have ended if this article had not been ratified; and the terms of their successors shall then begin.

Section 2. The Congress shall assemble at least once in every year, and such meeting shall begin at noon on the 3d day of January, unless they shall by law appoint a different day.

Section 3. If, at the time fixed for the beginning of the term of the President, the President elect shall have died, the Vice President elect shall become President. If a President shall not have been chosen before the time fixed for the beginning of his term, or if the President elect shall have failed to qualify, then the Vice President elect shall act as President until a President shall have qualified; and the Congress may by law provide for the case wherein neither a President elect nor a Vice President elect shall have qualified, declaring who shall then act as President, or the manner in which one who is to act shall be selected, and such person shall act accordingly until a President or Vice President shall have qualified.

Section 4. The Congress may by law provide for the case of the death of any of the persons from whom the House of Representatives may choose a President whenever the right of choice shall have devolved upon them, and for the case of the death of any of the persons from whom the Senate may choose a Vice President whenever the right of choice shall have devolved upon them.

Section 5. Sections 1 and 2 shall take effect on the 15th day of October following the ratification of this article.

Section 6. This article shall be inoperative unless it shall have been ratified as an amendment to the Constitution by the legislatures of three-fourths of the several states within seven years from the date of its submission.

Amendment XXI

(1933)

Section 1. The eighteenth article of amendment to the Constitution of the United States is hereby repealed.

Section 2. The transportation or importation into any state, territory, or possession of the United

States for delivery or use therein of intoxicating liquors, in violation of the laws thereof, is hereby prohibited.

Section 3. This article shall be inoperative unless it shall have been ratified as an amendment to the Constitution by conventions in the several states, as provided in the Constitution, within seven years from the date of the submission hereof to the states by the Congress.

Amendment XXII

(1951)

Section 1. No person shall be elected to the office of the President more than twice, and no person who has held the office of President, or acted as President, for more than two years of a term to which some other person was elected President shall be elected to the office of the President more than once. But this article shall not apply to any person holding the office of President when this article was proposed by the Congress, and shall not prevent any person who may be holding the office of President, or acting as President, during the term within which this article becomes operative from holding the office of President or acting as President during the remainder of such term.

Section 2. This article shall be inoperative unless it shall have been ratified as an amendment to the Constitution by the legislatures of three-fourths of the several states within seven years from the date of its submission to the states by the Congress.

Amendment XXIII

(1961)

Section 1. The District constituting the seat of government of the United States shall appoint in such manner as the Congress may direct: A number of electors of President and Vice President equal to the whole number of Senators and Representatives in Congress to which the District would be entitled if it were a state, but in no event more than the least populous state; they shall be in addition to those appointed by the states, but they shall be considered, for the purposes of the election of President and Vice President, to be electors appointed by a state; and they shall meet in the District and perform such duties as provided by the twelfth article of amendment.

Section 2. The Congress shall have power to enforce this article by appropriate legislation.

Amendment XXIV

(1964)

Section 1. The right of citizens of the United States to vote in any primary or other election for President or Vice President, for electors for President or Vice President, or for Senator or Representative in Congress, shall not be denied or abridged by the United States or any state by reason of failure to pay any poll tax or other tax.

Section 2. The Congress shall have power to enforce this article by appropriate legislation.

Amendment XXV

(1967)

Section 1. In case of the removal of the President from office or of his death or resignation, the Vice President shall become President.

Section 2. Whenever there is a vacancy in the office of the Vice President, the President shall nominate a Vice President who shall take office upon confirmation by a majority vote of both Houses of Congress.

Section 3. Whenever the President transmits to the President pro tempore of the Senate and the Speaker of the House of Representatives his written declaration that he is unable to discharge the powers and duties of his office, and until he transmits to them a written declaration to the contrary, such powers and duties shall be discharged by the Vice President as Acting President.

Section 4. Whenever the Vice President and a majority of either the principal officers of the executive departments or of such other body as Congress may by law provide, transmit to the President pro tempore of the Senate and the

Speaker of the House of Representatives their written declaration that the President is unable to discharge the powers and duties of his office, the Vice President shall immediately assume the powers and duties of the office as Acting President.

Thereafter, when the President transmits to the President pro tempore of the Senate and the Speaker of the House of Representatives his written declaration that no inability exists, he shall resume the powers and duties of his office unless the Vice President and a majority of either the principal officers of the executive department or of such other body as Congress may by law provide, transmit within four days to the President pro tempore of the Senate and the Speaker of the House of Representatives their written declaration that the President is unable to discharge the powers and duties of his office.

Thereupon Congress shall decide the issue, assembling within forty-eight hours for that purpose if not in session. If the Congress, within twenty-one days after receipt of the latter written declaration, or, if Congress is not in session, within twenty-one days after Congress is required to assemble, determines by two-thirds vote of both Houses that the President is unable to discharge the powers and duties of his office, the Vice President shall continue to discharge the same as Acting President; otherwise, the President shall resume the powers and duties of his office.

Amendment XXVI

(1971)

Section 1. The right of citizens of the United States, who are 18 years of age or older, to vote, shall not be denied or abridged by the United States or any state on account of age.

Section 2. The Congress shall have the power to enforce this article by appropriate legislation.

Amendment XXVII

(1992)

No law varying the compensation for the services of the Senators and Representatives shall take effect until an election of Representatives shall have intervened.

U.S. Constitution Time Line

1142 Iroquois Confederacy formed

1215 King John forced by English nobles to sign the Magna Carta at Runnymede

1620 Mayflower Compact signed

1692 Salem Witch Trials

1735 Peter Zenger acquitted in a jury trial; found not guilty of engaging in seditious libel

1765 The British adopt the Stamp Act

1767 The British adopt the Townsend Act

1770 The Boston Massacre

1773 The Tea Act is adopted

The Boston Tea Party

1774 The First Continental Congress meets

1775 The Second Continental Congress meets

Battles of Lexington and Concord

Battle of Bunker Hill

1776 Declaration of Independence

1777 Second Continental Congress writes the first draft of the Articles of Confederation

1781 Articles of Confederation adopted

1786 Shays's Rebellion begins

1787 Northwest Ordinance adopted

Constitutional Convention

Delaware becomes the first sate to adopt the new constitution

Federalist Papers run in New York newspapers

Anti-Federalist *Brutus* and *Letters from the Federal Farmer* run in newspapers and appear in a pamphlet.

1788 Constitution ratified by requisite number of states

George Washington elected as the first president of the United States

1789 Judiciary Act of 1789 establishes the Supreme Court with six members, and allows for cases from a state's highest court to be appealed to the United States Supreme Court

President Washington appoints the first six justices

John Jay becomes the first chief justice

1791 First 10 amendments to the Constitution, known as the Bill of Rights, are ratified

1793 In *Chisholm v. Georgia,* the Supreme Court rules that a citizen of one state can sue a different state in federal court

1796 Oliver Ellsworth becomes chief justice

1798 In *Calder v. Bull,* the Supreme Court declares that the ex post facto clause applies only to criminal matters.

Congress adopts the Sedition Act

The Virginia and Kentucky Resolutions, authored by Thomas Jefferson and James Madison, challenge the constitutionality of the Sedition Act

The Eleventh Amendment overturns *Chisholm v. Georgia*

1800 John Marshall becomes chief justice

Thomas Jefferson defeats John Adams for the presidency, but only after the House of Representatives selects him over his running mate Aaron Burr to become president

1803 In *Marbury v. Madison,* Supreme Court states it has the power to declare laws unconstitutional

1804 The Twelfth Amendment changes the presidential election process so that the president and vice president run as a ticket

1810 In *Fletcher v. Peck*, the Supreme Court declares it has the power to review the constitutionality of state laws

1811 Samuel Chase is the only Supreme Court justice impeached by the House of Representatives; the Senate refuses to convict him

1816 In *Martin v. Hunter's Lessee*, the Supreme Court overturns a Virginia law, affirming the power of the Supreme Court to declare state laws unconstitutional

1819 In *McCulloch v. Maryland*, the Supreme Court upholds the constitutionality of the Bank of the United States and indicates that the federal government has expansive powers under the "necessary and proper" clause

In *Dartmouth College v. Wooodward*, the Supreme Court rules that the contract clause prevents a state from changing the charter of a private college

1820 Missouri Compromise adopted

1824 In *Gibbons v. Ogden*, the Supreme Court upholds expansive power for the United States government to regulate commerce

1831 In *Cherokee Nation v. Georgia*, the Supreme Court issues the first of several decisions regarding the status of Native Americans in the United States

1833 In *Barron v. Baltimore*, the Supreme Court states that the Bill of Rights does not apply to the states

1836 Roger Taney becomes chief justice

1837 In *Charles River Bridge v. Warren Bridge*, the Supreme Court rules that the contract clause does not preclude the state of Massachusetts from allowing a new bridge to be incorporated and built next to an existing one that had received a charter from the state

1851 In *Cooley v. Board of Wardens*, the Supreme Court affirms the power of states to regulate local navigation issues despite restrictions imposed by the commerce clause

1854 Kansas-Nebraska Act adopted

1857 In *Dred Scott v. Sanford*, the Supreme Court declares the Missouri Compromise unconstitutional and also rules that blacks are property, not citizens

1860 Abraham Lincoln elected president

1864 Salmon P. Chase becomes chief justice

1865 The Thirteenth Amendment, abolishing slavery, is ratified

Reconstruction begins

1866 In *Ex parte Milligan*, the Supreme Court affirms the power of Congress to remove its jurisdiction to decide a habeas corpus after the Court had already had oral arguments in the case

1868 The Fourteenth Amendment is ratified, overturning *Dred Scott v. Sanford;* the amendment prevents states from denying the privileges and immunities of U.S. citizens, granting equal protection of the law or due process of law

1870 The Fifteenth Amendment is ratified, prohibiting discrimination in voting on the basis of race

1873 In the *Slaughterhouse Cases*, the Supreme Court limits the meaning of the privileges and immunities clause of the Fourteenth Amendment

1874 Morrison R. Waite becomes chief justice

1875 Supreme Court rules in *Minor v. Happersett* that states may deny women the right to vote

1876 In *Munn v. Illinois*, the Supreme Court upholds the regulation of grain elevators

1877 Reconstruction ends with the withdrawal of federal troops from the South

1883 In the Civil Rights cases, the Supreme Court declares that Congress lacks the authority to prevent discrimination in private establishments

1887 In *Mugler v. Kansas*, the Supreme Court strikes down a state law prohibiting intoxicating beverages, ruling that it (the Court) has the right to review the reasonableness of legislation

1888   Melville W. Fuller becomes chief justice

1895   Supreme Court upholds the use of injunctions to halt labor strikes in *In re Debs*

Supreme Court narrows the application, the Sherman Antitrust Act and the power of Congress to regulate commerce in *United States v. E.C. Knight Company*

Supreme Court declares federal income tax unconstitutional in *Pollock v. Farmers' Loan*

1896   In *Plessy v. Ferguson*, the Supreme Court upholds segregation and the "separate but equal" doctrine

1897   In *Chicago, Burlington & Quincy Railroad Company v. Chicago*, the Supreme Court begins the process of incorporating the Bill of Rights to the states by holding that the Fifth Amendment just-compensation clause applies to the states

In *Allgeyer v. Louisiana*, the Supreme Court strikes down a state law regulating a private contract

1905   In *Lochner v. New York*, the Supreme Court strikes down a state law regulating the working hours of bakers, holding that it violates the due process clause of the Fourteenth Amendment

1907   The Tillman Act is passed, preventing corporations from expending money to influence federal elections

1908   In *Muller v. Oregon*, the Supreme Court upholds laws limiting working hours for women; Louis Brandeis introduces the famous "Brandeis brief" in the case

1910   Edward D. White becomes chief justice

1913   The Sixteenth Amendment passes, overturning *Pollock v. Farmers' Loan*

The Seventeenth Amendment passes, providing for direct election of U.S. senators

1914   Supreme Court declares the exclusionary rule to be part of the Fourth Amendment

in federal proceedings in *Weeks v. United States*

1916   Louis Brandeis, the first Jewish Supreme Court justice, is sworn in

1917   Bolsheviks seize power in Russia

Congress adopts the Espionage Act

United States enters World War I

1918   In *Hammer v. Dagenhart*, the Supreme Court strikes down child labor laws as an unconstitutional regulation of commerce

Congress adopts the Espionage Act

1919   The Eighteenth Amendment is adopted, banning the sale and manufacture of alcohol for consumption

Justice Oliver Wendell Holmes, Jr., develops the "clear and present danger" test in *Schenck v. United States*

In *Abrams v. United States*, the Supreme Court upholds the convictions of five Russian immigrants who circulated antiwar leaflets

1920   Nineteenth Amendment ratified, giving women the right to vote

1921   Former president William Howard Taft becomes chief justice

1923   In *Adkins v. Children's Hospital*, the Supreme Court strikes down as unconstitutional a federal minimum wage for women

1925   In *Gitlow v. New York*, the Supreme Court incorporates the First Amendment free speech clause to apply to the states through the due process clause of the Fourteenth Amendment

In *Pierce v. Society of Sisters*, the Supreme Court declares that parents have a right to send their children to private religious schools

1927   In *Buck v. Bell*, the Supreme Court upholds a law requiring the forced sterilization of a mentally retarded woman

1930   Charles Evans Hughes becomes chief justice

1931   In *Near v. Minnesota*, the Supreme Court rules that the First Amendment prevents states from engaging in prior restraint; in this case, the Supreme Court also incorporates the First Amendment freedom of the press clause to the states

1932 In the Scottsboro case of *Powell v. Alabama,* the Supreme Court rules that the state must provide legal counsel to those accused of capital crimes; it incorporates this Sixth Amendment right to the states

Supreme Court upholds the power of states to issue a moratorium on mortgage repayments in *Home Building and Loan Association v. Blaisdell*

1933 The Twentieth Amendment is adopted, changing the dates for terms of the president, vice president, and members of Congress

The Twenty-first Amendment is adopted, repealing the Eighteenth Amendment

1935 Supreme Court building completed and the Court moves into it

In *Schechter Poultry Co. v. United States,* the Supreme Court declares a trade rule adopted under the National Industrial Recovery Act to be an unconstitutional violation of the commerce clause

1936 In *Carter v. Carter Coal,* the Supreme Court invalidates a federal law seeking to regulate coal production, ruling that it violates the commerce clause

1937 President Roosevelt issues his "court-packing plan"

In *Palko v. Connecticut,* Justice Benjamin Cardozo develops the doctrine of "selective incorporation" and fundamental freedoms

In *NLRB v. Jones & Laughlin Steel Co.,* the Supreme Court invalidates portions of the National Labor Relations Act as a violation of the commerce clause

In *DeJonge v. Oregon,* the Supreme Court incorporates the freedom of assembly clause to apply to the states

In *West Coast Hotel v. Parrish,* the Supreme Court upholds a state minimum wage law for women, overturning *Adkins v. Children's Hospital*

1938 In the famous footnote number four of *United States v. Caroline Products,* the Supreme Court through Harlan Fiske Stone indicates that it will no longer give heightened scrutiny to economic legislation, but instead will afford more protection to civil rights; this case marks the beginning of the "New Deal" Court

Hatch Acts adopted, placing restrictions on the political activities of federal employees

1940 In *Minersville School District v. Gobitis,* the Supreme Court upholds a compulsory flag-salute law

In *Cantwell v. Connecticut,* the Supreme Court incorporates the free-exercise clause to apply to the states

Franklin Roosevelt elected to a third term as president of the United States

1941 Harlan Fiske Stone becomes chief justice

United States enters World War II

In *United States v. Darby Lumber,* the Supreme Court upholds the Fair Labor Standards Act of 1938 and, in effect, overturns *Hammer v. Dagenhart*

1942 In *Wickard v. Filburn,* the Supreme Court rejects the broad commerce clause power of Congress to regulate wheat production for personal use

In *Betts v. Brady,* the Supreme Court creates the exclusionary rule that prevents the use of illegally obtained evidence in federal court to convict an individual

The Court declares in *Skinner v. Oklahoma* that individuals have a fundamental right to procreate

In *Chaplinsky v. New Hampshire,* the Supreme Court declares that fighting words are not protected by the First Amendment

1943 In *West Virginia v. Barnette,* the Supreme Court holds that compulsory flag saluting in school is unconstitutional; this decision overturns *Minersville School District v. Gobitis*

1944 In *Korematsu v. United States*, the Supreme Court upholds the forced and mass detention of Japanese Americans; in the same case, the Court also declares that any policy that categorizes individuals by race is suspect

1946 Fred M. Vinson becomes chief justice

In *Colegrove v. Green*, the Supreme Court says it will not hear reapportionment cases

1947 In *Everson v. Board of Education*, the Supreme Court rules that the establishment clause does not bar the use of public school buses to transport students to parochial schools; in this case, the Court also incorporates the establishment clause to apply to the states

1948 In *McCullum v. Board of Education*, the Supreme Court rules that the establishment clause bars religious instruction in public schools

In *In re Oliver*, the Supreme Court incorporates the Sixth Amendment right to a public trial to apply to the states

1949 The Federal Communications Commission adopts the Fairness Doctrine

In *Wolf v. Colorado*, the Supreme Court incorporates the Fourth Amendment, but not the exclusionary rule, to apply to the states

1951 In *Dennis v. United States*, the Supreme Court upholds the conviction of 11 members of the Communist Party for violating the Smith Act

The Twenty-second Amendment is adopted, limiting presidents to serving two terms

1952 In *Youngstown Sheet & Tube Co. v. Sawyer*, the Supreme Court declares that President Truman's seizure of the steel mills during the Korean war was unconstitutional

In *Beauharnais v. Illinois*, the Supreme Court rules that the First Amendment does not protect group libel

In *Zorach v. Clauson*, the Supreme Court upholds a release time program to allow public school students to attend religious education classes

1953 Earl Warren becomes chief justice

1954 "Separate but equal" doctrine declared unconstitutional in *Brown v. Board of Education* and in *Bolling v. Sharpe*

1957 Supreme Court seeks to define obscenity in *Roth v. United States*

In *Watkins v. United States*, the Supreme Court places limits on congressional investigations

1958 Supreme Court declares it is the final word on the meaning of the Constitution in *Cooper v. Aaron*

In *NAACP v. Alabama*, the Supreme Court declares that states may not violate the right of freedom of association

1959 In *Barenblatt v. United States*, the Supreme Court rules that Congress may compel witnesses to testify about their past political associations

1961 In *Mapp v. Ohio*, the Supreme Court extends the exclusionary rule to apply to the states

The Twenty-third Amendment is adopted, giving the District of Columbia three electoral votes in the selection of the president

1962 In *Baker v. Carr*, the Supreme Court reverses its decision in *Colgrove v. Green* and rules that reapportionment challenges can be heard in federal court

In *Engel v. Vitale*, the Supreme Court declares that state-sponsored prayer in public schools is unconstitutional

In *Robinson v. California*, the Supreme Court incorporates the Eighth Amendment cruel and unusual punishment clause to apply to the states

1963 In *Gideon v. Wainwright*, the Supreme Court rules that individuals accused of felonies must receive an attorney if they cannot afford one

In *Ferguson v. Skrupa*, the Supreme Court declares the doctrine of substantive due process for economic legislation to be dead

In *Sherbert v. Verner*, the Supreme Court rules that a state must give unemployment benefits to a person who was fired from a job for refusing to work on her sabbath

In *Abington v. Schempp*, the Supreme Court declares Bible reading in public schools to be unconstitutional

In *Edwards v. South Carolina*, the Supreme Court effectively incorporates the First Amendment right of petition to apply to the states

1964   The Civil Rights Act of 1964 is passed by Congress

In *Heart of Atlanta Motel v. United States* and *Katzenbach v. McClung*, the Supreme Court upholds the constitutionality of the 1964 Civil Rights Act

In *New York Times v. Sullivan*, the Supreme Court establishes a higher standard that must be met for a public official to sue libel

The Twenty-fourth Amendment is adopted, outlawing poll taxes

In *Aguilar v. Texas*, the Supreme Court incorporates the warrant requirements of the Fourth Amendment to apply to the states

In *Malloy v. Hogan*, the Supreme Court incorporates the Fifth Amendment privilege against self-incrimination to apply to the states

In *Reynolds v. Sims*, the Supreme Court establishes the "one person, one vote" standard for redistricting

1965   The Voting Rights Act of 1965 is passed by Congress

In *Pointer v. Texas*, the Supreme Court incorporates the Sixth Amendment right to confront witnesses to apply to the states

In *Griswold v. Connecticut*, the Supreme Court declares unconstitutional a state law making it illegal to sell contraceptives to married couples

1966   In *Miranda v. Arizona*, the Supreme Court rules that those suspected of a crime must be read their rights when they are taken into custody

1967   Thurgood Marshall becomes the first African American on the Supreme Court

The Twenty-fifth Amendment is adopted, creating a line of succession to the presidency in the event of a vacancy

In *Klopfer v. North Carolina*, the Supreme Court incorporates the Sixth Amendment right to a speedy trial to apply to the states

1968   Supreme Court decides in *Flast v. Cohen* that taxpayers have standing to challenge some religious funding under the Constitution

Congress adopts the Indian Bill of Rights

In *Duncan v. Louisiana*, the Supreme Court incorporates the Sixth Amendment right to a trial by jury (for significant offenses) to apply to the states

1969   In *Brandenburg v. Ohio*, the Supreme Court rules that mere advocacy of violence is protected under the First Amendment

In *Stanley v. Georgia*, the Supreme Court rules that individuals have a First Amendment right to view pornography in their own homes

In *Tinker v. Des Moines Independent School District*, the Supreme Court rules that students have a First Amendment right to wear black armbands in school to protest the Vietnam War

In *Benton v. Maryland*, the Supreme Court incorporates the Fifth Amendment right against double jeopardy to apply to the states

In *Red Lion Broadcasting v. FCC*, the Supreme Court upholds the fairness doctrine

Warren Burger becomes chief justice

1970   In *Oregon v. Mitchell*, the Supreme Court declares unconstitutional a federal law lowering the voting age in state elections to 18 years old

1971   In *Lemon v. Kurtzman*, the Supreme Court issues a constitutional test to determine when state aid to parochial schools violates the establishment clause

In *Swann v. Charlotte-Mecklenburg Board of Education*, the Supreme Court upholds the use of busing to achieve racial integration of schools

In *Cohen v. California*, the Supreme Court rules that the First Amendment protects the right of an individual to depict profanity on a piece of clothing in a court to protest the Vietnam War.

In *New York Times Co. v. United States*, the Supreme Court affirms the First Amendment right to publish the Pentagon Papers

The Twenty-sixth Amendment is adopted, overturning *Oregon v. Mitchell* and lowering the voting age to 18 years

1972 In *Furman v. Georgia*, the Supreme Court strikes down all death penalty laws as unconstitutional

In *Eisenstadt v. Baird*, the Supreme Court strikes down a state law preventing the sale of birth control devices to single individuals

1973 Laws outlawing abortion are struck down in *Roe v. Wade*

Supreme Court establishes a new test for obscenity in *Miller v. California*

Four justices in the Supreme Court case *Frontiero v. Richardson* declare "sex" to be a suspect classification

Supreme Court declares, in *San Antonio Independent School District v. Rodriguez,* that education is not a fundamental right and that wealth is not a suspect classification

Congress adopts the War Powers Act

1974 In *United States v. Nixon*, the Supreme Court orders President Nixon to turn over his private, tape-recorded White House conversations to a special prosecutor

1976 In *Buckley v. Valeo*, the Supreme Court upholds portions of the new Federal Election Campaign Act that regulate campaign contributions; the Court strikes down the regulations on campaign spending

In *Gregg v. Georgia*, the Supreme Court upholds the Georgia death penalty law

In *Craig v. Boren*, the Supreme Court states that a higher level of scrutiny is needed when individuals are classified by gender

1977 In *Carey v. Reproductive Health Services*, the Supreme Court rules that the Constitution protects the right of minors to receive birth control

In *Coker v. Georgia*, the Supreme Court declares that the Eighth Amendment bars the execution of individuals convicted of rape

1978 In *Regents of the University of California v. Bakke,* the Supreme Court upholds the use of affirmative action in education admissions so long as race is one of several factors used in evaluating candidates

In *Zurcher v. Stanford Daily*, the Supreme Court upholds the issuance of search warrants to search a student newspaper office

In *FCC v. Pacifica Foundation,* the Supreme Court affirms the power of the FCC to fine a radio station for the broadcast of George Carlin's "Seven Dirty Words" routine

1981 Sandra Day O'Connor becomes the first woman on the Supreme Court

1982 In *New York v. Ferber,* the Supreme Court declares that child pornography is obscene and not protected by the First Amendment

1983 In *INS v. Chadha*, the Supreme Court declares a one-house legislative veto to be an unconstitutional violation of the presentment clause

1986 William Hubbs Rehnquist becomes chief justice

In *Bowers v. Hardwick*, the Supreme Court rules that private, consensual homosexual sodomy is not protected by the Constitution

In *Bethel School District v. Fraser,* the Supreme Court rules that public school officials can regulate student speech that is vulgar

In *Meritor Savings Bank v. Vinson*, the Supreme Court declares sexual harassment to be sexual discrimination

In *Bowsher v. Synar,* the Supreme Court strikes down the Budget and Emergency Deficit Control Act of 1985, ruling it to be a violation of separation of powers

1987   In a contentious confirmation process, United States Senate refuses to confirm Robert Bork to the Supreme Court

1988   In *Hazelwood School District v. Kuhlmeier,* the Supreme Court rules that public school officials can regulate school-sponsored student speech

In *Morrison v. Olson,* the Supreme Court upholds the constitutionality of the special prosecutor law

1989   In *Texas v. Johnson,* the Supreme Court declares unconstitutional a law making flag burning illegal

1990   In *Cruzan v. Director, Missouri Department of Health,* the Supreme Court rules that individuals have a right to withhold medical treatment and to die

In *Employment Division v. Smith,* the Supreme Court affirms the unemployment benefits to two Native Americans who were fired from work because they tested positive for the use of peyote during an Indian religious ceremony

1991   Clarence Thomas is confirmed as a Supreme Court justice after allegations of sexual harassment by Anita Hill

1992   In *Planned Parenthood v. Casey,* the Supreme Court reaffirms *Roe v. Wade* but also upholds several restrictions upon women seeking abortions

In *Lee v. Weisman,* the Supreme Court bans public prayer at public school graduations

The Supreme Court strikes down a cross-burning law as a violation of the First Amendment in *R.A.V. v. St. Paul*

The Twenty-seventh Amendment, originally proposed in 1789, is adopted, providing that any changes in compensation for members of Congress cannot take effect until after the next election

1993   Congress adopts the Religious Freedom Restoration Act in an effort to overturn *Employment Division v. Smith*

1995   In *United States v. Lopez,* the Supreme Court strikes down Congress's authority under the commerce clause to regulate guns near schools

In *Rosenberger v. Rector & Visitors of the University of Virginia,* the Supreme Court rules that the University of Virginia cannot deny student activity fees to religious groups

1996   Congress seeks to regulate the content of the Internet with the adoption of the Communications Decency Act

1997   In *City of Boerne v. Flores,* the Supreme Court strikes down application of the Religious Freedom Restoration Act to the states

In *Reno v. ACLU,* the Supreme Court strikes down two provisions of the Communications Decency Act of 1996

In *Printz v. United States,* the Supreme Court declares that Congress lacks the authority under the commerce clause and the Tenth Amendment to require local officials to perform mandatory background checks on gun purchasers under the Brady Handgun Violence Protection Act

1998   In *Clinton v. New York,* the Supreme Court strikes down the presidential line-item veto

2000   In *Bush v. Gore,* the Supreme Court halts the Florida presidential recount, making George Bush the winner of the 2000 presidential race

In *Santa Fe Independent School District v. Doe,* the Supreme Court rules that a high school's practice of announcing prayers over the loudspeaker at high school football games violates the establishment clause

In *Boy Scouts v. Dale,* the Supreme Court rules that the First Amendment protects the right of the Boy Scouts to exclude gays from their organization

2001   Terrorist attacks on the United States

The PATRIOT Act is adopted

In *Cooper Industries v. Leatherman*, the Supreme Court incorporates the Eighth Amendment right against excessive fines to apply to the states

2002 Congress passes McCain-Feingold, the Bipartisan Campaign Reform Act, to regulate money in politics

In *Atkins v. Virginia*, the Supreme Court declares that the Eighth Amendment bars the execution of individuals who are mentally retarded

2003 Supreme Court overrules *Bowers v. Hardwick* in *Lawrence v. Texas*

In a pair of cases, *Gratz v. Bollinger* and *Grutter v. Bollinger*, the Supreme Court upholds the use of affirmative action to promote educational diversity

In *Virginia v. Black*, the Supreme Court upholds a state cross-burning law as constitutional

In *McConnell v. FEC*, the Supreme Court upholds the soft money ban in the Bipartisan Campaign Finance Reform Act of 2002

In *United States v. American Library Association*, the U.S. Supreme Court upholds the Children's Internet Protection Act

2004 In *Hamdi v. Rumsfeld*, the Supreme Court rules that an American citizen cannot be held indefinitely on American soil without a right to habeas corpus review

In *Rasul v. Bush*, the Supreme Court rules that aliens being held in confinement at the American military base in Guantánamo Bay, Cuba, are entitled to have a federal court hear challenges to their detention under the federal habeas corpus statute

2005 John G. Roberts, Jr., becomes chief justice of the Supreme Court

In *Roper v. Simmons*, the Supreme Court declares the imposition of the death penalty on individuals under the age of 18 to be a violation of the Eighth Amendment

In *Kelo v. City of New London*, the Supreme Court affirms as a valid public use for eminent domain the taking of private property for economic development purposes

2006 Samuel Alito replaces Sandra Day O'Connor as justice on the Supreme Court

The U.S. Supreme Court upholds a Ten Commandments monument display in a Texas public park in *Van Orden v. Perry* and strikes down displays of the Ten Commandments outside two Kentucky county courthouses in *McCreary County v. ACLU of Kentucky*

2007 In *Gonzales v. Carhart*, the Supreme Court upholds a federal law banning partial birth abortions

In *Parents Involved in Community Schools v. Seattle School District*, the Supreme Court rules that race may not be used in school placement/enrollment decisions

In *Morse v. Frederick*, the Supreme Court rules that school officials can censor/punish student speech seen as advocating illegal drug use

In *FEC v. Wisconsin Right to Life*, the Supreme Court rules that McCain-Feingold restrictions on advertising are unconstitutional as applied

2008 In *Boumediene v. Bush*, the Supreme Court rules that the foreign terrorist suspects held in Guantánamo Naval Base in Cuba have the right of habeas corpus (to challenge their detention in a U.S. court), which was previously denied to them by the Military Commissions Act of 2006

The Supreme Court rules in *District of Columbia v. Heller* that the Second Amendment protects the rights of citizens to own a firearm for private use. This case was the first in Supreme Court history to directly address the issue of gun control for individuals

LOCATING COURT CASES

This encyclopedia cites hundreds of Supreme Court and other court cases. To find them, one needs to know some basic rules about how these cases are referenced.

All court cases cited are reported or published in a similar way. The general citation format is the name of the case printed in italics or underlined, followed by a comma, and then a citation to the volume number of the reporter it is in, the abbreviation of the name of the reporter the decision is in, the page number the decision starts on, and then the date of the decision in parentheses. The name of the case includes the two parties to the case.

For example, take a case such as *Baker v. Carr,* a famous case that dealt with reapportionment. There are several ways that one can look up this case. Baker represented the plaintiff, the person appealing or bring the case, and Carr was the defendant or respondent, the party against whom the court case was brought. The "v." is an abbreviation for "versus." *"Baker v. Carr"* is thus read as "Baker versus Carr."

Court decisions can be found in many public libraries. County courthouses, state law libraries, and college and law school libraries are other places where court opinions may be found.

The Word Wide Web has many sites where court decisions can be found. The federal government, as well as many states and specific courts, also have their own Web sites where many decisions are located.

United States Supreme Court Decisions

United States Supreme Court cases are published in three different volumes. The official publication for the Court's opinions is *United States Reports,* abbreviated as "U.S." The official citation to *Baker*

v. Carr would thus be *Baker v. Carr,* 369 U.S. 186 (1962). What this citation means is that this decision can be found in volume number 369 of *United States Reports,* with the decision starting on page 186. The information in the parentheses, 1962, refers to the year the decision was issued.

The first 90 volumes of *United States Reports* also contain the name of the specific court reporter in the citation. It is important to note that, for most people and lawyers, specific reference to that reporter is not needed.

United States Supreme Court Reports, abbreviated as "L.Ed" or "L.Ed.2d.," is a second place where Supreme Court decisions are reported. This is a private and unofficial reporter, but it is a very good and widely used source to cite and look up Court decisions. There is both a first and second edition of this volume, with the first edition cited as "L.Ed." and the second edition cited as "L.Ed.2d." *Baker v. Carr* is cited here as *Baker v. Carr,* 7 L.Ed.2d. 663 (1962).

Finally, the *Supreme Court Reporter,* abbreviated as S.Ct., is a third privately published source of Supreme Court opinions. *Baker v. Carr* is cited as *Baker v. Carr,* 82 S.Ct. 691 (1962).

Sometimes one might see a citation such as *Baker v. Carr,* 369 U.S. 186, 195 (1962), where a second number is cited after the beginning page number of the decision. That second page number refers to a specific page or reference in that decision; the "195" refers to some citation on page 195 of the *United States Reports* decision in *Baker v. Carr.*

Other Federal Court Decisions

United States Federal Court of Appeals decisions are published in the *Federal Reporter,* abbreviated as "F.," "F.2d.," or "F.3d."

United States District Court opinions are published in the *Federal Supplement*, abbreviated as "F.Supp."

Both federal court of appeals and district court decisions, as well as all other federal and state cases, are cited the same way as Supreme Court decisions, with the name of the case printed in italics or underlined, followed by a comma, and then a citation to the volume number of the reporter it is in, the abbreviation of the name of the reporter the decision is in, the page number the decision starts on, and then the date of the decision in parentheses.

There are many other federal court decisions for speciality courts, such as bankruptcy and courts of claims. Each of them has their own books or volumes where their decisions can be found.

State Court Decisions

State court decisions can be located in the same way as federal court opinions.

Most states have their own official reporters for their opinions. However, West Group, a private legal publisher, has created a series of nine different books where one can find state court opinions. New York court opinions are found in the *New York Supplement,* cited as "N.Y. Supp." or "N.Y.S. 2d.," and California decisions since 1960 are located in the *California Reporter,* cited as "Cal. Rptr." or "Cal. Rptr. 2d.," etc. The rest of the states are found in one of seven different volumes, grouped by geography, with each volume having its own abbreviation.

SELECTED BIBLIOGRAPHY

Adler, David Gray, and Robert George, eds. *The Constitution and the Conduct of American Foreign Policy.* Lawrence: University Press of Kansas, 1996.

Alley, Robert S. *Without a Prayer: Religious Expression in Public Schools.* Amherst, Mass.: Prometheus Books, 1996.

Alonso, Karen. *Korematsu v. United States: Japanese-American Internment Camps.* Springfield, N.J.: Enslow Press, 1998.

Amar, Akhil Reed. *The Constitution and Criminal Procedure.* New Haven, Conn.: Yale University Press, 1998.

Atwell, Mary Welek. *Equal Protection of the Law? Gender and Justice in the United States.* New York: Peter Lang, 2002.

Babst, Gordon A. *Liberal Constitutionalism, Marriage, and Sexual Orientation.* New York: Peter Lang Publishing, 2002.

Bailyn, Bernard, ed. *The Debate on the Constitution: Federalist and Antifederalist Speeches, Articles, and Letters during the Struggle Over Ratification.* 2 vols. New York: Literary Classics of the United States, 1993.

Baker, Leonard. *Back to Back: The Dual between F.D.R. and the Supreme Court.* New York: Macmillan Company, 1967.

Baker, Liva. *The Justice from Beacon Hill: The Life and Times of Oliver Wendell Holmes.* New York: Harper Collins, 1991.

———. *Felix Frankfurter.* New York: Coward-McCann, 1969.

Bancroft, Frederic. *Calhoun and the South Carolina Nullification Movement.* Baltimore: Johns Hopkins Press, 1928.

Bartlett, Irving H. *Daniel Webster.* New York: Norton, 1978.

Baum, Lawrence. *The Supreme Court.* Washington, D.C.: CQ Press, 2000.

Baxter, Maurice G. *One and Inseparable: Daniel Webster and the Union.* Cambridge, Mass.: Harvard University Press, 1984.

Beard, Charles. *An Economic Interpretation of the Constitution of the United States.* New York: Macmillan, 1925.

Bedau, Hugo Adam, and Paul G. Cassell, eds. *Debating the Death Penalty: Should America Have Capital Punishment? The Experts on Both Sides Make Their Best Case.* New York: Oxford University Press, 2004.

Beer, Samuel H. *To Make a Nation: The Rediscovery of American Federalism.* Cambridge, Mass.: Belknap Press of Harvard University Press, 1993.

Behuniak, Susan M., and Arthur G. Svenson. *Physician-Assisted Suicide: The Anatomy of a Constitutional Law Issue.* Lanham, Md.: Rowman & Littlefield, 2003.

Berger, Raoul. *Impeachment: The Constitutional Problems.* Cambridge, Mass.: Harvard University Press, 1973.

Bernstein, R. B., and J. Angel. *Amending America: If We Love the Constitution So Much, Why Do We Keep Trying to Change It?* New York: Times Books, 1993.

Best, Judith A. *The Choice of the People?: Debating the Electoral College.* Lanham, Md.: Rowman and Littlefield, 1996.

Beth, Loren P. *John Marshall Harlan: The Last Whig Justice.* Lexington: University Press of Kentucky, 1992.

Bickel, Alexander. *The Least Dangerous Branch: The Supreme Court at the Bar of Politics.* New Haven, Conn.: Yale University Press, 1962.

Bickel, Alexander M. *Politics and the Warren Court.* New York: Harper & Row, 1965.

Blasi, Vincent. *The Burger Court: The Counter-Revolution That Wasn't.* New Haven, Conn.: Yale University Press, 1986.

Bloom, Allan, ed. *Confronting the Constitution.* Washington, D.C.: AEI Press, 1990.

Bork, Robert. *The Tempting of America: The Political Seduction of the Law.* New York: Touchstone Books, 1990.

Breyer, Stephen. *Active Liberty: Interpreting Our Democratic Constitution.* New York: Alfred A. Knopf, 2005.

Brigham, John. *The Cult of the Court.* Philadelphia: Temple University Press, 1987.

Cardozo, Benjamin N. *The Nature of the Judicial Process.* New Haven, Conn.: Yale University Press, 1964.

Carter, Dan T. *Scottsboro: A Tragedy of the American South.* Rev. ed. Baton Rouge: Louisiana State University Press, 1979.

Chernow, Ron. *Alexander Hamilton.* New York: Penguin Press, 2004.

Choper, Jesse. *Judicial Review and the National Political Process: A Functionalist Reconsideration of the Supreme Court,* Chicago: University of Chicago Press, 1980.

Citizenship. New York: Hill and Wang, 2000.

Clinton, Robert L. *Marbury v. Madison and Judicial Review.* Lawrence: University Press of Kansas, 1989.

Collier, Christopher. *Decision in Philadelphia: The Constitutional Convention of 1787.* New York: Ballantine Books, 1987.

———. *Roger Sherman's Connecticut.* Middletown, Conn.: Wesleyan University Press, 1971.

Cortner, Richard. *Civil Rights and Public Accommodations: The Heart of Atlanta Motel and McClung Cases.* Lawrence: University Press of Kansas, 2001.

Corwin, Edwin S. *The Higher Law Background of American Constitutional Law.* Ithaca, N.Y.: Cornell University Press, 1955.

———. *The President: Office and Powers.* 5th revised edition. New York: New York University Press, 1989.

———. *The Commerce Power Versus States' Rights.* Princeton, N.J.: Princeton University Press; London: H. Milford, Oxford University Press, 1936.

Cox, Archibald. *The Court and the Constitution.* Boston: Houghton Mifflin, 1987.

———. *The Role of the Supreme Court in American Government.* New York: Oxford University Press, 1976.

Currie, David P. *The Constitution in the Supreme Court: The First Hundred Years, 1789–1888.* Chicago: University of Chicago Press, 1985.

———. *The Constitution in the Supreme Court: The Second Hundred Years, 1888–1986.* Chicago: University of Chicago Press, 1990.

Curry, Thomas J. *The First Freedoms: Church and State in America to the Passage of the First Amendment.* New York: Oxford University Press, 1986.

Cushman, Barry. *Rethinking the New Deal Court: The Structure of a Constitutional Revolution.* New York: Oxford University Press, 1998.

Cushman, Clare. *Supreme Court Decisions and Women's Rights.* Washington, D.C.: CQ Press, 2000.

———. *The Supreme Court Justices: Illustrated Biographies, 1789–1995.* Washington, D.C.: Congressional Quarterly, 1995.

Davis, Michael D., and Hunter R. Clark. *Thurgood Marshall: Warrior at the Bar, Rebel on the Bench.* Updated and rev. ed. New York: Citadel Press, 1994.

Delgado, Richard, and Jean Stefancic. *Must We Defend Nazis? Hate Speech, Pornography, and the New First Amendment.* New York: New York University Press, 1997.

Douglas, William O. *The Court Years 1939–1975.* New York: Random House, 1980.

Downs, Donald Alexander. *Nazis in Skokie: Freedom, Community, and the First Amendment.* South Bend, Ind.: University of Notre Dame Press, 1985.

Eisler, Kim Isaac. *A Justice for All: William J. Brennan, Jr., and the Decisions that Transformed America.* New York: Simon & Schuster, 1993.

Elliott, Orrin. *The Tariff Controversy in the U.S., 1789–1833.* Palo Alto, Calif.: Stanford University, 1892.

Elsmere, Jane Shaffer. *Justice Samuel Chase.* Muncie, Ind.: Janevar Publishing, 1980.

Ely, James W., Jr. *The Guardian of Every Other Right: A Constitutional History of Property Rights.* New York: Oxford University Press, 1998.

Ely, John Hart. *Democracy and Distrust: A Theory of Judicial Review.* Cambridge, Mass.: Harvard University Press, 1980.

Epstein, Lee, and Joseph F. Kobylka. *The Supreme Court and Legal Change: Abortion and the Death Penalty.* Chapel Hill: University of North Carolina Press, 1992.

Fairman, Charles. *Reconstruction and Reunion: History of the Supreme Court.* New York: Macmillan, 1971.

———. *History of the Supreme Court of the United States: Reconstruction and Reunion, 1864–88.* New York: Macmillan, 1971.

———. *Mr. Justice Miller and the Supreme Court 1862–1890.* Cambridge, Mass.: Harvard University Press, 1939.

Fallon, Richard H., Jr. *The Dynamic Constitution.* New York: Cambridge University Press, 2004.

Farrand, Max. *The Records of the Federal Convention of 1787.* New Haven, Conn.: Yale University Press, 1966.

Fehrenbacher, Don. *The Dred Scott Case: Its Significance in American Law and Politics.* New York: Oxford University Press, 1978.

Finkelman, Paul. *African Americans and the Right to Vote.* New York: Garland, 1992.

Fireside, Harvey. *Plessy v. Ferguson: Separate but Equal.* Berkeley Heights, N.J.: Enslow Publishers, 1997.

Fisher, Louis. *Presidential War Power.* Lawrence: University Press of Kansas, 2004.

Fiss, Owen. *The Civil Rights Injunction.* Bloomington: Indiana University Press, 1978.

Frankfurter, Felix. *The Commerce Clause under Marshall, Taney and Waite.* Chicago: Quadrangle Books, 1964.

———. *Mr. Justice Holmes and the Supreme Court.* 1938. 2d ed. Harvard, Mass.: Harvard University Press, 1961.

———. *Felix Frankfurter Reminisces.* New York: Doubleday, 1962.

Friendly, Fred W. *Minnesota Rag: The Dramatic Story of the Landmark Court Case that Gave New Meaning to Freedom of the Press.* New York: Random House, 1981.

Fuess, Claude M. *Daniel Webster.* 2 vols. Boston: Little, Brown, 1930; reprinted, 1968.

Furer, Howard B. *The Fuller Court, 1888–1910.* Danbury, Conn.: Grolier Educational, 1995.

Garrow, David J. *Liberty & Sexuality: The Right to Privacy and the Making of* Roe v. Wade. New York: Macmillan, 1994.

Gillman, Howard. *The Constitution Besieged: The Rise and Demise of Lochner Era Police Powers Jurisprudence.* Chicago: University of Chicago Press, 1993.

Gottlieb, Stephen E. *Morality Imposed: The Rehnquist Court and Liberty in America.* New York: New York University Press, 2000.

Graber, Mark, and Michael Perhac, eds. *Marbury versus Madison.* Washington, D.C.: CQ Press, 2002.

Greenberg, Jack. *Crusaders in the Courts: How a Dedicated Band of Lawyers Fought for the Civil Rights Revolution.* New York: Basic Books, 1994.

Gross, Robert A., ed. *In Debt to Shays: The Bicentennial of an Agrarian Rebellion.* Charlottesville: University of Virginia Press, 1993.

Gunther, Gerald. *Learned Hand: The Man and the Judge.* New York: Knopf, 1994.

———. *John Marshall's Defense of* McCulloch v. Maryland. Stanford, Calif.: Stanford University Press, 1969.

Haines, Charles Grove. *The Role of the Supreme Court in American Government and Politics, 1789–1835.* New York: Russell & Russell, 1960.

Hall, Kermit L. *The Magic Mirror: Law in American History.* New York: Oxford University Press, 1989.

Hasen, Richard. *The Supreme Court and Election Law: Judging Equality from Baker v. Carr to Bush v. Gore.* New York: NYU Books, 2003.

Henkin, Louis. *Foreign Affairs and the United States Constitution.* Oxford: Clarendon Press, 1996.

———. *Constitutionalism, Democracy, and Foreign Affairs.* New York: Columbia University Press, 1990.

Heumann, Milton, and Lance Cassak. *Good Cop, Bad Cop: Racial Profiling and Competing Views of Justice*. New York: Peter Lang, 2003.

Higginbotham, A. Leon. *Shades of Freedom: Racial Politics and Presumptions of the American Legal Process*. New York: Oxford University Press, 1996.

Hitchcock, James. *The Supreme Court and Religion in American Life*. Vol. 1: *The Odyssey of the Religion Clauses*. Princeton, N.J.: Princeton University Press, 2004.

Hobson, Charles F. *The Great Chief Justice: John Marshall and the Rule of Law*. Lawrence: University of Kansas Press, 1996.

Hofstadter, Richard. *The Age of Reform: From Bryan to F.D.R.* New York: Alfred A. Knopf, 1955.

Hofstadter, Richard, ed. *The Progressive Movement (1900–1915)*. Englewood Cliffs, N.J.: Prentice-Hall, 1963.

Holmes, Oliver W., Jr. *The Common Law*, ed. Mark DeWolfe Howe. Boston: Little Brown, 1963.

Howard, J. Woodford. *Mr. Justice Murphy: A Political Biography*, Princeton, N.J.: Princeton University Press, 1968.

Hughes, Charles Evans. *The Supreme Court of the United States*. New York: Columbia University Press, 1938.

Hurst, James Willard. *The Law of Treason in the United States: Collected Essays*. Westport, Conn.: Greenwood, 1978.

Hutchison, Dennis. *The Man Who Once Was Whizzer White: A Portrait of Justice Byron R. White*. New York: Free Press, 1998.

Jeffries, John C., Jr. *Justice Lewis F. Powell, Jr.* New York: Charles Scribner's Sons, 1994.

Johnson, John W. *Griswold v. Connecticut: Birth Control and the Constitutional Right of Privacy*. Lawrence: University Press of Kansas, 2005.

———. *The Struggle for Student Rights*. Lawrence: University Press of Kansas, 1997.

Kahn, Paul. *The Reign of Law: Marbury v. Madison and the Construction of America*. New Haven, Conn.: Yale University Press, 1997.

Kahn, Ronald. *The Supreme Court and Constitutional Theory*. Lawrence: University Press of Kansas, 1994.

Kalman, Laura. *Abe Fortas: A Biography*. New Haven, Conn.: Yale University Press, 1990.

Kalven, Harvey. *A Worthy Tradition: Freedom of Speech in America*. New York: Harper and Row, 1988.

Kaplan, Lincoln. *The Tenth Justice: The Solicitor General and the Rule of Law*. New York: Vintage Books, 1987.

Kelly, Alfred H., Winfred A. Harbison, and Herman Belz. *The American Constitution: Its Origins and Development*. 2 vols. New York: W.W. Norton, 1991.

Kens, Paul. *Justice Stephen Field: Shaping Liberty from the Gold Rush to the Gilded Age*. Lawrence: University Press of Kansas, 1997.

Kerber, Linda K. *No Constitutional Right to Be Ladies: Women and the Obligations of Citizenship* New York: New York University Press, 1983.

Killenbeck, Mark Robert. *McCulloch v. Maryland: Securing a Nation*. Lawrence: University Press of Kansas, 2006.

Klarman, Michael J. *From Jim Crow to Civil Rights: The Supreme Court and the Struggle for Racial Equality*. New York: Oxford University Press, 2004.

Kluger, R. *Simple Justice: The History of* Brown v. Board of Education *and Black America's Struggle for Equality*. New York: Knopf, 1975.

Krieger, Linda Hamilton, ed. *Backlash against the ADA: Reinterpreting Disability Rights*. Ann Arbor: University of Michigan Press, 2003.

Kutler, Stanley. *Judicial Power and Reconstruction Politics*. Chicago: University of Chicago Press, 1968.

LaFave, Wayne R., Jerold H. Israel, and Nancy J. King. *Criminal Procedure*. St. Paul, Minn.: Thomson/West, 2004.

Langran, Robert W. *The Supreme Court: A Concise History*. New York: Peter Lang, 2004.

Latham, Frank Brown. *The Great Dissenter: John Marshall Harlan, 1833–1911*, New York: Cowles Book Company, 1970.

Leuchtenburg, William E. *The Supreme Court Reborn: The Constitutional Revolution in the Age of Roosevelt*. New York: Oxford University Press, 1995.

Lewis, Anthony. *Gideon's Trumpet*. New York: Random House, 1964.

Lutz, Donald S. "Connecticut." In *Ratifying the Constitution,* ed. Michael Allen Gillespie and Michael Lienesch. Lawrence: University Press of Kansas, 1989.

Malcolm, Joyce Lee. *To Keep and Bear Arms: The Origins of an Anglo-American Right.* Cambridge, Mass.: Harvard University Press, 1994.

Maltese, John Anthony. *The Selling of Supreme Court Nominees.* Baltimore: Johns Hopkins University Press, 1995.

Marcus, Maeva. *Truman and the Steel Seizure Case: The Limits of Presidential Power.* Durham, N.C.: Duke University Press, 1994.

Margolis, Lawrence. *Executive Agreements and Presidential Power in Foreign Policy.* New York: Praeger, 1985.

Mason, Alpheus Thomas. *Harlan Fiske Stone: Pillar of the Law.* New York: Viking Press, 1956.

Mayer, Kenneth R. *With the Stroke of a Pen: Executive Orders and Presidential Power.* Princeton, N.J.: Princeton University Press, 2001.

McCann, Michael W. *Rights at Work: Pay Equity Reform and the Politics of Legal Mobilization.* Chicago: University of Chicago Press, 1994.

McClellan, James. *Joseph Story and the American Constitution.* Norman: University of Oklahoma Press, 1990.

McKitrick, Eric. *Andrew Johnson and Reconstruction.* New York: Oxford University Press, 1988.

Mezey, Susan Gluck. *Elusive Equality: Women's Rights, Public Policy, and the Law.* Boulder, Colo.: Lynne Rienner, 2003.

Millis, Harry A. *From the Wagner Act to Taft-Hartley.* Chicago: University of Chicago Press, 1950.

Morris, Richard Brandon. *John Jay, the Nation, and the Court.* Boston: Boston University Press, 1967.

Muir, William K., Jr. *Prayer in Public Schools: Law and Attitude Change.* Chicago: University of Chicago Press, 1967.

Murdoch, Joyce, and Deb Price. *Courting Justice: Gay Men and Lesbians v. the Supreme Court.* New York: Basic Books, 2001.

Murphy, Bruce Allen. *Wild Bill: The Legend and Life of William O. Douglas.* New York: Random House, 2003.

Murphy, Paul L. *The Constitution in Crisis Times, 1918–1969.* New York: Harper and Row, 1972.

Nelson, William. Marbury v. Madison: *The Origins and Legacy of Judicial Review.* Lawrence: University Press of Kansas, 2000.

Nowak, John E., and Ronald D. Rotunda. *Principles of Constitutional Law.* St. Paul, Minn.: Thomson West, 2005.

Onuf, Peter S. *Statehood and Union: A History of the Northwest Ordinance.* Bloomington: Indiana University Press, 1987.

Orfield, Gary, and Susan E. Eaton. *Dismantling Desegregation: The Quiet Reversal of* Brown v. Board of Education. New York: Free Press, 1996.

Pacelle, Richard L., Jr. *The Transformation of the Supreme Court's Agenda.* Boulder, Colo.: Westview Press, 1991.

Pederson, William D., and Norman W. Provizer. *Leaders of the Pack: Polls & Case Studies of Great Supreme Court Justices.* New York: Peter Lang, 2003.

Perry, H. W., Jr. *Deciding to Decide: Agenda Setting in the United States Supreme Court.* Cambridge, Mass.: Harvard University Press, 1991.

Peters, Shawn Francis. *The Yoder Case: Religious Freedom, Education, and Parental Rights.* Lawrence: University Press of Kansas, 2003.

Pound, Roscoe. *The Formative Era of American Law,* Gloucester, Mass.: Peter Smith, 1938.

Pringle, Henry F. *Life and Times of William Howard Taft.* 2 vols. Hamden, Conn.: Shoe String Press, 1965.

Pritchett, Charles Herman. *The Roosevelt Court: A Study in Judicial Politics and Values, 1937–1947.* New York: Macmillan, 1948.

Provine, Doris Marie. *Case Selection in the United States Supreme Court.* Chicago: University of Chicago Press, 1980.

Pusey, Merlo L. *Charles Evans Hughes.* 2 vols. New York: Macmillan, 1951.

Rakove, Jack N. *Original Meanings: Politics and Ideas in the Making of the Constitution.* New York: Knopf, 1997.

Reagan, Leslie J. *When Abortion Was a Crime: Women, Medicine, and Law in the United States, 1867–1973.* Berkeley: University of California Press, 1997.

Rehnquist, William H. *The Supreme Court: How It Was, How It Is.* New York: Quill, 1987.

Remini, Robert V. *Daniel Webster: The Man and His Time.* New York: Norton, 1997.

Richards, Leonard. *Shays's Rebellion: The American Revolution's Final Battle.* Philadelphia: University of Pennsylvania Press, 2002.

Rosenberg, Gerald N. *The Hollow Hope: Can Courts Bring About Social Change?* Chicago: University of Chicago Press, 1991.

Ross, William G. *The Chief Justiceship of Charles Evans Hughes, 1930–1941.* Columbia: University of South Carolina Press, 2007.

Russomanno, Joseph. *Speaking Our Minds: Conversations with the People Behind Landmark First Amendment Cases.* Mahwah, N.J.: Lawrence Erlbaum Associates, 2002.

Ryden, David K. *The U.S. Supreme Court and the Electoral Process.* Washington, D.C.: Georgetown University Press, 2002.

Salokar, Rebecca Mae. *The Solicitor General: The Politics of Law.* Philadelphia: Temple University Press, 1992.

Savage, David G. *Turning Right: The Making of the Rehnquist Supreme Court.* New York: John Wiley, 1992.

Saxton, Alexander. *The Indispensable Enemy: Labor and the Anti-Chinese Movement in California.* Berkeley: University of California Press, 1975.

Scalia, Antonin. *A Matter of Interpretation: Federal Courts and the Law.* Princeton, N.J.: Princeton University Press, 1997.

Scher, Richard K., et al. *Voting Rights and Democracy: The Law and Politics of Districting.* Chicago: Nelson-Hall Publishers, 1997.

Schneider, Elizabeth M. *Battered Women and Feminist Lawmaking.* New Haven, Conn.: Yale University Press, 2000.

Schultz, David A., and Christopher E. Smith. *The Jurisprudential Vision of Justice Antonin Scalia.* Lanham, Md.: Rowman and Littlefield, 1996.

Schwartz, Bernard. *The New Right and the Constitution: Turning Back the Legal Clock.* Boston: Northeastern University Press, 1990.

———. *Super Chief, Earl Warren and his Supreme Court: A Judicial Biography.* New York: New York University Press, 1983.

———. *A History of the Supreme Court.* New York: Oxford University Press, 1993.

Schwarzenbach, Sybil, and Patricia Smith. *Women and the Constitution.* New York: Columbia University Press, 2004.

Scotch, Richard K. *From Good Will to Civil Rights: Transforming Federal Disability Policy.* Philadelphia: Temple University Press, 1984.

Segal, Jeffrey A., and Harold J. Spaeth. *The Supreme Court and the Attitudinal Model.* New York: Cambridge University Press, 1993.

Seidman, Louis Michael. *Constitutional Law: Equal Protection of the Laws.* New York: Foundation Press, 2003.

Sickels, Robert J. *John Paul Stevens and the Constitution: The Search and the Balance.* University Park: Pennsylvania State University Press, 1988.

Silverstein, Gordon. *Imbalance of Powers.* Oxford: Oxford University Press, 1997.

Silverstein, Mark. *Constitutional Faiths: Felix Frankfurter, Hugo Black and the Process of Judicial Decision Making.* Ithaca, N.Y.: Cornell University Press, 1984.

Simon, James F. *What Kind of Nation: Thomas Jefferson, John Marshall, and the Epic Struggle to Create a United States.* New York: Simon & Schuster, 2003.

———. *The Center Holds: The Power Struggle Inside the Rehnquist Court.* New York: Simon & Schuster, 1995.

Sorenson, Leonard R. *Madison on the "General Welfare" of America: His Consistent Constitutional Vision.* Lanham, Md.: Rowman and Littlefield, 1995.

Storing, Herbert J. *What the Anti-Federalists Were For.* Chicago: University of Chicago Press, 1981.

Strum, Phillippa. *Louis D. Brandeis: Justice for the People.* Cambridge, Mass.: Harvard University Press, 1984.

Swisher, Carl Brent. *Stephen J. Field: Craftsman of the Law.* Hamden, Conn.: Archon Books, 1963.

———. *Roger B. Taney.* New York: Macmillan, 1935.

Tribe, Laurence. *Abortion: The Clash of Absolutes.* New York: Norton, 1990.

Tribe, Laurence H., and Michael C. Dorf. *On Reading the Constitution.* Cambridge, Mass.: Harvard University Press, 1991.

Tushnet, Mark, ed. *The Constitution in Wartime.* Durham, N.C.: Duke University Press, 2005.

Urofsky, Melvin I. *Money and Free Speech: Campaign Finance Reform and the Courts.* Lawrence: University of Kansas Press, 2005.

Uviller, H. Richard, and William G. Merkel. *The Militia and the Right to Arms, or, How the Second Amendment Fell Silent.* Durham, N.C.: Duke University Press, 2002.

Vallely, Richard M. *The Two Reconstructions: The Struggle for Black Enfranchisement.* Chicago: University of Chicago Press, 2004.

Walker, Samuel. *Hate Speech: The History of an American Controversy.* Lincoln: University of Nebraska Press, 1994.

Walker, Samuel, et al. *The Color of Justice: Race, Ethnicity, and Crime in America.* Belmont, Calif.: Wadsworth, 2000.

Warren, Charles. *The Supreme Court in United States History.* 3 vols. Boston: Little, Brown, 1924.

Wasby, Stephen L. *The Impact of the United States Supreme Court: Some Perspectives.* Homewood, Ill.: Dorsey Press, 1970.

White, G. Edward. *The Marshall Court & Cultural Change: 1815–1835.* New York: Oxford University Press, 1991.

———. *Creating the National Pastime: Baseball Transforms Itself.* Princeton, N.J.: Princeton University Press, 1996.

———. *The Constitution and the New Deal.* Boston: Harvard University Press, 2000.

Wiecek, William. *The Guarantee Clause of the U.S. Constitution.* Ithaca, N.Y.: Cornell University Press, 1972.

Witte, John, Jr. *Religion and the American Constitutional Experiment.* Boulder, Colo.: Westview Press, 2000.

Wood, Gordon. *The Creation of the American Republic, 1776–1787.* New York: W.W. Norton, 1969.

Wood, Stephen. *Constitutional Politics and the Progressive Era: Child Labor and the Law.* Chicago: University of Chicago Press, 1968.

Woodward, Bob, and Scott Armstrong. *The Brethren.* New York: Simon & Schuster, 1979.

Woodward. C. Vann. *The Strange Career of Jim Crow.* Oxford: New York, 1966.

Wormuth, Francis, and Edwin Firmage. *To Chain the Dog of War: The War Powers of Congress in History and Law.* 2d ed. Chicago: University of Illinois Press, 1989.

Yarborough, Tinsley E. *John Marshall Harlan: Great Dissenter of the Warren Court.* New York: Oxford University Press, 1992.

Yoo, John. *The Powers of War and Peace: The Constitution and Foreign Affairs after 9/11.* Chicago: Chicago University Press, 2005.

Index

Note: **Boldface** page numbers indicate main entries; *c* refers to the U.S. Constitution Time Line appendix.